POLICE FIELD OPERATIONS

Fourth Edition

Thomas F. Adams

Professor Emeritus
Criminal Justice Department
Santa Ana College
Santa Ana, California

Former Lieutenant of Police
Santa Ana, California

Prentice Hall
Upper Saddle River, New Jersey 07458

Library of Congress Cataloging-in-Publication Data

Adams, Thomas Francis, 1927–
  Police field operations / Thomas F. Adams. — 4th ed.
    p.   cm.
  Includes bibliographical references and index.
  ISBN 0-13-266362-7 (case cover)
  1. Police patrol—United States.   I. Title
HV8080.P2A397   1998
363.2'32'0973—dc21   96-48358
                                             CIP

Acquisitions Editor: *Neil Marquardt*
Production Editor and Interior Designer:
  Adele M. Kupchik
Managing Editor: *Mary Carnis*
Director of Manufacturing
  and Production: *Bruce Johnson*
Manufacturing Buyer: *Ed O'Dougherty*
Editorial Assistant: *Rose Mary Florio*
Marketing Manager: *Frank Mortimer, Jr.*

Formatting/page make-up: *Clarinda
  Company*
Printer/Binder: *R. R. Donnelley & Sons,
  Harrisonburg, VA*
Cover Design: *Miguel Ortiz*
Cover Photos: *Courtesy of the Metro-
Dade Police Department and the North
Carolina Highway Patrol*

©1998, 1994, 1990, 1986 by Prentice-Hall, Inc.
Simon & Schuster / A Viacom Company
Upper Saddle River, New Jersey 07458

Printed in the United States of America

10   9   8   7   6   5

ISBN 0-13-266362-7

Prentice-Hall International (UK) Limited, *London*
Prentice-Hall of Australia Pty. Limited, *Sydney*
Prentice-Hall Canada Inc., *Toronto*
Prentice-Hall Hispanoamericana, S.A., *Mexico*
Prentice-Hall of India Private Limited, *New Delhi*
Prentice-Hall of Japan, Inc., *Tokyo*
Simon & Schuster Asia Pte. Ltd., *Singapore*
Editora Prentice-Hall do Brasil, Ltda., *Rio de Janeiro*

CONTENTS

PREFACE

As a peace officer it is your responsibility to preserve the peace and tranquility of your community and to protect the lives and property of the people who live in—and visit—that community. There are few individuals in society who have a more sacred trust than yours. There will be times when you will have to decide whether or not to arrest a suspected offender, and that decision will have a profound influence on many lives and reputations. In less than a second, you may have to decide whether or not to use deadly force, to take the life of someone who you believe is presenting an immediate threat to your life or that of someone else. You will make wise decisions, and you will make mistakes as well. There will be times when you will have overwhelming support and other times when you will be all alone, with no one willing to give you moral or physical support. Because of these considerations, service as a peace officer is one of the most selfless and courageous career choices you could make.

Police Field Operations, Fourth Edition has been developed over a period of several years from literally hundreds of sources. Training bulletins and course outlines from many police academies and college course offerings, dozens of hours in the classroom and in the field as a working police officer and supervisor, student, administrator, and college professor plus the input of colleagues throughout the world in the criminal justice professions have all been utilized to produce this text. It is my fervent hope that it serves you well and aids you in developing your own base of police knowledge that will enable you to become a true police professional. I have learned a great deal from others; so shall you.

All the information and techniques presented in this book are the culmination of the collective wisdom and experience of my colleagues, both past and present, and represent the best that I could compile and put into this one volume. In the interest of space, we had to leave out many things that should have, or could have, been included. Space constrictions, however, demanded that we include what we considered most important for the well-rounded field police officer.

Once you have settled down into your field duties, you are going to develop a better way to handle some of these procedures, more suited to your own personal style. In the meantime, while you are finding those special ways of doing things your way, may I suggest that you try these. Then as you prove these methods are no longer suitable for your style, discard them. As we move into policing for the twenty-first century, we cannot stand still or we will stagnate.

Once in a while you will read or hear offhand remarks such as "we are going to teach you how police work should be, and not how it has been for many years"— obviously not spoken or written by someone who has been "in the trenches," so to speak. Although it is true that many procedures have changed and many new scientific instruments and techniques have been introduced in recent years, many of the old ones still work. Change just for the sake of change is fruitless; changes must be for improvement of the system. As a former vice-chancellor of the college where I teach said more than once, "If it ain't broke, why fix it?" One of the temptations for the professor and the author who are no longer in the field is to change procedures in one's own special environment far removed from reality. I, too, have been tempted to present the ideal solution to many of our unsolved problems only to find that the problems continue to be unsolved despite my brilliant attempts to set the world right. What I aspire to do in this book is to present what I believe to be the best techniques in the real world of police work today.

Sources of information and ideas for this book number literally in the hundreds, and most of the credit should go to those individuals in the profession whose unselfish devotion to our dream of professionalism has motivated them to share their "trade secrets" with their fellow professionals. None of this material has been taken verbatim from any source. You will note the limited use of footnotes and references, the reason being that this is a procedures book, not a compendium of information sources or a survey of the literature, as are some academic publications.

To you, my fellow professionals, I present this material. I challenge you to improve upon it, even render it obsolete, if you must.

I wish to express my special thanks to two very fine gentlemen—Jack Pritchard and Bob Howland—who were responsible for getting me involved in writing for Prentice Hall in the first place, and to the many colleagues in the teaching and policing business who have inspired and mentored me for more years than I would like to admit.

T. F. Adams, Santa Ana, California

LAW ENFORCEMENT CODE OF ETHICS

As a *Law Enforcement Officer,* my fundamental duty is to serve mankind; to safeguard lives and property; to protect the innocent against deception, the weak against oppression or intimidation, and the peaceful against violence or disorder; and to respect the Constitutional rights of all men to liberty, equality, and justice.

I will keep my private life unsullied as an example to all; maintain courageous calm in the face of danger, scorn, or ridicule; develop self-restraint; and be constantly mindful of the welfare of others. Honest in thought and deed in both my personal and official life, I will be exemplary in obeying the laws of the land and the regulations of my department. Whatever I see or hear of a confidential nature or that is confided to me in my official capacity will be kept ever secret unless revelation is necessary in the performance of my duty.

I will never act officiously or permit personal feelings, prejudices, animosities, or friendships to influence my decisions. With no compromise for crime and with relentless prosecution of criminals, I will enforce the law courteously and appropriately without fear or favor, malice or ill will, never employing unnecessary force or violence and never accepting gratuities.

I recognize the badge of my office as a symbol of public faith, and I accept it as a public trust to be held so long as I am true to the ethics of the police service. I will constantly strive to achieve these objectives and ideals, dedicating myself before God to my chosen profession . . . law enforcement.

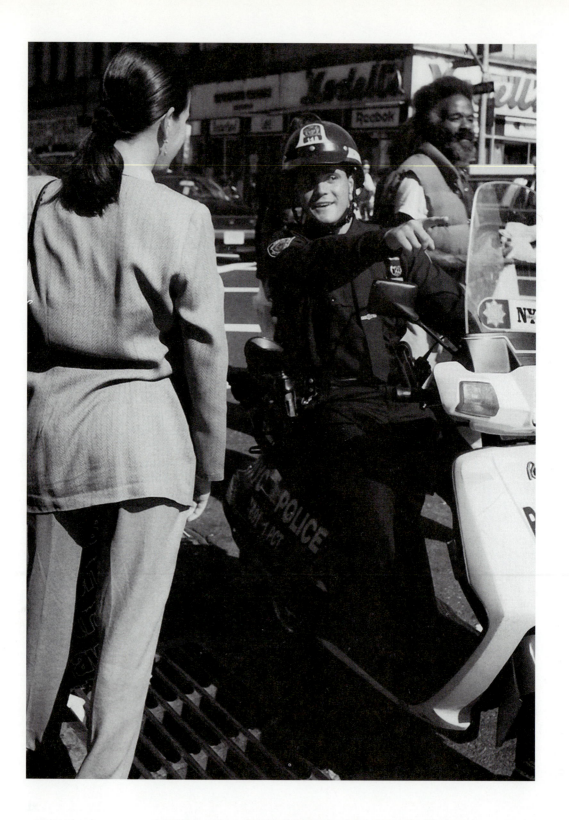

C H A P T E R   1

INTRODUCTION TO PATROL

INTRODUCTION

As a uniformed field officer for the local police or sheriff's department, you are the most visible representative of the government; to many people you *are* the government and the law enforcement establishment. All of those other government people, such as the mayor and the city councilpersons, the state legislators, and all the bureaucracies they represent, are essentially invisible to the people you contact on an everyday basis. Therefore, you will take the wrath and criticism on their behalf. You are also the goodwill ambassador representing your government to those people.

The majority of the people with whom you and your colleagues come into contact on a regular professional basis know and respect the police as protectors, and will work with you to accomplish your common goals of a society reasonably free of crime and a community where they are willing to keep it a safe place for themselves and their children. Others, however, see the uniformed officer as a nuisance, while still others consider the police the *enemy*. It is your sworn duty to serve all members of the community with equal dedication, respect, and with a sense of justice.

Approximately one half of all the local police departments in the United States employ fewer than 10 officers; almost 1000 of those departments have only one officer. About 90 percent of all departments serve populations of less than 25,000 persons and employ fewer than 50 officers. The sheriff's departments for thousands of counties and parishes (such as in Louisiana) are similarly made up primarily of small departments. Half of the sheriffs and their deputies serve populations of less than 25,000, and their sworn ranks number fewer than 25 in two thirds of all departments, with about one third of that number employing 10 or fewer deputies. Because of the vast differences in numbers of officers in the thousands of police and sheriff departments throughout the country, it is very difficult to develop standardized training programs that would fit them all. In other words there is no "one size fits all" formula. Specialization is also a problem in the smaller departments because with so few officers each officer may have specialized in more than one special detail in addition to patrol. For example, one officer may be responsible for crime scene investigation and the community policing program, another may be required to coordinate traffic enforcement and handle juvenile offenders and victims.

At the other end of the spectrum, we have 34 police departments and 12 sheriff's departments that are quite sophisticated and highly specialized, employing more than 1000 officers and deputies each. These are the agencies that we see represented in movies and television, with each officer assigned a specific line of duty, such as detective, juvenile detective, burglary detective, auto-theft and accident investigator, crime scene investigator, fingerprint expert, photographer, and on without end to the list.

The smaller departments will assign all but a few to the task of patrolling and responding to calls for service as well as doing most of the investigative work. In the smallest departments, all officers are on patrol, with some assigned the added responsibility of taking on a specialty, such as identification, or dealing with juvenile victims and offenders, performing those duties on an as-needed basis. Consider the one-officer department, with that officer performing every one of the duties performed by dozens of different specialties. In addition to investigating crimes and traffic collisions, responding to all types of calls for service, and running the administrative responsibilities, he or she must find spare time to make the necessary speeches on the "rubber chicken circuit" to all the local service clubs to fulfill community relations obligations. He or she will spend the greatest amount of on-duty time on patrol assignments, of course, but will be called "chief" or "sheriff."

As the department grows to keep up with the increasing population, expanding geographical boundaries, and growing diversity of the jurisdiction, the chief will begin to add on to the force of officers, then will hire office personnel to take over the secretarial and record-keeping functions to free the officers for their field responsibilities. As the department continues to grow, officers are taken out of the field to specialize in traffic investigation and control, juvenile victims and perpetrators, plainclothes detective activities, and all the other specialized functions, each time adding to the patrol force to replace the specialists. All the while, the patrol force continues to be the principal functioning unit of the department.

The sheriff has additional duties, such as keeper of the county jail and bailiff in the superior court for the county. Patrol may actually be the smaller operating unit in the sheriff's department, depending on the size of unincorporated parts of the county. In a county that is composed of nothing but "wall to wall" cities with no unincorporated areas at all, the sheriff would have no patrolling responsibility, except in cases where cities enter into a contractual agreement with the sheriff to provide all their police services, thereby negating the need for the creation of a city police department.

Evolution of Patrol

The patrol function originally began many years ago as a volunteer force made up of residents and merchants, who gave their time and efforts to protect their own properties and that of their neighbors. In early America the night watches were merged into one police force under government control and on the government payroll. Training and supervision of police officers became necessary to assure effectiveness of their efforts. In order that police officers and sheriff's deputies could be held accountable for their responsibilities, it was necessary to use men and women who would devote their full time to policing instead of trying to get the job done by unpaid and untrained volunteers who would also pose control problems because—after all—they were contributing their services free, and there was no threat of any type of disciplinary action, except to ask them to resign.

With the development of professionally trained police officers, the city and county governments could exercise more control over their officers. Moonlighting on outside jobs was forbidden entirely, or their hours and the types of part-time jobs they held were limited to types of work that did not conflict with their policing responsibilities. This reduced the splitting of loyalties that one experiences when one has more than one master. It would make no sense to have the owner of a "fringe-type" business, such as a bar which allowed prostitution, gambling, and other vice activities to flourish in and around his or her establishment, also serve as a police officer with the responsibility to arrest people for vice crime violations. Nor could you expect a police officer to be very effective if the off-duty job is owning or managing the type of business described above.

The "professionalization" trend that gained momentum following World War II in the later 1940s and early 1950s involved a surge of officers to go to college and earn degrees in criminology, criminal justice, police science, and master of science degrees in criminology, social ecology, criminal justice, and on to earn doctorate degrees in their chosen field. Simultaneously, there came a dramatic surge in development of police academies that grew in numbers and length of attendance. At the same time, these emerging "professional" police officers became more aloof and isolated from the publics they served. These were well-educated and -trained men and women who could command salaries that were no longer at the unskilled labor level. They began to see themselves as detached professionals, as doctors and lawyers saw themselves, no longer public servants who were considered lower on the social scale than the average citizen.

The elitist attitude on the part of these new professionals led many of them to see themselves as separate and apart from the masses they served. Some developed an "us versus them" attitude and a "siege" mentality, often considering the public as their enemies who had to be kept in line. While not all officers who considered themselves as professionals held themselves above and apart from their constituents, many did. What we are seeing now is a movement by police leaders and the rank and file beginning to adjust attitudes in the police professions, and the police and sheriff's officers see themselves as viable movers and shakers within the communities they serve. This shift in attitudes and activities has led to what we are now seeing as community policing and proactive policing. Officers are more permanently assigned to small sections of their community and work out of storefronts, houses, and apartments right in the middle of the district to which they are assigned. The officers meet and work with various people in the district to identify problems that need to be addressed for the improvement of the entire community, not only devoting their attention to crime problems. The officers serve as ombudsmen who cut through the bureaucratic red tape of so many government agencies and work with representatives of the public to get the neighborhood cleaned up, the streets and street lights repaired, the trash picked up, and the graffiti cleaned off the walls and fences.

The officers and the children know each other by name, and juvenile delinquency problems tend to become less insurmountable when the police and the kids are not strangers to each other. As a police officer, you must care about your community and what's to be done to make it not only crime-free but also safe, friendly, and productive. Prevent the crimes before they are committed, making it more difficult for the criminals to function when you have a partnership with the residents and businesses in the district and a commitment to develop a better standard of living for everyone.

For many years police and sheriff's departments were made up exclusively of sworn male officers with full police authority. Office and communications duties were performed by uniformed officers, who could be called into the field for full service should the need arise. The prevailing attitude was that only police officers could do police work, no matter what type of work it was. This also assured the administrators that officers could be pulled off the desk or away from the typewriter to pick up a shotgun or a nightstick and go out into the field when necessary. Women were added to do "woman's work," such as searching and guarding female arrestees, dealing with juvenile problems, and doing clerical jobs around the stationhouse, but not what their supervisors considered "real," or confrontational, police work. As time passed, that too passed, and women officers are doing the same tasks as their male counterparts. Office and other nonconfrontational duties are now assigned to nonsworn, or civilian, personnel.

In this chapter we take a look at the basic field unit, which is usually known as the patrol division. What are the objectives of the police or sheriff's department? Whatever they are, so are the objectives for the patrol unit, which is the primary operating unit for the entire organization. We list those objectives and discuss each one briefly; then we describe the many activities that the officers perform to meet each of those objectives. Next, distribution of the patrol force is explained, along with the administrative considerations that influence such distribution.

In the past, administrative evaluation of the field activity reports of patrol officers included a goal of *absence of activities* amounting to the optimum of 50 percent of each officer's duty day. Minutes devoted to arrests, transporting prisoners, answering calls for service, and conducting routine and special investigations were tallied and subtracted from the 550-minute day (8½-hour day, including lunchtime), with the goal of having each officer's log show 200 to 300 minutes *not* accounted for. This was interpreted as *patrol time,* when the officer ostensibly was checking out the neighborhood, looking for crimes in progress—or recently committed—and being visible to the public and ready to take whatever action a situation called for. Of course, this never has been verifiable; perhaps an officer was just simply *doing nothing,* sleeping, reading, or visiting a friend.

With ongoing austerity programs brought on by budget constraints, expensive fuel, skyrocketing criminal activity related to the drug epidemic, rapid urbanization, cutbacks on personnel, and cost-effective analyses, there must be some hard decisions made as to whether "reactive patrol" (driving around the district waiting for something to happen) is still affordable or sensible. The alternative is "proactive patrol," which puts the field units in their districts with prescribed objectives and verifiable tasks scheduled for the day to augment the calls and other on-sight activities that round out the officer's day.

During those times between called-for services when the officer would otherwise be "patrolling," the proactive officer would be making burglary prevention inspections of businesses and residences, going to the residence or workplace of known drug dealers or burglars and "tailing" them for a while to see if they are plying their unlawful trades, making follow-up contacts with victims and witnesses of crimes and traffic collisions previously reported and currently under investigation. We shall come back to proactive patrol from time to time throughout this chapter, and it will pop up elsewhere whenever "routine patrol" comes up.

Additional topics we will cover in this chapter include discretionary prerogatives of the field officer, police ethics, civil liability problems attendant to field police work, and peace officer rights.

OBJECTIVES OF POLICE FIELD OPERATIONS

Protection and Defense of Lives and Property

The slogan "To Protect and Serve," which is attached to the stationery and doors of black and white cars of many agencies throughout the country, is intended to notify the public that we are dedicated to those objectives and that it means more than just words. The protection function is accomplished in a variety of ways that include both reactive and proactive patrol. The reactive aspect is covered by the officers responding to calls for service and investigating complaints of criminal or antisocial behavior. The proactive aspect begins with your investigation of the incident and bringing it to a successful conclusion. Then you will have some problem solving to do, such as determining that the problem arose out of turf warfare among street gangs, for example. Your job just begins when you and your colleagues work with the schools, the community leaders, the business owners, the residents, and the many government agencies to clean up the blight and other conditions that engender gang activity.

Participative Law Enforcement

Attitudes of the people about how effective the police are in protecting them in their homes, on the streets, and wherever they may go in the city or county are extremely important. Opinion polls taken by media such as television or national magazines tend to take on the appearance of contests, listing which city is most dangerous for shopping in the malls—which has the greatest number of thefts from autos. Many people are impressionable and pay heed to what they read in those reports, making decisions about where to move the home office of their major corporation, or their drug laboratory, and where they want to raise their children. Although the surveys may accurately reflect the exact results the reporters wish to report, people may be misled because they not only want security but also want to be told that the security is better than the city from which they are moving. For example, a gate, a high fence, and a security guard at the gate do not necessarily assure absolute safety. Rather, they create an *illusion* of security. Also, you are going to be hard-pressed to convince a family that has just been tied up in their home and robbed by a bunch of thugs that the city they live in is actually safer statistically than any of six other cities in which they might choose to live.

In a letter written to me by Police Chief C. R. Meathrell of Salem, West Virginia, dated April 27, 1992, we get a glimpse of small-town community policing that appears to work:

> Police Field Operations and Police Community Relations are one and the same if you are a police officer in Salem, W. Va.
>
> We are the typical small city police agency. While we do have crime and investigation, it is . . . small in scope. As you doubtless know, West Virginia ranks very low in the crime rate. I am forced to believe that there are some solid reasons for that.

The Chief goes on to say in his letter:

> People have a way of looking after one another. We had a form of the Crime Watch long before it was a national deal. It came of general concern for their neighbors. If your neighbor was gone for vacation, then you watched his place. If someone was seen near the place that did not belong, then you called the police.
>
> As Police Chief of what is now a 3 man department, I have become a clearinghouse for everyone's problems. It doesn't matter if the question is on the law or not, they bring the problem to me. If I don't have an answer, then I find someone who does, or at least send that person in the right direction. . . .

Teamwork between the public and the police is not a luxury; it is mandatory if we are to perform effectively. It is not a new concept. The teamwork concept just seems new to those of us who have forgotten the basics. In the small, intimate community, there is a constant interchange of ideas and vocalization of needs between the police and the people. In our drive to "professionalize," the police service has, in many respects, removed itself from the people you are to serve. Get back to the basics, and make a constant and deliberate effort to know your district and the people in it.

What they have done is to break the large and impersonal police departments into small units, creating a series of small "home-town" police departments that are responsive and responsible to smaller parts of the city as though they were separate cities. The citizens and the police work together to reduce crime, prevent delinquency and criminal behavior, maintain the peace, and reduce local problems that are the *mutual* responsibility of the police and the people.

The field officer's responsibility is to ensure that this one-on-one relationship between themselves and the public yields maximum results. There must be a constant effort to use every available opportunity to allow the people personally to know the officers and their enforcement philosophy, and to become familiar with the overall attitudes of the department toward its general and specific responsibilities. Unfortunately, far too many people have formed attitudes based on their impressions of certain motion picture and television police personalities, or on what they have read in biased newspaper and magazine stories about the police, or on what they may have personally observed in isolated or unrelated incidents on occasions when certain police officers did not exemplify the professional image. There is no better opportunity for the police officer to cultivate attitudes toward the police—positive, it is hoped—than through personal and informal contacts.

Prevention of Criminal and Delinquent Behavior

This police objective is particularly aimed at ways and means of reducing the desire to commit crime. Sometimes you will succeed, but most of the time when you are influential in causing someone to "go straight," or decide not to commit a crime, you will probably never know it and will have no way to measure how much crime you prevent. It is going to be virtually impossible for you to convince the successful burglar who nets thousands of tax-free dollars per month that crime does not pay and that a job in a fast-food restaurant at the minimum wage is the better way to go. Nevertheless, it is worth the effort. One objective must be to cause the burglar's net income to diminish through careful planning and effective law enforcement. Actually, some surveys have revealed that the average thieves and robbers could make a more profitable living by working at slightly higher than minimum wage at the local fast-food restaurant or the corner convenience store. And they would get to wear a uniform, too, instead of jail clothes for a large portion of their lives.

Rehabilitation and redirection of the criminal offender is the responsibility of parole and probation officers after those offenders have been identified and brought to trial by the police. The police responsibility is to identify those offenders, delinquents, and near-delinquents before an arrest becomes necessary. This is more regularly carried out by the field officer in contacts with juveniles whose behavior patterns are not so indelibly impressed and who might be amenable to change. Through keen observation and diligent investigation, the officer attempts to locate and detain the first-offending juvenile either before or during the commission of a criminal act and then take steps to help the child to redirect energies into lawful and socially acceptable channels.

Repression of Criminal and Delinquent Behavior

Repression of crime is generally accomplished either by having police officers present at specific locations maintaining a highly visible profile or by publicizing a highly active undercover operation. In both cases, the objective is to cause people to decide not to commit crimes for fear of being caught in the act. The theory is based upon the assumption that people will not commit crimes if they believe they are certain to be arrested when they do. Uniforms and distinctively marked vehicles immediately and unquestionably identify the police. As a field officer, your repressive activities are accomplished by making your presence known in such a way that, even when you are not at a specific location, the would-be miscreant will refrain from misbehaving because of the likelihood that you will suddenly pop out from nowhere and nab him, or her. We usually refer to this phenomenon as *police omnipresence*.

Actually, the uniformed police comprise only a small percentage of the overall force of individuals responsible for enforcement of public health and safety laws. Fire marshals, building inspectors, occupational safety and health investigators, health officers, fish and game wardens, the Coast Guard, harbor police, agriculture investigators, weights and measures examiners, investigators for the multitude of licensing agencies, and all types of referees and umpires and other investigators are constantly looking into the behavior of the people in the community. Other people responsible for the enforcement of police powers include social welfare investigators, probation and parole officers, prison guards, school principals and attendance officers, college administrators, driver's license examiners, highway patrol and animal control officers, customs inspectors, airport security, border patrol, secret service, the various federal and state investigative units. The list goes on. But it is you, the uniformed field police officer, who represents them all.

For the crime and delinquency repressive objective of the police to be successful, it is imperative that the vast majority of the people comply with the law, be it out of fear of being caught or simply a desire to do what is right. Your role is to help those people continue to obey the law. Crime repression by police patrol is to try to create an impression of total and continuous presence without creating an air of oppressive dominance. In New Amsterdam (now known as New York), the night warden walked down the streets and alleyways shaking a noisy staff that sounded like a rattle, warning any criminals that he was in the area and that they should behave, at least while he was in the neighborhood. This "rattle watch" was less sophisticated than our present methods of using distinctively painted vehicles with light and siren bars extending across the roof and wearing readily recognizable uniforms. A continuous and unpredictable patrol by the field officer is an attempt to create this feeling of omnipresence. This repressive patrol activity may become a luxury that cannot be justified on the basis of cost-effectiveness because of the increasing cost of fuel for the vehicles and the higher salaries of the officers.

One of the most effective activities of the crime repressive role of the police is the field interview program, which consists of making actual field contact with individuals you encounter in your district when their presence causes you to have reasonable suspicion as to their identity and motive for being where they are under the circumstances that call for further inquiry. The program has proven to be highly effective.

Identification and Apprehension of, and Conviction of, Offenders

This objective is addressed by the field officers knowing their districts and the behavior patterns of the people in them. As one of those officers, you will be in a position to readily identify obvious or suspected violations of the laws and to take immediate enforcement action when possible. When you are assigned to investigate a complaint of a crime in your jurisdiction, it is first your responsibility to know what is a crime and what is not. You must initiate the investigation immediately, locate and question victims and witnesses, protect the crime scene against further contamination, and make every effort to locate and apprehend the suspect.

For misdemeanors not committed in your presence, and for other crimes requiring further investigation, it is your responsibility to make the decision *not* to arrest at that time, but to carry through with the investigation as fast and as far as you can before taking the case to the prosecutor for a warrant, or turning it over to your investigation unit in the department for follow-up and completion.

Your responsibility also extends to include exoneration of the wrongfully accused, as well as conviction of the guilty. Your participation in this process does not end until you have presented evidence and testimony in court as required by the prosecution, and have gained the eventual outcome of the case: conviction of the accused when that person is guilty, or freedom of the innocent.

The *due process* provisions of the Constitution of the United States and the respective states have been interpreted by the various courts, and their decisions have served as controlling influences on such police procedures as field interviews, stop and frisk, arrest, search, seizure of evidence, impounding contraband, storing vehicles, interviewing the suspect, use of force, and various other activities. It is your duty to work within the framework of the many laws and guidelines and to assure fair presentation of evidence in court to assure a conviction that will withstand the test of constitutionality.

Traffic Flow and Collision Reduction

Pedestrian and vehicle traffic must be free-flowing and collision-free so that people may move safely from one place to another in your jurisdiction. The police objective is to determine the causes of congestion and to relieve it, which involves investigation and the Three E's: enforcement, engineering, and education. Enforcement is the most highly visible aspect of these three aspects of the police traffic responsibility, and engenders the greatest amount of antipathy from traffic law violators. Intelligent enforcement of traffic law violations, focusing attention on those violations that cause the most number of injuries and property damage and citing according to a set of priorities designed to significantly reduce those violations and corresponding collisions does yield significant results that even the most severe critic cannot dispute.

Engineering at first does not strike one as a police responsibility, but it is. For example: Analysis of the collision statistics show that an inordinate number of unlawful left turns at a certain intersection are listed as the cause of collisions. Officers issue a lot of citations to the violators of those violations at that location, and the collision rate goes down. But did they solve the problem? The reason for the collisions may be that many drivers are frustrated because there is no left-turn lane and traffic is so heavy that they cannot make a left turn without taking a chance and cutting in when they see a break in opposing traffic. What they need is a left-turn lane and a traffic signal with a left-turn green sequence so that the people turning left can do so without having to play "chicken" with opposing traffic. Officers in the field can recognize this problem because they are dealing with it on a daily basis, and they should pass this information on to the city traffic engineer or public works department.

The education aspect of traffic control can significantly reduce collisions by requiring violators to attend classes where their specific types of violations are discussed, and they may go through a retraining process to reduce their citations and lower their insurance rates. During the past few years we have seen a revolution by the outraged public against drivers who operate their vehicles while under the influence of alcohol and other drugs. Education of the driving public is aimed at changing the behavior and attitude of people who use those drugs and have been driving motor vehicles as a matter of routine, but who are now changing their behavior to avoid arrest and tragedies that they might cause.

Maintenance of Order and the Public Peace

This is one of the broadest, most variable, and sometimes most misunderstood of all the police objectives. It is in the "all other" category, because this category includes not only those activities that have been legally delegated to the police but also those that have been traditionally assigned, and sometimes those that your department may have assumed simply because there was no one else to do them. A free society such as ours is characterized by its relatively small number of controls when compared with other forms of governed society. Yet to permit the majority of the people in the country to enjoy their own pursuit patterns for comfort and happiness, certain controls are necessary. One person's freedom to listen to loud music must be restricted when the sounds interfere with another person's freedom to enjoy the absence of sound. To balance the two, the police must maintain a constant and vigilant patrol, frequently making direct contact with a number of people to demonstrate their presence in a peacekeeping role and responding to called-for services to referee disagreements in family and neighborhood situations that would erupt into full-scale combat situations without their presence.

You will be required to attend places where large numbers of people congregate, such as meeting halls, stadiums, theaters, and places of political rallies and demonstrations to maintain order and prevent violations of the laws. At the same time, you will be required to enforce the people's rights to assemble peaceably and express their opinions and beliefs. Most people are peaceable. You will be called upon to deal with the unusual situation, such as the boisterous party, loud radio or television, or the public gathering that grew into a riot.

The "order maintenance" process includes many other responsibilities, such as directing traffic at fires or collision scenes, controlling crowds and preventing panic at disaster scenes, and providing a stabilizing influence in times of emotional upset. Most breaches of the peace are settled merely by firmly suggesting that the violators desist and comply with the law. In those cases when the violators do not comply, you must take immediate and decisive action, which may lead to arresting and prosecuting the violators.

Crisis Planning. As a professional public safety officer you must plan for the unexpected event that is likely to happen in your jurisdiction. The earthquakes, fires, riots, floods, hurricanes, tornadoes, oil spills off the coast, airplane and train crashes, and hundred-car pileups on the expressways may be more of a probability where you live and work; but the West Coast is not the only place that has earthquakes, South Carolina has no monopoly on hurricanes, nor does the Mississippi Valley have the only floods. One or the other is more likely in your "neck of the woods," but you should plan on all other types of man-made and natural disasters, no matter how remote their possibility. Your agency should have evacuation and disaster plans, special preparations for all anticipated and unanticipated crisis situations so that there will be less panic and pandemonium when such an event does occur.

Problem Solving. You and your colleagues in the department should frequently meet and discuss not only the problems of law enforcement but also all the problems in your jurisdiction that affect the quality of life of the entire population. Housing projects where there are crack houses and meth labs very directly affect law-abiding families and children, and must be shut down. A park where gangs rule and keep out other children of the neighborhood must be kept open and safe for the entire community through the cooperative efforts of the police, probation and parole agencies, recreation leaders, teachers, neighbors, local business operators, and virtually everyone.

Abandoned buildings make excellent gathering places for criminals, gangs, and other unwanted activities. Owners must be contacted and required to fence off properties and board up or otherwise secure the buildings, or have them destroyed. Overcrowded residences are those such as single-family apartments designed for no more than six residents that have sixteen or more people living in almost every apartment in the complex. Zoning enforcement officials and property owners need to cooperate in reducing the population in those buildings. Accumulated trash must be removed from the alleys and sidewalks, and you must see to it that the trash is removed. Just simply making a report and forgetting about a problem does not solve it. As a field officer it is your responsibility to take a personal part in solving all these problems.

ACTIVITIES OF THE PATROL DIVISION

Routine Patrol and Observation

Basic patrolling activities are usually referred to as "routine," although even the most mundane of your tasks should never be taken so lightly as to be considered routine. As a matter of fact, it should be your "routine" not to patrol your district the same way twice. Once you establish any sort of pattern or schedule for your patrolling duties, your effectiveness in repressing any sort of criminal or delinquent behavior is virtually eliminated. Many intelligent and wealthy criminals have attributed their phenomenal successes to their ability to work around the time schedules of the field officers. They learn the shift hours, district assignments, and number of officers on patrol at any given time, and then they analyze the patrol methods employed by the officers working the districts where they intend to commit their crimes. Look at your own patterns. Do you always drive the same route in the same sequence when you leave headquarters? Do you spend the first hour making a one-time sweep of the district and then devote specific times to the same activities day after day?

When you do not have a fixed pattern for patrolling your district, the criminals must take greater risks when attempting to commit crimes while you are on duty. The routine of patrol, therefore, should be one of *routine avoidance.*

Preventive Attendance at Public Gatherings

Wherever people gather in sizable numbers, the police should be visibly present. This presence should alert anyone inclined to break the law that there would be a greater probability of arrest. This presence will also assure a peaceful assembly and provide protection for those who wish to exercise their rights to peaceful assembly and free speech. There should be no indication that you intend to control or dominate the people who are in attendance. Your purpose is to prevent—if you can—any unlawful activity by individuals or by the crowd as a whole. Riot *prevention* is much better than riot *control*. Once a riot begins everyone loses. Freedom of assembly is a basic freedom assured by the First Amendment to the Constitution. Your prime duty when arriving at the scene of an assembly is to determine that it is lawful. Your responsibility is then to remain present to assure everyone that you are going to ensure that the assembly continues to be peaceful. Although it is true that you must remain on location where there is a continuing need for police presence, such as an organized demonstration attended by opposing interest groups, congregations of opposing street gangs, open-air concerts, a county or state fair, or any event where violence or other criminal activity is anticipated, it is good police practice to leave once you determine that your energies could be better spent elsewhere.

There are times and places where anything more than a casual police presence and departure could be misinterpreted as oppressive. Consider the polling place on election day. Officers standing around for the purpose of keeping the peace could be perceived as government intervention into the free-election process, not unlike elections in a native country from which our new voters escaped to become citizens of this country where they may vote as they choose.

Benevolent and Community Services

Because the police are always available and on duty, they are often called upon to perform many services that do not appear on any list of job specifications for police officers, but they perform them nevertheless. Although not required by any law or ordinance, many of these tasks have become traditional simply by the officers' own willingness to do them as a service to the people who ask for them, or they may have become a social custom in a particular community. You will be called upon to perform midwife duties at childbirth or to render first aid to collision or disaster victims, even though those activities are generally the responsibility of paramedics and other medical service personnel who are far better trained and qualified to perform the task. There will be times when you must arrange for emergency shelter and subsistence for the homeless and destitute, getting them in touch with welfare and social service people who provide them the means and services they so desperately need. Sometimes officers have been known to dip into their own pockets to help less fortunate people on their beat.

You will be called upon to referee neighborhood or family quarrels when they have probably reached the violent stage, and people there will look to you for spiritual or psychological counseling, which you must avoid doing because you are not licensed to do so. Nevertheless, you still have to defuse the situation to avoid later having to take someone to the hospital or to jail. You will deliver death messages when the appropriate spiritual counselors cannot be located. There are times when you will be called upon to help people get into their homes or autos when a locksmith is not available. Be careful when playing Good Samaritan. I know of a time when a beat officer helped a citizen push his car to get it started, then found out later that he had actually helped a thief steal that car, not knowing he was doing so.

A dilemma is created and perpetuated by the traditional acceptance of various duties that should not be provided by the police. There seems to be no other agency that is geared to cope with the unusual and unexpected. One of the more blatant misuses of police personnel and equipment is the ego-boosting practice of providing chauffeur service for visiting dignitaries and local officials. If the transportation is for the purpose of providing protection, then it is a police responsibility. Usually, however, it is transportation that should be provided by a local taxi service. Even a limousine would be more economical than would taking the officer and the police unit out of service for that period of time. In the absence of a realistic evaluation as to what constitutes police work, you will probably continue to perform these services as though they were required of you.

Business and Property Security

Security of personal and business property is the responsibility of the people who have legal custody of that property. It is also your responsibility to protect that property. Therefore, it becomes a joint responsibility of both owner and the police. Since this is a partnership, you should take it upon yourself to advise your so-called "partners" on how they might make their property as secure and crime resistant as possible. It is not unusual for property owners to install elaborate alarm systems and expensive locks to protect against intrusion through flimsy doors and windows, and their walls are so thin that they may be penetrated by a mere kick and a well-placed foot. Sometimes, in the interest of "economy," property owners will shortchange themselves in the area of security. Another serious problem is that even after installing elaborate protective devices and alarm systems, one of the occupants will leave for the weekend without activating the system or will leave doors and windows open and unlocked.

As a field officer, your responsibility is to check out thoroughly the security of residential or commercial buildings and properties as best you can within the constraints of time and your other responsibilities. If it were possible to educate successfully all these would-be victims of the need for security, you would make your job much easier. Frequent and unscheduled visits to the property for security checks will further reduce the likelihood of criminal activity at those locations.

Inspection Services

Inspections for security against theft are obvious responsibilities of the patrol force. But there are additional types of inspections that you perform. One of the more important is to look for fires and fire hazards at the same time you check for security against crimes. It is not feasible for local government to provide another patrol force that would duplicate the police patrol and that would travel the same routes as the patrol units. Since the officer is already on the streets, it is most efficient to extend the inspection responsibilities of the police and then require the officers to report the law violations or unsafe conditions to the appropriate agencies.

Included in the various types of inspections the field officer performs are utility outages, streets and sidewalks in need of repair, building code violations, health and safety violations, unsanitary conditions in restaurants and grocery stores and butcher shops, obscured traffic signs and signals, professional and business license violations, and leash law violations. Your initial action might include issuing citations or making arrests for criminal violations and/or submitting a comprehensive report to be forwarded to the responsible agency for further investigation and follow-up to correct the problem.

In this area of inspection services your role will be expanded considerably. You will be expected to concern yourself about every facet of life in your district. Your interests go beyond the traditional police scope, because your responsibility includes doing your share of improving and maintaining the quality of life in your community. If you see a problem, do what you can to solve it, whatever it is, and call upon other people and agencies to do their share. Did you ever notice how much better children behave when they are wearing their nice clean clothes than they do when they are dirty and "grubby"? Well, the same principle applies to your district. Keep it clean and safe, and take care of the little problems before they get too big to handle.

Responding to Calls for Service

The great majority of calls for police service do not involve matters that lead to an on-the-spot arrest or any other action beyond what the officer handles at the scene. Neighborhood children damage fences or border plants along property lines, or the children get involved in a fight that eventually leads to a squabble between their parents; then the police officer arrives and everyone agrees to shake hands and make up. A husband and wife begin to fight over finances, which leads to a bitter debate about each other's in-laws and an airing of previous arguments that had never been settled; the police arrive, and all grievances are postponed until the next argument. The ritual is quite common in many families, and the postponement is sometimes the best the officer can hope for. Sometimes you will be called upon to scold a neighbor child for some sort of real or imagined misconduct. There are other times when you may convince the combatants that fighting is no way to settle an argument. On several occasions in neighborhood and family disputes, a relative or neighbor will demand that the police officer "beat up the husband and teach him a lesson." Eventually, nothing will surprise you when it comes to the variety of demands as to what action you are expected to take, many of which will be inappropriate. In these civil disputes, your presence is legal principally because you have been invited or because the disturbance is in public and your primary responsibility is to preserve the peace and ascertain whether anyone has broken the law. Most of the time, your action will consist of reminding the participants that their problem is a civil one and that they will have to seek a solution to their problem through one of the many services that you will refer them to, and of advising them to settle their differences amicably so that you may return to your other duties.

The task of responding to calls for service may be regarded as a matter of disposing of *minor complaints,* although none of them is minor to the participants. The problems confronting these people are obviously beyond their capacity to cope with by the time they call for police intervention. It takes a tremendous amount of tact and diplomacy to handle these so-called "minor" problems. The child who fails to respond to a parent's discipline in a demonstration of contempt for an authority figure may be a family problem today but a police problem tomorrow unless some solution can be worked out today. The unethical, though legal, business transaction in which the unsuspecting consumer buys a $5 burglar alarm for $400 may not in itself be a violation of any criminal code, but if the consumer's complaint is reported correctly and there are sufficient other such complaints, an investigation may ensue that will reveal false representation and fraud.

Many matters involving repossession and property rights, landlord–tenant arguments, employer and employee relations, arguments about property lines, poorly constructed dikes and levees resulting in floods, late garbage collections, and a multitude of "gripes" about various government services will be laid in your lap. Although you have little or no authority over any of the principles in these matters, you will be expected to solve the problems, whatever they are. You must deal with them intelligently and with diplomatic persuasion.

People commit suicide. The police are called. A woman is having a baby. The police are called. An elderly bedridden person falls out of bed and needs help getting back into the bed. The police are called. An explosion destroys the three lower floors of a hotel. The police are called. A sonic boom causes windows to rattle as though a burglar were trying to get in. The police are called. A distraught student who has just received a report card with three F's climbs up on top of a clock tower and threatens to jump unless the professors reconsider. The police are called. You respond to each of these calls. You take appropriate action, whatever it is, prepare the ubiquitous report, and then resume patrol.

Animal Control

There is probably a separate agency in your jurisdiction that handles problems of lost, stray, abandoned, or injured animals. It is either a government-supported agency or a privately funded organization, such as the Society for the Prevention of Cruelty to Animals. The police department will be called in to investigate and enforce violations of animal abuse. Because of the constant availability of a police patrol unit, it will not be unusual for you to have to round up an occasional dog or cat or panther that strayed away from its home. As if you did not have enough problems with domestic pets, there are those people whose ideas of pets are somewhat diverse (or perverse) and who insist on keeping exotic—often dangerous—pets on their premises which are either unlawful to keep, or at least unwanted by the neighbors. You may have to take some action based on your own judgment before you are able to consult wildlife specialists on the best way to handle the critters. You will also be called upon to provide for the treatment of injured animals and disposal of those less fortunate ones that are killed in traffic or by back-yard hunters.

Traffic Direction and Control

The police field unit may have both patrol and traffic responsibilities, but even when there is a separate traffic unit, your responsibility as a field officer is to assure safe and efficient movement of vehicular and pedestrian traffic in your district (see Figures 1–1 and 1–2). Traffic control and collision prevention require constant vigilance. In addition to responding to collisions and protecting the scene from further damage and injury, you will frequently be called upon to provide traffic control services at scenes of fires, large crowds and gatherings at public events, rush-hour traffic in school and business zones, and traffic tieups caused by inclement weather or unusual road conditions. Whatever the problem, you will be expected to take the initiative to address the problem the best way that you can and to call for whatever assistance is necessary to protect the scene and restore it to normal.

Information Services

You—the field officer—and your department are expected to be the wellspring of information about everything in your jurisdiction: where everything is and whatever is happening, and where it is happening. You should know the street-numbering plan for your city: even numbers on the north and east sides of the streets and houses numbered in multiples of 10, so that you will know that 1940 is the fourth house from the south cross-street on the east side of the street. This will obviate the need for you to search for the house at night when responding to a "burglary in progress" call and

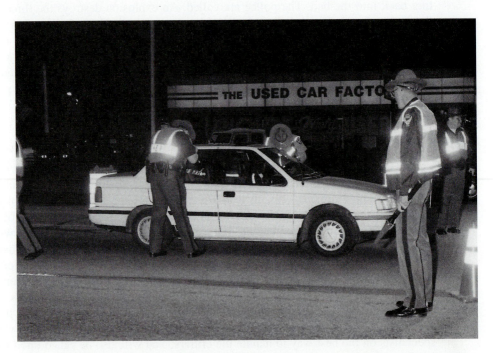

Figure 1–1 Traffic control often involves setting up roadblocks to check for unsafe drivers and vehicles. (Courtesy Ohio State Highway Patrol.)

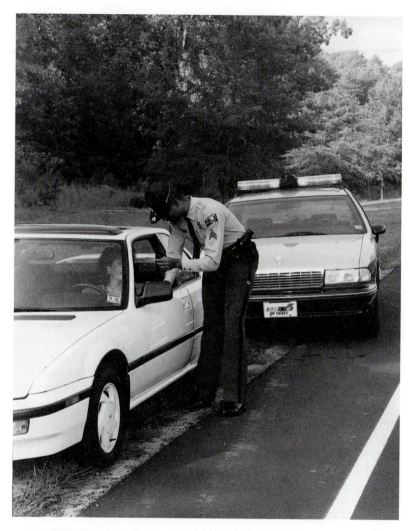

Figure 1–2   (Courtesy North Carolina State Highway Patrol.)

you will probably be able to describe the house to an inquirer about the location of 953 West Pine Street.

It should be in your personal encyclopedia where the all-night service stations are located, which pharmacies stay open late and provide emergency all-night services to the ill, and the locations of the variety of ethnic restaurants in the area. If someone asks you where one may get the best lobster dinner for the money, or the best steak or fajitas, be prepared to recommend more than one lest you should be accused by competitors of playing favorites. Of course, if there is only one Chinese restaurant within 10 miles of your town, that's the one you're going to name. People will ask about the old-fashioned ice-cream shop, rare book store, sheet music store, bicycle repair shop, a "respectable" tavern where one may take an out-of-town guest, or a place to have film developed while they wait. You should be prepared to give directions and at least know where to look to help these people. As the most visible representative of your local government, you should be prepared to answer such questions as what is the population? the altitude? the average year-round temperature? What are the names of local politicians and famous residents? You are the weather bureau, the chamber of commerce, but hopefully not the local gossip. You will be expected by your department to be the community's goodwill ambassador.

You should also be the best source of information for your fellow officers and other emergency services as to the location of road closures and other hazards, street parties, hotly disputed athletic events, and other occasions where it appears there will be trouble later if you let it get out of hand during the evening.

Developing Contacts

This is a departmentwide activity. Actually, if a community–police partnership is to succeed, there should be open and free-flowing lines of communication between the police and all segments of the community. The department should zealously guard against showing any favoritism for any particular segment of the community, either in actuality or in the eyes of others. That would only lead to more bitterness and rivalry within the community. You should not be satisfied with just doing a good job. If there are effective lines of communication open to all segments of the community, it will make your job so much easier. People outside the department must know enough about the police responsibilities and methods of operation that they may observe and judge for themselves whether their police officers are doing the excellent job they say they are. Then you will have the enthusiastic support that you need to be a successful field officer. Such openness will tend to squelch unfounded rumors, reduce friction, and enhance support.

As a field officer, you are responsible for the development of informants. We are not talking about the character who talks out of the side of his mouth and looks over his shoulder while giving you the information you are seeking in return for a "fiver." Of course, that character will probably be among your reservoir of informants. But we are talking about certain "fringe" businesspersons—those who are operating just inside or outside the law but who seem to conceal their criminal behavior successfully—who will give you information that will be intended to put their competitors out of business. There are the violators you catch but cannot prosecute because of some technical difficulty with constitutional exclusion of evidence, but who will willingly provide you with information concerning narcotics traffic or stolen property operations either to get themselves off the hook or to divert attention away from themselves.

When developing leads from informants whose own prosecution was hampered because of contaminated evidence, keep in mind that any evidence emanating from these sources may likewise be inadmissible. The "fruit of the poisoned tree" doctrine is often referred to by the courts when excluding evidence gained as a result of unconstitutionally gained information, such as a confession that officers obtained without advisement of the Miranda rights. The court usually views the evidence as "tainted," and thereby inadmissible, similar to the theory that one rotten apple in a barrel will cause other apples in the same barrel to become rotten. Although vice and narcotics detectives are credited with their success in relationship to the volume and quality of their informants, officers in all divisions develop informants, including the newest rookie in the department. When developing these informant relationships, be careful to keep them at arm's length if they are involved in the criminal world, and avoid compromise. To understand how dogs behave, you do not have to sleep with them and share their fleas.

Sometimes you will actually encounter the patriotic person who will provide you with information because "it is the right thing to do." There are others who have served their time for previous violations but as a part of their rehabilitation believe that they must inform on other criminals. You should seek out people from a wide variety of occupations and professions and cultivate them as sources of information.

Jewelers are the best source of information as to actual value of diamonds and other precious stones. They also hear through their own channels which jewelers are honest and which ones will buy stolen merchandise, and they can recognize each other's work in cutting and setting stones and repairing jewelry. People in the construction industry are the best source of information concerning individuals and companies involved in legitimate and illegitimate dealings in the construction industry. Doctors know about other doctors, pharmacists know about other pharmacists, cooks know other cooks, and so on. Everyone who sincerely believes that honesty and ethical practice are the only way to conduct one's business may voluntarily assist you in your investigations of other people in their respective fields who are making "a bad name" for the legitimate practitioners.

Establishing rapport with citizen participants (or informants) in law enforcement should yield mutual benefits to the police department and the participants. Gratuities should not be involved in any of these information-seeking relationships. There are exceptions, of course, as when certain information is rewarded according to established procedures or when a cash reward has been advertised. You may repay the debt in other ways, such as suggesting ways in which the informant may burglarproof his office. Your irregular and unannounced visits to shops may discourage would-be shoplifters and robbers. Using taxicab and truck drivers and their own commercial or citizens band radio networks as an extension of the police radio network may cause a more satisfactory working relationship, and you may, in turn, make a little extra effort in educating them on how to avoid committing so many traffic violations. When dealing with informants, consider their motivations.

Develop a resource file of all public and private services in and around your jurisdiction where you can go to solve the problems of spousal and child abuse, abandoned vehicles, zoning violations, money laundering, truancy problems, and on ad infinitum. You not only should have a file and know who and where they are but also should make it a point to get acquainted with all of these people and their services. Health and building departments, the fire marshall, all the local, state, and federal agencies, and the services they provide should be at your finger tips.

Preliminary Investigations

Field patrol officers are constantly available and on the street, ready to take immediate action, and such action involves performing preliminary investigations of traffic collisions and criminal law violations. Providing that the field officers are adequately trained and that there are sufficient officers to perform the work, the patrol division is actually in the better position to handle these initial investigations. There are certain exceptions, such as continuing investigations and those that involve undercover work over a period of time in matters involving narcotics or vice or intelligence gathering. That does not mean that uniformed field officers are not involved in those types of activities. Quite the contrary. In many departments, the majority of arrests for narcotics and vice activities are made by the patrol officers.

As the first officer on the scene, you must look after the safety of the victim and witnesses, and you will apprehend the suspect if one is at the scene. You will be required to take immediate steps to protect the scene from any further contamination and then immediately establish communication with headquarters to broadcast information about wanted suspects and vehicles, and request whatever additional assistance that you need.

As the first person on the scene, no one is better prepared than you to take immediate action. While the scene is still fresh and victims and witnesses still caught up in the spontaneity of the situation, your job is to observe carefully all evidence before anyone has had a chance to contaminate it—to reflect or to change their stories or to fabricate alibis. You will probably be assigned to continue with the investigation until all leads are exhausted and any further investigation would take you out of your district for too long a period of time. You will question the victim, the witnesses, and any suspects that you may encounter. You will collect the evidence and catalog and file it; then you will prepare the reports. At some point, the follow-up work on the investigation may be continued by an investigator and other specialists. At other times, you will handle the entire case on your own with no follow-up being necessary. The key to the success of any follow-up investigation is usually attributable to your skill as the one who handles the initial investigation.

In many agencies, initial response and investigation of traffic collisions is the responsibility of the field patrol unit, with the follow-up handled by traffic specialists from a traffic division. Some departments have merged traffic and patrol into a single uniformed field unit. Regardless of the category in which your department belongs, you as the first field officer at the scene will be the first to protect the scene from further collisions, check for injuries and administer first aid, locate and identify drivers and witnesses, and handle the initial phases of the investigation. You are probably the most logical person to perform the initial investigation for the same reason that you would perform the initial criminal investigation. You are in a position to observe the scene before it has been contaminated, see the vehicles before they have been moved, observe short-lived evidence that might be destroyed before the arrival of other police units, and talk with the participants while the incident is fresh in their minds, free of fabrication or exaggeration.

Somewhere along the way in the traffic investigation, as with the criminal investigation, you will have to complete your records and get back to your district, and a follow-up investigator will continue and "wrap up" the case. The *primary* consideration as to just how far you investigate and how long you continue before turning over the investigation to others is *time*. You have other responsibilities and must move on to provide the entire spectrum of services to the people in your district.

As a field patrol officer, you will also conduct investigations into alleged unethical or unlawful business transactions, suspicious persons such as door-to-door canvassers and salespersons (not all these street people are criminals, but daylight residence burglaries go up when there are more of them around, particularly those who move from city to city), and other persons whose presence calls for some sort of explanation. Additionally, you will investigate vagrants, loiterers, streetwalkers, and suspected vice operants. You will conduct field interviews with people whose presence in a particular place and under certain circumstances cause you to have a reasonable belief that they should be checked out. You will investigate vehicles that appear to be abandoned and conduct literally thousands of other investigations into matters that pose real or imagined threats to the health, welfare, and safety of the people and property in your district.

Collection and Preservation of Evidence

Inherent in the investigation process is the proper handling of evidence for the purpose of assuring a fair trial of the accused. From the moment you arrive on the scene until you complete your testimony and presentation of evidence in court, you will be directly involved in this process. You must be careful to avoid contaminating any more evidence than is necessary. Your responsibility is to assess carefully the situation when you arrive and then methodically collect and prepare the evidence for transportation and storage and laboratory analysis. After storing the evidence, or forwarding it to the laboratory, you will be required to prepare the necessary reports. When the time comes for the court appearance and presentation of the evidence, you will usually be the same person to withdraw the evidence from storage and account for its continuity of custody. This should be standard department procedure.

For many of the investigations you conduct, you will be required to prepare sketches and diagrams, using them for more effective coordination of the information you put in your reports and for orientation purposes. You may be one of those officers who will be specially trained in the collection and preservation of evidence and carry the added responsibility of being assigned as a crime scene investigator (CSI). Whenever the need arises, these specialists are taken out of their regular field patrol assignment and are dispatched to the scenes of crimes and collisions to collect evidence, dust for latent fingerprints, take photographs, and generally provide a little more expertise to assist in the initial investigation.

Some departments have selected and trained permanent nonsworn men and women to perform CSI as Police Service Officers, or Community Service Officers. Many have found that people who aspire to make a career of this job with no visions of advancement into—and out of—this assignment as a career step do an excellent job, although they are not classified as police officers.

Arrest of Offenders

Second only to caring for the injured or wounded, the field officer's primary responsibility at the scene of a crime is to locate and arrest the offender. Once you effect the arrest, you may use one of several alternative methods to introduce the arrestee into the criminal justice system. The alternative methods are described by the laws, the courts, and the procedural manuals prepared by your department.

In virtually every felony case, you will take the arrestee to jail, where the "booking," or processing, begins. Except when provided for by law, every arrestee is entitled to post bail, which is a guarantee assuring his or her later court appearance after release. In some situations, the arrestee may be taken directly before a magistrate in lieu of booking and bail, although such procedure is not routine. In misdemeanor arrests, the violators are booked into jail, or they are issued a citation and are allowed to sign a promise to appear in court on or before a specified date. The citation method has been used extensively in traffic cases for many years, and in some states more recently, it has been extended to cover most misdemeanor violations when immediate release poses no threat to life or property.

Roll call training sessions and various publications constantly disseminate information about current crimes and wanted criminal offenders. It is your responsibility to search diligently for those wanted persons and to seek information as to their whereabouts and get them into court to answer the charges against them. In many cases of minor violations, you will issue written and oral warnings rather than make arrests and issue citations. Most of those cases will relate to traffic violations.

Traffic laws—as with criminal laws—are separated into felonies, misdemeanors, and (in some states) infractions. The felonies and misdemeanors we have already discussed. The infraction usually carries no punishment other than a fine. The recipient is sometimes required to correct an equipment failure, such as replacing a tail light. When the individual fails to correct the equipment violation and/or appear in court to show that the situation has been resolved, the infraction becomes a misdemeanor violation for failure to comply.

Preparation of Reports

Nearly everything you do while assigned as a field patrol officer will be committed to some sort of a written or printed report. It may consist of merely checking a box or two or recording the names and addresses of the principals involved and adding a cryptic phrase such as "miscellaneous service." However, you will also be required to prepare a detailed report on precisely who was involved in an incident, what were the circumstances, and when and where did the crime or incident occur, and to provide sufficient information so that the reader will know exactly what took place and what further action, if any, is warranted. Preparation of reports is one of the most time-consuming of all police activities and one of the most demanding. The reports that you will prepare are used as the basis for determining whether to charge an individual with a crime and, if so, what specific charge will be made. In many cases, the reports that you prepare will be the only source your supervisors have to determine your decision-making ability and to evaluate your performance. Your reports must be complete and accurate, since they are usually the only written record of what transpires.

The importance of accuracy, honesty, and efficiency in reporting cannot be overemphasized. In addition to the prosecuting attorney, the defendant and defense attorney have a right to review the reports under the rules of *discovery*. Judges and juries—if the report is placed into evidence—all read the reports. Not only do they evaluate accuracy, but they will not resist the temptation to assess the intelligence of the writer of the report. A poor report will be interpreted as a poor job.

Although this may appear at the end of the list of things to do in a criminal or traffic investigation, it will seem to be just the beginning in a very complicated case. Once you receive the subpoena to appear in court, you must go back and retrieve all the reports in the file as well as all of your personal notes. Conferences with the prosecutor are extremely important. Be absolutely candid and honest with the prosecutor. Consider the untenable position the prosecutors were in when it came to Detective Fuhrman in the Simpson case. Fuhrman had previously spent many hours with a would-be screenwriter laying out scenarios of police abuse and other unethical behavior. Perhaps this was just for the purpose of building a fictional character and a fictional police department where violation of the rules ran rampant. When it finally came out in court, however, largely because of the diligent work of the defense investigators, the many hours of taped conversations between Fuhrman and the writer caught the prosecutors completely off guard. Fuhrman testified under scathing examination by attorney F. Lee Bailey about whether he had ever used the "N word," to which he emphatically replied that he had not. When the tapes were played, the entire world heard the detective use the word many times. That lack of communication between the officer and the prosecutors was probably one of the deciding factors in the jury returning a verdict of "not guilty," and Mr. Simpson is free. Tell the truth even if it hurts.

Not only must the truth be presented in court by the prosecutor, but the strategy of how and in what manner it is delivered may determine the outcome of the case. You are the primary source of information about a case if you were the first on the scene, and you should work very closely with the prosecutor until the case has been concluded. Then do not relax because there may be appeals and follow-up actions, which may include civil cases arising from the criminal case. Remember that you are not an advocate; that is the role of the attorneys. Your role is that of a dispassionate, objective witness who is merely presenting the facts honestly. However the case turns out is up to the judge and/or the jury.

PRIVATE POLICE ACTIVITIES

Although this text is primarily directed toward field procedures for the public police agency, it would be negligent to overlook the valuable services provided by private patrol and investigative agencies. Because of the limitations on time and resources available to city and county police agencies, many private companies and individuals have security needs that exceed those provided by the services of the government's police. They employ private police agencies to provide those services, which include the following:

Perimeter and Access Control

To protect the premises against intrusion of thieves or spies (of the international or local variety) and to slow down the incidence of theft, guards are posted at various places of ingress and egress and around the perimeter of the property involved. This is accomplished by continuous patrol or spot inspection or with the aid of electronic surveillance equipment, such as remote video cameras operated from a central control room. Only authorized persons with specific clearances are allowed access to those locations where patent secrets or secret government information is located. This may actually be required by a government-contracted manufacturer.

Asset Protection and "Inventory Shrinkage". Theft from the business establishment goes out both the front door and the back. Dishonest "shoppers" are matched in skill and ingenuity by dishonest employees. Spotting and surveilling shoplifters require special training and skills, and the successful store detective learns that one must think the way a thief does in order to catch a thief. One-way mirrors and connecting "catwalks" above the ceiling provide observation platforms from where the investigator may watch and photograph suspected activities by shoplifters and dishonest employees. Strategically placed videocameras are also utilized for observation of several locations simultaneously by a single operator, who can radio to a fellow investigator on the floor where to go and what (and whom) to look for.

Catching the employee who steals includes many of the same surveillance techniques, plus the use of undercover operatives who fit in as fellow workers, utilization of informants, and professional "shoppers" who act as spotters to look for discrepancies in sales procedures. Use of the polygraph has lost favor during recent years, but it is still an effective tool.

Security and Safety Consulting

Occupational Safety and Health (OSHA) regulations and general employee safety and health, as well as building and personnel security, just make good sense. Many private security and detective agencies do consulting in these areas.

Background Preemployment Screening

Many private companies employ specialists who conduct extensive investigations into the past lives of their potential and current employees for bonding, entrusted positions with trade and company secrets, and preventive maintenance.

Personal/Executive/Celebrity Protection

The bodyguard business utilizes men and women who have had extensive training and demonstrated skills in weaponless defense, as well as some specialists with weapons, and many agencies have combined forces with limousine services, providing both the means of transportation and the personnel. (See Figure 1–3.) Escort vehicles are utilized when there is an enhanced anticipation of a kidnap or assault attempt. Sometimes evasive maneuvers are necessary, which may give the protected person the feeling of being transported via a Magic Mountain ride. This has become almost routine of late, because a ransom for a kidnapped superstar of sports or television or some corporations would finance a small war, and terrorist acts are not uncommon.

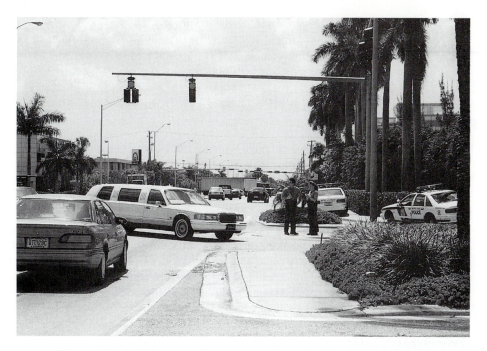

Figure 1–3 Celebrity protection is the responsibility of both public and private agencies. (Photo by Lynn Scrimshaw; Courtesy Metro Dade Police Department.)

Location and Recovery of Stolen Children

Children who are the victims of kidnapping receive the full attention of all segments of the police system: federal, state, and local. The probability of a homicide following the kidnap is great. Although private investigation agencies may be hired by the victim's family in kidnap cases, they are utilized more extensively in child-stealing cases, where the noncustodial mothers or fathers violate court orders and take the child to lavish their own form of love and care, with less likelihood that they will harm the children. In these cases, the matter is both civil and criminal, sometimes involving conflicting laws among nations. The role of the private investigator in these types of cases is to locate the child, then do whatever possible to protect the child and parent by having court papers verifying legal custody, and to manage the retrieval of the child. Investigators without government affiliations are sometimes more effective than the local police because there are fewer restrictions on their professional behavior and their financial resources are restricted only by the parent's ability to pay the tariff.

Disturbance Prevention and Crowd Control

At large athletic or entertainment functions, the promoters of the event and the property owners are concerned with keeping the peace as well as protecting their investment in property and equipment. Security is principally provided by the promoters within the perimeter of the event and by the local police outside the perimeter. Labor–management disputes usually involve heavy reliance on private police agencies. Shopping centers and colleges are equally concerned with protection of people and property and will augment local police protection with their own police forces.

Special-Purpose Police

There is yet another type of police agency that is neither public nor private, or is both. Special quasi-governments such as park districts or housing authorities are created. To protect their property interests and the people who live in, or traverse over, their properties, special police forces are created. Depending on the conditions, these agencies are public or private.

Private agencies would be employed by large residential communities operated by a corporation or association of owners, an industrial park, or large private recreational parks such as Disneyland and Disney World. Government agencies in this category would include public college districts or universities and state colleges, which have their own government-sanctioned police officers with authority restricted to students, properties, and personnel of such institutions.

DISTRIBUTION OF THE PATROL FORCE

No one knows exactly how many crimes are actually committed every year, but it is generally agreed that considerably more are committed than are reported. How many crimes the patrol force will prevent, if any, is another figure that we can only speculate about. Of the crimes that are reported each year, the numbers that are cleared by arrest are much lower than we care to acknowledge. It is apparent that whatever the patrol forces are doing is not enough to show a statistical improvement. The police department is charged with prevention, repression, and solution of crimes within the framework of limitations of funds, human resources, and equipment.

Selectivity of assignment and referral to other agencies seem to be the only realistic approach to the problem of distributing the patrol force so that it may do the most good. Even if two police officers were placed on every one-block square area of the jurisdiction, it would not assure any better patrol results than we are getting at the present time. As a part of participatory management of the police department, in which the citizen representatives take part in making critical decisions as to which calls for service will be designated greater priorities, there must not only be some agreement on priorities but, eventually, a recognition that some of the traditional police services will be given lower priorities or no priority at all.

Policy Decisions Concerning Distribution

When developing a priority sequence on field assignments, certain questions must be answered. For example,

1. Which calls for service will be handled completely by telephone, and which ones will require an officer to be sent to the caller's address? The guiding factor in answering this question is: What can or should the officer do following arrival? Is a suspect still at the scene, or is there evidence available that might lead to conviction for a criminal law violation?

2. Which calls will be "counseled out" by advising the calling party that the matter can better be handled by another agency? Many types of calls fit into this category. A referral directory could be used with the complaint operator providing the appropriate telephone numbers or dialing and diverting the call directly.

3. To what extent will the patrol officers become involved in neighborhood quarrels and family disputes; advise children regarding their school attendance and other behavior patterns; give advice on interpersonal relationships; and undertake peacekeeping functions? While some of these situations call for some sort of police intervention, many could probably be handled better by psychological counselors.

4. What portion of the crime investigations will be handled by patrol officers, and at what point will cases be turned over to the specialists? One factor to consider is that there is often a natural inclination for the specialist to start at the beginning and reinvestigate, which is a flagrant waste of time and resources.

5. What is the patrol officer's role in traffic accident investigation and traffic law enforcement? Will the officers be solely responsible, or will there be supplementary assistance and coordination by traffic specialists? There is also the option of utilizing civilian specialists in taking reports, thereby costing less and freeing police officers for other assignments. Many reports can be taken at the police building.

6. To what extent will the officers be responsible for building security in their districts that will necessitate their being away from their patrol units for extended periods of time? Perhaps the police have spoiled the property owners by doing some of their security checking for them. Flourishing private patrol operators usually sell this service on the grounds that the local police either cannot or will not perform well in this area.

7. How much of the public relations function of the department will directly involve the patrol officers? Will they be required to eat lunch and play basketball with the children? Will the field officer be assigned to crime prevention activities, such as inspecting buildings for burglary security, or will that be done by civilian specialists and volunteers? There must be a limit. The question is: Where is that limit?

8. What will be the reporting responsibilities of the field officers? How detailed must their reports be? Where will they go to make the reports—to headquarters? to a telephone? Or will they carry portable dictating units? What forms will be used—fill-in, checklist, or all prose? Will the officers be required to type or print out their own reports? How often must the officers return to headquarters to turn in their reports? This entire area is very important. In the author's opinion, many departments require far too many reports, many of which could be disposed of by checking a box indicating that the matter was handled and that no further action is warranted—two checkmarks at the most instead of two or three paragraphs. Perhaps many can be closed out by computer from the car.

9. How will priorities be established to give precedence to certain types of calls over others? If units are not available, which calls will not be assigned? Each type of call could be given a weighted point value, such as 5 points for a robbery in progress and 1 point for a burglary that occurred last night. A citizen advisory committee would be invaluable when it comes to making this list.

10. How are the supervisors and administrators used for management of the field officers? Are they going to provide field supervision and leadership? Are they going to handle calls? Are they going to be augmented by senior officers or training officers? Are they going to be used to perpetuate a lot of unnecessary administrative paperwork?

11. What types of forms and other documents must be maintained as supervisory control devices over the patrol officers—daily logs? tally sheets? Are only necessary forms going to be required? Many in use today have no value other than tradition.

12. To what extent will the department be involved in other affairs of the community? Is the department fully involved in community policing, proactive policing, and problem-solving philosophies and activities? What are the time requirements compared with the available personnel?

Once your department has developed a manual of procedures concerning all anticipated police activities and attached priorities, which should be developed by representatives of all levels of the department, not just management personnel, it should be presented to the people in the community. Your department head will, no doubt, discuss it with the council or board of supervisors and the city or county administrator, but the final discussions should be held with various citizen groups throughout the jurisdiction. Expectations of your services will affect the perception of your effectiveness by the public.

This is where proactive patrol takes place. Your department may have decided that whenever a caller reports that his or her home was broken into sometime during the owner's absence between 7:30 A.M. and 5:30 P.M. and that a suspect is not in sight, the police response to the call will be on an appointment basis at the mutual convenience of the victim and a nonsworn crime scene investigator. Many calls for service may be handled just as well by having the victim drive the vehicle into the police station to be dusted for prints when a stereo has been removed from the car sometime during the weekend. By scheduling report taking and crime scene investigations that do not require urgent response, personnel work-load schedules both in the field and in the office may be equalized somewhat.

Factors That Determine Patrol Deployment

How to make maximum use of human resources and equipment is the responsibility of the police chief, particularly when deploying the patrol force. There are never enough people authorized to accomplish all the police objectives. When arranging workdays and hours, vacations, holidays, days off, and the unexpected sick or injury days, the object is to meet realistically the community's demands of their police department for service when needed. When planning deployment of personnel, the chief and administrative staff must take into consideration a great many variable factors, some of which are listed here. You as a field officer should be aware of these considerations as well so that you will better understand the reasoning behind the assignments that you receive.

1. Resident and transient populations, particularly in business and tourist centers. A beach community may be 100 times its resident population during the daytime. The county seat or industrial center may have a daytime population a dozen times its nighttime population, whereas a "bedroom community" may be virtually empty of people during working hours on weekdays.

2. Numbers and types of crimes and arrests.

3. Locations of crimes and arrests.

4. Traffic collision statistics and patterns.

5. Locations of "frequent incidents" or hazards requiring concentrated police coverage. Such places as sports arenas, stadiums, popular night spots, singles bars, theaters, transportation terminals, or other gathering places.

6. Disproportionate concentrations of population, such as widely separated single-family residences versus heavily concentrated high-rise multiple-family dwellings. A small area comprising one tenth of the geographical size of your city might house one-half the population.

7. Socioeconomic factors. Higher-income families may seek their recreation outside the area, whereas those less fortunate must stay home. Some people never stray more than a mile or two from where they live for an entire lifetime, whereas the average person today is considerably more transient. Vehicle ownership also leads to greater mobility.

8. Zoning plan of the city (relative locations of business, industrial, residential, and other types of zoning). By their very nature, certain types of businesses and industries call for higher volumes of police service.

9. Size of the jurisdiction (in square miles) and shape.

10. Geography and topography. Are there widely separated strips and islands in your jurisdiction? Mountains, bays, ravines, rivers, lakes, or various other barriers may make it impossible to patrol both sides of the barrier at the same time.

11. Parks and recreational facilities. Consider locations, size, proximity to residences, access roads, and special characteristics, such as a forest area versus rolling, grassy hills.

12. Streets and highways. Consider total mileage and configurations, traffic flow patterns, state of repair and construction.

13. Locations and number of "attractive nuisances," including abandoned wells and mines, deserted buildings, swimming pools, open holes, woods, sandpits, rock quarries.

14. Age ratios of the population. Consider juveniles versus adults and the various age categories: preschool, adolescent, teenage, young adult, middle-aged, and seniors.

15. Male–female ratios and married couples versus unmarried population.
16. Homogeneity and/or mixture of various ethnic-cultural populations.
17. Modes of transportation and locations of transportation terminals.
18. Restaurants and theaters; volume and types of clientele, hours.
19. Known locations where criminal offenders live and go for recreation.
20. Number and qualifications of officers available for field duties.
21. Amount of trust and confidence of the people in their department, which may influence the frequency and types of calls for police service.

Designation of Districts

Taking into consideration all the preceding factors, the chief must apportion the jurisdiction into patrol districts that can be equitably handled by the assigned officers. With the aid of electronic data processing methods, it is now possible to separate the jurisdiction into very small segments known as "reporting districts," to maintain complete records on each district, to group the reporting districts into contiguous "patrol districts," and then to assign the officers proportionate to the indicated proportionate needs of the districts. Frequent evaluation conferences may cause fluid and frequent changes in the district boundaries to assure maximum utilization of personnel. The days are gone when a city or county can be divided into equal sections, just as a pie is cut, as a basis for work-load distribution.

Police patrol is a serious game of chess. The district officers must be armed with current and valid information concerning the crime and other police activity potentialities in their respective districts, and then attack each problem through a systematic patrol approach by being at various places in their districts at unpredictable and irregular times. The goal is to minimize the successes of criminals through strategy based upon knowledge and experience.

Rotation of Assignments

In municipal law enforcement, assignment to administrative duties has been traditionally a promotion in exchange for some years of devoted service. Once assigned and given the title "detective," the officer could then plan on spending the remainder of a career in that assignment. The only alternative was to be promoted to a higher rank, which necessitated a return to uniform or some other assignment. Many detectives chose not to seek promotion specifically to avoid having to return to uniformed patrol duties.

Lately, however, administrators have begun to realize that many of their better patrol officers are lost forever from the patrol division through this promotion policy. And some forward-looking administrators have started to experiment with planned rotational assignments similar to those used in business management programs, in which young business employees are rotated throughout the organization. When certain police officers are rotated throughout the various divisions of the police department and eventually are returned to patrol duty to serve as senior officers, or instructors, to the newer officers in departments where this procedure is followed, it is recommended that those senior officers be proportionately assigned to assure the most advantageous use of their talents.

Rotation of working hours may cause serious health problems if changes are made too frequently. Sleep cycles cannot be changed on the spur of the moment, and other bodily functions also need some stability to sustain good health if officers are to maintain peak efficiency. For special types of assignments, such as vice and narcotics, there is a high rate of burnout if officers stay on the assignment too long. In addition to the tremendous drain on family relationships are the constant temptations regarding "monopoly money" profits and the proverbial offering of the "apple" in the Garden of Eden, which destroy officers who yield to the temptations.

PROACTIVE VERSUS REACTIVE PATROL

The police can no longer indulge themselves in nonproductive and meaningless patrol. The cost of the vehicles, their maintenance, and other operational expenses have pushed into history the days when patrol time was considered correctly proportioned only when the officers could show 50 percent of a watch as being "on patrol." Cruising and looking for the unexpected and unusual is no longer a legitimate agendum.

There has been a trend toward development of a closer working relationship between the police and the public, such as neighborhood watch or community-oriented policing programs. Residents and merchants are expected—and encouraged—to watch more closely the activities that are going on around them and to report any suspicious persons or activities to the police department. There has been an increased awareness that the so-called "omnipresence" of the police simply does not prevent and repress crime. The police patrol cannot be everywhere or see everything, and the police administrators and the press must make the public aware of that reality. There must be a working partnership between the police and the people they serve.

Rather than stake out 847 drugstores because there is a very active drugstore burglar operating in town, it makes more sense to stake out the burglars suspected of working drugstores. Investigators and patrol officers make use of the records division data on past and present drugstore burglars. They then locate the burglar and maintain surveillance on the individual. They may watch him or her continuously for awhile, or their surveillance might only be during those times when the burglaries are occurring. Then, if the burglar appears to be "reformed" or inactive at the time, the officers drop that burglar and pick up surveillance on another. The officers do not harass anyone. They make contact with the burglar only if they observe a criminal act. A great many officers are highly successful in investigating crimes this way instead of randomly patrolling and hoping to be at the right place at the right time. This is proactive patrol.

Proactive patrol may reduce the occurrence of serious traffic collisions if officers visit the various drinking establishments in a district and greet the patrons as they leave. The obviously intoxicated and disorderly individuals may require arrests or some other alternative for their safety and continued prosperity. Those who appear to have impaired ability to walk will probably be in no condition to operate motor vehicles. A gentle reminder that they should, perhaps, have someone drive them home or take a taxicab may prevent a collision later. Bartenders and cocktail waitresses should be encouraged to pay more attention to their customers when they appear to be drinking beyond the limits of good judgment, and to encourage them to slow down and not drink for a while before leaving the establishment. By making occasional bar checks, you will also be in a better position to observe the potential hazards and call them to the attention of the manager or bartender. Such proactive patrol might save some lives, not to mention the loss of property and the humiliation of DUI (driving under the influence) arrests.

Analysis of problem locations and neighborhoods and more realistic selective enforcement practices may aid you in knowing where to be at certain times of the day and night so that your presence may have more effect in prevention and repression of criminal activity. Identify the problem locations; then direct a proportionate part of your patrol time to the places where the problems are.

Reactive patrol involves getting to the scene of the crime or collision after the fact. Through proactive patrol you might actually be there when the event unfolds before your eyes. Although it might be less exciting, you might actually be able to prevent the incident altogether.

Police Discretionary Prerogatives

In its 1967 report, *The Police*,[1] the President's Commission on Law Enforcement and Administration of Justice reported that there is considerable variance in police practices throughout the United States, particularly in tactical field problems and arrest situations. It was the consensus of that group of observers that police agencies exercise little or no control over the discretionary decision-making process in the form of operational guidelines.

In 1973, the *Report on Police* by the National Advisory Commission on Criminal Justice Standards and Goals[2] recommended that every police agency

> should adopt comprehensive policy statements that publicly establish the limits of discretion, that provide guidelines for its exercise within those limits, and that they eliminate discriminatory enforcement of the law. . . . Every chief executive should establish policy that guides the exercise of discretion by police personnel in using arrest alternatives. . . . Every police chief executive should formalize procedures for developing and implementing the foregoing written agency policy.

With all due respect to those observations and recommendations, there are some problems. As we have discussed elsewhere in this book, it may be possible to provide the field officer with general guidelines, but specifics are difficult. Some problems in enforcement, for example, include the following:

- The investigator locates the assault suspect, but once the suspect is in custody, the victim refuses to talk about the assault and no witnesses are available.
- Three separate traffic violations are committed in the presence of an officer, but the officer can get to only two of the violators and not the third. The officer alone must decide which ones to stop and cite.
- An officer arrests a suspect for a crime for which the police chief has demanded full enforcement, but every time such a case comes before the local judge, it is

dismissed, which indicates that someone in the system does not agree with the police chief.

- The officer knows that the suspect is guilty of a crime but also knows that there is not sufficient cause to justify an arrest, even though the guidelines state that the officer should make the arrest. Only the officer will know exactly when there is sufficient evidence to make that arrest.
- A crime violation occurs at the same time as an incident requiring an immediate rescue.

Consider these situations as being similar to surgery being performed in the hospital. The attending physician-surgeon examines the patient and takes the case to a meeting with a staff of other doctors. A consensus is reached that the surgery is necessary. Later, when the surgeon is operating, a complication arises that makes the removal inadvisable because of certain facts known only to the surgeon. The ultimate decision can rest only with the surgeon on the scene. In police work, too, there are many field situations in which the field officer with the total picture is the only person who can make the critical decision.

Use of discretion in field police work is absolutely essential. There is a continual development and modification of priorities, depending on availability of time, department strength, demands for service, and activities of the public. We are continually reacting to changing situations. A decision to clean up a parking problem can suddenly be changed by an airplane falling out of the sky. Ask a police chief about law enforcement. Is there any truth to the rumor that only certain laws are enforced with greater diligence than others? You will be told that all laws are enforced with equal vigor. Ask a fellow officer about total enforcement and you are likely to receive a similar response. But when a number of laws are violated and only some of them receive attention, ask the investigating officers and the answer you will get is, "We can't be every place at once." What is happening, of course, is the exercise of discretion in which cases to work and which to postpone. It is as predictable as popcorn at the movies.

Within the organized structure of law enforcement agencies, each of the thousands of individual officers functions as a virtually independent agent when it comes to routine as well as extraordinary police activities. The chief and top staff of the department may develop policies as to what will be done and in what manner, but they are not in the field when the time comes to make the critical decisions. Personal value systems as well as training and enforcement policies determine the actual parameters of law enforcement practices of the police as a professional body of individuals.

The broad discretionary powers entrusted to you as a field officer include such matters as dealing with traffic law violators, handling disturbances of the peace involving lone individuals or hundreds of people, enforcement of the criminal laws, apprehension and detention of juvenile delinquents and near-delinquents, regulation of private morals through enforcement of vice laws, and the performance of myriad other duties in the course of a normal day. You will function with little guidance except for the laws and the department manuals of procedure. You will have some field supervision, but when the time comes, most critical decisions—when to arrest, when to pursue, and when to shoot—will usually be left for you alone to decide.

Operational Guidelines for Discretionary Decision Making

The system of criminal justice abundantly provides for broad use of discretion by its law enforcement officers and all others similarly involved in the system. Setting the standard when the California Penal Code was introduced on February 14, 1872, the legislature provided for such discretion by the wording of Section 4:

> The rule of the common law, that penal statutes are to be strictly construed, has no application to this code. All its provisions are to be construed according to the fair import of their terms, with a view to effect its objects and to promote justice.

A leading case that further elucidates the intent of law and those who enforce it has been described in the California Supreme Court's ruling in *People* v. *Alotis,* 60 Cal. 2d 698 (1964):

> When language reasonably susceptible to two constructions is used in a penal law, that construction which is more favorable to the defendant will be adopted. The defendant is entitled to the benefit of every reasonable doubt as to the true interpretation of words or the construction of language used in a statute.

As a police officer you have the responsibility and authority within existing laws to act in a variety of ways when you encounter what, in your opinion, constitutes a violation of the law or other action requiring your official intervention. You may contact the violator and admonish with no arrest, or you may arrest and release the violator because you believe there is not sufficient evidence or other cause for further action. You may merely issue a citation and release the offender when he or she signs a written promise to appear later in court, or you may take the arrestee directly to jail. Once you have introduced the offender into the system by arrest and booking or by citation, other individuals in the system will make their own discretionary decisions, such as prosecuting attorneys and judges. A large percentage of the cases you handle will be disposed of informally, with no charges filed. Regarding the decision to arrest or not to arrest, you must be judicious in your use of discretionary power.

Specific sections of the criminal codes involving police discretion include such wording as "searching for weapons on *reasonable cause,*" "*reasonable* restraint when making an arrest," "*reasonable* force to effect an arrest, prevent escape, or overcome resistance." The basic arrest laws state that the officer *may* arrest when there is *reasonable cause* to believe a person is committing a crime in the officer's presence or there is *reasonable* cause to believe a person has committed certain crimes, although not in the officer's presence, *whether or not such a crime has in fact been committed.*

Wording of other criminal code sections indicates that the use of discretion is in order. Examples of these words are "specific intent," "reasonable" or "probable cause" (again), "malicious," "unsafe," "too close," "unfit," "unnecessary," and "reliable." Each of these words involves value judgments by individual officers.

ETHICS AND INTEGRITY

Public trust is not to be taken lightly. You are expected to be completely honest in all of your relationships with the people you serve. Trust involves someone expecting you to step into an unlocked bank vault with millions of dollars that has not been counted to be completely safe while in your hands.

You are not a thief because you arrest thieves and put them in jail. You are not a moocher because you chase moochers out of town. A police officer is paid well and has no need to ask for a charity discount on meals or other purchases from any of the business in your districts. Real estate people and truck drivers pay for their coffee and donuts; so should you. When you speak, it is understood that you do not lie or exaggerate the facts to make yourself look better in the eyes of your superiors at the expense of some innocent person's freedom or loss of reputation. These are just a few of the things expected of you and taken for granted because you are "the law."

It is very disappointing to hear a police officer lie while testifying in court. I believe that to be no less sacrilegious than a priest or minister blaspheming God from the pulpit. The court is our temple of law, and we are the disciples. Having worked internal affairs, I am not proud to say that I have known of many officers who lie and cheat and exaggerate and steal, but in my experience I have found those officers to be part of a small minority.

CIVIL LIABILITY OF THE FIELD OFFICER

In today's lawsuit-conscious society, it is not unusual for you as a police officer to report to work one day and be formally notified that you are being sued. Financial support for the suit is provided by false arrest and other types of insurance carried by your agency. The prospect of an award of some of those funds, however, often encourages people with weak cases to sue.

Police work is an adversary occupation in many respects. Very few people will thank you for arresting them. Even fewer will thank you for using force on them, even if you did believe that it was necessary to prevent injury to yourself. "After all, a police officer has to expect to get hurt once in a while. It goes with the territory. Right?" Wrong, but who are you going to convince? Whenever you arbitrate a dispute, both sides cannot win. Someone is going to be unhappy about whatever you do in such matters. Who is to blame? In other words, lawsuits are a real part of your work, and you might as well expect them and be prepared to present a defense if and when you are sued.

Another aspect in the defense of a lawsuit is money. Even for defense against a false or spurious charge, it will cost your department and its insurance carrier several thousands of dollars before the case ever gets to court. If there is any possibility of your losing, there may be a decision to settle out of court even though you are not at fault.

Bear in mind the fact that you are personally responsible for everything you do in the line of duty. You—and not a fellow officer or your supervisor—will ultimately stand alone in the lawsuit. Constantly evaluate and reevaluate your performance, particularly in the sensitive areas of arrest and the use of force, and remember to be your own counsel. The ultimate test will be the "reasonableness" of your actions and the propriety of your official conduct. Carefully record for future reference any incident that you believe might someday become a contested issue. Your constant awareness might well be the deciding factor in the court's deciding that you were right or wrong.

You are not always left out on a limb with no support. Many agencies have review committees, who evaluate reports, interview witnesses, investigate all aspects of the case, and make a concerted effort to get to the truth of a situation to determine if an officer's actions are defensible and "reasonable." Prosecuting attorneys have roll-out teams to investigate all police-involved shootings for the purpose of determining civil and criminal liability. Officers' unions and associations also come to the aid of their members when there is need for moral or financial support, even in some cases of criminal prosecution of the officer.

There is another side to the coin: There have been some successful cases where wrongfully accused police officers have sued their accusers. Turning the other cheek is sometimes okay, until you run out of cheeks to turn. A police officer must expect to take some "flak," but there is no rule that says the officer should be a masochist.

CRIMINAL LIABILITY OF PEACE OFFICERS

Peace officers are not protected from criminal culpability by some shield that makes them immune from their legal responsibilities. Officers must operate within the law to enforce the law. It is not unusual for some people to become enraged at times to see what appears to be a "whitewash" or "cover-up" whenever officers appear to get away with breaking the law when the average citizen would be hauled down to the "slammer" and booked and prosecuted to the fullest limit of the law. We also see what appear to be times when nonpolice people get away without being prosecuted for their crimes. There should be no cover-ups, and when the evidence can be constitutionally proven in court, then officers should be prosecuted and punished for their crimes the same as anyone else. There are many police officers who have lost their jobs and gone behind the bars of jails and prisons. Of course, as citizens of the United States, peace officers are guaranteed protection under the same rules of criminal procedure and the constitutions of the state and federal governments, as are all the other people accused of crime in our courts.

POLICE OFFICERS' BILL OF RIGHTS

Within the past few years, legislators have been asked to look at the rights of the police officers who selflessly serve their communities, sometimes at great personal and financial risk. In an effort to address some of the concerns of their officers in California, Government Code sections 3300 through 3309 were enacted. We have quoted the sections verbatim in this chapter, citing what is known as the Public Safety Officers Procedural Bill of Rights Act (enacted 1980).

SEC. 3300

This chapter is known and may be cited as the Public Safety Officers Procedural Bill of Rights Act.

SEC. 3302

a. Except as otherwise provided by law, or whenever on duty or in uniform, no public officer shall be prohibited from engaging, or be coerced or required to engage, in political activity.

b. No public safety officer shall be prohibited from seeking election to, or serving as a member of, the governing board of a school district.

SEC. 3303

When any public safety officer is under investigation and subjected to interrogation by his commanding officer, or any other member of the employing public safety department, which could lead to punitive action, such interrogation shall be conducted under the following conditions. For the purpose of this chapter, punitive action is defined as any action which may lead to dismissal, demotion, suspension, reduction in salary, written reprimand, or transfer for purposes of punishment.

a. The interrogation shall be conducted at a reasonable hour, preferably at a time when the public safety officer is on duty, or during the normal waking hours for the public safety officer, unless the seriousness of the investigation requires otherwise. If such interrogation does occur during off-duty time of the public safety officer being interrogated, the public safety officer shall be compensated for such off-duty time in accordance with regular department procedures, and the public safety officer shall not be released from employment for any work missed.

b. The public safety officer under investigation shall be informed prior to such interrogation of the rank, name, and command of the officer in charge of the interrogation, the interrogating officers, and all other persons to be present during the interrogation. All questions directed to the public safety officer under interrogation shall be asked by and through no more than two interrogators at one time.

c. The public safety officer under investigation shall be informed of the nature of the investigation prior to any interrogation.

d. The interrogating session shall be for a reasonable period taking into consideration the gravity and complexity of the issue being investigated. The person under interrogation shall be allowed to attend to his own personal physical necessities.

e. The public safety officer under interrogation shall not be subjected to offensive language or threatened with punitive action, except that an officer refusing to respond to questions or submit to interrogations shall be informed that failure to answer questions directly related to the investigation of interrogation may result in punitive action. No promise of reward shall be made as an inducement to answering any question. The employer shall not cause the public safety officer under interrogation to be subjected to visits by the press or news media without his express consent nor shall his home address or photograph be given to the press or news media without his express consent.

f. The complete interrogation of a public safety officer may be recorded. If a tape recording is made of the interrogation, the public safety officer shall have access to the tape if any further proceedings are contemplated or prior to any further interrogation at a subsequent time. The public safety officer shall be entitled to a transcribed copy of any notes made by a stenographer or to any reports or complaints made by investigators or other persons, except those which are deemed by the investigating agency to be confidential. No notes or reports which are deemed to be confidential may be entered in the officer's personnel file. The public safety officer being interrogated shall have the right to bring his own recording device and record any and all aspects of the interrogation.

g. If prior to or during the interrogation of a public safety officer it is deemed that he may be charged with a criminal offense, he shall be immediately informed of his constitutional rights.

h. Upon filing a formal written statement of charges, or whenever an interrogation focuses on matters which are likely to result in punitive action against any public safety officer, that officer, at his request, shall have the right to be represented by a representative of his choice who may be present at all times during such interrogation. The representative shall not be a person subject to the same investigation. The representative shall not be required to disclose, nor be subject to any punitive action for refusing to disclose, any information received from the officer under investigation for noncriminal matters.

This section shall not apply to any interrogation of a public safety officer in the normal course of duty, counseling, instruction, or informal verbal admonishment by, or other routine or unplanned contact with, a supervisor or any other public safety officer, nor shall this section apply to an investigation concerned solely and directly with alleged criminal activities.

i. No public safety officer shall be loaned or temporarily reassigned to a location or duty assignment if a sworn member of his department would not normally be sent to that location or would not normally be given that duty assignment under similar circumstances.

SEC. 3304

a. No public safety officer shall be subjected to punitive action, or denied promotion, or be threatened with any such treatment, because of the lawful exercise of the rights granted under this chapter, or the exercise of any rights under any existing administrative grievance procedure.

Nothing in this section shall preclude a head of an agency from ordering a public safety officer to cooperate with other agencies involved in criminal investigations. If an officer fails to comply with such an order, the agency may officially charge him with insubordination.

b. No punitive action, nor denial or promotion on grounds other than merit, shall be undertaken by any public agency without providing the public safety officer with an opportunity for administrative appeal.

SEC. 3305

No public safety officer shall have any comment adverse to his interest entered in his personal file, or any other file used for any personnel purposes by his employer, without the public safety officer having first read and signed the instrument containing the adverse comment indicating he is aware of such comment, except that such entry may be made if after reading such instrument the public safety officer refuses to sign it. Should a public safety officer refuse to sign, that fact shall be noted on that document, and signed or initialed by such officer.

SEC. 3306

A public safety officer shall have 30 days within which to file a written response to any adverse comment entered in his personnel file. Such written response shall be attached to, and shall accompany, the adverse comment.

SEC. 3307

No public safety officer shall be compelled to submit to a polygraph examination against his will. No disciplinary action or other recrimination shall be taken against a public safety officer refusing to submit to a polygraph examination, nor shall any comment be entered anywhere in the investigator's notes or anywhere else that the public safety officer refused to take a polygraph examination, nor shall any testimony or evidence be admissible at a subsequent hearing, trial, or proceeding, judicial or administrative, to the effect that the public safety officer refused to take the polygraph examination.

SEC. 3308

No public safety officer shall be required or requested for purposes of job assignment or other personnel action to disclose any item of his property, income, assets, source of income, debts, or personal or domestic expenditures (including those of any member of his family or household) unless such information is obtained or required under state law or proper legal procedure, tends to indicate a conflict of interest with respect to the performance of his official duties, or is necessary for the employing agency to ascertain the desirability of assigning the public safety officer to a specialized unit in which there is a strong possibility that bribes or other improper inducements may be offered.

SEC. 3309

No public safety officer shall have his locker, or other space for storage that may be assigned to him, searched except in his presence, or with his consent, or unless a valid search warrant has been obtained or where he has been notified that a search will be conducted. This section shall apply only to lockers or other space for storage that are owned or leased by the employing agency.

SUMMARY

In this chapter you have been introduced to the world of police patrol and the overall responsibilities of that unit referred to in this book as the police field unit. There are several objectives of field operations, which include (1) defense of life and property, (2) participative law enforcement, (3) prevention of criminal and delinquent behavior, (4) repression of criminal and delinquent behavior, (5) identification, apprehension, and conviction of offenders, (6) traffic flow and collision reduction, and (7) maintenance of order and the public peace. To accomplish those objectives, the many activities of the police field unit are described as follows:

1. Carrying out routine patrol and observation
2. Performing preventive attendance at public gatherings
3. Engaging in benevolent and community services
4. Maintaining business and property security
5. Providing inspection services
6. Responding to calls for service
7. Providing animal control
8. Performing traffic direction and control
9. Providing information services
10. Developing contacts
11. Conducting preliminary investigations
12. Collecting and preserving evidence
13. Arresting offenders
14. Preparing reports

15. Testifying in court

16. Saving lives and maintaining the quality of life of a free society

Private police and special-purpose police and some of their activities were covered as well in this chapter because of their close working relationship with public police.

Next, we covered distribution of the patrol force and factors that determine patrol deployment, as well as some of the administrative decisions that go into distribution of the field patrol unit by times, days of the week, and district distribution. Although the types of patrol vary from one department to another, many are universal, and these were outlined for your consideration.

Integrity is a major requisite in the personnae of police officers. Their integrity and ethical behavior are constantly tested to the breaking point. Once an officer goes beyond that point, his or her professional career should be over.

In addition to the pervasive problem of civil liability claims against the field officer, the spectre of criminal charges also looms overhead for the officer who is negligent in carrying out the job or is negligent or guilty of outright criminal behavior in violating the sacred trust conferred upon police officers. Officers should be mindful of the fact that they are not above the law.

When the time comes to make the decision of whether to arrest or to use force or to use your weapon, that decision will be yours. You will be guided by your department's rules and regulations, by the laws, and by your training as well as by your supervisors and administrators. As we discussed in this chapter, your ultimate guidance will be within yourself. As a companion to that discussion, we followed discretionary prerogatives with a commentary on civil liability, which expands on the concept that you are ultimately going to be held responsible for your own actions. The ultimate test of your actions will be whether or not those actions were reasonable. Finally, the chapter concluded with the Public Safety Officers Procedural Bill of Rights Act, which is designed to clarify police officers' rights vis-à-vis those of the citizens they serve.

EXERCISES AND STUDY QUESTIONS

1. List and explain the main points of the Law Enforcement Code of Ethics.

2. Compared to the *professional police officer* of the 1950s and 1960s, how would you describe the current police philosophy?

3. Give an example of *participative law enforcement*.

4. What types of problems should the police officers attempt to solve in their problem-solving meetings?

5. What is a *benevolent service?*

6. If someone were to ask, how would you describe *routine patrol?*

7. What is the difference between *proactive* and *reactive* patrol?

8. What is the difference between *community* and *public* relations?

9. What are the six objectives of police field operations?

10. What is the difference between crime *repression* and *prevention*?
11. As a field police officer, what is your *primary* responsibility at a large gathering of people?
12. List at least five *benevolent services* performed by the patrol officers of your local police department/sheriff's department.
13. What is the role of a police officer at the scene of a marital dispute?
14. What is the police responsibility for animal control in your jurisdiction?
15. List at least five items of information that every police officer should be able to answer when asked by a tourist.

REFERENCES

ADAMS, THOMAS F. *Law Enforcement: An Introduction to the Police Role in the Criminal Justice System,* 2nd ed. Englewood Cliffs, N.J.: Prentice Hall, 1973.

———. *Introduction to the Administration of Criminal Justice,* 2nd ed. Englewood Cliffs, N.J.: Prentice Hall, 1980.

ADAMS, THOMAS F., GERALD BUCK, and DON HALLSTROM, *Criminal Justice Organization and Management.* Pacific Palisades, Calif.: Goodyear, 1974.

CHAPMAN, SAMUEL G. *Police Patrol Readings.* Springfield, Ill.: Charles C. Thomas, 1964.

NATIONAL ADVISORY COMMISSION ON CRIMINAL JUSTICE STANDARDS AND GOALS. *Proceedings of the National Conference on Criminal Justice.* Washington, D.C.: U.S. Government Printing Office, 1973.

PRESIDENT'S COMMISSION ON LAW ENFORCEMENT AND THE ADMINISTRATION OF JUSTICE. *Task Force Report: The Police.* Washington, D.C.: U.S. Government Printing Office, 1967.

FOOTNOTES

1. The President's Commission on Law Enforcement and Administration of Justice, *Task Force Report: The Police* (Washington, D.C.: U.S. Government Printing Office, 1967).
2. National Advisory Commission on Criminal Justice Standards and Goals, *Report on Police,* Standard 1.3 (Washington, D.C.: U.S. Government Printing Office, 1973), p. 21.

CHAPTER 2

BASIC FIELD PROCEDURES

*I*NTRODUCTION

Patrol, observation, and *participation* are the three words that describe the patrol function most comprehensively. Your assignment will principally consist of patrolling a district, or "beat," in a distinctively marked vehicle with the word "POLICE" or "SHERIFF" emblazoned on both sides, the trunk, and the roof, and you will wear the traditional uniform of your department. There will be no mistaking who you are and whom you are working for. Although the police in the United States did not wear standardized uniforms until about 150 years ago (it was considered un-American, in the opinion of some émigrées from oppressive countries in the Old World), your uniform will be immediately distinguished from that of the various airlines, fast-food restaurants, real estate sales offices, and a multitude of other professions and occupations. You will probably be wearing the traditional blue or suntan or forest green uniform of the police, sheriff's, or other agency you choose to work for. Of course, there is a purpose for the uniform: immediate recognition.

Assuming that the great majority of the population is honest and law abiding, the mere presence of the police officers as they appear at various places throughout their jurisdiction will remind those people that the officer is present and will protect them as well as arrest the law violators. The would-be violators theoretically will not continue with their criminal intentions, at least not while in the officer's presence. The active criminal is less likely to ply his or her criminal trade if the police are also active and seemingly always present.

In this chapter we cover the so-called "routine" aspects of police patrol. In the preparation section of this chapter, we discuss the process of getting ready for your tour of duty as well as the psychological aspects of that tour, which include going out on patrol with a positive and nonjudgmental attitude. This is followed by some rudimentary pointers on patrolling your district, your district responsibilities, and the various inspections that you will perform while on routine patrol. A section is devoted to crime prevention follow-up, which should help the crime victim avoid being the victim again. Other topics addressed in this chapter are patrol hazards, the processes of surveillance and stakeouts, specialized patrol, and the concept and practice of community policing.

TYPES OF POLICE PATROL

Police patrol should involve as much ingenuity and innovation as possible for it to be effective in the aggressive attack on crime. Regardless of how sophisticated it may become, however, its most important function is to serve as the police department's actual field contact with the people—law abiding and criminal alike—on a personal one-to-one basis. The types of patrol refer to the various means of getting from one place to another in the district. None of them are intended to isolate the patrol officers from the people they serve and protect.

Foot Patrol

Foot patrol is probably the original type of police patrol. Although it confines the officer to small areas and limits the scope of activities, foot patrol is still among the most effective of the various types of patrols. The methods of foot patrol consist of the fixed post, line beat, and random patrol. Foot patrol is restricted to small areas and is used to deal with special problems of prevention and repression that cannot be adequately handled by the officers in radio cars. Fixed foot patrol is usually used for traffic, surveillance, parades, and special events. Moving foot patrol is used where there is considerable foot traffic, as in business and shopping centers, bars and taverns, high-crime areas, and special hazard areas and on streets where there are many multiple-family dwellings.

Horse Patrol.   Horses may be used for certain patrol problems in jurisdictions that contain large park areas or similar places where automobiles either cannot go or may be forbidden. Motorized officers cannot be expected to race across lawns, wooded areas, or pedestrian malls. Horses fulfill the need for greater mobility in these situations (see Figure 2–1). They also work quite well for moving crowds of people, hostile and otherwise. Search and rescue in wild, undeveloped terrain is accomplished with considerable success by a well-trained team of officers on horseback.

Motorcycles.   Primarily used for traffic enforcement, the motorcycle can also be used for fair-weather patrol assignments and for maneuvering in and around heavy traffic and accompanying pursuit on bicycle, horse, and jogging trails where the automobile cannot go.

Figure 2–1 Mounted Patrol Officer Bill Eades. (Courtesy Metro-Dade Police Department.)

Bicycles. Foot patrol officers may be assigned to cover greater areas such as sporting venue and mall parking lots, bike trails, gated apartment and other residential complexes, parks, pedestrian-only streets that have been blocked off to cars, amusement parks, and other places where other types of vehicles are either not allowed or cannot go (Figure 2–2). Bicycle patrol preceded the automobile in many countries, such as Great Britain and Germany, and is still used today in those and many other countries. When we used bicycles for special problems such as early evening residence burglaries and break-ins back in the 1950s, newspaper stories were written about this new police innovation. The bicycle is so indispensable that it will probably never completely disappear from our repertoire of vehicles. Officers can carry more gear on their bikes than they can while on foot. Weapons, communications and rescue equipment, additional clothing, and so many other items may be packed onto the bicycle. Also, police officers on foot or on the bicycle can get closer to the people in the neighborhoods, and can see and hear things that they might miss if they were inside that steel and glass shell we call a police car.

Small Vehicles. All-terrain vehicles with giant balloon tires, golf carts, motor scooters, hovercraft both on the beach and over the water, jet skis, and motorboats all have a function in the police department, particularly the coastal departments and

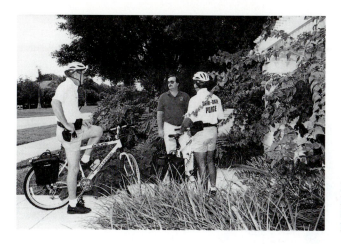

Figure 2–2 Hammocks District Bike Patrol. (Photo by Lynn Schimshaw, courtesy Metro-Dade Police Department.)

those that contain forests, wilderness areas, and open stretches of rural territory. Snowmobiles and dogsleds come in handy in snowbound regions where the automobile cannot go. Officers wearing casual street clothes will blend in more with the neighborhood when they use vehicles other than the traditional police cruiser, and then can identify themselves at the appropriate time.

Fixed-Wing Aircraft

Fixed-wing aircraft obviously need an airport with adequate runway and maintenance space. There is also the problem of locations to set the plane down in case of an emergency. For that reason ultralight aircraft and STOL (short takeoff and landing) equipped aircraft are used by the department. Fixed-wing aircraft are excellent for patrolling long stretches of highways or expanses of undeveloped or wild land, for transportation of people and equipment, for surveillance, and for search and rescue.

The first airborne police unit in the United States was created in New York City in 1930, when daredevil pilots were flying and doing stunts above the city, sometimes crashing into densely populated areas. The New York City "Air Police" were put into operation to catch and arrest these daredevil violators.[1] The fleet started out with one amphibian plane and three biplanes and operated well into the 1950s, when the airplanes were replaced with a fleet of helicopters.

Helicopters. The helicopter has been added to complement the air capabilities of the airplane, but it has the advantage of being able to travel at slower speeds, to hover when necessary, and to land in otherwise inaccessible places because of its vertical takeoff and landing capabilities. It is a virtual platform in the sky (see Figure 2–3).

The helicopter may also be flown at lower altitudes than can the fixed-wing airplane, and it may be used when marginal visibility conditions exist. A true champion as a police vehicle, the helicopter is used for rescue, medical evacuation, traffic control, general patrol, criminal apprehension, crime prevention and repression, emergency transportation, surveillance and searches, and other activities.

Figure 2–3 Aviation Unit—
Helicopter Pilot Jeep White. (Photo by
Brian Clay; Courtesy Metro-Dade
Police Department. Pilot Jeep White.)

Automobile Patrol

The automobile is the most extensively used and the most effective means of transportation for police patrol. On the beach it may be a Jeep with four-wheel drive and balloon tires. Usually, for general street patrol, it is an efficient late-model car with high-performance capabilities. It may be designed like a dune buggy for desert patrol or like a safari-type vehicle for mountains and forest areas. In the urban community, the vehicle is the distinctively marked late-model automobile.

For all practical purposes, the police car is a mobile police station. Equipped with the latest in radio gear and various types of rescue and restraining devices, it provides a rapid, safe, and efficient means of transportation under average operating conditions. All modern law enforcement agencies use the automobile as a patrol vehicle and many of them use no other means of transportation.

Boats and Amphibian Vehicles

In jurisdictions that patrol beaches, shorelines, and inland waterways, various types of deep-water and shallow-water boats are put into service. In many areas, a separate harbor or waterway patrol unit may be utilized, or field officers may be assigned to boat patrol on a rotational basis. Smuggling of people and contraband from coastal waters into inland harbor areas is a constant problem. Investigation and apprehension can be accomplished only with the aid of boats and helicopters.

Fixed Surveillance

Although not a means of transportation, when we are discussing various types of patrol we cannot overlook fixed surveillance. This is accomplished in person or with the aid of television cameras or stop-frame photography. The occasional stakeout at the place where a crime is anticipated is less likely to turn up a suspect than is installing surveillance on a permanent or semipermanent basis. With the use of monitors at a central location, it is possible to watch several locations at the same time and dispatch a field unit to whichever location is in need of immediate response. At one time used almost exclusively for intelligence operations and by the various governments spying on each other from their respective embassies, various types of listening and viewing devices are now being used to supplement routine patrol. This is in line with the proactive patrol concept.

The fixed surveillance, or stakeout, is utilized when you have information about a certain individual or group of people or a specific location that there is illegal activity going on (such as a suspected "meth lab" because of the odors emanating from a house or motel room), but you have no concrete evidence with which to go to a judge and get a search warrant. Your surveillance will yield the evidence you need to convince a judge to issue a warrant. You should have special vehicles and equipment for this, such as a van with video and motion picture cameras to record your observations.

PREPARATION FOR PATROL

General Preparation

There are many intangible factors related to an officer's preparation for patrol duty. First and foremost is that of attitude preparation. Your attitude must be positive. So many things that happen and so many of the people around you will be so negative that you will find yourself becoming negative and depressed, which will destroy your personal life if you let it. Attitudes will be affected by your social and psychological maturity, the nature and quality of your education, and physical conditioning. Your personal value system must be in harmony with the objectives of law enforcement and a sense of fair play. You must go to work each day with an attitude of confidence in the honesty and decency of most of the people you will encounter in the course of your work (see Figure 2–4). Because of the nature of your assignments, you may encounter only that small percentage of individuals who are dishonest and hence may judge everyone in those terms. For example, if you associate with only 100 people in your entire lifetime and all hold the same views, you may believe that the whole world thinks as you do because you do not encounter anyone who disagrees. You cannot believe that everyone is a thief just because all you see are thieves. To counteract this feeling, you must get involved in your off-duty hours with other people like yourself who are not violating the law. With this "anchor" in reality and the normal pattern of society, you will be better able to maintain a more accurate perspective on life and your fellow human beings.

As a police officer it is an attribute if you have a healthy curiosity and suspicion of everything around you, and are able to recognize that which is unusual or out of synch with the rest of the surroundings. Skepticism causes you to check out the

Figure 2-4 Formal inspections are morale builders. The uniform is to be worn with care as well as pride. (Courtesy Police Department, Costa Mesa, California.)

truthfulness of statements people make and events that do not appear as your sense tells you they should. Be careful that you do not go overboard and get to the point that you don't believe or trust anyone under any circumstances. If the activities around a house that would normally harbor a family or two with a few children running in and out look to you as though there are about six different pregnant women whose dress and mannerisms suggest that they are in a strange place, you might just have six single pregnant women living together. On the other hand, you might have an adoption business going on, with the resident of the house bringing women from another country to bear their children so that they may be sold to a black market adoption operation, then paid well for the baby and returned to their native country.

A broad base of experiences in education, occupations, and social interaction will prove to prepare you better for the role of police officer than if you were to have lived a one-dimensional cloistered life. As a child, you probably had no choice but to live and grow according to the plans of others. Now that you have had a choice prior to and following your entrance into police work, you should seek out and communicate with people who fill the entire spectrum of social standards, educational and occupational backgrounds, political philosophies, and moral and religious codes.

We did not have the opportunity to go to a supermarket and pick out the parents we wanted in what we believed their financial and/or social situation in the community should be. Neither did all of the other people that you deal with in the normal course of your patrol activities. Cultures and traditions vary considerably, and you may encounter many things that seem foreign to you. So will the people from other places see us and the things we do as strange. Keep this in mind whenever you meet new people and situations.

You must be objective, empathetic, and friendly, yet nonjudgmental. As a police officer, you may enforce certain behaviors, but you may not force your personal beliefs on the people you encounter, whatever their views. Your role is that of diplomat and protector of all the people you serve, a public servant who does not serve with obsequious servitude but who firmly and fairly enforces the laws and rules of the society you serve. People with very fervent belief systems have a tendency to be intolerant of others who do not believe the same, so they will try to proselytize others to their point of view. Be careful to harness your own personal belief systems, and strive to avoid acting as a missionary. If that's your goal in life, then go for it and study theology to become a minister. As a police officer, your goal is to enforce the law and ensure peace in your community. You will be a servant to the *public,* not to individuals or their personal whims and desires. Although you deal directly with individuals on a personal basis, your responsibility is to handle each situation for the overall good of the community. To function intelligently and effectively, you must continually assess your role as a police officer in this dynamically changing society.

Prepatrol Preparation

Prior to going out on patrol, you must arm yourself with both knowledge and equipment. Only a few of the essentials are covered in this chapter because they vary from department to department and from day to day. As for the knowledge to do your job each day, there is usually some type of "roll-call training," which is devoted to providing you with specific assignments, such as your vehicle and partner (if any), break and meal times, and district in which you will be working. Other items of information will include changes in laws and court decisions affecting field activities, new tracts and streets, changes in jurisdictional boundaries, such as the addition of a tract to a city, or formation of a new city, thereby reducing the size and changing the shape of the unincorporated county jurisdiction, general and special orders from administration, and new techniques for improvement of your field performance.

Keep in touch with current events in your own community and the world around you by reading the newspapers, news magazines, and watching television news programs on the national networks and cable news. No matter where we are, we are affected by what we see and hear around us, and attitudes toward the police may change because of what happens on the streets or in the courts anywhere in the country. Although the officers in Wichita had absolutely nothing to do with the car stop and beating of a young black man in Los Angeles in 1991, or the state or federal trials and riots that followed, my bet is that the Wichita officers were affected in more ways than one by those events many hundreds of miles away. People will make comparisons between your actions and those hyped by the media to enhance their ratings and advertising revenue.

What's new? One of the first things in the order of business for your day is to get updated from computer-generated lists of recent crimes in your district, individuals wanted for questioning and/or arrest and stolen vehicles. Runaways and missing persons should be on your list of people to look for. You should keep up with the local and national news and computer online and television programs about unsolved crimes and wanted persons. Many people who live in your jurisdiction watch such shows as *America's Most Wanted* and *Unsolved Mysteries,* and a very large percentage of those cases are solved through the public's help, by people calling in to their local police agencies. Keep current on those shows through your roll call meetings and training sessions so that you will be able to respond appropriately when one of the many "armchair auxiliaries" calls in with offers of assistance and information that will help solve those cases.

Investigators from traffic, juvenile, vice, narcotics, and Detectives should visit your meetings and share with you information that will enable you to help solve their cases as well as those of other jurisdictions. If a serial rapist or child molester is operating in neighboring jurisdictions, you can bet that your district might be next. You may be asked to watch certain people and look for particular types of behavior so that you may build on the information those special officers may have. Oftentimes, there is a strong suspicion about someone and there is not sufficient evidence to arrest, but additional information that you might develop may be just what an investigator needs to put a case together and make an arrest. Many cases of all types are cleared by observant field officers.

Frequently, when new laws and ordinances are passed, some interpretation as to their intent is necessary for the field officer. Following passage of a new law, except when there is an emergency clause calling for immediate enactment, there is usually a 60- or 90-day delay before the legislation is enacted. This is to allow time for publication and for study by the police, attorneys, and judges who will be dealing with it from various angles. In addition to the wording or the "letter" of the law, there is the additional agenda of the "spirit" or intent of the law. Although the word and spirit should be the same, how many times have you written something and then had to tell someone "let me explain what I meant when I wrote that"? Following passage of new laws, your training will consist of someone—possibly a prosecutor who handles arrests made by your department—discussing with you and your fellow officers the laws as written and as it was intended they should be enforced. The instruction will also include suggestions on what kind and amount of evidence will be required to sustain convictions for those law violations.

An occasional visit by a prosecuting attorney and a judge would be a real bonus for your roll call training sessions. The prosecutors have to work with your "screwups" in court and out of the sight of your supervisors and administrators. Judges, of course, watch officers while they are on and off the witness stand and will have a lot to offer you about the way you present yourself when on the stand and officer behavior in and around the courtroom. You will be subpoenaed more often than you will actually be called upon to testify, so it is not unusual for you to get rattled and self-conscious while testifying. It's not very often that an "officer cool" does everything absolutely perfectly in court.

Under a community policing plan, you and your special team of officers will be semipermanently assigned to work the same district so that you will get to know the people and places in your district as you know the inside of your own living room. Become familiar with street addressing plans, such as even numbers on the south and east sides of streets, odd numbers on the west and north; every house jumps two numbers from 1002 to 1004 or ten numbers from 1010 to 1020, and so on. Most cities have some sort of plan for numbering houses and buildings, and also for naming streets, such as the first avenue generating away from the center of the city begins with each successive letter of the alphabet—Ash, Birch, Cherry. Then, when you know the fronts of the buildings, get acquainted with the same houses and buildings from the rear as you traverse along the alleyways. If you have helicopters and other aircraft in your area, there should be a system of identifying places and addresses from the air. This should be worked out as part of your problem-solving duties.

Where are the gates allowing entry into certain residences? What are the floor plans of the buildings in your district? When you receive a robbery call at a jewelry store in your district, you should be able to have instant access to information about the doors and windows, skylights, inside and outside stairways, so that you and your colleagues can work out a plan of action to rescue hostages and arrest the robbers or burglars.

What gangs operate in your district and surrounding jurisdictions? What are their graffiti tags, the names of their members, distinctive tattoos, hand signs, slogans, colors? Tagging may be done by individuals whose sole objective is to tag their name in as many places as they can, such as freeway signs, but gangs use their graffiti to mark their territorial boundaries as a cat marks its territory by urinating on a tree or structure. Graffiti is used to identify the various members of the gangs, and the different gangs communicate with each other and make challenges through the use of their graffiti shorthand. Get acquainted with all of these things about the gangs in your area so that you may be aware of impending conflicts and disputes over territory.

Additional facts that you should have available prior to going out on patrol are such items as where streets are closed because of construction or weather, what new hazards are in effect (e.g., power lines down across a street you might use to pursue someone), which business establishments are closed for vacations or repairs and might need some additional protection, who is on vacation and wants a house checked, where special events are taking place, what is the traffic collision and congestion situation, and at what locations have there been family and neighborhood disputes that the officers who responded earlier are convinced will require your attention later. In other words, get to know your district and the people in it, and each day prior to going out on patrol make a deliberate effort to get an update from reports and fellow officers who have just returned from spending the previous several hours in the same district (see Figure 2–5).

While preparing for field duty, you will often receive orders to complete assignments begun by the earlier shift. Jobs that await your arrival may include locating and securing additional information from witnesses and victims of incidents that have occurred earlier, or relieving another officer on a surveillance or stakeout or conducting special patrol inspections at certain times of day. Warrants may be issued and you will go out and arrest wanted persons on the warrants. You may have to serve subpoenas and notify people whether or not they will be required in court the next day. Because of the heavy case load of the earlier shift, you may have to answer calls that have not yet been assigned.

In-Field Preparation

Whenever possible, one of your first responsibilities when you go out on patrol is to have a "debriefing" conference with the officer whom you are relieving and who has just spent the previous several hours in the district. If you cannot meet the person you are replacing, you should attempt at least a rendezvous with one or more of the

Figure 2–5 Prior to going out on a tour of duty, the officer should compare notes with the officers who have been on duty during the preceding shift. (Courtesy Police Department, Detroit, Michigan.)

officers from the previous shift. Conferences between shifts will tend to assure some continuity in coverage of the district and, it is hoped, more continuity in overall field activities. If you want to know what has been happening, such as pending disturbances, crowds, parties, and traffic conditions, your best source of information will be the officer who has been on top of the situation. It is not unlike the pilot en route to Chicago checking with another pilot who just arrived from Chicago as to weather conditions en route. Military units have used the debriefing process with considerable success.

Some items and bits of information will not be included in the reports; for example, the recent return of a burglar from prison whom the beat officer ran into at the donut shop, observation that two known narcotics dealers just happened to be at the same auto repair shop at the same time, or the family fight that was supposedly settled but the officer has a nagging feeling that nothing was really settled. Officers have "feelings" or "hunches" about certain things they see or hear, but they cannot— and should not be required to in many cases—commit the information to a formalized report that requires documentation. Such nuances of information should be passed on to other officers, however, for follow-through and to see if anything substantial develops.

These are some of the observations that the officer going off duty may share with you so that you may follow up: A strange station wagon is parked in back of a dress shop and no driver or passengers were observed; two men known to be on parole for armed robbery have been observed loitering near three different convenience stores, which are the types of places they have "hit" before; a middle-aged man sitting in a car with a newspaper on his lap was paying an unusual amount of attention to a junior high school girls' outdoor dancercise class and reluctantly left, but will probably return; there appear to be an unusual number of youths from opposing gangs who are congregating at a park where a "rumble" appears to be in the making.

Vehicle Inspection

At the time you assume control of the assigned vehicle for your tour of duty, inspect it for clean windows and windshield, a full tank of gasoline, and correct oil level. Check the tires and the brakes. Start the engine and listen for any perceptible malfunctions. Never overlook special weapons and equipment that are kept in the trunk of your vehicle, including rescue and first-aid equipment and a fire extinguisher. It may sound unimportant to mention such routine items, but my personal experience tells me that it is not unusual to overlook the obvious. Check out all the emergency lights and sound equipment, including the siren. Experienced pilots use checklists prior to flying their airplanes; why not devise and use your own checklist?

During the first few minutes while you are driving the vehicle, other possible problems may become apparent, and you should not hesitate to report the problems. A walkaround should become routine so that you might look for any obvious problems, such as a missing fourth wheel, but also look for structural damage and—using a preprinted diagram of the vehicle—sketch the location and appearance of the dent or other damage. The emergency nature of your work demands that the vehicle you drive be in the best condition possible. Except when absolutely necessary, you should not accept a vehicle for patrol that is not adequate for the demands of both routine and pursuit driving. Since you are responsible for the vehicle, be sure to complete the required faulty equipment forms and follow up to see that the malfunctions and deficiencies are corrected.

District Orientation Tour

Once in the field, take a general familiarization and inspection tour of your assigned district to orient yourself to the sights and sounds and the "normal" patterns that present themselves to you. Use a different route each time you cross the district, and vary your technique so that no one can predict with any accuracy the sequence of your tour or see any resemblance to a timetable. Check for streets closed or under repair and note holes and ruts that may cause traffic accidents or congestion. During a high-speed pursuit later, it will be good to know the condition of the streets you will be traveling.

In the initial cursory tour you may observe many circumstances or people that arouse your curiosity but not your suspicion that there is any criminal involvement. Perhaps there is an automobile parked in an unusual location or a small group of people gathered where such a group has never gathered before. If you believe that you may have stronger suspicions if the situation is unchanged upon your return visit, make notes and plan to return later. Write down license numbers, descriptions of objects, vehicles, and people. These notations may later prove worthless; they may prove priceless. Carry a camera and take photographs.

In addition to noting your existing and potential police problems, be sure to look for—and record—abandoned vehicles, graffiti, and old advertising signs for long-past sales and political campaigns that still fill the fences and walls and utility poles in your district (which, in the opinion of the author, are just as much a blight on the community as those signs and symbols "tagged" by feuding gangs). Be sure to include on your list buildings that have been abandoned and/or have lost their doors and windows, unattended lots that have overgrown with weeds, and other conditions you observe that negatively affect the quality of life in your community. Front and back yards and driveways that have been converted into junkyards should also be cleaned up. Keeping the city cleaned up is not unlike the philosophy of dressing the kids up in clean clothes and watching how careful they are not to get them dirty. Contact the property owners and have them clean up the properties.

If you use a daily log, and if your department's policy—and form—provides for such a procedure, notations regarding your initial observations during a district orientation tour may be written directly on your log. In any event, make liberal use of the field notebook for information that you believe may be of some value later. During this initial tour, there will undoubtedly also be some items requiring more formal attention and reports. In such cases, take care of whatever demands your immediate attention; then continue the tour.

There are several good reasons for taking an orientation tour of your district. One is that it may allow you to establish time elements. For example, you may note that a particular location appears normal at 10:13 P.M., but when you return at 11:37 P.M., you find a window smashed out. The initial tour of the district allows you to narrow down the times within which the window was broken considerably more than some time between 5:30 P.M. and 11:37 P.M. Another reason for the orientation tour is to acquaint yourself with the entire district in its current condition to gain an impression of what is "normal" and what appears "abnormal." A third reason for this patrol technique is to put the deterrent forces of your presence in the district to work. Any individual bent on committing a crime should know that you are in the district and that you are likely to show up at virtually any unannounced time or place. The optimum result would be that the would-be criminal does not perform his crime.

PATROLLING THE DISTRICT

There are two basic methods of police patrol: foot and vehicle. Both are usually performed in uniform, but either may call for street clothing under unusual circumstances. Use may be made of horses, motorcycles, bicycles, scooters, or aircraft, depending on the individual and special needs of the agency involved. The techniques of patrol are essentially the same regardless of the mode of transportation employed.

The following discussion deals with police patrol from three primary angles: foot patrol, vehicle patrol, and plainclothes patrol. In the discussion of foot patrol, it should be understood that any means of transport may be used to get the officer to the district to be covered on foot. It should also be clear that the discussion of techniques of patrolling a district by automobile may apply equally well to other types of vehicles.

Foot Patrol Tactics

The cop on the beat in the "good old days," whenever that imaginary time existed, seems to be remembered as the sustaining symbol of law enforcement. Depicted in fiction stories and the motion pictures, he was the friendly but firm fatherly type who walked the streets in his small beat, nearly always on duty and always in uniform and always a man. He maintained order and control in his district by chiding, scolding, cajoling, and sometimes arresting the violators. He visited the shopkeepers and residents, exchanged anecdotes with the street vendors, and performed numerous benevolent services. Some communities have utilized foot patrol continuously since the beginning of police patrol, but many discontinued it because of its prohibitive cost and extremely limited use of the work force. During recent years, there has been a trend back to foot patrol in downtown and high-density neighborhoods where there is a lot of pedestrian traffic and at times when officers will have a greater opportunity to deal with the people on the streets on a one-to-one basis. The objective is to establish a bond of trust and respect between the people and the officers on patrol.

In addition to performing your duties as a professional police officer while on foot patrol, you will be performing invaluable community relations tasks for your department. Through your personality and your actions, you will demonstrate to the people what all police officers are like, because you will be the model they can see and touch. By your friendly and understanding attitude, you should make every effort to develop a feeling of confidence and respect in *you and your department* within those individuals whom you encounter. Your assignment to a foot beat might have been without a thought to selectivity, or you may have been assigned because your supervisor believes that you have certain qualities that will enhance the image of the department. Although you should be conscious of the community relations responsibility that you have whenever performing any police task, it will be more demanding when you are on foot patrol and in constant, direct contact with the people.

Whenever you are on foot patrol, take advantage of every opportunity to get to know as many of the people in the district as you can. Make a deliberate effort to meet and talk with people, and use a notebook to keep notes on those contacts. For example, the manager of a dress shop on your beat has a child with a certain medical problem and another in college. You keep notes so that when you stop in to visit the store again you will remember to ask about the children. You and your department will have a friend and supporter for life just for taking a little extra time to show an interest in the people you serve.

At the same time you are getting to know the people, you must also perform all other functions required of the patrol assignment. There will be fewer demands on you because you lack the mobility and other advantages of having a vehicle at your disposal. You will have a portable radio or cellular phone, but you will have greater autonomy to carry out your responsibilities. You may have fewer assignments from headquarters, but you will encounter and handle more "on-sight" incidents while on patrol.

Every district has a distinctive personality, and it is important that the assigned officer get to know that personality. Wanted persons may live in the area. Known felons and narcotics users may habitually loiter around the local nightclubs or family recreation center, which is also frequented by many juveniles and young adults who are not criminals or narcotics users. Certain business establishments fall prey to specific crimes, such as armed robberies and burglaries. These locations should be given close attention in an effort to prevent criminal occurrences or reoccurrences. When you are assigned to the foot beat, get to know it and the people in it, then give it personalized service.

When walking through the district, most experts recommend that you walk close to the curb during the day and close to the buildings at night. They reason that the objective of daytime foot patrol is to contact and to be seen by as many people as possible, and the objective of nighttime foot patrol is to be seen by as few people as possible and to catch criminals in the act before they are aware of your presence. However, others suggest for nighttime patrol that you consider the time of night and the lighting conditions, evaluate your objectives while covering the particular part of the district in which you find yourself, and then work accordingly. There should be no standard place to walk depending on the relationship of the sun to the earth any more than there should be a standard schedule to follow.

Keeping in mind the fact that police patrol means service as well as protection, never hesitate to take the initiative when practicable to offer your services in whatever way is consistent with the purposes of law enforcement. For example, probably no duty manual will be found that requires an officer to give a distressed motorist a little advice on how to start a flooded car or to call for a tow service for some mother who cannot leave her stalled car containing four preschool children. An elderly lady may have difficulty getting across a busy street because she walks so slowly and no one will allow her to take advantage of a break in a seemingly endless flow of traffic. Stopping traffic to assist the lady or a person in a wheelchair across the street would be a typical foot patrol service. These activities are hallmarks of the distinguished police officer who sees the occupation as something more than "just a job."

One of the problems that confronts the foot beat officer, and sometimes comes to the attention of the radio car officer, is the sidewalk showroom. Not having enough room or attention for their products, some merchants move out onto the sidewalk to display their wares. Also look for the scam artists with their shell games. This use of the public walk is unlawful in most cities, and it causes congestion of foot traffic. Maintaining a free flow of pedestrian traffic is just as important as keeping vehicular traffic moving.

Sometimes the street merchant has no vested interest in the neighborhood and has only the wagon or truck to sell from instead of a store or market. These wandering merchants may have no business license or health department or zoning enforcement agency controls to abide by, and may also be inflicting hardships on the merchants who have to pay rent and follow the rules. Unlike the merchants in the mall who have little kiosks or wagons or stands placed in open areas, the street merchants do not pay rent and have no reason to take pride in being a part of the community. They simply move to where the money is. You should check on these merchants to be sure that they are in compliance with all zoning, health, and license laws.

When walking the beat, do not develop a routine, yet be sure to give the area adequate coverage. Walk with a purpose and look at the people. Speak with them when it is natural to do so, and encourage them to feel as though they can talk with you. Do not hesitate to smile when the occasion warrants it. Maintain a professional posture by being friendly and firm, not aloof and unapproachable. Never "mooch" by soliciting or accepting special discounts, free merchandise, or free refreshments. One practice that is absolutely intolerable is paying bills or otherwise tending to personal business while on duty, especially stopping to get a haircut. An old-timer once told me "my hair grows while I'm on the job, so I don't see anything wrong with getting it cut while I'm on the job." The entire on-duty time belongs to the department and the people. It should be spent accordingly.

Walk from one place to another so that it appears to the observer that you are *patrolling* the district, not loitering. Stop frequently to observe the people and the things around you. Change your routine, sometimes retracing your steps, and do not neglect the alleys or areas behind buildings when patrolling your district. When walking, look behind and under things, and inside trash containers. You are looking for safety hazards and stolen property as well as wanted persons and crime incidents. Look for scuff marks on walls alongside telephone poles and drainpipes. As a matter of routine, get to know those buildings that are most vulnerable to attack, such as those with skylights and rooftop entryways. Determine through observation what is normal for the district, then look for the unusual and deal with it accordingly.

At nighttime when you are patrolling for possible burglars, approach each building with caution, assuming the possibility that someone may be inside the building, or hiding in the doorway. Stop momentarily, stand in a darkened area to avoid being seen, and listen for unusual sounds. At nighttime when there is almost absolute silence, it is possible to hear the sound of breaking glass, or walking, or a dog barking from hundreds of yards away. Sounds seem to be magnified by silence.

When you are satisfied that there are no unusual sounds, continue with the routine. Check the doors and windows, feel the glass for heat that may indicate a fire inside, then move on to the next building. Watch the rooftops and any means of access to the roofs of the various buildings. Roofs are a popular means of entry among some professional burglars. By entering through the roof, the burglar delays the discovery of his crime and is sometimes able to work inside without detection even with an officer standing outside.

Vehicle Patrol Tactics

The vehicles used for patrol should not be used as shells, but merely as means of transportation and protection. When you are on vehicle patrol, one of the first rules to follow is to get out of the car frequently. Never use it as a means of isolating yourself from your patrol duties. In fact, you will probably have few opportunities to remain in the vehicle very long because, due to their high mobility and access to rapid communications, officers assigned to automobiles handle virtually all calls for service as well as the bulk of assigned activities.

For automobile patrol, solo patrols or two-officer teams are used for various times of the day and types of districts, depending on department experiences. When solo patrol is utilized, there is a need for closer coordination of the field officers' activities with communications personnel, and the field units must frequently follow up to other field units. The solo patrol concept is not intended to place lone officers at locations where two or more officers are needed. The patrol officers should work in teams for purposes of field contacts, citations, checking open doors, and responding to most calls. Only the patrolling should be done solo.

Operate the vehicle at normal speeds, consistent with traffic conditions. If the traffic is moving faster than you believe necessary for adequate surveillance of the people and places along the way, stop, turn around, or go around the block and retrace your route. If the traffic is too fast for effective patrol, stop frequently and wait, then move on. Patrolling heavily traveled streets is virtually impossible at times. Move around the district on all the streets rather than just a few. A patrol officer is of no value when driving at high speeds.

Open the windows of the police car whenever consistent with weather conditions, and turn the radio down low so as not to drown out the sounds outside. Patrol the district so that the vehicle will be seen by the greatest number of people, frequently turning corners and covering the side streets as well as the main thoroughfares.

Several types of patrol patterns have been variously described, such as the "zigzag," "quadrant search," and the "clover leaf." The design is meaningless as a technique in itself and merely describes the driving pattern that resembles what the title suggests. Whatever pattern you decide to use should be irregular and unpredictable. Move around the district. Start at one side and work to the other, or work out from the center, or go across the district, turn around, and immediately retrace your route. The entire district should receive attention with emphasis on those places that require special attention because of the frequency of crimes and arrests. Never develop a time schedule for patrolling your assigned district, and always consider the possibility that a burglar or thief will commit crimes in the most illogical places and at the most unusual times of day.

Patrol Driving. Most patrol driving consists of stop-and-start, slow-speed driving with frequent backing (see Figure 2–6). The majority of accidents involving police units occur during this type of driving, and a large percentage of them involve the backing process. Fatigue and inattention to driving are other patrol accident factors. Seat belts/shoulder harnesses and other safety equipment installed in the vehicle for your safety are absolutely essential. Not only are they installed for your personal safety, but if people who have been cited for failure to wear safety belts and children see that you are breaking the law, your credibility goes out the window!

Keep awake. Driving at nighttime and during the early morning hours often becomes monotonous, particularly when you have not had adequate rest and the patrol routine at that time of the day presents no novelty to you. Open the car window for fresh air, talk out loud occasionally, and move your eyes around frequently while driving along a straight stretch of road. Stop the car occasionally, get out, and flex your muscles. Never use pills or medication to stay awake on the job. It is better to use adequate rest than to use a chemical "crutch" to stay awake.

Set an example by obeying all traffic laws, including boulevard stops, speed laws, and the general rules of the road. The vehicle operated in this manner serves as much of a purpose as the officer driving it by encouraging compliance with the laws by example.

Special skills are required for driving in rain, snow, and slush. In an article entitled "New Facts about Skidding: They May Save Your Life," E. D. Fales, Jr., outlines some excellent suggestions for driving at times when skidding is possible.[2] Fales points out that studies by various agencies have revealed that the front tires of an automobile moving at higher speeds actually leave the surface, or hydroplane, when moving across rain, snow, or slush. At speeds above 30 miles per hour, the tires begin to lose contact with the road. At a speed of approximately 55 miles per hour on top of a water-covered street surface, there is only slight tire contact with the surface, and at higher speeds there is none whatsoever.

Figure 2–6 Some agencies, including the Pennsylvania State Police, have comprehensive vehicle operation training for their new officers. Skill development should not be left to chance. (Courtesy the Pennsylvania State Police.)

Fales suggests that adding air pressure to the tires and driving more slowly may improve maneuverability. The depth of the tread and the depth of the water on the road surface have a direct bearing on the hydroplaning phenomenon. One other way to reduce the occurrence of hydroplaning in inclement weather is to drive in the tracks made by preceding vehicles, which may be relatively dry because of continuous friction and water displacement.

Skidding occurs under various conditions, and it has been discovered that the skid itself perpetuates the problem. As the vehicle goes into the skid, the tire temperature rises, the rubber melts, and the tire lays down its own thin layer of melted rubber, which makes a slideway. When the vehicle begins to go into a skid, use all the driver training techniques, including braking the vehicle with short, rapid-sequence braking motions instead of the usual steady pushing motion. The brakes are less likely to lock the wheels in a skid when they are applied in this manner.

Parking police vehicles is a frequent problem. Upon arrival in response to an emergency call for service, there may be no readily available space and little time to look for a place to park. The circumstances must dictate the action. There can be no strictly enforced regulations concerning the parking of police vehicles, except that they should always be parked legally unless an emergency condition exists. The vehicle should be parked in a legal manner and the key to the ignition should be removed. Sometimes it is wise to lock the vehicle completely to protect it against vandalism. Instead of taking the ignition key away from the unit, officers working as a radio car team will take the key out of the ignition and place it in a hiding place that is convenient and known to both of them. Either officer thus has immediate access to the unit regardless of his or her partner's location. Better yet would be to assign a key to each officer and avoid the problem of having to worry about where the keys are.

Plainclothes Patrol

Unusual conditions may necessitate patrol officers' special assignment to perform their patrol operations in regular street clothing and to operate department vehicles or privately owned vehicles that are not identifiable as police cars. This type of assignment is particularly effective for "saturation coverage" of high-crime areas. It provides extra coverage without alarming the occupants or signaling the culprits with an unusual number of patrol units. The burglars or robbers may possess a false feeling of security because they lack knowledge of the plainclothes patrol. The result may be successful apprehension of some "long-time wanted" felons and the clearance of many cases.

For plainclothes patrol, dress to fit the occasion and wear whatever clothing is the mode of the day and fits the type of activity you will ostensibly engage in as a "cover" for your presence in the neighborhood. Use a vehicle that similarly matches the occasion. Sometimes it may be wiser to use a rented car or borrowed used car than to use a so-called "undercover" unit belonging to the department.

Situations calling for plainclothes patrol vary with current problems. Within the department, it may be used to supplement any existing or "standing" assignment, such as vice or detective assignments, when a particular situation requires more attention than the responsible division can devote to the problem. At the beach or the amusement park in a resort community, plainclothes patrol may be the most effective way to deal with seasonal problems. In the city, there may be several locations where large numbers of juveniles "just fool around" or seek meaningful recreation, and plainclothes patrol may be used to give those locations extra police coverage without fanfare and without giving the juveniles the impression that they are being "over-policed."

Rallies, sporting events, or other occasions when large numbers of people gather for a variety of reasons may best be patrolled by the police department with an officer or two in uniform and others not in uniform. The latter mingle with the crowd and make themselves available in case of a need for their assistance. A team of plainclothes patrol officers can move about from place to place throughout the city inconspicuously and quite effectively.

Picture this scenario: It is an open-air concert with about 60,000 in attendance. Most of the crowd is orderly and enjoying the performance. Down in front near the stage two young men appear to be under the influence of an intoxicant and are making complete fools of themselves, causing a disturbance and starting to pick fights with half a dozen other people. Unless someone neutralizes the situation, we are soon going to have a riot. There are a couple of uniformed officers nearby. If the officers go down and try to arrest the two culprits, they might exacerbate the problem. Out of the crowd emerge four "friends" of the two unruly hoodlums. They take their "buddies" out of the crowd and the rest of the crowd goes back to enjoying the event on stage. Actually, the four "friends" were police officers in plainclothes, but no one was the wiser and what might have led to forcible action by uniformed officers and the inevitable angry crowd getting angrier was defused quickly and effectively. These same officers may be assigned to check on transient vice conditions or virtually any other type of problem not requiring uniformed officers. Plainclothes patrol should be a normal part of the patrol division's repertoire of techniques, and it in no way infringes on the privileges or obligations of the other operating units in the department.

One of the many problems you will encounter in working a plainclothes assignment is that of positively identifying yourself as a police officer once the need for such identification becomes necessary. The less you look like an on-duty police officer, the more effective you are on the detail you are working. Suddenly the need arises for you to identify yourself and state "I am a police officer." A handgun displayed by itself means only that the bearer is armed and may appear to some people as an immediate threat to be overcome. The identification card by itself may look like a driver's license, or a badge carried may have a worn-out appearance and look more like a toy badge than the real thing when presented by an officer in a polo shirt and jeans. Whatever the arrangement made by your agency for your identification when the need arises, you must make it in a positive manner and the credentials and/or badge should have an official-appearing configuration. The person you are confronting in an arrest situation, or some other form of official business demanding proof of your authority, must know that you *really* are the police officer you say you are. Another officer might not recognize you either.

Recognition of an Officer in Plainclothes.   Whenever you encounter another officer out of uniform, you are confronted with a problem. That officer may be on an undercover assignment and the last thing he or she wants is to be recognized as a fellow police officer or deputy. Probably the better policy of a department is that you make it a practice for the officer in plainclothes to first greet the uniformed officer. If there is no greeting, then it is probably a signal that you should go on about your business as though the encounter were between strangers. There is the old story about the uniformed officer who greeted a plainclothes officer who was in deep cover and walking along with a member of the mob that he had taken several months to infiltrate. When the uniformed officer grabbed his hand, started pumping it, and stated that they had not seen each other since the academy, months of hard work went down the drain and the officer's life could have been lost.

DISTRICT RESPONSIBILITY

Your assigned district is the area of the city entrusted to you for a specified period of time to answer calls and to patrol at all times except while otherwise engaged. During your tour of duty, you may leave the district to eat lunch, to go to headquarters for reporting or prisoner transportation, to handle an assigned call outside the district, or to pursue a known or suspected violator. The reason for assigning specific units to designated districts is to assure at least minimum patrol coverage of each district. When you are assigned to a district, give it your full attention and provide its people with the best possible police service.

Under the community policing plan, you may be permanently assigned to a specific district until you are promoted or transferred out of the patrol unit. Such an assignment will give you greater incentive and opportunity to get to know your district and the people in it and unique problems that may exist in that district, such as which gangs claim which turf and who are their members, and all of the business operators and residents. Many departments maintain a resource center or mini substation right in the district so that you have a base to work from as well as a place for the people to call upon you and your fellow officers.

INSPECTIONS ON PATROL

During a tour of duty, the patrol officer performs a succession of inspections for a variety of purposes and to assist various other agencies and individuals as well as the police department. Fundamentally, the inspections of buildings and other places are for the benefit of the owners and operators themselves, for building security, and for early discovery of fires and other hazards. Additionally, the inspections serve as a crime prevention tool, and there is always an extra deterrence factor during the actual presence of the officer. Other inspections may be for the benefit of building and safety departments, the health officer, license department, public utilities, and environmental protection agencies.

Building Inspections

While you are on patrol, get out of the patrol unit frequently and physically check the buildings. From the front seat of a patrol car with the aid of a powerful spotlight, it is possible to check windows and the ground below for broken glass. Some glass does not reflect.

By getting the right angle of the light on a space between double doors it may be possible to see the locking bolt where it locks the doors together. One technique used by officers for building security is to get out of the car, try the doors and windows of the building, and then place a small piece of paper in the crack above the door. The officer returns periodically during the tour of duty and shines a light on the slip of paper, assuming that the building is secure. Some enterprising burglars have been known to pry open the door bearing the small piece of paper, then tape the paper to the top of the door, enter, commit their crime, and leave. The paper never leaves the doorway, but the building security has been violated.

Other methods of indicating whether someone has intruded are to string thread or fine wires across the entranceway that will be broken on contact; or attach invisible or transparent tape stretching from door to door frame in more than one location in hopes that the intruder will not see any or all of them. Whatever device you use should be creative and be changed from time to time. Burglars are going to be imaginative and resourceful, like the true professionals many of them are.

Plan to check out the entire group of buildings when you approach a shopping center or complex of buildings. Although you may use a spot-check technique, you should be reasonably sure of the security of the entire area. In most districts it is virtually impossible to provide all of the police protection that you should because of the heavy demands on your time and attention. To compensate for this lack of complete coverage, work out some sort of unpredictable spot-check procedure, giving the greatest attention to those places most likely to be subject to burglary or similar crimes.

During your "routine" building checks, it would be wise to plan for the time when you might have to attack the building in a hostile situation, such as a raid, a barricaded felon, and/or a hostage situation. If not on paper, at least have a sketch in your mind of the building's entrances and exits, skylights and windows, and types of locks or latches and locations of the keys or names and addresses and phone numbers of people who can assist you in gaining access. Know where the master switches for electricity and shut-off valves are for the water and gas, and the piping systems for heating and air conditioning. Keep notes also on the proximity of emergency services, such as fire stations and hospitals.

When approaching a location where a suspect may be inside, turn off your headlights and turn the volume down on your radio so as not to signal your arrival. When applying the brakes, use the hand brakes to avoid flashing the brake lights. Park your unit some distance away, and walk, being sure not to slam the car door. When you approach on foot, there is less likelihood that the burglar—if there is one—will hear you. Move silently without keys rattling; walk flat-footed (heels and soles down at the same time) and you will find that your footsteps are much quieter. Take advantage of the natural cover of darkness and the shadows. Do not use the flashlight except when absolutely necessary, and then only when holding it to one side away from your body. Walk close to the buildings and avoid silhouetting yourself in doorways or in front of windows.

Plan your approach so that you are not walking in the glare of headlights or other light or casting shadows that signal your presence. If you work in a team, you and your partner should plan your strategy to complement each other, and both of you should know the whereabouts of the other at all times. One effective means of communicating with other officers is by tapping short code signals on the pavement with the police baton. Other methods of communication include flashing a light on a high object that may be visible to officers on two sides of a building or flashing a signal directly toward another officer with the hand covering all but a small "pinhole" of light emanating from the flashlight. Consider carrying a small penlight in your shirt pocket with your writing pens. There are many times when it will be more convenient than your large flashlight. If you must talk, whisper. To reduce the hissing "sibilant explosion" sounds that accompany whispering, first take a deep breath and let out half of your air before making the first sound.

Every building that you approach may have someone inside, either a burglar or someone legitimately there, such as office or cleanup personnel, or the proprietor. Since none of them will be wearing labels, you should expect to find a burglar or two. Using that logic, some training officers recommend that you make every approach with your handgun in your hand ready for immediate use.

Other training officers recommend that you vary your practice depending on time of day, whether you have a backup, whether you have to have a flashlight in your hand, and if there are doors that you have to open by turning knobs first. Some officers have very strong opinions about this specific procedure and state that they *never* enter any place where they might encounter a dangerous felon without their weapon in a ready position in their hand. You will have to make your own decision, but consider how many hands you have free to move things and to struggle with a suspect should you encounter one. One alternative is to hold the flashlight and gun in the same hand and keep the other hand free.

When you come to a door that opens inward away from you, turn the knob, step back, and kick the door open with your foot so that it swings all the way and hits the doorstop when it is completely open. You then know that no one is hiding behind the door. Reach in for the switch and turn the lights on. Then you can keep your flashlight in your pocket and have the gun in one hand with the other hand free. There are some training officers, however, who keep their guns in their holsters for routine open-door situations unless there is reason to believe that an armed felon is inside. Their belief is that they can draw and fire a weapon as quickly as if it were in their hand. I recommend that you practice what works best for you in various situations. You only live once.

While approaching the building, look around for vehicles that seem to be out of place and sacks or suitcases that might have contained burglar tools for roof and safe "jobs." Check for footprints in the mud or loosely packed earth beneath doors and windows that may have been the point of entry or exit. Inspect the sides of the building where it is adjacent to utility poles, piles of boxes, ladders, or some other means of access to the roof. It is possible that the burglar—if there was one—might have scuffed his shoes on the building when climbing.

Make a serious game out of building inspections, varying your technique and starting point each time, and generally causing confusion for anyone who might attempt to analyze your methods. The rear doors and windows are most vulnerable to attack by burglars, but some burglars prefer the front because they may believe officers check only back doors. Never overlook the possibility that there may be some person inside who has a legal and legitimate reason for being there, but consider everyone suspect until you have completely checked them out. Also consider the possibility that a lookout accomplice may be standing, or sitting in a parked automobile, somewhere outside the building and that he or she may appear to have a perfectly logical reason for being at that location. The lookout may have some unique method for signaling your presence to the burglar inside, which may indicate to you possible complicity in some type of criminal activity.

When checking out a door, look first to determine which way it opens. Some burglars close the door just far enough so that when someone carelessly grabs it to see if it is locked, the bolt locks into place. The clicking sound of the bolt serves as a signal device for the burglar. Do not stand directly in front of the door, since the intruder may shoot through the door. Standing directly in front has proven a fatal mistake for many police officers. Hold the door steady, take hold of the knob and turn it to take up any slack that may exist, then attempt to open the door in whichever direction it opens. If it is secure, check for pry marks and then move on to the next door or window.

Whenever you check out the interior of any building that appears to have been forcibly entered and you believe there is a possibility that the culprit is still inside, wait for backup officers and proceed as though it were a crime in progress. Make liberal use of lights, turning them on and leaving them on as you proceed with the search. The eyes adjust to lighting changes that you should use to your advantage.

For example, if your eyes are adjusted to the light and you are entering a dark room, reach inside and turn on as many lights as you can find switches for. If there is someone inside the dark room, that person's eyes will take about 20 to 50 seconds to adjust to see in the light. You might check this phenomenon by stepping out into bright sunlight for a few minutes, then walk back into a dark room; or stand in a lighted room, then turn off all the lights. What happens to your vision? It takes quite a while for your eyes to adjust to the change, like going from a positive to a negative photo print. It actually involves a change in functions of the rods and cones in the eyes. Of course, if you want this test to work correctly and get the full effect of the dramatic changes in vision capability, be sure to go from the sunlight into a room that is totally dark and does not have light shining through partially opened blinds.

In your real-life situation when you are checking out a building and you have turned on the lights, you will have that time to see the culprit and make a decision about what you are going to do about his or her presence. Also, when you are opening the door, give it a firm shove so that it will strike the doorstop or a wall. If it strikes something soft, there might be a person standing behind that door. (Figure 2–7 illustrates an alternative to the solo patrol.)

Inspecting windows usually involves first checking for any broken glass, pry marks, or latent prints before touching any portion of the window, to avoid contamination of possible evidence. Make sure that glass is actually in the window. It may

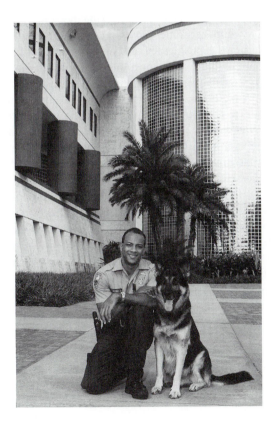

Figure 2–7 Canine Officer Brian Callaway. (Photo by Orlando Mendez; Courtesy Metro-Dade Police Department.)

have been completely removed by some careful burglar. Touch the glass to feel for any unusual heat inside the building, which may indicate the presence of a smoldering fire or a faulty heating system. Determine the way the window opens; then attempt to open it by applying reasonable pressure. If there is some evidence of entry, check the wall below for scuff marks and the sill for dust disturbance. Sometimes the window may prove to be one that was broken earlier but never repaired. At first it may appear to be a burglar's point of entry, but a closer inspection may reveal a substantial quantity of dust and the presence of spider webs, which would have been destroyed if entry had been made recently.

If you find the door and/or window of any building open, consider that it might be the result of a criminal act. Check it out in the same manner whether the person in charge had left the door open and had neglected to lock up for the night or if there had been a burglar inside. Sometimes there is no way for you to determine whether or not a crime has been committed—or is in progress—without investigating further.

Crime Prevention Follow-up

Whenever repeated instances of crime hazards are inadvertently caused by the potential victims, as when doors or windows are carelessly left open or company trucks are parked overnight with the keys left in the ignition, it is your responsibility to encourage the potential victims to correct the situation.

Because your duty hours may preclude your making personal contacts with many of these people, there should be some provision for follow-up contacts by another officer, preferably during the business hours of the places to be visited. If time does not permit personal contacts, an inspection form may be prepared with notations for suggested improvements in security precautions, and it may be mailed to the business in question. This is an excellent job for the community service (nonsworn) people to perform, if your department is fortunate enough to have the luxury of such supplementary personnel. Block captains in your community-oriented policing program or your local community college, or senior citizen programs of the city or county, may choose to assume these community relations–oriented programs.

This follow-up procedure serves two purposes: public relations and crime prevention. It is important that you let the public know of the work that you are doing and the attention that is given to their establishments. By expressing your concern over the security of their property, we hope that those contacted will follow your advice and at the same time have increased confidence in the value of having such an efficient police department. The crime prevention aspect, of course, will tend to reduce your increasing work load. There is always the possibility that the crime rate will increase, but perhaps you may be effective in causing the increase to be less than if you made no effort at all to reduce crime.

House Inspections

As part of an overall crime repression program, it may be wise to institute a house inspection service for people on vacation if your community does not already have such a service. Some people may be absent from their homes for weeks or months, and a crime committed during their absence may go undetected and unreported for all that time. The greater the time between the occurrence of the crime and its discovery, the greater the culprit's chance of escaping apprehension.

Some burglary victims will remember that they actually provided the burglars with valuable information. A wife may inform the local newspaper that her husband has won an award for being the salesman of the month and that he and his family who live at 1327 Lonely Lane will be on a month-long, all-expense-paid vacation in the Bahamas. A society couple whose home is known for its works of art hanging on the walls may let their friends and suppliers know that they are going on a goodwill mission to a remote Indian village for three months. In both cases, the individuals are indirectly providing burglars with a wealth of information. In either case, the burglars may hire a moving van and take the entire contents of the house.

Residents may be asked to report their anticipated absences to the department so that its officers can instruct them on a few methods of burglary prevention. The officers may request that the people announce their good news to the press upon their return rather than at the time of their departure. Arrangements may be made for "house sitters" to take up residence during an extended absence or to have friends or relatives check the house periodically and report to the police department that they have found it still secure. Some plans should be made to eliminate signs of vacation, such as long grass, dry flower beds, accumulated circulars and sales brochures, milk, newspapers, and other objects strewn about the premises. People should be advised to leave a light or lights on in the house, possibly a radio left playing, and some shades or drapes not drawn all the way; this will leave a burglar guessing as to whether there is anyone inside or not. Timers may be installed to turn electrical appliances and lights on and off at normal times rather than continue to operate during daylight hours. Even electronic equipment goes bad sometimes. I am reminded of the people who left for a month, whose lights turned on and off alternately about every hour for the full month because of a malfunctioning timer, with no friend or relative checking the place. A friend or neighbor should also be given a key and should be present to assist the officer in checking out the residence in the event that a crime has been committed.

During the day, house inspections for those on vacation should include a thorough check of the entire premises for security and freedom from vandalism (see Figure 2–8). Ask the neighbors if they have seen anything at all that might strike them as suspicious and to report to the department if they do see something out of the ordinary. During the nighttime, make occasional and unscheduled inspections. Use your flashlight liberally to avoid injury at the hands of a neighbor who might believe that you are a prowler or burglar. It is also wise to make liberal use of the lights inside the house, turning them all on as you go through the house or business establishment. After all, you are not hiding from anyone.

I have been told by several officers of larger departments that this service is no longer offered by their departments, and that they recommend the services of private security companies. Another option is to make use of the neighborhood watch program, with neighbors performing these functions. Within the department, the task could be performed by college students who serve without charge as interns in exchange for college credits, or this might be yet another function of community

Figure 2–8 People who leave on vacation often forget such things as locking doors or closing a window. In this case, the family may have forgotten to secure the place, or there may be a burglar inside who forgot to close the door after he or she broke in. (Courtesy Police Department, Bismarck, North Dakota.)

service officers. It may be a trade-off, using time to prevent burglaries in lieu of the time it takes to investigate burglaries.

Miscellaneous Inspections

Each jurisdiction has a widely varied set of regulations and procedures for many other inspection services that are required of the patrol officers in their respective jurisdiction. Some cities require their police officers to make quarterly business license inspections. The building codes in some communities may specify that any building department inspector or police officer who observes a construction job in progress must check for the necessary permits. When they go into cafés or any place where food is served, officers in some jurisdictions are required to look for unsanitary conditions and to forward a report to the health department whenever they observe violations. When venereal disease may result from some promiscuous activities of juveniles, the health department may require that a form be forwarded to them for follow-up treatment.

Depending on the city or county policies, police officers or sheriff's deputies are expected to perform a variety of additional types of inspections, including an examination of all liquor licenses and dance hall or entertainment permits. It is not unusual for certain operators to stretch the limitations of their permits beyond what has been permitted, such as dancing in a place that is licensed for entertainment only, or using a ten-piece band in a saloon licensed for only a three-member group. As a part of your community policing program, you are also concerned with quality of life of your constituents.

"ATTRACTIVE NUISANCES," OR PATROL HAZARDS

The "attractive nuisance" doctrine is that one maintains on his or her premises (business or residential) a condition, instrumentality, machine, or other agency that is dangerous to young children because of children's inability to appreciate peril, which may reasonably be expected to attract children to such premises, and that one therefore has a duty to the children (and society in general) to exercise *reasonable care* to protect against the dangers of such an attraction *(Schock* versus *Ringling Brothers and Barnum and Bailey Combined Shows,* 5 Wash. 2d 599, 105 P.2d 838, 843).

The doctrine also applies to creating such a condition on the premises of another, or in a public place which may be a source of danger to children, and states that one has a duty to take such precautions as a reasonably prudent man (or woman) would take to prevent injury to children of tender years whom he or she knows to be accustomed to resort there, or who may, by reason of something there that may be expected to attract them, come there to play *(Atlantic Coastline Railroad Company* versus *O'Neal,* 48 Ga. App. 706, 172 S.E. 740, 741).

One cannot apply this doctrine to a natural condition or common dangers existing as a part of nature (such as a free-flowing creek or stream running through an open field or forest) *(McCall* versus *McCallie,* 48 Ga. App. 99, 171 S.E. 843, 844). What does apply, however, is that the attraction must be visible from a public place where children have a right to be *(Rokiski* versus *Polish Nat. Alliance of U.S. of North America,* 314 Ill. App. 380, 41 N.E. 2d. 300).

The term "patrol hazard" is frequently used to describe a specific condition or place that requires the patrol officer's special attention. The hazard may be a bar where gang fights occur frequently. It may be an old dump site that has filled up with stagnant water and is now being used as a swimming hole by the neighborhood children. A hazard location might be an abandoned building, a "haunted house," or a secluded area that a child might consider a "secret place" because it is a place to hide. Although this may have no direct bearing on the character of the operators, virtually every place that attracts large numbers of people is a patrol hazard because of the potential problems inherent whenever large numbers of people are thrown together for any purpose. Places where tourists stay and congregate are high hazard areas because there is usually a disproportionate number of people on foot, and many of them carry larger than usual amounts of cash on their person. Tourist attractions and places of entertainment and shopping also attract hookers and hustlers. You will also find pickpockets, muggers, carjackers, and other criminals large and small.

When you are on patrol, give these "frequent incident" or "hazard" locations more than average attention and attempt to prevent any criminal activity by your frequent and unscheduled attendance. Develop a professional relationship with the owners and operators of the places that require more frequent patrol coverage, and impress upon them the fact that your occasional visits are for their protection as well as that of the other people in the community. Encourage them to call for your assistance if they should need it, and generally develop their respect for your ability to perform your duty in a fair and objective manner. Develop informants in the neighborhood, or among the people who work or visit these places, and encourage them to let you know of any potential problems that may be developing so that effective police action may actually prevent the occurrence of any large-scale criminal activity. Maintain a list of these places and continually update your information regarding the names of the owners, operators, and other key people whom you should be able to locate whenever necessary.

SURVEILLANCE AND STAKEOUTS

Surveillance is the process of keeping under observation a place, a person, or an object for the purpose of identifying persons, developing information, discovering relationships between people and places or objects, and discovery of evidence.

The object of surveillance is usually suspected of being related to criminal activity one way or another, either from the standpoint of victimization, or as a suspect. Through the means of a surveillance it is possible to determine who is meeting with whom, who a person's friends and associates are, where certain people go and what they do and for what purposes, where they might be hiding certain things, and what they might be saying to each other. Activities, identities, contacts, and virtually every facet of a person's life are under scrutiny, usually with the purpose of solving a crime and gaining a conviction of the guilty persons.

A loose surveillance is one in which an officer follows or observes a person on an occasional basis, such as after work for a few hours to see if the person may be planning a robbery for this evening. A close surveillance might be an open convoy to protect a person or to let the person being "tailed" know that he or she is being watched very closely. A fixed surveillance is usually referred to as a "stakeout," such as when officer(s) secrete themselves inside a convenience market they anticipate might be robbed at the approximate time the officers are present.

A convoy is a type of surveillance that is performed either to protect the subject or to keep the subject purposefully under observation with his or her knowledge as a means of letting the subject know that he or she is being continually watched. This technique is quite effective when a known organized crime "enforcer" comes into town for what you believe to be a secret visit or to perform a specific task, such as make a collection or pay a debt. Although it may seem to be a form of harassment, the "convoy" technique actually involves no harassment at all. It is merely a form of preventive maintenance. While the subject is being watched, there is little likelihood that he or she will commit any crime, and if the subject commits no crimes, the officers make no attempt to contact him or her or to restrict his or her movements. Sometimes the airport detail of the intelligence unit may even greet an undesirable character on his arrival, greeting him by name and acknowledging his presence. This is usually accompanied by a suggestion that he mind his manners while in town because he will be under constant surveillance.

Objectives of a Surveillance

These are some of the principal objectives for initiating and maintaining a surveillance.

1. Obtain sufficient evidence to make a physical arrest or secure an arrest or search warrant.

2. Locate and apprehend suspects or wanted persons.

3. Locate the residence, hangouts, or other places that the subject of the surveillance and his or her contacts frequent.

4. Identify the relationships between known and suspected criminals.

5. Prevent—or attempt to prevent—the commission of crimes.

6. Check out informants and the reliability of their information.

7. Prepare for a raid of a gambling or vice establishment.

8. Determine the best way to accomplish an arrest or to rescue a person being held as a hostage.

9. Locate missing persons or runaways, adult and juvenile.

10. Obtain background information for an interview or interrogation.

11. Locate hiding places, fences, unethical businesspersons, relay points for criminal transactions, or headquarters for various criminal or espionage activities.

12. Protect persons, places, or objects.

Preparation for Surveillance

Prior to starting surveillance, secure as much information about the subject as possible. Check the files of your own records system and every other available source of information to help you get to know the subject, his or her habits, and acquaintances. If available, secure a copy of a recent photograph of the subject and familiarize yourself with his or her general appearance as well as distinctive features.

If you have any advanced information concerning the specific location or general area where you will be maintaining surveillance on the subject, thoroughly familiarize yourself with that area. Get to know the street names, their relative locations, and the tract configuration. Check records and other officers to identify the people in the area who may assist you in the surveillance or who may assist in the transmission of information to headquarters when regular means are not available.

Foot Surveillance

For an effective surveillance operation, more than one officer must be used. It will be necessary to alternate the sequence and relative locations of the surveillants, or "tails," so that the subject does not become aware of their presence unless they intend that the subject know they are there. When the subject turns a corner, the surveillant immediately behind the subject should continue across the street at the intersection, then turn and walk parallel to the subject down the same street. The next surveillant in line should turn the corner and take the lead position immediately behind the subject. If there are three surveillants, the third officer can be used for relief or can assume the lead if one of the other officers is identified, or "made" by the subject. This "leap-frogging" technique should continue so that a single officer is not continually following the subject.

When on surveillance, you should work out a signal system with your partner so that it will not be necessary to get together in frequent huddles, or to make obvious signals to each other. If you are conducting a surveillance in street clothing, avoid chameleon disguises. Minor changes in appearance can work wonders at times, such as a baseball cap that can be worn or removed and placed in a pocket, a reversible jacket, or removing a necktie or jacket somewhere (and returning later to pick it up). Look natural while operating a "tail." You may find it to your advantage occasionally to wear eyeglasses or sunglasses and to vary the distance between yourself and the subject, but avoid any "private eye" melodrama. The key to your success as a surveillant is to look as inconspicuous as possible and to fit into the surroundings naturally.

Watch out for the subject's methods for testing whether he is being "tailed." Avoid eye-to-eye contacts or any other direct confrontation. There must always be some plausible explanation for you to follow the subject for an extended period of time. Frequent alternation of surveillants will ensure that no solo officer is following the subject for too long a period of time.

When turning a corner, walk naturally and continue moving at the normal rate of travel. The subject may have stopped immediately after turning. If this is the case, your sudden appearance around the corner should not be followed by a sudden, obvious stop. Keep on walking, even though it necessitates walking past the subject. If the subject makes a telephone call, you or your partner should also do something natural during the same period of time. There is little likelihood that you will find adjoining phone booths. If you do, perhaps a call of your own would be in order. When the subject enters a building or an elevator, follow if it is natural to do so. Otherwise, it may be better to wait until the subject returns to the street before resuming the surveillance.

Testing for surveillance is executed in many ways. The subject may stop suddenly for no apparent reason and look around or may suddenly reverse direction of travel and meet his or her surveillants head-on. If either of these things happens, the first officer has been "made" and should be replaced, if a replacement is available. The subject may take a short taxi ride, or get on a bus for a block or two, then get off just before it starts to move after a stop. The subject may watch a "tail" in store windows. To bait the surveillant, the subject may discard some unimportant piece of paper and then watch to see whether the person following stoops to pick it up.

Auto Surveillance

Before beginning an auto surveillance detail, be sure that you have plenty of gasoline. As with the foot method, it is best to have two or more surveillants (vehicles) so that you may use the same leapfrog technique discussed in the previous paragraphs covering foot surveillance. Be sure not to follow the subject's vehicle too closely. If possible, try to keep a "cushion vehicle" between yourself and the object vehicle. Keep the headlights on low beam, and drive naturally without arousing the suspicions of the subject by attempting to maintain a constant interval between your unit and the subject's. The subject may "test for a tail," as described earlier and may also drive alternately fast and slow to watch the car following. The subject may slow down as if to stop at a changing signal, then speed through the intersection just at the moment the light changes to red, leaving the surveillant behind. The subject may make frequent U-turns or take other types of evasive action.

The Stakeout

A stakeout is usually for the purpose of waiting for the anticipated arrival of a suspect who is either wanted for investigation or expected to commit a crime at the location being "staked out." When working such an assignment, be sure to preplan carefully. Get adequate food and rest before entering the place, and take a sufficient quantity of food with you in case it is necessary to spend some time. Arrange for efficient communications with other units and with headquarters.

Deliver your equipment, such as a shotgun, binoculars, or other special equipment, inconspicuously to avoid arousing suspicion. Dismantle the gun, and carry it in a case or container that would normally be carried by someone who works at that location. Wear the same type of clothing that would be natural for the establishment.

When working a stakeout in a place of business where other types of crimes may occur that are not related to your purpose, be sure to advise the store owner or other people in charge that they are not to reveal your presence to handle the matter. For example, a stakeout for an anticipated armed robbery will be rendered ineffective if the manager observes a shoplifter and calls to the officer to arrest the petty thief at just about the same time the potential armed robber steps into the store. The manager or others could also destroy the value of the stakeout by announcing to some of the customers that an officer is protecting the place.

Basic Guidelines for a Stakeout

1. Operate in a businesslike manner.
2. Be natural and avoid melodrama.
3. Do not use phony disguises.
4. Be on the alert for a subject "testing for a tail."
5. Be adequately prepared for surveillance, particularly a fixed post where you may have to stay for some time.
6. Prepare a "cover" reason for being in the area while on a surveillance.
7. Keep sufficient money and supplies on hand.
8. Avoid direct eye contact with the subject.
9. Prepare for adequate communications with other officers and with headquarters.

SPECIALIZED PATROL

At one time or another, your department may have to create a specialized patrol unit that is separate from the regular patrol force. The everyday demands of routine calls for service and all other activities of the patrol unit make it virtually impossible to address special problems. Using a great amount of ingenuity and imagination, a separate unit will be able to concentrate on one problem at a time or perhaps on several different activities. Some of the types of special problems include street muggings, sexual assaults, burglaries in a concentrated area or of a certain type, narcotics trafficking, theft and fencing on a wide scale, pilfering from autos, prostitution, and street walking.

For the unit to enjoy any degree of success, the officers must have the freedom to develop their own skills and techniques while working within the framework of good police practice. They should be relieved of any responsibility for generalized patrol, follow-up investigation, and regular crime prevention and repression activities while assigned to this special unit. Another factor that helps such a unit to succeed is to publicize its existence and success rate but keep the actual identities of the officers anonymous. Publicizing the existence of a special team of officers working as decoys in the downtown area to combat the problem of sexual assaults on the streets may reduce the number of such crimes because the responsible offenders know that they run a higher risk of getting caught.

Specialized patrol may or may not acquire some title, such as "Metro," "Spec. Enf. Bureau," saturation patrol, or "the sting," and the officers will be assigned to wear uniforms or special equipment for some assignments, plainclothes for others, sometimes costumes and special makeup, and disguises for other assignments. Male officers may be dressed as females and serve as decoys. Negative effects of specialized units include jealousy among officers who are not accepted in the program, an "elitist" attitude among assigned officers, credit being given to the special unit at the expense of the work of the regular patrol, empire building by the assigned officers, hostility from citizens, and problems of coordination and cooperation between specialized details and regular units with a drain on human resources from the regular units.

Advantages of specialized units may overshadow the negative aspects, however. There is a specific designation of responsibility on the special team to get a certain job done effectively. The officers seeking assignment would have something to strive for, and the officers assigned would have the special feeling of being part of the "elite" group. Training and skills development in certain areas, such as special weapons or techniques, will give the officers goals to work for. If all goes well, and the specialized unit is successful, the publicity and positive reactions from the public will greatly enhance the image of the department.

The decision whether to create specialized patrol units depends on such factors as nature and volume of certain crimes, the current effectiveness of current patrolling methods, history of success with special units in saturation patrol or decoy operations, or special methods of surveillance. Some officers might have to change their physical appearance and length and amount of facial and head hair, adjust their mannerisms and speech patterns, and isolate themselves from the police department so that they are not known as police officers while performing special assignments. Deployment of the specialized units would depend on need, and those needs might change daily. For example, the recent release of an unusual number of burglars who have served their time in prison and have returned home on parole, many of them to return to burglarizing, would cause the department to want to maintain close surveillance on those individuals to determine which ones were truly rehabilitated.

Undercover Assignments

Because of the delicate nature of this type of work, your role is to develop information and determine whether someone is committing criminal or disloyal acts. You cannot form bonds with your "fellow employees" or "fellow students" because you are there in an investigative role, and when you finish your job you are not leaving as a "snitch." Also, should you later leave the police or sheriff's department and look for another job, do not apply anyplace where you have worked undercover.

Who knows who you really are and what your role is? In some instances you may be introduced to the manager or supervisor, who will hire you and will be your contact away from the job. In other instances, the manager or supervisor may be the subject of your investigation, and you will have to apply "cold" for the job and then assume the role you are hired for while you continue your undercover assignment. You may be one of several investigators who apply for the job; then the one who is hired assumes the role.

When you apply for the job, your résumé and application should have information that can be verified. This will require planting of phony work histories and school records where necessary and will call for cooperation from the people who will verify your imaginary past. You may list places of employment that are no longer in business and former supervisors who are deceased. You may have to establish a phone answering service that will provide your cover references, perhaps from a fellow officer at the office with special instructions how to answer the phone and what to say about you. High school and college records, birth certificates, drivers' licenses, and certain documents may also have to be prepared, depending on how elaborate your cover must be. This, of course, depends on the seriousness of the case and how much time and money there is to do the undercover job.

Memorize your personal history so that you can play the role in a convincing manner. Make sure that your vehicle, clothing, wallet, schoolbooks, and all other paraphernalia related to the role you are playing are consistent with that role. Play your role to the hilt and do not "blow your cover," no matter what happens. You may have to watch petty crimes committed in your presence and do nothing because if you were to act like a police officer, your job would be over. A suspicious person you are investigating might actually try to bait you to see if you are a police officer. Your reading material and music on your Walkman[tm] should be consistent with the role you are playing. Never confide in anyone that you are actually an undercover officer working on a job. Believe it or not, I actually had a young lady who was operating for my private investigation company and posing as a customer watching a bartender suspected of stealing and gambling as well as selling drugs. He was finally found out and fired (and later arrested), no thanks to our operator. Another customer in the bar invited her to go with him to another bar for a drink, and she replied that she could not leave because she was working. When questioned, she said that she was actually working undercover. The man then walked over to the bartender, who happened to be a friend of his, and told him that the young lady he had been buying drinks for was probably someone from "beverage control" who was watching the place. That blew her cover. She never worked again for my company.

Make personal and written reports as required by your supervisors, but stay away from police officers and police headquarters. You are on your own. Do your job, develop your information, then quit or get yourself fired or laid off, and leave. Wrap up your case by completing the necessary reports and coordinating the evidence you may have collected and prepare for grand jury and other legal proceedings.

You eventually will have to go back to your patrol job, which may be quite a letdown in comparison. Recently, a policewoman returned to patrol after having posed as a streetwalking prostitute for about 10 years. What a change that must have been!

TEAM POLICING

Team policing is approached differently by different departments, but essentially it means that the city or county is broken down by area, and officers are assigned on a permanent or semipermanent basis to those areas. The large department is broken down into several smaller departments, and the local teams work more closely with the people in their respective areas, on the grounds that the police can be more effective if they have the support, confidence, and assistance of the people they serve. The administrators and supervisors in these team areas are given more autonomy and local responsibilities for field activities, investigation, community relations, and overall police performance.

Team policing is not for every department. As a matter of fact, if your department is one of the smaller ones, with fewer than 50 to 75 officers, you already have team policing. In the larger police jurisdictions, this grass-roots approach is undertaken to bring the people and the police closer together in a more cooperative situation. The local substation or storefront headquarters is a place the local citizens can visit to meet with the local police commander and staff to discuss mutual problems. In team policing, a greater effort is made to involve the assigned officers in participative management, identifying problems, setting objectives, and developing methods to meet those objectives. There is more flexible scheduling and flexibility in assignments, and the officers have greater opportunity to follow up investigations they have started. The officers are also encouraged to develop and work with neighborhood "watch" groups and encourage the people to report suspicious circumstances, and to take a greater interest and more responsibility in preventing and repressing crimes.

In a team-policing environment, you may find that supervision is somewhat less formal because you are working closer with your team, but the operation must have discipline if it is to operate effectively. You cannot have four drivers in the same car, all going different directions. Discussion and negotiation will have to be undertaken to determine the direction in which all are to go. So it is with team policing. According to Whisenand, the role of the team policing supervisor is to (1) support subordinates, (2) facilitate interaction, (3) emphasize goals, and (4) facilitate work.[3]

COMMUNITY POLICING

Although the team policing concept is not practiced by some departments and has given way to community policing, there are some similarities, but team policing has gone further. It is more of a community–police partnership where the officers are more permanently assigned to specific districts and more closely identify with their districts. Storefronts in the districts are converted into mini-stations, and there are frequent problem-solving meetings and follow-up activities. The officers are expected to be more proactive in addressing the problems of the community in a more "hands-on" manner. For example, instead of fretting over children not being properly strapped into their safety seats in their parents' automobiles, the officers bring the errant parents into the police headquarters and teach the parents how to attach the seats. People who attend seminars like this often have their citations dismissed because they have agreed to provide for the safety of their children, which is the most important aspect of this program.[4]

A humanitarian group may operate a soup kitchen for homeless people, whose presence in a certain neighborhood around schools and parks where children play causes concern for the parents. Rather than close down the kitchen, the police officers may assist the group find a place where the people may still be fed, but the children can play in their park without having to stumble over people rolled up in their blankets waiting for their next meal. A particular complex of apartments becomes the congregating place for large groups of nonresidents whose drunken behavior night after night causes concern for some of the residents who want to have peace. Officers not only send the party goers away and make the necessary arrests but also follow up by contacting the owner of the apartment complex, who is in a position to determine the identity of the hosts for the unruly parties, and takes legal action to evict them.

Gangs are formed by children who need to be loved, many who feel disoriented in a dysfunctional family, and need to belong to something that will give them self-esteem. Officers work with groups of boys and girls and get them involved in organized sporting events and other activities that compete with gang membership. Other people from the community who were gang members themselves take part in these activities alongside the police officers, and redirect these children toward law-abiding lives. Graffiti is quickly removed by volunteers and public works employees as well as some of the "taggers" who have been ordered by the courts to clean up their mess. There is no "art" in graffiti that costs property owners hundreds and thousands of dollars to paint over and remove time and time again.

Abandoned vehicles and other junk left to rot in front and back yards are a blight on the entire city. They are cited and quickly removed, as are the other clutter and overgrown weeds handled in other abatement programs. Homeless squatters who move into empty buildings create fire hazards and health hazards. These properties are boarded up and fenced in, or ordered destroyed at the insistence of the officers who work the district.

In general, community policing is just that: *Community Policing*. All of these activities are directed toward improvement of the quality of life for all residents and their guests in your jurisdiction instead of just the privileged few.

SUMMARY

This chapter has been designed to introduce you to the basics of police patrol, beginning with attitude preparation and going on to actual preparation and the preliminaries prior to commencing patrolling activities. In the sections on patrolling the district, district responsibility, and inspections on patrol, we outlined the many functions and responsibilities of the field officer. A constant and alert as well as imaginative officer is required for this task, and one's principal responsibility is to maximize one's efforts by seeking the willing cooperation of the constituents, the people in the district.

Crime prevention follow-up should be directed toward educating victims on ways in which they might prevent a reoccurrence of the crime. Inspections of houses of people on vacation should be handled conscientiously, recognizing that this gives you an opportunity to ply your skills as a community relations specialist. Patrol hazards include attractive nuisances that may involve criminal and civil liability, but they also include any place or activity that requires more of your attention than other aspects or areas of your duties.

The topics of surveillance and stakeouts are sometimes thought of as the responsibility of more sophisticated police officers, such as the more experienced follow-up detectives. Actually, these are more often assigned to field patrol officers. There are some aspects of the "cops and robbers" game to these activities, but there are hazards and there are rules.

Specialized patrol involves assignment of officers with special talents and skills to units that may be temporary or permanent, their major objective being to address a problem that for some reason cannot be handled successfully through the more traditional police methods. Team policing also involves specialized assignments, but the objectives are to accomplish the police task through perhaps a greater variety of activities. Participative management and public cooperation are the secrets of successful team policing, and the newer approaches to policing: problem solving and community policing.

EXERCISES AND STUDY QUESTIONS

1. What is the purpose for the police and sheriff's field officers wearing distinctive uniforms?
2. Do you have any conflict between your personal value system and the basic police philosophy of law enforcement and community policing?
3. List the personal characteristics you believe make a good police officer.
4. For what reason does the author suggest that you develop relationships outside the department and your own circle of police friends?
5. In what way is a police officer a *public servant*?
6. Do officers always enforce the law exactly as written?
7. What is the *debriefing process* discussed in the text?
8. Why should you begin your shift with a district orientation tour?
9. What is the advantage of foot patrol over vehicle patrol?
10. For what type of assignment would you use bicycle patrol?
11. What is a disadvantage of using fixed-wing aircraft in the city?
12. For what types of assignments would you use plainclothes patrol?
13. Describe the procedure for two officers to check out a building with an open door.

14. How would you and your partner cover a building when you suspect a burglar might still be inside?

15. What does your instructor recommend that you do with your gun when checking out a building when you have found an open door?

16. Does your local police and/or sheriff's department utilize local public access television for public information programming?

17. Why should you not be the first to acknowledge an old academy buddy when meeting him or her in public when you are in uniform and the other officer is in plainclothes?

18. Are there any attractive nuisances in the neighborhood where you live?

19. How would you perform a crime prevention follow-up with the victim of a residence burglary? a commercial burglary?

20. After you have worked undercover at a shoe store, why should you not go back and ask for a part-time job?

21. What is the purpose of a *vacation house inspection,* and how and when would you carry it out?

22. Describe two types of problems for which you would set up a stakeout.

23. What is the difference between a *close* and a *loose* surveillance?

24. Describe how you would use three officers to survey one subject.

25. Describe *community policing* as you see it.

REFERENCES

CHAPMAN, SAMUEL G. *Police Patrol Readings.* Springfield, Ill.: Charles C. Thomas, 1964.

HALE, CHARLES D. *Police Patrol Operations and Management.* New York: John Wiley, 1981.

IANNONE, N. F. *Principles of Police Patrol.* New York: McGraw-Hill, 1975.

LOS ANGELES POLICE DEPARTMENT. *Daily Training Bulletins,* Vol. I. Springfield, Ill.: Charles C. Thomas, 1954.

___. *Daily Training Bulletins,* Vol. II. Springfield, Ill.: Charles C. Thomas, 1958.

McCREEDY, KENNETH R. *Theory and Methods of Police Patrol.* Albany, N.Y.: Delmar, 1974.

WHISENAND, PAUL M. *Police Supervision: Theory and Practice.* Englewood Cliffs, N.J.: Prentice Hall, 1971.

WILSON, ORLANDO W. *Police Planning,* 2nd ed. Springfield, Ill.: Charles C. Thomas, 1958.

Various training bulletins and related materials from the police departments of Glendale, Los Angeles, Riverside, and Santa Ana, the California Highway Patrol, and other agencies.

FOOTNOTES

1. Joan Potter, "Aviation Units: Are They Worth the Money?" *Police Magazine,* Vol. 2, No. 4, July 1979, p. 22.
2. E. D. Fales, Jr., "New Facts about Skidding: They May Save Your Life," *Law Enforcement Bulletin* (Washington, D.C.), May 1965, pp. 13–16. Reprinted from *Popular Science Monthly.* Copyright © 1964 by Popular Science Publishing Co., Inc.
3. Paul M. Whisenand, *Police Supervision: Theory and Practice* (Englewood Cliffs, N.J.: Prentice Hall, 1971), p. 394.
4. Much of this chapter was developed with the information provided by several administrators responsible for community policing in their respective departments. Thanks particularly to Lieutenant John Higley of the Orange (CA) Police Department.

CHAPTER 3

OBSERVATION AND PERCEPTION

*I*NTRODUCTION

One of the most critical factors in the police officer's work is the eyewitness's ability to communicate accurately what he or she actually witnesses. Sometimes we don't always see or hear, feel or taste, or smell what we believe we have perceived. At other times we have trouble communicating our perceptions to others because of our differences in understanding what another person means. We are influenced by learning and conditioning, by our ability to interpret what we perceive, and by what others believe about our perceptions based upon their own learning and conditioning, which is different from ours. The statement "As unreliable as an eyewitness" holds true in all too many cases.

Most people are not trained observers. They see people, yet they do not actually *see* them and cannot describe physical characteristics such as the color of their eyes, shape of a nose, stature, color, and style of clothing. If the observer likes or dislikes or recognizes something in what he or she sees, that observer is more apt to be able to give a better description than if the event or any part of it has no meaning at the time of perception. For example, a jewelry designer might notice the style and design of a necklace worn by another person, whereas a dental technician might see a perfect set of dentures in the wearer's mouth and not even be aware of the necklace.

When you are seeking out and questioning witnesses, bear in mind that most witnesses will describe their observations in their own imperfect ways. You must find out as much as you can about the witnesses and their perceptual abilities, likes and dislikes, and the meanings behind their statements, and then interpret accordingly what they tell you. In this chapter we study some witness characteristics and discuss some of the techniques you may develop to utilize more effectively those witnesses in your investigations.

BASIC REQUIREMENTS OF A WITNESS

When you encounter a witness to any event you must establish five facts about that witness, which must be taken into account when determining whether or not to use that person as a witness in court, or whether you can assign any credibility to the information you glean from him or her.

1. *Was the witness present?* "Presence" may be defined for the purpose of this discussion as being at a place of vantage to gain knowledge of a particular fact through perception with one or more of the senses: sight, sound, taste, smell, touch. Some witnesses have been considered "present" when they have (a) watched two people standing side by side exchange money for a package containing what appeared to be a white substance, making the observation with the aid of binoculars and from a distance of a half mile across the river; (b) smelled marijuana smoke through an open car window while standing alongside the vehicle, such as while issuing a traffic citation; (c) overheard a hooker and her prospective "john" negotiating a price while sitting in an adjacent diner booth; (d) listened to a death threat delivered by telephone from several thousand miles away; (e) felt the cold steel blade of a knife or the warm wet blood in the darkness, having stumbled over a body without seeing it; (f) tasted a beverage that contained what had the characteristics of a carbonated beverage; or (g) watched a person shoot another from point blank range while in the same room. All qualify for "presence," and the annals of the courts abound with similar examples.

2. *Was the witness consciously aware of what took place?* Not only must the person have been within range to perceive, but was it a cognitive perception? A person may be present in the same room as an old friend and frequently look in the friend's general direction yet never actually be conscious of the friend's presence because of his own occupation or preoccupation with some other phenomenon that he is observing. Two officers may have been sitting in a patrol car parked near an intersection when one officer said: "Say, did you see that violation? That yellow Oldsmobile went through the stop sign." The second officer may have looked up immediately and seen the yellow Oldsmobile traveling east across the boulevard. Only one element is missing: The second officer did not see the actual violation at the moment it occurred and cannot testify to the fact. The officer can, however, testify to the identity of the driver of the car and all other circumstances surrounding the pursuit and citation. As the investigating and reporting officer, it is dangerous to assume that since two people were standing side by side when an event took place, they both saw the same things.

3. *Was the witness attentive as the event took place?* To have been present and to have seen something may not be sufficient for an individual to actually have been cognizant of what took place. A witness may actually observe a man holding a revolver up to another man's chest during the commission of an armed robbery and be so inattentive that the action seems to him to be some form of friendly play among friends. When asked about the event, the semicompetent witness who almost observed the event may respond by saying, "Yes. I saw a couple of guys over there but I was not aware that a robbery was taking place." How many times have you been deeply engrossed in watching television or studying your homework when a family member starts talking to you and you merely grunt in response without actually hearing what he or she had to say? Then you have to ask the person to repeat while you change the focus of your attention. Many times we look at something—or so it seems—without actually seeing it. Your potential witness may not have been focused and would, therefore, be incompetent as a witness.

4. *Was the witness physically and mentally competent to perceive and assimilate the information and events as they occurred?* What was the wake state of the witness at the time of the event? still sleeping, or just awakened and clearheaded, or groggy from the sleep? What is the subject's mental and emotional state? oriented as to time and space? aware of the date and time of the event when relating the information to you? Does the person communicate with you in a normal and mature level equal to his or her chronological age? How about the person's health? A case of the flu or a bad cold could affect one's perceptive capabilities. Was the witness drunk or sober, angry or upset at the time over some unrelated event? In your observation of the subject, do you see any signs of hearing or sight impairment, such as a hearing aid or eyeglasses or the telltale impressions on the bridge of the nose caused by constant or frequent wearing of glasses? Ask other witnesses about the capabilities of the others.

5. *What is the person's ability to communicate effectively when relating the information to you and what will be the probable ability to communicate the information in court?* (Later background checks will possibly reveal other problems, such as a criminal record or history of mental illness or alcoholism.) Some people simply cannot function when speaking in public, such as when giving testimony in court. They become blabbering idiots under the intensive cross-examination of well-meaning attorneys who zealously fight for their clients, even if it means tearing down the character of an otherwise competent witness.

FACTORS IN PERCEPTION

When considering the perceptive faculties of a witness, many factors must be taken into account. These may be divided into two broad categories: (1) external factors and (2) internal factors.

External Factors

Distance, or Proximity. The closer an object or event is to the observer, the greater likelihood there is that he will direct some of his attention toward it. Something that occurs nearby more directly involves him than does something that may occur in a remote location.

Phenomena That May Affect Perception, Such as Differences in Lighting, Various Weather Conditions, and Sounds. The eyes function differently under different lighting conditions through the medium of the cones and the rods, and colors appear quite differently under different kinds of light. Some people are night blind. Artificial lighting in darkness causes shadows, which may appreciably affect an individual's powers of perception. Rain, snow, wind, and fog may cause a significant difference in an individual's perceptive abilities. Distortions of vision are not unusual. Noises directly affect one's perception. Loud and unusual noises may cause distractions that divert the observer's attention completely away from an object he may be looking at. An event may be meaningless without sound, but pleasant or frightening with the appropriate sounds. For an example of this phenomenon, watch a horror film on television with the sound off; then turn it on and compare your reactions. Certain illusions also occur when color is introduced. For example, compare a red object with a blue object of the same size. The blue object will appear smaller. The object that makes more noise will appear larger. An object speeding toward you will appear larger than the same object speeding away from you.

Intensity and Size. If something is louder and larger than other things about it, it will receive the attention of observers more rapidly and with greater intensity than the things around it.

Contrast. Something unusual or out of the ordinary will receive more attention than will common or ordinary things. For example, the golfer in a funeral home will receive about as much attention as the tuxedoed undertaker on the golf course.

Repetition. A person or object that appears—under certain conditions—more than one time will attract much more attention than if he or it appears only once. This factor is probably one of the reasons why an individual who appears to be loitering attracts more attention than the individual who seems to be moving with a purpose and a destination.

Movement. A stationary object will soon appear as if it belongs where it is and will blend in even with contrasting objects. The moving object attracts and holds the attention. For example, consider the attention that a running man on a downtown street receives as opposed to all of the other walking men.

Similarities. A woman who looks like Cousin Dalmation is likely to receive more attention than is one who is completely strange. For example, when a witness with missing teeth observes a suspect with missing teeth, that characteristic will probably be the most outstanding one the witness will remember having noticed.

Sounds. Size perception will be affected by sounds. For example, an attacker who is shouting at the same time is more frightening than is a similar attacker who is silent. The person making the noise will appear to be larger, and numbers of people will appear greater when they are making loud and menacing noises. Depending on weather and other atmospheric conditions, the distance from which a noise is coming may be grossly miscalculated, and the direction may not be accurate.

Odors.   According to William S. Cain, in a *Psychology Today* article: "When it comes to identifying odors, people are strangely inconsistent and often imprecise. When exposed to a smell whose origins are not obvious, they may feel on the verge of identifying it . . . but they often cannot come up with the name without prompting."[1] Cain points out that people may improve their ability to identify odors through practice, stating that one of the problems we have in describing odors is that we have trouble finding the correct words to describe our olfactory experiences. Cain reported that 80 common substances were chosen and 103 young women wearing blindfolds were asked to identify them. On the average, the subjects were successful in identifying only 36 of them with 10 most often identified (5 by brand name). Among those most identifiable were (1) Johnson's baby powder, (2) chocolate, (3) coconut, (4) Crayola crayons, (5) mothballs, (6) Ivory soap (bar), (7) Vick's VapoRub, (8) Bazooka bubble gum, (9) coffee, and (10) caramel. Keeping this information in mind, be careful not to place too much reliance on a statement by a witness that he or she smelled beer or whiskey on a person's breath, while actually it could have been any type of alcohol or might not have been alcohol at all. We have expectations, and sometimes the witness might smell what he or she expected to smell.

Internal Factors

Personal Characteristics about the Witness.   People's perceptive abilities depend on their physical condition. Eyesight is one sense that is relied upon most heavily, and the individual's capabilities with respect to acuity and perception should be the subject of inquiry. Some people should wear corrective lenses but do not for reasons of vanity, as in the following case when an identification depended entirely upon the single eyewitness.

One evening after dark, the witness arrived home and was walking along the corridor of the semidark apartment house approaching his front door. At that particular moment a form that appeared to be a man pushed past the witness and hastily departed down the corridor and down the stairs. The witness only glanced at him for a moment, commenting to himself about the rudeness of some people. As he started to enter his apartment, the lady from the apartment across the hall screamed that someone had been attempting to break down her door. She did not see the culprit.

The witness was the only person who saw the suspect. The woman called the police department and reported the attempted entry, and the gentleman witness described the suspect. Shortly thereafter a young man was stopped for questioning in the neighborhood, and he was invited to return to the scene of the crime for a possible elimination as a suspect. The witness looked at the young man and stated that he could not be sure, but that there was a strong resemblance to the suspect he had seen in the hallway. The young man's name and address were recorded and he was allowed to continue whatever he had been doing. Two days later, an investigator contacted the same witness and asked him to look at some photographs of suspects. He replied that he would be glad to, and then took out a pair of glasses with lenses that were as thick as soda bottle bottoms, indicating an obvious case of myopia. The man could not help with the identification. The investigator asked him if he had an eyesight problem, and he replied, "Oh, yes, I'm blind without my glasses." The investigator asked him if he had been wearing them on the night of the crime, and he replied, "No, I never wear them when I'm driving. I usually leave them home."

Although the case just cited is unusual, there are many degrees of disability that people experience and do not talk about. Some people have no night or peripheral vision, some have color perception problems, and others have difficulty with depth perception. People who are tone deaf cannot hear some sounds, and even someone who hears well can have his perception of sounds to which he is listening altered by distracting noises. Taste, touch, and smell are similarly affected.

Emotional and Psychological Considerations. Under various types of stress, people react differently from when they are in complete control of their faculties in a relaxed state. Some senses may be sharpened by the increased state of agitation of the body functions; others may be rendered ineffective because of preoccupation with a single incident, such as a suspect pointing a gun at the victim. Exaggeration and elaboration are commonplace. A revolver pointed at the face may actually be a .22 automatic, but takes on the appearance of a .45 automatic. A boisterous and belligerent attacker may appear to be taller and heavier than he actually is. A crowd or five people may appear more like ten.

The personal drives of sex, hunger, and comfort may play a part in a witness's perception, as indicated by some events that seem to occur at various times which are described in minute detail. For example, someone who has just eaten a meal may not remember any food odors, whereas a hungry person may recall them more accurately.

Some people who suffer from handicaps such as a malformed or missing finger, harelip, missing teeth, or some congenital birth defect, are naturally more sensitive to similar problems experienced by others and would be better qualified to describe such irregularities. Personal interests in occupations and hobbies stimulate greater attention in objects and events that may be peculiar to those particular interests. Compare the number of errors you see in a police movie or television show with the observations of your nonpolice friends.

Experience and Education. The witness's conditioning to certain observation experiences through learning help him to perceive, remember, and communicate his observations and impressions. Conversely, a lack of experience or training may cause problems in communications, such as difficulty in interpreting what was seen into meaningful symbols and expressions. There may be a language barrier.

Prejudice or Bias. Most people tend to see what they want to see. Strong feelings toward or against an object tend to influence the amount of attention one pays to any particular event or object. In his role as the collector of information from the witnesses, the officer's task is not to change such attitudes, but to be aware of them and their effect on the ability of the witnesses to recount a reasonably accurate and objective picture of what actually took place.

Point of View.   When considering the statements of witnesses, ask yourself this question: Could they actually have observed what they say they have seen from their respective vantage points? Some well-meaning people may actually be lacking bits of information and will sometimes fill in the gaps with what they *believe* happened rather than what they *saw*. All people see things through different sets of eyes and experiences, interpret with different combinations of interpretation processes, and then communicate differently using their own unique methods of conveying thoughts and ideas. Your function is to coordinate all these bits of information and interpret them into terms that are meaningful to your superiors, to the prosecuting attorney, and to the courts to assure the accused of due process of the law.

Moods Affected by Color.   In the July 1982 issue of the *Reader's Digest,* Lowell Ponte reports:

> According to Swiss psychologist Max Lüscher, lecturer at the University for Artistic and Industrial Design at Linz, Austria . . . colors arouse specific feelings in people. Blue conveys peace and contentment, but those who favor dark blue are motivated by a need for security. Blue is widely used in the symbols of banks and automobile manufacturers. Yellow, says Lüscher, is associated . . . with modernity, achievement, and the future. Red conjures up power, an urge to win, vitality . . . Green and red together stir feelings of strength, reliability and incorruptibility. Greenish-blue invokes a sense of security and self-esteem.[2]

Ponte further points out that in some tests violent prisoners were put in pink cells. The results showed that a particular shade of pink was "sufficient to tranquilize and to replace aggressive impulses with passivity." Exposure to blue serves as an antidote in that the blue color tends to restore the power drained from the person when in the pink room.[3]

Memory.   Bower[4] reported that in one of his studies he found that persons in a sad mood recall more accurately and vividly their sad experiences, and when in a happy mood they recall a greater amount of their happy experiences. If that proves to be true, then it will tend to show that recall will possibly be better if the person at the time of recounting an experience is in a mood similar to that at the time of the experience. Returning the witness to the scene of the crime may stimulate both the mood and the memory.

James McGough reported[5] that massive amounts of the hormones epinephrine and norepinephrine "released by the adrenal medulla when the body is excited . . . appear to enhance the organism's ability to remember." He also reports that memory can also be impaired by drugs, such as amphetamines. Elizabeth Loftus, a psychologist at the University of Washington at Seattle, reports that "booze and pot seem to affect information storage more than retrieval." That is, memory may work well at the time, but some things that occur while a person is under the influence may not be recalled. Senility works in a similar way, eroding ability to store new information.[6]

In the Leo article, he points out other findings made by Loftus:

[Loftus] has a sobering message for grownups: their memories are almost as unreliable as children's—so encrusted with experiences, desires, and suggestions that they often resemble fiction as much as fact. In Eyewitness Testimony [a book by Loftus], . . . Loftus made a strong case against the reliability of remembrances of court witnesses. In Memory [another Loftus work] , . . . she indicts human recollections in general.[7]

Leo continues:

One problem with many, says Loftus, is that people do not observe well in the first place. . . . People forget some facts and "refabricate" the gaps between the ones they do not remember accurately; they tend to adjust memory to suit their picture of the world. . . . We fill in the gaps in our memory using chains of events that are logically acceptable. . . . Our biases, expectations, and past knowledge are all used in the filling-in process, leading to distortion in what we remember.[8]

Benderly discusses a phenomenon known as the "flashbulb memory." He states:

They are simply there, ready to appear in stunning detail at the merest hint. It's as if our nervous system took a multimedia snapshot of the sounds, sights, smells, weather, emotional climate, even the body postures we experience at certain moments.

We remember the exact look, sound, and feel of a traffic accident, the midnight phone call bringing word of a loved one's death; the voice, manner, and surroundings of the doctors who broke the news of a serious illness, the fleeting twinge of pain that appears on a president's face as he is hit by an assassin's bullet and just before he is pushed to the floor of the limousine by a bodyguard.[9]

According to Benderly, a University of California, San Diego, professor of neuroscience, Robert Livingston, in the late 1960s called this phenomenon "print now" and later changed the term to "now store," as if by a computer.[10] Livingston stated that two criteria determine such a response: (1) novelty and (2) biological significance. If a highly novel event were accompanied by pain and sorrow or some other strong emotion, then the event would be instantly stored.

Benderly states: "The contents of the flashbulb accounts, although apparently random, fall into a handful of categories—place, ongoing event, informant, affect in self, and affect in others—and a residual category of unclassifiable information, such as the weather, the brand of cigarettes just lit up, or the color of a garment.[11] This may explain the problem we sometimes run across when a witness can vividly recall certain events relevant to the crime but has no memory whatever of other events that occurred at the same time.

In personal discussions with memory specialists, I have been told that the sense of smell corresponds closely with one's emotions, and that once you smell something and identify it, you will probably always remember it. For example, the narcotics officer will describe the odor of burning marijuana as "distinctive, like nothing else." Animals and babies find their mothers by using their sense of smell. Since the visual process takes up a large portion of the brain, you are more apt to remember a person's face long after you have forgotten the name. Memory may also be enhanced by involving as many senses as possible, such as by repeating a name out loud, by writing it down, and by looking at the person while using his or her name as often as you can during the conversation.

Forgetting. On the down side of memory is the process of not remembering, or forgetting. Consider these factors in the process:

1. *Passive decay.* This is the "use it or lose it" theory. The information is stored in the memory, but it must be "called up" once in a while. Did you at one time speak a foreign language fairly fluently, and now remember just a few words and phrases? If you want to remember a specific investigation, go back to your reports and review them occasionally.

2. *Interference.* The filtering process in remembering can get clogged up by having too many types of input at the same time. Try watching a basketball game while you are studying for a promotional exam and carrying on a conversation with several members of your family.

3. *Storage failure.* For some reason you might have simply forgotten because the event did not get stored, such as a name you did not quite hear and which you did not ask to have repeated.

4. *Amnesia.* This is a medical and/or psychological problem.

5. *Repression.* You might not want to remember the event. It may be something you have done that is out of character, or does not meet your self-image requirements. We sometimes block out very undesirable events.

6. *Motivated forgetting.* Did you ever forget an appointment with a dentist? Sometimes you may say "I have a bad memory for names," or "I know I am going to forget this." Then you do forget them, don't you?

7. *Distortion.* The filtering process involves your prejudices and various other emotions that edit what you remember, and you forget the rest. Everyone's filter is different, and it involves morals, ethics, culture, and many other elements of individual personality.

8. *Chemical interference.* Alcohol, antihistamines, blood pressure medicines, and many other substances contribute to the process of forgetting.

DESCRIPTIONS OF PERSONS

Standard formats have been established and are in general use for the purpose of communicating brief but accurate messages regarding descriptions of people and property. When asking a witness to describe an individual, it is usually a good procedure to ask the person to first describe something about the suspect that "stood out" or to recall some similarity between the suspect and anyone that the witness knows. This technique calls into play the witness's ability to recognize objects that are familiar. After having recalled the familiar features, go back and obtain as much detailed description as possible, using the following format and the outline given in Figure 3–1.

1. *Name, if known.* Include the nickname or "monicker." List also all aliases or "aka" (also known as). Include first, middle, last name, plus any additional designation, such as Jr. or III.

2. *Sex.*

1. Name
2. Sex
3. Race
4. Age
5. Height
6. Weight
7. Hair
8. Eyes
9. Complexion
10. Physical marks, scars, other identifying characteristics
11. Clothing
    a. Hat or cap
    b. Shirt and tie
    c. Jacket or coat
    d. Dress or trousers
    e. Shoes
    f. Jewelry
       (1) Ring
       (2) Watch

Figure 3–1 Standard descriptions of persons.

3. *Race and nationality descent, if known.* "W" for Caucasian, "N" for Negro, "O" for Oriental. Except when representatives of other racial origins are indigenous to the area, spell out the origin to avoid misunderstanding. The nationality descent tends to reduce the field of suspects by identifying hair and eye color and certain similarities in facial features, and it should be used when known.

4. *Age.* Either an estimate or exact age, if known. If such information is available, list date of birth.

5. *Height.* Exact, if known. A male suspect is short if he is less than 5′6″, medium if 5′6″ to 5′10″, and tall if over 5′10″. Women are short if less than 5′2″, medium if 5′2″ to 5′6″, and tall if over 5′6″. Victims and witnesses will usually overestimate height.

6. *Weight.* Men are light up to about 150 lb, medium if from 150 to 180 lb, and heavy if over 180 lb. The weight and height ratio largely determines the body build. Women are similarly classified. In addition to the approximate weight, indicate whether "slim," "stocky," or other general build.

7. *Hair.* Color, type of hair style, length, and any baldness.

8. *Eyes.* Color, shape if other than Caucasian configuration, and any distinctive characteristics.

9. *Complexion.* Color and shade, plus any other characteristics, such as freckles, pockmarks, acne, birthmarks, blotches, suntan or burn, skin grafts.

10. *All other features and accessories.* Describe facial hair and sideburns, unusual shape or appearance of some facial feature, any disfigurement, scars, marks, or visible tattoos. Include any unusual characteristics about any other visible part of the body.

11. *Eyeglasses and jewelry, if any.* Although eyeglasses may be worn as a partial disguise, the wearer may be required to wear them. Look for any distinctive characteristics about them, such as extra thickness or unusual appearance caused by the way they are ground.

12. *Clothing worn.* Start at the top and work down in the following order: headgear, shirt, tie, jacket, coat, dress or trousers, shoes and socks. Include style, color, material, and any characteristics that will identify the clothing article. On headgear, indicate whether it is a hat, cap, uniform cap, helmet, beret, or scarf. The necktie is usually most distinctive and the shape, style, design, and colors should all be described. The shirt should be described by color and style, such as sport, dress, uniform, and the material should be given if it can be determined. On the coat and trousers, or dress, describe the material, design, and colors. Sweaters or other overwear are quite distinctive and can often be described in detail. Shoe style and color should be indicated, if known; also any heel pattern, if known, for possible surface prints.

13. *Personal characteristics.* Anything about the subject that will tend to distinguish him from any other person should be listed, such as a speech impediment or accent, or a distinctive tonal quality or pitch of the voice. Note any habits or unconscious movements he may be making, such as twitching, chewing fingernails, scratching the face, cracking knuckles, whistling, making unusual sounds with the teeth, picking at any part of the body or clothing, and generally any other observation about the individual that would aid in later identifying him.

EYEWITNESS IDENTIFICATION

There are essentially three types of lineups commonly used by the field officer: the field identification, the photograph identification, and the formal in-station lineup. Each of them has its special place in the process.

Field Identification

A primary consideration when using this method of identification is fairness to the individual whom you are holding for the possible identification. Immediately following any type of crime, when the suspect is probably still nearby, you will search for the suspect. The instant the broadcast is sent out, or immediately following your notification that a suspect is wanted, you will be operating on very vague and uncertain descriptions of the suspect. For a short time until witnesses have been more thoroughly interviewed and a better description is known, virtually anyone you encounter in the proximity and who could logically be a suspect should fall within your scrutiny. In some cases, you will have the true culprit; in others you will have an innocent person whose only relationship to the crime is that he or she just happens to be at a location where a suspect might logically be found.

For the field identification, or "showup," always bring the witness to the location where you are holding the suspect to be identified unless (1) you are sure that there is probable cause to make an arrest without the identification, or (2) the suspect validly consents to the movement to where the witness is, or (3) there is some compelling practical reason why you cannot move the witness to the suspect's location. Your witness may be bedridden or injured, for example.

This one-to-one confrontation is automatically suggestive to the witness because of the fact that the person shown to the witness is in police custody and there is only one person to look at. Despite this problem, the courts make an exception to the general rules concerning lineups because the field showup is held within a reasonable time following the crime—not more than one or two hours at the most, and the witness has the suspect's image clearly in mind. The person who is not identified as the suspect is free to go immediately, and the investigation can continue so that the true culprit may be found.

Unless it is necessary for security reasons, do not have the subject to be identified in handcuffs, as it implies that you have more information than you do and the witness might feel compelled to make a positive identification even though he or she is really not sure about the person being presented. If you had probable cause to detain the subject, you no doubt had cause to perform a cursory patdown for weapons, and restraining devices might not be necessary at this point.

Be careful to avoid making the showup too suggestive. Consider the competence of the witness, the circumstances under which the witness observed the suspect, the accuracy of the witness's description, the certainty of the witness in making identification at the showup, and your own conduct at the showup. Never tell the witness that you have caught the right person, that contraband was found, or that the person to be identified has made incriminating statements or a confession. Do not call the person you are showing to the witness the "suspect," and if there is a positive identification, do not state that he or she picked out the right person.

Be sure to tell the witness that he or she should keep an open mind and just because you brought the person to the place for an ID is in no way meant to suggest that the person is guilty. When the witness makes an identification or does not make an identification, follow the same reporting procedure as with a lineup.

When making a field identification, be sure to point out to the witness who is about to make the identification that you are not requiring that the person you have in custody be identified. Attempt to re-create the lighting and visibility as similar to the way they were at the time of the crime. If the witness observed the suspect in a dim light through a window, simulate the same situation for the identification. If the suspect and victim or witness were 15 feet apart, place them an equal distance for the field lineup. Be careful to keep them separated to avoid allowing the witness to make some sort of retaliatory attack on the person in custody in the event that you have the true suspect. At the same time, make your own personal observations and determine whether such an identification actually could have been made under those conditions. For example, at 50 yards at that time of day under those weather conditions, it may have been physically impossible to see a face of any color or shape clearly.

It must not be unnecessarily suggestive,[12] and it must be able to stand the scrutiny of the court afterward. One 1968 and two 1970 cases cited situations in which a "confrontation" or on-the-scene lineup can be performed. Those situations include (1) when the evidence is weak that you have the right person; (2) when several suspects have been collected, and there was only one perpetrator; (3) when a suspect is found near the crime scene within a reasonable time after its commission; (4) when it is necessary to take the suspect to the hospital if the victim witness is in danger of dying and might not live until a more formal lineup is arranged; and (5) when the subject is exhibited without restraints, if practicable, unless the person is combative or uncooperative.[13]

This is a field identification admonition format that you may choose to read to your witness at the time you show your possible suspect(s) to your witnesses:

> "We are detaining a person for you to view who may or may not be the person who committed the crime now being investigated. The fact that this person is detained, and may or may not be handcuffed, should not influence your identification. You are not obligated to identify this person. It is just as important to free innocent persons from suspicion as it is to identify guilty persons.

> "Please look at the detained person carefully. If you wish to see him (her) walk or stand or move in any particular way, please tell an officer. Also, if you wish to see the person under different lighting conditions, please tell an officer. If you wish to hear the person speak certain words or phrases, tell an officer.

> Please do not talk to anyone other than police officers while you are viewing the detained person. Do not consult with or talk to other persons who may also be witnesses or have knowledge of the crime. You are to make up your own mind whether or not you can identify the detained person.

> "After you have had enough time to view this person, please tell an officer whether you can or cannot make an identification. Please use your own words to tell the officer how certain you are of any identification you may make. Remember, you are not obligated to make an identification merely because this person is detained, and it is just as important to free innocent persons from suspicion as it is to identify guilty persons."

Photographic Identification

Armed with a description of a suspect, you may also have been able to locate other leads by checking the modus operandi file (covered in Chapter 5) and any other source for names of possible suspects. You may have known offender photo collections at your disposal or offender "mug" books. To have a fair selection process, you should have at least six photographs to show the witness. Follow these guidelines:

1. Use the most recent available photo of the suspect. If the suspect is in custody, take a photograph.

2. Number each photograph by putting the number on the back, and make a list of all persons whose photos you are using. You must keep the photos and the list when an identification is made so that you can present the entire collection in court to show fairness.

3. The photographs shown to the witnesses should be selected to ensure fairness and impartiality to the suspect.

4. Fairness and impartiality of this means of identification depends on many circumstances. As much as practicable, select photographs using guidelines similar to those you would follow in selecting subjects for a formal in-person lineup. Be sure that there are several individuals depicted that have similar facial features, hair color and style, and skin texture and pigmentation. If your suspect is in a group photograph, be sure to include several other group photographs in the collection. Consider the possibility that the witness may be somewhat inaccurate in describing the suspect. In other words, just because the witness states that the suspect had a brown mustache and a mole on his nose does not mean that you should restrict the collection to men with brown mustaches and moles on their noses. Use common sense and be reasonable.

5. Have only one witness view the photographs separately from other witnesses. Do not let them discuss the photographs among themselves—if there is more than one witness—either before or after looking at the photographs.

6. Give these instructions to each witness (unless your own prosecuting attorney has a different set of instructions for you to use):

In a moment I am going to show you a group of photographs. This group of photographs may or may not contain a picture of the person who committed the crime now being investigated. The fact that the photos are being shown to you should not cause you to believe or guess that the guilty person has been caught. You do not have to identify anyone. It is just as important to free innocent persons from suspicion as it is to identify those who are guilty. Please keep in mind that hair styles, beards, and moustaches are easily changed. Also, photographs do not always depict the true complexion of a person—it may be lighter or darker than shown in the photo. You should pay no attention to any numbers or markings that may appear on the photos. Also, pay no attention to whether the photos are in color or black and white or any other difference in the type or style of the photographs. You should study only the person shown in each photograph. Please do not talk to anyone other than police officers while viewing the photos. You must make up your own mind and not be influenced by other witnesses, if any. When you have completed viewing all the photos, please tell me whether or not you can make an identification. If you can, tell me in your own words how sure you are of your identification. Please do not indicate in any way to other witnesses that you have or have not made an identification. Thank you.

7. If the witness picks out a photo, have the witness initial the back of the photo, and place your initial alongside.

8. Regardless of which photo the witness chooses, do not discuss the choice with the witness.

9. Place all photos in evidence, and handle as any other item of evidence.

10. When you have several witnesses and one or two of them are able to make positive identifications from the photographs, consider discontinuing the photograph identification phase and have the other witnesses make their selection from the in-person lineup. Whenever you have a physical lineup following a photographic identification, there is always the danger that the witness will identify the suspect from having seen his or her photograph instead of remembering the person from the scene of the crime.

The Lineup

The lineup is the more formal method of identifying a suspect. Although the witnesses should be reminded that just because a person is being displayed, it is not an accusation or a statement that he or she is guilty of any crime. Some people are put through a lineup following an arrest when they were discovered in possession of the loot from a robbery or some other evidence that substantially ties them in with the crime in question. The person may already have been tentatively identified in a field showup or in a photo lineup, or perhaps recognized by an officer with the aid of a composite sketch or videotape taken at the time of the crime. While the *Miranda* rule applies when it involves questioning, a person may or may not have the right to the presence of an attorney during a lineup.

There is some variance from state to state and in the federal rule. In the 1967 *Wade* case[14] a person was arrested and charged with robbery. The court ruled that because he had been charged, Wade was entitled to the presence of an attorney during the lineup. In 1972, the U.S. Supreme Court ruled in *Kirby*[15] that the accused has a right to an attorney only if the lineup occurs *after* formal charges have been filed. But, they added, such presence does not entitle the attorney to do anything but observe.

A suspect may not refuse to stand in a lineup, nor can he or she refuse to speak words or phrases for voice identification, or wear certain articles of clothing, put on a wig, walk, or show tattoos on his or her body, provided that the lineup is fair and free of overzealousness on the part of the police. In *Simmons* v. *United States,*[16] the Court stated: A violation of due process occurs if the pretrial identification procedure is "so impermissibly suggestive as to give rise to a very substantial likelihood of irreparable misidentification." It is a violation of the 5th and 14th Amendments to suggest in *any way* to a witness that the suspect to be observed in a lineup or showup is guilty of anything.

Prior to conducting the lineup you must decide whether or not to advise the person of his or her right to have an attorney present, depending on your own state's current requirements. If the person does have an attorney there to observe, you should have a prosecuting attorney or department attorney present to represent the state's interests. You may have a printed form for the suspect to sign, waiving the right to an attorney. The top part of the form would read as follows: "You will be placed in a lineup for identification purposes. You may not refuse to participate in the lineup. You have the right to have an attorney present during the lineup to observe the proceedings. If you cannot afford an attorney and want one, a lawyer will be provided you without cost." The waiver portion would read as follows: "I have read the above statement and am fully aware of my rights. I do not desire the presence of an attorney for the lineup. This statement is signed of my own free will, without any promises or threats being made to me." It would then be signed, dated, and witnessed by you or a disinterested third party, if available.

The lineup procedure should be approximately as follows to assure fairness and effectiveness:

1. At least six persons, including the suspect, should be included.
2. Advise the suspect that any type of noncooperation may be commented on in court as an indication of guilt.
3. All persons should be of the same sex, same general coloring, same racial characteristics, and about the same age. Height, weight, skin color, and hair color should be reasonably close to that of the subject as described. Take into account the possibility that there will be some variance between actual appearance and the description provided by the witness. A suspect described as being of Latin origin might have actually been a dark-haired person of Irish descent.
4. The suspect should choose where in the lineup to stand.
5. All persons in the lineup should be dressed similarly. A suspect in a light-gray three-piece business suit with red necktie should not be in a lineup where everyone else is wearing open-collar knit sports shirts.
6. All persons in the lineup must be strangers to the witness if the suspect had been described as a stranger.
7. Attempts should be made to duplicate the lighting, visibility, and relative distances between witness and suspect as much as possible to recapture the identification problems as they existed at the scene.
8. Witnesses should be kept separate from each other and not be allowed to compare notes or arrive at a "jury decision" in the identification.
9. Subjects in the lineup should be required to make the same statements, put on the same jacket, and act the same as the others.
10. Make a photographic or videotaped record of the lineup in case of later charges of improper conduct or unfairness.
11. Interview each witness carefully following the lineup, particularly if a positive identification is made, and make a complete report on the interview. Comments such as "I vividly remember that look in his eyes" or "I couldn't mistake that triangular-shaped scar on his chin and the little red birthmark beneath the left ear" tend to validate the identification.
12. Keep a list of all participants in the lineup and all other persons present during the event. This will come out later during the trial when laying the groundwork to introduce the results of the lineup.

Always tell the witnesses who are about to observe the lineup (remember that each witness does this as a solo effort):

1. To keep an open mind
2. That the person who committed the crime may or may not be among those present

3. That just because the person is in custody does not mean that he or she is guilty of a crime
4. Not to discuss the identification with any other witness

Never tell the witness:

1. That you have caught the person who committed the crime or whom you believe to have committed it
2. That the suspect had the victim's property in his or her possession
3. That the suspect had made confessions or admissions
4. That the persons to be observed in the lineup are suspects

STANDARD FORMULA FOR DESCRIBING PROPERTY

Many people in law enforcement and its related agencies have devoted considerable time and effort to developing a uniform method for describing property. The following material represents some of their work toward establishing such uniformity. For maximum results in the effort to return stolen property to its owner, the formula presented here should be followed as closely as possible when preparing reports, teletypes, and in any other way describing lost, stolen, pawned, purchased, or sold property.

Number of the Article in the List.   In each itemized list, use a numbering system to facilitate references to a specific item for teletypes or correspondence.

Quantity of the Article.   For example,

(3) watches . . .
(1) television set . . .

Kind of Article.

Watch (or ring, or tire, or . . .)
For whom or for what purpose the article is designed. For example:
     watch, man's (or woman's or child's)
     saw, keyhole
     tire, bicycle
Trade name and manufacturer

Identifying Serial and Model Numbers.

Material or Type of Metal.   For example, yellow metal. Indicate the kind of metal claimed by the victim, such as "WM, platinum claimed." The officer's report does not verify the actual material or its value. His report merely reflects the claims and statements of the victim.

     Gold
          Solid gold is 24-carat gold. Carat, when used to describe gold, is a unit of quality. In 24 carats of gold, there are 24 grains of gold to the pennyweight.

Filled gold and *rolled gold* are both veneers of gold on a base metal. The processes involved in applying the gold are the same; however, the gold used on a filled gold article is of greater carat value than that used on a rolled gold article. A filled gold article has gold of 0.03 carat or more, and a rolled gold article has gold of 0.015 to 0.03 carat.

Gold-plated or *gold-washed* articles are electroplated with gold of below 0.015-carat value.

Other metals or minerals.

In the case of jewels, follow the same procedure: red stone, green stone. Indicate the kind of stone claimed by the victim. Diamonds are designated as white stones.

Other Materials. It is necessary to question the victim closely to get the correct material.

"Silk" may be rayon, bemberg, taffeta, pongee, shantung, satin, crepe, or nylon.

"Leather" may be artificial leatherette, cowhide, horsehide, sealskin, ostrich, alligator, snakeskin, calfskin, or a number of others.

"Wool" may be all wool, half wool, virgin wool, or reclaimed wool.

Physical Description.

Model, size, shape, color, pattern, measurements, style

A picture of the article from a catalog or from advertising material is useful.

A sketch of the article may be drawn by the victim.

Clothing size may be determined from the owner's height, weight, and build.

Identifying Marks.

These include *initials, marks put on by the owner, dents, scratches,* and *damage repairs.*

In the case of watches when the numbers are known to the owner, find out what jeweler last repaired the watch. If it has never been repaired, find out where and when it was purchased and whether it was bought on credit. Every jeweler keeps a record book of the work he has done. In the book will be found the date the work was done, a description of the watch, the owner's name and address, the watch case and movement numbers, and the jeweler's own number. If the watch has never been repaired, the dealer may have a record of its sale.

Flat silver, or *table silver,* has a pattern name. Specify which company made the set, since there are duplications of names among the various lines. List whether the set is sterling or plate. If the silver was in a chest or box, include a complete description of it as well.

Silver services, silver dishes, and *silver trays* have a number on the bottom and usually a hallmark or trademark. Their patterns will also have a name.

Expensive jewelry will often have a jeweler's scratch mark.

Age and Condition.

When purchased, whether new or used when purchased
State of repair
Shabby, dirty, worn, mended, patched, clean, new

Market Value.   The current market value should be determined by an expert in the values of the specific items stolen. The value may distinguish the difference between petty or grand theft.

Order for Listing Items in the Report.

1. Articles bearing numbers
2. Articles bearing initials or personal marks
3. Articles bearing identifying marks
4. Articles bearing identifying characteristics
5. Articles without market value

DETAILED DESCRIPTIONS OF COMMONLY STOLEN ITEMS

Jewelry

Novelty Jewelry.   Figures, charms, scatterpins, bracelets, necklaces, rings, etc. Of little value, usually gaudy and set with cheap rhinestones of various colors.

Costume Jewelry.   Generally the same as for novelty jewelry except that the material and workmanship are better and the value is somewhat greater.

Jewelry Such As:

Pins
Clips
Earrings
   Kinds:
   Clip
   Screw
   Hoop
   Styles:
   Teardrop
   Dangle
   Petal
   Button
   Novelty

Cuff buttons, cuff links, and studs
Necklaces

> *Kinds:*
> *Chain (size and design of links)*
> *Snake*
> *Lariat*
> *Pearl (simulated, cultured, seed)*
> *Crystal (artificial, tin cut, rock)*
> *Stones (artificial, synthetic, genuine); note number of stones and space between stones.*

> *Number of strands and length:*
> *Knotted*
> *Choker*

Lavalieres (on necklace)
Lockets

> *On chain, fob, pin, or bracelet*

Bracelets

> *Kinds:*
> *Expansion*
> *Link*
> *Bangle*

> *Settings:*
> *How mounted*
> *Distance between sets*
> *Number of sets*
> *Kind and color of sets*

Rings

> *Parts: shank, mounting, and set*
> *Size*

> *Engraving:*
> *Outside and inside*
> *Trademark and carat designation inside*
> *Scratch marks*

> *Kinds:*
> *Men's, women's, baby's*
> *Emblem (lodge, fraternity, class, school)*
> *Signet (initials and type of letters)*
> *Dinner rings*
>> Number, kind, and size of settings
>> Baguettes, chip and cut stones
>> Ornamental colored stones

Wedding rings
Width, engraving inside and out

Styles:

Diamond (how many, size, and spacing)
Antique
Modern
Unusual (chain or two that fit together)

Mountings:

Belcher: an old-type mounting, 8 to 12 prongs, deeply scalloped
Bezel: may extend all around or be on corners or sides only
Gypsy: set directly into ring with bezel
Tiffany: set high on 6 or 8 prongs; named after jeweler who designed it
Claw: any prong set other than Tiffany
Basket: filigree work around the stone

Settings:

Diamonds

  Color
  Shapes and cuts
    Size has no bearing; may be small, decorative, or the large main stone
  Facets
    58 on brilliant, round full cut, emerald cut marquise
    24 to 32 on Swiss cut
    18 on single cut
  Chips
    Just what the name implies
    Used for decoration

Cameos and intaglios

Cameo is a carved, raised figure, usually a head; intaglio is a figure carved into a stone
Cameos and intaglios are used in earrings, pins, fobs, and cuff links, as well as in rings

Birthstones and other colored stones

Garnet, amethyst, bloodstone, aquamarine, emerald, moonstone, ruby
May be genuine, synthetic, or artificial

Gemstone cuts:

Cabochon cuts have a domed top of either high or low curvature, and the base may be the duplicate of the top or it may be concave shaped, or any cut between. This cut is used for emeralds, rubies, sapphires, opals, turquoise, starstones, cat's eyes, and other precious stones.

Rose cuts have a flat base with triangular facets, either 12 or 24, terminating in a point. Small diamonds and pyrope garnets use this cut.

Brilliant cut is the most common cut for the diamond. It has 58 facets, with 33 above the girdle and 25 below. The Marquise and Pendeloque are variations of the brilliant cut.

Zircon cut is similar to the brilliant cut with more facets on the lower portion of the stone.

Briolette is an oval- or pear-shaped diamond with its entire surface cut in triangular or rectangular facets.

Step, trap, or emerald cut are cut according to a plan shape of square, oblong, or baguette and have a series of rectangular facets arranged parallel to the girdle.

Scissors or cross cut is similar to the step cut with the exception that the side facets are made up of four or more triangular facets.

Other cuts include the kite, lozenge, triangle, and obus.

Clothing

Suits, Women's and Men's.   Women's tailored suits and coats have the same general identifying characteristics as men's suits and overcoats. The word "tailored," when applied to any article of women's wear, *means* plain, or without decoration. Men's suits come in three lengths—short, medium, and long—plus a size number. For instance, size 40 will be found in short, medium, and long.

Color and material

Be as exact in color as possible.

Get a description of any pattern in the weave.

Whipcord, serge, gabardine, flannel, tweed, broadcloth. Most other materials are known as worsted.

Labels

Manufacturer's inside of inside coat pocket.

Retailer's outside of inside coat pocket or at nape of neck.

Coats

Suit coats

Overcoats

Sport coats

    Single or double breasted, number of buttons

Lapels

Pockets

    Patch or inset; with or without flaps

    Number and locations of inside pockets

Lining

    Color and type of material

    Full, half, or quarter lined

Back
    Vented: single or double, or no vents
    Straight
    Tapered, form-fitting

Trousers, Women's and Men's.

Some women's trousers are tailored the same as men's with fly front.
Fly front, no fly front
Zippers or buttons, locations
Waistband
Pleats, if any; how many?
Cuff or not

Overcoats.

Men's or women's—buttons and buttonholes are reversed.
Trim
Length
Removable lining
Reversible

Women's Clothes Generally.

Size
Labels
Material
    Kind
    Color
Trim
    Color
    Buttons
    Braid or piping
    Embroidery or cut work
Skirts
    May be part of a suit
    Length
    Fit (flared, full, or tailored)
    Slashed or slitted (location and length of slit)
    Pockets
    Number of panels

Jackets, Men's.

Size

Material

Color and design of weave

Pockets

Number of (inside and outside)

Kind

Slash, inset, patch, muff type, flap

Fastenings (zipper and button)

Front fastenings (zipper or button)

Collar

Knitted, also cuffs as in leather jackets

Fur, pile

Lapels

Detachable

Parka hood

Lining

Color

Rayon, quilted, sheepskin, blanket

Back

Plain, half-belt, swing shoulders

Sweaters.

Man's, woman's, child's (size)

Coat (button or zipper)

Pullover

Neck (crew neck, turtleneck, V-neck, roll collar)

Sleeve or sleeveless

Furs.

Kinds

Generally the name of the animal, but may have a more exotic name to correspond with the price.

Color (dyed or natural)

Lining

Material: dull or shiny, color, bindings or pockets

Pockets

Labels

Wear and repairs

If custom-made or if ever repaired, the owner might have written her name on reverse of skin.

Length

Measured from bottom of collar down back

Three-quarter, fingertip, chubby

Fasteners

Frogs (size)

Hook and eye (size)

Buttons (kind and size)

Snaps (number and size)

If a neckpiece, number of skins

    Heads and/or tails sewn on

    Fasteners

Any repairs, and what furrier used

Hosiery.

Kinds
Material
Size
Weight

Sheer, medium, other

Color
Cotton tops or feet
Support hose

Men's Shirts.

Color, pattern, brand, collar style
With or without collars
Size

Collar and sleeve length

Sport shirts come in small, medium, and large

Kind

Sport, dress, work, cowboy

Material

Cotton, wool, rayon, rayon-gabardine, nylon

Buttons

Number on cuffs if more than one

Buttondown collar

Number of buttons down front

Pockets

Number

With or without flaps

Cuffs

Regular

French cuffs

Handbags.

Style

Women's handbags are of five basic styles: pouch, box, envelope, underarm, shoulder strap.

Handles

Fasteners

Zipper, turn lock, lift lock, snap lock

Material

Leather

    Patent leather, suede, sealskin, ostrich, calfskin, cowhide (any of which might be imitation)

Plastic (may look like patent leather or enamel)

Cloth

Reptile: alligator, lizard, snake

Inside

Lining (material and color)

Label

Number of divisions

Attached or loose coin purse and/or mirror

Contents

Complete list

Radios and Televisions

Kind (portable, table model, etc.)

Brand

Dials

Bands

AM, FM, stereo

Number of control knobs

Color and material of case

Measurements

Television—brand

Size of screen

Control knobs

Description of case and cabinet

Portable, console, table

Serial numbers (do not confuse with model numbers)

Tools

Tools are frequently the objects of theft. Since there are so many kinds, types, and manufacturers, it is necessary to depend upon the victim for details.

Private marks
Damage
Description of the chest or box if one was taken, and of the tools inside
Serial numbers on certain tools
Electrically operated tools

Luggage

Suitcases
Describe inside
   Lining and color
   Number of partitions, pockets
Material
Handles and fasteners
Trunks
   Foot lockers (with or without tray)
   Steamer or wardrobe trunk (number of hangers, drawers)
   Box trunk
   Describe material, inside, fasteners
Briefcases and brief bags
   Describe material
   With or without straps
   Single or double handles
   Fasteners
   Number of compartments

Cameras

Two numbers appear on the more valuable cameras, one on the lens and one on the camera itself. Camera lenses are interchangeable. Speed of the lens is important. Owner's description is usually dependable.

Binoculars

Power and size
   First number indicates magnification and the second number indicates the size of the lens in millimeters (8×30).
Type of focusing (central or single eye)
Hinged or solid bridge
Barrels (length and covering material)

Coated lenses
Carrying case

Firearms

Make, caliber, and serial number
  Hidden numbers and parts' numbers
  Foreign guns without serial numbers; also have proofmarks as a rule
  Complete description
Finish
  Nickel-plated
  Blue
  Anodized
  Rough or sandblasted
Length of barrel
Grips
  Material and color
Condition
  Marks
  Damage
  Repairs
  Signs of wear
Loaded or unloaded
Where and when purchased

Musical Instruments

Kind, make, and serial number
Pitch
  Most wind instruments are made in varying pitch (e.g., saxophones are in C,
    E flat, B flat, tenor, and B-flat baritone; clarinets are in A, B flat, tenor,
    and bass). The same applies to many stringed instruments.
Finish
  Brass, silver, or gold
  Rough or sandblasted
  Gold or brass with silver design or vice versa
  Silver with gold bell
Condition
  Signs of wear
  Dents and scratches

Case
  Complete description
  Attachments and other articles in the case
Where and when purchased

IDENTIFICATION OF AUTOMOBILES AND ACCESSORIES

Automobile manufacturers bank their sales futures on how uniquely they can design their new models each year and make them more attractive than the competition. For that reason, it should be part of every investigator's mug files to have dealer- and manufacturer-provided photographs of their automobiles from all different angles each year. Their colors are distinctive and run the entire spectrum and then some. Color charts from each of the manufacturers would help.

Do not overlook the dashboard configurations of each car, which a kidnap victim might be able to identify more readily than the exterior. Cassette and compact disc players and AM-FM radios all have their own unique characteristics. An excellent project for interns or cadets as well as students involved in criminal justice studies would be to load all of these images onto a CD-ROM, which could hold thousands of makes and models of both domestic and foreign vehicles.

When a child-molestation victim states that her abductor took her away in a gray van with purple stripes, your should be able to search the files for the vehicle that would match the victim's description that you could then print in color and distribute to your officers, the media, and put online in the World Wide Web. We have the capability. Thousands of people throughout the country would have access to your descriptions of such vehicles and their interior accessories. Criminals do not restrict themselves to just one area of the country, as you know. Two days ago the perpetrator might have been in New Hampshire and is now in Idaho plying his or her nefarious trade.

SUMMARY

In this chapter we covered three major topics. First, we studied some of the various factors involved in observation and perception and the problems involved, including internalization of perceptions as well as the external factors. Because of the high degree of tentativeness in the qualifications and accuracy of the eyewitness, you must be extremely careful to validate any descriptions of suspects presented by witnesses and victims. The second topic was that of the identification process, be it in the field, by a photograph, or in the more formal in-station lineup. The key to accurate identification is to pay attention to the details and reasonableness in assuring yourself—and the courts eventually—that any positive identification of persons responsible for crimes be made in a fair and objective manner. The third topic was devoted to the actual process of identifying persons and property. Accurately describing items that have been stolen or people you are searching for will enhance your chances of successfully locating either one.

EXERCISES AND STUDY QUESTIONS

1. Describe some of the factors that make an eyewitness unreliable.

2. Considering the examples cited in the text as to who might better describe an item of jewelry or a person's false teeth, who would you expect to give a good description of a person's eyeglasses? make of an automobile? hair style? unusual looking facial feature?

3. What are the three basic requirements of a witness?

4. List and discuss at least five of the external factors that influence perception by a witness.

5. Which will appear to be larger—a blue object or a red one—considering the fact that they are actually the same size?

6. Of the perceptive senses of a witness, which one is considered the least reliable?

7. Can a trained witness distinguish between the odors of whiskey and beer?

8. Test yourself by choosing a dozen edible items. While blindfolded, identify each one by taste. Then identify each by odor. How did you do?

9. If you want to check out the perceptual ability of a witness, what would you do to make sure the witness actually did see an event under certain lighting and weather conditions, and from a specific distance?

10. List and discuss at least three internal factors that influence perception by a witness.

11. According to Ponte, what color would you paint a jail cell that holds violent prisoners?

12. What effect do alcohol and marijuana have on memory, if any?

13. Describe the phenomenon known as "flashbulb memory."

14. Give an example when such an event occurred in your lifetime that you vividly recall in precise detail.

15. When asking a witness to describe another person, which sequence would you follow?

16. What height is medium for a man? a woman?

17. List and describe the three types of lineups described in this chapter.

18. May an attorney legally advise a client not to take part in a lineup? May the client legally take the advice of the attorney and refuse to take part in such a lineup?

19. Describe the wristwatch you are wearing, if any; a ring, a necklace.

20. Describe the clothing you are now wearing.

21. Describe the television set that is now in your home.

22. Describe as best you can the various parts of a trumpet, guitar, sewing machine.

23. How would you describe a metal that appears to be gold? silver?

24. According to the theory of color influencing specific feelings, what does the color blue do for people?

25. Explain the procedure for preparing a witness for a lineup.

FOOTNOTES

1. William S. Cain, "Educating Your Nose," *Psychology Today,* July 1981, pp. 56, 58.
2. Lowell Ponte, "How Color Affects Your Moods and Health," *Reader's Digest,* July 1982, p. 96.
3. Ibid.
4. Gordon H. Bower, "Mood and Memory," *Psychology Today,* June 1981, p. 60.
5. James L. McGough, "Adrenalin: A Secret Agent in Memory," *Psychology Today,* December 1980, p. 132.
6. John Leo, "Memory, the Unreliable Witness," *Time,* January 5, 1981, p. 89.
7. Ibid.
8. Ibid.
9. Beryl Lieff Benderly, "Flashbulb Memory," *Psychology Today,* June 1981, p. 71.
10. Ibid., p. 72.
11. Ibid., p. 74.
12. *Stoval* v. *Denno,* 388 U.S. 293 (1967); *Gilbert* v. *California,* 388 U.S. 263 (1967); and *United States* v. *Wade,* 388 U.S. 218 (1967).
13. *Bates* v. *United States,* 405 F.2d 1104 (1968); *Arizona* v. *Boens,* 8 Ariz. App. 110 (1970); and *Martin* v. *Virginia,* 7 Cr. L 2147 (1970).
14. *United States* v. *Wade,* 388 U.S. 218, 87 S. Ct. 1926 (1967).
15. *Kirby* v. *Illinois,* 406 U.S. 682, S. Ct. 1877 (1972).
16. *Simmons* v. *United States,* 390 U.S. 377 (1968).

CHAPTER 4

POLICE COMMUNICATIONS

INTRODUCTION

Some of the most dramatic progress in law enforcement has been made in the various areas of communications. Radio and telephone communications and computer and facsimile systems make it possible for the field officer to be in virtual constant contact with fellow officers, headquarters, and a wide variety of data resources. The old comic book character Dick Tracey was ahead of his time with his wrist radio back in the 1940s, but time has caught up with him.

Telephone and radio transmissions not only carry the voice around the universe instantaneously, but with the aid of modems and computer systems, reams of data can be instantaneously faxed throughout the law enforcement system and on through to the mobile computer in the police car. The field officer can run a record check and in a matter of minutes find out that a person is wanted in a town two or three thousand miles away. With the transmission of fingerprints of that person by fax, identification can be verified, a warrant transmitted to the asylum state, and the suspect booked into jail.

No longer is it necessary to go off the air while checking an unknown circumstance or an open door; you will carry your portable radio or cellular phone with you at all times. Many agencies now have vehicle tracking, which makes it possible for each field unit's position to be displayed on a tracking map in the communications center. It has only been a few short years, historically speaking, since the only means of communication the officers on foot in the field had with other officers or the police station was by means of a signal light posted on top of a tall building in the center of town; when the radio appeared on the scene in the early 1920s, headquarters would utilize the assistance of local broadcasting stations to break into their regular programming and send messages to the field units whose radios were tuned to the commercial station. Call boxes used railroad telegraph "clickers," then telephones to report in to the station while they were in the field. Compared to those "good old days," technology has significantly improved.

In this chapter we study police communications from an operational standpoint, beginning with interpersonal communications, which include body language, unspoken words—and departmental administrative communications. We follow with a survey of the department's intra- and inter-agency systems and how they work. The balance of the chapter is devoted to general guidelines for traditional radio operations as they continue to function.

INTERPERSONAL COMMUNICATIONS

Many of the problems in society today relate to our communicating with one another. Breakdowns in communications or lack of communications altogether or misunderstandings in our communications are at the root of the breakdown of family, marital, social, and a variety of other relationships. As a field officer, it is imperative that you develop the skills essential to communicate effectively with the people with whom you come in contact. If asked to rank order the skills necessary for effective performance of your job, this author would list "the ability to communicate effectively" right at the top of the list next to "must be breathing."

Through the various means of communications we transmit information and ideas, we change behavior or convince or persuade others, and we generally interact socially. We transmit messages, and with luck, the receiver gets the same message that we sent. Your success in communicating will actually depend on how well your messages are received. We hear what we want to hear, and how we receive the message is influenced by our own interpretative system, which is influenced by our language skills, prejudices, fears, and various emotions as well as through the nonverbal communications that accompany the spoken word, such as facial expressions, gestures, movements, and posture, known as "body language."

We miss a lot when we speak with someone by telephone. What is the person on the other end of the line doing while we are carrying on what you or I believe to be an important conversation? He or she might express interest verbally but out of our sight is looking up words in a dictionary to complete a crossword puzzle. It is so much more effective when we can make our contacts in important police matters in person and face-to-face.

Barriers to effective interpersonal communications are perceived attitudes, basic conflicts in language usage—perhaps by differences in cultural interpretations in exactly what some words and phrases mean—thinking processes tempered by differences in life experiences between the two, and negative reactions to the signals being transmitted by the other person, whether consciously or subconsciously transmitted. For example, you might approach some construction workers on the job and evoke a negative spoken response to your questions because of what to them appears to be an attitude of arrogance or superiority on your part. President Franklin D. Roosevelt gave the people the impression that he was looking down at them from his "aristocratic perch," while he was actually trying to see them better through the lower portion of his bifocal eyeglasses.

To overcome those barriers, you must develop a technique in encoding and decoding your messages in languages that both you and the person with whom you are communicating agree upon as being the same. To better accomplish that task, it will be necessary that you establish some rapport prior to trying to convince or persuade. Look for the areas in verbal communications where there seem to be some difficulty and try to improve, but also devote some time and attention to the messages you deliver "MOS." (In the early days of motion pictures, several well-known German directors in Hollywood would direct their actors to deliver their feelings or emotions "mitout sound.")

In nonverbal communications you might be mouthing the words "I am interested in what you are saying," but your body is turned away from the speaker and you are looking at an object beyond the person, which is actually delivering the message *"I'm not going to listen to you"* or *"I really don't care about what you have to say."* Gestures indicating openness and a receptive attitude include open hands, unbuttoning and/or removing a jacket or coat, opening up the body by uncrossing the legs and leaning forward, or outstretching the arms and leaning back, similar to the trusting animal who will lie on its back and spread its legs so that you may rub its stomach. Its defenses have been lowered to accept your expression of kindness. The defensive or nonreceptive person will cross the legs and fold the arms, or both, and physically assume the attitude of "closing up" and shutting you out. The folded arms are telling you that your advice is falling on deaf ears and that the product you are selling is going to go without a closure. Finally, you are showing the other person that you are in charge of the situation and are shutting off communications when you rise to your full height and fold your arms. This means that you are in charge and are going to do the talking, not the listening.

People who are interested in each other's conversation look at each other, but not intently. Most of the time when people are in a normal conversation, you will note that they look at each other only about half of the time. The listener will look at the speaker longer than the speaker will look at his or her listener. Usually when you see two people gazing intensely at each other, it is an indication that the interest is more on the person than on the conversation, such as when two people are extremely angry with one another, or when one or both are in love. Depending on cultural differences, the person who looks directly at the other person when telling the truth will usually avert the other's eyes when telling a lie, when trying to hide something, or when on the defensive.

Listening is one of the most important facets of the art of communicating. Many of us hear what another person says to us, but we are really not listening to what the person means by what he or she is saying, *how* the words are being spoken, and if there is a hidden agenda. Statements made with a smile and under the guise of feigned sarcasm may actually be hiding intense anger and hatred. Listen to comedians on the comedy channel of television sometime for an hour or two and *listen* to the anger expressed by some under the guise of "humor." Although people say, "I see what you are saying," they may not actually understand the unspoken message that accompanies the spoken message. I have seen people laugh hysterically while they are actually being insulted because the words sound funny but the message is not.

Most people will look at you while listening, then look away when answering a question that causes them some embarrassment or when they are about to embark on a tale of fantasy or when they are fabricating a story, such as a witness who will tell you what he or she would like to have seen rather than what actually happened. The person who sits with a leg draped over an arm of the chair or who sits astride the chair with the back of the chair facing you like a shield may be displaying an attitude of competitiveness or superiority. When you see one person walking at a certain pace and somewhat in the lead, and the other people with that person are keeping the same pace and slightly behind that person, you are usually looking at the leader of that group, such as a mother hen with her chicks.

Frustration is sometimes indicated by rubbing the hands, taking deep and short breaths, scratching an imaginary itch, alternately clenching and unclenching the fists, sighing, kicking dirt or sand, making clucking sounds, wringing the hands. Nervousness evokes throat clearing, adjusting clothing when it is not necessary, humming to oneself as if to drown out sounds from others, and fidgeting. The nervous person may also be picking at imaginary lint on the clothing, picking on the fingernails, or picking up and putting down objects for no apparent reason.

Boredom is sometimes indicated by drumming the fingers on the table, tapping the feet, holding the head in one's hands, and doodling on any available piece of paper. Is the person actually listening to you and considering what you have to say? If so, here are some of the signs: hand goes to the cheek, strokes the chin or beard, toying with eyeglasses or other objects in his or her hands, or leaning back in the chair and "opening up" by putting the arms on the back of the chair or hands clasped behind the head.

Shaking hands with the person may give you a clue to that person's state of mind. A firm handshake with the palms interlocking with yours indicates self-confidence, while a tentative shake with sweaty palms indicates nervousness and reluctance to enter into a conversation. Suspicion may be indicated by the individual avoiding looking at you or giving you a sideways glance, as a boxer moves to parry a blow from another boxer.

When lying, the individual may inadvertently put a hand to the mouth as if to shut off the lie, then may move the hand to the nose to "cancel out" the hand-to-mouth signal. A similar type of move would be when you start waving at someone and halfway through the wave you realize that the object of your wave is not that person at all; you then change the waving motion into something else so you won't feel foolish for waving at a complete stranger.

When things are going well, individuals will unbutton their coats, loosen a collar or necktie, uncross the legs, and move toward the leading edge of the chair and lean closer to the other person at the table or similar barrier that separates them. Gestures that indicate a defensive or noncooperative attitude are buttoning the coat, crossing the legs, folding the arms, clenching the fists, or sitting astride a chair as described previously.

Be aware of your own body language and use it to your advantage when necessary, but be careful not to send a false signal. When you intend to put the other person at a psychological disadvantage, lean into his or her "personal space," which is somewhere around two to two and a half feet (an invisible bubble) surrounding the person. It varies from culture to culture; for example, in some parts of the world, friends may actually appear to be so close that their noses are touching. When you travel to other countries, watch for the differences in personal space required by different peoples.

If you wish to demonstrate respect and politeness to the persons in your contact, stay outside the "personal bubble" and avoid touching except to shake hands. When you move in and touch someone, you are silently "taking charge." Although the "position of interrogation" that you learned in the academy is to stand at arm's length from what you believe to be the other person's strong hand (right or left, sometimes indicated by the wrist watch being worn on the "weak" hand), you will probably develop the habit of moving into the other person's personal zone to maintain the advantage once you have determined that the immediate danger has passed.

Another way to put a person at a psychological disadvantage is to tilt the head back and look down at the person as though you were looking through the lower portion of your bifocals.

By carefully observing people while they are demonstrating certain emotional involvement, you may be able to determine when in your contact is the best time to shift to another phase in your conversation, such as when the person will probably listen to your advice. You may be getting across to that person if he or she puts a hand to the cheek, or with an elbow on the table puts the chin on a hand, or slightly cocks the head to one side, or the hand begins to stroke some parts of the face.

All of these indicators are merely clues to look for, but if you look carefully while you are talking with people, you will be well on your way to enhancing your communicative skills. These are some of the modes of body language communications.

1. *Facial expressions.* People may show fear, anxiety, love, hatred.
2. *Eye contact.* Determine a person's style, then look for changes.
3. *Motion and gestures.* Walking, standing, tapping a hand or leg.
4. *Touching others and themselves.*
5. *Use of space, or "body bubble."* Intimate space is usually from 18 to 30 inches. Social space is at least at arm's length, and a hostile distance might be more or less, with the angry argument at nose-to-nose distance, extending outward until the person begins to assume a fighting stance at about arm's length.
6. *Silence.*

ESSENTIALS FOR A POLICE COMMUNICATIONS SYSTEM

The police and sheriff's departments are emergency services and are regarded as such on a 24-hour year-round basis, even though many of the services are of a non-emergency nature. The communications system must be ready to function efficiently and effectively at any and all times. In addition, secondary backup systems must be ready for immediate implementation without loss of time or human resources. Under most conditions the actual routine of meeting the emergency and routine demand upon the various communications media will function smoothly and efficiently. However, contingency plans should be in place to cover all the potential "unexpected" situations that can be foreseen as well as those situations that occur frequently.

To assure maximum efficiency in carrying out those plans, certain criteria must be met.

1. *Training.* As much as possible, most types of messages should be committed to standard handling procedures. Any conceivable type of situation should be worked out in hypothetical "role play" sessions and communications procedures worked out accordingly. Once standard operating procedures are established, they should be made well known to all operating personnel, and these personnel should be instructed and rehearsed in as many different types of situations as possible. The training must coincide with the planning, and both must be constant in the dynamic environment of the law enforcement milieu.

2. *Dependability.* The police communications system must be totally dependable under both emergency and routine conditions. Secondary systems must be available on a standby basis, and they must be totally operational. Frequent inspections and operations testing should be done frequently so that they can be up and running in a moment's notice. Not only should radios and computers have online backups, but there should also be backup power sources.

3. *Security.* The police communications system must be secure from attack in the event of any criminal action directed toward destruction or neutralization of any part of the police agency's vital functions. It must also be secure from any foreseeable natural or accidental disaster, such as fire, flood, earthquake, tornado, hurricane, or airplane crash.

4. *Accessibility.* All operational units of the organization must have convenient access to every type of communications medium that is essential to its efficient operation. Mail delivery, extension telephone systems, and computer terminals usually accommodate most of the basic needs of a police organization, but there may also be a need for radio broadcast and monitoring equipment at remote locations, and for computers in locations separate from the battery of units maintained in a communications center. It is also quite feasible to install remote terminals for electronic data processing systems that tie in with centralized information storage banks. Access must be commensurate with utilization.

5. *Speed.* Radio and telephone and interfacing computers provide immediate access to other persons or agencies, assuming that the line or air is clear to transmit the message (see Figures 4–1 and 4–2). One method to assure maximum utilization of all forms of communications for law enforcement agencies is to develop a language that is clearly understandable to all its users but that can appreciably shorten the time it takes to deliver the message. Radio codes are primarily designed for such

Figure 4–1 The modern police communications systems involve computer to computer as well as radio, the old standby. (Courtesy New York City Police Department.)

brevity as well as clarity and, to some small extent, possibly some confidentiality. Redundancy in police correspondence or teletype messages should be avoided.

6. *Confidentiality.* Police communications should not be made public as a matter of course. Much of the information in possession of the police agency is private and personal as it relates to suspects and victims, and it is essential that this information be guarded to protect the innocent. Although radio codes are known by virtually anyone who is involved in law enforcement, there is some degree of privacy in using the codes because they are not universally known. Teletype and computer systems used by law enforcement agencies are on private lines with accessibility only through coordinating agency authorization. For some transmissions by radio or telephone, it may be feasible to use scrambler systems that transmit garbled sounds and "unscramble" them at each end. For certain types of unusual police operations, unpublished frequencies may be utilized. It is a simple matter for eavesdroppers to listen in on any unscrambled radio transmission you make with the use of sophisticated scramblers that many amateurs have for personal entertainment. Remember, also, that wireless phones within a building and cellular phones are nothing more than radios, and people with scanners may listen in on those, too. A truly secret message should be whispered into the other person's ear, or at least by telephone line, using a code and a scrambler.

INTRA- AND INTERDEPARTMENTAL COMMUNICATIONS

Two other aspects of police communications that should be defined are intra- and interdepartmental communications. Intradepartmental communications involve the formal and informal transmission and exchange of information throughout the various

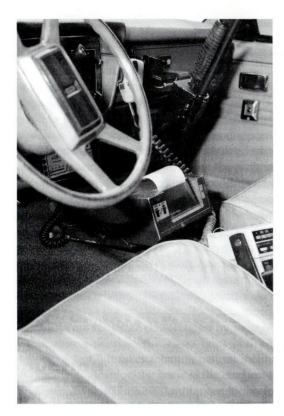

Figure 4–2 Police cars are equipped with mobile data terminals and have unlimited communication capabilities. (Courtesy Santa Ana, CA Police Department.)

divisions and subdivisions within the agency. The interdepartmental communications system involves the interchange of information among the members of two or more agencies. Both these systems will be briefly reviewed.

Intradepartmental Communications

With a quasi-military organization such as a police department, there are several methods for the formal transmission of directives, orders, ideas, and information to be conveyed through the various levels of the organizational structure in a downward, upward, or lateral direction. There must also be provisions for an informal interchange of ideas and information in all directions throughout the department. Without this informal flow of communications, there is the danger that incentive will be destroyed, mediocrity will be perpetuated, and eventually the effectiveness of the department will be totally neutralized.

For the purpose of presenting to the public an image of unanimity within the agency, all news releases and general information emanating from the agency should "clear" through the office of the agency head—the chief of police or sheriff or a press relations officer. This increases the possibility of getting out information that is accurate and complete, and reflects the true philosophy of the department. Incoming communications should be received by a central office so that it may be routed correctly.

Personal and confidential mail should be so labeled and routed, but mail addressed to a specific person within the department might not get appropriate attention concerning urgent matters if not opened and routed to someone who can give the necessary immediate attention.

General and special orders usually originate in the office of the chief. *General orders* are long-lasting policy statements or standardized procedures that affect all members of the department. *Special orders* have a shorter effective length, or they involve matters of interest to some number of employees rather than the general membership. Time limits should be placed on all orders, whether intended to be long-lasting or not. This will make it mandatory to have periodic review and evaluations of such orders and modifications as necessary.

A variety of other types of directives or information bulletins may emanate from the chief's office or other divisions within the department in accordance with the system established by the chief and the staff. Conformity to some sort of system assures consistency and predictability.

In addition to the written message that the chief or sheriff must continually originate and update, there should be a more informal system for the interchange of ideas as well as the delivery of orders. The chief usually meets with immediate staff on a daily basis, sometimes several times during the day. The immediate staff consists of those ranking officers who are in the direct line of command in the organization and report directly to the chief indicated on the organizational charts. The chief holds less frequent meetings on a formal and informal basis at irregular or scheduled times with command and supervisory officers. The general purposes of such staff and command meetings are to articulate policies, to maintain some uniformity in the interpretation and execution of the department's responsibilities, and to provide for a continual, free flow of communications and feedback essential to the management process.

Following the lead of the chief, all supervisory employees and ranking officers should have both formal and informal meetings with their subordinates to discuss the same general policies, philosophies, and ethics, but also to work out ways and means to perform their jobs with the greatest degree of efficiency. There should also be provisions within the organization at all levels of supervision up to—and including—the chief for an open door into that person's office to discuss any personal matter that directly affects the department. Naturally, it is not possible for the chief of police or the sheriff of a large agency to personally visit with each of the members of the department, or the entire day would be consumed by such visits and the chief could not accomplish the other responsibilities of the office. However, there must be some system of unstifled flow of information to allow feedback and also to provide a safety valve for the officers and other employees to communicate their emotions, their ideas, and their complaints.

Within the ranks and between the various working units in the department there must also be an established system for the free flow of information without the unbending restriction that everyone go through the "chain of command" to exchange information. There is a particularly acute need for such a continuous flow of information between the field officers and the investigators, for example. A field officer may develop some good leads on a case and pass them on to the investigator assigned to the follow-up investigation of that case. It is imperative that the investigator later send back word to the officer who originally uncovered the leads, preferably by telephone or a personal note in a department mailbox, to let the officer know the information helped in the case. The investigators should frequently visit the patrol roll call sessions to discuss their cases and to seek assistance in locating wanted individuals or information that the field officers may be in a better position to find because of their continuous presence in the field.

Accident investigators may ask for patrol assistance in a hit-and-run case in which the only leads they have are that the suspect drives a light-blue car and that he might drive on a certain street every night about the same time. Vice detail officers may request that a particular house be watched for unusual activity or more than the average number of automobiles in the vicinity. These are just a few examples of the many instances when the cooperative efforts of two or more operating units are enhanced by informal communications.

Rumors will usually fill the gaps left by the lack of information, and police departments are not exempt from rumor-passing situations. To counteract the dissemination of rumors, it may be necessary to point out the true facts of a situation, such as the purpose for disciplinary action. Rules and regulations should be published and distributed. Policies, procedures, and other types of information should be passed on to the employees. Additionally, there should be some provision for the release of information that is newsworthy to the many members of the department. Although there are some items of information that must remain confidential, they should be kept to a minimum to keep the air clear of intrigue and rumor-producing conditions.

Interdepartmental Communications

There is an acute need for a free flow of communications between the various law enforcement agencies throughout the country and, in many cases, with other law enforcement bodies in foreign countries. Nonpolitical and nonreligious organizations that are directly involved in the law enforcement or investigative process serve as one means of assuring this interdepartmental exchange of information and ideas. Through membership in national and international organizations, the chief meets other chief administrators from the United States and the rest of the world. They and their intelligence details and community relations officers also develop valuable contacts outside their own jurisdictions. These contacts facilitate the flow of information that is essential for the successful operation of police units in cases having national and international aspects and far-reaching effects. They may be extremely useful, for example, in cases involving safe burglars or clothing store burglars, who often work many cities across the country.

Another instance of interdepartmental communications is when the officer-specialists in several different departments meet under formal organization meeting situations. Through such organizational relationships they form friendships that facilitate frequent informal contacts for social reasons as well as for discussion of cases in which they are mutually interested. It is not unusual for the officers from several departments in contiguous jurisdictions jointly to solve a series of cases through the medium of their organizational ties. Otherwise, they might solve only those crimes that a culprit commits in one jurisdiction.

The World Wide Web and the Internet have opened up a myriad of possibilities not only for interagency communications on a continuous basis but also for interaction on the Net with millions of people outside the system. This broadens the scope of possibilities in identifying unknown dead persons held in limbo in the morgues, and developing information sources for unsolved crimes. Witnesses or possible witnesses to events surrounding criminal activity can contribute what they know directly to the investigating officer without leaving the comfort or safety of their homes. Investigators from different departments can compare their cases for similarities in a matter of seconds. Fingerprints, composites, photographs, and descriptions of evidence from their desktop and laptop computers, and field officers can be included in this communications loop by way of their mobile data terminals.

EXTERNAL RELATIONSHIPS

Isolation is not a favorable situation for any single segment of society, and you should avoid developing an insulated barrier between yourself and the other members of society. You should make a diligent effort to diversify associations among as many different special- and general-purpose organizations as possible, consistent with your work schedule and other responsibilities. These include school–parent organizations, church clubs, fraternal organizations, youth groups, and others that you encounter in the course of the many roles that you play. If you focus all your attention on those organizations related to law enforcement, you may develop a narrow, ethnocentric outlook.

Politics and religion are often causes for debate when a police officer is involved. As a private individual, you should be encouraged to take an active part in exercising your right to vote and expressing your freedom to worship in any way that you choose. When on duty, however, you should be as objective as possible and remain aloof from intense religious or political discussions so that you do not become identified as one who attempts to foist personal points of view on others under the guise of your official position.

On duty, never be so vocal in your beliefs that it can be said that you arrested an individual, or used your official position to coerce another person to comply with a certain request, because of your differences in religious or political beliefs. A police force should not be used as a tool to extort votes for a particular individual, or the people have a political police force, which is contrary to the American system of government. Keeping this neutral posture while on duty is a must, but if you wish to take an active part in your private life by affiliating with a church and political party of your choice, you have every right to do so as a first-class citizen. You also have the right not to affiliate if that is your wish.

With the increased development of community policing programs in so many departments, it is much more convenient to stay attuned to the community's needs and the many personalities who make up the community. The storefront (or next-door apartment) neighborhood police substation is putting the officers and the people they serve in closer proximity in so many different ways. When officers are closer to the people they serve, they are more likely to take it personally when problems arise in the community, such as streets that need repair, trash collection problems, absentee landlords neglecting their properties and allowing their tenants to live in rat- and roach-infested dwellings, as well as the formation of violent street gangs, illegal drug trafficking, and other traditional police problems that they must deal with. The problems are no longer "yours" and "ours," but "all of ours collectively."

Although you may live with your family in another community miles away from the community you serve as a police officer, your involvement in the community policing aspects of your job make you so much more personally committed to the goals of overall improvement of the living and social conditions of the community.

GUIDELINES FOR COMMUNICATIONS MEDIA

U.S. Mail

Mail is one of the oldest and most durable forms of communication used by law enforcement. Virtually every type of police business is transacted by mail, from the routine letter of verification for delivery of a shipment of ballpoint pens, to a special delivery, airmail letter to the detective division advising of the whereabouts of a possible robbery suspect. Individual patrol officers may not be directly involved in the routine use of the mails; but whenever it is necessary to send a letter related to the department's business, it should be in accordance with an established procedure. Outgoing mail should usually be sent over the signature of the chief of police or the division head, and returns should be requested in the same manner. The primary purpose of this procedure is to present the image of a single agency rather than a haphazard conglomeration of individual operators. Also, if an individual has been transferred or is off duty, the mail will be processed immediately.

Nightsticks, Whistles, and Hand Signals

Prearranged signals with either or both of these standard items of police equipment may be used for a variety of worthwhile purposes. At nighttime a nightstick rapped on the sidewalk pavement may be heard with a distinctive sound for several blocks. Short blasts of the whistle may also be heard, yet be considerably less noticeable than an officer's voice shouting a command or call for assistance. Whenever working with other officers under conditions when it will be necessary to be on foot, set up two or three distinctive hand signals. These may be particularly effective when attempting to surround a building to apprehend a burglar who is hiding inside.

Recall Signal Devices

Prior to the advent of portable two-way radios, some police departments set up systems of signal lights located throughout the areas covered by officers on foot beats. The lights were connected directly to the station houses, and messages were sent to the beat officers by means of coded combinations of light flashes. In other cities, small signal lights were installed atop a building in the center of town, and they signaled the officers downtown to report immediately to the station to take out a car for a service call in the outlying areas, or to come in for lunch relief.

The old days of the signal light are gone forever. Sophisticated recall methods have taken their place. The beeper and cellular phone are now commonplace accessories for the officer who is in the field and away from the office. Completely portable radios that you carry when away from your vehicle, and the mobile data terminal (MDT) in the vehicle keep you in constant touch with other officers, the communications center, and data resources throughout the country. The communications operator assigns you to the next call by typing it into your MDT, ready for you to read upon return to your vehicle. Verbal radio assignments are made simultaneously so that you will not have to ask for a repeat, but merely read the correct information. Your records of the calls were first retained on large reels of tape, but now are carried on computer discs so small that they may be stored for years.

Telegraph

Before the implementation of the teletype, one of the more common means of police communication was telegraph. Telegraph wires were linked to the police headquarters and the various precinct stations. They were also wired from one police department to another. Telegraphers were employed for the purpose of maintaining communications between stations. One disadvantage to the system was that police officers had to be specifically trained in operating the telegraph equipment and using the Morse code, which consists of combinations of clicks made by activating an electromagnetic key. The alternative was to employ trained telegraphers for the specialized job and to keep them on duty around the clock, which they apparently did. The system was used for many years but has been virtually obsolete since the 1940s.

Radio and Teletype

Following, and concurrent with, the phasing out of Morse Code sent over telephone lines, the new International code beamed across telephone lines and wireless radio was not only broken into sounds of dots and dashes but also printed visually on narrow strips of paper ribbon and guided along a track atop a typewriter so that the operator could type out the message. Typewriters were also connected to telephone lines and wireless radio and the receiver teletypewriter printed out the received message. Developed by Western Union and Postal Telegraph and Mackay Radio Companies, the teleprinter gained widespread use by the military and police services for long-distance communications. This assured greater accuracy in transmission and permanent record-keeping capabilities. Facsimile made it possible to transmit entire images by telephone and wireless transmission, and gained widespread use along with the progression of television through the 1950s and 1960s.

Computers

Although computers had been used by most major industries and some law enforcement agencies for many years, it was not until the 1960s that they gained widespread use in law enforcement. The Omnibus Crime Bill of 1968 passed by Congress made it possible for the federal government to pump money into the system to purchase hardware, equipment, and technology that local taxes could not buy. For the next 14 years the Law Enforcement Assistance Administration authorized the infusion of approximately $5 billion to modernize and professionalize law enforcement, the courts, and corrections agencies. A large portion of that money was used to enhance computerization of the system.

With the merging of radio, teletype, television, and facsimile into the police communications systems, and with their continuing improvement, there is now a highly efficient interconnected network of information storage and retrieval, which holds great promise for the future. Centralized records of stolen automobiles, criminal records and outstanding warrants, fingerprints, crime reports, pawned and stolen items, gun sales, and many more related data are maintained in centralized state and federal clearinghouses. Computer networks make it possible for almost instantaneous transmission of information from agency to agency and on down to the officer in the field in his mobile data terminal (MDT) and the desk of the investigator.

In addition to the statewide networks and information systems, the U.S. Department of Justice established in 1967 a central computerized information clearinghouse that provides instantaneous information retrieval and storage services for virtually every police agency in the country. Known as the National Crime Information Center, or NCIC, the system is operational and functioning as an integral part of the police information system.

NCIC serves all FBI field offices, all 50 of the United States, the District of Columbia, and Canada. It contains computerized files on wanted persons, stolen vehicles, license plates stolen and related to wanted persons, firearms transactions, stolen identifiable articles, securities files, aircraft, snowmobiles, dune buggies, and stolen boats. The system also contains criminal history files that allow an interchange of information concerning personal descriptions of arrested persons, total times arrested, charges and convictions or other dispositions, the number of times arrested in each offense category, the latest arrest and current status and/or disposition, appeal information, custody status, and change in status, such as probation on parole.

Any person whose name is contained in the NCIC files has a right to see and challenge any of the information contained therein to assure accuracy. The confidentiality and integrity of NCIC is assured in the following manner: (1) Terminals are available only to criminal justice agencies; (2) security provisions at the sites of the terminals are required; (3) there is a limit on the number of people who have access to terminals; (4) all personnel who have access to terminals and at the data center are carefully screened; (5) logs and other appropriate records are maintained to identify the users of the file; and (6) there are editing procedures implemented to assure file accuracy.

Secretaries, stenographers, and other clerks regularly employed by the various police departments may be easily trained to use computer equipment. Established uniform message formats should be followed closely to assure brevity, clarity, and maximum benefit from the exchange of information in accordance with a uniform sequence and style.

Facsimile (Fax) and Computer Interface

When we wrote the first edition of this book several years ago, fax and computers were new to criminal justice. Although computers have been around for decades, it was often difficult to get them to talk to each other because of their incompatibility. Now the process is quite commonplace and routine for records and investigative information to be shared throughout the world by computers and telephone connections. The same is true of fax, or "facsimile" as it was called when first used by major communications companies during the 1940s. Smaller than a copy machine of the portable variety, and connected to a telephone line, the exact duplicate of a document can be sent immediately to any other fax machine in the world.

Investigators are able to compare fingerprints by means of sophisticated fingerprint identification systems (in California it is called CAL-ID), to search the files, and to identify the culprit by his or her fingerprints in a matter of seconds. Just a few years ago, the process of identifying some of our more notorious wanted criminals—including some mass murderers—would have taken dozens of experts months or even years to do. Now the same job may take as few as 10 or 15 minutes, including human verification by experts at either end of the line. While a suspect is being booked in jail in Montgomery, Alabama, his or her fingerprints can be sent to the central clearinghouse in Washington, D.C., then on to various other states where the suspect is known to have been. Before the booking is completed, Montgomery will be notified by the Sacramento, California, department that it wants the suspect for burglary, and Charleston, South Carolina, will be sending a message that the suspect is probably in violation of parole in that state. Sketches, diagrams, composites, ransom notes, and forged checks can all be duplicated and sent via fax. The possibilities are limited only by your imagination. Mug shots and crime data are now exchanged with other agencies and the general public via the Internet and the World Wide Web.

Television

Sight and sound transmissions by means of television are an excellent adjunct to the other communications media employed by police departments. Television is popular because of its economy and ease of operation. As employed by the field officer in the patrol division, it is possible for the investigating officer at the scene of a crime to record the entire scene by means of videotape. Use of a videographer at major crime scenes is necessary and not a luxury.

Use of television makes it possible for lineups to be held at a central location while witnesses who are unable to travel view the suspects at some other location. The chief of police, the sheriff, or other officers may address a maximum number of officers and other employees who are located at various places throughout the jurisdiction either "live" or on videotape, thereby assuring the greatest possible coverage without interfering with normal operations or the off-duty time of the many employees.

Remote television cameras and transmitters carried in a helicopter, or located at various key places in a city, such as a heavily used intersection of two major arterials, make it possible for officers to view many places simultaneously, providing greater patrol coverage. A single officer can visually observe as many places as there are television cameras, and can dispatch a patrol unit to whichever one of the various locations requires the physical presence of a patrol officer. Using television to supplement patrol, it is possible to observe on a continuous basis many high-hazard or high-crime areas that otherwise might be checked only occasionally for a minute or two at a time once or twice a day.

We should not overlook the invaluable assistance provided by commercial and cable television. On public access TV it is possible for your agency to develop and produce your own programs to cover wanted persons, lost children, video shots of suspects captured on the victim store's video, and community policing matters. The possibilities are as endless as your imagination. We should also recognize the excellent cooperation by network and local commercial television programs, such as *America's Most Wanted, Unsolved Mysteries, American Detective, Highway Patrol,* and others that dramatize real cases and broadcast photos and descriptive data on wanted and missing persons. Utilizing all these electronic aids in the past few years has added the equivalent of several million additional at-home detectives to our rosters. Those programs can rightfully boast about their clearance rates with enviable statistics. The bartender watching the show recognizes the newcomer to town who just moved into the motel next door; unknowing new "marks" for a con artist can see the story of a new friend who bilked some poor unsuspecting widow out of all her survivor's insurance money and who happens to be working on his new victim, who can call the police instead of being his next victim. Their success rates are enviable.

Telephone

The most common means of communication between police departments and the people they serve will always be personal contact. The first contact—and sometimes the only one—usually consists of the telephone call requesting advice or assistance from the police officer. No type of police operation is transacted without frequent use of the telephone. Many members of the department literally spend their entire duty time on the telephone, answering questions for information or advice, questioning people concerning their identities, where they are, and their reasons for calling the police.

The telephone is a convenient, economical, and rapid means of communicating with others. Your department may have a central switchboard (PBX, Private Board Exchange) or Centrex system that allows calls to be made directly between the offices and the public without going through a central operator. This substantially reduces operator time. Because the telephone is so intimately involved with the role of law enforcement in the lives of people during times of great need and tragedy, the department members must be constantly mindful of the sensitive part they play in that role. It is just as important that the representative of the police department answer every call with a pleasant attitude as it is that the representative of an insurance company respond to each call as if it were from a new customer.

Telephone Techniques. Every telephone call must be answered with a pleasant voice, never in such a way that the caller gets the feeling that he or she is interrupting someone's sleep or that the person answering the call would rather be doing something else. The brusque or rough-sounding voice has no place in an operator's methods of response to calls. A good telephone voice should be similar to that of a radio announcer. The voice should be clear, distinct, evenly paced, pleasant, and natural. Speak directly into the mouthpiece. If you wear a headset with a small tube-shaped mouthpiece, be sure it is in front of your mouth when you talk.

Always answer the phone promptly or transfer the call to someone who can answer. Be attentive to the caller and attempt to determine from the tone of voice the urgency of the call for services. Keep the length of all incoming calls short. Be polite, but discourage the marathon conversation. If the caller must talk longer than you have time for, perhaps it may be possible to transfer the call to a clerk who will advise the caller that the officer was required to move on to another call and inquire whether there is additional information that should be passed on to the officer. Such a tactic should not be designed to discourage callers, but it is necessary if the lines are to be kept reasonably clear for an emergency call that may come in at any moment.

Any incoming phone call to the police department may be a request for help in a life or death situation. It may not be such a call—most calls are not—but law enforcement is an emergency service organization and must be geared for emergency at all times. The next call may be the most important call of the day, and a minute saved may mean the difference between an individual's life or death. The phone must not be allowed to continue ringing unanswered, and there should be a standard procedure for immediate response when the telephone operator is busy. One method for handling all incoming phone calls is to have the principal operator respond to as many calls as possible and immediately connect other calls to other persons who have desk assignments in the building. The call may be handled by that person, or if it is a nonemergency call for service or a request to speak with a particular individual within the building, it can be returned to the operator when the earlier surge of overloading calls has subsided.

One effective method for handling many calls at once is to answer each call with "Police Department. Is this an emergency?" If the person at the other end of the line states "No," go to the next call, handling only the emergency calls. Then go back to the calls that were not in need of immediate attention. By using this method it is possible to give all callers the attention they expect of their police department and at the same time give them priority attention. If you use this procedure, the key to success is to wait for a reply when asking, "Is this an emergency?" Otherwise, the purpose is defeated.

There is nothing worse for the caller with an urgent message to have the police operator open the line and say: "Police Department. Is this an emergency?" followed by an immediate click and to be placed on hold without the operator having listened for an answer to that critical question.

Another technique is to utilize a complaint board and tape recorder combination. Any request for service can be switched to the tape recorder on a delayed-action arrangement, which allows you as the operator to switch to an extension after the caller has already begun talking. You can listen to the recorded conversation at high speed and catch up with the slower pace at which the caller is talking. This is a time-delay device that phone-in radio and television talk shows use when taking incoming calls so that they may block out obscene or profane words or slanderous comments before they are broadcasted. When the complaint desk is at normal load, you will answer incoming calls directly. It is good practice to use the tape recorder and record all telephone conversations. There may be a need to study the tapes for voice identification or to establish who said what to whom and under what conditions for a variety of reasons.

However you answer the phone, or when you must put the caller on hold, or if you transfer the call to another station, check back frequently to be sure that the caller gets the call completed as intended.

Incoming calls of an emergency nature should not be referred to another phone number. The operator should take the information and relay it to the agency that can respond to the situation by virtue of jurisdiction or nature of the requested service. If the call is for service or information that does not require immediate attention, the caller should be referred to the correct agency and provided with the correct name, address, and telephone number. "It's in the phone book" is not an appropriate retort.

The 911 telephone system has been a tremendous boon to the emergency services. A free call from any telephone, including a pay phone, immediately links the caller with the service desired and the geographical location of the caller.

An excellent method for disseminating information about a "hot" call such as a robbery in progress or a hostage situation that will need many available units beyond the usual assigned field unit is for the telephone operator, in this case the 911 operator, to ring all concerned units (Watch Commander, SWAT, Crime Against Persons Detail, and others) on a conference line so that the call can be broadcast over a loudspeaker in each office. At the same time as the call is assigned to the field unit by radio, the data is transmitted to that unit and other units in the field on their MDTs. Updates on the call will then continue to be sent out to the mobile computers.

Whenever a private person takes the time to call the police department about some need for police service, it is usually one of the most important events in that person's life at that particular moment. Very few people call for police aid with any regularity, and they are sometimes unfortunately referred to as "chronic complainers." With due respect for the officers who use this term, we would agree that there are some persons who fit that category because their requests are for the police officers to perform false arrests or to "put a scare into" someone. On the whole, however, most callers are sincere and justifiably want the police to perform some action that falls within the purview of our responsibilities. When such is the case, it should be a matter of routine courtesy for you to take a few extra minutes when possible after responding to the call to phone or visit the callers to bring them up to date on the action you took. There is no need to disseminate tidbits of gossip for the rumormongers; just state what is sufficient to satisfy the caller that you did perform your duty.

Whenever an alarm company calls in that a silent alarm has been set off at some location in your jurisdiction, they go through a series of procedures to verify that the signal was probably not a false alarm, in some cases, and that it was a possible burglary or robbery. At stormy and extremely windy times, many of those alarms turn out to be false. Until that fact is determined, however, the call is handled as a hot crime in progress and appropriate backup is provided for the assigned field units. Other units should also be alerted in case the situation develops into an "in-progress" call.

Police Radio

It is difficult to imagine a modern, efficient law enforcement agency without the use of radio. Now it is taken as a matter of course, with little thought to the fact that police radio was nonexistent until about 1929. The first radios were quite cumbersome and considerably different from those in use today. The transmitter was located at headquarters and the police cars were equipped with receivers only. In many agencies there was no transmitter, and it was necessary to send emergency calls to the police cars in the field by using the facilities of local broadcast stations.

By 1938 the use of one-way radios in police cars had become fairly widespread, and it was during that year that some departments began installing transmitters in their vehicles, making two-way radio communication possible. The system involved use of a common frequency for all transmissions from both the station at headquarters and the mobile units. This simple configuration is called a *simplex system*. The next step was to provide separate frequencies so that the station was using one frequency and the mobile units another. This double frequency system is known as the *duplex system*. As it progressed, police radio added a third frequency for car-to-car transmissions, and the triple frequency system was named the *triplex system*. Variations of all three systems are presently in operation. Some police units are equipped with scanners that allow interception of messages over other frequencies in addition to the "priority channel" they are regularly assigned.

GUIDELINES FOR RADIO OPERATION

Utilization of the radio frequencies for many purposes by hundreds of different types of organizations and individual operations has made it necessary to have very strict limitations on frequency allocations and on the actual use of those frequencies that are allocated. Along the spectrum of sound wave frequencies, only a portion of the frequencies may be used by radio. Other frequencies are used for ultraviolet and infrared transmissions, for X-ray, diathermic, and ultrasonic therapeutic devices and for television and both private and commercial radio. As a result of all of these demands on the existent frequencies, which cannot be expanded, the frequencies are constantly being narrowed and exploited more efficiently through the use of highly sophisticated equipment.

Air time on the police frequency is as valuable to the police officer as the most valuable gem is to the jeweler, and you should use it accordingly. Even though there may be silent gaps during the day, it is just as desirable to save the silent moments as it is for the jeweler to preserve every scrap of the precious gem or metal and get maximum use of the leftovers in producing other items. With the radio, the object is to use only that time that is necessary to deliver the message, no more. Each transmission must be brief, but not so brief that it must be repeated for explanation or clarification, and it must be accurate. Through the use of standardized radio codes, it is possible to cut sentences down into numbers, such as "code seven at 14," which means, "I am going to stop for a few minutes for lunch at the coffee shop to which we gave the number '14' sometime previously, and I may be reached at that phone number—also listed previously—if you need to get in touch with me while I am eating."

Operating Laws and Regulations

The Federal Communications Commission is charged with the responsibility for the legal and efficient use of the radio frequencies. Profanity, obscenity, and superfluous transmissions are unlawful and are prosecutable offenses. It is your responsibility to follow the recommended procedures discussed in this chapter and to avoid the use of profanity, obscenity, and superfluous transmissions. All other matters will be handled by the engineers and those people who are appropriately licensed as the principal operators for the various radio stations.

Microphone Technique

Prior to broadcasting by radio, depress the button to turn the microphone on and wait for a moment to allow the transmitter to be at full power when you are speaking. Hold the microphone about two inches from your mouth and in such a position that the sound is going past the microphone rather than directly into it. Using this technique will reduce the distracting sounds that occur when spitting the P's and hissing or whistling the S's. Some high-quality broadcast microphones filter these sounds out, making it possible to speak directly into them.

Use radio codes as much as possible for clarity and brevity, and speak in an evenly modulated tone of voice, slowly and distinctly. Exaggerate the diction slightly, such as the consonants at the end of the words, and the vowel sounds. For example, the word "police" should sound like "po lees" rather than "plece." As much as possible under the circumstances at the time of broadcast, try to make every transmission free of emotion. Any expression of anger, impatience, rudeness, or excitement may be exaggerated during the radio transmission, and its contagion will negatively affect most of the people who are listening to that particular frequency.

Volume control is essential. Keep the volume evenly modulated. Shouting will cause a distorted transmission, and an important request for help may be so distorted by shouting that it is unintelligible. Outside noises from sirens, racing motors, overhead aircraft, and other sources all interfere with the transmissions, but shouting over the noise will not correct the problem. If at all possible, time your broadcasts so that they occur at times of least interference. If there is outside noise and you must transmit, try talking with the microphone directly against the throat at the larynx.

Broadcast Procedures

Listen to the radio for a few seconds before broadcasting to be sure that you are not interfering with another exchange of transmissions. Use this time to quickly think out your message before you say it. Depress the microphone button and begin talking after a brief pause, keeping the transmission "moving." The pause allows time for the transmitter to turn on because there might be a delay from the remote location of the activating switch. If you start talking at the same time you depress the switch, your first word or two might be lost. If you must stop to think or secure additional information, clear the air and return a minute later rather than stutter or stammer as a stall for time. The air time is valuable; use it as if it were gold dust.

Be articulate in your broadcasting style, carefully pronouncing every syllable in each word, including the final syllable instead of mumbling toward the end of each sentence. Be careful not to distort your voice by shouting, making it unintelligible. Emotional outbursts have no place in police radio communication. Not only is it difficult to understand the distorted sounds, but the outburst affects those who listen to the broadcast at the time. Later, when the tape is played, it might prove embarrassing to all concerned with the call. I am reminded of communications operators in particular. One would get so emotionally involved that she would start crying and her transmission was totally garbled. Another former air controller for the military whom you would think could handle about any emergency would start throwing up into a nearby trash basket between transmissions whenever he got emotionally involved in the situation. Both were very sensitive people, but no more effective than would be a doctor whose tears would drop into the open wounds while operating on a patient in the emergency room.

If the transmission is long, stop occasionally and secure an acknowledgment of the message so far before continuing. The break will ensure clear communication, and it will also permit another unit with an urgent message to interfere when essential. Wait briefly for an acknowledgment before repeating the message or asking for an acknowledgment. The person at the other end of the message may have received the message, but may have been momentarily called away from the microphone by some other matter. If you do not wait, you may be broadcasting at the same time the station is broadcasting its acknowledgment, and with both transmitters on simultaneously, neither of you will hear the other. Unfortunately, impatience for a response sometimes causes considerable confusion.

Do not repeat messages unnecessarily, as occasionally portrayed on television or in the movies. A well-executed message given once is usually sufficient. If the receivers did not get it all, they will ask for a repeat of that portion they missed. There is no need to transmit a message and then ask for an acknowledgment in the same manner as the individual who asks after every sentence, "Do you understand?" or "Did you get that?" Whether he is asked or not, the receiver is required to acknowledge a transmission. Therefore, the request for acknowledgment is superfluous.

Pay attention to other transmissions on the radio that do not directly affect you, such as open-door discoveries or car stops. Although the officer may not request a follow-up unit, it should be a matter of course for the nearest unit to follow up to assure adequate protection for the lone field officer. When another unit calls in a license number and auto description when the officers make a car stop, copy it down. In the event that an officer is attacked or the vehicle flees the scene, or both, you already have the essential information and do not have to wait for a general broadcast to take action.

Acknowledgment of Calls

Respond to all calls as quickly as possible to avoid the need for a repeat or a second call to ask you if you received the first one. When acknowledging a call, respond with the appropriate code, but also give your location. The dispatcher and the other units that are listening to your transmission will know the distance you will have to travel to respond to a call and they can estimate your probable route of travel. Follow-up units, if necessary for the occasion, will know how they should proceed. In some cases, it may be possible to reassign a call to a closer unit, which is particularly important for injury accidents and "crime in progress" calls. If you are operating the follow-up unit and intend to respond, broadcast your intentions and the location from where you are responding.

Station Broadcasting and Assignment of Calls

The communications center is the authoritative voice of the agency. Radio and MDT transmissions assigning calls are the most authoritative, or so say your department's procedure manuals. You are to accept the assignment as given whether it is in your assigned area or not, regardless of whatever your negative feelings may be about the call. There is usually a provision for a supervisor or command officer in the field to countermand that assignment if he or she has more valid information, such as a closer unit or an officer with specific qualifications who could better handle the situation. When the countermanding order is given, the person giving it is usually required to justify the decision, and will notify the dispatch center of the change in assignment with the authority to do so.

The dispatcher and the field officer are partners and are dependent upon each other to complete the mission of the department. Avoid vitriol and anger when communicating with dispatch or other units by radio or MDT. Transmissions must be impersonal, station-to-station broadcasts, and not a social party line. The transmissions are permanently recorded and may be called up for presentation in court and a myriad of purposes. Be careful not to transmit any message that would reflect negatively on you and your agency.

If you are assigned to the 911 board, as a dispatcher you have the added responsibility of determining in as short a time as possible the precise nature of the problem and the best way to address that problem. Once you have dispatched the field unit(s), ambulances, fire department, and other help to the scene, your work has probably just begun. It is the 911 operator who must continue to draw developing information about the ongoing situations, such as a recent holdup I am aware of. Four robbers were inside a Home Depot, one of them pistol-whipping the manager, while at the same time one of the hidden employees was using a cellular phone and keeping up a running dialog with the 911 operator, providing information for the SWAT officers outside to successfully carry out their mission, while the operator was keeping those inside informed of what was happening outside the building. Many emergency childbirths and CPR procedures have been accomplished with the aid of the 911 operator giving instructions while emergency equipment was still on the way to the scene.

As the station operator in the dispatch center, you are responsible for maintaining order on the airways and reminding the comedians and practical jokers on the air that they should take their antics to a comedy club. Humor will naturally enter into virtually all facets of life, including police communications, but usually the type of humor that causes one to raise an eyebrow or smile. It is a natural reaction to stress for some people to cope by looking at a situation with a somewhat macabre sense of humor. It is not my suggestion that individuals should not act and react with human responses. The point is that the players in these life scenes are not auditioning for character roles in a television sitcom.

General Broadcasting Rules

Whenever using the police radio, use the following rules as guidelines for effective broadcasting results.

1. Practice courtesy. It is contagious and will make their work much easier for everyone who uses the radio as well as those who must listen to it constantly during their entire tour of duty.

2. Broadcast station-to-station only. "Mike to Joe" transmissions are not allowed and should be held for personal meetings or telephone calls.

3. Humor and horseplay have no place on the police frequency. Rude sounds and sarcastic comments emanating from anonymous users of the radio frequency may sound funny for the moment, but they are immature, unlawful, and they may someday interfere with a transmission that could mean the difference between whether an officer lives or dies. Leave the humor to the commercial broadcasting clowns, who are employed specifically for the purpose of entertainment.

4. Avoid any use of the radio for personal conflicts, such as "chewing out," arguments, or sarcasm.

5. Keep all transmissions brief and to the point. Use the telephone for lengthy messages.

6. Profane and indecent language are unlawful.

7. Transmit only essential messages. Avoid asking for the time of day just to hear the radio, and secure routine information, such as time to eat lunch and other scheduled matters, either before going out in the field or by telephone.

8. Be completely familiar with your department's radio procedures and the individual items of equipment.

9. Assume a personal responsibility for correct and intelligent use of the radio by your department.

10. Use radio code for brevity and accuracy when practicable.

Radio Codes for Emergency Services

10-1	Receiving poorly
10-2	Receiving well
10-3	Stop transmitting
10-4	OK, or acknowledge
10-5	Relay
10-6	Busy
10-7	Out of service

10-7-B	Out of service at home
10-8	In service
10-9	Repeat
10-10	Out of service, subject to call
10-11	Transmitting too rapidly
10-12	Officials or visitors present
10-13	Weather and road conditions
10-14	Escort or convoy
10-15	Enroute with prisoner
10-16	Pick up prisoner
10-17	Pick up papers
10-18	Complete present assignment quickly as possible
10-19	Return or returning to the station
10-20	Location, or what is your location?
10-21	Call your station or dispatcher by telephone
10-21-A	Advise my home I will return at _____
10-21-B	Call your home
10-21-T	Reply via teleprinter
10-22	Cancel last message or assignment
10-23	Stand by
10-25	Do you have contact with _____?
10-27	Check _____ computer for warrants
10-28	Registration request
10-29	Check for stolen or wanted
10-30	No records or wants your subject
10-31	Subject has record, but not wants
10-32	Subject wanted. Are you clear to copy?
10-33	Standby. Emergency traffic only
10-34	Resume normal radio traffic
10-35	Confidential information
10-36	Correct time
10-37	Name of operator on duty
10-39	Message delivered
10-40	Is _____ available for telephone call?
10-40-A	Is _____ available for radio call?
10-42	Pick up officer
10-45	Service your equipment
10-46	Stand by. I am moving to a better location
10-48	I am now ready to receive information
10-49	Proceed to _____

10-86	Traffic check (Do you have any messages for this unit?)
10-87	Meet _____ at _____.
10-88	What phone number should we call for station-to-station call?
10-96	Request test of selective call equipment
10-97	Arrived at the scene
10-98	Completed last assignment
NO CODE	Handle calls routinely
CODE 1	Routine, take this call next
CODE 2	Urgent. Expedite, but obey all traffic laws. No red light/siren
CODE 3	EMERGENCY. Proceed immediately, using red light and siren
CODE 4	No further assistance needed
CODE 4-A	No further assistance needed, but suspect at large in area
CODE 5	Stakeout. Other units stay away unless ordered there
CODE 6	Out for investigation
CODE 7	Out of service to eat
CODE 8	Fire box pulled
CODE 9	Jail break
CODE 12	Patrol assigned area and report extent of disaster damage
CODE 13	Activate major disaster plan, or perform major disaster duties
CODE 14	Resume normal operations (used only following CODE 12 or 13)
CODE 20	Notify news media
CODE 20-D	Request department photographer
CODE 99	EMERGENCY situation. The emergency button in mobile unit has been depressed. No voice contact.

SUMMARY

In this chapter, we covered basic procedures in telephone, radio, and other communications, as well as a discussion of some of the many types of communications equipment available to the modern police agency, such as computers, television, speed photo and facsimile, the mails, whistles and nightsticks, and recall signal devices, and some of their uses. One of the most important aspects of police communications is how to deal with each other interpersonally. Addressing that aspect, we discussed both verbal as well as nonverbal communications and some of the problems and responsibilities attendant to those ways that you, the field officer, communicate with the people you serve.

1. What factors influence how we interpret what we hear?

2. Give two examples of how body language may contradict what a person might be saying.

3. If a person you are questioning sits back on the chair and opens up his arms while answering your questions, would you interpret the body language as that of a cooperative person?

4. How would you shut off a conversation and let it be known by body language that you are in charge?

5. When two people are gazing very intently at one another, what type of conversation are they likely to be having?

6. Describe how a person's body language will say that he or she is nervous.

7. Describe a sign of frustration.

8. Six items were listed as being essential for a police communications system. List and explain all six.

9. Interview one or more of the old-timers in your department, and write a brief synopsis on how officers handled communications prior to the advent of the police radio.

10. What is the reason for putting a time limit on all orders, including general as well as special orders?

11. What is the purpose for a chief executive officer to have an "open-door" policy?

12. Do you believe that a peace officer should have the freedom to actively practice partisan politics while on duty? Why? (or) why not?

13. What is the basic reason for having official department correspondence addressed to the department rather than to an individual officer?

14. What is NCIC, and what type of information may be found through its use?

15. What is the correct way to answer the police telephone when you are overloaded with incoming calls?

16. Of what value is the tape recorder to the police complaint board operator?

17. What is the "911 system," and how does it work?

18. What is the purpose of a telephone hot line?

19. What is the correct technique for speaking into a microphone?

20. What is the principal purpose for using radio codes?

21. What is the recommended technique for speaking into a microphone when outside noise, such as a wailing siren, makes it almost impossible to be heard over the sound?

22. What does the author say about personal conversations over the police radio?

23. What is the radio code for "received your message"?

24. Using radio code, how would you say "Please repeat your message"?

25. What is Code 1? Code 2? Code 3?

26. How would you report a structural fire by radio?
27. What is the radio code for "everything is OK"?
28. What is the distance of your own *personal space?*
29. Does your local department have an Internet or Web Site?
30. When a group of boys or girls are walking in a group across the campus, how do you determine who the leader is of that group?

REFERENCES

ADAMS, THOMAS F. *Training Officers' Handbook.* Springfield, Ill.: Charles C. Thomas, 1964, Chap. 5.

FEDERAL COMMUNICATIONS COMMISSION. *Rules and Regulations* (annual).

LOS ANGELES POLICE DEPARTMENT. *Daily Training Bulletins,* Vol. I. Springfield, Ill.: Charles C. Thomas, 1954, Chap. 9.

———. *Daily Training Bulletins,* Vol. II. Springfield Ill.: Charles C. Thomas, 1958, Chap. 25.

LOS ANGELES SHERIFF'S DEPARTMENT. *Communication Procedure (Daily Training Bulletins 1–8),* Vol. 1. Los Angeles: Los Angeles Sheriff's Department, n.d.

MORRIS, DESMOND, *Manwatching: A Field Guide to Human Behavior.* New York: Abrams, 1977.

C H A P T E R   5

REPORTING AND RECORDS

*I*NTRODUCTION

As a novice, you may look upon the preparation of reports and the maintenance of comprehensive records as a relatively unimportant part of the total police role. These tasks may not hold much interest. However, as you gain experience and as cases are won and lost in court, personal evaluations are discussed with superior officers, commendations for outstanding performance of duty are awarded, and reports are sent back for rewrite, the tremendously important part played by officer-prepared records becomes quite evident. They are vital to the continued efficiency of any police agency. Their effectiveness is your responsibility.

This chapter covers the subject of reporting and records maintenance in three parts. The purpose of this format is to emphasize the relative importance of each of the three parts with respect to the other two. Basic to all three sections is the premise that no police action is performed correctly unless the report accurately recounts such action exactly as it happened in clear, concise, and objective language. Section One deals with field notetaking. This is where it all begins. Accuracy at this stage will often set the tone for an entire investigation and will be the determining factor in the eventual success in prosecution. Section Two covers basic report writing techniques, including report dictation, which is actually the most logical method for recording reports. It also presents a collection of forms

Figure 5–1 Computers play an important role in the management of police organizations. Shown here at his PC is Police Chief David L. Snowden. (Courtesy Police Department, Costa Mesa, California.)

that can be completed by checking the appropriate statements concerning routine calls that have been handled in accordance with standard operating procedures. Section Three, "Getting the Most Out of Records," is intended to stimulate the field patrol officer to do just that: get the most out of the police records system (see Figure 5–1). It is a gold mine of information providing, of course, that it has been filled previously with "gold" as indicated in Sections One and Two in this chapter.

Section One: Field Notetaking and Crime Scene Recording

INTRODUCTION

Of all the various types of notes you make regarding day-to-day activities, the most important are field notes. They are made specifically for the purpose of compiling facts in the order in which they present themselves to you. As viewed by the observer at some later time, it is apparent that the officer making the notes had no reason, no desire to alter the notes in any appreciable way. They are likely to be highest on a credibility scale if there were to be such a measuring device. It is probably for this reason that the rules of evidence provide that a witness may refer to notes while giving testimony if those notes were made by the witnesses themselves, or by someone under their direction at the time the fact being recorded was actually occurring, or was still fresh in the memory of the person recording it.

Field notes should be limited to names, addresses, and other pertinent data relevant to the identities of persons mentioned in reports and their relationships with the incident, and short succinct statements relating elements of the situation being recorded in the sequence as they occur and come to the attention of the recorder. Any opinions should be clearly explained and substantiated by facts and be kept to an absolute minimum. Departure from facts should occur only when inferences could be made by any other reasonable and prudent person with the same collection of information. *Never* fabricate or fictionalize reports to make a better case or for self-aggrandizement.

WHAT CONSTITUTES FIELD NOTES?

Field notes are actually the index to your memory. They are generally limited to brief notations entered into some type of book, or a collection of notes on cards or papers you carry for the purpose of recording notes. They may include letters or diaries, log books, or complete reports prepared in the field after you complete the call. Principal characteristics of field notes are accuracy and proximity in time to the actual incidents recorded.

NOTETAKING

You may use your field notebook for a general collection of notes concerning the many aspects of your job, such as new orders or policies emanating from the administrative sections of the department, work schedules, court appearance calendars, notices of changes in laws, and any other bits of information that you wish to have at your immediate disposal in your pocket. The key to maintaining a good notebook is to determine what notes *not* to keep. Selectivity is necessary to ensure that only essential data are recorded but it is important not to exclude any information that will later prove to be critical to a case.

When to Take Notes

At the beginning of the workday, it is advisable to start a new page. List the date and time worked, partner (if any), unit number, and district worked. It should be a matter of routine to jot down notes on each incident as soon as possible after arriving on the scene. It would not seem appropriate to approach the calling party with notebook in hand or to approach a suspected law violator with your hands full. You should make your initial approach with your hands free to respond to any immediate need for action, such as rescue or apprehension. Once you have taken whatever action is necessary, it should then be a practice to take out your notebook and start recording brief but succinct notes.

Include the date and time of the incident, weather conditions if relevant, and location of the incident—not only the street address but also the character of the neighborhood (industrial, residential, transitional) if the incident and the neighborhood for some reason should be recorded. You may find it an excellent adjunct to your memory to write down any impressions you may have to indicate reasonable cause to interview an individual at a particular moment. You may later find yourself hard put to define your impressions at the time of the interview. When walking into a crime scene, you may detect a peculiar odor, hear unusual noises, or see something that just does not seem right for that particular place or time of day. Such an impression is a fleeting one and will almost as quickly be forgotten if not recorded as perceived. It is also a factual situation, not mere opinion.

Avoid editorializing when you make your field notes—or any other notes for that matter. You are making a record of what you perceive and what may be deduced from those perceptions. If the reader sees from your notes that a witness makes contradictory statements, one may guess that some of the information is false or exaggerated, but you should not write that in your notes. Let the facts speak for themselves. One officer reported in his field notes that the "African fairy" appeared to be snooping around behind a building. That very same individual had occasion to check his own record in an unrelated situation, and his attorney discovered the officer's personal observation on the form. A threatened lawsuit led to an out-of-court financial settlement and some embarrassment to the department. All statements, comments, and observations are "on the record," no matter what someone may say to you. Consider for a moment the O. J. Simpson case and some "private" conversations between Officer Fuhrman and the erstwhile screenwriter whose tapes received worldwide distribution, and permanent damage to the officer's (now retired) reputation. The best way to avoid being quoted is to avoid writing or speaking words that will later come back and haunt you.

When taking information concerning routine complaints, the notes you enter in your notebook may later prove quite important. For example, in a routine neighborhood quarrel, you respond to the call. After contacting the calling party and serving as a referee while the persons present settle—or at least air—their differences, you determine that no crime is being committed in your presence and that nothing seems to have occurred prior to your arrival but hot debate. You record in your notebook the names and addresses of all the people you contact, and jot down a few statements concerning the actions you observed and whatever action you took or advice you offered, and then leave. Some time later you are dispatched to the same scene to investigate an aggravated assault or worse. Armed with the notes you made at the earlier incident involving the same principals, you will be far better prepared to carry the investigation through to a successful conclusion.

When you first arrive on the scene of a crime, it would be ideal to have a portable television recorder with attached microphone. As you walk up to the scene, you simply record the scene visually while simultaneously narrating your observations, pointing out and describing each item of evidence, and generally attempting to reconstruct the crime as it probably occurred. But the ideal is usually not practical or economical. The next best arrangement is to prepare a rough sketch and jot down notes in your notebook in the same manner as if you were going to later narrate the investigation from start to finish. A miniature tape recorder should be a standard item of your reporting equipment. Record all statements made by the victims, witnesses, suspects, and anyone else you question concerning the incident, and generally record brief notes on everything that you will later commit to more formal reports. Tape as much as possible, especially verbatim statements of witnesses as long as they do not refuse to speak into the microphone and object to the recording. It is advisable to first ask the person you are talking with: "Do you mind if we record this? I want to make sure that I get it all right." Gather as much information as possible. Actually, even if the individual objects to the taping, there will be no problem because at this point your objective in the taping is to be accurate. It is always better to be open and aboveboard, especially when dealing with a voluntary and cooperative witness.

Value of Field Notes

There are many valuable aspects to field notes and the notebook, some of which we have already covered. Consider a few more. During your busy day, you respond to many demands for service. It is impossible to remember all that you should about each incident that involves you. Your notebook serves as your memory bank, and the brief entries serve as your index of "landmarks" in your memory.

The notes provide valuable leads to investigations, data about certain items of evidence that should be checked out more thoroughly, and invaluable bits of information necessary to conduct an intelligent interview with witnesses or suspects. The notes actually serve as a self-discipline tool, forcing you to be accurate and thorough, and to organize your thoughts in logical sequence.

Sometimes when an attorney is questioning you in court, you may be asked about peripheral information to check out your powers of recall. If you are candid and forthcoming in your responses generally, your occasional "fuzzy" memory may be explained because you were not focused on those particular matters at the time while you were focused on the events you were required to record. The opposing attorney will try to use your memory problems as indications of "selective memory," but the attorney who called you as a witness will be able to have you recover by bringing it out that no one remembers everything 100 percent accurately.

Because of their admissibility as "past recollections recalled" and "recorded impressions," the set of well-prepared notes provides a medium whereby you may quote exactly entire statements by the principals in the investigation rather than fragments and sometimes inaccurate bits of statements. Good notes thus prepare you to deal in specifics rather than generalities. The notes will "remember," whereas the human mind may not remember efficiently. Needless to say, testimony based upon an excellent set of notes will make a more favorable impression in the courtroom and will be weighed against testimony presented by persons who did not take notes and whose memory on key points may be sprinkled with "I don't recalls" and similar excuses for not having all the facts.

What to Record

Selectivity is essential for field notes. Experience in the field and in the courtroom will be the principal teachers in this important matter; however, both take time. Foremost in your mind should be the elements of the corpus delicti if you are investigating a crime. All of those elements are going to have to be substantiated if you are to lead the case to a successful conclusion. The Five W's and the H of every case—When, Who, Where, What, Why, and How—are

W-1: When?	When did the event occur?
	When was it reported?
	When did the problem begin that is now being reported?
W-2: Who?	Who are the principal characters in this scenario?
	Who else is present?
	Who are all these other people?

	Exactly who did what in the event, including the investigating officers?
	Who has information concerning the details of this problem?
	Who has information about the background of this problem?
W-3: Where?	Where are the victims?
	Where are the witnesses?
	Where are the suspects?
	Where is the evidence?
W-4: What?	What appears to have happened?
	What do the people tell you happened?
	What *really* happened?
W-5: Why?	Why is the informant telling you this?
	Why is the story people tell you "too perfect"?
	Why did the crime occur? (Look for motive.)
H-1: How?	How did the crime occur? Was it possible?
	How did the burglars remove six tons of gold bullion in two hours with a pickup truck?
	How did the burglarized store have the window glass smashed from the *inside?*
	How could the culprit get in through that little opening?

When you record names and descriptions of victims and witnesses, be sure to use correct spelling as the people themselves spell their names, not as you guess they might spell them. List the names of other officers who are involved in the event, describe their activities, and indicate that they, too, are preparing reports (if, in fact, they are). Describe in detail the chain of custody of evidence that you handle.

At all times when filling out your notes, bear in mind the kind of report you will probably be making. Most form reports require that specific information be entered into the appropriate spaces. If it is a crime report of a particular nature, the information should justify the corpus delicti of that crime or those crimes. Your victim or other reporting party may claim that the crime is a rape, but your evidence shows only a sexual battery; the *facts* must guide you, not the demands or expectations of the reporting party. If a victim claims a break-in is accompanied by a grand theft of certain claimed missing property, but your investigation reveals no evidence of a break-in and the actual verifiable loss adds up to a petty theft, your report should reflect the product of your investigation. If your investigation contradicts unverified claims of the informant, point out the discrepancy to the informant and ask for an explanation of why the facts contradict the claims.

Don't be surprised to see more on these items of reporting again and again throughout your instruction. Your job as a police officer includes looking beyond the statements of the witnesses and surface appearances, and to get to the *truth*. Never take anything for granted when investigating any type of police incident. While compiling the information in the field and the courtroom, you will have to attempt to anticipate all the questions that will be asked (and the spaces to be filled out in the report forms) by the supervisors, the prosecutor, and the court; and then you must set about recording the answers to all those questions in your notebook. You may choose to keep a separate notebook on debriefing data and significant impressions that you would rather not make public but need for a convenient reference.

Retention or Destruction of Field Notes?

Department policy may decide this question for you, and require that either you retain or you destroy your field notes once you have committed the information to a formal report. Certain internal affairs and intelligence assignments may require the destruction of all notes to assure that the formal report you submit to the chief is the only report in existence. My recommendation is that you retain your original notes for at least a year or two except for one or more of the reasons listed above.

The courts have held that it is proper to throw away your field notes as long as (1) you destroy them in good faith; (2) you incorporate them into a formal report; (3) the formal report accurately reflects the contents of the notes; and (4) the prosecutor turns over a copy of the formal report before trial.[1]

The Notebook

Although some departments are quite specific about the type of notebook officers carry, the type of book is secondary to what you put inside (see Figure 5–2). Some "experts" recommend that only loose-leaf books be used, allowing the insertion or removal of pages in any desired sequence. I prefer the bound or spiral notebook, because it is immediately apparent when a page has been removed. Most legally required log books and ledgers are bound to avoid the problem of "page juggling." The least efficient type of notebook is the standard clipboard with a collection of loose sheets of paper held together only by a spring clip at the top of the board.

The argument against the bound notebook is that when an officer once refers to the notebook in court, the defense attorney may inspect the book, presumably to challenge its authenticity. The argument then points out that the rest of the book is laid bare for the inspection of the attorney and that the attorney will go on a "fishing expedition" reading passages from other cases and perhaps reading aloud in the courtroom some statement that might prove embarrassing to the author, thereby serving as a means to attempt to impeach the officer's reference to the notes in question. If that is the case, where is the prosecutor? The officer who plans to refer to a notebook in court should make that fact known to the prosecutor and show the portion of the book that includes notes relevant to the case at hand. Any other portion of the notebook is "off limits" because it is totally irrelevant and immaterial to this case. Introduction of any of that extraneous material to the case by either side would be inadmissible, as would be any other extraneous material. The judge may order those portions of the book closed, or stapled shut, and inadmissible.

The book should bear some identifying data on the cover, such as the name and badge number of the officer and perhaps a notebook number. After the book has been filled with information, it is a good practice to keep it for a reasonable period of time. Keep the books at the very least two or three years, which should extend beyond trial

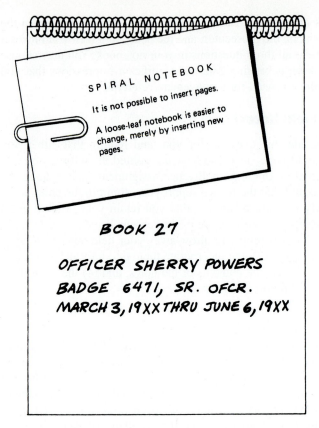

SPIRAL NOTEBOOK

It is not possible to insert pages.

A loose-leaf notebook is easier to change, merely by inserting new pages.

BOOK 27

OFFICER SHERRY POWERS
BADGE 6471, SR. OFCR.
MARCH 3, 19XX THRU JUNE 6, 19XX

Figure 5–2 Sample notebook.

and appeals deadlines. In some homicide cases, this time may extend several more years. The book should be numbered and maintained in some semblance of sequence for quick retrieval in the case of a call to court to testify in some case whenever it comes up for trial, or retrial. To reduce the possibility of any charge of "doctoring," the pages can be numbered.

FORMAT OF THE BOOK

The specific style of keeping notes should be a personal matter, with each notebook differing from one officer to another. However, for the sake of some continuity, the department should establish broad guidelines to cover what should and should not be included, and there should be some sort of uniformity so that others can decipher your notebook.

The style of notes will vary with the situation, and several styles may occur while recording facts in a single event. The *narrative* style is a shortened version of the events as they are going to be recounted in the more lengthy report. It may include information that is only indirectly related to the incident and is included because it provides a series of memory "landmarks." For example, when a suspect states that he was attending a motion picture, it may be immaterial to the case at hand, but it will be significant to the investigation if the suspect is asked about the title of the picture and the story line. Other people he saw, or memory enhancing incidents that may have occurred during his attendance at the theater, such as the traffic accident that occurred just outside the theater as he and his date were enroute to the ticket booth to purchase tickets, may be necessary for inclusion in a narrative account recorded in the field notebook (see Figure 5–3).

Another notetaking format is the *question-and-answer method.* An excellent example of this format is the advisement of a suspect's constitutional rights against self-incrimination and right to an attorney before and during questioning and the suspect's verbatim responses to both the admonishment and his or her exercise or waiver of those rights. Instead of writing "I advised the subject of his rights," indicate the exact words used and the exact response by the subject to tell the officer that he knows exactly what his rights are and that he still chooses to confess; this may prove quite significant when later referring to those notes in court, leading up to the introduction of the actual confession. Use of the question-and-answer format in this instance may make the case because it demonstrates the professional approach of the officer to a delicate situation involving an individual's constitutional rights in our democratic society.

A third format for recording notes is the *chronological approach,* which may consist of a series of notes, each preceded by a letter or number to indicate the

P.27

JUNE 1, 19XX TEMP. 78   8:30 P.M.
FULL MOON, SLIGHT OVERCAST.
REC'D CALL BY RADIO THAT A BROWN
MAVERICK WAS LOST OR STOLEN
IN THE VICINITY OF COLLEGE
PARKING LOT. I OBSERVED
BRN 78 MAVERICK W/B ON
UNIV. DRIVE, CAR "JACK RABBITING"
FROM 1/S AS THOUGH DRIVER
WAS UNFAMILAR W. CAR. OFFICER
QUINCY — BADGE 4512 — AND I
STOPPED THE CAR. 1 MALE CAUC.
23, BLONDE, GREEN, 5-8,
DOB 8-14-XX WAS DRIVING.
NO PASSENGER.

Figure 5–3 Narrative style. Used to substantiate "probable cause" and to record events in logical sequence.

exact sequence of events as they occurred and as they presented themselves to the recorder.

Numbering pages in the notebook is a matter of choice for the keeper of the book. The advantages have been pointed out, but there may be no actual need for this extra procedure. As a general guide, when you come to the end of information concerning one case before reaching the end of the page, you should draw a line or several lines from the bottom of that information to the bottom of the pages to clearly indicate that there is no more information to be entered. The lines also show to the observer that nothing has been added since the drawing of the lines.

Each new case or incident should begin on a new page in the book, with the identifying data somewhere on the page. Using a fresh page makes it easier to keep information on several cases separate, and it will also serve to keep the nonrelated material out of the courtroom. The data on each case should include the date and time the notes are being entered, the weather conditions (if relevant), the location, names and addresses of persons contacted or mentioned, and their respective relationships to the incident. It may later be to your advantage if you also write a brief description of each individual named to serve as an additional memory jogger. This description should be followed, of course, by whatever information is provided about or by each individual named.

A word to the wise when you are preparing any report, particularly when describing individuals. Avoid the use of "trigger words" that make one's hair on the back of the neck stand on end when they are used in public. You are not writing to entertain your supervisors or others who read your reports (which may be the entire world and CNN), but your reports are to accurately *report*. Keep in mind the experience of the officer who thought he would be cute referring to what he believed to be the sexual preference of a field interview subject. You are not writing for the Humor in Uniform section of *Reader's Digest*.

"Creative report writing" refers not only to lies and exaggeration but also to officers who embellish their reports and take literary license by trying to turn it into a docudrama to make an otherwise boring saga read like a Robert Ludlum thriller. Stick to the truth and "just the facts, man (and woman)."

Techniques in Notetaking

One of the predominant pitfalls in recording statements by various persons contacted during the course of an investigation is to represent paraphrased information provided by witnesses or victims as exact quotations. A simple rule to follow is to identify quotations with quotation marks and then record the verbatim statements in precisely the same words used by the subject. Never violate that rule. If one word is changed or missing, do not use quotation marks.

Whenever you are questioning people, be sure to speak with them separately so as to get individual impressions from each witness. Avoid the "jury description" of people or of events. This is particularly important when securing descriptions of suspects, since the differences between descriptions may lead to a quicker apprehension. The individual with the stronger personality may be wrong and yet be able to con-

```
MARCH 14 - TUESDAY  8:14 A.M.
GILES NORTH CONVICTED FOR RAPE LAST
FALL, OBSERVED IN THE COFFEE SHOP
OF HILL ST. HOTEL.  HE WAS WITH
BLONDE CAUC. FEMALE APPROX 22-25,
MED. BLD. WEARING LT. GRN. SWEATER
AND GREY PANTS. THEY WERE GONE
WHEN I RETURNED AT 8:32 ——
10:32 A.M. '82 PONTIAC TRANSAM
BLACK L/C TEP 1GSL352   OBS.
CRUISING BANK OF TOKYO  FOUR
TIMES.  I DID NOT F. I.  OCCUP.
1 MALE CAUS.  THICK "WALRUS"
MUSTACHE DRIVING.
```

Figure 5–4 Recording impressions.

vince his fellow witnesses that he is right and they are wrong. Be sure to get facts, not suppositions, about what might have happened.

Too much information in the notebook is usually better than too little, but be careful not to overdo it. If you include too little, your notes may have no value later because you left out information that you later found was important but did not know was important when you were taking notes. Use all the space you need for the notes, but keep the language understandable and the writing legible (see Figure 5–4). One instructor may say that you should make your notes illegible and use a shorthand that is understandable only to yourself, so that you can testify in your own style without having to slavishly stick to your notes. Use of such a system seems foolish and unnecessary. If there is some question as to the veracity of your notes, then perhaps they should not be used at all. Deliberate efforts to keep notes are difficult enough without the added complication of deliberate illegibility. Also, *absolute honesty in reporting is paramount.*

There should be some sort of general uniformity throughout your notebook that will develop as you identify the elements that are essential to good reporting. Consistency in your reporting format and style will make it much easier for you to use your notes intelligently for later testimony and report preparation.

Officer's Daily Log

In addition to the field notebook, it is essential that you maintain a daily log or some form of accounting system to keep track of your on-duty field patrol activities (see Figure 5–5). With a data processing system, it may be possible to maintain accurate records without a log by using "activity record cards" that are made out and time-stamped for every accountable activity in which you take part. In lieu of the computer method, which is standard with law enforcement agencies throughout the country, you must keep a log.

The purposes of a log are manifold. One obvious purpose is that the log actually serves as a chronological diary of the field officer's working day. You may use it for reference at some later date to supply specific information, it may serve as a memory jogger, and it can be relied on to show where you were and what you were doing at particular times of the day. In addition, supervisors use the log as a control device, for guidance in counseling officers on the types of activity with which they concern themselves and to discuss their work in general. The log is good for documentation of an officer's activities; for example, when a burglary was committed in the officer's area, the supervisor may ask: "Where were you when the burglar was breaking into a building in your district?" The log can also be used for cost accounting, tabulating actual time spent on various types of activities, and interpreting the information in matters of actual cost for each activity. Other uses for the log are as a source for tabulating volume of work and percentages of time devoted to various tasks on the job.

The daily log should contain columns for each of the following entries for each separate activity: source of call (radio, supervisor, private person, or observation by officer), time started, time completed, and time consumed in performing the activity.

OFFICER'S DAILY LOG

Name _____ Rank_____ Badge_____ Date_____

Day of the Week_____ Duty Hours: Start_____ End_____

Weather_____ Visibility_____ Unit #_____ Partner_____

Assignment_____ Mileage: Begin_____ End_____Total____

Citations_____F.I.'s_____ Arrests: Fel._____ Misd._____ Open Doors_____

Recov. Veh. _____Calls_____ Reporting Time_____ Patrol Time %_____

Time Start	Time Compl.	Time Cons.	Case No.	Incident	Dispo. & Comments

Figure 5–5 Daily log.

Next in line should be a space for a brief statement of the nature of the call and names of principals. The disposition is next, and the final space calls for any numbers related to the incident, such as case, citation, or warrant numbers.

If necessary for management or planning purposes, the various amounts of time could easily be totaled at the end of the day. The breakdown would vary with individual department needs, such as criminal versus noncriminal activities, time spent on incidents observed at your own initiative, miscellaneous time spent in delivering or servicing vehicles, actual patrol time, and reporting time. The recapitulation portion at the top of the log could include spaces for tabulating such activities as citations issued, field interviews conducted, open doors investigated, vehicles recovered, and any other type of activity for which a number count would aid in supervision or planning.

Each log should be headed with your name, district assignment, unit number, and any other pertinent information. If it would serve a purpose, a space for starting and ending vehicle mileage could be provided as well as a place for statements on the condition of the vehicle and any conditions on the beat requiring some attention but not a separate report.

Section Two: Report Writing

INTRODUCTION

Reports and other police records provide the basis for the many different activities carried out by the field officers, the investigators, the many specialists in the organization, the supervisors, and the administrators.

Nearly every service you perform, each crime or accident you investigate, and any other police operation you participate in calls for the initiation of a permanent record of some type or other. The record may range from a single terse entry on a line in a daily activity log to a detailed document several pages in length.

Your skills as a police officer are evaluated largely on the basis of your reports. How you do a job or perform a service is of tremendous importance and is actually the real test of your abilities as a police officer. How you report what you have done indicates your skill not only in doing the task but also in transmitting that information to your readers. To the majority of people affected by your actions, your report is accepted at face value as an accurate account of what you did. A supervisor may have been present when you performed your task but probably was not (at least during the majority of occasions he or she will not be). The ranking officer in the office who reviews your reports and passes judgment on your abilities through your reports, will not have been present. The various people to whom the report is sent for appraisal, action, or filing will have only the report to go on.

Beware of getting too smug. Although you may not be aware of a supervisor's presence, always bear in mind that the eyes and ears of the media might be looking over your shoulder, and they certainly will if your report ends up in a high profile case that might even be on *Court TV.* Any "creative reporting" that tends to creep into police reports all too frequently will surely come back and bite you. This is not to infer that you should not use variety in your selection of words, such as more than one way to write "said," or to insinuate that it is your practice to fabricate facts to enhance your report. However, from many years of experience, I know there is a tendency to exaggerate or build on one's actual role in the event, and to avoid embarrassment or the ire of a supervisor to include information that should have been included, such as a statement to the effect that an attempt was made to contact witnesses to no avail, then a later follow-up investigation reveals that no such effort was made. It is only human that we want to look good in the eyes of our readers. In my rookie days my police chief complimented me on some excellent work that he knew about only through my "excellent" reports.

Your supervisor checks the report to make sure that you operated in conformance with department policies and procedures. Follow-up investigators of your department and other agencies determine what you have done on the case to date (based upon what you relate in your report) and what they must do next to bring the case to a successful conclusion. You should include in the report a statement of what you did not do and the people you did not contact, and give the reasons, such as "works nights, home during the day," or "did not have sufficient information to establish that he was the perpetrator."

For example, assume that during a routine crime investigation you collected evidence, interviewed witnesses, and performed hundreds of minor related acts, thoroughly investigating the case. During the investigation, several of the people whom you contacted had nothing of material value to add to the case. Several leads resulted in dead ends. When preparing the report, you omit the information that led to dead ends because it is of no evidential or material value to the case; and you also omit any mention of the names or identities of the many persons you contacted who had no information to offer. By omitting this information you have streamlined the report. However, when the follow-up investigators get the case and set out to wrap up loose ends, they will probably experience many hours of wasted motion. They will retrace your footsteps without knowing it, come to the same dead ends you did, and gain the same lack of information from the many nonwitnesses you had contacted earlier. What a tremendous loss of time! It would have been of far greater value to the investigators if your report had been a page or two longer and had included all the negative information—which is also essential to an investigation—as well as the positive. It is also possible that the follow-up officer's re-contact with some of those people you contacted earlier may bear fruit. Records searches and prior knowledge of some of those individuals may give the investigation a "leg up" on their re-contact.

In an office far removed from the scene of the crime, the prosecutor reviews the report and the many factors that constitute the circumstances surrounding the crime: dramatic moments of confrontation between officer and suspect, weapons, sounds, and other factors. The prosecutor must often use the report as the sole criterion for determining whether the elements of the crime are all reflected accurately and firmly so that the charge will be sustained. "Is there sufficient information to show that the evidence will prove the case?" The answer must be "yes."

Confession or admissions by the suspect are valueless in themselves. If they are to be of value, certain other factors must be shown in the report: Was the suspect admonished regarding his or her rights to remain silent and to have an attorney present while questioned? Were those rights waived intelligently? What language was used to admonish the suspect and what language did he or she use to convey his or her waiver? Were you acting on reasonable cause when you made the stop or conducted the search of the suspect? What were the circumstances? What was the exchange of dialogue between the suspect and you? If you read the *Miranda* admonition from the card, your report should state that you did. (You do use the card, don't you?)

The prosecutor can assume nothing but must have accurate facts to plan strategy for the courtroom. All decisions concerning the preceding questions must be made in the absence of the reporting officer and be based exclusively on the officer's report. If any questions remain unanswered, the prosecutor must act on the premise that the reporting officer probably did not perform a specific function, such as admonishment of rights. Absence of information in the report does not indicate that it was done. Absence of information in the report indicates absence of action in the field.

After conviction of a defendant, the judge must determine the most appropriate punishment within the framework of the law. The judge relies upon reports from probation officers who investigate the background of the accused. That background includes information from the many police reports they may review and summarize for the judge. The judge may also review the actual report itself. Even though the defendant may have been found guilty, if the judge finds that the report is an extremely poor one, he or she may determine that the investigation was equally poor. The punishment may then be lessened because of the judge's sympathy for the defendant who apparently was not handled by a professional police officer.

When the guilty party is sentenced to prison in states having the indeterminate sentence, a committee of responsible citizens may review all the facts surrounding the subject and the crime committed, including a copy of the reports, from which they make their determination as to whether or not they will schedule an early date when the subject may apply for parole. The police report may or may not be used. What type of impression would it make upon them if they were to find the report full of misspelled words and grammatical structure reflecting a sixth-grade education, although the officer preparing the report is alleged to have attended college for some time? If the report also lacks critical information about the crime and the criminal, it will be virtually worthless.

Many other situations may present themselves when the officer's reports are reviewed in an effort to know the person preparing them. Transfers into choice assignments may be on the basis of how well you can express yourself in the written and spoken word, and promotions may also take into account your ability to prepare reports. Policies are formed, police action is planned, command decisions are made, and cases are won and lost on the basis of single police reports. Finally, but certainly not to be discounted, is the fact that suspects, witnesses, and victims may have an opportunity to review your reports. If they contain misinformation, or untruthful information, there may be damaging repercussions. Your integrity and reputation of credibility are at stake.

When preparing your report, be sure to include the names and addresses of people who you were not able to contact but who should be contacted during a follow-up investigation, as well as the identities of the people you interviewed but from whom you gained no relevant information (or did not strike you as relevant at the time, and later review may lead to a change of opinion). Later contact by a plain-clothes officer when the situation has calmed down somewhat may yield valuable information. If, however, these people are not listed in the original report, the follow-up investigators may not have a clue and might miss crucial information.

CHAIN OF CUSTODY

Your report should accurately document the precise route and timing of the movement of evidence from the moment it is collected—and be specific—as to exactly who collected what (not the editorial "we" or "undersigned") and who transported each item, describing every step of the route. How was it collected, handled, packaged, and transported? Was it left in an unlocked vehicle or an unguarded location for a while? (If so, you have a broken chain.) From the vantage point of a defense attorney, this chain of custody is one of the more vulnerable parts of an investigation.

If you take photographs, report where the camera was positioned and aimed and what each photo is expected to display. In a "busy" photo of a cluttered crime scene, it may be difficult to see what it is that the photographer intended that the viewer see. The report should explain what to look for so that the viewer does not need a personally guided tour.

PURPOSES FOR POLICE REPORTS

The report file and all of its related indices serve as the memory bank for the police department. This file provides for the members of the department a compilation of written records of all department transactions for which policy requires that reports be made and maintained. How extensive and detailed the system must be is a matter for the administrator to decide. What you expect to get out of it is, of course, the determinant as to what is going to have to be put into it.

Allocation of Resources

Reports are administrative tools. Budgeting decisions are made through a series of interpretations involving translating personnel and material needs into realistic money amounts. Various types of plans, long and short range, are made on the basis of compiled reports. Most plans involve establishment of a system of priorities for the order in which certain police operations will be performed or the amount of stress to be placed upon each operation. Officers' reports of past experience in performing those various tasks will be used as the basis for planning future activities. In some cases, certain types of police service traditionally relegated to the police for no apparent reason, particularly those involving noncriminal matters, may be discontinued. The decision to discontinue the service will be backed up by a collection of reports involving police officers' actions in that type of situation in the past.

Department personnel will be distributed to the various shifts, or watches, of the day, days of the week, and even the various separate operating divisions, on the basis of the reports compiled by the department and its members. If there is not sufficient personnel to cope with the problems confronting the agency, or if the existing force is performing in substandard fashion because of insufficient personnel, the reports should also indicate a need for a decision as to whether additional workers are to be added or whether certain services are to be discontinued. For example, it has been traditional for officers to respond to every call by going to the place where the call for service originated. A car parked on the street that has been broken into and a compact disc player or air bag removed will lead to no better solution to the crime than if the victim drives the vehicle to the police station by appointment and gives the information to a clerk or intern. Seldom is there any evidence found at such a scene in this type of crime of opportunity. The only hope for solution to the crime is if the thief sells or pawns the stolen merchandise. Traffic collision reports are similarly reported at a reporting center to a report taker, as opposed to an investigating officer at the scene. This is a necessary break in tradition.

Policy Changes

Long-lasting department policies often go unchallenged because of apathy, lack of interest, a desire to avoid conflicts with stronger personalities, or a "don't rock the boat" philosophy. Properly prepared reports recounting department activities utilizing means prescribed by department policies may actually point up the need for revision, or at least review, of those existing policies. In defense of tradition, it might be added that some long-standing policies are still valid and workable; often, however, the officers may have developed habits and actually be performing in violation of the existing policies.

Lack of efficiency may actually be due to the fact that officers are not abiding by policy. Any change in procedures will be long-lasting and will affect a great many people. Such change must be for improvement, not merely for "furniture rearrangement." Statistics and crime trends are indicated through the medium of police reports. Data are compiled as well for annual or semiannual reports.

Investigative Source

The reports serve as an information exchange device between the officers in different divisions and between officers on different shifts in the same division. They provide leads for investigation and a common pool of information available to all who have access to the files. Compare this method of relaying information with a system in which each officer has a separate series of information sources and resources. To find what information each has, you must first guess which officer has the information you are seeking. Once you have found the correct one, you must meet and compare notes at your mutual convenience, considering days off, sick leaves, vacations, holidays, and work schedules. When the reporting system is complete and accurate, the common pool of information is instantly available regardless of all those considerations. The reports, if kept current, will accurately reflect work that has been done and things still to be done. It serves as an aid to preparation for court and prosecution.

Information Resource for Other Agencies

Police reports provide prosecutors and the courts with a ready source of information regarding current or past cases. Probation and parole officers make decisions and recommendations regarding their probationers and parolees using every possible source of information, including police reports. Even innocuous types of reports may have an appreciable influence on their actions.

The various media have access to most police files for the purpose of assuring accuracy in reporting. Cases under investigation usually are not open to anyone, but some agencies find that by frankly presenting considerable information to the press concerning a specific case and then pointing out how the release of certain information will hinder the investigation, ethical press people will respect a confidence and are less apt to release critical information.

Although police records are generally private records of a public agency, because much of the information they contain is relevant and useful to other agencies, these agencies may be given access to the information that affects their operation.

PREPARATION OF REPORTS

Background Preparation

Before proceeding with the actual preparation of a report, spend a few minutes gathering and arranging the information in a logical sequence, thus outlining the report before you start. Although it takes more time in the initial stages, preparing a rough outline is more than worth the time and actually results in a net saving of time. Working from an outline reduces the likelihood of your finding it necessary to later insert out-of-sequence statements such as "It should be noted that . . ." or "We failed to mention in the preceding paragraph. . . ."

Arrange all your notes, evidence, and exhibits in the same order as you intend to present the information in your report. When you come to the part of the report in which you refer to a certain item of evidence, you will not need to look for it. You can simply pick it up or otherwise examine it, determine how you are going to discuss it in the report, and then continue with the report.

Before starting with the report, also eliminate any superfluous information and excess verbiage. Mere words to fill space have no place in a police report. This does not imply that valuable information should be sacrificed for space purposes, but rather that the report should be used as a medium for transfer of information and not as an entry for a literary award. Include all information that is relevant, even if it has a negative effect on the investigation. If you omit negative information, and if it is found later that you withheld it, the court may rule that you suppressed valid evidence.

If there is to be more than one officer taking part in the preparation of the report, in one continuous document, or if you are to prepare a summary of your own part in the case, be sure to correlate the information before beginning your work. In addition, be sure that the reports refer to each other and that they are correlated in such a way that readers will have no difficulty in maintaining continuity of thoughts when reading the reports and taking follow-up action on them.

Report Style

For some reason, normal, reasonably articulate young people who become police officers stop talking in a normal manner; instead of getting out of a car, they "alight from said vehicle." A car becomes a "unit," and "we" becomes "officers" or "under-signed." Instead of running after a suspect, they "pursue the alleged perpetrator." Instead of running west, they "proceed rapidly in a westerly direction." The dead man becomes "the deceased," Jones becomes "victim number one," and whenever an officer watches someone, the officer's report states that he or she "maintained visual control." The possibilities in this strange police language are endless and for the most part do nothing but obfuscate.

What happened to good "olde" English? If the novice and the old hand alike would just write the way they talk, there would be far less trouble with the police reports. As a watch commander, I spent many days and nights in the office discussing reports with officers. They would come into the office and discuss the circumstances and merits of the case, lay out the scenario, and seek advice from the "master." Then they would go off to their chores of wrapping up the investigation, booking the suspect, "lodging the evidence" (which is similar to putting it into the evidence locker), and preparing their reports. By the time the report got to my office, the only similarity between the report and the earlier conversations that I had with those officers were the names and the places. The "gobbledygook" characteristic of the police report would often change the circumstances of the event and result in great confusion for the prosecuting attorneys who had to read the reports and sort out the facts.

A police report should be simple, brief, descriptive, factual, and to the point. Adherence of the Five W's and H are essential. By all means the police investigative report should very clearly enunciate the WHO—who did what to whom or who are the players in this life drama; the WHAT—what happened, what was the means to commit the crime, what was the weapon or tool used to commit the crime, what was the object of the theft or assault; the WHY—the motive or reason for the crime; the WHERE—the location of the crime, where the weapon or tool came from, where the tool or weapon was found after the crime; the WHEN—the time of day, day of week, month, year; and the HOW—how the perpetrator went about committing the crime.

Tell the story as you would tell it to a fellow officer. There are few officers who pass the entrance exams and the academy training without being able to express themselves in at least an average articulate manner. They have little trouble in their daily discussions about their day on patrol and the interesting events. Your report should be written in the same style as your conversation. Explain the events in the report using the same style that you would use to explain it to your sergeant or fellow officer when you take time out from your reports and bring each other up to date on what has been happening. Take a tape recorder to the coffee shop and record your explanation of the incident while discussing it there, then play it back when you get ready to prepare your report, and you will probably discover that your report will be much better than if you succumb to the urge to write in the outdated language of the police reports of 30 years ago when we were told that we must write about the things we do as police officers in a detached third-person language so as to avoid giving our readers the impression that we are egotistical by using the big "I" too often in the report.

Use a free-flowing and uncomplicated reporting style to describe the action and investigation and other information in logical sequence as it presented itself to you. Be sure to write to *express,* not *impress.* If you use the same language you use in normal conversation, and know the meaning of the words you use, there will be little likelihood of confusion. The reporting style should reflect your individual personality. If you are not quite sure of the meaning of a word that you want to use, don't use it.

Resist temptations to exaggerate or to model a report on someone else's work. There is sometimes a desire to prepare an outstanding report on an individual's physical appearance, as when someone is under the influence of narcotics or dangerous drugs. The temptation is also great to memorize the case number of a report that was brilliantly executed by another officer at some time in the past, to refer to it for guidance in preparing similar reports, and then to either consciously or unconsciously plagiarize the material because it reads so well and can be used to apply to the specific case at hand. Incongruity between the officer and his or her reports will indicate whether this may be the case.

Do not copy the reporting style of other officers. If you do resort to such chicanery, consider what happened to one of my officer colleagues. One report in the department was very popular for its description of a suspect while under the influence of an opiate. Several officers had the case number, and whenever they wanted to write a good description of their suspects under the influence of opiates, they used the sample report as a guide. One officer who copied the sample report verbatim to describe the suspect he had just arrested ran into trouble when the report was presented later in court. The defense pointed out that the defendant's eyes could not have reacted to light the way the report said they did because the defendant was *blind in one eye.*

Follow a logical sequence when preparing the report. The sequence of events as reported to you will probably be the most common method of presentation. In a very complicated case, the events that occurred may be presented to you entirely out of sequence through several disconnected accounts from a series of people. If that is the case, it will be necessary for you to reconstruct the information, and the various bits and pieces of information, and report it in logical sequence without showing a lack of continuity in the investigation. It may be necessary to list the many people who provided information, describe briefly what each person had to offer to the case, and then bring together all the information in the report.

If you are reconstructing the crime on the basis of your investigation as it progresses, you may have to step back briefly, look at the entire sequence of events, and attempt to reconstruct the crime as you believe it *probably* occurred. If you use this method, be sure your report reflects a statement to that effect.

Be careful when you do this, and be sure to present the information as "supposition." Your investigation may later turn up evidence and reveal information that discounts your suppositions, making your original and supplemental reports look as though they are contradicting each other.

Use variety in your vocabulary. It will reduce reader fatigue as well as the possibility of each of your reports developing into a carbon copy of each preceding one on a similar matter. A person may state, he may reiterate, retort, reply, say, or do any number of things when he responds to a question. The English language is designed to express many shades of meaning when appropriately used.

Unless your own department head has established a policy that prohibits it, try using the first-person singular when reporting what you did, whom you questioned, what you observed. It seems more sensible to write that "I" did something than for you to write the "undersigned" or "officer" did this or that. Suppose that you and another officer jointly investigate a case and that one discovers a piece of evidence while the other questions a witness. The alternatives might be: "Officer Jones discovered a crowbar with a 2-inch bite under the left front seat of the suspect's car while I was questioning the suspect. The suspect told me that he had used the crowbar to force entry into the drugstore just a few minutes before I had observed him running down the alley." Or "Undersigned and Officer Jones conducted a search. Officer Jones (who is also undersigned, by the way) found the crowbar while the suspect told the undersigned that he had used the crowbar just a few minutes before he was discovered by the undersigned." Which way do you talk when recounting the situation to your supervisor or how will you relate it in court?

There are some proponents of the traditional third-person style who will say that third person makes the case more impersonal and unbiased. They also feel that it reduces the possibility that personal aggrandizement will creep into the account of the story, maintaining that too frequent use of the word "I" does not belong in a police report. I say that this argument is invalid. The personality of the reporting officer, and not his or her style of writing, will determine whether or not bias will creep into the picture. An egotist will not be stifled by mere elimination of the use of the word "I." If the word "I" may be used in court, why not in the report?

In the infamous O. J. Simpson murder trial, Los Angeles Police Department criminalist Dennis Fung testified that he had personally collected evidence, but he later admitted under cross-examination by defense attorney Barry Scheck that the actual collection was done by his partner, who was new on the job. My guess is that the report was nonspecific as to exactly who did precisely what during that crime scene search. If the report clearly lays out the specific role of each investigator and lists which item is collected by which one of the two (or more), this should not happen when it comes time to testify. A quick reference to the report would negate any confusion whatsoever. This could have been cleared up during the prosecution's lengthy pretestimony preparation of Mr. Fung long before his appearance on the witness stand. Mr. Scheck would not have had the occasion to shout: "How about that, Mr. Fung?" after drawing his litany of errors bit by bit during some excellent cross-examination. Judge Ito was compelled to ask: "Is that a question, Mr. Scheck?" From that point on, Mr. Fung had humiliated and disqualified himself as a competent witness, much less an expert witness in the eyes of the jurors.

If you have prepared in advance and have arranged the sequence of events in the report, it will seldom be necessary to use statements such as "It should be noted" and "We failed to mention" or to preface a statement with "The information gained was substantially as follows." If the information substantially follows, why preface it with worthless words?

CONSTRUCTION OF THE REPORT

Many police reports have been reduced to forms and filling in numbered boxes or spaces with single words, symbols, or checks. This is ideal for the common types of reports, when it is necessary to report only that certain procedural requirements have been met by the reporting officer. The time saved by maximum utilization of this type of form amply justifies the creation of the separate form it may require. If you have put the information in the spaces at the heading of the report, it is not necessary to report it again in the prose portion. Do not include such statements as "on above time and date" or "at above location." It is already there; there is no need to say it again.

Many reports require that the officer recount the information in prose form and in longhand. As in an essay or other form of written communication, the report should have an introduction, a body, and a conclusion. The introduction usually consists of a synopsis of the report and an announcement of what the reader may expect to find in the body of the report. The conclusion consists of a reiteration of the body of the report in capsule form and some recommendation for further action, or a statement that this particular case requires no further action. The following deals with these basic components in more detail.

The Synopsis, or Introduction

Designate the type of report according to the agency's classification system. List all the names of persons mentioned in the report for whom there are no specific "boxes" in the standardized portion of the form, if there is such a section. Be sure to indicate the relationship to the case each named person plays. Enumerate and describe any evidence, exhibits, or other information you intend to bring in during the body of the report. In a paragraph, summarize briefly the information you are going to recount in more detail in the following paragraphs.

The Body

Use short sentences and short paragraphs in your reports. Describe the sequence of events and information in concise and understandable terms. Either recount the events as presented to you, or, if necessary for continuity and if possible without compromising the authenticity of the report, lay out the body of the report in a logical sequence either as the events occurred or as you believe they might have occurred.

Be *completely honest* and *objective*. Be sure to include all information developed, even though some of it may be detrimental to the case from your point of view. The purpose of the report is to report information accurately as it presents itself, not to distort it to make a more convincing case against anyone named in the report.

When taking and recording statements by various informants, bear in mind the fact that victims and witnesses are not always unequivocally correct. Suspects may offer rationalizations and defenses that may be wholly or partly true. Any opinions you may have to advance as the report progresses should be clearly identified as such, and they should be included only when the opinion has a substantial bearing on the case. Never express an opinion as fact. It is more appropriate to label and recite observations and impressions that present themselves to you, and to leave any opinion making to the reader. Whatever reporting method you choose, be sure that you do not employ any device that serves to communicate any prejudice or bias that you may entertain about any of the persons named in the report.

When recording statements made by the many persons in the report, identify verbatim statements with quotation marks and correct punctuation. Never paraphrase a statement and present it as a direct quotation. Identify all sources of information. Avoid statements such as "one of the witnesses stated. . . ." Name the witness. Your police report is not an authentication of fact. A witness states something as "fact," but you are simply recording that statement, which the witness may be required to repeat in court. The court may choose to accept the statement as fact, but at best your report is "hearsay." It is important to point out to all who have access to police reports and who would use them for any purpose that what a witness tells you and what you then recount in your report does not authenticate the accuracy or truthfulness of those statements. Some people seem to hold the belief that whatever is published by the police is 100 percent correct. That is certainly not correct.

Answer all the questions that must be answered in any police report, or at least all those to which you can obtain answers. The Five W's (who, what, when, where, why) and How should be the object of your investigation, and as many as possible should be answered. Sometimes the absence of certain answers are just as significant as their presence. If you observe behavior by a suspect or witness that causes you to believe there is going to be a "diminished capacity" or witness qualification problem at the trial, describe the behavior you observe without making a statement of your opinion or conclusion.

Report all the investigative leads you have followed, including those that did not bear fruit. It is just as important to report that you contacted five named potential witnesses and gained no information as it is to enumerate only the names and information provided by those who present positive leads and information. Without the unsuccessful leads, the follow-up investigator will have to pursue leads that you have already checked out. If you obtain identical information (or lack of it), it is correct to summarize by reporting that witness Jones stated substantially the same as witness Izenthall, if that is the case.

If you have information that tends to point toward the innocence of the suspect although all of your other information points toward guilt, you must include all of the information in the report. While it is true that you are responsible to the prosecutor to aid in the prosecution, it is also your responsibility to clear the innocent.

Explain delays in the investigation. For example, why did you wait three months before interviewing a key witness? If it was because the witness had been out of the country, say so in your report.

Use of Names

The first time you use a name in a report, list it in full, including the title, such as Mr. Jonathan Quincy Forthright. During subsequent references, use the last name only. If there are two or more persons with the same name, such as Mr. and Mrs., or John and Georgia, it will be necessary to use the different first names or titles to continue to distinguish the two different players. Avoid the use of labels, such as "victim number 1" and "witness number 13." Such labeling adds to the confusion that is already prevalent in what is usually a complicated case, and readers have to prepare a cast of characters for themselves so that they can continuously refer to it while reading your report. Use of the names lessens the confusion.

In addition to the names, use date of birth and description of the named person. Two people in the same place of residence may have identical names, such as father and son who do not use the "junior" or "senior" labels. Also, you should include a statement as to any obvious impairment that might alter the value of his or her statements, such as "speech slurred, and odor of alcohol indicates that he is under the influence of alcohol" or "wearing hearing aids in both ears," or "wearing eyeglasses that appear quite thick."

The tenor of your report should indicate the nature of the follow-up necessary. Sometimes the results you achieve will be far more productive if you provide the readers with sufficient information to determine the need for urgent action as a result of their own thought processes rather than tell them that they should perform their jobs in the manner you suggest. The message is the same, but the method is more effective. If there is an urgent reason for following a certain lead, the wording of your report should indicate the priority it should receive. In most agencies, cases are handled in accordance with some system of priorities. The priorities are usually established by the follow-up officers on the basis of the information they glean from the reports, except for those cases that fall into specific report classifications.

The Conclusion

Before preparing the conclusion of the report, go over the synopsis and body at least cursorily, then "wrap it up" with your conclusion. If the case is cleared or closed, indicate that fact so that record-keeping requirements may be fulfilled. Any unfinished work should be listed and presented in such a manner that the reader can make his or her decision to pursue the investigation according to an independent priority system. Generally summarize what you have done and what is left to be done on the case. In some cases, policy may require that you make a recommendation for further action. If that is the case, any recommendation you make should be based upon information that the reader may find in the body of the report.

Abbreviations

Some standardized forms make it necessary to abbreviate to get all the relevant data in the undersized space provided. Only in that case is it wise to use abbreviations. Too often the time that may be saved by using them is lost in later attempts to decipher some of the abbreviations that may be employed by the economy-minded reporter. If in doubt, do not abbreviate except for use of the very commonly accepted forms that are listed in any standard dictionary, and avoid the use of police jargon.

Avoid Ambiguity

Following is a list of words and phrases that are commonly used in police reports which cause more confusion and raise more questions than if they had been left out of the report. After each word or phrase, we shall attach a comment or list some of the unanswered questions posed by use of those words. Bear in mind that the readers are not going to be able to have you around when they don't understand what you meant when you wrote the report.

"was contacted"—how? by whom? in person? by telephone?

"she (or he) indicated"—how? by saying something? by a gesture?

"we responded"—was the response in person? an emotional response? did you drive there? or walk? or call back?

"proceeded to"—started to? went to? Better to write: We went . . .

"observed"—in what manner? by which of the senses?

"detected"—by what means? odor? smell? brilliant police work?

"it should be noted"—an unnecessary statement

"it was determined"—by whom? how?

"we failed to mention earlier"—plan ahead and you will. Delete.

"residence"—what kind of residence? a house? apartment? motel?

"related"—did he or she tell you something?

"articulated"—was this done by word of mouth? by telephone?

"verbally related"—the word "verbal" means either orally or in writing, or by the use of words

"informed"—told? wrote? sent a secret message by telegraph?

"altercation"—why not just say they had a fight?

"verbal altercation"—do you mean to say they had an argument?

"in reference to"—a lot of words to say ". . . about . . ."

"at that point in time"—a lot of words to say ". . . then . . ."

"utilize"—use?

"the bottom line"—just what does that really mean?

"maintained visual control"—how can you control with your eyes?

"exited the vehicle" or *"alighted from vehicle"*—got out

"maintained surveillance over"—did you watch? or listen?

"officer (or undersigned) verbally advised"—I told him . . .

"a knife was found"—who found it?

"a sound was heard"—by whom?

With a little imagination, your own list could grow extensively. Try to make every word mean exactly what you want it to mean. As you can see from the preceding list, some words may have more than one meaning.

Second only to the video recording of both sight and sound, one of the more accurate methods of assuring accuracy in reporting is to use a tape recorder on the spot and tape everything. That is hardly possible in all circumstances, but you should attempt to make extensive use of such a device whenever practicable. Verbatim accounts of any event are valuable when you are analyzing the activity later and are evaluating what went wrong, or right, and how the situation might be handled better the next time. It also is a tremendous aid when preparing your reports, and it is difficult to remember everything that happened and who said what. Once you get away from the scene, immediately record whatever it is that you want to remember. Then review the tape while the events are still fresh in your mind.

Dictating the Report

An encouraging trend during the past few years has been the attempt to reduce the time required for report writing without reducing the efficiency of the reports. Short forms have been developed for many of the "routine" reports, such as miscellaneous service, calling for insertion of a series of X's in appropriate boxes on the form. Other forms have been streamlined and designed so that you may write or print out your report in its entirety while still in the field, and turn it in at your convenience when you return to headquarters for some other purpose. Some reports have been virtually eliminated, and the information they once contained is now recorded in a terse statement as a single line entry on an officer's daily log. Despite such developments, however, many reports cannot be streamlined by use of any of these methods. The crime report must include a detailed narrative account of exactly what took place during the commission of the crime and during the investigation. In cases when the report must recount actual words used and verbatim accounts of things done by the principals, the narrative report is still the only efficient method for recording the necessary information.

Stenographers have been used for police reporting for many years as have several types of dictating and transcribing equipment been used by reporting officers and clerical assistants as a team. The results have been rewarding in many cases. Reports have improved, and officers have increased their ratio of field time to report time. In other cases, the results have been tremendously disappointing. I suggest that the concept is sound but that the system must be well planned and executed. The people using it must be willing to sit down together and work out the details of how to make it work.

Individual department needs vary, as do their financial resources and facilities. However, every department must have some provision that will allow you to stop occasionally and listen to a partial playback (or readback in the case of an in-person stenographer), so that you may edit when necessary and maintain continuity in your reports.

Whether you dictate your reports in person to the stenographer in the office, telephone in the reports, use a dictating instrument, or carry your dictating unit in the field with you, there are a few basic rules that must be followed.

1. Organize your thoughts in advance. You should have developed the report from start to finish before you begin dictating. Random notes may suffice, but an outline may prove more useful.
2. Dictate your report while the information is still fresh in your mind.
3. Dictate the report in clear, concise language. Exaggerate the consonants so that they are heard, and avoid slurring words together. Whenever there is any possibility of misunderstanding in the pronunciation of a word, particularly when listing, spell it out. The person transcribing the information you dictate cannot be expected to guess what it is that you meant to say or how a particular name should be spelled.
4. Dictate the report in the same language and style you would use if you were telling it in person. First-person singular reads most naturally, and I recommend its use.
5. Avoid redundancy. Do not ramble, repeating yourself in several different approaches. This is to be avoided when dictating a report rather than typing it yourself.
6. Have all names, addresses, and phone numbers to be included in the report close at hand.
7. Do one thing at a time. While dictating, do not perform other tasks, such as making out a log, shuffling papers, or carrying on a conversation with another person.
8. Make maximum use of your field notes, which should provide a good foundation for accurate and complete reports if they have been compiled as recommended earlier in this chapter.
9. Keep your sentence structure simple and correct.
10. Check the report after it has been typed, and compare it with your dictated tape to assure accuracy. Retain the tapes until you are able to make the comparison.
11. Never expect the person who is preparing the actual typewritten draft of the report to alter it in any way from the way in which you dictated it.

THE MISCELLANEOUS INCIDENT REPORT

Every agency has a standard procedure for reporting actions and incidents for which there is no specific form. In fact, such a miscellaneous classification may have a standardized form. There are two basic kinds of formats for this type of form. One consists of a series of statements with adjacent blocks for insertion of X's or checkmarks for indicating basic information that is so standardized that no value could be derived from narrative response. For example, you might respond to a call on a family disturbance. Upon your arrival you determine that no law had been broken. You contact the principals in the case, separate them, and get a brief account of the nature of the problem. You determine that the matter is entirely civil in nature and that if you were to give advice, it would be unethical and extralegal. You arbitrate the matter because your role is to prevent crimes. After calming the people down and making sure that the likelihood of a crime occurring after your departure is not apparent, you leave.

In this case, you might use a *forced choice* form. You merely have to fill in the date and time of the incident, the names and addresses of the principals, the identity of the calling party, and the location of the incident. You then go down the list of choices and mark the boxes adjacent to the statements to the effect that (1) the call was a neighborhood dispute; (2) it was noncriminal in nature; (3) the people were advised to contact attorneys in any civil law question; or (4) you kept the peace and advised the parties that someone could be arrested for any law violation.

The second type of form for miscellaneous incidents is more common. It calls for brief statements concerning the nature of the call and any action taken by the officer, a summary of the circumstances leading up to the demand for police service, and a synopsis of any other relevant data that might later be of some value in criminal investigations.

In completing this report, indicate the names of all principals involved in the call, and indicate by a brief statement the relationship of each named individual to the call, such as "our presence was requested to keep the peace" and "involved in neighborhood disturbance." The report should briefly recount the facts in an informative fashion and contain only relevant data. What occurred while en route to the call and the fact that you "resumed patrol" are examples of irrelevant data.

THE ARREST REPORT

Many departments use a form that serves as a combined booking slip and arrest report (see Figure 5–6). The information required is mostly self-explanatory, and only a very small space is reserved for any narrative that may be necessary. Listing the name of the arrestee may seem relatively unimportant because it is so routine. Yet this is probably the most important part of the report. When spelling out the name, be sure to check all the identification materials and documents that the subject has in his or her possession. Ask the arrestee to explain any discrepancies, and be sure to record all different spellings as aliases. Many times a name has not been assumed at all; it has merely been misspelled.

Of the many sources of information about the identity of a subject, the arrest report is—or should be—the best. Take extra care to fill out the form completely. Add any items of information that come to your attention, such as various organizations and unions in which the subject holds membership cards and physical deformities or other distinguishing characteristics, that would help a later identification even under an assumed name or after an attempt at altering his or her appearance.

THE CRIME REPORT

Usually the crime report form consists of a series of standardized, required bits of information to establish jurisdiction for the case, questions that must be answered to reflect all the elements of the corpus delicti—or body—of the offense and all the required data to serve as a base for the investigation and, ultimately, the successful prosecution of the alleged perpetrator (see Figure 5–7).

The heading of each report calls for a title. In a crime report, the title includes the specific law that has been violated. The balance of the report must substantiate

Figure 5–6 Arrest report.

that fact. When more than one law violation is listed, the report must also reflect all of the elements of each separate offense.

The date and time of the occurrence and the date it is reported may provide clues to the investigator as to the possible motive of the reporting party, particularly in cases where personal animosity may be involved. The occupation and age of the victim, and the location and type of premises where the crime occurred, might lead to a specific suspect who specializes in some type of crime. Every question has a purpose and should be answered as thoughtfully as possible.

Spaces are provided for the name, address, and phone numbers of the victim, the person reporting the crime, the person who originally discovered its occurrence,

MISCELLANEOUS COMPLAINT OR CRIME REPORT

VICTIM'S NAME (Last-first-middle. Firm name if business)	DR
WEAPON, FORCE OR MEANS USED (Describe cal., type, etc.)	TYPE (Mur-Stat. Rape-Batt., etc.)
APPARENT MOTIVE	LOCATION OF OCCURRENCE / REPORTING DIST.
VICTIM'S COND. (HBD, normal, etc.) SUSPECT(S) NO. - SEX - DESCENT	DATE AND TIME OCCURRED / DATE AND TIME REPORTED TO P.D.
TRADEMARKS OF SUSPECT(S) (Actions or conversation)	TYPE OF PREMISES
VEHICLE USED BY SUSPECT(S) - (Yr - make - body - col - lic. no. & I.D.)	INVESTIGATIVE DIVISION(S) OR UNIT(S) NOTIFIED AND PERSON(S) CONTACTED
CODE: V—VICTIM **R**—PERSON REPORTING CRIME **W**—WITNESS	LIST ANY CONNECTING RPT(S). BY TYPE AND D R NO.
VICTIM'S OCCUPATION - SEX - DESCENT - DATE OF BIRTH CODE	

NAME	RESIDENCE ADDRESS (Bus. add. if firm)	CITY	RES. PHONE	X	BUS. PHONE	X

IDENTIFY SUSPECT(S) BY NO. (Name-address-sex-descent-age-ht-wt-hair-eyes-complexion-clothing-identifying characteristics. If arrested, include bkg. no. & charge.)

1.

2.

(1) IDENTIFY ADDITIONAL SUSPECT(S).   (2) RECONSTRUCT THE CRIME.   (3) DESCRIBE PHYSICAL EVIDENCE, LOCATION FOUND, AND GIVE DISPOSITION.   (4) SUMMARIZE OTHER DETAILS RELATING TO CRIME.   (5) TIME AN D LOCATION WHERE VICTIM/WITNESS CAN BE CONTACTED BY DAY INVESTIGATORS IF NO AVAILABLE PHONE NUMBERS.

CRIME CLEARED BY ARREST ☐ YES ☐ NO	If additional space is required, use Continuation Sheet, Form 15.9.
SUPERVISOR APPROVING SERIAL NO.	INTERVIEWING OFFICER(S) - SER NO. - DIV. - DETL. PERSON REPORTING CRIME (Signature) X
DATE & TIME REPRODUCED - DIVISION - CLERK	CLEARED BY MULTIPLE
	FOLLOW-UP **DR** INDEXED CHECKED

Figure 5–7   Miscellaneous complaint or crime report.

and other witnesses. When listing this information, be sure to secure additional information concerning where each of these persons may be contacted when they are not at their places of residence, such as business addresses and phone numbers. If they are planning to be absent from the area for some period of time, be sure to include that information in the summary portion of the report.

The crime report should include a "modus operandi" section for recording in easy-to-locate spaces certain distinguishing characteristics about the crime that provide keys to the investigatory leads and to the possible identification of the culprit. At times the criminal will say and do certain things during the commission of crimes that are almost as effective in identification as fingerprints. The experienced investigator can sometimes compare the reports of two different crimes and see similarities in the "MO" section that indicate that both crimes may have been committed by the same individual. Filling in those spaces in the report should be done very carefully.

In crimes against property, such as burglary (see Figure 5–8) or breaking and entering, and in some crimes against persons, the point of entry and the point of exit must be identified and an effort should be made to reconstruct the crime as it probably occurred. In some cases, the nature of the force—or lack of it—used to gain entry serves to prove intent. This is particularly important in specific intent offenses.

Figure 5–8 Burglary report.

The weapon or tool used should be identified. If not known, marks made by tools may serve to indicate the type of weapon probably used. Be sure to include in the report a statement that the weapon or tool was *probably* whatever you believe it was if you do not know for sure. A positive statement could be disastrous to the prosecution if it later developed that an error had been made. Only when you have positive facts should you make a positive statement.

The location of the property stolen or damaged is always significant, but it is more so when the property had been in a concealed or out-of-the-way location. The apparent ease with which the culprit found the item may indicate familiarity with the place. The nature of the object attacked, such as a safe, may indicate the skill of the thief.

It is not necessary to prove motive to prove the elements of the case or to establish the identity of the culprit, but when you ask yourself "who would have benefited from this?" the motivation may lead to an indication of intent and eventual identification of the suspect. In a property crime, the motive is usually to gain possession of the stolen property. The motive in a sex crime may be revenge, or to inflict serious injury, and is usually not to achieve sexual satisfaction. An attack with a deadly weapon may be for the purpose of committing another crime, such as robbery or rape, or it may be a matter of revenge. When attempting to determine the motivation for the crime, it is sometimes possible to come up with one or more suspects. To know the motive is also an insight into the personality of the perpetrator.

Each crime report calls for a "trademark." Whether it is discernible depends on the case, but most criminals do something that is just a little unusual that distinguishes them from all others. Some individuals make a habit of using exactly the same words each time they assault a victim; others use a specific technique that seems to work each time they force entry into a place of business. The trademark thus becomes as distinctive as the persons themselves, and it may immediately identify a known criminal to the follow-up investigator. An example of a burglar's trademark is found in the case of the thief who steals an item of some value from a teacher's drawer in a classroom and then causes so much destruction that it appears to be the act of several juvenile vandals. One case presented such an appalling sight that we immediately approached the investigation from the standpoint of malicious mischief. It was just by accident that we found a pried drawer that was usually kept locked and discovered that some prescribed medication the teacher had kept in that drawer had been stolen. Because of the outrage, the teacher herself had actually overlooked the theft. Several trademarks may be present in the following case of robbery.

The bandit walks into the savings and loan office precisely at 12:15 P.M., walks up to the cashier, hands her a brown paper bag, orders her to place all the money she has in the drawer into the bag, then smiles and apologizes for the inconvenience, and leaves through the front door. Both the time and the brown paper bag may be significant. Another unusual factor is the smile and the apology. The eventual solution in a similar case established that the robber always committed his crimes during his lunch hour and that the bag was actually the one in which he brought his lunch to work. Unusual? So is the idea of committing armed robberies.

Suspect

Whenever you describe, or name and describe, a person in the "suspect" box of the crime report form, there must be a sufficient substantiation of the subject's responsibility for the crime to justify an arrest. If there is enough information in the report reflecting evidence pointing toward an individual as the culprit, and if a judge would issue a warrant on the basis of that information, the individual should be named as a suspect. If there is some doubt, or if there is no proof but circumstances indicate that a particular individual's possible relationship to the crime is more than casual, list and discuss him or her in the narrative portion of the report as a *possible* suspect.

Descriptions of Property and Other Relevant Information

Additional spaces in the crime report form call for complete descriptions of the property stolen, the vehicle used by the culprit, and any evidence collected during the investigation. Several spaces are also provided for administrative handling of the report and its accompanying material. In addition to these special information spaces, there is usually a substantial portion of space for the narrative account of the crime as reported to you, as you observe it, and as it develops during the investigation. This section often continues on a second page. It is in the narrative portion that the entire case should be explained in prose.

SPECIAL REPORTS

In addition to miscellaneous incident reports, crime and arrest reports, and traffic accident reports, each department has a wide variety of special forms. Some departments create separate forms for every conceivable type of incident, while others have a few basic forms and instruct their officers to adapt the information in each situation to fit existing forms. A few of the items for which special forms are often used are missing persons, dead body, lewd or annoying phone calls, impounded vehicle, evidence report, checks, intoxication, advisement of rights, and abandoned vehicle (see Figure 5–9). Other special forms may be made to fit virtually any need of some unit within the department with a special interest.

DISCUSSION

Every agency has a different set of reporting policies. For a crime report to be prepared, all the elements of a corpus delicti must be evident and reportable. For a traffic accident report, the vehicle must be moving, or there must be a minimum value damage. A missing person report will depend on the person who is missing and any attendant circumstances that indicate some criminal behavior as well. The missing child calls for an immediate investigation and report, and broadcasting the information as quickly and as thoroughly as possible. The errant husband or wife who left work at 5 P.M. and has not shown up for dinner at 7 P.M., who has a history of stopping at a pub on occasion before going home, will be reported differently from the missing child.

Some people may request that a specific report be made, such as a theft report for the benefit of an insurance or tax deduction claim. Exactly which form you as the

DRIVING UNDER THE INFLUENCE ARREST REPORT DR No.

VISIBLE SCARS, MARKS, DEFORMITIES—EVID. OF NARCOTIC USE	ARRESTEE'S NAME (Last, First , Middle)		BOOKING NUMBER

RESIDENCE ADDRESS	CITY	CHARGE (Section No., Code and Definition)	☐ MISD. ☐ FEL. ☐ OTHER

EMPLOYED BY	OCCUPATION	LOCATION OF ARREST	R.D.	DIV. & DET. ARREST

NICKNAME, ALIAS	SOC. SEC. NO.	DATE & TIME ARRESTED	DATE & TIME BOOKED	DIV. BKG.	EVIDENCE BOOKED ☐ YES ☐ NO

DRIVER'S LIC. NO.	STATE	BIRTH PLACE	SEX	DESCENT	AGE	HEIGHT	WEIGHT	HAIR	EYES	BIRHTDATE

COMPLAINTS OR EVID. OF ILL. OR INJ.—BY WHOM TREATED	LOCATION CRIME COMMITTED	PROB. INVEST. UNIT

LIST CONNECTING REPORTS BY TYPE & IDENT. NUMBERS	DISPOSITION OF ARRESTEE'S VEHICLE	HOLD FOR

VEHICLE USED (Year, Make, Body Style, Colors, Lic. No., Identifying Marks)	DRIVING VEHICLE (Direction and Name of Street)

AT OR BETWEEN STREETS	CLOTHING WORN

CODE: V-VICTIM   W-WITNESS   P or G-PARENT OR GUARDIAN

NAME	CODE	RES. BUS.	CITY	PHONE	X
		RES. BUS.			
		RES. BUS.			

JUV. ONLY:	PARENTS NOTIFIED BY	TIME	PLACE JUV. DET.	DIV. OF APPEAR. DATE/TIME	BKG. APPROV. BY	DETEN. APPROV. BY	PRINTED?
							PHOTOS

ADMONITION IF RIGHTS: The arrestee was "warned" that he had the right to remain silent, AND that if he gave up the right to remain silent, anything he said can and will be used against him in a court of law, AND that he had the right to speak with an attourney and to have the attourney present during questioning, AND that if he so desired and could not afford one, an attorney would be appointed for him without charge before questioning.

ADMONITION IF RIGHTS GIVEN BY:	FIELD SOBRIETY TEST GIVEN BY:	CHEMICAL TEST GIVEN BY:

FIELD SOBRIETY TEST ADM. ☐ YES ☐ NO	ATTITUDE	BREATH	COORDINATION	EYES	FACE	SPEECH

Walking Line Test: ○ R. Foot △ L. Foot	BALANCE	PUPIL REACTION RIGHT EYE ┃ LEFT EYE	○ Right Index △ Left Index
TURN	WALKING		
	TURNING	TIME TEST ADMIN.	

Are you sick or injured? ☐ Yes ☐ No   Are you under care of doctor or dentist? ☐ Yes ☐ No
Are you diabetic or epileptic? ☐ Yes ☐ No   Are you taking any medicine or drugs? ☐ Yes ☐ No
Do you take insulin? ☐ Yes ☐ No   Do you have any physical defect? ☐ Yes ☐ No
If answer to any of the above is "Yes", explain completely on Continuation Sheet, Form 15.9.

WHAT HAVE YOU BEEN DRINKING?	HOW MUCH?	WITH WHOM?	WHERE?

NAME OF LAST DRINK	WHAT TIME IS IT NOW?	WHERE ARE YOU NOW?	WHERE ARE YOU GOING?

WHAT HAVE YOU EATEN TODAY?	WHERE?	WHEN?	WHEN DID YOU LAST SLEEP?	HOW LONG?

Arrestee was requested to submit to a chemical test of his blood, breath, or urine, and was informed of his failure to submit to such chemical test of his choice would result in the suspension of his privilege to operate a motor vehicle for a period of six months.

CHEMICAL TEST ADMINISTERED ☐ BLOOD ☐ URINE ☐ BREATH ☐ ALL TESTS REFUSED	BREATHALYZER TEST NO. %	LOCATION	TIME ADMINISTERED	IF NOT BOOKED STATE REASON

In the opinion of the arresting officer(s), arrestee was intoxicated and unable to safely operate a motor vehicle.

Use a Continuation Sheet, Form 15.9, for circumstances of the arrest. Include statements of arrestee's understanding of his rights, manner of operating motor vehicle, unusual actions during field sobriety test, and any other information necessary in the completion of this report.

SUPERVISOR APPROVING	SERIAL NO.	ARRESTING OFFICER(S)	SERIAL NUMBER DIVISION—DETAIL	VACATION DATES
DATE & TIME REPRODUCED	DIVISION	CLERK		

Figure 5–9 DUI arrest report.

reporting officer use is strictly a department matter and should be of no concern to the complaining party. It is of absolutely no value to the overall effectiveness of the department to tell a distraught wife, "Sorry, but your husband has not been gone long enough for us to make a 'missing person' report." What matters is that (1) you have taken the information, (2) you will make some sort of report, and (3) you and the department will take some action on the basis of that report.

Section Three: Getting the Most Out of Records

INTRODUCTION

The records system is the nerve center, the memory bank, and the control center of the police department. The nerve center characteristic of the records system is seen in the fact that virtually all the functions of the department involve maintenance of records, constant reference to them, and sometimes total dependence upon them. The memory bank aspect is apparent. As with any other memory system, it is only as accurate as the information fed into it, and its indexing system must be as comprehensive and as easy to understand as possible to assure complete and instantaneous access to the contents of the files. The control center aspect is best illustrated by the fact that the personnel responsible for the system will not accept faulty or incomplete records for inclusion in the system—whenever they receive it through channels— because it "does not compute." Reports prepared by field officers constitute the majority of the records for the system. Accuracy is a must. The most useful and efficient system will be the one that receives the most complete and the most accurate bits of information for its files.

The greatest advancement in police records systems has been made in more extensive utilization of computers. Filing cabinets full of thousands of cards and paper reports have been replaced by hard and soft discs, compact discs, and microfilm, which are far more efficient and space thrifty. Forms that had to be filled out in multiple copies and sent to each of several different agencies can be sent directly to a central file and be retrieved on demand by the other agencies who have a need for such information. For example, warrants may be stored in one agency's files and called out via the data transmitter in the police car. The abstract will be sent via modum, and then the officer merely has to go to the single file source for the warrant instead of having to search for its whereabouts at any one particular time. Gun sales forms and slips made out by pawn shops go to the central state file, and there is no need to keep separate files of the same materials in several different locations. In other words, many duplicate files are no longer necessary with all the computer systems interfacing with one another.

USES OF RECORDS

Records information provides the basis for interchange of such information among the various units of the department, and between the department and numerous other individuals and agencies with whom it communicates. Officers working together during the same hours of the day are in a relatively good position to keep each other informed because of their rather frequent contact with each other. Personal contacts provide the major means of communication. But what about these officers and the rest of the department? They have no direct line of communication beyond their own sphere of contacts. Their written reports and related documents serve as their major means of communication with all others.

Other members of the department, or some other agency, who must take follow-up action, such as continuing an investigation or returning to a specific address to verify that a dog that has bitten a child has been correctly placed under quarantine by its owner, must act upon the report on the assumption that all the information has been recorded accurately in its entirety. The information in the initial report provides the base for the follow-up work.

Because all officers are required to complete their reports during the same working day or within a very short time afterward, it is possible for one officer to assume an investigation inaugurated by another in the event that the original officer does not continue for some reason. The reports filed to date, together with their accompanying data from related files, are available for review. They allow the investigation to continue without interruption.

Records of filed reports provide a factual record of work performance: work that has been done and work to be done. The officer who not only performs well in the field but also prepares complete and factual reports accurately reflecting good work is a double threat in the competitive service. In addition to serving as a tool by which the quality of your work may be evaluated, your reports provide a means by which to ascertain the quantity and the nature of the work you have performed.

BASIC RECORDS AND THEIR USES

Every police agency has a different structure for its records system. Special needs and interests of the many persons involved in the evolution and development of the systems have made them as distinctive and original as a set of fingerprints. There are several basic files that are more or less standard, with minor variations, of course. They include the master—or alphabetical—index of all named persons, places, and things listed in reports; the report files in which the original reports are maintained; stolen and pawned object files; and several other files.

The Master Index

At one time a massive bank of filing cabinets holding 3 × 5 cards serving as the alphabetical reference point for every person, place, and object listed anywhere else in the system, the file is reduced to a few thousand floppy and compact discs. No longer is it necessary for officers and others from throughout the buildings of several different agencies and their members in the field to pay a personal visit to the Records Division information counter. They have instant access from their own desktop, laptop, and mobile data terminals. The files are used strictly as an index, although some agencies will actually carry in the "alpha file," as it is sometimes called, some original and complete records, such as field interview cards. By searching through the master index, it is possible to find a wealth of information in the various other files for which it serves as the index.

Some of the many bits of information that will be found in the master index will be names of victims, witnesses, suspects, wanted felons, and persons who died under circumstances when the police were notified of the death, such as suicides, individuals who have made purchases of concealable firearms from local dealers, and others who have licenses or permits to carry concealed weapons. Some "alpha files" contain nicknames of persons who are known to the majority of their friends and neighbors only by those partial names, or "monickers." The index also includes the names of persons who repossess vehicles and the purchasers from whom they are repossessed, and the names of individuals who have been interviewed under a variety of circumstances in the field. This is only a partial description of the contents of the master index. The only limitations to the extent of the master index in the police department are space and the imagination of the people using it.

The Report Files

The originals of all reports are filed for a period of time. In some cases they are microfilmed and permanently stored in compact form; the filmed copies become the originals, and the bulky letter-sized originals are destroyed. The reports may be filed under a single numbering system, in chronological sequence as the incidents were reported to—or came to the attention of—the department, or they may be separated under several different categories with different numbering systems and stored in various places.

As a management tool, a case number is assigned by the dispatcher at the time of assignment of the call. As a matter of policy, the department may have a system whereby every complaint, incident, and case that will probably generate a report will be assigned the next number in sequence. Many years ago, yours truly assigned the title "C-I" to such numbers, standing for Complaint-Incident. Some departments use the designation DR for Daily Record. The first two numbers are the year, such as 96 for 1996, followed by the case number. This system provides a supervision tool for the various managers to follow up on each case assignment to assure completion of the appropriate investigation and report(s). Many of these cases will carry a number followed by the designation that there will be no report because the officer assigned determined that no action or report was required. Many times certain types of miscellaneous service are handled by giving someone directions or advice and nothing more.

The Crime File

Each reported offense is classified according to the Uniform Crime Reports classification system. Since 1930, the Federal Bureau of Investigation has served as the central clearinghouse for crime statistics in the United States. With very few exceptions, virtually every police agency in the country contributes information concerning their statistics to the system. The information is cataloged in a variety of ways and published annually in booklet form. Each contributing agency maintains its own collection of bits of information to satisfy the reporting requirements of the system, usually in the form of a 3 × 5 card file or computer bytes.

The crime file is an excellent source of leads for an investigation, providing that the modus operandi portion of the original report has been accurately filled out by the reporting officer. The file is separated by crime classification and then divided into "cleared" and "uncleared" categories. Although the primary purpose of this file in most agencies is statistics, it doubles quite efficiently for a "modus operandi" file.

Crime file information cards contain the case number of each offense, the type of crime, date and time of occurrence, description of the property stolen and its market value, the location of the crime and the type of real estate attacked (market, parking lot, city street, or private residence). The card also gives the name, address, and occupation of the victim, and any "trademark" or unusual circumstance about the case that may serve to identify the culprit. If the name or description of the suspect is known, or if a person has been arrested, that information will also be indicated on the card.

Serial Number File

Serial number files are maintained by local departments and by state agencies that have centralized clearinghouses for criminal information. Whenever the serial number of a stolen item is known, the number is included in this file. The method of filing may vary, but it is usually in numerical sequence according to the last three digits of the number. For example, an item bearing serial number 7Z09253 would be filed in the 253 file. Also filed in the same location are serially numbered items that have been pawned or sold to secondhand dealers, who are required to report such transactions to the police department and a state agency.

By placing both stolen and pawned items into the same file according to serial number, the hope is that the two may meet in the files and thus arm the investigators with sufficient data to investigate the circumstances surrounding the sale or pawn transaction, solve the crime, apprehend the thief, and return the stolen property to its owner. In addition to cards on stolen and pawned items, the serial number file might contain cards on new dealer sales of handguns or any other item bearing serial numbers on which the local jurisdiction requires report of transactions.

Stolen Object File

This is another file that is common to many police departments. Any identifiable object that has been stolen is carded and filed according to its classification. There is considerable dependence upon the thoroughness of the reporting officers for this particular file to serve any practical purpose. A stolen radio, for example, would be filed as a transistor, subfiled again by name of manufacturer, and possibly filed again into another subcategory of style or band name. Watches are subfiled under "man's" or "woman's," calendar, yellow or white metal, manufacturer's name, and popular name. Accuracy in describing the object may be the determinant as to whether it will be recovered and returned to its owner.

Pawned Object File

As in the case of serially numbered items, the local department or a central clearing-house may classify and file stolen objects in one file and pawned objects, plus others that are sold to secondhand dealers, in another, with the ultimate objective of matching the items in the file and causing an investigation to be conducted that will eventually end in return of the stolen property to its lawful owner. The clerical personnel in the records division should check cards destined for one file against the other, and vice versa, whenever the opportunity presents itself, as a matter of routine. This check is simplified to a great extent when the information is committed to an electronic data processing system that has an automatic matching procedure built into its program.

Location File

The location file may be designed according to either one of two plans: the street and number system or the grid system. Cards are prepared for each crime and/or arrest for any of a number of specified offenses, or they may be made for all crimes and arrests, depending on the administrative decision made by the individual department head. For maximum utilization, the information is cross-referred to the object file, serial number file, and crime file. In the grid system, the police agency's jurisdiction is divided into reporting districts, which consist of square blocks, groups of blocks, specific streets, single locations (frequent incident bars, recreation centers, and other places determined by the operator of the system to require special attention), or the reporting districts may correspond to census tract boundaries. In the street and number system, the file is arranged according to numbered streets and lettered streets in logical numerical and alphabetical sequence. This file can be used quite conveniently in conjunction with spot or pin maps, which show special problems or types of crimes by location.

HOW TO USE THE FILES

The files discussed in this chapter comprise only a small portion of some records systems. Some agencies create separate files for literally dozens of different uses, and they are usually cross-indexed for efficiency. But consider the possibilities of just those files covered in the preceding pages.

Case 1.   You respond to a burglary call. While investigating, you discover that the culprit entered through an unlocked back door during daylight hours while the occupants of the house were away. The culprit very carefully ransacked the house, taking care not to destroy any property, and took only money. While in the house, the culprit turned on a different radio station from that ordinarily selected by the owner of the house, indicating that the burglar had a particular desire to listen to a certain type of music while he worked. The investigation reveals no other information. There are no latent fingerprints to be found. Actually, the culprit left behind a trademark although he left very little evidence. There is no known suspect in this crime.

Probably the first place you should go upon arriving at the office to prepare your report on this case, if time and departmental procedure allow, is the record bureau. Check the crime file for daylight residence burglaries, both the solved ones and those that have yet to be solved. Other crimes with similar circumstances, such as the method of entry and the selection of music on the radio, may indicate the possibility that they have been committed by the same person. Perhaps there is a similar one or two that had been cleared by arrest some time in the past. If the latter situation occurs, you may have at least a possible suspect, because most people—including burglars—are creatures of habit. If there are other cases with similar MOs, you should include this information in the report. The investigator who follows up on the case will attempt to determine whether the burglar follows some sort of pattern, such as always committing his crimes in a specific area, or on a particular day of the week, or at the same time of the day. He will also consider the strong possibility that a firm lead on one crime will result in the eventual solution of all of the similar offenses.

Case 2. You arrest a young man for theft of a stereo tape deck from a car parked on the parking lot at the football stadium. While questioning him, the subject admits to stealing other items of a similar nature, but he cannot remember when or where. A check of the stolen object file may reveal a series of similar thefts of stereo tape decks. By retrieving the original reports and discussing the cases with the subject, you may be successful in clearing up a series of thefts rather than just one. Other sources of information to check while conversing with this willing confessor are a map and the location file. By discussing the various locations where he may have committed theft, you may find that he is a parking lot specialist. Check similar crimes that have occurred in parking lots throughout the city, and again you may strike pay dirt.

Case 3. This case may be a little different. During a routine field interview of a person observed under suspicious circumstances, you discover that he is in possession of several objects, such as transistor radios, household appliances, and a television set. He is unable to provide a reasonable explanation for such possession. By searching the stolen object and the serial number files, you discover that one or more of those items had previously been reported stolen.

The greatest limitation on your imaginative use of your records system will be imposed by the time that may be involved. There are occasions when the pressure of other field responsibilities will prevent your maximum utilization of those records, but there are other occasions when the time is available and should be put to use.

SUMMARY

This chapter is divided into three major sections: field notetaking, basic report writing techniques, and getting the most out of records.

Field notes must be comprehensive and accurate. Many times you will find that incomplete notes will result in incomplete reports and the appearance to all who judge your work that your work was incomplete. We cannot overemphasize the importance of well-prepared reports to the overall effectiveness of a police department. It should become routine for you to take notes on virtually everything you do while on patrol, including casual observations that may seem insignificant to you at the time. For example, when you are called upon to testify in a traffic case, you may be asked to describe the weather and lighting conditions at the time you wrote the citation.

Whenever you are making field notes that will later be typed onto standard forms, be sure to have in mind all the information that the form will require. Later, when you are filling out the report and discover that you forgot to record certain essential information, you will be hard-pressed to explain why you neglected to record that information in your field notes. You may have to go back and reinvestigate the case all over again.

In the report writing section, we placed a heavy emphasis on the importance of complete and accurate reports. Throughout your career you will find that you will be judged by the reports you prepare. Decisions are made by supervisors, investigators, prosecutors, and dozens of other people on the basis of what your reports say you did and saw during your investigation, which should be the same as what you actually did do and see.

In the records section of this chapter, we reviewed many of the various records that are maintained by most police agencies. Effective use of records will result in thorough police work, providing that the information contained in those files is accurate and complete.

EXERCISES AND STUDY QUESTIONS

1. What is the value of accurate field notes?
2. What type of information would you include in your field notes?
3. What type of notebook do you believe best for field notes? Why?
4. Give an example of how you might use a TV camcorder at a crime scene.
5. Give an example of how you would use a micro-tape recorder in an investigation.
6. What is the value of field notes as "past recollection recalled"?
7. How do you think a jury would react to an officer's reference to field notes compared with recollection from memory only?
8. What does the author mean by the term "debriefing"? Of what value is it?
9. How would you go about preparing for a trial and assure that only those portions of your notebook related to the case at hand be open for inspection by counsel for the defense?
10. What type of notes would you use to record an interview of a burglary suspect?
11. Give an example of a narrative report, a question-and-answer report.
12. In your notebook, how would you record your conversation with a suspect who waives rights to an attorney and against self-incrimination?

13. When quoting verbatim statements in your notes and reports, how do you distinguish between actual quotes and paraphrasing?

14. What is a *jury description,* and how might you avoid getting one?

15. List and discuss at least three purposes for an officer's daily log.

16. What types of information should you record on a daily log?

17. Why should you report negative leads, or lack of information, as well as those that prove fruitful?

18. Of what value is your report to the prosecutor?

19. For what purpose would a judge review a police report?

20. To what extent is your department's record system computerized?

21. In your opinion, how broad should the access of the press to your department's files be?

22. In the discussion regarding report preparation, how were the Five W's and H explained?

23. What is the advantage, if any, of writing a report in first-person singular?

24. What is the argument against using the pronoun "I" when you are preparing a report?

25. What is the purpose of outlining your report before dictating or typing it?

26. Prepare a list of phrases that confuse, rather than enhance, a report. (Please send a copy to the author.)

27. Into which part of the report will you insert your opinion as to the honesty or integrity of a witness?

28. What is the purpose of beginning a report with a synopsis or summary?

29. What is a good basic rule concerning abbreviations of words in reports?

30. Add at least 10 phrases to the ambiguous list. (Send a copy to the author.)

31. List and discuss at least 10 of the 11 rules presented in this chapter regarding dictating reports.

32. Collect a copy of each type of form used by your department, and make a set of model reports. (You may use the samples included in the text.)

33. List and explain how each of the several types of files are used by your records system.

34. What is the function of an alpha file?

35. In your records file, how are serial numbers indexed for rapid retrieval?

36. When you recover a suspected stolen car stereo, how do you check your department's records to see if it has been stolen?

37. What is the purpose for a location file?

38. Describe how you would check a vehicle and its driver for wants.

39. How would you go about identifying a burglar by his or her modus operandi?

40. If you had the authority and financial resources, what would you change about your department's record system?

REFERENCES

DIENSTEIN, WILLIAM. *How to Write a Narrative Investigation Report.* Springfield, Ill.: Charles C. Thomas, 1964.

FEDERAL BUREAU OF INVESTIGATION. *Manual of Police Records.* Washington, D.C.: U.S. Government Printing Office, 1966.

————. *Uniform Crime Reporting Handbook.* Washington D.C.: U.S. Government Printing Office, 1966.

INTERNATIONAL CITY MANAGERS' ASSOCIATION. *Municipal Police Administration,* 5th ed. Chicago: International City Managers' Association, 1961.

U.S. ARMY. *Criminal Investigation FM 19-20.* Washington, D.C.: U.S. Government Printing Office, 1951.

————. *Police Planning,* 2nd ed. Springfield, Ill.: Charles C. Thomas, 1957.

WILSON, O. W. *Police Records: Their Installation and Use.* New York: Public Administration Service, 1951.

————. *Police Administration.* New York: McGraw-Hill, 1963, Chap. 18.

Special thanks to Ms. Anita Barrett, manager of the Santa Ana Police Records Division for her in-depth discussion of current records practices and procedures.

FOOTNOTES

1. *Gary, G.* 115 Cal. App. 3D 629 (1981); *Seaton,* 146 Cal. App. 3D 67 (1983); *Angeles,* 172 Cal. App. 3D 1203 (1985); *Trombetta,* 467 U.S. 479 (1984); and *Youngblood* 109 S. Ct. 333 (1988).

CHAPTER 6

INTERVIEWING TECHNIQUES

INTRODUCTION

The best sources of information about people are the people themselves. And probably the best means of getting information from people is to ask them for the information. As a police officer, if you expect to be effective and successful, you are going to have to become proficient in the art of interviewing people. Actually, there are two basic methods for getting information: interviewing and interrogating. Since the *Miranda* rule was written by the Supreme Court,[1] the term "interview" has come to mean obtaining information by asking questions, whereas the term "interrogation" seems to have acquired some sinister meaning. When one interrogates, one asks questions in a prying manner, sometimes getting answers that the person being questioned did not intend to provide voluntarily. The *interviewer* is assumed to have a willing respondent, whereas the *interrogator* has an unwilling respondent. Basically, the definitions fit, but that does not necessarily mean that one is good and the other is bad.

You are going to be talking with, and asking questions of, a variety of people for many different purposes. Most of the people you will be interviewing are not criminal suspects, but many of them will be as reluctant to talk with you as though they were guilty of some crime. Contrary to some of your instructors' teachings, you are going to be interviewing and interrogating many people during the same encounter. You will be talking with victims, witnesses, informants, complainants, interested participants, disinterested parties, women, men, children of both sexes, professional people, blue-collar workers, white-collar workers, no-collar workers, people who arouse your curiosity, those who bore you to death, people who behave in a civil manner, and those who do not. You will occasionally interview a suspect, which may lead you to other suspects or may evolve into a full-scale interrogation. The purpose of this chapter is to introduce you to the art of interviewing people no matter who they are.

The chapter is divided into two parts: one addressing the art and principles of interviewing and the other addressing the propriety and process of the field interrogation, or interview. Using the recommended procedures contained in the pages that follow should enhance your techniques in the art of questioning with the purpose of getting answers and also the art of listening, which is critical to success in interviewing.

Section One: *Interviewing*

THE "ART" OF INTERVIEWING

Of the many police activities you must perform, interviewing truly approaches the category of "art." It takes talent, a natural inclination to perform the task well, study and practice to develop the basic skills, and continual self-analysis and cultivation of the talents and skills involved in the questioning process. To be adept at interviewing, you will first study yourself; then you will adapt your own personality to the various situations and the personalities of the people whom you question. You should develop a style that is distinctive and improve with studied experience. No one is a "born" interviewer any more than one is a born marksman. You must have an intense interest in human nature, a desire to develop the skill, and the ability to learn from each interview experience.

Human beings are gregarious; they like to talk. They like to talk about their successes, their failures, their good and bad luck, their ambitions, themselves and others, and—quite significantly—they feel a compulsion to talk about their crimes when they commit them. Many experts theorize that it is the intense desire to share experiences with others that causes criminal law violators to confess their crimes. Theodor Reik, a student of criminal psychiatry and a protégé of Freud, advanced the theory that an individual who commits a crime is haunted by the guilt feelings caused by violating personal ethical standards, and the terrible truth of the crime begs to be let out through confession. Reik called this the compulsion to confess. This is congruous with the beliefs of many skilled police interrogators, who have often encountered individuals who demand to be heard and who freely and voluntarily confess to atrocious crimes that are so repugnant to the confessors that they must purge themselves of the terrible secrets or suffer a lifetime of torture. Once they tell of their crimes, they show distinct signs of relief, and they seem to look forward to whatever punishment society has prescribed for them. The penance of punishment may help to cleanse them of their crimes.

A key to your development as an interviewer is your ability to see each person that you interview as an individual with a distinct set of values and a personality quite different from that of all other humans. Be constantly mindful of the individuality of the people you question and guard against letting yourself oversimplify a problem by stereotyping individuals into "categories" that may seem to you to be all alike. Once you begin to generalize in this manner, the "artist" fades and the "report taker" emerges. Your responsibility as a professional police officer is to strive to perform as the "artist."

Objectives of the Interview

There are four basic objectives of an interview and of an interrogation: (1) secure complete and accurate information, (2) distinguish fact from fantasy, (3) proceed according to a well-thought-out plan, and (4) have *truth* as your target.

Information.   It is important that your investigation reveal the real truth. You may be able to verify the statements of one person by interviewing several other people who witnessed the same event. As we discussed in our earlier discussion of perception, you know that not everyone sees the same things through the same set of eyes or experience, or any of a number of factors that influence perception, memory, and articulation of those observations in a later discussion with a police officer. The fact that two eyewitness accounts differ does not necessarily mean that one person is lying, nor is it impossible for two witnesses to tell stories that sound quite similar. You should also test the information that a witness gives you by actually visiting the scene of the observation and placing yourself at the exact spot occupied by the witness at the time, and then see (or hear or smell) for yourself if it was possible to perceive what the witness reported.

Fact versus Fantasy.   Check out the witnesses for honesty and reliability. Check records and what other people who know them have to say about their sobriety, emotional level, and reputation for truthfulness. Compare statements of the several witnesses and walk through the event as it had been described to you to determine what *could have happened* and what *could not have happened.* People who remember events have "landmarks" in time because they actually happened. They will remember the sequence, the people present, and attendant items that tend to verify the witness's statements. For example, the witness describes an event, names other people who are present, and may even be able to tell you what show was on television at the time. Witnesses will remember these things even if they are asked to recount their observations in reverse, or to skip around and go back and forth to their various observations. A fabricated story will sound different every time and will probably fall apart when the witness is asked to recount certain observations out of sequence.

Plan.   If you have examined the crime scene and have learned all that you can about the crime and the person you are about to interview, you will have a fairly good idea as to which questions you are going to ask the witness. Make an outline of your questions, have your reports (if they have been prepared yet), and have a sketch of the crime scene.

Truth. This is the ultimate focus of every crime or collision or other investigation that you are going to conduct. Although you may have certain information that makes you believe that you know what a suspect or witness is going to tell you, it is imperative that you keep an open and nonjudgmental mind. A preconceived notion that certain people are innate liars, or that others speak nothing but the truth, will get you into trouble. As an internal affairs investigator, I have even—on rare occasions—run across police officers who have lied, others who have exaggerated, and still others who have fallen into the habit of being careless with the truth. None of these is acceptable for a police officer, but the fact that they do have such imperfections further illustrates the fact that you are going to have a job on your hands ferreting out the truth from the information you collect during your interviews and interrogations. Do not hesitate to ask people to tell their stories more than once, and challenge them by pointing out discrepancies with their own earlier statements or those of others.

DEFINITIONS

Interview. An interview is the process whereby an officer seeks, obtains, and evaluates information given to him or her willingly by persons who have personal knowledge of the events or circumstances of a crime, accident, or other matters of interest to the interviewer. The word "interview" implies cooperative consent to give information.

Interrogation. An interrogation involves the process by which an officer endeavors to obtain information about a case from someone who is reluctant to provide that information, and in most cases does not have to provide such information. Generally, the word "interrogation" is applied most often to persons suspected of crimes themselves, but may apply as well to reluctant victims or witnesses.

Confession. A confession is a direct acknowledgment of guilt on the part of the individual offering the information, either by a statement of the details of the crime or an admission of the ultimate fact. When a defendant pleads guilty to a charge in court, that person is making an acknowledgment of the ultimate act. The guilty plea in court is known as a judicial confession, and outside court is called an extra-judicial confession. In addition to the guilty plea in court, the judge also calls for a statement by the defendant as to how he or she committed the crime so that the judge will have no doubt that the confession is valid. Outside of court the officer will also seek inculpatory statements that will unequivocally implicate the confessor.

Admission. An admission is a statement by the accused of a fact or facts pertinent to the issue that tends to prove his or her guilt when coupled with other facts brought out during the investigation. A shooting, for example, may elicit a statement by the accused that he did, in fact, shoot the victim. That's an admission. But it would not be a confession if the next sentence coming from the suspect's mouth includes an exculpatory explanation, such as the shooting was in self-defense. An admission will not sustain a conviction.

COMPONENTS OF THE INTERVIEW/ INTERROGATION

The Case. Before you can conduct an intelligent interrogation of the suspect, you must have as much information about the case as you can possibly acquire. You should visit the crime scene, examine all of the evidence, and talk with the people who have any information about the crime. As the initial investigating officer, you have a distinct advantage that no one else may have. You were probably the first officer to arrive on the scene and your observations of the crime scene involve all of the sensory perceptions.

The atmosphere of the crime surrounded you, such as the sounds, the odors, the impressions that all play a part in the crime scene, however insignificant they may seem individually. If you did not arrive immediately, you probably arrived very shortly after the crime was reported. The suspect and victim as well as many of the witnesses may still have been at the scene, who continue to live out the drama, especially if the crime was a violent one. There has been less time for witnesses to compare and change notes and for the information to deteriorate with time.

If you were not so fortunate to visit the crime scene, then you should by all means have appropriately prepared yourself for the interview by reading and examining all materials available to you concerning this case. Hopefully, you have been able to develop a sense of the crime and all its attendant features so that you may conduct an intelligent interview. Be careful not to insert your own assumptions and guesses as to what might have happened, because of what you may have remembered from other similar cases. This case is unique. Keep it so.

The Subject. The subject is your unknown quantity of each case. Using all the resources at your disposal, find out as much about the subject as you possibly can. Check records and make discreet inquiries as to his or her honesty and reliability. Do not make conclusions about the individual's integrity and accuracy, but keep that person's reputation in mind when conducting the interview.

General Interviewing Techniques

Preparation. Whenever possible, arrange to have a private area for the interview to take place, free from outside interference, telephone calls, or interruptions by children or friends of the witness. The best location is a specially furnished interview room at police headquarters. Set aside enough time to conduct the interview, and take into account any time commitments that the person you are about to interview has. It is very distracting to be at a crucial time during an interview when one or both of the participants start fidgeting and looking at their watches. Be sure to have all the facts that are available to you. If you are interviewing the victim or suspect in a crime, it will certainly enhance your effectiveness if you had visited the crime scene and if you have all the facts straight in your mind as to time and location of the event, weapon used, location and nature of injuries, evidence left at the scene, and items removed from the scene. Without this information, you would not even know if the suspect were telling the truth while giving a full confession.

Seating Arrangement.   Depending on the effect you wish to create, you may choose to have a table or other barrier between you and the interviewee, with the chair you sit in bigger and better to give you an unspoken psychological advantage. Size and design differences in furniture are traditionally used to indicate relative importance or superiority. Look around the offices of the captains and sergeants in your own department, or the offices of the instructors and the president or chancellor of your local college.

If you want to show the person you are interviewing that you do not intend to take advantage of your obvious position of advantage, move away from your desk to another chair of the same size as the one occupied by your subject. This will have a tendency to indicate an air of openness and trust between the two of you.

Comfort and Social Necessities.   You are responsible for the safety, health, and comfort of the person you are interviewing if the interview takes place where you control the environment. Provide for restroom facilities, water, or other refreshments if the interview is prolonged, and food if the interview extends beyond normal limits. When you are interviewing a suspect, it is particularly important that there is no indication of duress or psychological abuse that influences a confession or admission. Treat everyone with the same respect as you would expect yourself. Smoking is not only unhealthy, but it can be a distraction. If you smoke during the interview, you must allow the subject to smoke. A better alternative would be to simply state: "I'm allergic to smoke, so I would rather that you not smoke."

Opening the Interview.   Establish some sort of rapport between yourself and the subject of the interview. This is principally to determine that you are both speaking the same language, so to speak, or talking on the same "wavelength." You want to make sure that the words you are using have the same meaning to each other or that at least you know what the differences are. Determine the other person's interests, language level, and value standards as much as possible so that you will be able to communicate. You can determine a person's truth-telling style while going through the preliminaries so that you may later be able to see any differences in style that may indicate an attempt at deception or holding back information. If there is any personality conflict or for some reason you cannot effectively communicate, arrange to have another person conduct the interview. If you are interviewing a suspect, be sure to abide by the *Miranda* rule, which will be covered later in this chapter.

If you intend to get information from the subject, be careful not to take on an adversary role or to show contempt or displeasure with the person. Stay calm and maintain a professional posture throughout the interview. Whether you work alone or not will depend on department policy, but recognize that no one likes to talk to a crowd, especially when relating something embarrassing, or, if you are interviewing the suspect, to confess to a crowd the commission of some cruel or inhuman crime. In addition, some victims feel guilty, particularly in sex crimes. They are not guilty, of course, and they need to be reassured that responsibility for the crime is not theirs.

GENERAL TECHNIQUES IN INTERVIEWING

There are basically two approaches to questioning, which you may use one at a time or simultaneously: the direct approach and the narrative approach. The direct approach usually consists of asking questions and getting answers, and the narrative response consists of you asking a question and then allowing the respondent to give an answer by recounting the event with interruptions for new questions, or to get the storyteller back on the subject, or to help the person remember. Your attitude should generally be aloof. Variations may consist of a sympathetic approach and a logical approach.

Sympathetic Approach

The sympathetic approach is usually more effective than the direct approach, because the person who has committed the crime usually feels remorse and guilt for having done something that he knows is wrong. To call him a thief or a liar will surely end the interrogation before it begins. Accidental offenders and first-time criminals respond to this approach most readily. Others who will usually respond to sympathy are sex offenders, persons who have committed crimes of passion involving intense emotional feelings, and people who have sensitive personalities.

The technique in the sympathetic approach is to indicate an interest in the person as an individual. Show him that you can understand why he would have done whatever it is that he did. Be kind and considerate to the person, who is entitled to your respect. His crime may have been indicative of animalistic tendencies, but if you are to gain his confidence and respect, and his confession, it is imperative that you appeal to his human qualities in a rational and understanding manner. Be friendly in a professional way. Your role as the interrogator is not to scold or punish the criminal violator.

Logical Approach

The direct approach is most likely to work with preadolescents, recidivists, and those types of law violators who commit crimes against property, which indicates their disregard for the property of others. Some people commit crimes in defiance of the law or because they do not agree with the law and see no reason why they should obey the law. White-collar crimes, vice operations, and organized crime offenses are hardly likely to be committed by amateurs, and whenever a violator of one of these types of crimes is questioned, the best results will probably be obtained by telling the individual what he is being questioned for, presenting him with the facts, and then soliciting from him any statements he wishes to make. Although I doubt that there is any individual who is totally without emotional feelings, except perhaps the sociopath, the people who respond to the logical approach seem to be those whose crimes involve intelligence or cunning, rather than emotional involvement as in the crimes of passion and sex offense.

Techniques for the logical approach generally consist of keeping the interrogation simple and to the point. State why the subject is being questioned and give him sufficient information to show him that you have reasonable cause for the arrest, while avoiding giving him more information than you hope to receive. You may give him some of the details of the case, then simply state that you believe he has a "side" to tell and that you want to hear it to determine the true facts of the case. Occasionally, this technique proves so effective that the suspect cooperates fully, and when he does give his "side" of the story, it becomes apparent that there has been no crime. If his story consists of lies and discrepancies, point them out to him and ask for an explanation. While using this technique, never assume that the suspect is lying and that the victim or witnesses are entirely correct. Many times the suspect will speak the truth, and the truth may bear no resemblance to the account of the crime as presented by the accusers.

Operational Suggestions

If in doubt as to which approach to use, try the sympathetic technique first, then direct questioning. Once the suspect indicates that the interrogation is over, it is. Beware of the confession that is too easy to obtain. As long as the suspect is willing to speak about his crime freely, have him prove his points by describing all the elements of the crime, plus whatever additional information may be necessary to prove his actual guilt. There will be fewer suspects to interview than witnesses and victims. You will have more flexibility in questioning witnesses than suspects because of the constitutional restrictions involved in questioning your suspects. Never underestimate the subject of your questioning: he or she may be quite deceptive and difficult, or uncooperative. Another piece of advice is: Never overestimate your own abilities. No one "bats 1000," not even the multimillion-dollar baseball player.

INTERVIEWING THE SUSPECT OF A CRIME: THE INTERROGATION

Constitutional Guidelines

Before you may begin custodial police interrogations in which you intend to question suspects about their involvement—or suspected involvement—in any criminal act, you must advise them as follows:

> You have the absolute right to remain silent. Anything you say can, and will, be used against you in court. You have the right to consult with an attorney, to be represented by an attorney, and to have one present before I ask you any questions. If you cannot afford an attorney, one will be appointed to represent you (free of charge) before you are questioned, if you desire.

Most prosecuting attorneys will recommend that you carry this warning on a printed card and that you read it to the suspect so that you will remember every word of the admonishment, and also so that you may present it in court when describing how you discussed the admonishment with the suspect.

The suspects must understand and communicate to you their understanding of the wording of the admonishment and its significance as it relates to them in their present predicament. If they do not understand any of the words, or their meanings, they must be explained. Once you have an agreement that they understand the words and their meanings, the Supreme Court has ruled: "the defendant may waive effectuation of these rights, provided the waiver is made voluntarily, knowingly, and intelligently." You may proceed with the questions only if the suspect understands the admonishment and you gain an affirmative response to this question:

With these rights in mind, are you ready to talk with me about the charges against you?

The suspect must give an oral waiver and consent to continue with the interview. A mere lack of response in the form of silence does not constitute a waiver. Once the suspect exercises the right to remain silent and indicates that there is no desire to answer any of your questions, you must discontinue the questioning because they will not be admissible in court. Do not persuade the suspect to change his mind or engage him in any "games" in an effort to trick him into changing his mind or giving you information inadvertently.

On June 13, 1966, the U.S. Supreme Court, in its *Miranda* rule,[2] delivered a decision dealing with the "admissibility of statements obtained from an individual who is subject to *custodial police interrogation* [italics added] and the necessity for procedures which assure that the individual is accorded his privilege under the Fifth Amendment to the Constitution not be compelled to incriminate himself."

A "custodial interrogation" is one that is conducted under circumstances when the subject of the questioning process is "significantly deprived of his freedom" in the words of the court, and under circumstances when the investigation is forced on the subject at an accusatory stage of the investigation. The crime may be a felony or misdemeanor.

To qualify as a "custody" situation, the suspect (1) must have, in fact, been deprived of his or her freedom in a significant way (cannot leave), and (2) must be personally aware of his or her lack of freedom or reasonably believe that it exists. Consider the situation and the location: Was it taking place in a police car or at the station, or was it in the suspect's home or car? Was it late at night, or during the day? Was more than one officer present, or did the questioning take place in the presence of the suspect's friends and family? How long did it last? How accusatory did you get during the questioning?

Victims and witnesses are not in custody and not in an accusatory stage, meaning that they are not suspected of a crime. There are many occasions on which you may question people in field interviews to ascertain their identities and the nature of their business in a particular location at an unusual time or under suspicious circumstances or to determine ownership of certain unexplained property in their possession. In most of these cases, the questions are asked and satisfactory answers received without incident and the interviewer never reaches an *accusatory* stage when you would focus on the subject as a suspect in a specific crime. Under most of these investigatory situations, it would be a personal affront to the subject of the questioning to advise him of his constitutional right to remain silent and to have an attorney with him, because to do so would be insinuating that he is suspected of having committed some sort of criminal act. In some situations, of course, the field interviews do lead to accusatory circumstances, and at those times it is necessary to lead into the *Miranda* admonition, as described earlier.

Once advised of these rights, the subject may exercise them, say nothing, and request the presence of an attorney. He may waive the rights by stating that he does fully understand them but that he still wishes to talk and answer your questions. Once he waives the rights he may reconsider at any time. In the words of the *Miranda* decision:

> If, however, he indicates in any manner and at any state of the process that he wishes to consult with an attorney before speaking, there can be no questioning. Likewise, if the individual is alone and indicates in any manner that he does not wish to be interrogated, the police may not question him. The mere fact that he may have answered some questions or volunteered some statements on his own does not deprive him of the right to refrain from answering any further inquiries until he has consulted with an attorney and thereafter consents to be questioned.

If a person is not actually the subject of a custodial interrogation, as when you are on the scene conducting the preliminary investigation (including most field interviews), and he makes any spontaneous declarations of any type—including what may amount to admissions or a confession—his statements are admissible in court regardless of whether you advised him of his rights to remain silent and to an attorney. There is no way of predicting circumstances under which a person will make such spontaneous declarations, and there can be no insinuation that you obtained statements of this nature under "custodial conditions."[3]

Miranda was certainly not the case that single-handedly changed the entire police interrogation/interview process, but it proved to be the "flagship case" and the lightening rod for thousands of subsequent related matters. One case that stands out preceding *Miranda* was when small-time burglar Danny Escobedo was arrested for a murder in the Chicago area. As the story goes, while he was being questioned in one room in the police station and asking to see his lawyer, his interrogators told him that his lawyer did not want to see him. At the same time, Danny's lawyer was standing on the other side of the door leading into that room demanding to see his client, and he was told that Danny did not want to talk with him. The lawyer filed a protest over not being able to see his client and left. Escobedo confessed, but the court later overturned his conviction on the basis of denial of his Sixth Amendment right to see his attorney (*Escobedo* v. *Illinois,* 1964, 378 U.S. 478).

Although the prosecuting attorneys usually ask that you recite the *Miranda* admonition verbatim and that you read from the card on which it is printed to assure your accuracy and completeness, the Court has stated in *California* v. *Prysock* (1981, 453 U.S. 355, 359): "This court never indicated that the rigidity of *Miranda* extends to the precise formulation of the warnings given a criminal defendant. Quite the contrary. *Miranda* itself indicated that no talismanic incantation was required to satisfy its strictures." This decision served as a validation of an ad-libbed variation of the advisement of rights.

Another question was answered in *People* v. *Braeseke,* (1973, 25 Cal. 3d 691, 701–702): "Does a suspect have to be re-advised before conducting a second, or subsequent interrogation after he has once been advised of his *Miranda* rights?" The answer is: "If the suspect waives his rights and officers later want to question him further about the same case, a second advisement is not necessary unless substantial time has passed (possibly 24 hours)." In the *Braeseke* case, it was about one and a half hours between interviews.

In the Linda Sobek murder, the photographer who had taken her to the desert for some modeling work, then killed her, and buried her body in the Angeles Forest was not—he declared—allowed to consult with an attorney and claimed he was denied his *Miranda* rights. His point may be countered by *People* v. *Dean* (1974, 39 Cal. 3d 875, 882), in which the court opined: "While life hangs in the balance, there is no room to require admonitions concerning the right to counsel and to remain silent."

In another similar case—*People* v. *Riddle* (1978, 83 Cal. 3d 563, 578)—officers thought that a missing woman left for dead in a remote area might still be alive, the incriminating statements made by the suspect without *Miranda* compliance were allowed. The Court stated: ". . . under circumstances of extreme emergency where the possibility of saving a life of a missing victim exists, noncoercive questions may be asked of a material witness in custody, even though the answers to the questions may incriminate the witness. Any other policy would reflect indifference to human life."

Here are some examples of invocation of the *Miranda* rights:

"I guess we need a lawyer." (*People* v. *Superior Court—Zolnay,* 1975, 15 Cal. 3d 729)

"Maybe I should talk to my attorney." (*People* v. *Munoz,* 1978, 83 Cal. 3d 993)

"Have you got an attorney here, present, close?" (*People* v. *Duran,* 1982, 132 Cal. 3d 156)

Examples of noninvocation of *Miranda* rights:

"Well, I need one, but you can go ahead and ask me questions." (*People* v. *Smith,* 1982, 136 Cal. 3d 961)

"Yeah, if I want an attorney, I got to wait all day." (*People* v. *Smith,* 1982, 136 Cal. 3d 961)

If a person is arrested and there is to be no questioning, there is no need to admonish him regarding his constitutional rights at the time. In some situations it is the wiser course of action to wait until after the heat of the situation has cooled down to the point where it is possible to rely on a rational discussion. Consider the following as an example of a time when it would hardly seem suitable to perform the advisement rites:

You are parked on a side street near one of the city's main boulevards when you hear from a radio broadcast that a green, two-door sedan containing two occupants has just left the scene of an armed robbery. The victim attempted to thwart the robbery by shooting at one of the suspects, but the victim was disarmed and beaten. You are alone and about three blocks from the scene of the crime, and suddenly a car matching the description of the wanted one appears. You negotiate a turn onto the street in medium traffic and are about five cars behind the suspect car. You radio in for a cover unit and decide to follow the suspects until they are out of the way of other cars and your follow-up unit is near to cover you. Suddenly, the driver spots you and begins a high-speed attempt to escape. You radio in this new information, then turn on the red light and siren, and take up the chase.

The chase involves high speeds through medium to heavy traffic, including going against several signals and signs, barely avoiding some serious accidents. Finally, after about two miles of pursuit, you edge the suspect car to the curb. The driver stops, and you jump out and approach the suspect car to get to the suspects before they gather their wits and use any weapons that they might have.

You know that this is not the academy-recommended procedure, but you believe it is better under the circumstances because there are so many other cars and pedestrians around that you believe you can avoid gunfire. You grab the door handle, open the door, and tell the suspects to get out. Shocked by your fast action, the suspects get out of their car with no struggle. As you quickly search the suspects for weapons, one of them tries to attack you. You subdue the one suspect and you are met by some resistance from the other. You regain control of the suspects just as the follow-up unit arrives. You take both suspects back to the other car, thoroughly search them this time, and place them in the back seat of the car.

At that particular moment when the action has calmed down at the scene, would you advise the suspects of their right to remain silent and to have an attorney present when they are being questioned? Are you prepared to begin an interrogation at that time and under those conditions? It is not difficult to imagine what the response would be from the suspects at that moment if you were to ask them, "Do you want to talk with me?" If you believe that an on-the-scene interrogation is essential to clear up some vital facts of the case or that it would be tactically wise to question the suspects at the time, then it is imperative that you proceed with the *Miranda* admonishment.

If you have sufficient evidence to lead to an arrest based on reasonable cause, and the tactical decision is to wait before any questioning, then do not advise the subject of those rights at that moment. When you make an arrest solely on a warrant, make the following determinations prior to admonishing the subject or questioning him: Are the officers who investigated the case and who should conduct the interrogation available? If so, contact them and follow their instructions. If the warrant is from another jurisdiction, do not admonish the arrestees or attempt to conduct any interrogation, as you have no information to prepare you for an intelligent interview.

Consider this interesting 1977 case, in which the subject—not a suspect at the time—was *invited* to go to the station for questioning.[4] Mathiason, a parolee, was named by the victim of a burglary as a possible suspect, but there was no hard evidence. The officer went to Mathiason's apartment and left a card and a note stating that he (the officer) would like to discuss something with him. Mathiason later called the officer and accepted the invitation to come to the office and talk. Mathiason arrived and the officer went into an office and closed the door.

The officer told Mathiason that he was not under arrest but that he had been called in to talk about a burglary. The officer then said that if Mathiason told the truth, it would help him with the district attorney or the judge. The police officer then told Mathiason that he believed Mathiason was involved in the burglary and that his fingerprints had been found at the scene of the crime (actually they had not been found).

Mathiason remained silent for about five minutes and then admitted to the burglary. At that point the officer advised Mathiason of his *Miranda* rights and took

Mathiason's confession, which required about five minutes. The officer told Mathiason that he would not be arrested at that time and then released him. Mathiason went home. The case was referred to the district attorney. Mathiason was tried and convicted for the burglary. On appeal, the Oregon Supreme Court overturned the conviction and ruled the confession inadmissible, saying that the "environment was coercive."

The state of Oregon appealed the reversal to the U.S. Supreme Court, which reversed the ruling and reinstated the conviction. By a 6-to-3 vote, the Court said that *Miranda applies to a custodial interrogation in which a person has been taken into custody or deprived of his or her freedom "in any significant way."* The Supreme Court noted:

> Any interview of one suspected of a crime by a police officer will have coercive aspects to it, simply by virtue of the fact that the police officer is part of a law enforcement system which may ultimately cause the suspect to be charged with a crime. But police officers are not required to administer *Miranda* warnings to everyone. Nor is the requirement of warnings to be imposed simply because the questioning takes place in the station house or because the questioned person is one whom the police suspect. *Miranda* warnings are required only when there has been such a restriction on a person's freedom as to render him "in custody." It was that sort of coercive environment to which *Miranda* by its terms was made applicable, and to which it is limited.

The warning regarding the individual's constitutional rights and his or her exercise of those rights, or waiver of such rights, only affects the admissibility of the subject's statements when later used against him or her in court. One exception to this provision is that in some states laws have been enacted that require any minor who is arrested to be admonished regarding certain rights, including those to an attorney and against self-incrimination, whether the subject is to be questioned or not. A child may waive those rights in the same manner as an adult, but when the child does, the question arises as to whether he or she could actually comprehend the true meaning of the admonishment to make a value judgment and, then, whether he or she could make an intelligent waiver with that limited knowledge. This is a matter for the interviewing officer to decide at the time and the courts to rule on later.

When a police officer stops a car and asks the driver for identification and a vehicle registration slip, and upon receiving unsatisfactory answers, further asks the driver's destination and business, no "in-custody" interrogation, as discussed in *Miranda* takes place, according to a 1969 case.[5] In subsequent cases, it has been affirmed that traffic stops in which the officer routinely asks for a driver's license and registration were specifically excluded from the *Miranda* rule.

Miranda warnings need not be given in cases when the suspect is required by "implied consent" laws involving driving a vehicle while under influence of alcohol to submit to a blood or breath or urine analysis for the purpose of determining blood-alcohol percentage. The suspect need not be admonished prior to giving handwriting exemplars, before having his fingerprints or photograph taken for identification purposes, or before standing in a lineup. An individual may require his attorney to be present for the purpose of observing the lineup to assure his client that it is being handled correctly, but he need not be advised of his rights as provided in the *Miranda* rule for that purpose. He may be asked to speak during a lineup for identification purposes, and that is not a violation of the court's rule. The *Miranda* rule applies strictly to the admissibility of an individual's statements in court when used against him in his trial, and those statements that were elicited from the individual during a custodial interrogation.

Independent of the *Miranda* considerations, the test of "voluntariness" applies. Any threat or promise of any kind will nullify the admissibility of any statements or admissions made by a suspect. Threats or promises may be real or implied. The actual test is whether the court perceives an officer's conduct as meeting those criteria.

In certain cases when a person has exercised his rights against self-incrimination, he later indicates of his own volition that he wishes to resume the interview and that he wishes to voluntarily make statements or a confession. Under these circumstances such statements will be held admissible. The subject must initiate the action, however, and there can be no attempt on the part of the officer to take the initiative to gain the statements under conditions when it would appear that the subject was coerced or enticed to subsequently waive those rights.

Confessions and Admissions Made to a Private Person

The basic question is whether the person doing the questioning is doing so as a private person or acting as an agent of the police. If it is as a person acting on direction by, or as an agent of, a police officer, the *Miranda* rule would apply. The individual would then become a person *in authority* as the *Miranda* rule specifically stated: "When an individual is taken into custody or otherwise deprived of his freedom *by the authorities* [emphasis added] in any significant way and is subjected to questioning. . . ."[6] However, in some situations, certain statements were excluded in the "person in authority" premise, such as (1) questioning by a pier gateman employed by a private detective agency,[7] (2) questioning by a person making a private person arrest,[8] or (3) questioning by a supervisor of a gambling casino.[9]

Although private citizens need not Mirandize a suspect they interrogate, according to *Berve* and *Haydel*,[10] their use of threats or force to obtain a statement will render the statement involuntary and inadmissible. As a police officer, be sure to follow the rules carefully, but also be sure to advise other people who are in the private security and retail business particularly that any means they might use to gain statements might negatively affect the admissibility.

Here are some examples of a person not being in custody and, therefore, not covered by the *Miranda* protective blanket:

1. An officer arrives on the scene and asks each person present, "What's going on?"

2. Was the person being questioned free to leave? The prosecutor should ask the officer if the person was told at any time that he or she was *not free to leave.*

3. An investigatory temporary detention that is not in an accusatory mode is not custody (*People* v. *Patterson,* 1979, 88 Cal. 3d 742).

THE QUESTION OF VOLUNTARINESS

Long before *Miranda,* the courts have always been concerned about the voluntary nature of statements made by people being questioned by the police. (Watch a few segments of police television shows, and you will see many examples of statements given under duress, such as after being thrown up against a wall and questioned with the television cop's hands around the suspect's throat, or having one's head slammed onto the table in the interrogation room.) Three questions that must always be answered are (1) whether the suspects have the capacity and opportunity to make an intelligent and knowing waiver of rights, (2) whether such waiver was given free of any police misconduct or intimidation, and (3) following a valid waiver was there any police misconduct that led to an involuntary—and therefore invalid—confession?

Examples of voluntary waivers:

- A person under the influence of drugs gave coherent answers (*People* v. *Taylor,* 1982, 112 Cal. 3d 348).
- The suspect had a 0.20 blood alcohol level (1982, *People* v. *Missin,* 1982, 128 Cal. 3d 1015).
- Although this was unknown to officers, the suspect claimed he had had no food or sleep for 32 hours (*People* v. *Murtishaw,* 1981, 29 Cal. 3d 733).

Examples of involuntary waivers:

- Use of force to obtain a waiver is prohibited (*People* v. *McElhenny* 1983, 137 Cal. 3d 396).
- Implied threats, intimidation, and express and implied promises of leniency used to obtain a waiver (*People* v. *Clary,* 1980, 20 Cal. 3d 218; *People* v. *Haydel,* 1974, 12 Cal. 3d 190).
- Using deception or tricks such as untrue statements, to get a waiver: "We found your prints on the flashlight" (*People* v. *Keithly,* 1979, 13 Cal. 3d 406).
- Prolonged interrogation in the absence of counsel (36 hours with interrogators working in 8-hour shifts) (*People* v. *Alfieri,* 1979, 95 3d 533, 546).

Deception to Gain Confessions

Although the police cannot use trickery or deception in getting a waiver, they may be used to get a confession, providing the deception is not such as to be "reasonably likely to procure an untrue statement" (*People* v. *Atchley,* 1979, 53 Cal. 2d 16-, 171). Although this should not be misinterpreted to imply that you may circumvent the law, neither should you meekly give up and be intimidated by some court ruling that possibly had not been made yet. A great deal of the court's evaluation of a situation depends largely on an officer's good-faith intentions.

Examples of admissible statements gained by 'trickery or deceit."

- Telling a wounded man he might not live to the hospital (*People* v. *Walker,* 1978 10 Cal. 3d 764).
- Falsely telling a suspect his prints were found at the crime scene (*People* v. *Watkins,* 1978 6 Cal. 3d 119).

- Falsely telling a suspect his accomplice has confessed (*Frazier* v. *Cupp*, 1969 394 U.S. 731).

S*ection Two:* *Field Interviews*

INTRODUCTION

One of your basic responsibilities is to do whatever is within the scope of your duty and authority to maintain your assigned district as free from crime and disorder as possible. In fact, one of the principal factors considered in evaluating your efficiency and effectiveness is the *absence* of crime in your district. The well-trained officer knows that field interviews are among the most useful "tools of the trade," because it is largely through their use that the officer prevents and represses criminal activity. You are most productive in activities such as arrests and crime clearances when you aggressively make personal contact with the people you observe during the course of your patrol activities, particularly those who arouse your suspicions, and when you conduct thorough field interviews with those people.

You should know the character and nature of business of as many people in your district as possible. You should also know the identity and character of those who are occasional and frequent visitors to your district. In many instances, it is your responsibility to know what you can about certain "first-time" or "one-time-only" visitors to the district you patrol. The only effective means whereby such identification and character determination can be accomplished is by *observation* and *interrogation.* One of the most immediate ways to get an answer to your question, "I wonder who he is and what he is up to?" is by making contact with that person and asking him. Although this is the most obvious method, *too few* officers choose to use it as a matter of routine, which it should be.

OBJECTIVES OF FIELD INTERVIEWS

There are three principal objectives of having a department-wide, organized field interview program. These objectives are (1) identification, (2) prevention and repression of crime, and (3) centralized records of field contacts. Let's cover each of these three separately.

Identification. As we mentioned earlier in the chapter, you are responsible for knowing the people who live, work, and pass through or seek recreation in your district. You should know the identity and places of residence of people with criminal records and criminal tendencies as demonstrated by their past actions, which are a matter of record. You should likewise know the identities and any unusual hours or habits of the residents, such as the milkman who leaves home at 3:00 A.M., the person who works in the post office until 2:00 A.M., or doctors or other professionals whose work takes them out of the house at all hours of the day and night. You should know the businesses in your area and be aware of their irregularities in business practices and hours, such as overnight inventories, restocking the shelves between 2:00 A.M. and 10:00 A.M., or deliveries made at night to avoid parking problems. By having made previous personal contact with literally hundreds of people on your beat, you know who has the criminal records, who are the burglars or thieves, and who is peddling narcotics. Armed with such information, you are better prepared to take appropriate action, such as a cursory search, surveillance, utilization of an undercover officer, or immediate arrest whenever the circumstances call for police response.

Prevention and Repression of Crime. An active and alert police patrol with an objective field interview program creates a continuous awareness of the omnipresence of the police. Law-abiding citizens have the feeling of security in knowing that their safety is assured, and criminals know that they have a greater chance of getting caught at their illicit activities or when they are in possession of contraband. The criminals who know that the police know them and their records, their addresses, their methods of transportation, their crime specialties, and the names and addresses of their associates are less likely to commit their crimes under circumstances when they also know that you are aware of their presence in the immediate or general vicinity.

Records. Every field interview or field contact (which may include mere observation of known criminals under circumstances that merit a record of time and place but no necessity—or opportunity—for a conversation) should be made the subject of a permanent or semipermanent record entry in the department files. A printed card the same size as the standard 3×5 cards used for a master alphabetical file is ideal, because it can be placed directly in that file along with other cards pertaining to the same individual. If your department feeds "FI" data into the computers, it is a good idea to build in a time limit for retention of the data, because people change appearance, residence, vehicles, and associates often.

The field interview cards provide a ready source of information about physical description, times and locations of contact, vehicle description, associates, employer or school, and circumstances surrounding such contacts (see Figure 6–1). The cards showing records of field interviews are most helpful in locating possible suspects and witnesses. Lovers in the park may later develop into victim and suspect in a rape case. The employee moving inventory from one store to another at 2:00 A.M. may turn out to be someone who was fired for theft two weeks previously who is stealing a former employer's inventory. There are many examples we can use from personal experience, such as the "student" with the stolen portable typewriter, a car thief driving a "borrowed" car, a "witness" to a hit-and-run accident later identified as the suspect, and known burglars observed in the area at about the same time a burglary was reported. Quite often a field interview card in the police file is more current than is a telephone directory published 10 months earlier. The advantages of maintaining a permanent record of field interview records far outweigh the disadvantages. For the individuals who are interviewed rather frequently, it would probably be advisable to maintain only those cards related to the most recent two or three years.

FIELD INTERROGATION CARD

JR. No.	FIELD INTERROGATION CARD		DATE & TIME

NAME (LAST NAME FIRST) — NICKNAME

RESIDENCE ADDRESS — RESIDENCE PHONE

CLASSIFICATION — DRIVER'S LICENSE NO. — DRIV (X) | PASS (X) | PED (X)

LOCATION OF OCCURRENCE — PLACE OF BIRTH

SEX	DESCENT	AGE	DATE OF BIRTH	HEIGHT	WEIGHT	HAIR	EYES	COMPLEXION

MARKS, SCARS, TATOOS, ETC.

CLOTHING WORN

YEAR AND MAKE OF CAR	BODY TYPE	COLOR(S)	LICENSE NO.	YEAR

SUSPECT'S BUSINESS ADDRESS (PH. NO. & SHIFT) (IF JUVENILE, NAME OF SCHOOL & GRADE)

NAMES OF PERSONS WITH SUSPECT AT TIME OF INTERROGATION

REASON FOR INTERROGATION

DISPOSITION

OFFICER(S), REPORTING (LAST NAME AND SERIAL NUMBER) — DIVISION — DETAIL

Figure 6–1 Field interrogation card.

LEGALITY OF THE FIELD INTERVIEW

For many years, the courts throughout the United States have held that police officers have the duty to protect themselves and the people who live in, and visit, their jurisdictions, and that they may stop and question any subject who arouses the officer's suspicion if the conditions at the time warrant such inquiry (see Figure 6–2). In one of the two early leading cases in California, the California Supreme Court stated

(a.)

(b.)

Figure 6–2 Whatever your jurisdiction, the field interview is an essential function of the police. [(a) Courtesy Ohio State Highway Patrol; (b) Courtesy Delaware State Police.]

The duty of every good citizen is, when called upon, to give all information in his power to the proper officers of the law as to persons connected with crime; and this should be held to require that all proper information should be given on request of a personal nature, as affecting the one of whom inquiry is made, when the circumstances are such to warrant an officer in making an inquiry. A police officer has a right to make inquiry in the proper manner of everyone upon the public streets at a late hour as to his identity and to the occasion of his presence, if the surroundings are such as to indicate to a reasonable man that the public safety demands such identification. The fact that crimes had recently been committed in that neighborhood; that the plaintiff at a late hour was found in the locality; that he refused to answer proper questions establishing his identity, were circumstances which should lead a reasonable officer to require his presence at the station, where the sergeant in charge might make more minute and careful inquiry.[11]

Recognizing the need for legal justification of the field officer's participation in a program of conducting field interviews in circumstances warranting such inquiry, many states have followed a trend of enacting laws requiring that certain people cooperate with the inquiring officers whenever public safety demands both the inquiry and the cooperation. Some of the laws, such as those in New Hampshire, Delaware, and New York, authorize the police to stop and question persons who they "reasonably suspect" are committing, have committed, or are about to commit a felony or serious misdemeanor. In many of these cases, the detention is not considered an arrest, but if the officers reasonably believe that they are in "danger of life or limb," they may search the subject to ensure that he does not possess any weapons or other items which would imperil the officers' safety. Providing that reasonable cause exists for the original stop and inquiry, some cases have indicated that this search may also extend to items under the immediate control of the persons searched, such as a woman's handbag or a man's attaché case. If the officers find weapons when conducting such a search, they may make an arrest for the violation and conduct a thorough search incidental to the arrest.

WHEN TO CONDUCT A FIELD INTERVIEW

A good police officer is suspicious by nature, always alert for anything that appears out of the ordinary. What is ordinary, of course, depends on where you are, the time of day, and the culture and habits of the people where you are. You notice people and events that are incongruous with the "norm." Some of the factors that should be taken into account when establishing reasonable cause for temporary detentions for field interview contacts are hours of darkness, a place where crimes of a particular nature are frequently and currently taking place, a neighborhood where there has been a recent rash of burglaries, particularly within the same shift or previous day or two, or when the individual observed at such a time and place has a record of criminal activity that has been occurring in that particular neighborhood where the contact is to be made. Other factors might be cases in which the subject is driving in an erratic manner, two persons are sitting in a parked car at a time and place that does not fit the circumstances, or individuals are overtly violating a traffic law or criminal code. A sharp robber may run away from the scene and then, when the officers begin arriving in response to the in-progress call, turn around and begin walking casually back toward the scene of the crime.

Going back to the laws, consider the individual who—because of circumstances—appears as if he is committing, did commit, or is about to commit a felony or misdemeanor. Consider the following factors as general grounds for a temporary detention for a field interview:

1. There must be a rational suspicion by the officer that some activity out of the ordinary is occurring or has taken place.
2. Some indication must exist to connect the person under suspicion with the unusual activity.
3. There must be some suggestion that the activity is related to crime.

The circumstances must be sufficiently unique to justify your suspicions, and you should be prepared to explain the circumstances causing you to choose to conduct a field interview. You are an acknowledged specialist as an observer, and the court will expect you as that officer to call upon your expertise, your training, and past experiences with similar circumstances to "lay the foundation" justifying your cause for conducting the field interview.

There need not be sufficient cause to justify an arrest or a search, but there must be sufficient cause to indicate to you that your failure to make inquiry into the matter would amount to a dereliction of duty as a conscientious police officer.

Whenever there is sufficient cause to detain an individual temporarily for a field inquiry, there may be sufficient cause to perform a cursory "patdown" of the individual for any weapons with which he or she may attempt to inflict violent injury upon you or some other person. Although there are many occasions when a field interview situation may not call for a search for weapons, certain factors may indicate the need for a patdown. Consider these points when deciding your course of action:

1. The nature of the suspected criminal activity and whether a weapon would be used
2. Your situation: Are you alone or has assistance arrived?
3. The number of subjects and their emotional and physical state (angry, fighting, intoxicated)
4. Time of day and geographical surroundings
5. Prior knowledge of the subject's reputation and/or any police record he may have
6. The sex of the subject or subjects encountered
7. The behavior and apparent agility of the subjects
8. The circumstances as they present themselves to you at the time and as you evaluate them

FIELD INTERVIEW PROCEDURE

Use this procedure as a general guide for making field contacts, but always adjust your procedure to fit the person contacted and the circumstances involved.

Location to Choose for Field Interview

If you are in a well-lighted business area, or an industrial complex where there are many high fences and buildings with few open driveways, try to make the contact near a streetlight in the middle of the block. If you are in a residential area where there are many driveways and open areas, choose an intersection for the contact. The reason for selecting these contact locations is to make it easier for you to pursue the subject if he should *decide* to run. It is easier to chase a subject down a street than through backyards and alleys. Also, consider your own safety when selecting the spot for the contact.

The Approach on Foot[12]

If you are walking toward the subject and you meet him head on, let him walk past you, then turn toward the subject facing his right side. If you approach him from the rear, have him turn so that you are initially on his right side. As soon as you can determine whether the subject is right- or left-handed, take a position of advantage closest to the "dominant" hand.

Depending on the circumstances leading to the field contact, you may order the subject to stop and place his hands on the back of his head or someplace where you can see them. If you do not wish to alert him to your suspicions, you may simply state that you wish to speak with him. The person may be deaf or not understand your language, which may lead you to believe that he is not paying attention, while he is actually unable to do so. Avoid offensive terminology when directing the subject to submit to a field interview. Do not place your hands on the subject except to frisk, search, or control him. Be aware of every person's "personal space." When you get so close that the person pulls back, you will know the boundaries of that "space."

The Position of Interrogation

Stand slightly forward and to the right of the subject at slightly more than arm's length away. If he appears to be left-handed, stand to the side of his left hand. Look for the wristwatch, which most people would wear on the weaker hand. Stand at about a 90-degree angle from the subject. From this position, it is possible to grab the subject's arm and ward off a blow that he may intend to wield. Some weaponless defense instructors recommend that you assume a head-on position slightly out of range for the suspect's hands or feet to be used as offensive weapons against you. Your own training and experience will determine which stance you will assume.

If there is more than one subject, attempt to separate them as soon as practicable before questioning them to prevent them from preparing standardized answers to your questions. Keep them separated until you have completed questioning both of them. Until assistance arrives, stand in the position of interrogation next to the leading subject and have the others stand on the other side, all in plain view.

If there are two officers and one subject, the officer who will conduct the interview should stand at the position of interrogation while the second officer stands to the rear and the opposite side. If there are two officers and more than two subjects, use the same basic posture with the subjects between the officers. Once you have searched them, if necessary, separate them and question them separately.

Ask questions to satisfy your curiosity and your suspicions. Ask positive questions to secure positive responses, such as "Where is your car?" or "When was the last time a police officer questioned you?" Do not make the mistake of providing the subject's answers for him by asking questions such as "You don't have a car, do you?" or "You have never been questioned by the police before, have you?"

When you do not wish to alert the subject to the fact that you may suspect he is a wanted felon or that he matches the description of a person observed at a crime scene, it is advisable to use subterfuge while making the initial contact. The purpose of the deception is to avoid alerting him to your suspicions until you are in a position of advantage. It may appear natural for you to ask the subject if he has seen a car you are looking for or if he is the person who called to report an abandoned car.

If the subject's answers and his behavior continue to pique your curiosity and suspicions, you may change your line of questioning as soon as you have a position of advantage.

If the subject's answers, attitude, or other behavior indicate that there is no further cause for action or detention, complete the form or notebook entry required by your department and conclude the interview. If the circumstances indicate the need for further inquiry, continue the interview. Never lower your guard and "assume" that the subject presents no danger to you. He probably does not, but you do not know that.

1. Check for identification. Be sure that the documents describe the subject. Indicate on your field interview card or notebook the types of documents you used for the ID, and list any numbers found on the documents. A card with a photograph, such as a driver's license, is far better than a social security card, which is virtually worthless as identification.

2. Ask the subject to repeat the nature of his business in the area. Does this actually make sense to you, under the circumstances?

3. Secure a statement as to where the subject is going and where he has been. Is this actually on the way? Ask the subject where he is now. The answer may surprise you. The subject may have no idea where he is.

4. Check out the story when possible. If two persons are providing different information, compare notes and get a reason for the differences.

5. Fill out a complete description on the subjects, including
   a. Visible scars, marks, tattoos. Draw a sketch, if practicable.
   b. Deformities, unusual characteristics. Describe carefully or sketch.
   c. Membership data as indicated by cards presented for identification, car club jackets, car plaques, business cards, gang insignia. Take photographs when practicable.
   d. Design of shoe and heel prints and shoe size, particularly those whose records indicate a history of burglary arrests.
   e. Subject's statement regarding past criminal record and/or prior contacts with the police. Check records and record the information.

The Interview

1. *Maintain a friendly, yet not overly familiar, attitude.* The attitude of the subject of the interview may be a reflection of that of the officer (see Figure 6–3).

2. *Identify the subject.* One of the first questions to ask him is where he lives. He may be anticipating your asking him for a name and he may be prepared with a fabricated one, but he is less likely to have thought of a false address.

3. *Take out your field interview card or notebook only after you have identified the individual.* Some people tend to become uncooperative when confronted with something that indicates the imminence of a permanent written record.

4. *Determine the nature of the subject's business at the location where you contact him.*

5. *Ask the subject where he is going and where he has been.* The story should logically relate to his explanation for being where he is when you contact him.

6. *Determine how familiar the subject is with the neighborhood if he claims to be a frequent visitor.*

7. *Use the radio or a telephone—if available—to check records on the subject for a prior record and to ascertain if he is wanted.*

8. *Arrest or release the subject, depending on the circumstances as indicated by your investigation to this point.*

9. *Conduct a patdown or cursory search.* If circumstances warrant your field contact with the subject, the same conditions may justify the patdown for any offensive weapons with which the subject may attack you. The timing depends on the circumstances of the individual case, but the search should occur early unless a brief interview indicates to you that you do not wish to further restrict

Figure 6–3 Interrogation is an art. One of the most important factors is to establish rapport and maintain a friendly atmosphere. (Courtesy Hawaii Police Department, Hilo.)

the subject's movement. If you do pat down the subject, do it early to avoid later regrets.

10. *Complete filling out the field interview card or the notebook entry.* When writing your reason for the field interview, indicate *what it was about the subject and/or the circumstances that caused you to first decide to proceed with the field interview.* Be specific, as this justification should be considered reasonable cause for the interview, the detention, and any other action you should take. Without this information, it is conceivable that you might lose an otherwise good case.

11. *Conclude the field interview promptly.*
   a. To the "legitimate" subject, a word of caution about recent crimes in the area, a brief explanation of the field interview program and its necessity, and a "thank you" for his cooperation.
   b. To the "suspicious" subject, a word of advice pertaining to the process of the field interview and its possible significance to him, depending on the circumstances of the contact and the character of the subject.
   c. If the interview and accompanying circumstances lead to the need for more intensive investigation and discussion of the matter at hand with the subject, you may have "focused" on him as a suspect in a specific offense and a custodial interrogation may follow.

Several years ago, a team of officers from several departments spent several weeks interviewing a burglar whose arrest cleared more than 800 burglaries. The purpose of the interviews was to understand better how a burglar thinks and operates to help the field officer prevent the crime more effectively and to apprehend the burglar. Whenever you question an individual whom you find to be responsible for certain types of crimes, listen to the answers that you get about method of entry, object of the crime, and other factors. Then add your findings to this list, which includes some of the observations made by the burglar of several years ago, plus additional comments by other burglars.

1. *Clothing worn by burglar:* Whatever fit the neighborhood being worked.
2. *Tools:* Seldom anything that resembles "burglar tools"; more often has a three-bladed pocket knife, plastic card, and penlight.
3. *Vehicle:* Stolen cars that had been stolen some time ago and were replaced on the hot sheet by more recent vehicles stolen. Plates were removed and replaced with those stolen from stored vehicles, usually from another state.
4. *License plates:* Same age and state of repair as the cars, such as new plates for new cars, beat-up plates for beat-up vehicles.
5. *Selection of victims:* Comfortable middle class observed in restaurants and bars during "happy hours" who used cash rather than credit cards.
6. *Casing the victim:* Try ringing the doorbell. If no answer, try the phone in the garage. Dial the ring-back number and if no one is home, go into the house. Avoid barking dogs, but if dogs continue sleeping, they are no threat. Snoring sleepers no problem.

7. *Casing the police.* To find out how many officers and units on the air, go to the station at shift-change time and count the officers as they depart for patrol, listening on radio for their unit numbers. Watch officers on patrol and figure out their patterns. Usually one pass per shift is all they would make in any neighborhood. Look for discarded hot sheets and other valuable information in trash cans outside and behind police station.

8. *Field shakedowns:* Act naturally and give all correct information from the stolen driver's license used (date of birth, etc.) and registration information about the car; know contents of trunk and glove box. If the burglar received a citation using another person's car and license, he would pay it to avoid it "going to warrant." Suspect always had a ready answer why stolen merchandise was in car, such as moving to another apartment. Acted "cool" because officers are suspicious of people who are nervous and "appear to be hiding something."

9. *Logical reasoning:* Most officers follow fixed patterns of patrol; they are creatures of habit. An officer may be taken off guard and not be able to react suddenly when there is an unusual event, such as the traffic violator waiting for the officer to get out of the car and approach, then the violator suddenly "digs out." "Officers seldom look up when looking for suspects and other items."

10. *The crime:* Best object of attack are glass patio doors, which can be lifted out of their tracks, whether locked or not, even with broomstick handles in the track while door is left ajar. Lots of people leave doors and windows open and unlocked. Burglars who find one fruitful house in the neighborhood will often return to the same house and to the same neighborhood. Burglars take stolen "loot" to bushes along the curb, attack another house and others, and then get their cars and go along the street and pick up all the loot.

11. *Flight:* When the police started closing in, subject sometimes approaches the officers and asks what is going on and offers to help; sometimes burglars climb trees, or crawl into attic crawl hole in resident hall. Burglars may flee over fences and bushes knowing that some officers don't want to get their uniforms dirty. Officers do most of their searching without getting out of their vehicles.

12. *Searches:* It appeared that officers search as though they do not expect to find anyone.

SUMMARY

Implementation of an active and objective field interview program is essential to the successful and effective operation of the modern law enforcement agency. The program not only gives you an opportunity to prevent and repress crime by meeting and counseling the actual or potential criminal law violators but also provides you an additional vehicle for contacts with the law-abiding people in his district.

Indiscriminate field interviews and accompanying searches for weapons are not warranted. They must be based on reasonable cause factors and you must be able to articulate them. You must check into any individuals or circumstances that appear at the time to be deleterious to the good order and the peace of the community. Your diplomacy may ease the strain in situations that appear to you at first to be quite suspicious but after the contact turns out to be strictly legitimate and aboveboard. If you handle it correctly, the field interview will result in a favorable contact with someone who will appreciate your diligence and efficiency in looking after his or her safety by making such field inquiries, particularly at times and places where suspicious circumstances warrant it. The law-abiding person will appreciate you for your interest in keeping the streets free of undesirables and criminals, and the people who are intent on breaking the law may choose somewhere else to ply their trade.

When interviewing or interrogating anyone, be it the suspect, the victim, the witness, or some disinterested bystander, bear in mind your responsibility to seek the truth, whatever that is. Through perseverance, tenacity, and a great deal of skill and native ability, you will find that your success as a police officer will be greatly enhanced if you can interview and interrogate effectively.

EXERCISES AND STUDY QUESTIONS

1. Define "interrogation."
2. Define "interview."
3. Describe the difference, if any, between an interview and an interrogation.
4. What is Reik's theory regarding confession?
5. Why does the author refer to the process of interviewing as an art?
6. List and discuss the five basic objectives of interviewing and interrogating.
7. If you had a choice, where would you choose to interrogate a suspected child molester?
8. How would you go about opening an interview to establish rapport?
9. Give an example of the logical approach in interviewing.
10. Give an example of the sympathetic approach.
11. Explain the *Miranda* rule, and recite verbatim the admonishment.
12. How must the suspect respond for you to testify that you received an intelligent waiver?
13. Describe a custodial interrogation.
14. What do you do when a suspect has waived *Miranda* rights and talks freely about the crime and then suddenly has a change of heart and stops talking?
15. Describe what happened in the *Mathiason* case that caused the Supreme Court to rule as it did.
16. When you stop to cite a traffic violator, must you warn the offender of his or her *Miranda* rights before asking for the reason for not stopping at the intersection for the crossing pedestrian?
17. Are private security officers bound by the *Miranda* rule the same as city police officers? What makes the difference, if any?

18. What gives the peace officer the right to conduct a field interview?
19. What are the objectives of a field interview program?
20. Describe the legal basis for a field interview in your jurisdiction.
21. Design a field interview card that would be an improvement over the one depicted in this chapter.
22. List at least 10 different situations that you believe would justify a field interview.
23. Describe the difference between a confession and an admission.
24. Give an example of an *involuntary* statement.
25. Does the use of trickery or deceit by the interrogator during an interrogation always render any statements by the suspect inadmissible?

REFERENCES

COLEMAN, JAMES C. *Abnormal Psychology and Modern Life,* 5th ed. Glenview, Ill.; Scott, Foresman, 1976, Chap. 4.

FREUD, SIGMUND. *Psychopathology of Everyday Life.* New York: Mentor, 1951, pp. 102–108.

GILBERT, JAMES N. *Criminal Investigation.* Columbus, Ohio: Charles E. Merrill, 1980, Chap. 6.

INBAU, FRED E., and JOHN E. REID. *Criminal Interrogation and Confessions.* Baltimore: Williams & Wilkins, 1962.

REIK, THEODOR. *The Compulsion to Confess: On the Analysis of Crime and Punishment.* New York: Farrar, Straus & Giroux, 1959.

SCOTT, JAMES D. *Investigative Methods.* Reston, Va.: Reston, 1978.

STOKKE, ALLAN H., and ROBERT W. FERGUSON. *Legal Aspects of Evidence.* New York: Harcourt Brace Jovanovich, 1978, Chap. 8.

WADDINGTON, LAWRENCE C. *Criminal Evidence.* Encino, Calif.: Glencoe, 1978, Chap. 11.

WESTON, PAUL B., and KENNETH M. WELLS. *Criminal Evidence for Police,* 2nd ed. Englewood Cliffs, N.J.: Prentice Hall, 1976, Chap. 13.

———. *Criminal Investigation, Basic Perspectives,* 3rd ed. Englewood Cliffs, N.J.: Prentice Hall, 1980, Chaps. 9, 11.

FOOTNOTES

1. *Miranda* v. *Arizona,* 384 U.S. 438 (1966).
2. 384 U.S. 436, 457.
3. See *Maxey,* 172 Cal. App. 3d 11 (1985).
4. *Oregon* v. *Mathiason,* 97 S. Ct. 711 (1977).

5. *Lowe* v. *United States,* 407 F. 2d 1394, 9th Cir. (1969).
6. 384 U.S. 436, 478 (1966).
7. *United States* v. *Antonelli,* 434 F.2d 335, 2d Cir. (1970).
8. *State* v. *LaRose,* 286 Minn. 517, 174 N.W. 2d 247 S. Ct. (1970).
9. *Shoumberg* v. *State,* 83 Nev. 372, 432 P.2d 500 S. Ct. (1967).
10. *People* v. *Berve,* 51, Cal. 2d 286 (1958); *People* v. *Haydel,* 12 Cal. 3d 190 (1974).
11. *Miller* v. *Fano,* 134 Cal. 106 (1906).
12. For the vehicle approach, see the section "Car Stops" in Chapter 11.

CHAPTER 7

FREQUENT PATROL ASSIGNMENTS

*I*NTRODUCTION

Under perfect conditions, if such were possible, you would come out of the academy with a specific operational plan for every type of anticipated police activity. You would be able to begin your long and eventful career with a fistful of answers to all of the situations that you would encounter while on patrol. Academy training and simulated experiences in role-play training would have prepared you for every conceivable contingency. But we don't live in a perfect world, and there are no magic formulas for circumstances that have not yet happened. The variables are beyond imagination.

What you have done in the academy and in your field training, which continues throughout your career, is to study past actions and to attempt to formulate some general guidelines for as many different types of assignments so that you will have some clue as to how to proceed legally, ethically, and as humanely as possible. In this and other texts, we continue to strive for the same goals; that is, to develop some plans to assure some degree of continuity and uniformity in how you and other police officers carry out your duties. This chapter is devoted to some of the types of assignments that you will be given more frequently than others. You should never consider your assignments as "routine," although they may seem so after several years on the job. Bear in mind that no two situations are ever the same, no matter how familiar they may appear to you.

This chapter is devoted to the following types of assignments: (1) the lost child, (2) missing persons, (3) intoxication cases, (4) civil disputes, (5) crisis intervention, (6) domestic violence, (7) mentally and emotionally disturbed individuals, (8) alcoholic beverage control and enforcement, (9) abatement of abandoned vehicles, (10) nuisances—attractive and otherwise, (11) parades and special events, (12) fire scenes, (13) rescue and first aid, (14) courtesy services, (15) public utility assistance, and (16) handling animal calls. As you can see, this chapter is a variety act, and we will cover some basic techniques for each assignment category.

LOST CHILD

This is one of the most important of all police activities and should involve maximum personnel assignment at the earliest opportunity after the parent reports the child as missing (see Figure 7–1). There has usually been some lapse of time prior to the parent's report. Therefore, time is of the essence because of the distances the child may have traveled or the length of time the child may have been exposed to the many hazards he or she might encounter and possibly not be able to cope with.

Some children may have been taught to fear the police uniform and may hide from the searching officers without realizing that the police are trying to reunite them with their parents. Some children who are the object of a search may hide and play games with their searchers.

Figure 7–1 Searching for a lost child is one of a police department's most responsible functions. Dogs are excellent aids in this type of activity. (Courtesy North Carolina Police Department.)

Secure any information you can regarding any earlier case in which the child ran away. The parents can sometimes provide valuable information, although they may be somewhat reluctant to do so because of embarrassment. If the child has run away or wandered off before, ascertain where he was discovered on the earlier occasion. Check your records and those of surrounding jurisdictions for any similar incidents of lost or kidnapped children—or attempts to pick up kids—about the same age and sex as your case. You may have a situation far more serious than a child who has merely strayed from home.

Consider the age of the child. Where would you go if you were that age? What type of entertainment or adventure would you pursue if you were on your own away from the sometimes prohibitive control of parents who may disagree with a five-year-old boy's concept of fun and excitement?

When you begin the search, start as though there had been no previous search by anyone. *Do not take anyone's word that a certain place has already been searched.* Search the immediate premises, including any containers that might conceivably contain the child and also smaller containers. Children, both alive and dead, have been found in suitcases, freezers, dresser drawers, clothes hampers, and the most unlikely of places. The child may have gone into hiding to avoid some form of punishment, yet he might not want to stray too far from the security of home. The child may have left the home and the premises earlier, but may have returned and may now be hiding under a bed, in a closet, or somewhere else in or near the house. Is one of the child's vehicles missing, such as a skateboard or bicycle? Look for the child at a favorite place to play or one that is a curiosity to a child, an attractive nuisance, school grounds, or a park where older children play.

Who are the child's friends and relatives? Check them out to see that the child is not paying a visit without having asked permission of his or her parents to do so. Sometimes the host parent or relative may not ask the child if permission was granted for the visit, or the child may not be entirely truthful if asked.

Establish the exact time and location at which the child was last seen. Set up a grid pattern on the jurisdiction map, and divide the search area into well-defined areas with specific assignments to assure complete coverage. Consider the maximum distance the child may have traversed during that period of time, then add more distance for additional coverage. Each assigned officer should then start at the outermost point and search the assigned area in a zigzag or cloverleaf manner, working in toward the center, or the location where the child was last seen, then working back out to the perimeter.

Use the loudspeaker on a police unit and consider having the parents, a relative, or a close friend of the child broadcast the appeal to the child to come out of hiding. Their voices may have a greater value than that of the searching officer. Also consider the use of plainclothes officers and civilian volunteers for extra help because the child may be hiding from the police uniforms, which the child may perceive as a threat.

Never overlook the possibility of kidnapping, and begin an early search for any evidence of such an event. Question parents and other adult family members about the possibility of a custody problem. A common form of child stealing is by a non-custody or limited-custody parent who chooses to defy a court order and establish his or her own custody rights. Sometimes you will encounter a childless woman who will steal a child to adopt unlawfully as her own; and there are people who steal children to sell in adoption businesses. An earlier contact with someone who has paid particular attention to the child may be recounted by the parent; such a person may be a good suspect.

Check the files for any known or suspected child molester or registered sex offender who may live or be suspected of performing crimes in the area. Locate and question him or her, if available. Rather than harassment, this procedure is actually an assurance to him. It gives him an opportunity to exonerate himself early in the investigation. Continue a relentless search until you find the child.

Do not overlook the possibility that the child may have run away from an abusive situation that he or she is afraid to tell anyone about. After the child is found, discreetly look for any signs of trauma, physical or emotional, and report any suspicions to your department's juvenile specialist. Listen to what the child has to say that might give a clue about any cause for his or her disappearance. But do not make the mistake of suggesting to the child anything that may inspire the child's imagination and lead to a witch hunt.

If the child has wandered away from home out of curiosity to see what's out there in the world, or perhaps wanted to revisit a favorite or familiar place, question the child about the places he or she went while on the adventure. Include the information in your report. Sometime in the future, the child may repeat the adventure, as they sometimes do. Subsequent searches might prove fruitful by looking for those places the child visited previously. There might also be other places with a similar attraction that could be added to the list of places to look.

MISSING PERSONS

Many times friends and family members report someone missing. In most cases, that person has isolated himself for a purpose. Relatively few of the reported missing persons are actually the victims of amnesia or have become confused and lost. They are missing by choice. If the missing person is a juvenile, the matter will be handled as a juvenile case, with the child referred to his parents and possibly—in serious cases—to the juvenile court. In the case of missing adults, there is a somewhat different procedure.

Whenever a person is reported missing within a few hours beyond the time when he should have arrived home from work, or is overdue on some sort of trip, it is good practice to take whatever information the reporting party wishes to provide and to advise the person how to go about checking with hospitals where unidentified injured persons may have been taken. In addition, it is advisable to attempt to reassure the reporting party with what information you have about the lack of serious freeway accidents or aircraft crashes or with the information that your department has no unidentified victims of any crimes of violence reported during the time that the person has been missing. Beyond that first phase of taking the report and assisting the reporting party, the next step is to use the resources you have to locate the person and to put the case to rest as soon as possible, hopefully with the location and/or return of the missing person. We must keep in mind the mature adult's right to be missing by choice, and it is the police responsibility to respect that right, provided that such a case does not involve an attempt to evade legal responsibilities.

If there is some evidence or strong reason to believe that the missing person has met with some type of forced absence or violence, an immediate investigation should begin. You should not automatically assume that the person is missing by choice, although that is the case in a large percentage of missing adult situations. In other missing person cases, after a reasonable time has elapsed and the party has not yet returned to his expected destination, a concerted effort should be made to locate him. Once the person is located, if he or she is an adult and indicates a desire not to have his whereabouts made known, your own department police may require that you notify the reporting party that you found the missing person in good health and that he does not wish his whereabouts made known. In the event of a missing husband, consider the possibility of an impending nonsupport situation with the husband absenting himself. If this is the case, the matter will be a criminal one. Every missing person case should be given adequate attention, but it must be carefully handled within the framework of department policy and law. Whatever you do, however, when taking a missing persons report, avoid getting into an argument about what type of report you are going to make or that the investigation will not be conducted for whatever reason you may have. This is a serious matter to the reporting party, and you should not trivialize the situation by suggesting that the reporting party is getting hysterical over nothing.

INTOXICATION CASES

Traditional police responsibility for arresting and incarcerating the drunks, alcoholics, and other persons whose actions in public indicate their apparent lack of ability to care for their own welfare, rests with the patrol officer. The primary reason for taking such persons into custody is to protect them from themselves and from the dangers of the elements, from traffic, and from any other hazards that they may be exposed to while in an intoxicated state.

Intoxication is relative, and the officer's discretionary powers are great in this area. The laws vary, but those concerning intoxication in public cover persons who are intoxicated to the degree that they are unable to care for their own welfare and are in that state as a result of overindulgence in alcohol, drugs, or other intoxicating or stupefying substances. One of your first considerations is to determine if the subject's condition is caused by some type of illness, poisoning, injury, or other condition, brought about by some situation other than voluntary ingestion by the subject, knowing that the substance used had intoxicating or stupefying affects. A smell of alcohol on the breath may not be alcohol at all. Look for the identification bracelet that many diabetics wear to warn anyone finding the victim of diabetic shock that the subject needs immediate medical attention and look for other signs of injury or illness that may or may not be accompanying the presence of alcohol. Question and examine the subject very carefully.

Since alcoholism is considered to be a disease as well as a criminal offense, many jurisdictions will take the person into custody for a specified period of time (four or five hours), then release him or her, and retroactively classify the arrest as a detention. In many jurisdictions that have the resources, the drunk is taken to a detoxification center for "drying out" and treatment. This makes more sense, especially when the jails are so badly overcrowded with more serious criminal violators.

How to handle the common drunk or the intoxicated person in public depends on your own department's philosophy about the disease or the condition and enforcement policies. For coverage of the tactics and techniques involving the person who operates a motor vehicle while under the influence of alcohol or other drug, see Chapter 11.

By getting the intoxicated person off the street, you are performing a valuable service for others, if not the individual, who may consider your action as nothing but harassment. The individual might be too helpless to defend himself or herself in case of an attack or mugging, or worse. Or the subject may get into an automobile and jeopardize the lives of countless others while driving intoxicated, and is quite likely to go home and get involved in a fight and commit serious crimes of domestic violence against innocent loved ones. You may joke that there is no glory in arresting drunks, but you may be wrong.

CIVIL DISPUTES

Civil disputes frequently escalate into full-blown criminal behavioral problems before the police arrive to intervene and possibly mediate (see Figure 7–2). At this point we are dealing with the problem hopefully before the escalation takes place. Most of the domestic disputes you will be called on will involve landlord–tenant arguments about unpaid rent or undone improvements or necessary repairs that must

Figure 7–2 The officer is often called upon to mediate disputes of both major and minor natures. (Courtesy Chicago Police Department.)

be done; property boundaries, arguments or fights among their children, dismissal or disciplinary action taken against an employee, labor–management disputes over money or working conditions, large layoffs caused by a company downsizing, and, of course, the family disputes.

You are usually called upon by one or more of the participants, who will expect you to be their advocate because it was they who called you. You may receive the call from a neighbor who may or may not be identified. One aspect is nearly always certain: The crisis stage will have arrived, and conciliation is going to be extremely difficult because emotions are at their highest peak.

Some of the participants or interested bystanders expect you to work miracles when all other efforts have failed. Once you arrive on the scene, your primary responsibility is to the safety of the participants. The next responsibility is to prevent any ongoing assault from taking place and to arrest the criminal offenders. Once you have determined that all urgent action has been performed, your role changes to that of invited arbiter and you must defuse the volatile event. You are going to be asked for advice, and what counsel you do give must be strictly within the scope of your authority. Be careful not to give spiritual or psychological advice, or legal advice, because you are neither licensed nor qualified for the role.

Diplomacy and tact are put into play almost constantly during these "referee" sessions. Occasionally you will be reminded by the calling party that it was he who called and that you should enforce his side of the argument, regardless of all other considerations. You are not—nor should you be—the "big bad officer" who is "going to get someone who is naughty," or the "cop who is going to take the bad child into the dark room and beat him up with a big stick," or any other type of demon described by some adults to get their children to behave.

You will often find yourself in what appears to be a "no-win" situation when you are dealing with family or other disputes when love and respect have turned sour. You will have people demanding that you punish the offender—"slap him around" like some of the motion-picture stereotype "tough cops" they envision. They will become angry with you when you refuse. Your role is to rise above the bickering and not be "sucked into" a partisan argument. It is necessary to maintain a professional aloofness.

The telephone operator or dispatcher who receives the original call for police presence at the scene of a civil dispute sets the tone for your initial response. From the details of the situation provided by the calling party, and from the tone of voice and sense of urgency transmitted through the telephone to the dispatcher, the dispatcher determines how many units will be assigned the call, and with what speed they must respond. They should be trained to screen calls, such as "the lady reports they have guns," because some zealous "safety consultant" may have told people that if you want the police to respond to your call and not take their time getting there, the thing to say is that firearms are involved. Irresponsible calls such as that have caused negative results. For example, my younger son and his girlfriend were sitting in his car for what a neighbor believed to be too long for "lawful" persons and called in that there were two suspicious people with guns in a car in front of her house. She got the response she wanted, because within a short time my son and his girlfriend were confronted by three police officers with guns drawn, one of them cocked and stuck in my son's ear. When I called the watch commander for an explanation of such behavior, he explained that the calling party set the tone for the officers' response.

The dispatcher may refer the call to another agency, such as a mental health unit that may be better qualified to handle the problem at hand. The dispatcher may advise the people to come into the police station the next working day and discuss the problem with a juvenile officer or some other specialist. These are some guidelines for the dispatcher to follow when taking the call and deciding the appropriate response (this may be at the same time unit[s] are on the way):

1. Find out exactly what is happening, or as nearly as possible. Listen to the background noises as well as to the voice of the calling party.

2. Determine if someone has been injured and is in need of immediate medical attention.

3. Determine if there is an immediate and imminent danger confronting someone who is on the scene.

4. If there is such a danger, who or what is it?

5. If someone is armed with some sort of weapon, find out what type of weapon, the present whereabouts of the armed subject, and the individual's state of emotionalism and/or sobriety. Is the person using the weapon for self-defense or to assault another person?

6. Find out from the calling party—if possible—and by checking the records files if this is a recurrence of some similar activity that has occurred in the past. What happened that time? (Check records if time permits.)

7. Keep the caller on the telephone as long as necessary.

8. As any new developments arise while you are still talking with the calling party and the assigned officers have been dispatched, keep the officers updated on any information that will assist them in responding to the call.

9. Dispatch enough officers to handle the situation effectively.

10. If the situation calls for response from another police agency, such as in a contiguous jurisdiction, or from an organization or agency that is specifically geared for this particular problem, advise the calling party that another agency should handle the matter. What they may actually need instead of—or in addition to—the police might be paramedics or the fire department. Instead of instructing emotionally involved callers to dial another telephone number, either help them transfer the call or take what information you need, then instruct them that you will call the other agency and handle the matter. Do not add to the caller's frustration and/or anger by stating: "Sorry, ma'am, that's not our jurisdiction. Try the sheriff's office. . . . No. I don't know what their number is, but I'm sure they are in the book."

11. Send backup cars, if necessary. Consider the specific location of the call, the individuals involved, experience with the nature of the call and the principals, the neighborhood characteristics—which may be hostility toward the police in general—and the information you receive by telephone.

12. Call off the units that are no longer needed if there is a change in the circumstances at the scene as reported by the first officer to arrive and other officers.

As the officer assigned to handle the call, your responsibility is to handle the case as well as possible under the circumstances. Any advice that you give should be kept to a minimum. Your role is to restore order, to protect the combatants from themselves and each other, to arrest for violations of the law when necessary, and to give instructions or take whatever action the circumstances dictate to settle the matter during your first visit. Whatever advice you give should be presented in such a manner that they will accept it and act upon it. Any warning you give concerning future arrests should the situation recur must be soundly covered by the law, because if it does continue and you do return, you are committed to make the arrest you promised. It is virtually impossible to make everyone at the scene happy, but they must be placated sufficiently to heed your advice and discontinue the disturbance. Following are some of the more commonly encountered civil dispute situations and a few basic guidelines to use when taking effective police action.

CRISIS INTERVENTION

A crisis as seen by the patrol officer is any event that involves individuals—usually two or more in conflict—who have reached such a debilitating mental state that they seem to have lost the ability to cope with a situation through what one would consider normal methods, such as discussing or negotiation. The event that precipitates such a crisis may be a problem that the individual cannot cope with, such as loss of a loved one, dismissal from a job, an unwanted or unexpected pregnancy, notification of divorce, or marital unfaithfulness. Other situations that may lead to a crisis situation include interpersonal relationship breakdowns, notification that someone has a fatal or incurable disease, a sudden loss of position, or situation that will cause irreparable damage to one's reputation. Excessive use of alcohol or drugs may cause the person to lose ability to reason things out. The crisis occurs when the individual reaches that point when there seems to be no way out of the problem, whether the event occurs instantaneously or whether it has been building up over a period of time.

As a field officer, you will usually be dealing with the symptoms and the crisis itself rather than the causes. Your role will be to intervene and defuse the situation and then attempt to arrange for some sort of immediate assistance with referral for professional assistance. If your department has a crisis intervention team, or a staff psychologist who is specifically trained and assigned to crisis intervention, you will have support available to you. In some jurisdictions a mental health unit may be available for field follow-up to crisis situations. In other jurisdictions, it will be you alone, with a possible follow-up by the family minister or rabbi or family doctor.

Since this book is not intended to prepare you to be a crisis intervention specialist, but is merely a guide in how to proceed with the initial stages and what to do until the specialist arrives, here are a few basic guidelines.

1. *Assess the situation.* Immediately upon your arrival, attempt to identify the cause of the crisis and what you may do to defuse the hostilities or high emotionalism. Is there a crime being committed that will require immediate enforcement action? Is there a severe medical problem, such as wounds or injuries that must be treated? Are adversaries still in confrontation who must be separated? Is there someone present who appears to be making the problem worse by continuing to harass or agitate the disturbed individual?

2. *Take immediate corrective action.* Separate the combatants and isolate them sufficiently that they cannot see or hear each other. If arrest is warranted, do so and immediately have the offender removed from the vicinity. If medical help is needed, see that appropriate help is provided. If the crisis is an impending suicide, attempt to defuse any contributory factors, such as distraught friends or relatives whose presence and actions are making matters worse. Get those people out of the area. Taking a minimum of risk for your own safety, attempt to disarm or neutralize any individual who is intending immediate violence to self or another.

3. *Listen and observe.* In a crisis situation, one of your most effective techniques is to make a deliberate effort to see exactly what is happening. At this point, attempt to be totally nonjudgmental, and devote your full attention to what the principal actors in this crisis are saying and doing. You may be confronting a self-blaming victim of a sex crime who believes that the only way to preserve his honor is to kill himself. A person may have been disgraced by discovery of fraud by the auditors at the person's bank. If the crisis stems from a situation that has been exaggerated in the person's mind, you may be able to discuss the matter and bring it back into a more rational perspective.

4. *Employ crisis diffusion techniques.* When you are attempting to diffuse a crisis situation, there are a few suggestions for you to consider:

a. Keep your voice at a low volume and speak slowly. With an agitated adversary, your own attempts to outshout or dominate the conversation are not likely to work. Calmly repeating words of comfort or assurance or understanding may have a soothing effect on the agitated individual. If the individual wants to argue with you, it will be necessary for that person to quiet down to listen to what you have to say.

b. Nonverbal communications should indicate openness and willingness to listen. A posture of folded arms in a dominant position will not get the same positive results that you are likely to get by keeping your arms open and your gestures indicating that you are willing to negotiate. Consider your earlier exposure in this book to body language.

c. Make eye contact with the person you are addressing. This tends to underline your sincerity and willingness to listen. It also indicates to the subject that she or he has your full attention.

d. Touching the person you are talking with may help to keep the lines of communication open. This one you are going to have to play by ear. Some people will interpret your touching them as overly dominant or sexually aggressive. With others, there seems to flow the energy of a positive contact, and the person you are touching on the arm will probably give you more attention because there is physical contact as well as visual contact.

e. Attempt a compromise. If the person you are addressing feels that there is some dignity even to the situation of being taken into custody, you will probably have more success in keeping the person under physical control as well as emotional control.

5. *Follow-up.* Even if you have defused the crisis situation, you have probably not solved any problems. At best, you have more than likely only postponed a problem. At your earliest convenience, make follow-up reports and arrange for professionals in psychology or family counseling, or spiritual guidance, or whatever other need there appears to be, to pursue the matter so as to avoid any repeat performance of the crisis you have just addressed.

DOMESTIC DISPUTES AND VIOLENCE

Prior to police intervention, tensions and disagreements and violent behavior have more than likely been escalating for some time. There are usually deep-seated emotional problems that lead to conflict and disagreements, then escalate into violence of spouses against each other and then abuse of the children. If your response leads to nothing more than advising the parties to split for the night and then try to patch things up another day, you are not addressing the problem. In the past, everyone in the justice system, from police officer in the field to prosecuting attorney to judges, was reluctant to interfere with what seemed to all of us as "family matters." The approach today instead is when you see evidence of violence by one person against another, especially a child, take immediate action and arrest the perpetrator. In cases where there is no evidence of violence or behavior that warrants an immediate arrest, then it may be handled as a civil matter. But bear in mind that such a so-called "civil matter" still needs some attention and cannot be swept under the rug.

Upon arrival at the scene of a domestic dispute, do not take on the role of marriage and family counselor, or spiritual adviser or attorney. Your role is that of peace officer, and your primary responsibility is to preserve the peace. Watch and listen very carefully not only to what is happening in your presence but also to the undertones of what has been happening before your arrival. If the husband comes to the door and states that his wife and children are in bed asleep, you should ask to see them and satisfy yourself that there are no signs of physical abuse. Look around the premises for signs of fighting or objects having been thrown around. You are not searching, but merely taking advantage of the opportunity to survey the view in your plain sight.

If your observations indicate that the noise and shouting described by the neighbors has been an argument and there is no sign of physical abuse, then you might spend a little time with the participants to defuse the situation. Crisis intervention is another matter that requires special training and more time, but your purpose at this point is to de-escalate heightened tempers and to prevent the situation from getting worse. Suggest to the disputants that they consult an attorney or a family counselor, and do not leave until you are satisfied that you do not have a more serious problem.

At best, you have probably merely addressed the symptoms of more serious problems that exist in that family. Be careful not to take sides and make the problem worse than it is. Since the O.J. Simpson murder case, greater attention has been directed by the courts, legislatures of many states, certainly the police and prosecutors, and a great many people to the problem of domestic violence. More stringent laws have been passed and assertive enforcement directed at violations of those laws and others that have been on the books for decades but that received little or no attention. Publicity slogans, such as "spousal abuse is now against the law," have shown up around the nation on billboards and on television. In situations in the past the police would ask the victim of an assault whether or not she or he wished to prosecute, and if there was no affirmative answer, the officers would leave the victim to fend for herself (or himself). The buzzword was "If there is no complaining victim, there is no crime."

You have complete authority to arrest for suspicion of felonies whether they were committed in your presence or not. In some states, this latitude for suspicion arrests has been extended to include domestic violence misdemeanors. Warnings and no follow-up have failed in the past, and the current attitude is book and prosecute the offenders, even if the victim is unwilling to prosecute. "Don't ask for the victim's consent to make a domestic violence arrest. You don't ask a murder victim if he or she wants to prosecute, do you?"

Separate the protagonists and speak with them separately and privately, preferably out of sight and hearing distance from each other. Be careful not to make any movement or say anything that might be used against you in a claim of sexual harassment or physical abuse should that person later complain about your behavior in any way. (This is where a small tape recorder would come in handy.)

In a domestic dispute situation, you may find that you will become the object of attack. Love and hate are strong emotions and they do not seem to be entirely unrelated. One spouse may be verbally and physically abusing the other spouse until a third party comes along and attempts to defend the person under attack. Suddenly the third party—in this case a police officer—becomes a mutual threat, and both spouses join together to overcome that threat. This phenomenon occurs with alarming regularity.

Children may develop antipolice attitudes out of some domestic quarrel in which you as a police officer become involved because you have been called upon for help. This antagonism probably occurs through a transference process. The father may come home drunk and beat the mother. The children become emotionally involved because their security is threatened, or their father may find some reason to punish them in an unusually cruel manner. Eventually the mother calls the police because she cannot defend herself or the children.

You arrive and assess the situation. The mother consents to the arrest of the father, may even demand it under these conditions, because she fears for the safety of the children and herself. The man goes to jail, sometimes after a violent struggle with the arresting officers. Unfortunately, this often occurs in the presence of the children. Through this twist of fate, the police officers—not the father—become the hate objects of the children, because the officers further threatened their security by taking their father out of the home. The financial difficulties relative to posting bail or losing salary for the time in jail—possibly the loss of a job—are sometimes also blamed on the police officers.

Whenever possible during family fight situations, attempt to have the children removed from the scene. Whatever action that ensues is then less likely to involve them so emotionally. A violent arrest scene is not savored by anyone and perhaps it can be avoided altogether. During your assessment of the situation on your arrival, you may determine that a crime such as felonious spousal or child beating had taken place or was occurring during your arrival. Or you may observe that the environment is detrimental to the health and safety of the children, which may call for the arrest of one or both parents for maintaining an unfit home, for being intoxicated, or for performing lewd acts in the children's presence. In many situations, arrests will not be made, but many times such action is imperative.

Child protective service agencies and other agencies involved with possible domestic dispute cases should be alerted to your visit and actions taken at the scene so that they might investigate further, in case the situation signals a problem for them to check out. Their experience and training equip them with the ability to recognize trouble signs.

In an emotion-paced domestic quarrel, it is not unusual for one or both of the principals to demand the immediate arrest and incarceration of the other party. At this point, your discretionary powers come into play. Analyze the situation. What is the present physical and emotional state of the participants? What signs are there of physical injury? What evidence is there that the purported action took place? What do the witnesses—if any—say? What is likely to happen after you leave? Is a crime being committed in your presence? Do you have reasonable cause to arrest for a felony that did not occur in your presence? If you believe that an arrest is warranted and can be effected in a legal and ethical manner, then by all means make the arrest. If you believe that the arrest is not the answer to the problem, you may refuse to accept an arrest by a private person if you do not believe there is legal justification for the arrest.

The age-old problem of convincing an abused wife or child to actually go through with the arrest of the abuser is still very real, although victim-witness and abused persons support groups have met with some success in advertisements stating that "wife beating is now against the law," and "if you really love him, have him arrested so that he can get help." You are on the horns of a dilemma when you witnessed nothing but you are sure that you are going to make a return trip if you do not settle the matter on your first visit. You and your fellow officers should confer with your local prosecuting attorney for advice on how to proceed in this type of a situation. You may be preventing a more serious crime, even a homicide.

Another frequently used alternative is to advise the parties to come into the office of the police department or the prosecuting attorney (depending on your own department practices) during the next business day and to discuss the matter at that time. Then, if it is determined that an arrest should be made, steps will be taken to secure a warrant and effect the arrest. This procedure gives the principals some time to reflect on the matter and to make a rational decision that will have long-lasting effects. If you use this alternative and so advise the principals, you may still need to warn them that if you have to return, you will be compelled to reassess and will have to make some arrests after all. Remember, though, do not make a promise that you cannot keep. Once you have made such a statement, you may be committed to take action or lose your effectiveness. Idle threats are more devastating than is taking no action at all.

Landlord–Tenant Disputes

You are not a bill collector. You do not have the authority to evict tenants from other persons' homes or apartments unless you are the civil division deputy from the sheriff's department or marshal's office who does so by court order. You act as an agent of the jurisdiction for which you serve in your official capacity, not as a personal representative of any landlord or tenant. As with any other incident requiring your attendance, your role is that of police officer to preserve the peace.

When responding to a dispute involving property rights and eviction notices or similar disturbances, approach both adversaries and advise them that your presence is to keep the peace and to prevent the commission of a crime. If they ask for legal advice other than an explanation of the criminal laws they may be contemplating violating, refer them to an attorney of their choice. Legal services are generally available to indigent persons at nominal costs, and small claims court actions for lawsuits involving amounts of money that would probably include the cost of rent may be instituted at a cost of just a few dollars.

There are certain times when a landlord may lock a tenant out of a room or apartment and hold certain luggage and other property to enforce payment of rent. Sometimes one of the people involved—either landlord or tenant—may be guilty of trespass, depending on the rental or lease agreement and other considerations. Keep the peace and advise the disputants to contact their respective attorneys. Even though you may know the correct answers to their various questions about the law, you are not an attorney and cannot give legal advice.

In some disputes in which tempers flare and the participants appear to be at an impasse, it may be necessary to order an end to the argument to avoid more serious problems that would inevitably lead to an arrest of one or both of them. The landlord may seek assistance through the courts, with eviction proceedings, and secure the services of the sheriff or marshal. Either party may seek legal advice. Both must be advised to discontinue their argument.

Mechanics' and Innkeepers' Liens

An auto mechanic or service station operator may retain custody of an automobile until the costs of repairs are either paid for or some arrangement agreeable to mechanic and owner is worked out for payment. Operators of hotels and rooming houses may hold certain belongings of the tenants to enforce collection of rent. All merchants, business owners, and others who provide goods and services are entitled to just payment for those goods and services. Many times you will find that the business operators have had similar problems more than once and that they have had sound legal advice, but occasionally you will encounter the businessperson who will take every opportunity to fleece unsuspecting victims under the guise of legitimate business.

When you are called to the scene at which the matter appears to involve nonpayment of charges for merchandise or repairs, or some other type of service, question all participants and witnesses carefully. Although you may not act as a bill collector in a civil matter, many nonpayment situations are nothing more than flagrant acts of theft or "defrauding an innkeeper" violations. If there is some dispute regarding charges, they may involve an amount that the party refusing to pay claims is too high. Whatever their statements, advise them that certain property may be held to enforce payment of debts. Also advise them of the laws concerning theft. If the matter cannot be amicably settled by the participants in your presence, advise them to seek legal advice. In the meantime, they should usually pay the bill to gain possession of the property being held and to avoid a charge of theft. If the charges are too high, a judge or jury would have to decide that point. Remind them that small claims courts are available for deciding matters such as fairness of charges for facilities and services.

Repossession Disputes

Modern conditional sales contracts have been standardized and designed to meet most conditions that one comes across in a contractual sale. They have been modified and clarified so many times that many of them are quite standard and free of "loopholes" that might render them invalid. About the only method that can be used to nullify the average contract is to show that some type of fraud was involved to induce a person to enter the agreement.

The title of the property covered in most sales contracts rests with the seller until the total debt is paid. Any default in payment is generally covered in the contract, which provides for repossession. There are only three persons who may legally repossess: (1) the seller and his full-time employees, (2) a successor in interest (buyer of the contract from the original seller) and his full-time employees, or (3) licensed repossessors acting on behalf of their clients who are either sellers or successors in interest.

If a repossession is made peaceably, but in violation of the conditions of a sales contract, there is civil recourse. If the person in possession of the property does not peaceably accede to the repossession, the repossessor must go to the courts for judicial direction. At that stage, any legal repossession will be made by the bailiff of the court. The bailiff may use whatever force is necessary to enforce the court order, as directed by the court and by guidelines for repossession. The repossession may be made prior to a court hearing if the possessor waives the right to a hearing. Otherwise, a hearing must be held with the judge making a decision as to repossession rights during the hearing and then issuing an order as to whether or not there will be a repossession.

The repossessor cannot enter private property to repossess and cannot use force (this does not refer to the bailiff, who acts by court order). Usually, a repossession is made surreptitiously. If the repossessor is able lawfully and peaceably to gain possession of the property (dominion and control), the repossession is complete, and any effort to retake the property would not be lawful. The buyer who is in possession of the property to be repossessed has a right to object to the repossession at the time it is taking place either orally or physically. If the objection is made before the repossession is accomplished, then the repossessor must discontinue the act of taking the property in dispute. The repossessor should also report the action to the police department as soon as possible to avoid the risk of being charged with theft.

Other property, which is not subject to repossession, but happens to be inside a repossessed vehicle, for example, is the property of its owner and must be returned to that owner on demand. If a third person is in possession of property to be repossessed at the time the repossession is attempted, that person has the same rights as the buyer. If the property is in storage, or in a commercial parking lot, the person in charge may not give permission and cannot allow the repossession.

MENTALLY AND EMOTIONALLY DISTURBED INDIVIDUALS

Civil laws usually provide for temporary custody of individuals who appear to be in need of immediate emergency observation because of some emotional or mental breakdown. They are called to police attention usually through some erratic behavior or act of violence that the subject's friends or relatives cannot handle without assistance.

In some states, the patrol officer is empowered to take people suspected of being in need of emergency care to a psychiatric clinic and have them held for observation by psychiatrists, if the officer believes such action is necessary to the health and safety of the subject or other persons. In some cases, it requires more formal action, such as court hearings similar to a trial, which will require testimony of witnesses as to aberrant behavior and other actions of the person alleged to be in need of psychiatric care.

When responding to a call involving an individual who appears mentally or emotionally disturbed, be extremely careful to handle the person with understanding, diplomacy, and tact. Symptoms may include such things as dramatic and sudden changes in behavior; loss of memory; mistreatment of a loved one; a sudden, impulsive act of theft; extreme depression; or anxiety that is out of proportion to the circumstances that appear to be causing the anxiety. There may suddenly be a strong dependence on someone to make simple decisions or an intense suspicion or distrust of theirs or an intense feeling that someone is plotting against the individual. The individual may talk to himself or hear voices, or he may be displaying dangerous or belligerent behavior for no apparent reason. The mentally or emotionally disturbed individual may be in a very docile mood for a while and then become extremely violent without any apparent cause. For that reason, whenever you believe you have such a person in custody, use ample restraining equipment as a precautionary measure for his protection as well as your own. Be aware, also, that certain symptoms may be mistaken as indicators of mental or emotional disorders; for example, the sweating or twitching of a diabetic, the delirium that accompanies fever or severe infection, the irritability of the person suffering from meningitis, or the violence or confused state of an epileptic.

When arrested, some felons may feign mental illness in an attempt to avoid punishment for their crime, using the pretense of disorientation as a defense against the claim that they formed specific intent to commit their crimes. To place such a suspect in a psychiatric ward might provide the subject with his defense. He can, for example, show that you were obviously impressed with his lack of mental or emotional control because you placed him in a psychiatric ward for mental observation. If there are obvious manifestations of mental or emotional upset, you have no choice but to place him under mental observation. But if there is some doubt and the case is an extremely important one, it might be sounder to place him in an isolated cell and immediately consult with the prosecuting attorney. The attorney may decide to have a psychiatrist conduct an immediate examination and make his evaluation, to assure proper care and treatment for the suspect if he is truly in need of psychiatric care. Some jurisdictions have a standing procedure that requires an immediate psychiatric evaluation at any time a criminal homicide suspect is arrested. This policy allows the officer to obtain a determination as to the suspect's mental state as soon after the commission of the crime as possible. At the same time, the act of causing the psychiatric evaluation carries with it no reflection of any opinions the arresting officer may or may not have had.

As an aid in understanding the mentally and emotionally disturbed, the following descriptions and definitions are presented from a layperson's point of view. They are merely items of information, and in no way should they ever be used as a guide for making any type of diagnosis.

A *psychosis* is a gross and persistent falsification of conventional reality that leaves the person unable to manage conventional reality with any degree of effectiveness. The major components of psychosis are delusions and hallucinations. A *delusion* is a faulty belief that is motivated primarily by the individual's needs or wishes and has no basis in fact. An *hallucination,* conversely, is usually manifested in a visual image that is quite vivid and real to the individual who experiences it. The hallucination does not actually exist, but there is probably some correspondence between the hallucination and some actual sensory input, and the individual is willing to take some action based upon that perceptual experience. Many people have hallucinations when encountering unusual situations and are not necessarily suffering from psychosis, but the hallucinations do not recur once the situations have passed. Hallucinations include those visions that appear in the middle of a desert highway as puddles of water or an oasis in the middle of sand dunes. Another hallucination might be something that looks like a prowler, which is actually a hibiscus shrub brushing against the screen. Psychoses are mental illnesses.

Paranoia is a set of fixed delusional beliefs that are accompanied by clear and orderly thinking outside the delusion system. The true paranoid, or "classical paranoid," as some psychologists prefer, may be highly intelligent and so persuasive that he will successfully recruit other persons to help him in his war against his enemies. He may not be identified as easily as the individual with a *paranoid reaction,* who does not handle the problem with as much logic or intelligence as the true paranoid. Paranoia manifests itself in inferences and beliefs that the subject is "being talked about," "being made fun of," or "is the object of a hate campaign," or that someone is trying to get rid of him. The paranoid has been described as "vigilant, suspicious, distrustful, insecure, and chronically anxious." According to some theorists, the paranoid may justify his intense hatred of some object, such as Hitler's hatred of the Jews, by stating, "I hate you so intensely because you hate me and you are trying to get rid of me."

Schizophrenia is a thinking disorder. According to some experts, approximately 80 percent of the mentally ill population is schizophrenic. There are several subcategories of schizophrenia, such as the catatonic state, demonstrated by the patient's rigidly held position for sometimes interminable periods of time, and the hebephrenic state, in which the subject continually acts childlike and silly. Indications of the schizophrenic condition appear in three different ways: (1) The subject's language may be rambling or tangential; he may make up meaningless rhymes, or echo everything he hears. (2) The subject may show his split personality by an incongruence between his expressed ideas and his emotional responses, which indicate two thought processes operating simultaneously. (3) The subject may isolate or alienate himself from the rest of society and pull himself into his personal shell.

A person who is suffering from a *psychoneurotic condition,* or a *neurosis,* is most likely to be observed in a continuous state of anxiety. The erratic behavior would more than likely be displayed by reaction to the anxiety in the form of rationalization, projection, or displacement. The individual may be shaking uncontrollably. Another symptom of the neurosis is depression without explanation. Reaction to a police contact might be exaggerated by a psychoneurotic condition, and the person might react violently to an arrest or a field interview or some type of personal confrontation.

As a field officer, you will not be expected to diagnose the individual, nor are you expected to distinguish between the many variations of psychoses and neuroses. Your principal concern is for your own safety and then that of the individual, and making an effort to see that the person receives appropriate professional attention.

You are likely to encounter the mentally or emotionally disturbed individual under almost any type of circumstances. Many people are emotionally upset for the moment because of the nature of the situation, such as an intense family fight or a repossession confrontation, but they return to a state of relative normality fairly quickly. Whenever you encounter a person who appears to exhibit a mental or emotional problem more deep-seated than the immediate circumstance warrants, the following guidelines may assist you:

1. Approach the subject with extreme caution. Maintain a calm and casual manner.
2. Speak to the subject by name, if you know it. Your tone of voice should be soothing, but firm and businesslike.
3. Say or do nothing that might threaten or intimidate.
4. Avoid arguing or scolding the subject, and don't allow anyone else to do so.
5. Make use of friends or relatives who know how to talk to, and deal with, the subject, unless there is friction between them. The subject might have more trust and confidence in you if you appear to be getting along with the friends or relatives.
6. Whenever possible, try to stall until you have a follow-up officer on the scene. This type of situation might be more volatile than a routine arrest.
7. If the situation warrants it, and you take the subject into custody, do so carefully. Avoid pain-producing holds, if possible, and keep your gun and other weapons out of the subject's reach.

8. When you transfer custody to psychiatric personnel, give these people as much information about the symptoms you observed and all the details about their behavior. This will help in the diagnosis. Do the same when you prepare your reports.

ALCOHOLIC BEVERAGE CONTROL INVESTIGATION AND ENFORCEMENT

Among the states there is considerable variety in the laws and their application. Laws generally prescribe the conditions under which alcoholic beverages are dispensed and distributed, the people who may serve and be served the beverages, and numerous license regulations. Licensed premises must abide by certain rules of decorum to assure against their becoming "disorderly houses," and the hours of sale are also regulated.

Rather than address the specific laws, which might not apply in the same manner from one state to another, or from one jurisdiction to another, this section deals with the general investigative techniques of alcoholic beverage control violations. The format and information contained in this section is based on an enforcement manual of the California Department of Alcoholic Beverage Control.[1]

Liquor Violations: General Investigative Techniques

Identification, Preservation, and Examination of Evidence. Adequate evidence must be collected to prove a violation and sustain a conviction.

1. Seize and book into evidence the alcoholic beverage (in the original container when possible).
2. Mark for evidence the same as any other item of evidence.
3. Seal the bottle in the presence of the person from whom seized, if possible, or in the presence of a witness.
4. Present a receipt for the evidence seized.
5. If the drink is a mixed one, immediately remove ice, pour the drink into an evidence bottle, and seal.
6. If necessary to establish alcoholic content, such as if you did not observe the bartender pour from a labeled bottle, taste and smell the beverage. Use a small straw and beware of the danger of germs or other harmful matter.
7. As soon as practicable, have the laboratory analyze the beverage to establish alcoholic content.

Establishing Age and/or Identity. For a licensee or employee:

1. Obtain name, age, address, telephone number, length of time with this establishment, and length of time in the liquor business.
2. Obtain the hours of duty for the person identified.
3. Observe and record the physical condition of the licensee or the server (or both), including vision, hearing, and state of sobriety.

4. Observe and record the condition of other individuals served by this employee or licensee, such as for a violation of serving to an obviously intoxicated person or an underaged person.

For minors:

1. Determine what documents were shown for identification, and examine them.
   a. Check carefully for alterations.
   b. Seize all false identification documents.
   c. Look for additional identification documents. Many minors will use a false ID for alcohol purchases, but will use authentic documents for all other occasions.
2. Question the minor on his or her age and determine if the server checked for identification prior to service.
3. If possible, verify the subject's age with a relative (by phone, if necessary, but by follow-up investigation prior to the court date).
4. A birth certificate may be used to establish age only; supplemental documents are necessary for establishing identity.
5. Carefully scrutinize all documents for validity, and ask the subject such questions as middle name, home address, and date of birth, and compare photographs with the subject.
6. Marriage status does not affect minimum legal age, and statements by other persons present do not legally verify age. Documents are required.
7. A person who refuses to present proof of age will be assumed by the server to be underaged. The establishment is authorized to demand documentary evidence.
8. Note the appearance and clothing of the minor.
9. Thoroughly search for other identifying documents.
10. Secure and record names and addresses of witnesses and prepare a complete report.

Essential Facts for Your Report

1. Condition of the premises: lighting, size of crowd, size of the bar, and general demeanor of the crowd.
2. Number of employees present.
3. Appearance and demeanor of the buyer/patron in violation.
4. The order as written (secure the actual check, if one is used).
5. Identify the type of beverage or name the cocktail, including the ingredients.
6. How was the beverage served? in a bottle? in a glass? packaged?
7. Indicate the time the order was served.
8. Where did the beverage come from (back bar, speed rack, shelf, or refrigerator)?
9. Cost of the merchandise. Secure the receipt, if there is one.

a. Amount requested by the seller.

b. Type and amount of money presented by the buyer.

c. Amount of change, if any.

10. If the license covers sale but not consumption on premises, wait and observe consumption on the premises.

11. Citation of arrest of the subject(s).

12. Search the premises thoroughly.

13. Secure signed statements when possible (remember *Miranda*).

14. Inspect and verify liquor license (type, number, and expiration date).

15. Note the correct time.

    a. Compare this with the clock on the premises.

    b. What time does the watch of the server indicate?

16. Note whether the licensee was on the premises and whether he or she took part in the violation.

17. Establish whether the licensee was in a position where he or she should have observed the violation. Was the person exercising correct management control, or is there criminal responsibility?

ABANDONED VEHICLE ABATEMENT

Trash should be removed from the streets, and from both public and private property, even if it carries a license plate. The idea of this type of activity is to keep vehicles off the street and out of public view when it is apparent that the owners have abandoned them or when it is apparent that there is no intent to make them operable again. Other purposes of vehicle abatement are to reclaim salvageable metals, dispose of neighborhood eyesores and attractive nuisances for children, reduce rodent and insect infestations, and reduce health hazards.

Certain legal proceedings are required, which usually consist of notification of the owner, waiting out specific periods of time to show noncompliance, having the property towed to government-subsidized locations, and holding public auctions, the proceeds of which go to the general fund. Your primary consideration should be public safety and the general welfare of the community.

NUISANCES

There are two general types of nuisances that require the attention of the police department: the public nuisance and the attractive nuisance. Both may involve criminal code violations—and they often do—but they also involve civil, nonpolice matters.

The public nuisance often involves misdemeanor crime violations such as disturbance of the peace, boisterous conduct, loud and unusual noises during prohibited hours, drunkenness, assaults, delinquency of minors, vagrancy, and vice violations. It encompasses a multitude of encroachments on the peace and dignity of the community at large as well as the many individuals who are disturbed.

General public nuisances involve law violations such as offensive advertising signs that are too large or placed in locations where ordinances prohibit them, disagreeable odors caused by abandoned refuse in a vacant lot, automobiles that are either abandoned or placed on blocks in the street for repairs that never seem to get done, and the maintenance of an excessive number of animals for the size of the house or lot. An abandoned building that becomes the residence of drunkards and vagrants may soon present itself as a public nuisance.

One type of public nuisance that presents a special problem is the "party house." It is usually occupied by two or more people who legitimately pay the rent and then have parties involving more people than the place can accommodate. These often become too raucous and noisy. The place might become a gathering place for people to violate liquor laws ostensibly under the guise of "private property asylum" or a place for numerous narcotics and dangerous drug law violations. In some jurisdictions, it is possible to cause the owners and occupants of the homes or apartments involved to discontinue the nuisance or to vacate the premises. This action is possible if it can be shown to the court that the "party house" threatens and generally disturbs the "public" in the persons of the surrounding residents and others who are disturbed.

An attractive nuisance is usually given that designation because it is a condition or place that attracts children and poses an imminent threat to their health and safety (see Figure 7–3). The nuisance may in itself be entirely legal or innocent, but by its own nature it attracts young people who cannot understand the significance of the threatened danger. A legal definition of "attractive nuisance" has been presented as "an unnatural condition that attracts infants who do not understand the danger, and injury results because of the condition." Here is a list of what might be considered attractive nuisances under certain conditions:

1. Building under construction
2. Abandoned or unoccupied buildings that have not been adequately secured to prevent entry
3. Swimming pools without adequate fencing, gate locks, and reasonable means of prohibiting swimming without responsible persons in attendance
4. Accumulations of water of unknown, or excessive, depth
5. Piles of dirt, sand, or gravel
6. Excavations
7. Ladders and scaffolding
8. Dead trees and accumulations of dead foliage
9. Telephone and power poles with cleats close to the ground, making it possible for easy climbing
10. Unattended construction machinery or farm implements that can be started without an ignition key

Some attractive nuisances are prohibited by specific criminal laws, such as an abandoned refrigerator with the locking mechanism left intact, or an unattended motor vehicle with the motor running. They should be diligently investigated and the laws

Figure 7–3 Children are always attracted to the water. (Courtesy Metro-Dade Police Department.)

enforced. Most of this conduct is prosecutable under civil law, in tort actions. There are three types of conduct that may be considered cause for action: (1) intentional, (2) negligence, and (3) acts of peril. The third type involves certain situations when the defendant may be considered liable without fault, or culpability. Nevertheless, the loss of the lawsuit means two things: someone—probably a child—suffered the loss of life or some form of injury, and the defendant suffers the loss of money.

Your role in this matter is twofold. You should attempt to protect children by frequently checking the locations of such attractive nuisances, and you should remind the owners or other persons in charge of the nuisances of their existence and the possibility that they may suffer losses in tort actions. Whenever children or other persons are found at those locations, they should be told to leave, and the parents of the children should be notified of your action so that they may attempt to exercise appropriate controls to prevent tragedies from occurring. When notifying the owners or other responsible persons of the existence of nuisance conditions, prepare reports to permanently record the fact that you fulfilled your responsibility at that point. If the hazardous condition continues to exist, more formal action may be taken in the form of registered letters directed to the offenders or, possibly, civil action filed by the city attorney on behalf of the people to protect the lives and limbs of their children. Of course, private individuals will probably also take action on their own in aggravated situations.

PARADES AND SPECIAL EVENTS

The primary police responsibility at any special event, such as a parade, festival, or other occasion involving a greater than usual number of people, is to expedite vehicular and pedestrian traffic, and to keep the traffic lanes open for emergency vehicles. Spectator safety is paramount, particularly the safety of young children who may not be capable of looking after their own safety. Direct your full attention on the people, utilizing crowd and traffic control procedures.

FIRE SCENES

A fire scene is the responsibility of the fire department commanders and their personnel. They handle the rescue operations and extinguish the blaze. The police responsibility is the same as at any other location where crowds of people congregate: vehicle and pedestrian traffic and crowd control.

Upon your arrival at the scene, contact the fire commander, who will be in charge of the overall operations. Divert traffic away from the scene to prevent any further damage or injuries that might have already occurred. Keep the streets open to allow for the ingress and egress of fire vehicles, ambulances, and any other vehicles and equipment required by the fire department. Above all, protect the water hoses against tampering and do not allow any vehicles to run over them. Look out for, and interview, suspicious persons who might have started the fire, if it later turns out to be a case of arson. Instruct passersby and casual spectators to leave the immediate area of the fire to prevent any major disaster. Once you have handled the matters required of you in your police officer capacity, contact the ranking fire department officer and determine if there is any need for your assistance in rescue operations or any security matters involving the fire equipment or valuable property at the scene. If the situation warrants it, you may find it necessary to declare the area of the fire a disaster area and then to enforce the area control diligently as long as the emergency exists.

RESCUE AND FIRST AID

A police officer is authorized and—in some states—legally required to administer first aid and to perform rescue operations whenever the need arises. One of the prime considerations to bear in mind relative to that statement is that first aid does not mean to practice medicine or in any way to exceed the limitations of "first aid" treatment. Once you assume such treatment, you are liable for exercising reasonable care, which has clearly been defined and described in your training. Any rescue operations are subject to the same requirements.

Some people carry identification bracelets or necklaces or cards in their wallets that indicate a special problem that rescue personnel should be aware of (see Figure 7–4). Problems might be allergies to bee stings or certain medications, such as penicillin, sulfa, or antihistamines. The individual may be suffering from hemophilia, a heart condition, diabetes, or epilepsy; be wearing contact lenses or taking anticoagu-

Figure 7–4 Medical identification bracelet.

lants; or be breathing through a hole in his or her throat. Several organizations provide such bracelets and other devices and maintain a 24-hour call service for special notifications. One of the more widely known of those services is Medic-Alert. Whenever you encounter anyone who appears to be in need of medical attention, look for the special identification.

COURTESY SERVICES

There are a number of types of what I call "courtesy services" that have been performed by police officers for many years, principally because they have seemingly always been doing them. These services consist of such activities as providing bodyguard protection to satisfy a politician's ego more than for protective reasons, escort services for dignitaries when no security hazard exists, taxicab service to take politicians and other government officials to airports and other places mainly to signal to all who watch that these are important people.

It is a physical impossibility for the police department to provide all the services that would be requested once the service is started. Policy decisions should be made by your department as to which services will be provided; this listing should be communicated to all members of the department. Then those services should be uniformly provided by all officers. Personalized service for certain individuals merely opens the door for a long series of "modifications" in policy and procedure for certain individuals on a favoritism basis.

Merely having police officers on duty and on constant patrol throughout the various parts of the city encourages some people to believe that the officers are there to serve their whims. Such people do not consider any of the myriad other responsibilities with which they are charged. "They are on duty already, so why not have them do it?" may be asked by a councilman who has no idea of the full extent of the burden already carried by the police department. A simple reply to that question is: "Why not, indeed?" Using that oversimplified logic, why not assign certain of those services to the fire department, recreation leaders, license and building inspectors, or anyone else who is "on duty already"? The duties of the police department are defined, and they must be limited if the department is to be held responsible for the safety of the people in the community and their property. Escort service, messenger service, and a wide variety of other services are regularly provided by private enterprise for profit—or loss. Taxicabs are in the business of transporting persons for hire. Is it equitable for the police department to compete with private enterprise by providing free services to some people, while most others utilize the facilities of private businesses? Many of these services are not police responsibilities, and their perpetuation should not be tolerated. Tradition may be a safe answer to the question "Why are these services performed?" However, tradition does not necessarily offer the correct answer. Consider the advisability of performing these courtesy services; then respond to them in accordance with the policies of your own department.

Many courtesy services are performed by the patrol officer as a matter of routine, most of them because it has "always been done." Whichever of these services your department performs should be executed with tact, diplomacy, and courtesy. They are free services, and there should be no expectation of anything in return.

1. Check a house to see if the vacationer, who is calling from about a hundred miles away, did remember to turn off the gas furnace and lock all the doors.

2. Deliver a message to someone who has no telephone but who is needed in the office because of a company emergency that cannot wait.

3. Deliver a death message to the wife of a laborer who had been buried alive in a landslide. In such situations, consider stopping along the way to pick up the family minister, rabbi, or priest for spiritual guidance to the survivors. Neighbors may lessen the strain. Sometimes it may be wise to notify the fire department rescue team that you are going to deliver a message in the event that that unit is needed for an emergency in case of a cardiac arrest or other side effect from the shock. If the person to receive the message is known to be gravely ill, it may be advisable to call the family doctor to accompany you when you deliver the message or have him or her make the delivery.

4. Help a bedridden invalid who needs immediate assistance in securing an emergency delivery of medicine, or in being lifted back into bed after falling out. One serious problem that could result from giving such assistance is the creation of a dependence by the invalid on the service provided on a few occasions by the district police officer. If such a dependence becomes a habit and is allowed by the department, the invalid might someday call for emergency service that the department cannot provide because all the officers are busy, and because of such failure to respond, the invalid's condition may worsen or he or she may die. The question may be asked in court: "Why was the police department negligent in not responding to that individual's call for help?"

5. Escort a frightened or cautious woman or child down a darkened alley to her apartment in a high-crime area when a sex killer is at large.

6. Give directions or provide other informational services for guests or tourists in town. In many cases, the police officer on the street represents the entire community to the inquirer, and that officer's attitude is interpreted as the attitude of the entire community.

7. Help someone who has locked himself out of his home or automobile to break in. Some burglars and thieves have actually been assisted by unsuspecting

police officers who have been entirely innocent of any criminal involvement. Some persons have sought the assistance of the police in gaining entry, then complained about the method used by the officer who assisted them. This type of service should be strictly on an emergency basis. Occasions when there is clearly an indicated need for your assistance would be when a person's life may be endangered, which might be the case when a child is locked inside a car with the motor running, or when a person who has locked himself inside a house has indicated his intention to commit suicide.

Whenever you assist a person in gaining entry in a routine problem situation, be sure to get satisfactory proof of identification and ownership of the property, and limit your participation to advice except in unusual cases, as with elderly persons or invalids. When you actually assist in such matters, consider the advisability of having the persons assisted sign a waiver relieving you from liability. This procedure may help to avoid a later complaint.

ASSISTING PUBLIC UTILITIES AND SERVICE AGENCIES

Following are guidelines for responding to utility or other public service problems:

1. *Street lights out or damaged.* The lighting is to provide people with sufficient illumination to assure them of safety on the streets. The lights should be replaced as quickly as possible. Look for malicious damage, which may indicate some purpose to use the darkness as a cover for illicit activities.

2. *Electricity out and electric wires down.* The line that is out may be providing electricity for a kidney machine or an emergency surgery, as well as for hundreds of homes and apartments. Locate the wire that is down or the place where the cable has been cut and notify the power company immediately. While waiting for the arrival of the repair crews, keep curious onlookers at least 10 feet away (the farther the safer), and take whatever precautions that are necessary to protect the area. Electric power is energy in motion, as are moving automobiles or flying bullets. It travels like water through a hose, but it is deadly power, sometimes fatal.

Have the dispatcher contact the power company and ask for instructions on what it would prefer that you do to keep the wires under control and to prevent serious injury to yourself as well as to others. While waiting for the crew to arrive, (a) keep the area lighted if during the hours of darkness, (b) keep yourself and others clear of metal or water, and (c) avoid being between any two wires or between a wire and the ground.

3. *Damaged water mains or fire hydrants.* When water mains or fire hydrants are broken, there are two dangerous effects that should be overcome as soon as possible. One is an almost sudden drop in water pressure in that area; the second is extensive soil erosion, particularly on a hillside. Either could be disastrous if not handled as an emergency situation. It may be wise to evacuate homes on hillsides below the broken main because of possible earth movement problems.

4. *Telephone lines down.* Telephone repair crews should be notified as soon as the broken line or cable is discovered. Many emergency services depend on the telephone as their only means of communication and cannot function effectively without it. Watch for electric wires that might also be present.

5. *Broken gas pipes.* Domestic natural gas has odor-producing gas added and it is easy to detect if present in any quantity. The natural gas itself is odorless and may not be detected as easily, but lines extending within populated areas usually have the easily detected odor. If possible, locate the source and extent of the leak. Immediately notify the gas company and ask for any special instructions it may wish to give you pending the arrival of repair crews. Immediately evacuate persons from the vicinity of the broken line. Instruct the people to turn off all fires or flames, to refrain from smoking, and to avoid doing anything that might cause a spark, including turning electric switches off or on. If the gas leak seems to be inside a building or confined space, do whatever you can to allow maximum ventilation.

6. *Defective streets and sidewalks.* Holes and broken places in cement or asphalt may not be readily visible to the pedestrians who use the sidewalk or the drivers who use the street. Any defects in either of these surfaces should be reported as quickly as possible to the street department so that they may be repaired. If they are allowed to go unrepaired or with no warning barricades or lights of some type, the city might be held civilly liable in the event a lawsuit is initiated.

7. *Traffic signs, signals, other controls.* There is obviously a purpose for these various traffic control implements. Allowing any one to go for any length of time in a state of disrepair, or to be missing altogether, could result in traffic congestion or a serious traffic accident. Some signs lose their painted surface or their reflective quality, or they become illegible because of overhanging tree branches or shrubbery. If there is a need for them where they are, the traffic control devices should be functioning fully as intended.

HANDLING ANIMAL CALLS

How to handle stray animals, if this is a police department function in your jurisdiction at all, varies with local laws and policies. Animals that are suspected of having rabies require special handling and quarantine for a required period of time. If it is necessary to dispose of an animal suspected of having rabies, the head should not be destroyed, since the brain is used for analysis. If you must dispose of an animal, never do it in the presence of children.

SUMMARY

Although the activities covered in this chapter are handled frequently by patrol officers, none can be considered "routine." The people and places are different and each situation is unique.

Each lost child and missing person may not be lost at all, except to those who are searching. Leaving home or another place may be by choice and for a reason, such as mental or physical illness or abuse. Finding the lost child or adult may be no small task, but you should also inquire into the underlying circumstances of his or her departure.

Civil disputes and domestic violence may involve people with severe emotional problems, or drug or alcohol abuse. Crises arise because of conflicts between people with psychological or emotional problems. Each situation involves a different set of dynamics.

Alcoholic beverage control presents an entirely different set of demands on you as a field officer. Children or other innocent victims may be involved. The "over-poured" drunk or the person who abuses these drugs with the sole objective of getting drunk becomes the batterer or the DUI, or both, and you can see that many problems are interrelated.

The most important lesson to learn in this chapter is to approach each incident with open eyes and ears—and an open mind to something you may never have encountered before.

EXERCISES AND STUDY QUESTIONS

1. How would you search for a child who may be hiding from the police?
2. When searching for a child who is missing from his or her home, where should you begin the search?
3. Where would you go if you were a child who had decided to run away from home?
4. Look around your own home and list all those places a small child might hide in each room.
5. What is the purpose for questioning people with records as child molesters who happen to live near a missing child's home?
6. What is the routine procedure for handling a missing adult in your department? Under what conditions would you delay the search, and for how long would you delay?
7. How does your department deal with nonbelligerent drunks?
8. From what other ailments might a person be suffering who appears to be intoxicated?
9. List at least five additional indicators that might lead to a drinking driver arrest but are not listed in the text.
10. What is your principal responsibility at the scene of a domestic dispute?
11. What type of information should the telephone operator/dispatcher attempt to learn before dispatching a unit to the scene of a domestic dispute?
12. To what extent, if any, may a police officer give marital or legal advice?
13. If you must arrest someone at the scene of a violent domestic dispute, what should you do about the children?
14. What property may a landlord hold to enforce payment of rent?

15. What is a mechanic's lien, and how is it enforced?

16. What must the repossessor of an automobile do if the buyer who is home at the time refuses to allow the repossessor into the garage where the auto is parked?

17. Who may use force to accomplish a repossession?

18. How do you check for the authenticity of an identification card or a driver's license issued in your state?

19. How would you preserve the evidence if you were to arrest an underage person in possession of a rum and cola drink?

20. What type of document would you accept as valid proof of age?

21. If you arrest an underage person in a bar, may you also arrest or cite the person who served the drink?

22. What is the purpose for abandoned vehicle abatement?

23. What is the definition of attractive nuisance? List 10 places or conditions in your neighborhood that would fit that category.

24. What is your role as a police officer at a fire scene?

25. List 25 legitimate public courtesy services that your department should provide.

26. Give an example of how you would talk with an arguing couple to defuse the argument.

27. What is your primary role in crisis intervention?

28. What are the advantages of touching the person with whom you are talking during a crisis intervention situation? What are the disadvantages?

29. What is the difference between psychosis and neurosis?

30. Upon your arrival at the scene of a reported domestic dispute, you see that a woman or child shows signs of having been very recently beaten. What should you do?

REFERENCES

Abnormal Psychology, Current Perspectives. New York: Random House (Communications Research Machines, Inc.[CRM Books]). 1972.

AGUILERA, DONNA C., and JANICE M. MESSICK. *Crisis Intervention: Theory and Methodology,* 3rd ed. St. Louis, Mo.: C.V. Mosby, 1978.

COLEMAN, JAMES C. *Abnormal Psychology and Modern Life,* 5th ed. Glenview, Ill.: Scott, Foresman, 1976.

DAVISON, GERALD C., and JOHN M. NEALE. *Abnormal Psychology: An Experimental Clinical Approach.* New York: John Wiley, 1974.

DIXON, SAMUEL L. *Working with People in Crisis: Theory and Practice.* St. Louis, Mo.: C. V. Mosby, 1979.

"Facts about Suicide and Some Warning Signs." *Today's Health,* June 1967, p. 33.

LOS ANGELES POLICE DEPARTMENT. *Daily Training Bulletins,* Vols. I and II. Springfield, Ill.: Charles C. Thomas, 1954, 1958.

MATTHEWS, ROBERT A., and LLOYD W. ROWLAND. *How to Recognize and Handle Abnormal People: A Manual for the Police Officer.* New York: National Association for Mental Health, 1960.

STATE OF CALIFORNIA. Department of Alcoholic Beverage Control. *Enforcement Manual.* Sacramento, Calif.: State Printing Office, 1994.

FOOTNOTES

1. State of California, Department of Alcoholic Beverage Control, *Enforcement Manual* (Sacramento, Calif.: State Printing Office, 1994), pp. 11, 12.

C H A P T E R   8

CRIMES IN PROGRESS

*I*NTRODUCTION

There are few calls for police service that more directly involve the field police officer than the "crime in progress" call. The response must be immediate and with the precision of fine machinery. Time is precious. Response time is often the determinant of whether the victim will suffer death or serious injury. The element of time also determines whether the culprit will be apprehended at the scene or elsewhere, if at all.

Evidence is also disappearing and being destroyed as the minutes tick away. Many items are of a short-lived nature, such as wet footprints on a dry tile floor that will evaporate as the sun comes up or the fiber from a perpetrator's sweater snagged on a tree branch that will soon fly away. All too often, the arriving officers and other auxiliary personnel as well as the various media representatives all trying to get an "exclusive" for their particular media will destroy existing evidence and drag into the scene other items that will possibly be represented as evidence, even though they have no relationship to the crime whatsoever.

When possible, there should be some preparation and planning for the inevitable crime in progress to assure a fine degree of precision in handling the call and apprehending the suspect. During the planning process, locate those places within the city or county area of your jurisdiction that are potential crime hazards, such as banks and liquor stores for robberies, drugstores and restaurants for burglaries, and as many other places likely to fall prey to the criminal as can be anticipated. All of this preplanning can be done on computers for instant access when officers are dispatched to virtually any type of call.

This planning should be a normal part of your daily patrol routine. Blueprints or sketches of the structures should be collected and fed into the computers for easy access when the 911 call goes out. Whenever you have a spare minute, get out of your vehicle and study the building where you are parked. Is there access to the roof from outside the building? Is there access to the inside from the rooftop? Climb up there sometime and find out, or ask the occupants about the particulars of their building. Are there any skylights or doors giving light and other access to the building from the roof? Where are the air-conditioning ducts? What else is on the roof, such as water reservoirs, emergency generators, and utility equipment? If those items are on the roof, access doors or hatches will also be there. Are those entryways secured with good locks?

If you have done some proactive patrol work, you will have become acquainted with as many people in your district as possible. Some of those individuals might prove invaluable when you find it necessary to find out as much as you can about a building and its occupants.

Map out the surrounding areas, such as streets, alleys, dead-end streets, and cul-de-sacs. List and indicate the locations and numbers of entrances into the buildings. What are the most logical places where a burglar might enter? exit? Are there any low-hanging obstructions that will provide the culprit an additional means of escape by access to the roof, or that an officer may run into in the dark? Who are the informants in the neighborhood, and how will they act under stress? Ask yourself virtually every question about the crime that may occur at each location, the suspected criminals you may encounter, and the victims and what their reactions may be under various in-progress crime situations. In every way possible, work out the police coverage of the crime that may someday occur, although it may be only once. If not this location, there is little doubt that it will be another place with similar characteristics. Consider all possibilities of escape, including time of day and various related traffic factors. Planning should be a regular part of your routine while you are on patrol and there are momentary lapses in the demands on your time and energy.

In this chapter we cover some of the most frequently assigned "in-progress" types of crimes. In many cases, there is great similarity or commonality in responding to any type of incident that is in progress because of the urgency involved in responding to apprehend the culprit while still in the act, the safety of the victims and witnesses, and the immediate implementation of search and surveillance tactics. We also discuss communications procedures, field unit response, and specific types of crimes, such as crimes against person and crimes against property. Because the response required of the police is similar to in-progress calls, there is a discussion of gang activity. The chapter concludes with methods of coverage and search for suspects.

"IN-PROGRESS" COMMUNICATIONS PROCEDURE

When receiving the call that a crime is in progress, the dispatcher should immediately alert the various units and divisions that will be involved in the action, preferably by use of a "hot line," as described in Chapter 4. Impress upon the caller the importance of staying on the telephone or of at least keeping the line open, if it is at all practicable. When you begin the conversation with the calling party, state, "Don't hang up. Stay on the telephone!" Ascertain as quickly as possible the exact nature of the crime, whether it is a robbery, a burglary, or a theft that occurred three days ago. To some people, every crime is a robbery, and their emotions may be so involved that it is a "right now" situation even though the just-discovered crime may have occurred several days earlier.

Secure the precise address and location (i.e., apartment number, upstairs, building in the rear, guest house) where the incident is occurring so that you as dispatcher may give the assigned officer the best information possible. If this is an incoming *911* call, you will get a computer printout of the location of the caller's phone, but do not rely on that if you can possibly get the caller to provide an accurate location where the need is.

Secure the precise address and location within the building or place where the crime is occurring. Get as much descriptive data as possible about the suspect(s), including the number of suspects, distinctive clothing, the description of any hostages who might be taken away, any weapons, and the vehicle used, if any. Determine the location of the calling party and whether he is in any danger of being observed by the suspect or in danger of sustaining injuries if he should remain at the place. Broadcast the information and handle the essential preliminary assignments while keeping the caller on the open phone line; then go back to the telephone and secure any additional information that the caller may have to give about the initial event or any continuing sequence of events.

Be sure to instruct the caller to do nothing that will destroy or change evidence, such as "straightening things up" for fear the responding officers might be shocked to find such a dirty house. Victims of sex crimes understandably want to rid themselves of the "filth" inside them and on them by bathing and/or douching as quickly as possible. What they must do is to wait for a doctor to examine the victim, using a rape kit to capture any body fluids or tissues or other traces that the suspect has probably left behind. Blood types and DNA characteristics unique to each individual may be determined by examination of such fluids and traces, including pubic hairs that might have been left behind. Make this a very emphatic instruction to the victim so that the arriving officer will be able to have the victim taken for the necessary medical examination that may make or break the case.

When first receiving the call concerning an in-progress situation, alert all units in the area of the nature of the event. Once the alert is broadcast, the units in the immediate vicinity should acknowledge receipt of the call and give their respective locations. The unit closest to the scene should be assigned to handle the call. This may not be the unit assigned to that particular district, but the urgency of the situation may call for a deviation from normal procedure. If there is a department policy that requires the district unit to be assigned the call, a reassignment may be made after the initial response has been taken care of. At this moment the most important need is to have a police officer at the crime scene as quickly as possible. After assigning the unit that will handle the call, designate follow-up units, and direct all other units to proceed to key locations around the crime scene. These locations should not be so close to the scene of the crime that their effectiveness will be reduced. Although the call is in progress, there is a strong possibility that the suspects will soon be leaving—or may have been gone for some time—and too many units in the immediate vicinity will be a waste of time and effort for the officers responding.

If you are familiar with your district—as you should be—and you are one of the backup units, try to anticipate the movement of the perpetrator as if you were that person. Which direction would you go on which streets or alleys to avoid detection? Like the farmer whose mule had wandered into the woods who paused for a few minutes, then went out into the woods. Just a few minutes later, the farmer returned with the mule. When asked how he had succeeded in finding the animal in such short order, the farmer replied: "If you want to catch a jackass, all you gotta do is think like one." As a police officer you must think like the "bad guys" if you want to catch them. These people are determined that they do not want to get caught and will take desperate measures to avoid arrest. What would you do if you wanted to avoid going back to prison for the rest of your life?

FIELD UNIT RESPONSE

If it is possible that the suspect is still at the crime scene and that he or she is unaware that the police have been alerted, the objective is to get there as quickly as possible without signaling your arrival. Use red light and siren only if the dispatcher instructs you to do so. The factors that should be taken into consideration for a "code three" assignment are the urgency of the situation, the safety of any victim who may be under attack, the time of day, and traffic conditions for the responding units. Get to the scene of the crime as quickly as possible, but do not sacrifice your own safety or that of other people on the way. Know your streets and as much about your district as possible. There is usually some uniformity, some system in numbering the lots, all even numbers on one side, odd numbers on the other. The lapse between numbers may be in multiples of two, four, or ten, but whatever the configuration, it is probably uniform throughout the city. The naming and numbering system may also be according to some master plan. It is your area—you should know this.

Streets may be numbered or lettered in sequence or named with successive letters of the alphabet, such as A, B, C or Ash, Birch, Cash, then the next 26 streets going through the alphabet again with each name having two syllables. Or the naming of streets may have no logical system at all. *Know* your streets. Which ones start where? Does Chestnut start at Grand, which is 13 blocks east, and stop at Raitt, which is 21 blocks west, with Central Avenue being the north and south dividing line between east and west? Where are the cul-de-sacs, the dead ends? Which streets change names as they pass through different cities, such as Grand Avenue in Santa Ana, Glassell Street in Orange, then Kraemer Avenue as it enters Anaheim and Placentia (in Southern California)? These examples are some with which I am familiar. How about your jurisdiction? Perhaps you have the perfectly planned community, which is highly unlikely. Even tradition is broken sometimes. Boulevards, avenues, streets, lanes may have some reason for their specific designation; is it direction of travel or width or something else?

En route to the scene of the crime, be on the alert for virtually anything or anybody that appears to be in the area. It is possible that certain individuals may not fit the given descriptions of the suspects; there is a strong possibility that the descriptions were not accurate. Most of the people whom you will encounter will have perfectly legitimate reasons for being where they are, and some of those persons may have information concerning minor items surrounding the crime that may help you further identify the suspect and vehicle, if any, and possibly lead to other valuable evidence. Call for a follow-up unit to check these people out and take down their names, addresses, and telephone numbers and any other information about them that you may refer to later should you have reason to question them further. The field interview card is an appropriate device to use for this purpose. Your role as the responding unit is to go directly to the scene.

En route, if possible, you should jot down or dictate into your personal recorder the license plate numbers and descriptions of vehicles leaving the scene of the crime or merely driving around in the area. One of these vehicles may later turn out to be the suspect vehicle, or it may contain key witnesses to the event of surrounding circumstances. Also, consider the possibility that the suspect may have fled from the scene for a couple of blocks, then turned around and headed back toward the scene, believing that the police would never suspect someone going *toward* the scene of the crime.

Except when you wish to announce your arrival at the scene as a strategic move to distract the perpetrator of the crime in an effort to prevent serious injury to his victim, make your arrival as quiet as practicable. Use of the siren while approaching may be unwise, because it may alert a perpetrator, who might panic and hurt someone, or take hostages. Make your approach to the location by way of parallel streets to avoid letting any lookout who may be in the area see your unit until about the moment you arrive. Avoid squealing tires and the sudden braking sounds of your unit sliding into "home plate." The arrival of your unit should sound and appear the same as any other vehicle approaching and stopping in the neighborhood. Do not park directly in front of the location in question, or pull into the driveway, unless traffic is heavy and no other place is available either on the street or near the location of the crime. If time is on your side, park a few doors down and walk.

At this point you have some important decisions to make. For example, if there are victims and suspects inside, your arrival might cause the suspects to panic and take hostages. A jewelry store being robbed in Beverly Hills was built like a fortress. The officers could not see inside and upon arrival found the steel security gate and front door closed. The suspect held the hostages inside and the officers had no way to get in. The only way they could communicate with the suspect was by telephone. While inside he killed one hostage, and while attempting to escape with other hostages a police sniper shot and killed another, mistaking him for the suspect. It is impossible to go back and try another approach, but what would you have done differently? Would it have been better to wait outside silently until the robber had completed his act and then attempt to capture him as he left the building? But what would bystanders and the media have thought if the police officers had waited, and while they were doing nothing the robber had shot and killed his robbery victims anyhow? We have been criticized and condemned for acting both ways, when the result turns out as though the officers "should have" done it some other way. Monday morning quarterbacking is sure to happen, but your decision must be made *now,* and you must act *now.*

Once you are in position and can observe the exact location where the crime is believed to be taking place, determine whether it is in fact occurring. Upon your arrival, radio in your "arrived on the scene" transmission, and any other information that is of immediate significance. If it is evident that there is no need for the follow-up units that are on the way, advise communications to call them off. If you are immediately made aware of needed assistance, such as an ambulance or rescue equipment, broadcast that information as well.

Keep communications informed as to what is going on at the scene. The 10- to 15-minute delay that sometimes occurs between the original "there now" call and the next transmission from any of the units at the scene of the crime-in-progress call may seem an eternity to the concerned patrol commanders and the dispatcher personnel, not to mention the many other units on the same radio frequency who are following the events with considerable anxiety.

If the circumstances at the scene permit, attempt as soon as possible to establish a telephone connection with the communications center. Perhaps the dispatcher or desk officer who received the original phone call was successful in getting across to the calling party that the line should be kept open so that the caller would continue to feed information concerning the ongoing crime—if possible—and to hand the telephone instrument to the first officer to arrive on the scene.

Once you are on the scene and establish telephone or radio contact with the headquarters personnel, report on the current status and progress on the case. Continue passing on your instructions for follow-up units, and request whatever assistance you need from other police units and other emergency services. While you are questioning the victim and/or witnesses about the crime, relay by telephone such pertinent information as descriptions of suspects, the suspect vehicle, direction of travel, and any other information that will aid in the location and capture of the suspect if he has left the scene by the time you arrived at that location. While this is all going on, the dispatcher personnel will continue broadcasting the necessary information.

If you are the first follow-up unit, proceed directly to the scene. Determine whether your presence is required at that location. You will assist in the initial response to ascertain if the crime is still in progress and to take whatever immediate action is warranted. You will then assist in locating and interviewing the victims and witnesses, searching for the suspect and taking him into custody, and generally work as the partner to the officer originally assigned the call. Remain at the crime scene until you are no longer needed, and then take part in the area search for the suspect. The primary objective is to assure the safety of the victim.

TACTICS BY TYPES OF CRIMES

Crimes Against Person

First determine the nature of the crime and whether it is still in progress. A robbery involves the taking of another person's property from that person or from his presence by means of force or fear. If the crime is still in progress upon your arrival, make an immediate assessment and determine your course of action. Take a position out of the line of fire and as much as possible out of the suspect's line of sight as well. Use the police unit or part of the building as a shield against any impending attack by the suspect. Determine if there is any immediate danger to the victim, such as an ongoing attack, or obvious immediate need for medical aid.

Hostage situations may stimulate heroic yearnings of the police officer. You may be equipped with all the necessary protective equipment and weapons, but you are not omnipotent. Act with extreme caution to avoid losing your life and that of the hostage. If you are incapacitated, then both you and the hostage will probably be lost. Trained hostage negotiators have accomplished some pretty remarkable negotiations as documented by live television during recent years.

If the circumstances require your immediate confrontation with the suspect, approach him with extreme caution. It is at this point that many officers lose their lives either through carelessness or indecisiveness. Consider the possibility that your immediate approach may startle the suspect and lead him to take a hostage or to abuse his victim physically more than he may have already done. Under these circumstances, he may also attempt to kill or injure you as well as his other victim. If you must enter, do so quickly, moving to your left to make yourself a less conspicuous target and to compensate for any flinching the suspect may do if he fires a weapon at you. You are guessing, of course, that the suspect is right-handed. If the weapon is in the suspect's left hand, the flinching or jerking motion will probably be to the suspect's right, your left. In that case, your defensive movement should be to your right. Attempt to keep the suspect in sight and make every effort to gain physical control as soon as possible.

If you ascertain upon your arrival that there is no immediate additional danger to the victim, and if the suspect is not yet aware of your presence, remain outside at a vantage point and wait for help to arrive. There is no need to be foolhardy, and actions that are too hasty may cause serious injury or death to both yourself as well as the victim. If possible, wait for the subject to come outside so that the advantage will be yours.

There are several excellent reasons for waiting for the suspect to come outside. If the suspect is not aware of your presence, he may see no need to take a hostage. There may be less provocation to cause the suspect to inflict further injuries on his victim if the suspect's efforts to escape from the crime scene do not seem to him to be frustrated. While you are waiting for the suspect to come outside, your follow-up units may have additional time to arrive. They, too, should arrive as quietly as possible so as not to cause panic. When the suspect does come out, you have the advantage of cover provided by your vehicle, trees and shrubbery, walls of the building, and various other hiding places.

If the suspect has taken a hostage, be extremely careful to do everything possible to preserve the life of the hostage, but not at your own personal peril. While the robber is holding a hostage, if he were to demand that you give up your weapon, then he would have two hostages and you would have accomplished absolutely nothing to enhance the safety of the hostage or yourself. You will have increased the odds in favor of the robber. You are going to have a difficult decision to make under extremely stressful conditions, but your courage in not making a deal with a robber holding a hostage, and in not foolishly giving up your weapon so that you both may be killed, will probably save the hostage's life as well as your own. Survival is foremost on everyone's mind, and that includes the suspect, who must weigh the chances of living through the event.

Hostage negotiation takes a special talent and skill, and such a negotiator should be called into action if available. The negotiator is usually a father or brother or sister figure who can establish rapport with the hostage taker and form some sort of bond with the person to the extent that he or she will listen to reasonable arguments and yield to the logical approach that killing a hostage or prolonging the siege will be disadvantageous, or futile. The objective is to save the life of the hostage and to prevent bloodshed. Containment of the scene and talking and waiting out the situation may lead to an end to the problem. The hostage may escape or be released, and the desired result is that the hostage taker gives up without a firefight.

If you know that the suspect is gone when you arrive, immediately determine as best you can the condition of the victim. If there is no apparent urgency for rendering first aid, stop for just a moment and plan your action, trying under the circumstances not to destroy certain items of evidence that might be instrumental in securing a prosecution. Think of where the suspect might have walked and his possible point and method of entry, and then do what you can under the circumstances to preserve the evidence.

Proceed with as much deliberation and calmness as possible. The people you contact during the investigation of a robbery are inclined to be under severe emotional stress. Your leadership and display of courage and self-control encourage the victim and the various witnesses to remain calm. Consequently, they are likely to be far more effective in aiding the investigation.

Crimes Against Property

A burglar alarm is activated, an open door is found, or someone may actually be observed inside a building. Any one of these situations may prove to be a burglary in progress. Or they may not turn out to be any more than a faulty alarm system, a door left open by a careless employee, or the owner of the store taking an all-night inventory. Each must be handled by the patrol officer as if it were a possible burglary in progress.

The statutes defining burglary vary somewhat among the various states. In some jurisdictions, burglary may be the term used to define the crime of breaking into a building for the purpose of committing theft. In other states, including California, the crime of burglary involves any entry (whether a breaking into the building occurs or not) with the specific intent at the time of the entry to commit the act of theft or some other felony.

Burglars are felons. They must be apprehended and prosecuted. Every means possible should be utilized to take the burglar into custody with the least amount of force or destruction. When it is apparent, or when all appearances lead you to believe that a burglary is in progress, you should anticipate that at least one burglar is inside and immediately plan your strategy to block escape and prevent your capture.

Arrange for adequate assistance before entering a building that may be occupied by a burglar. Unless there is someone inside who may be in danger of attack from the culprit, you are at a tactical advantage by remaining on the outside with the suspect inside. Time is on your side. If a silent alarm system is utilized by the establishment, there is a possibility that the suspect inside is not yet aware of your presence. If possible, do not enter until your backup officers are in position and you have the entire building covered.

Do not overlook the possibility of calling for assistance from an adjoining jurisdiction to cover the building and to attempt capturing the suspect should he attempt to exit from the building. It is better to have too much help, if available, than too little.

While you are waiting for backup officers, place yourself in a position of advantage from which you may observe as much of the building as possible near the area where the suspect is most likely to exit. Look up at the roof, which is a popular hiding place for some burglars who believe that police officers do not look up. When the assisting officers arrive, place the first two officers at opposite corners of the building. In the event that the building is oddly shaped and difficult to cover from the opposite corners, consider placing the officers at opposite corners of the block. From these positions, they may not be in a position to apprehend the suspect, but they will see anyone who enters or leaves the area under their surveillance, which is important in this type of operation. Place additional officers at the places through which the suspect may exit. Be careful to prevent danger from cross fire in the event that shooting occurs.

Check for anyone in the vicinity who is on foot or in a vehicle. It is not likely that a lookout will linger for long after your arrival, but some people serving in that capacity have remained throughout the entire series of events. They were successful in not being detected because of the plausibility of their "cover" role and explanations for being where they were located. Lookouts may pose as a deliveryperson, construction worker, utility meter inspector, stranded motorist working on his automobile, a pair of "lovers" sitting in an automobile, or someone walking a dog in the neighborhood. Do not overlook the most obvious, the person who appears as if he is trying to get out of the area without your detection of his presence.

Another technique of some burglars is to approach the investigating officer, ask what is happening, and then blend in with the other onlookers. Some perpetrators have been known to step in and volunteer to help the police search for the "real thieves," drawing the attention away from themselves. Firefighters have often been approached and assisted by volunteers whom later investigation reveals as the arsonists. Then you may run into the police officer or firefighter who commits those crimes for whatever reason in his or her distorted mind.

If there are no readily visible signs of entry at any of the doors or windows, consider the roof. Many roofs are accessible by climbing on boxes, adjacent utility poles, drainpipes, fences, or other nearby roofs. Some merchants lock their ground floors and windows securely, but leave upstairs windows or skylights unlocked because of their apparent inaccessibility. There are many other methods of entry, such as a tunnel from another side of a fence and up through the floor or a hole broken through the wall from an adjoining suite in the same building.

Approach the place where you intend to enter very carefully and deliberately. It is preferable to have the burglar come out rather than to go in after him. Keeping this in mind, pause and give him the opportunity to come out at your invitation. If the suspect comes out with the merchandise he has stolen, it is easier to prove his intention to steal those items he is carrying, which is one advantage of waiting for the suspect to come out. The most important advantage in waiting is that there is less likelihood that someone will be injured in the ensuing action when you begin to make your entry into the building.

Determine in advance exactly who is going to enter the building. Never have officers at opposite sides of the building enter at the same time. They may meet inside in the darkness and each believe that the other is the suspect. The officers who enter should do so as a single team, and they should work close together while constantly keeping an eye on each other. Either work back to back or side to side, or alternately take the lead with one officer behind the other in a leapfrog pattern. The purpose of this method of coverage is to assure the officers that they know exactly who and where each other is in the darkened and deserted interior of the building. Without such a system it is possible that one officer could walk into the pointed barrel of another officer's revolver.

If the point of entry is a door, look at the ground or floor at the entrance for footprints or any other evidence the culprit may have left while entering. Consider the possibility that he may have left fingerprints on the door or doorknobs. It may be necessary to give first priority to apprehending the culprit, while obliterating some of the evidence you might have otherwise been able to collect. Preservation of life and property includes your own as well as that of the other people you serve and protect.

When you use a flashlight, hold it away from your body, preferably with your weak hand. Most inexperienced shooters have a tendency to flinch to their left while shooting directly at the light source. When entering the building try to avoid making a silhouette of yourself by standing in the center of the doorway and, at the moment you enter, consider turning off your flashlight. When you open the door, stand to one side out of the line of fire if the suspect should choose to attack you. Open the door by slamming it against the stop to make sure no one is hiding behind the door. Step in quickly and immediately to the side out of the doorway. Wait until your partner follows suit. Then stand and listen for a few moments to get accustomed to the new lighting conditions and the sounds inside the building. There are some noises characteristic to the building that can be quite disquieting if you are not accustomed to them. Refrigerators, freezers, electronics equipment, animals left inside for security, clocks, heaters, and air-conditioning devices all sound differently in a strange building.

Consider the use of building lighting. If you go from a lighted room into a dark room, each time you move to a new location, you will be blind for the several seconds it takes your eyes to readjust to the new lighting condition. For that reason, I suggest that once you prepare to leave a lighted area and move into a room or other area that is dark, turn on all the lights that you can before entering. As you continue moving about the premises, leave all the lights on. If anyone is hiding in the darkness, that person will be blind while his or her eyes are adjusting to the light. This will give you a few seconds with the advantage of seeing the suspect first. The time varies, depending on degree of darkness, but in total darkness, the time it takes for the eyes to adjust from darkness to light is from approximately 5 to 50 seconds. (This is not the same as checking for pupillary reaction to light of a person suspected of being under the influence of an opiate.)

If you use flashlights or other means of illumination in locations where there is no other source of lighting, make liberal use of whatever light that you have. Always maintain the advantage. Each time you enter another room, slam the door to the stopper or the wall to make sure there is no one standing behind the door.

Make a thorough and methodical check of the entire building to determine whether a crime has been committed and whether the suspect may still be inside. When people are hiding, they discover that they can literally shrink into spaces they never realized they would fit into. Look up! Burglars sometimes hide on closet shelves or in attics above closets where they may go undetected. Attics, large drawers, incinerators, storage cabinets, behind doors, under desks, and practically any place in the building is a potential hiding place. Once you have searched a particular room, or portion of the building, "clear" that searched area by closing the door and placing articles of furniture in strategic locations so that they would have to be moved for someone to pass through that area. If sufficient officers are available and if the area to be checked is large, an officer placed at a strategic location can guard closed and cleared areas.

As you proceed in the building search, make spot rechecks to compensate for the possibility that you may have a clever burglar who escaped detection or who sneaked past the searching officers. One morning, a team of officers who were checking out a building apparently overlooked one obvious place. After the officers had left the building, the burglar broke out and activated the alarm again. They were eventually able to catch the burglar in a nearby orange grove. When he was questioned about his ability to avoid detection, he stated that he had hidden under a desk in the office in the light manufacturing building. One officer had searched that room, discovered the phone, called the police station and conversed with the telephone operator for a few minutes, then had left the office and resumed the search with his fellow officers. The suspect stated that he had had a great temptation to untie the officer's shoelaces but decided not to.

If you find the suspect inside the building, search him or her immediately and use appropriate restraining devices. Never assume that he is working alone. Look for an accomplice either inside the building or nearby outside. This is one type of police activity for which the use of trained dogs is exceptionally valuable.

Be careful to make mental and written notes as to what you see when you check out a building. If time permits, take a few snapshots to memorize exactly how the building looks at the time. If time and circumstances permit, take a photograph or two to further document your observations. It is not unusual for claims to be made later that you tampered with—or stole—something. There are legions of attorneys who make their living handling lawsuits against the police. You may have been set up by someone determined to get even with the police for some longstanding grievance. Having worked internal affairs, I have some vivid memories of attempts by other people (in some cases other police officers) trying to frame members of my department (including me). Disappointing as it is, you will find out that everyone is capable of lying.

If it is determined that a crime was committed, proceed with the initial crime scene search and the preliminary investigation. If it turns out that the building had not been burglarized, but just left open, secure the building. In any event, contact the owner and advise him of your presence while requesting that he make an appearance. You may do this by phoning him direct from the office in his building if you can ascertain who he is, or you may have your communications personnel contact him. One method for determining the name of the owner is to check through records for a recent crime, such as a check case in which that business was listed as the victim. The report should reflect the names, addresses, and phone numbers of key company personnel. Business license files will reveal the same information. Perhaps your department has access to the computer containing that data. If it does, take advantage of it when necessary.

Questioning the Suspect.   If you are going to question the suspect at that time and expect to use his statements in court at his trial, be sure to admonish him of his right against self-incrimination and of his right to counsel and to have counsel with him when he is questioned. However, consider the fact that the burglar may be making statements during the actual commission of the crime prior to your admonishment that will be admissible under most circumstances because they are part of the *res gestae*. The *res gestae* encompasses the crime and the surrounding circumstances that all constitute the crime. Spontaneous declarations made by the suspect may also be totally admissible without the *Miranda* warning requirement.

What to Do with the Weapon.   What should you do with your gun while inspecting the interior of a building searching for the suspect? Ask yourself, "Where would be the best place to carry the gun so that it would serve its purpose most efficiently?" In the holster. By keeping your gun in its holster, you have it in a very accessible location, and your gun hand is free to handle doorknobs, to push aside obstacles that are in the way, to push the doors back to their stops, and to perform a variety of tasks while the other hand is holding the flashlight. If you practice regularly, you have no doubt found that it takes virtually no more time to draw your weapon from your holster and fire it than it does to fire a gun that is already in your hand. The time factor involves your reaction to the incident calling for your response. Your degree of alertness will determine how quickly you will react.

There is some disagreement with this philosophy among fellow officers. Some officers will tell you that they would never enter a building without a drawn gun. Of course, you will never see a television show or movie when an officer enters a building without his weapon in a two-handed grip looking as though he were searching an enemy village during wartime.

If you hold a gun in your hand, there is also a tendency to cock it unconsciously. On one occasion an officer did just that: He cocked his revolver while checking out a burglary scene, then replaced the revolver in his holster. He had not been aware that he had cocked the revolver and did not check it when he replaced it.

Several hours later, that same officer was working a traffic control problem when he placed his hand on his gun in a resting position. He pushed the hammer when he placed his hand on the gun and shot himself in the foot.

If the gun enters the room first, what is there to keep someone inside from using a baseball bat or chair leg to knock it out of your hand? The television version of officers always entering a room with their guns extended in front of them in a two-handed grip leaves the officers with little else to do with those hands but hold on to their guns.

During a raid in 1996 in Oxnard, California, an officer threw a flashbang grenade into the room as the officers simultaneously entered the room. In the excitement and confusion, the sergeant in charge of the raid shot and killed one of his own officers with the cocked gun he had in his hands. The tragic error is known as "friendly fire," but an officer died. Not having been on the scene or involved in the exhaustive investigation that followed, neither you nor I should guess what really happened, but I am reasonably sure the decision of the "rollout team" investigating the shooting will be that the sergeant who fired the gun made a terrible and tragic mistake and will be held blameless. I am also reasonably sure that the sergeant will retire on a stress disability after the dust has settled, so there are the lives of two officers destroyed.

There are many raids and similar situations when officers enter with guns drawn and ready to fire. Of those events, relatively few actually escalate into fire-fights. Is that because of the officers having their guns drawn, or would the situation have worked out with the drawn weapons? Actually, that is a question that cannot be answered with any degree of accuracy. I am not suggesting that officers should discontinue the practice of entering dangerous situations without having their weapons ready to use. I am merely saying that alternative tactics may be in order in different situations. Consider your options and be careful not to get into a rut by using the same routine every time and getting overconfident that your drawn weapon is positive life insurance.

A shotgun is impractical to use for checking out a building, except when there is a known felon inside, in which case one officer takes care of the door-opening and searching procedure, while the officer with the heavy armament stands back and "covers" the searching officer.

Prowlers. If you are familiar with the neighborhood where a prowler is reported, you have a tremendous advantage when responding to the prowler call. With such knowledge, it is possible to stop one or two houses short of the exact location of the prowler and approach silently on foot without warning the suspect of your arrival. It is also to your advantage to know how the numbers on parallel streets appear, so that you or the follow-up officer may park and wait on the next block in case the suspect chooses to hurdle fences or to run down alleys. There is usually a plan for street numbering, and you should know what it is so that you will know an address without even looking.

Approach the prowler's location quietly, driving the police car in the same manner as any local resident would drive home when returning from an evening out. Although your approach should not be too secretive, which in itself would arouse the suspect's suspicions, it should not be as though the occupation army had arrived. It may be to your advantage to stop some distance down the street, turn off the lights, then drive along the curb with the lights out for the last few hundred feet of your approach. Use the emergency brake to avoid activating the brake lights, which would broadcast your arrival. Locate the calling party's address by shining a light on the curb or some other place across the street from the calling party's address. Of course, if you know your district as you should, you will already know that the house is third from the north end of the block on the west side of the street.

While approaching the scene, observe all the people who are in the area, whether or not they are making furtive movements, or signaling by suspicious conduct that they are involved in some sort of criminal activity. Someone who is running or sneaking around a place where a prowler had been spotted will automatically be suspect, but do not overlook the possibility that the "cool" individual walking normally along the street may be the real culprit. At the initial stage of the investigation of a "prowler there now" call, question everyone you encounter for possible leads as to the identity and location of the suspect.

Once you have arrived silently without your presence being detected and have made the initial attempt to locate the prowler, it will be apparent to him that you are there. Use plenty of light and conduct a very thorough and systematic search for the prowler. Look for wires, chuckholes, booby traps, duck ponds, and other hazards, particularly when going through back yards.

Don't be surprised to run into the occasional clothesline stretched across the back yard. There are still some people who would rather dry their clothes in the back yard rather than the clothes dryer. Look out also for the croquet hoops and other game implements and toys left in the yard after play.

Avoid disturbing the residents in the area. Keep your radio on low volume, close the doors quietly, and keep the noise level of your activity down. While searching, do not assume that any place is too small to hide. Stealth is the key to a prowler's success. It will take persistence on your part to outthink the prowler and catch him or her in the act.

Once you have searched a particular area, post someone at that location to assure yourself that the suspect will not move to a place already searched to avoid apprehension. When using the flashlight, use it in the same manner as when you are checking out a building: out and away from your body. When you shine the light on a suspect, keep the light trained on his face to keep him at a disadvantage if he has intentions to attack you. Watch his hands for any movement that may signal anticipated actions by the suspect, such as an attempt to escape.

When you are searching for a prowler, you are looking for a misdemeanant. Use of a firearm is not justified unless the suspect would attempt to commit some felony or unless it were necessary under the "reasonable force" decision that you would make when meeting with his resistance to arrest. Keep your revolver in its holster and keep the shotgun in the car. Although there are exceptions, most prowlers are not dangerous.

When working in a team with other officers, be sure to use a rehearsed technique so that all officers will understand what their parts in the search for the prowler will be and will have an idea as to the location and activities of the other officers.

Discuss and rehearse your tactics and the various signals that you will use. Move in the shadows when you and your partner are aware of each other's whereabouts. Otherwise, stay out in the open to avoid meeting another officer in the dark who does not know or recognize you, even though you both may be wearing the same uniform. I learned my lesson by rounding the corner of a house while checking out a prowler and I found myself looking down the barrel of a cocked hair-trigger Smith and Wesson 6-inch revolver in the hands of a follow-up officer who did not anticipate my presence.

Interview the occupants of the homes on whose property the prowler was observed and ascertain whether the prowler might be a person who has any permission or lawful business on the property. Look for any evidence that the suspect may have left at the scene, such as footprints or semen on the ground beneath a window into which he may have been looking, articles that may have fallen from his pocket when reaching for an object in his pocket, or any other evidence that may have been left there. Look into nearby vehicles in an effort to determine the presence of anyone important to the case who may be hiding. Stand or park for a few minutes at various places while conducting the search to listen for any sounds and watch for any movements that are foreign to the surroundings and may indicate the presence of the prowler. Sometimes the culprit may gain confidence and believe that he may leave his place of hiding without detection and apprehension, and it is then that you may effect the arrest.

The calling party may have decided to have a friend or husband search the neighborhood for the prowler, and the searcher may have armed himself with a shotgun or a souvenir rifle. If at all possible, the telephone operator or dispatcher who receives the original call for police service should ascertain whether anyone is already involved in a search and if anyone is armed. If someone is armed, advise the calling party to invite the armed searcher back inside the house. When the officers search the premises and the general neighborhood, they will be less likely to encounter an armed individual, who may appear to be an armed suspect rather than a searcher. These "do-it-yourselfers" are sometimes far more dangerous than the prowlers or burglars you are looking for. Under stress conditions, it is sometimes impossible to tell the prowlers from the searchers, and someone could be seriously injured when people carry deadly weapons.

Some prowler calls involve nothing more than outside noises that may frighten the lone occupant of a house or apartment. Look for animals or shrubbery scratching the screens or rubbing against the buildings. Once you find the source of the sound, point it out to the calling party and recommend steps to eliminate the sound, for example, trimming or removing a bush or tree with long branches. Some "jungles" look pretty but are excellent hiding places for prowlers and burglars.

The prowler may be a burglar looking for a place to enter for the purpose of stealing. He may be a jealous husband or boyfriend who is intent upon doing some spying on his wife or girlfriend, or he may be a sex psychopath seeking out another unsuspecting victim so that he may satisfy his prurient desires. In most cases the prowler will be a curious adolescent or young adult with voyeuristic tendencies, seeking to expand his or her sexual awareness by peeking in on the private lives of others.

The average prowler is not dangerous, but he is a potential hazard. There is no way to determine in advance whether he is one of those "harmless" persons who wants only to look into other people's bedrooms or a burglar who intends to commit his crime in spite of any obstacles he may encounter.

In motion pictures and television sitcoms, do you ever notice how the actors always go to bed with the drapes and windows wide open at nighttime so the whole world can drop by outside and see the show from outside without having to come inside to the sound stage? A visit by your crime prevention people to the victims of burglaries and prowlers should be arranged so that they can receive appropriate instruction about how to shield themselves from prying eyes.

Usually when a person inside a house being "visited" by a prowler discovers the presence of that prowler, his or her actions alert the prowler that he or she has been discovered. By the time the calling party goes to the telephone and notifies the police that the prowler is in the area, chances of apprehending him are slight. If a young lady were to become aware of the admiring eyes of a prowler looking in from some point of vantage, there would be a greater probability that he would be arrested if the object of his attentions would continue with whatever she was doing, then casually go to the telephone and notify the police department, and resume the same activity until the arrival of the officers.

The prowler might continue to watch the young lady practicing her exercises or combing her hair while the police officers proceed to the scene and attempt to catch the suspect in the act of peeking into the window. If they are successful in making their arrival quickly and silently, they may succeed as well in effecting the arrest. Asking a woman caller to cooperate this way to apprehend a prowler is "beyond the call of duty," but if she insists on helping, this is one method by which we have met with some success in apprehending prowlers.

Whenever there is a chronic situation with a voyeur who continually visits the same places to watch what is going on inside, there should be some preparation for surveillance of those places. Planning to apprehend the prowler should be no less elaborate than planning for any other major crime. Some people use transparent curtains or draperies or window coverings that are so sheer that everything in a room is visible from the outside when the room is illuminated. Some people are so proud of their furniture and interior decor that they leave their windows undraped so that people can look in; others leave the view clear so that they can see the ocean or the mountains. All these households are potential prowler victims. From your own observation while patrolling your district, you will see these people as needing a little extra patrol attention.

GANG ACTIVITY

The open hostilities exhibited by youth street gangs—such as fights between opposing gangs in a neutral area or on the "turf" of one of the opposing gangs or the more frightening activity of "cruising," which consists of a carload of gang members cruising another gang's territory and firing several rounds of shotgun or rifle bullets indiscriminately into a randomly selected home—is at epidemic proportions in some cities.

No longer are we plagued by the small bands of street urchins who fight with each other over territory as the only gangs we have to worry about. While we still have those types of gangs, we now have organized and well-trained—and well-armed—terrorists who kill rival gang members for franchise rights to deal in cocaine or "crack" (a type of cocaine), marijuana, and other drugs in a multibillion-dollar operation throughout the world. These organizations make the Mafia look like campfire girls by comparison, and their methods include killing pedestrians and strangers at random, and firing automatic weapons into homes of innocent people totally uninvolved in their drug business or turf rivalry. This is a civil war with gangs that have greater financial resources than the police to carry on their warfare, and far more sophisticated weaponry.

Walter Miller reported that "in most cities, youth gangs today typically consist of small loosely organized groups of about a dozen teenage males. . ."[1] Not only do they protect their turf, or area in which they live and claim as their place to operate, but many of these gangs have terrorized entire neighborhoods, they have formed marauding teams of robbers, they operate "protection" rackets, and they have taken over entire schools and recreational facilities.

"Taggers" may or may not be affiliated with other gangs and gang activity. A recent phenomenon has been the emergence of graffiti "tagging" by individuals and groups of young men and boys who compete for space on freeway signs and over-passes, traffic signs, fences, and buildings throughout entire areas. Some of these "taggers" claim that it is an addiction with them to express themselves this way. When apprehended, they and their parents are fined and the offenders are required to do "community service" by painting over and chemically removing their own graffiti. Many of these gangs have violent confrontations and should not be considered as innocent kids "just expressing themselves."

Gangs are not new. Originally the Sicilian underground who preyed upon the hated French soldiers who occupied Sicily for so many years and retaliated in kind whenever any of their people were victimized by the French, the Mafia began preying on their own countrymen in Sicily and elsewhere in the world, branching out into all categories of organized crime. With the fall of Communist rule in the former Soviet Union, those countries are experiencing their own gangster activities.

In Rio de Janeiro and São Paulo, the favelas (shanty towns) spawn thousands of homeless children known as *meninos da rua,* who have formed gangs such as Comando Vermelho (Red Commandos) that rule the favelas in the hills of the cities and make their living by extortion and kidnapping. In southern California a group of high school self-styled "lovers" formed a gang they called a "posse," and their objective was to score points in competition to have sexual encounters with as many different girls as they could. There are many different ethnic street gangs that started out in the larger cities and have spread out throughout the country, for a variety of objectives, but they are all gangs.

The gangs that give the police the most trouble are not the small groups of neighborhood youths who put their graffiti on walls and fences and fight rival gangs; rather, they are the gangs that have objectives such as drug dealerships, robberies, muggings, shakedowns of merchants, and burglaries. The weapons they use are no longer "Saturday night specials," but are high-priced semiautomatic machine guns and pistols made by the world's best manufacturers.

Your responsibility as a field officer is to observe the people you contact on the street very closely. Look for signs of gang membership by hand signs or other signals they interchange, logos and insignia on their clothing and their vehicles, tattoos, and the graffiti they spray paint onto every blank space they can find. Try to determine their associates and their hangouts, their vehicles, their places of residence, their girl friends and relatives, and their organizational structure. Freely exchange this information with the specialists in your department who may be working a gang detail and also the investigators who are working the street crimes. In the field, be particularly wary whenever you see two or more gang members together who seem to have a purpose for being where they are or going wherever they are going.

GENERAL COORDINATION AND SEARCH

At the initial stage of an in-progress call, there is a tendency on the part of many officers to follow other police units in a "caravan" and to proceed directly to the scene, probably because of the intense desire to apprehend the culprit and to be on hand to "cover" a fellow officer. Both procedures must be avoided. The radio dispatcher should be responsible for assigning the units to proceed directly to the scene and coordinating all the other units by directing them to locations other than the immediate vicinity of the crime scene to take part in the search, if a search is necessary.

The assigned officer is in charge of the response, the investigation, and the search and continues to be in charge until the arrival of a supervisor, who will assume supervisory control. The supervisor will probably establish a command post at or near the crime scene and will coordinate the field activities from that location. At the time the field command post is established, the dispatcher at the communications center will discontinue the coordination activities and will provide subsidiary service to the field command post.

If you are not assigned the call, remain in your district unless assigned elsewhere, but move in the direction of the crime scene or to a point of vantage so that you can observe and be in a position to take up pursuit in the event that the suspect flees past the point where you are positioned. If you are on the outer fringe of the perimeter of the search, cover the logical avenues of escape from the scene, but also consider the illogical ones as well.

Be sure that if you are maintaining surveillance over a particular street or freeway that you have access to that route yourself, or that you are spotting for another unit that does have such access. Ask yourself, "If I were attempting to flee, where would I go and what would I do?" Consider the possibility that the suspect may run or drive very quickly away from the crime scene for a short distance, discard his distinctive clothing or other items he may have worn to confuse the witnesses, and abandon the vehicle. It is not uncommon for professional robbery suspects to have two or three alternate vehicles parked within a few blocks of the location of their crime, and switch to whichever of those vehicles they are able to escape to during the first few minutes before the arrival of the first police units. Once they switch vehicles and discard the incriminating clothing, they find little need to hurry from the scene. They may also have a confederate pose as the fleeing bandit to draw the attention of the police while the culprit with the loot gets away. When you stop the confederate, he will check out okay because descriptions of the suspect and the one you have stopped will not match.

Some robbers have been brazen enough to drive past the scene of the crime, then park and walk up to mingle with the small crowd of onlookers, and inquire of the officers the nature of the trouble and whether they have had any success in locating the robber. For that reason, you should not overlook the possibility that the robber may still be in the immediate vicinity and that he may not be running or speeding away from the scene.

METHODS OF COVER AND SEARCH

There are several methods of searching for suspects who may be at the crime scene or its proximity or who may have fled the scene and be some considerable distance away. The methods that we will discuss here are the foot, spot, leapfrog, and quadrant methods.

Foot Search

Park your unit some distance—possibly a block or two—from the crime scene or the place where you intend to search. Walk in, using natural cover provided by buildings, trees and shrubbery, or any other objects that will conceal your approach and protect you against missiles that might be aimed in your direction. Stop frequently to look and listen quietly for anyone who may arouse your suspicions. Once you have established the fact that the suspect is not immediately observable, begin contacting anyone whom you see, and secure from them as much information as you can as to what or whom they may have seen. Perhaps a lookout was loitering on the street corner for some time prior to the crime. One of the residents or workers in the neighborhood may be able to point out a car that is strange to the neighborhood and this may be one that the robber "planted" as a possible alternate escape vehicle. Perhaps a witness has seen the transfer from one car to another.

The foot search is very effective when searching for witnesses as well as evidence in the vicinity of the crime, and sometimes it pays off in the search for the suspect. The robber is usually busy looking for police vehicles and may be caught off guard if you carefully and methodically cover the area on foot.

Spot Cover

This is usually a fixed post, generally at an intersection or some other vantage point overlooking one or more possible avenues of escape. When you are assigned to this type of detail, place your unit in a location that allows constant communications with the dispatcher and with other units and access to the means by which you will pursue the suspect.

Leapfrog

The term "leapfrog" describes the method of search, just as other terms do: "zigzag," "cloverleaf," or "criss-cross." In the leapfrog method, you and your partner alternately take the lead in the search and cover each other as you progressively move on. You may find many variations of this type of search very effective.

Quadrant

Using the scene of the crime as the center of the quadrant grid, divide the area to be searched into four equal "pie-shaped" quarters generating from the center. Assign at least one unit to each quadrant. Each unit begins the search of its assigned quadrant at the outer perimeter, then moves in toward the center—the crime scene—in a zigzag pattern. The units should overlap each other's quadrant areas and work back outward to the perimeters of their assigned areas again. They continue this until the culprit is located or the search is abandoned.

PLAINCLOTHES ASSISTANCE

Whenever "plainclothes" officers assist in a police incident such as a crime in progress, a pursuit, or a similar incident involving high levels of emotional involvement, they must work in a capacity in which they may be immediately identified as police officers. They should affix their badges to the outside of their chests to aid in the identification. Some agencies now provide their officers with "jump suits" that they may put on over their street clothing, and which have the word *police* and the name of the agency inscribed in large letters across the back.

If someone is required to operate as a communicator or coordinator at a command post, a nonuniformed officer should be assigned to the task. Plainclothes officers may also be assigned to work in a team with uniformed officers or to assign them as drivers of police vehicles. An exceptionally good way to utilize plainclothes officers is to put them on the streets as decoys. When there have been unusual numbers of street crimes, such as rapes and muggings, placement of officers, in disguise, it is hoped, will draw the suspects away from helpless, unsuspecting vulnerable victims. When the mugger or rapist selects one of the decoys as a victim, the officers move in and make the arrest. There is no entrapment because the criminal intent is wholly in the mind of the criminal.

One example of how a plainclothes officer may be mistaken for a suspect occurred some time ago, but it could occur again unless the proper precautions are taken for its prevention. One afternoon an armed robbery occurred, and the chase began. As the chase progressed, several police units took part and it soon developed into a caravan. As the suspect vehicle approached each city in succession, a police unit or two from that city would move into place in the caravan and assume the lead in the chase. In this case, as the robbers entered the fourth or fifth city, a plainclothes officer in his unmarked unit fell in behind the suspect vehicle. The other police vehicles had fallen some distance behind. The detective unit was successful in making the stop, and the lone officer in that unit approached the suspect with his revolver in his hand. He opened the suspect vehicle door on the driver's side and, with his left hand, grabbed hold of the suspect's arm. The officer was turned in such a way, with his gun in his right hand, and with the left hand holding the suspect, that when the first "uniformed" car from another city arrived, it appeared to him as if the suspect were armed and getting out of the car. However, the officer in that first "uniformed" unit to arrive had seen the plainclothes officer pull into the caravan and recognized the armed man as an officer.

A second, third, and fourth car from various agencies rolled up to the scene, and several of the officers in those cars were not aware of the armed man's role in the action. To one of them, it must have appeared as if he were one of the suspects. As the plainclothes officer made a sudden move, a shot rang out. The bullet missed the officer, but it struck a wind wing on the car and shattered the glass. It was fortunate that the shot was not fatal. Unfortunately, however, the officer sustained a permanent eye injury from the flying glass particles and retired early from police service.

SUMMARY

In this chapter we covered the in-progress crime, including the crime against person and the crime against property. Critical to success in response to crimes that are in progress or believed to be while the officer is en route is effective and accurate communications. Responding officers should be kept totally aware of exactly what is happening with other responding officers and should be constantly updated on what is going on at the crime scene. If the officer who receives the call is able to keep the line open with the victim or witness, then the first officer on the scene gets to the telephone as soon as it is practicable and continues communicating. Once en route to the scene, be sure to be alert to people who are approaching or staying at the crime scene as well as those who might be hurrying away, because the suspect may not flee the scene as you might expect. If we were to wrap up this chapter with one word that would best describe possible success in apprehension of suspects at the scene of a crime, it would be "teamwork." You will be more aware of the value of good cooperative working relationships between officers when it is most important.

EXERCISES AND STUDY QUESTIONS

1. When a person calls in to report a crime in progress, what do you say to the person to keep him or her on the telephone?
2. What is the purpose for keeping the telephone line open?
3. What is the value of making a silent approach to the scene of a crime in progress?
4. Is there a standardized street numbering system in your town? What is it?
5. What should you be looking for while en route to the scene of a crime reported to be in progress?
6. Is it better to go into a building after a burglar or to wait for the burglar to come out?

7. What would you do if a robber who had taken a hostage asked you to trade yourself for the hostage or to surrender your weapons?

8. Explain how you and your partner officer would cover a building containing what you believe to be at least one burglar until your backup unit arrives.

9. Describe how you would assign two officers to search the interior of a building that showed signs of having been recently broken into.

10. In your opinion, where is the best place to carry your gun while checking out the interior of a building at nighttime and you expect to find a burglar?

11. How would you respond to a prowler call?

12. What is the extent, if any, of gang activity in the jurisdiction where you live?

13. List the names of the gangs in your own jurisdiction and describe their purposes (tagging, drugs, play), if known.

14. Is the ethnic composition of the gangs in your community mixed or single heritage?

15. Where would you set up a command post in proximity to a bank that had just been robbed?

16. Describe the quadrant method of search.

17. Describe at least five situations in which you would employ plainclothes officers as decoys.

18. Is there a plan for naming the streets in your city? What is it?

19. Collect newspaper clippings for the duration of the current semester regarding errors in policing made by the officers of your local police and sheriff's departments.

REFERENCES

The material for this chapter was devised for academy lectures in patrol procedures. Sources were numerous training bulletins and unpublished information memos from more than 20 different police departments, including Los Angeles, Santa Ana, Glendale, Riverside, and Oakland, California.

FOOTNOTES

1. Walter Miller, "The Rumble This Time," *Psychology Today,* May 1977, p. 52.

CHAPTER 9

PRELIMINARY INVESTIGATIONS

INTRODUCTION

As a patrol officer, you perform many types of investigations, rang-
ing from "investigate the woman screaming" to complicated multiple homicides and series of daylight residence burglaries. In some
departments, particularly the larger metropolitan agencies, it has
been customary for the field officer assigned to the district where the
crime occurs to respond to every call and then to call in specialists
for all but the "routine" nontraffic and noncriminal activities. Limits
were set on the officer's responsibilities primarily because of the
tremendous amount of time required just to keep up with responding to the calls. Once at the scene, the patrol officer would determine the nature of the problem, stand by to protect the scene,
administer aid and comfort to the victims, arrest the culprit, and wait
until the specialists arrived. In the large department, this procedure
continues to exist, but it is not practicable in the small or medium-
sized department. Even in the large departments, the problem of
overspecialization will have a tendency to render a department ineffective unless the specialization is kept to a minimum.

Whenever a crime occurs, or its earlier commission is discovered and reported to the police department, the first officer to arrive
on the scene is usually the patrol officer in whose district the incident has occurred. Because of your proximity to the scene, your
high mobility, and the fact that you are first on the scene, it is most

Figure 9–1   The preliminary investigation frequently involves a careful search for latent prints. (Courtesy Chicago Police Department.)

logical that you should be charged with the responsibility for the initial phases of the crime investigation (see Figure 9–1). This chapter covers some of the guidelines for this *preliminary investigation* process, which is normally handled by the field patrol officer. Investigations beyond that point will appropriately be covered in a good investigation techniques text.

PRELUDE TO THE INVESTIGATION

Investigations usually begin with personal interviews of people who are either witnesses or victims of the criminal acts of others. Sometimes the suspect is still on the scene, as is common in assault cases, and it is difficult to distinguish the respective roles of the participants in the action in an emotion-packed situation. In one case, two officers responded to the scene of what appeared to be a fight between some braceros. When the officers arrived, they discovered that no one at the scene could speak English and the officers knew no Spanish.

The officers immediately assessed the situation and found that two of the combatants were seriously wounded, one with slash wounds on his hand and the other with a cut throat that was bleeding profusely. The officers had to act fast. There was no ambulance immediately available, but the hospital was only six blocks away. Knowing that the two victims needed immediate medical attention, the officers placed them in the back seat of their unit, one officer driving and the other holding compress bandages on the wounded men.

Thanks to the quick thinking of the officers, both victims received emergency surgery and were on the road to recovery. It was only then that the officers discovered—with the aid of a Spanish-speaking doctor—that they had actually transported the combatants together, each having cut the other in the fight. The man with the slashed throat had averted a second blow, causing the second man to cut himself with his own knife.

This is an example of what could happen when an officer does not have all the facts at the beginning of an investigation. In an area where other languages are spoken, a valuable asset is to have officers who can communicate fluently in those languages. If none of your officers are so prepared, consider having a file in the office of people who have knowledge of many different languages. Your local college or university is an excellent resource.

One of the first and most important items on the agenda of the investigation is to assess the situation quickly and attempt to determine exactly what happened. Many questions must be answered. Determine what crime, if any, occurred, and respond accordingly. While making that determination, identify the principals. Who is the victim? Who and where is the suspect? If there is an immediate and imminent threat to the life of anyone at the scene, take steps to apprehend the suspect and reduce or eliminate the threat.

The victim of any type of personal attack should be the first object of concern. Is there any danger of further attack? What is the victim's condition? Is there someone present who can call for medical aid? If first aid is necessary, look after that need, and instruct anyone who is present to assist you. Even at the risk of destroying valuable evidence, the life of the victim has top priority. If the victim is dying, seek a declaration from the victim that will aid in identification and prosecution of the killer.

Quick apprehension of the suspect is high on the list of priorities, particularly if the crime is a personal attack and there is a likelihood that the suspect will repeat the attack unless taken into custody. Exactly which order of action you will follow will be determined by the precise facts as they present themselves to you. Regardless of the nature of the situation, use as much care as possible to preserve the evidence that will serve to establish the elements of the crime and the guilt of the accused (see Figure 9–2). Sometimes the destruction of evidence is inevitable when you are administering first aid or performing rescue services, or when taking the suspect into custody. If that is the case, do not overlook the possibility that some of the evidence may be salvaged even though partially destroyed.

At the time you arrive, stop for a moment. Look around. Does anything look unusual or "out of place"? Are there people sitting in cars when usually no one is around? Have members of the media arrived, such as a television crew? Where did they come from and how did they know about the event? Perhaps you have something more here than meets the eye. You may not know it, but the victim of this particular break-in is a basketball star. The murder victim may be a former motion picture actor. Or the suspect may be a celebrity of some degree, or perhaps a wealthy or very popular local person. Call for someone to come out to the scene and handle the media so that they can satisfy their program directors and the public and you will still be able to conduct the investigation very carefully.

Don't get "star struck" and get sloppy in your work. Stars in all walks of life are nothing but people who do "people things," such as beat their spouses, murder other people, lose their tempers, and do stupid things. Their celebrity status does not relieve them of any of the responsibilities of human decency, and when they break the law or commit social blunders, they should be expected to pay for their sins the same as you and I. Neither should you devote more attention to the case than any others of a similar nature because of an individual's star status.

Figure 9–2   This vehicle is being vacuumed for trace evidence, such as hair or fibers or residue from illegal drugs. (Courtesy Chicago Police Department.)

Try to make mental notes of the scene and various related factors during these initial stages, although you may have other important responsibilities for the moment. Try to remember if any articles of furniture were moved, doors opened or unlocked, lights turned on or off, or any footprints or traces of evidence visible. Some evidence is very short-lived and will disappear unless it is quickly collected or recorded.

As soon as possible, attempt to process the short-lived evidence. It will possibly consist of a footprint outside a building in the rain, which may be saved by covering it with a box or a piece of some type of weatherproof material. Sometimes during the night or early morning hours when the grass is wet, the suspect may leave wet impressions on a dry linoleum floor. This wet impression should be sketched and photographed as early in the investigation as practicable, because it will be forever lost once it dries.

As you are checking for short-lived evidence, look for traces of snagged clothing on tree branches and bushes, trampled down grass, signs of human blood on thorny rosebushes, and other items that are so often overlooked when you focus all your attention on "harder" evidence, such as footprints, fingerprints, and other larger items that are easier to see. Imagine your suspect as being about seven feet tall or less than four feet tall, and then look for evidence that might have been left behind by those individuals as well as average-sized people.

Once you have looked after the welfare of the victim, ascertained whether the suspect was present and accomplished the arrest if he was present, and taken the necessary steps to preserve and protect the short-lived evidence, the next step is to protect the entire scene against any further contamination. Define the perimeter and close it to the entry of anyone but those people who are actually essential to the investigation. Highly visible ribbon will probably work better than rope because the ribbon is easier to store and to attach to almost any surface. Several manufacturers produce the ribbon, and some have the words POLICE—DO NOT ENTER emblazoned across the surface of the tape every couple of feet. To put up the ribbon, tack or tape it to existing surfaces or use small sign sticks and staples. Call for whatever special assistance you may have available to you, which may include recruiting curious bystanders or the witness who discovered the crime; then proceed with the investigation.

In the very early stages of the investigation, you are going to be extremely busy looking after the health and safety of the victims and perhaps several witnesses whom you will want to interview once the dust has settled. Put the uninjured victims and the witnesses to work, assigning each one to a different task of guarding a piece of evidence—especially short-lived evidence that will soon disappear—or keeping other people away from the scene. This will keep them separated from each other so that they cannot form composite, or "jury," descriptions of suspects or of the events. What you want is each person's account of what occurred and a personal description of the suspect(s). If you have nothing else for them to do, hand them a pen and a sheet of paper and ask them to write down everything they can remember of the event.

You may have problems keeping two categories of curious onlookers away from the crime scene: fellow officers and the press. Neither has a license to contaminate the scene. Put them to work. Sometimes a posed picture or two, such as dusting a doorknob for prints, will appease a reporter for a while until your investigation is completed.

INDUCTIVE AND DEDUCTIVE REASONING

Inductive and deductive reasoning must be exercised in the investigative process. Taking specific facts and information, one employs inductive reasoning to attempt to arrive at general conclusions about what happened, causing one to take what is known and then attempt to reach a theory on what is unknown.

Bear in mind that a theory is just that: a theory. At times you will find that the leads are coming your way so fast and furiously that you will have a tendency to jump to conclusions. Guard against that tendency. You may have to work fast, but not hastily. The danger of haste is that when one gets locked onto a specific theory, there is a diminished interest in conflicting theories. A recent case was just overturned after 17 years. The victim was knocked senseless by her attacker, and when she came out of a coma, she recalled that her husband had assaulted her. He denied this at the time, stating that he had gone to a fast-food restaurant for a hamburger. When he came back, he saw someone running from his house, and when he got inside he found that his wife had been badly beaten and raped and her unborn baby killed in the assault. The victim was aided in "remembering" that it was her husband who must have caused the baby's death. The husband was prosecuted because the police did not believe his story even though the still warm hamburger was in the bag in the kitchen. He was convicted because the jury believed that the wife had remembered the details correctly, however hazy her memory was. Seventeen years later, in the spring of 1996, DNA tests, which had not been available in 1979, were conducted of preserved semen samples. The ex-husband had been convicted, divorced, given a dishonorable discharge from the U.S. Marine Corps, and turned down by parole boards on two or three occasions because the board members did not believe he was ready for parole because he would not own up to the crime for which he had been convicted. The true culprit was found, tied into not only that assault and murder of the fetus, but several other murders at about the same time with similar methods of operation. His DNA tested positive, and the accused man who had spent 17 years in prison for one of his crimes was freed in the summer of 1996.

Deductive reasoning involves the taking of general information and boiling it down to specific hypotheses. You take two or more premises and draw a conclusion from them as to what actually happened at the crime scene.[1] Deductive reasoning has the same restrictions: When you are working on one set of ideas, never give up the idea that there may be another explanation. Just because a man tells another that he is going to kill him someday is not proof that he is the murderer when the other man is found dead. It's highly possible, and perhaps a probability, but look at the other possibilities and probabilities as well.

THE INVESTIGATION

After all the immediate demands of the situation have been met, interview the people who are most likely to give you a preliminary description of the suspect and any con- traband that the suspect may have with him. Broadcast the information by radio or telephone for immediate general rebroadcast. If a telephone is available, use it for greater reception and less interference, *and* greater secrecy. Some professional crim- inals carry scanners so that they can hear what the police broadcasts are saying about them and the crime they just committed. Pause momentarily and briefly plan your course of action. Consider the type of case. Ask yourself what most likely happened. Where did the suspect go? What did the suspect do with the evidence? What was left by the suspect at the crime scene? What did the suspect take away from the crime scene? Generally attempt to reconstruct the crime scene. Make mental—or written— notes of your impressions and physical observations. This pause may give you time to look at the case more objectively. Proceed according to some logical plan that you have formulated during this pause.

Interview Witnesses

Separate the victims and witnesses. Interview them one at a time to secure as many individual viewpoints as possible. Sometimes a group interview will produce a *jury* description, one that is a composite resulting from a series of compromises between witnesses and one that will probably be incorrect. Remember that eyewitnesses are not always reliable, but they may be all that you have. Ask questions that compel the witnesses to give you their own information rather than a feedback of what you believe happened and their agreement that you are right, or nearly so.

Note First Impressions

Right from the start, you should be making written notes of information and evidence as the case develops. In these notes, include information on items that may be of incidental importance as well as of direct evidential value. List items such as your observation that the lights were on although the crime supposedly occurred in the daytime, a cigarette or cigar is still smoldering in an ashtray, a glass window appears to have been broken from the inside when it should have been broken from the outside. Note odors that may be foreign to the place, such as pipe or cigar smoke in a woman's apartment or the pungent smell of a particular aftershave lotion that you can identify. List your observations about any contradictions of witnesses or victims and various items of evidence or information that you collect. For example, the victim's statement that a shelf was full of merchandise may be refuted by the obvious presence of undisturbed dust on the shelf, indicating that nothing had been on that shelf that could have been removed. The loss may be an exaggeration or an outright lie for insurance purposes.

Collection and Preservation of Evidence

An officer cannot collect too much evidence. In your initial investigation, consider the possibility that virtually everything you encounter is potential evidence. Touch only those items that you must touch and touch them very carefully. Systematically collect every item that is—or might be—evidence. Sometimes the most seemingly inconsequential items turn out to be the most significant pieces of evidence when the case goes to trial. Consider what some investigators call the *theory of transfer*. If you subscribe to this theory, you will go into each investigation expecting to find that the perpetrator has left something at the crime scene and that he or she has taken something away. What the person may have left is an aura of body presence that cannot be measured or identified, and perhaps the only thing taken away from the scene is the memory of what had taken place.

According to the transfer theory, the suspect may leave behind his fingerprints, footprints, semen, blood, saliva, perspiration, hair, fibers, lipstick, stains, odors, sounds, or his physical description. He may take with him such items as dust or dirt; broken glass in his clothing; the victim's hair, blood, body fluids, tissue; stolen merchandise; contraband; or the victim himself.

During the entire investigation process, record accurate notes and field sketches, preserve and transport the evidence in accordance with recommended procedures, and take every precaution to substantiate your allegation that a crime was committed by proving the elements of the corpus delicti of each offense. Have sufficient evidence to establish the guilt of the suspect. If a camera is available, make it a general rule to always photograph prints, traces, or any other item of evidence before attempting to collect or otherwise process it.

Whenever taking clothing from the suspect that you intend to search for items of evidence, such as narcotics or broken glass embedded in the material, pack each item in a separate container. The laboratory expert may then testify as to which article of clothing yielded which item of evidence. Whenever taking items of evidence from the custody or presence of anyone, it is a good practice to prepare an itemized list of the articles taken and to leave a receipt with whoever is in charge of the premises.

Consider the following as a recommended policy regarding property and evidence:

> All property, regardless of value, the character or condition of the person from whom it is taken, or the circumstances under which it is acquired by the evidence section of the department, must be labeled and appropriately recorded. In all cases a receipt must be made for property taken or received. Whenever possible, this receipt should be made in duplicate, the original processed along with the evidence or property and the copy given to the person from whom the property is received. No member of the department shall assume a personal interest in, or possession of, any property that comes to him in his official capacity as a police officer.

TYPES OF EVIDENCE

When conducting the search for evidence, an appreciation of the various types of evidence and knowledge of the methods for collecting the evidence is necessary. This phase of the investigation may be conducted by the officer assigned the initial investigation or by a specially trained patrol officer designated "crime scene investigator." Regardless of whether you are the officer assigned to collect and preserve the evidence, consider the following information concerning the techniques involved in the process.

Fingerprints

Three types of fingerprints may be found at the crime scene: plastic, or molded, prints, visible prints, and latent prints. The plastic prints are those usually found in soft, pliable substances, such as putty, wax, soap, butter, or grease. Visible prints are those that need no development to be completely visible to the viewer. They may be found in items such as dust, blood, or any smooth and flat surface the suspect may have touched with the ridged parts of his hands or feet when they contained ink or some other substance that might serve as a "printing" medium when coming in contact with the surface. Latents are invisible to the naked eye and must be brought out of their hiding places be dusting them with dry or magnetic powder; or by fuming with cyanoacrylate (crazy glue), iodine crystals, ninhydrin, or other techniques that are being developed. In order for a successful development of latents, usually a nonporous surface lends itself to a greater degree of success. In recent years, however, the experts have met with some success in lifting prints off of human skin and articles of clothing, which some of the older practitioners will tell you is not possible. In your initial investigation, you will probably be restricted to searching for prints and using the basic dusting procedure with dry or magnetic powder.

Fingerprints that have the greatest value in a criminal investigation are those found in places where only authorized persons are allowed, such as in a cash box, the interior of a cash drawer, or inside some other container. Prints found on counters or desk tops, on the outside of a vending machine, or on an object that anyone could have handled during the normal hours of business may be of some value if the suspect claims that he was never inside or near the place where the prints appear. To help in locating these, turn off any glaring overhead lights and use a flashlight at an oblique angle. Consider items the culprit may have touched during the commission of his crime, then start your search by dusting or fuming the surface. If prints are possibly on items that can be removed to the laboratory, do so and then more time can be spent on the search under more controlled conditions. Also, if you believe that prints might be found on paper, such as valuable documents, or porous surfaces, have the specialist assist you in choosing the best approach and medium to use for the search.

Before dusting the surface where you anticipate finding latents, attempt to determine the direction that the ridges are most likely to run. Using a moderate amount of powder, brush with the grain or the lines of the pattern. Use powder that contrasts to the surface. Once you have developed the latent, or have discovered one of the other types of prints—plastic and visible—take photographs before attempting to transfer the prints to a tape or other lifting material, or before removing them in any manner for preservation. Consider also collecting samples of bare footprints, if there are any available. Some agencies, including the FBI, have done some work on classification of prints on toes and balls of the feet. It is worth a try.

Fingerprint Identification Systems. Computerized fingerprint identification systems now in use in many parts of the country and eventually throughout the United States have proven successful far beyond the expectations of their proponents. In California, the system, known as CAL-ID (see Figure 9–3), has already been utilized in locating and identifying several suspects in serious crimes, including multiple murderers. Taking a partial smudge or single print from the crime scene, the computer can search the files and make a tentative identification that is verified by

Figure 9–3 Fingerprints are one of the most positive means of identification. (Courtesy Chicago Police Department.)

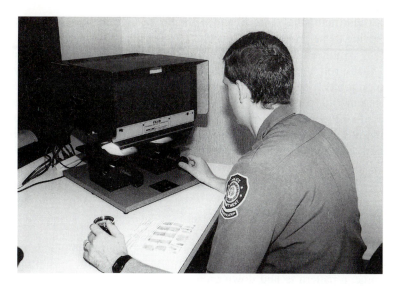

Figure 9–4   The Forensic Optical Comparator is used to compare a suspect's prints with latents found at the scene. (Courtesy Chicago Police Department.)

personal examination of a specialist (see Figure 9–4). Some estimates have included the claim that one fingerprint examiner would take about 100 years to do what this new system's computer can do in 20 minutes. Through the miracle of computers and facsimile communications, it is possible to query fingerprint files held in the archives of the FBI in Quantico, Virginia, as well as all other states and many other countries throughout the world. Many departments are doing similar work with footprints and palm prints.

Following is one method for lifting latents with fingerprint tape. Select tape that is free of bubbles; then pull a length of the tape free from the roll in one continuous movement to avoid creating a ridge at any point in the strip. Fold the tape back about ¼ inch on the end that is free of the roll. Place that end of the tape on the surface about 1 inch from the print that you intend to lift. Slowly press the tape down and move toward the print, keeping the free tape from touching the surface until you press it down. Continue pushing the tape smoothly until it is about 1 inch beyond the print. Cut the tape from the roll and rub across the entire surface to assure adhesion. Lift the tape slowly and place it smoothly on a card of contrasting color or on a piece of transparent plastic. There are many excellent materials available for this process.

You should be wearing clean gloves when collecting evidence, changing them frequently to prevent cross-contamination. Your next responsibility in the collection of visible and latent prints is to identify and locate all persons who have been at the location legally as well as anyone you suspect might have left those prints, including fellow officers at the scene. You are going to use these prints to eliminate suspects and to identify the maker of the prints that you have found. Finding the prints are not in themselves proof that the owner of the print-making fingers is guilty of anything, but that individual or individuals should be able to present a legitimate reason for leaving those prints where found.

You need fingerprint cards and an ink pad in your crime scene kit, or you may actually roll a person's prints onto the card without ink, although you will not have good prints. Use a flat surface and hold the subject's hand while you are rolling them onto the ink pad and then onto the fingerprint card, one finger at a time. Roll each print all the way from one side to the other with the ink, then move over to the card and roll the finger from side to side, getting all of the first joint of the finger on your card. Gently push the finger down onto the surface while you roll each finger, then for the four fingers and thumb you should not have to ink again, but just be sure to gently push down all fingers at the same time and each thumb separately.

DNA Analysis

At one time DNA testing was called "genetic fingerprinting," because when the lab technician analyzes bits of blood or tissue found on the victim or at the scene of a crime, a pattern is laid down on a chart that resembles a bar code like the one you find on most of the prepackaged items in the retail store that a scanner identifies and rings up on the sales register. This chart of characteristics found at the crime scene is compared with the DNA characteristics of a suspect's blood or tissue. The scientist who discovered this system of identification said that—except for identical twins, who have identical genetic codes—the chance of two people or two animals or other forms of life having genetic properties having the same DNA "fingerprint" is about one in 12 billion. For a world that has about 5 billion people, those odds are great. Another observer said that (except for identical twins again) no two people who have ever lived, now live, or will ever live on this earth will have identical DNA codes.

Discovered by Dr. Alec Jeffreys, a geneticist at Leicester University in England in 1986, this form of identification of individuals through analyses of the DNA characteristics cataloged from blood samples taken from literally every man of a targeted age group who was then, or ever had been, in the area where two brutal murders of young women that occurred three years apart, yielded the true murderer, who was convicted for the crimes. An innocent man who had confessed to one of the crimes was released as a result of the test. DNA, or *deoxyribonucleic acid*, is the most accurate means of identification in existence today. People who have been positively identified by eyewitnesses have been cleared and set free as a result of DNA testing.

In the celebrated murder case of former football icon Orenthal J. Simpson, DNA analysis identified convincingly that blood left at the murder scene was Mr. Simpson's and that blood taken away from the scene in his Ford Bronco and allegedly dropped by him on his property positively was the blood of the two victims, his wife, Nicole, and her friend, Ronald Goldman. The jury found Mr. Simpson not guilty anyhow. When asked about the DNA results, they largely dismissed them as irrelevant or thought that if the tests showed what was alleged, that the blood was probably planted by the police to make Simpson look guilty. Before and after the Simpson case, many people have been convicted and cleared on far less DNA evidence.

In April 1989, as reported in the *Los Angeles Times* (on April 20, 1989), Sheriff Brad Gates of Orange County, California, spoke of his state-of-the-art DNA laboratory, which is now fully operational and producing amazing results, as being like out of *Star Wars*. No longer is it science-fiction; it is here and now, and many people have been cleared of crimes after having been wrongfully accused and/or convicted, and many others are being convicted with the aid of DNA science. Gates' laboratory and others throughout the nation are building a massive library of genetic codes and cross-filing them so that the data bank will grow as murderers and rapists and other sex criminals are convicted and tested.

Shoeprints and Tireprints

In dust, dirt, mud, or plastic materials, you may find identifiable impressions of shoes or tire treads. They are often as distinctive as fingerprints, and the law of averages may be applied to show that the impression found at the scene of the crime was probably made by the shoes found in the possession of the suspect, or by the suspect's automobile. In one case, at the scene of a safe burglary, there were prints from two different shoes that indicated that they belonged to the people who removed the safe from the premises. Some distance from the scene of the crime, two men were questioned in a field interview, and the officer had the presence of mind to look at the bottom of their shoes. The comparisons proved that the shoes worn by those two men matched the impressions left at the crime scene, and the additional factor of the combination of shoe designs narrowed down the averages in favor of the prosecution. The combination of designs at the scene of the crime as well as at the field interview, when the two men were interviewed together, was attributed to more than mere coincidence. These types of impressions are first photographed; then plaster of paris casts made of the entire circumference of the tire or as many of the shoe impressions as possible.

The Federal Bureau of Investigation laboratory and others, mostly maintained by state Justice Departments and large cities around the world, have extensive files on various unique print characteristic of various brands of shoes and tires, and other items. In the Simpson case (again) an FBI criminalist found that shoe prints left at the crime scene were probably (nothing is absolute in scientific investigation, everything is stated in terms of probabilities) put there by a very large Bruno Magli shoe that was manufactured by only one shoemaker in a small town in Italy. There was not a similar design made by any other shoe manufacturer in the world. Of course, the defense raised the valid point that the FBI criminalist did not check with every other shoe manufacturer in the world, one of whom might have made shoe soles and heels with similar designs.

Tool Marks

Simple scratches, striations, and impressions are the most commonly encountered marks found at the scene of a crime, usually at the point of a forced entry. Simple scratches with no identifiable characteristics may occur on the inside of locks that have been picked with the aid of lock-picking devices. Striations and impressions are made by a variety of tools, and it is sometimes possible to match the marks and the tools. Whenever a tool is manufactured, it carries with it certain imperfections that are characteristic to only that tool. The tool-making tools are imperfect themselves and transfer their own imperfections to each new tool. Each time a tool is used, it undergoes an almost imperceptible change, but its distinctive markings can be identified by microscopic examination. It is impossible to classify and file in any organized manner tools and tool marks, but if the laboratory specialist has the tool and the mark it made, he may succeed in "making" the case on the basis of a single item of evidence.

Impressions are indentations made on a surface that is softer than the tool used to make them. They are usually found at the point of entry or at the hiding place of some object of theft. The most commonly used burglar tool is the screwdriver; some sort of pry tool is in second place. Hammers or any tool used to strike a surface will make impressions. Measure the impressions and allow for stretching of the material, which will actually make the impressions larger than the tools that made them. Take photographs and casts with material especially designed for this use, and take the actual impression whenever possible. This may necessitate taking out part of a door frame or windowsill for a courtroom presentation, but it is worth the trouble and expense if you are to prosecute the case successfully.

Keep the tool and the impression separate, and make the comparisons by measuring the tool and the impression rather than by contaminating the evidence by placing the tool in the impression possibly made by that tool. The laboratory specialist will make comparisons by making casts of the impressions and the suspected tool and matching them by microscopic examination and the comparison of photographs.

Striations are parallel scratch marks cut into the surface of some material that is softer than the tool or device that makes them. Any imperfections on the scratching surface of the tool making the mark, such as a slight nick or a blunted portion, will be transferred to the object scratched. Striations are made by a scraping, cutting, or glancing blow across the surface. Tools that may make striations are hammers, pry bars or screwdrivers used in a scratching motion, a chisel driven into metal, a bolt cutter cutting a padlock, a wire cutter, or a brace and bit.

Another common type of striation in criminal investigation is that made by the rifling and interior of a revolver, or other rifled firearm, on the bullet that travels through the barrel. Each time it is fired, the firearm changes, and it is imperative that the bullet and suspected gun be compared before it has been fired many times. Otherwise, the comparison will be worthless because of the change that has taken place.

The procedure for handling striations and the tools that are suspected of having made them is the same as that for handling impressions. They are usually compared by photograph and by microscopic examinations.

Soil as Evidence

Soil taken from the crime scene and that which is removed from the clothing or other effects of the suspect may be shown to have similarities that indicate that the suspect was probably at the scene. Different soils come from different source areas and include such distinctive items as seeds, fertilizer, building materials, insecticides, stones, minerals, and different types of soil. To collect soil, scrape the material onto a clean sheet of paper and fold it into a "bindle" or put into a clean plastic bag or bottle that locks or can be sealed on top. To collect it from the scene, such as where a footprint was made, take three or four samples from the immediate area and package in the same type of bag. Other types of containers may be a pill box or plastic tube with screw-top cap; .35 mm film containers, especially plastic ones, are excellent for evidence collection.

Biological Fluids

Stains such as those made by blood or seminal fluid may be classified by blood type and be subjected to other types of laboratory analysis if collected and handled correctly (see Figure 9–5). They may assume many colors by reacting to chemicals that may be on the surface where they are found, and often blood is found that does not resemble the reddish-brown color that one usually associates with dried blood. Seminal stains are usually found on articles of clothing in sex offenses. Collect this type of stain by handling the clothing as little as possible. If wet, allow the stain to dry without folding the clothing or covering it with any other article. Blood is found in various places and should be stored wet in a closed container if possible or be allowed to dry on clothing in the same manner as semen. Bloodstains may be found in the cracks of a freshly washed knife, in cracks in wood or tile floors, in carpeting, in towels or washcloths, in a clothes hamper or wastebasket, or in the drains of sinks or tubs.

When collecting bloodstains, photograph and sketch them first, showing their shapes and size, and the direction of the splash. Also indicate on the sketch whether they are dry, moist, or wet. Collect wet stains by placing the substance in a sealed container with a mild saline solution of 2 teaspoons of salt to 1 quart of water. About

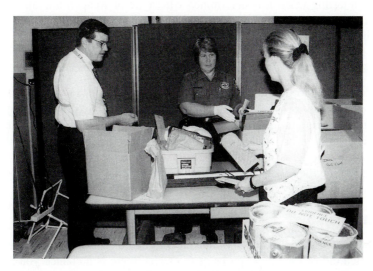

Figure 9–5　The careful handling of evidence is crucial to the successful conclusion of an investigation. (Courtesy Greensboro, NC, Police Department.)

10 cubic centimeters of blood is a desired minimum if it is possible to collect that much. If the blood is in soil, remove any insects before storing. Wet stains may be collected by use of a blotter, which is allowed to dry and is stored in the dry state. Collect dry stains by scraping them onto a piece of clean white paper and folding up the paper securely or by scraping them into a small glass or plastic container designed for the collection of evidence.

Blood groupings are the basic O, A, B, and AB, but may be further classified into M, N, or MN according to the M-N system or another system known as the Rhesus, or Rh, system. How well the classification can be done depends on age and condition of the blood or other body fluid. Approximately 80 percent of the population are secretors, which means that blood is secreted into other body fluids and blood type can be determined by examining those other fluids.

Odontology as an Investigative Tool

Teeth are used as weapons of attack in such crimes as physical assault or sexual abuse. Burglars sometimes bite into food and leave the remains at the crime scene. By examination of the tooth marks, it is sometimes possible to identify the individuals' bite marks by comparing with their teeth. If you encounter any item that appears as though it might contain bite marks, or any wound on a victim's body, it should be carefully examined to determine if it has tooth impressions. Photographs and laboratory examinations might yield some interesting results.

Gunpowder and Shot Pattern Tests

From tattooing on the victim's skin or clothing, it is possible to determine the direction from which a shot was fired and from what distance. This is determined by a study of the powder tattooing, if there is any present. The laboratory will do comparison testing when it is determined what type of weapon and ammunition were used. A suspect's hands and clothing will be tested for residue to determine if he or she has fired a weapon lately.

Fabrics as Evidence

Cotton and wool and other natural fabrics are easier to work with than are the synthetics, such as nylon and orlon. A sample of the victim's clothing compared with a piece of material that might have been left at the scene of a crime may be matched mechanically, as would be done with a piece from a jigsaw puzzle. The manner in which material is woven is characteristic of different mills, and it is also possible to determine the exact cloth content of the material. Dyes and other methods of coloring material may be determined by the laboratory.

Safe Insulation

Whenever a safe has been tampered with and the insulation has been taken out or has fallen out of the inner spaces of the walls, there is a chance you might find some of it in the clothing of the burglar. It is possible to determine that it is, in fact, safe insulation and from which safe manufacturer.

Wood Identification

Mechanical matches may be made if you have a broken piece of the wood and the object from which it supposedly came from. If a cutting instrument was used, matching striations may aid in more positive identification. It is also possible to determine the type of wood you have and also the various sealers, varnishes, and paints.

Paint Identification

All paints are different, but all contain (1) vehicles, which are used for drying, oils for mixing, and other substances that bind the pigments together; (2) pigments, which give paint a distinctive color and may include extenders; (3) driers, such as lead or cobalt; and (4) solvents and thinners, which adjust the consistency of paint.

Examination of dried paint may include a mechanical match of a chip compared with the automobile fender it was suspected to have come from. Layering will show the succession of colors that a surface has been painted, which aids in identification. How many 1968 Chevrolets, for example, have come from the factory with a metallic cherry red color, then were painted with a gray primer and a powder blue, followed by white, and finally a metallic black with gold glitter mixed in the paint? Make, model, and year of an automobile's production may be determined by examination of the original paint. Laboratory examination of paint will include spectrophotometry, X-ray, diffraction, and gas chromatography, which are covered in more detail in forensic texts.

Other Physical Evidence

At the crime scene, virtually any item may be evidence. Collect and itemize every article that in any way indicates that it may be used to aid the success of the investigation. Bullets or other projectiles are common to crimes against persons. Account for every shot fired and locate every projectile. If a bullet is lodged in a piece of wood or plaster surface, dig out the material surrounding the bullet and let the bullet fall out. Do not alter the markings made by the gun by prying directly on the bullet when trying to collect it for evidence.

Glass particles left at the scene of the crime may match those found on the suspect's clothing as a result of a search with a vacuum cleaner with a special filter. A button found at the scene may have been torn off the shirt of the suspect, and by matching thread or torn material, it may be possible to make an identification of the culprit. Tools and weapons are occasionally left behind. They may be examined for fingerprints as well as impressions or striations that they may have made. Sometimes the suspect will leave behind personal items without knowing it. At one armed robbery of a liquor store at night, two suspects walked in and selected some beer under the pretense of preparing to buy it. The clerk asked the men for their identification because of their youthful appearance. One of the suspects handed the clerk his driver's license, then took out a gun and told the clerk to give him all of the money in the cash drawer. The suspects fled, the one forgetting to take back his driver's license. Imagine his dismay when he remembered. At about the same time, the clerk was on the telephone telling the police that he had just been robbed by the person named and described on the license. Needless to say, he probably will never make that mistake again after he finishes "serving his time."

MARKING EVIDENCE

Mark, or in some other way identify, every item of evidence at the time you collect it. Make the mark distinctive enough so that you will later be able to examine the item and positively state on the witness stand that you made that exact mark and, therefore, that is the same item that you collected at the time of the investigation. Some items are of such a nature that it is impossible to mark the items themselves. In those cases, seal the items inside a container and place your mark on the outside of the container. If you use a sealing material, it will be possible for you to testify that you sealed the container and that it does not appear to have been broken.

Items that have serial numbers may not need marking because you may record the number. If in doubt whether to mark, do it. Make the marks very distinguishable, but small and in places where they will not destroy the value of the item you mark. Clothing may be marked with no damage to the material if you make the marks in places such as inside the waistband of trousers, on the manufacturer's label, or on the tail of a shirt. If you have several pieces of glass, sketch the outlines of the various pieces on a sheet of paper, and designate a number to each piece.

CHAIN OF EVIDENCE CUSTODY

When introducing an item of evidence at a trial, you must describe the location where you collected it and the manner in which you collected it. It is then necessary for you and the other people in your department to show the precise route of travel of that item of evidence, to assure the court that it has not undergone any change or other contamination between the time it was collected and the time it was presented in court. To be able to guarantee the most careful handling of evidence and its chain of custody, follow these guidelines when processing evidence.

1. Limit the number of individuals who handle the evidence from the time it is found to the time it is presented to the court.
2. Each time you handle the evidence, check its condition to assure yourself that it has not been damaged or altered.
3. If the evidence leaves your possession,
   a. Record the name of the person to whom it is given.
   b. Log the date and time the transfer of custody is made.
   c. Log the reason for the transfer of evidence, such as "to evidence man for analysis" or "for lab analysis."
   d. Log when and by whom it is returned, if at all.
4. Each person who handles an item of evidence should affix his identifying mark to the article so that he, too, may testify to the fact that it is the same item he handled earlier.

5. Obtain a signed receipt from the person accepting the evidence, or have some procedure for recording the transfer each time it is made.

6. When evidence is returned to your custody, assure yourself that it is the same evidence.

The handling and storage of evidence is one of the more vulnerable points in the chain of custody. It is critical to the evidentiary value of any items you send or take to the laboratory or to the evidence locker that everyone who handles the items does so with strict observance of the rules concerning chain of custody. Employees should be carefully screened to avoid such isolated incidents as the storage clerk selling three pounds of cocaine back to the suspect who was booked for its possession or the clerk who had his own auction of seized bicycles and firearms. Although such incidents are rare, and certainly are not representative of the thousands of honest workers for police departments, this news becomes a topic for debate in court when the chain of evidence custody is presented.

In addition to the need for tight security, attention should be given to the life expectancy of some evidence, which may be perishable. Correct marking and handling should make it possible to refrigerate and freeze those items that need it and to seal other materials. Perishables also include items that might not perish over time but whose value will, such as fashion clothing. Recovered fashion designer clothing that is held for months in an evidence locker will bankrupt the store owners. Consider photographing and otherwise documenting the lot; then hold a representative sample for evidence and present it and the photograph at the time of the trial. This will be matter for the prosecuting attorney to decide.

Whenever you send or take evidence to the laboratory for analysis, give the lab personnel as much help as you can by indicating what it is that you believe they should look for during the examination. You may not be correct, but it will at least give them a starting point.

PHOTOGRAPHS

The purpose of photographs is to provide visual aids to the case for the investigators, the prosecuting attorney, and, above all, the judge and the jury. A photograph must be an accurate representation of the scene as it appeared to someone who was present at the time the photograph was taken. If possible, photographs should be taken before anything at all is disturbed. This will make it easier to explain the scene because if anything has been moved, it will be necessary to explain why. If you must move evidence prior to the photograph, mark the location where it was located so that the photograph will show the mark where something had been removed. For example, in a homicide case, the victim may have been removed to the hospital because it may have appeared that he was still living. The body's location should be marked with a high-contrast material, such as a yellow marking crayon.

For closeup photographs, use a ruler or other marker of known size. When the print is made, it will be possible for the darkroom technician to use a ruler and reproduce the exact size of the item in the enlargement. When photographing flat surfaces, be sure to have the film exactly parallel with the surface. Any enlargement will be free of distortion that occurs when the photograph is taken from an angle. With each enlargement, the distortion is exaggerated if the film and the object are not parallel.

Take background, or condition, photographs to show general conditions at the scene. Orientation may include photographs of the exterior of the building, the hallway leading to the exact location where the crime occurred, and the exact location. These pictures take the viewer on a pictorial journey to the place of the crime. (See Figure 9–6.) Consider the use of Polaroid pictures for immediate review and evaluation, and other pictures if the earlier ones do not come out. The Polaroid camera is designed for snapshot quality, and it should not be used exclusively.

Color transparency slides are excellent investigative and evidential devices. They may be projected in a fully lighted room on a rear projection screen, or they may be projected in extremely large magnifications on a screen in a darkened room. The possibilities for using slides are several, particularly in the examination of minute bits of evidence.

For courtroom admissibility of photographs, the photographs must represent the scene as observed by the person who testifies to that fact. They must be material or relevant to the case, and they must be free of distortion. Photographs also cannot be of such a nature that would prejudice the jury against the defendant. Each photograph used should be one that adds to, rather than detracts from, the case. There must be some meaning to the picture, and it must depict what the accompanying testimony purports that it will depict.

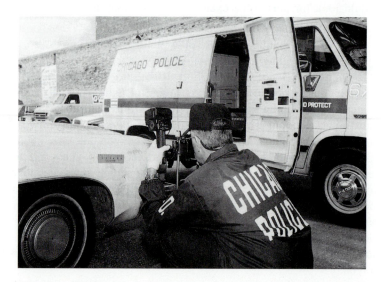

Figure 9–6 The picture that tells a story. (Courtesy Chicago Police Department.)

VIDEOGRAPHY

If time and circumstances permit, recording the entire preliminary investigation or particular phases of the investigation may prove invaluable for later reference. Items may have been overlooked by searchers but show up in the videotape, and the officers can go back and retrieve the materials while the scene is still intact and undisturbed. Be careful to make a decision before taping what sound you are going to record. If you are going to have the videographer narrate the tape, be sure that it coincides with the reports that are going to be prepared later and your field notes. If the videographer and the investigator are one and the same person, you are less likely to have such a conflict as contradictory observations of the scene. One extremely important task you or the videographer must perform before there is any taping: Check the date and time indicator and make sure that they are correct. It would be extremely embarrassing to testify that you took the videotape at 0715 on June 16, then play the tape for the jury and have them see May 22 2243 as the date and time. This has happened in some very important investigations and proven very embarrassing. It might possibly discredit the tape and/or the person giving testimony about it unless the explanation is very plausible.

ACCIDENT AND CRIME SCENE SKETCHING

A rough sketch is the simplest and most effective method of showing the scene as it relates to the crime or accident and the corresponding photographs. The two very rough sketches in Figure 9–7 illustrate how simple the sketch may be. When measurements are necessary to the case, they may be either paced or measured. When you do put in the measurements, indicate in your legend that the measurements are or are not exact and that the sketch is or is not to scale. Obviously, the sketch that you put in your notebook is not to scale if it looks anything like those in Figure 9–7.

Before you move anything, make every attempt to take photographs, and make a rough sketch so that you may reconstruct the scene with the aid of the sketch and photos, if necessary.

Police sketching falls into three types:

1. *Locality sketch:* view of the overall scene and its environs, including neighboring buildings, roads leading to the scene, and the location of the crime or accident in relationship to the surrounding geographical landmarks
2. *Grounds sketch:* scene of the crime or accident closer up, with its general surroundings

   Accident: point of impact, final resting place of vehicles, skid marks, and other evidence; nearby intersections, view obstructions, lighting devices, traffic controls, and related objects

   Crime: actual scene where the crime took place with its nearest surroundings, such as other rooms, house and lawn, garage, other floors in the building
3. *Detailed sketch:* immediate scene only, such as the room or place where the event occurred

Figure 9–7 Rough sketches for notebook.

Sketches are generally divided into two categories:

1. *Rough sketch:* made at the scene by the initial investigating officer. It need not be drawn to scale, but it should be in proportion, and the measurements indicated on the sketch or in the accompanying notes. Relative distances must be clearly indicated so that a finished drawing will show true perspectives.

2. *Finished drawing:* prepared primarily for court presentations by an experienced draftsperson (don't overlook your local public works department for an artist). This one is drawn to scale with exact measurements.

The materials you will need for sketching will be a pencil so that you can make erasures; graph paper, which will make it simpler to show distances; clipboard or other hard surface for drawing; small ruler for straight lines; a compass for accurate directions and true north; a steel tape that does not expand or contract with the weather conditions; and marking chalk or crayon.

Basic Rules for Sketching

Measurements must be accurate, and measured by the person preparing the sketch. If someone else is nearby, have him or her measure again to assure accuracy. Take all measurements the same way, either paced or measured, and so indicate in the legend. Recommended scales for sketches:

Detail sketches: ½ inch = 1 foot
Large areas or rooms: ¼ inch = 1 foot
Larger areas and houses: ⅛ inch = 1 foot
Larger buildings: ½ inch = 10 feet
Open areas, such as locality sketch: ½ inch = 10 feet

Your sketch must show essential items. Keep the sketch simple and uncluttered, free from unnecessary detail but including all objects related to the investigation.

Essential Elements for Crime Scene Sketch.

1. If in an open area, perimeter of crime scene, showing relationships to landmarks and permanent objects, such as trees and buildings
2. If the crime occurred inside, outline of the room, including doors, windows, and permanent objects
3. Point of entry and exit by the perpetrator, if known or indicated by evidence or witnesses
4. If it is a crime against person, location and position of the victim
5. Weapons and/or tools used in the perpetration of the crime
6. Stains, marks, and other traces related to the crime, including fingerprints and shoe and tire impressions
7. Furniture and fixtures relevant to the investigation
8. Objects attacked or damaged, such as desk, safe, dressers, or articles of clothing

Essential Elements for Accident Scene Sketch.

1. Point of impact by at least two measurements. For example, 8 feet north of south curb of Broadway, 68 feet west of east curbline of Main. This is determined by statements of witnesses and drivers, skid marks with abrupt change

of direction, or gouge marks or debris in the street resulting from sudden jolt of the vehicle.

2. Location where the vehicles came to rest by three measurements. For example, distance from point of impact to a specific part of the vehicle, such as the center of the wheel; distance from one wheel to the curb; and distance from another wheel on the same side of the vehicle to the curb. When no curbs or edges of the road are present, use the polar coordinate method of measurement.

3. Location of the injured or deceased, if out of the vehicle. Measure from a specific part of the body to the point of impact (POI).

4. Identification and labeling of the vehicles (V1, V2).

5. Direction of travel of vehicles and pedestrians and which lane of traffic they were in.

6. Names of streets, their widths, and number of lanes.

7. Type and condition of road surface.

8. Indication of weather and lighting conditions.

9. Locations of traffic signs and signals.

10. Vision obstructions.

11. Skid marks.

Essential Elements for All Sketches.

1. Compass directions: at least a north arrow.

2. Use a scale or draw in relative proportions.

3. Legend. Explain all symbols used in the sketch. Number or letter objects, with an itemized list, such as all numbered items are evidence and all lettered items are furniture.

4. Title block. List case number, date and time the incident occurred, date and time the sketch is prepared, description of the type of incident, the location, and name of the person preparing the sketch.

Measuring Methods.

1. *Coordinate method* (Figure 9–8a). The simplest way to locate objects in a sketch is by giving distances from two mutually perpendicular lines, such as two walls of a room.

2. *Polar coordinates* (Figure 9–8b).

3. *Triangulation* (Figure 9–8c). If the distance between two objects is known, a third object can be located and distance determined even though it cannot be reached (such as a point across a ravine or river).

INVESTIGATION OF SPECIFIC CRIMES

The next few pages are devoted to just a few of the dozens of different types of crimes that you will be required to investigate during the course of your career as a field patrol officer. Consider the pointers as a guide to your investigation. Many traf-

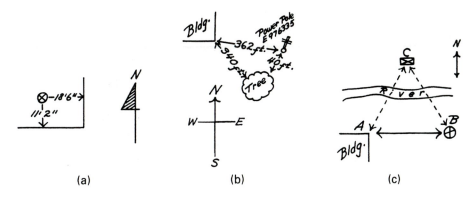

Figure 9–8   Measuring methods: (a) coordinates; (b) polar coordinates; (c) triangulation.

fic collisions are the result of criminal activity. Because of their special nature, collision investigation will be covered in Chapter 11.

Arson

A serious problem with arson investigation is that much of the evidence may have been destroyed in the fire. Although it may not lead to discovery of what or who started the fire, it would be helpful to know that just three days before the fire, the beneficiary of the insurance policy tripled the amount of insurance that will more than pay for any loss from the fire or water damage. This may show a jury that there was some type of incentive to suffer the loss. Another item of information, and this happened in a Newport Beach nightclub case, is that all the expensive liquor in the storeroom was removed to another location owned by the same people and was replaced with similar bottles containing water or some other liquid. Some of the bottles were not broken during the fire and firefighting efforts, and the arson investigator became suspicious of the broken seals on bottles that were allegedly unopened. Also, most of the good furniture was removed by someone before the fire and replaced with similar furniture purchased from a thrift store.

Investigation of the arson may be handled exclusively by a member of the fire department or the fire marshal. However, in some enlightened jurisdictions, fire investigation teams are made up of both police and fire investigators, the fire personnel for their knowledge of how fire behaves, and the police investigators for their knowledge of how people behave and for their investigative skill. As for your task when you first arrive on the scene, handle traffic control and crowd control, but pay particular attention to preservation of evidence, and look carefully at the faces in the crowd of spectators. It is not unusual for the arsonist to want to watch his or her handiwork or to actually volunteer to help put it out. Some firefighters have been known to also be firestarters. In one California city a bored police officer working the overnight shift would set fires in trash bins behind downtown shopping-center buildings, then he would supposedly be on patrol when he would "discover" a fire and start putting it out while waiting for the fire companies to arrive.

Look for the place where the fire is most intense if you arrive while the fire is still burning and you are standing by for the fire companies. That may be the point of origin. Look for evidence of any incendiary material, such as flammable liquids or oily rags or towels. Melted wax may be the residue of candles used to start the fire. Touch nothing until the fire is completely out, but point out to the fire supervisor on the scene any suspicious materials that you see so that special care will be given those items. Fire science has progressed considerably during the past few decades, and arson investigation has become a much more sophisticated undertaking than it was in the past. Arson fires are one of the major categories of losses from criminal activity, a great many fires being caused by insured people who seek to defraud the insurer or to break a long-term lease when business is bad.

Some arsonists use professional "torches," people who use very sophisticated devices and materials to start their fires, or throw several well-placed fire bombs to completely destroy a building and make it look like the work of hate groups or unruly crowds instead of a business venture for profit. Make it a habit to ask neighbors and others close to the business establishment, "How's business?"

Auto Theft

Special locking devices and alarms have slowed down amateur theft of automobiles, according to Bernard Edelman in "Auto Theft: For Police the Joyride Is Over": "The man geared to steal a car can steal one in minutes, no matter what safety or locking devices you put on."[2] The article points out that "chop shops," or professional car theft and stripping operations, are able to provide car parts at one-third the price that legitimate auto parts stores charge and can cut labor charges by 50 percent by selling preassembled units.[3]

Another type of auto theft is the insurance fraud perpetrated by the owners themselves, who contract with professional theft rings to steal their cars so that they may collect insurance. Some owners have more than one policy, so when a car is stolen, the owner is paid by each of the two or more insurance companies; a $5,000 stolen car can yield $15,000 in returns. Some insurance industry sources estimate that 25 percent of all reported thefts of automobiles are fraudulent.[4]

When taking the auto theft report, inquire about the payments that might have been missed; the car may have been repossessed. Sometimes the owner loaned the car to a friend or relative and now wants it back and will report it stolen so that the police will make a dramatic recovery. Such a false report may result in the loss of someone's life, possibly yours, in attempting to apprehend a car thief who knows that no theft is involved and will violently resist or might make a game out of the chase.

Cars with auto tracking devices such as LoJack will not stop or deter actual auto thefts, as the secret of successful recovery is not to advertise that the car has one installed. When the owner discovers that his or her vehicle is stolen, a 911 call to the police, giving the VIN, license number, and description of the vehicle then starts the process. The police or sheriff's department equipped with LoJack equipment remotely activates the homing device installed in the stolen vehicle. It then sends out a radio signal that is picked up by a satellite receiver, which relays the signal down to police vehicles equipped to find the location and direction of travel of the signal and meet the car thief at his or her destination before the car can be stripped or chopped. That's the way it works in demonstrations, as explained in television and radio commercials. When my car is stolen, I'll report on how well it works.

Whenever you stop a person who might be driving a stolen automobile, ask the person who claims to be the owner or the borrower who cannot find the registration slip a few questions that the person familiar with the car should know, such as mileage, contents of the glove box, contents of the trunk, brand of battery or tires, recent repairs or new wiring, or when the car was last serviced and where. Car thieves seldom take the time to check those things out, and they are likely to reveal themselves as thieves. There are also those car owners who don't know the answers to any of those questions either, but they are in the minority. Look for the "dummy key" in the ignition or the driver who is unfamiliar with the car or how the parts work, and remember that even car thieves remain calm while being questioned by the police.

Burglary

Burglary is entry of a building or any of a number of different types of structures, or a vehicle or a vessel with the intent to commit a theft or any felony, according to California law. The type of structure varies but usually includes any type of place that has a top and sides and is enclosed and has a door or flap or cover that—when closed—is intended to protect the contents against the elements or people from entry: a tent, a mine shaft with an entry door, a telephone booth that Clark Kent would change clothes in, or even a showcase. In some cases a partially enclosed carport may be classified as a "building" if it is attached to a house. A vehicle usually has to be locked. However, breaking into the locked trunk of an otherwise unlocked vehicle, or pushing open the broken wind wing of an otherwise locked vehicle will be a burglary. No force is necessary to constitute burglary of a building, but some sort of force is necessary for an auto burglary. For example, merely unsnapping the canvas top of a jeep would not be burglary.

There are essentially three types of burglars: the career criminal, the opportunist, and the juvenile. Of the three, the career burglar is the most likely to have an explanation for being in the area or for having the property that he has in his possession. The opportunist will take advantage of the open window or unlocked door and will take almost anything that suits his fancy. The juvenile will probably be someone who lives in the neighborhood. Although none of the three neatly falls into any category, you should be alert to all three who might be operating in your district. The opportunist may be a delivery person who takes advantage of the open door while making the normal rounds of his job, such as selling spring water or ice cream bars, or the transient magazine subscription salesperson working your city before moving on to another city next week.

You will usually receive notification of a burglary through citizen complaints or by burglar alarm, either silent or audible. Neighbors watching out for each other's property are probably the best protection against burglaries, and neighborhood watch programs should be encouraged. If you frequently check out unoccupied buildings for security, you will find the places that the owners make vulnerable and will require more diligent patrol. If you actively and aggressively interview all people in your district who arouse your suspicions, you will get to know the burglars who have criminal records and the other individuals who seem to have nothing better to do than to roam the streets at unusual hours.

Whenever responding to a burglary call, assume that the burglar is still inside until you establish otherwise. Do not enter any building alone or before assistance has arrived when you suspect burglary. You have the advantage from the outside; the burglar has the advantage when you go in. Look for point of entry and point of exit. Attempt to reconstruct the crime from statements of witnesses and from your own observations. You may find that the "victim" has made a false report if you listen and observe carefully. An entry or exit may be physically impossible when you try to duplicate the event, being careful not to disturb any evidence.

Dead Body Calls—Homicide

Whenever responding to a dead body call, approach it from the standpoint that it is a possible criminal homicide. Your investigation might establish that the death was accidental or natural or a suicide or caused by some other noncriminal means, but if you start out with the assumption that the victim died as a result of a criminal act, you are less likely to overlook valuable evidence.

Your first responsibility is to determine if death has, in fact, occurred. If there is any possibility whatever that there may be life in the victim, take immediate steps to attempt to preserve the life. This is your first responsibility. Some bodies indicate by their appearance that death has unquestionably occurred, and you may proceed accordingly. Look for the presumptive and positive signs of death when examining the body, and note the observations you make.

The presumptive signs, which indicate that death has possibly but not conclusively occurred, involve body temperature, heartbeat, and respiration. To determine if the person is breathing, look for any movement in the area of the lower border of the rib cage. Absence of any respiration indicates death or a condition that may be produced in drowning, electrocution, or narcotic overdose cases in which the respiratory process is arrested. For the heartbeat, feel for a pulse at the carotid artery on the right side of the throat, or at the heart itself. Body temperature decreases at a steady rate that varies with the individual. When death occurs, there may be a perceptible change in temperature. When examining the body for temperature, note any differences in temperature at the various parts of the body. If death has occurred not too many hours before your arrival, the differences in body temperature may help the medical examiner to determine the approximate time of death.

There are three positive signs of death: (1) postmortem lividity, (2) rigor mortis, and (3) absence of muscle tone in the eyelids. Bear in mind, however, that even though the person has obviously died and there is no question about it, you as a police officer have no authority to declare that death has occurred. Leave that task to the doctors, the coroners and their deputies, and other people who are authorized to make such a responsible determination.

Postmortem lividity appears on portions of the body that are closer to the surface on which it rests. It is a discoloration and appears something like a light-purple bruise with no obvious outer bruise on the skin surface. Lividity is actually a settling of all the body fluids by the pull of gravity to the lower parts of the body, and it begins about ½ hour to 3 hours after death. If it appears at some part of the body other than where it would be normally as a result of gravity flow, it may indicate that the body has been moved after death. Because of its resemblance to a bruise, do not overlook the possibility that it is actually a bruise.

Rigor mortis is a hardening, or calcifying, condition of the muscles throughout the body, usually beginning with smaller muscles and progressively developing in the larger muscles. For this reason, it appears to start at the face and head and work down to the feet. Actually, it is working in all parts of the body at the same time. Depending on the physical condition of the victim at the time of death, rigor mortis usually begins about 3 to 5 hours after death, is complete in 8 to 12 hours, then begins to disappear after about 48 hours. Sometimes a condition occurs that resembles rigor mortis and is misleading to the observer. This condition is known as a cadaveric spasm, which is an immediate rigidity of the entire body caused by an intense emotional situation that occurs at the moment of death. It is known to happen in crimes when the death occurs in a violent struggle or at an emotional peak. When examining the body, check various parts of the body to ascertain the presence of the rigor, but do not attempt to disturb the condition. Once the condition is "broken" by movement, it does not return.

The third positive sign of death is the total absence of muscle tone in the pupils of the eyes, the eye muscles, and the eyelids. This is also one of the first places that the decaying process in the human body begins. When checking for muscle tone, also look for a film that forms over the eyes, caused by the drying of the fluids that once were produced by the tear ducts.

Only a doctor or a coroner may legally declare death,[5] and until the arrival of such a person, it is your responsibility to make every effort to sustain what life may exist, except when there are such conditions as to positively establish the existence of death. The coroner takes charge of the remains and his possessions, and in cooperation with the office of the coroner, the police department investigates deaths as to their cause to determine what criminal law violations were committed, if any.

If there is a possibility that the death is anything other than "natural," by disease, or by accidental means, the investigation continues immediately. Except in departments that assign homicide investigators to take over the investigation immediately, your role as patrol officer is to assume the responsibility for the initial investigation. Specialists should be called in as early in the investigation as possible to handle laboratory and identification work, and the follow-up investigator may begin the follow-up at the same time you are conducting the initial investigation. Following is a list of guidelines for the investigation of any suspected death:

1. *Examine the victim.* Look for signs of life, or death. Make mental notes (write them in your notes as soon as practicable) about the variations in body temperature, state of rigor mortis, and other presumptive and positive signs of death that you observe. Consider the possibility of securing a dying declaration from the victim if he is still alive and coherent.

2. *Identify the victim.* Identification may be made during the victim's dying declaration, if there is one, and by examining the victim's personal effects. The property of the deceased is the responsibility of the coroner, but an officer may examine certain property to make an identification and to pursue the investigation. Sometimes the identity of the deceased will lead to the person who caused his present condition or to friends or relatives who should be notified of the death and may be of possible assistance in the investigation.

3. *Determine the cause of death.* The cause may be obvious, but do not overlook the not so obvious. For example, a known heart patient was found dead under what appeared to be "natural" conditions. The officer handled the case as he would handle any other heart patient until the ambulance had taken the victim to the morgue, and it was discovered that two puncture wounds were in the victim's chest. There was very little bleeding. Had there been, it would have given the officers a clue as to the cause and nature of the wound. It was not until during the autopsy that the cause of death was determined to be two bullet wounds. The bullets were still inside the victim's chest. Sometimes the coroner or medical examiner has to investigate extensively to ascertain the cause of death.

4. *Protect the scene.* The scene includes the place of the death and the immediate surrounding area. Every death that occurs under unusual circumstances must be considered a possible homicide until the investigation establishes that it is not.

5. *Question witnesses.* Separate the witnesses and question them about the identity of the victim and any other matters that seem pertinent to the investigation. Ask about anyone who might have had a reason for killing the victim, such as a dismissed employee or an estranged spouse or some other relative. More than half of all homicide victims knew their killers, according to statistics compiled over the last several decades. The seemingly respectable or shy person should not be overlooked any more than the sinister or suspicious looking person should. The innocent-looking witness may be the killer.

6. *Draw sketches and take photographs to memorialize the scene before you remove any of the evidence or the body.*

7. *Remove the body.* Prior to the body's removal, arrange to have photographs taken, and prepare a field sketch. Specific parts of the body in relationship with fixed objects at the scene will aid in the preparation of the sketch. Note the exact location of the body, its position, and any relevant information. If there was an immediate removal of the body because of a belief that life may have existed, make notes of your recollections of the scene at your arrival.

8. *Search.* Search the immediate and general area for any evidence that may lead to the eventual solution of any crime that may have occurred or that may aid the investigation in any appreciable manner.

9. *Reconstruct the occurrence.* By organizing the statements, the facts, evidence, and whatever else is available, attempt to determine the cause of death and the circumstances surrounding it. Establish a motive for the homicide, if one is apparent.

The motive is not necessary to prove guilt of the accused, but it often leads to the identification of the guilty party.

Laws in your state will specify which deaths must be reported to the coroner. Once the coroner or a deputy arrives, that person is responsible for custody of the deceased and all personal belongings. When evidence is involved, the coroner will not keep those items from you. California Government Code Section 27491 designates the following as cases for the coroner:

1. No physician in attendance
2. Wherein deceased has not been attended by a physician in the 20 days prior to death
3. Physician unable to state the cause of death
4. Known or suspected homicide
5. Known or suspected suicide
6. Involving any criminal action or suspicion of a criminal act
7. Related to or following known or suspected self-induced or criminal abortion
8. Associated with a known or alleged rape or crime against nature
9. Following an accident or injury (primary or contributory, occurring immediately or at some remote time)
10. Drowning, fire, hanging, gunshot, stabbing, cutting, starvation, exposure, alcoholism, drug addiction, strangulation, or aspiration
11. Accidental poisoning (food, chemical, drug, therapeutic agents)
12. Occupational diseases or occupational hazards
13. Known or suspected contagious disease, constituting a public hazard
14. All deaths in operating rooms
15. All deaths where a patient has not fully recovered from an anesthetic, whether in surgery, recovery room, or elsewhere
16. All deaths in which the patient is comatose throughout the period of physician's attendance, whether in home or hospital
17. In prison or while under sentence
18. Solitary deaths (unattended by physician or other persons in period preceding death)
19. All deaths of unidentified persons
20. All deaths of persons who are charges of the state (Fairview or Lanterman patients)
21. Fetal deaths where the attending physician cannot state an underlying cause of death

Drug and Bomb Laboratories

Many ingredients used to manufacture bombs and to mix drugs and other chemical formulas are highly flammable and volatile. Once you have identified the problem, isolate the room or building, perhaps even the entire neighborhood, depending on the size of the operation and the substances being manufactured. Secondly, evacuate all people from the area, including fellow officers. Once you are sure the area is clear, the more prudent choice would be to call upon the bomb or hazardous material people to neutralize the area and collect the evidence while you continue to keep the tourists away. You are certainly going to be in charge of evidence collection, but the Fire Department HazMat Team is outfitted with appropriate clothing and training to collect the materials, and you are going to call out the specialists to take the investigation further than you will have time to handle. State and federal agencies will also be involved in cases of sizable proportions, and your nearby military component will probably have a bomb squad available.

Many terrorist targets are federal establishments, such as federal buildings and post offices. If your problem is located at one of those establishments, you will be required to immediately call upon the Postal Inspection Service (PIS), Alcohol, Tobacco, and Firearms (ATF), and the Federal Bureau of Investigation (FBI), who have a terrorism task force to roll out on any situation involving terrorist or suspected terrorist activity. As for the drug laboratories, your target may be producing materials that are transported out of the country or from state to state. Therefore, you will no doubt be calling upon agencies beyond your own personnel right from the start.

Forgery and Suspected Documents

Whenever searching the suspect and his or her property, look for anything that the person may have written under regular everyday conditions. Next, get sample writings while in your presence so that you will later be in a position to testify that you observed the suspect actually doing the writing or printing. These are a few guidelines:

1. If a handwritten document is in question, get the suspect's handwriting and attempt to get approximately the same type of writing. For example, if the suspected document is a check, have the suspect write out a check.
2. If all was done in capital letter printing, get capital letter printing.
3. If written in pencil or if written with ballpoint pen, use a similar instrument.
4. If written on lined paper or unlined paper, use a similar type of paper.

Dictate the wording if you are attempting to approximate the original document, but do not spell the words for the suspect, as the misspelling might be a clue. For the same reason, do not allow the suspect to copy another document.

Gambling

Undercover investigation and the use of informants are usually required to succeed in gambling cases. There is a brotherhood among gamblers and their bookies and other participants, a "we're in this together" conspiracy. Unless there is some cheating involved, it is difficult to find a complaining witness. Although a certain gambling operation might have the appearance of being a small-time operation among friends, it is hard for any gambling operator to survive without underworld connections or protection—any successful operator, that is.

Look for inconsistent situations, such as people coming out of a shoe repair shop with shoes that have not been repaired, or a barber shop without haircuts, or a butcher shop without meat. There may be an unusual number of people involved that could not be handled by the number of service personnel present, such as one barber who could not possibly trim 27 heads of hair in a half hour.

When approaching a suspected gambling operator, such as a bookie, look for water-soluble paper inserted in the mouth or a cigarette glowing next to flashpaper, which instantly melts and burns on contact with a flame. Once the suspect is in custody, and if the bookie had been near a telephone, you might find that by answering the phone for the next several minutes you will collect evidence that will establish the business nature of the calls, which may be used as evidence to establish that the suspect is a bookie.

Receiving Stolen Property

Mere possession of property that your record check reveals is stolen is not sufficient for an arrest of the person in possession of that property. You need to develop more substantial indicators that the person knows that it is stolen. The possession must be accompanied by what the courts will recognize as "suspicious circumstances." The following behaviors might indicate a guilty mind under the right circumstances:

1. Attempt by the person to flee when you approach him or her and you wish to interview
2. False statements offered by the subject as to how the property came into his or her possession.
3. Use of a false name and inability to establish the existence of the person(s) from whom the property was supposed to have been received
4. Sale of the property under a false name and at an inappropriate price (i.e., far too low)
5. Sale of the property with identification marks removed
6. An attempt to throw away or hide the property

Robbery

Consider your personal safety above that of all others, including hostages. A dead police officer will be of no assistance to any victim, regardless of age or sex. If you are able to negotiate with a robber, do so by telephone or through some remote means so that you are not exposed to possible gunfire. Determine as quickly as possible if the situation is actually a robbery and if the suspect is still on the premises at the time of your arrival. If the suspect has left, consider what you might do if you were the robber. Look in the logical places, but also look in those places where you think it would be most unlikely to find the suspect.

When having the victim and witnesses describe the suspect, have them write down their impressions and keep them separate. Rather than ask for the hair and eyes and height and weight, you might first have them tell you what it was about them or their appearance, mannerisms, voice, or the way they moved that was distinctive.

What you are looking for is something that will set the suspect apart from all others. Did the suspect take anything away from the scene, such as a cola drink or a particular brand of beer? Whom does the suspect resemble that the witness knows? a brother? a fellow employee? Any idea at all will give you something more to work with.

Sexual Assault

In many kinds of sexual assault, you will find victims extremely defensive, sometimes because of strong moral-religious feelings that make them feel guilty and dirty at the same time. Victims might even show open hostility to you as an authority figure. Whatever your approach, you must be empathetic and nonjudgmental. Avoid at all costs making any statement or inference that would even indirectly imply that you are doubtful of the facts. At this moment of extreme emotional stress, it is possible for the victim not to remember details or for the entire situation to be exaggerated in the victim's mind. But there is no falsehood there. Be patient and understanding. What the victim needs at this time is someone who will offer reassurance and comfort.

Record your time of arrival and the condition of the victim. Have the victim do nothing to change the evidence, such as washing or changing clothes. If the crime is a rape, immediately have the victim examined by a doctor who is familiar with rules of evidence in rape cases and who has a rape kit. Your department may supply hospitals and clinics with the kits. All suspected body fluids, hairs, fibers, and inconsequential-appearing items of evidence might be the factor that will convict the accused.

In child molestations, be extremely careful not to suggest to the child the answers that you want. Ask the child to tell you in his or her own words exactly what happened. If a parent is present during the questioning, be sure that the parent understands that there is to be absolutely no interference and no leading questions. Children are very suggestible, particularly at a time of great emotional trauma, and should not be encouraged to say things that others want to hear. Question a child away from the parents, and have a witness present. You are dealing with a very sensitive situation, and hysteria is not unlikely.

Suicides and Attempted Suicides

You are responsible for protecting people against attempting suicide. You must take whatever steps you can to protect the life of a person who may want to end it himself or herself. Sometimes people with suicidal tendencies may attempt to bait you into a situation in which they hope you will shoot and kill them. Such people may cause the officer to fulfill their wishes.

When responding to an attempted suicide call, make every effort to preserve the individual's life. Although the person may not be "mentally ill" by definition, but experiencing a severe emotional crisis, he should be handled as a possible mental illness case and be subjected to an examination by a psychiatrist. Some jurisdictions provide for temporary civil commitment of people who attempt suicide until such time as they may be examined by a medical and psychiatric team and a determination made as to which treatment is best to prevent a recurrence.

Many fallacies exist concerning suicide, and some of these fallacies have been attacked by a Suicide Prevention Center at the University of California at Los Angeles Medical Center. Consider these views when responding to an attempted suicide call or when taking information concerning an individual's threat to commit suicide either immediately or some time in the future. One fallacy that has prevailed for some time is that a person who threatens suicide will usually not go through with it. It has been generally believed that such threats are bids for sympathy or attention, which they are. But it has also been shown through extensive study that the individual will commit suicide if he or she does not solve in some meaningful way whatever problem is the cause of the anguish.

Another fallacy about people who attempt suicide is the belief that they are so intent on killing themselves that they cannot be convinced to change their minds. This has been proven to be an invalid argument. Many people have been talked out of self-destruction, and, given proper treatment, they may permanently change their minds. They do not necessarily have to be suicidal for life. If they do not receive some counseling or other type of intervention, they may try again, and possibly succeed.

All people who attempt self-destruction are not necessarily mentally ill. The condition may be the result of complete despair or severe emotional problems caused by failure or unhappiness. Other causes of suicide may be a terminal illness, despair over losing a loved one, an extreme personal embarrassment, humiliation, depression, or loss of self-esteem. Once the crisis is past, the individual may realize how meaningful life may be, and he may never repeat his attempt to commit suicide.

Some university medical centers and medical associations have established "crisis centers" or similar services that provide psychiatric and psychological counseling by telephone for anyone who experiences an intense emotional or personal problem that he or she cannot cope with and who feels that there is no one else to turn to. There is no doubt that such centers have saved countless hundreds of lives.

SUMMARY

This chapter covered a variety of activities that we categorized as "preliminary investigations." As with your field notes, you will find that the preliminary investigation will usually determine the success or failure of the supplementary investigations and prosecution that follow. The field officer is the first to arrive on the scene of an accident or a crime, and it is critical that he or she immediately assess the situation, locate and preserve evidence that may later disappear or be overlooked, and protect the scene for the more complete investigation that follows.

The first officer on the scene not only protects the scene but also will look after the safety of victims, seek out and question victims and witnesses, look for the culprit if there is any chance that he or she is still in the vicinity, and also the field officer will call for the expert assistance of specialists who will continue with the investigation following the initial phase.

In this chapter, we covered a few of the basic rules of how to locate, identify, and preserve various types of evidence and how the laboratory might aid in the investigation. The last part of the chapter covered some of the basic procedures in handling the initial phase of various types of crime situations requiring investigation.

EXERCISES AND STUDY QUESTIONS

1. To what extent does the field officer in your department carry the initial investigation of property crimes? crimes against persons?
2. What is the advantage of having the district officer handle the preliminary phases of an investigation?
3. When you are making notes of your first impressions at the scene of a crime, what are some of the items you would list?
4. Describe the theory of transfer.
5. What is the purpose of photographing evidence before collecting it?
6. Name the three types of fingerprints that you may find at the scene of a crime.
7. Using the correct equipment, develop and lift a complete set of latent prints from two hands that someone has placed on a smooth surface.
8. Describe the procedures for collecting samples of wet blood from the scene of a crime.
9. How do you store for evidence certain items of clothing that contain wet bloodstains?
10. What is a striation? an impression?
11. How may tooth impressions be used as evidence?
12. Describe five types of evidence you might find at the scene of a burglary.
13. Describe five types of evidence (not listed in your answer to question 12) that you are likely to find at the scene of a rape?
14. Describe the method for collecting each type of evidence listed in your answers to questions 12 and 13. Explain how each type may be marked for evidence.
15. Why is the chain of evidence so crucial?
16. What is the value of using color slides in court rather than 8- by 10-inch prints?
17. What should you do first when you arrive at the scene and discover someone who appears to be deceased?
18. Describe postmortem lividity.
19. How long does it take for rigor mortis to set in completely after death?
20. What are the positive signs of death?
21. What are the presumptive signs of death?

22. Define inductive and deductive reasoning, and explain the difference between the two.
23. List at least 10 circumstances of death that must be investigated by the coroner.
24. Draw a rough sketch of a hypothetical traffic collision.
25. Draw a rough sketch of a hypothetical crime scene.
26. What is a burglary?
27. Give three types of behavior that would lead you to believe that a person was possibly guilty of "receiving stolen property."
28. Describe the recommended procedure for reassuring a sex crime victim that you are serious about apprehending the attacker.
29. Name two characteristics about a butcher shop that might give you a clue that the shop is actually a cover for a bookmaking operation.
30. List at least two reasons not listed in this chapter why people commit suicide.
31. What precautions would you take to reduce the possibility of having a crime scene become a media circus?
32. Explain the manner in which you would collect a latent print from a dusty table top.
33. Why wear gloves when searching for evidence? and why change often?
34. Where was DNA first a factor in a criminal investigation?
35. What is the probability that two people will have the identical DNA?
36. DNA is the abbreviation for what?
37. Describe the arson investigation unit in your city or county.
38. Describe how the LoJack works in an auto theft.
39. Describe how you would go about collecting evidence at a meth lab.

REFERENCES

ECKERT, WILLIAM G., ed. *Introduction to Forensic Sciences.* St. Louis, Mo.: C. V. Mosby, 1980.

GODDARD, KENNETH W. *Crime Scene Investigation.* Reston, Va.: Reston, 1977.

HORMACHEA, CARROLL. *Sourcebook in Criminalistics.* Reston, Va.: Reston, 1974.

O'HARA, CHARLES E. *Fundamentals of Criminal Investigation,* 2nd ed. Springfield, Ill.: Charles C. Thomas, 1970.

SCHULTZ, DONALD O. *Crime Scene Investigation.* Englewood Cliffs, N.J.: Prentice Hall, 1977.

SCOTT, JAMES D. *Investigative Methods.* Reston, Va.: Reston, 1978.

WILSON, O. W. *Police Planning,* 2nd ed. Springfield, Ill.: Charles C. Thomas, 1958. Emphasis on reprinted article in the Appendix by Don J. Finney, laboratory technician for the Wichita, Kansas, Police Department, entitled "Police Duties at Crime Scenes," From *American Journal of Police Science,* Vol. 27, Nos. 2 and 3, 1936.

FOOTNOTES

1. For a more detailed explanation of inductive and deductive reasoning, see Lynn Quitman Troyka's *Concise Handbook,* instructor's edition (Englewood Cliffs, N.J.: Prentice Hall, 1992), pp. 100–103.
2. *Police Magazine,* Vol. 3, No. 5, September 1980, p. 17.
3. Ibid.
4. Ibid., p. 18.
5. Laws vary, of course, but such a serious determination should be made only by the specialists.

CHAPTER 10

UNUSUAL OCCURRENCES

INTRODUCTION

During your entire police career, you might never encounter a major transportation disaster or a tidal wave or an earthquake or a hurricane or a fire of holocaust proportions. Chances are, however, that you will be involved in many events of disastrous proportions. A real problem for the police when such natural or human-made disasters do occur is that the department has not prepared for such a problem. For that reason, it is extremely important to plan and rehearse so that you and your colleagues will be ready for any contingency that should arise.

Planning for disasters and other occurrences of great proportions should be done with the complete participation of residents, business operators, and as many shakers and movers of your jurisdiction as you can get involved. This is community policing at its best, and problem-solving police work all rolled into one major operation. It is extremely important to involve all of these people in your planning for these events because they are going to affect large numbers of people. In addition to including many people in the planning, include them in your rehearsals as well.

Natural disasters, such as floods, hurricanes, tornadoes, earthquakes, or volcanic eruptions, are sometimes directly related to the weather and geological factors indigenous to your area. Other disasters, such as chemical or power plant explosions or fires in fuel tank fields or riots, may erupt for any number of reasons. These types of disasters may take priority in your department's planning activities because they are known hazards. Some disasters, however, may not even seem remotely possible, such as a collision of two aircraft heavily loaded with fuel and/or explosives or full of passengers over a quiet residential neighborhood in the suburbs. For that reason, no police agency should consider itself insulated from disaster or disaster planning.

In this chapter we devote our discussion to planning and techniques in carrying out those plans in major areas: disaster response, riot control, aircraft crashes, and bombing and bomb threats. The few times that you may be required to respond to these critical police problems will demand only the most precise performance from you because of the multiple problems facing you and the great numbers of human lives at stake.

Several aspects of disaster control directly involve the patrol officer. They include planning, training, and maintenance of a state of readiness. To some extent, the patrol officer is involved in logistics and public information when there is an impending problem about which advance information is available. Once the disaster occurs, the patrol officer is directly involved in all aspects of the disaster control activities. There is an immediate need for intelligence data to identify the nature and extent of the disaster, to notify persons to be warned and/or evacuated, and to contain the disaster area. Rescue operations, including medical aid for the injured, evacuation of survivors, and care for their property, are all tasks performed by the police in cooperation with the many other agencies similarly involved.

DISASTER RESPONSE

Rather than attempt to define and address each of several different types of natural and human-made disasters, in this section we cover the general problem of disaster response, which involves police planning and response whenever a disaster occurs. You should always anticipate the unexpected and be prepared for the inevitable.

In departments where participatory management is practiced, and in which you will have an opportunity to take part in disaster planning, you may participate in brainstorming, which is one of the more productive methods of gathering ideas during the preliminary stages of planning. During that time, everyone present is encouraged to contribute random thoughts, wild ideas, concrete proposals—anything that comes to mind—with no fear of being ridiculed or embarrassed because someone else thinks the idea is "stupid." Whatever the method for planning disaster response, it should involve you as the field officer.

Plan for the unexpected. Consider all the different things that could go wrong and develop alternative plans. Keep in mind the people who will be involved in certain parts of the activity, and capitalize on their individual strengths. It is usually impossible to predict who will be on duty at the exact moment any disastrous situation occurs. Therefore, plans should not be so complex that they will fail with the personnel on hand at the time of occurrence. Following the planning, or as a part of the planning, rehearsals and simulated problems should be worked out at training sessions. During some of those simulations, you may discover weaknesses in your plan that would hinder performance during the real event, but after more planning sessions and more rehearsals, you may refine your performance to more effective levels.

Disaster Control Procedures

1. *Identify the nature and extent of the problem.* Is it a single incident that has occurred, or is there a continuing hazardous condition that is going to repeat or extend over a long period of time? Determine if there is anything that may be done to prevent a recurrence of the situation. For example: An overturned and derailed train with many killed and others injured is the first disaster, but one of the overturned railroad cars contains highly explosive or flammable material that is likely to cause additional loss of lives unless something is done, such as evacuation. The fire company is reducing the hazard by neutralizing the volatility of the material. How much and what type of assistance do you believe you need immediately? What type of injuries have been sustained? Severe burn patients will need a different type of medical service than will victims of crushing, for example. If the disaster involves a public transportation vehicle, such as an airplane or bus, it will be necessary to notify the National Transportation Safety Board. If military vehicles or aircraft are involved, you will have to notify the nearest military base. You are going to need additional officers to control traffic, assist in evacuation of people in the hazard area, and help at the scene and elsewhere. At the time of your first assessment, it is better to overestimate the needs than to underestimate.

2. *Communicate with headquarters immediately.* Use all means available to get through as quickly as possible: radio, mobile data terminal (MDT), cellular phone, and/or landline phone, if available. The MDT and landline phone are less apt to alert the curious people with scanners who listen for police broadcasts, but get through as quickly as possible. In order to alert the people in headquarters of the emergency nature of your call, use the international distress signal MAYDAY a couple of times to get attention. Other officers who are on your frequency can also listen and make decisions as to what their part should be in the action. Supervisors and administrators can immediately start making plans and taking whatever action they deem necessary for the event.

State the nature and extent of the problem as you perceive it to be at the time, and your assessment as to the probability of continued and additional hazards. If you know there are deaths and injuries, report on approximately how many victims are involved so that the dispatcher may notify the coroner and medical and emergency service people with some idea as to the extent of the problems they will be meeting. Notify dispatch of the need for specialists, such as the armed services if some of their personnel or equipment is involved; the National Transportation Safety Board and Federal Aviation Authority if public aircraft or other transportation vehicles are involved. If the situation is on water, the Coast Guard or Harbor Patrol should be called. The railroad, bus company, or airline should be notified if one of their conveyances or personnel are participants in the event. In the event of an earthquake or a landslide, geologists will want to be notified, and bomb and terrorism teams will certainly be required if you have a disaster involving what appears to be caused by bombers or terrorists. Take into account all of the possible causes and effects of this particular situation, and be sure to let headquarters decide what additional personnel and equipment will be needed. If access routes to the scene are going to be a problem for those responding, try to provide information as to alternate routes.

While you are the only officer at the scene, it is usually better for you to remain at the location where you can maintain continuous communication with your headquarters to keep feeding new information and answering questions. An exception to this rule would be to save a human life when your presence will make the difference.

3. *Administer urgently needed first aid and other rescue activities.* At the initial stages of a disaster operation, your most critical duty requirement is to keep open the line of communication so that adequate help may arrive as quickly as possible. By leaving your radio or telephone post to start helping individuals, you will be far less effective than all the people you are summoning to the scene. For that reason, it may be more heroic of you to stay at the radio than it would be to rush in and single-handedly help a few individuals. If you were to lose your life or capability to communicate, you would become another victim and no longer be of any value to the overall operation.

4. *Establish a command post.* If you have no cellular phones at the time, set up your post near a fixed telephone such as a pay phone or, better yet, a house or building where telephones are available to you. This can be arranged through your community policing and neighborhood watch meetings, by asking for volunteers in each neighborhood who will agree to having their location available for police use in any emergency situation that may arise, including such occasions as a search for a lost child. You should have all of these locations indexed with the addresses, names of owners, numbers of telephones available, and hours when you are least likely to find people at that location. Your command post should be close enough to the action so that the officers in charge will not be isolated, yet far away enough so as not to be vulnerable to attack or interference.

As the field officer originally assigned the call, you will, no doubt, be in charge of the situation until otherwise notified. Depending on departmental policy, which should always be followed, you will be relieved after a superior or more senior officer arrives and advises you that he or she is taking over the director's duties. At that time, the command post may be moved to a more permanent location if the situation is of a more lasting nature than originally estimated. For the more permanent location, consider restrooms, dining areas, conference rooms, and adequate seating for all the workers, and rest areas for the alternate teams of officers to take their breaks. If you choose a school for your command post, try for a middle or high school or a college facility rather than a grammar school so that adults may be accommodated more comfortably. Temporary morgue and medical stations may be necessary. If there are many deaths and identification will be required, plans should be made to have refrigerated trucks or facilities available. The command post will have individuals assigned to coordinate such activities as personnel deployment, supplies and equipment, housing, meals and refreshment, weapons and ammunition, coordination of reserves and volunteers, issuance of identification cards or armbands, perimeter control, spiritual assistance for both officers and victims, and public information.

5. *Contain the area.* Once you have identified the nature of the problem and its extent, established communications, and summoned aid, looked after the immediate first aid needs of the victims that you could assist, and set up the command post, you should set up the perimeters of the area if you have not already done so. Have officers assigned to the outer limits of the perimeter, and instruct them to allow no one to enter except those engaged in the rescue operations.

There are several purposes for perimeter control. Chief among them is to keep the number of people exposed to any hazard to a minimum. Any disaster scene almost spontaneously draws crowds of curious people. They should be diverted away from the scene as soon as possible.

6. *Maintain open emergency lanes.* Certain streets should be kept open and free from congestion to provide for the free flow of emergency and other service vehicles into and out of the disaster area.

7. *Evacuate survivors and other persons in the area whose lives are in jeopardy.* People must not only be instructed to leave, but also be helped to leave in many instances. Seek the assistance of such organizations as the Salvation Army and the American Red Cross to assist in the movement of the people and their personal effects, and to provide temporary shelter.

The local transit authority may agree to provide emergency transportation in situations like this during your planning meetings, and there are many churches and companies that may have vans and other vehicles to use for the emergency evacuation of people.

8. *Provide public information services.* People who are directly involved should know of the incident. In addition to making personal contacts, local radio and television stations may broadcast warnings to the people to evacuate. Whatever information there is available should be released to keep residents who have evacuated informed as to the condition of their property.

9. *Provide for coordination with other agencies.* In your department's disaster plan, which should be constantly updated, arrangements will be provided for in advance of any need. Nearby military bases and colleges are excellent for human resources, temporary emergency housing, rescue and communications assistance, and many other contingencies. Volunteer organizations, such as those with citizens band radios, are sometimes well organized and constantly available for both fixed-based radio and field units on frequencies not cluttered with police emergency traffic. Service people—such as plumbers, electricians, and taxi owners—all have their own personnel with radio-equipped vehicles that may be called into service. Many charitable organizations that salvage clothing and furniture for rehabilitation of workers and fund raising, such as Goodwill Industries, Salvation Army, Veterans of Foreign Wars, and others, have their own personnel with radio-equipped trucks that could be used for emergency operations.

Tow services and ambulance companies are in rescue and salvage businesses, and there should be preplanned major emergency mobilization programs for those companies to cooperate in disaster situations. Other emergency departments, such as fire departments, civil defense, neighboring departments of police and fire, the state national guard, and youth organizations, such as Boy and Girl Scouts and Campfire Girls, and other focus groups should all be part of the master plan for disaster mobilization.

Wholesale grocers and restaurant chains and gasoline and diesel fuel distributors may provide their products and services as needed, hospitals and clinics and their doctors and nurses will be available according to their mobilization plans, and utility repair crews will work overtime. Not to be overlooked are citizen volunteers with no special service to offer—it may seem—but clothing, food, and shelter to victims and rescuers and who may be trained for disaster response. Hotels and motels sometimes also offer accommodations at little or no cost to displaced persons, and religious organizations provide their many services.

10. *Arrange for access into the area by authorized people only.* Some agencies have prepared for such contingencies by printing color-coded identification cards that are issued at the command post or some central location and are collected after the need passes.

11. *Record the event.* If the event is of some magnitude and continues for a period of time, a scribe or stenographer may be assigned to transcribe all information provided by the various officers, supervisors, and field commanders or other persons. In other situations, the many officers who take part in the action may prepare a report covering individual participation. One officer is then assigned to coordinate all the reports and to prepare one "cover" report that ties all the information together and caps it off with a summation. The report provides a permanent chronological record of the event and the department's participation.

The local transit authority may agree to provide emergency transportation is situations like this during your planning meetings, and there are many churches and companies that may have vans and other vehicles to use for the emergency evacuation of people.

12. *Evaluate.* Once the crisis event has passed and all emergency services and mop-up activities have been completed, your department and representatives of all other agencies taking part should begin debriefing all participants and evaluating what was done and what needs to be changed in case of a replay of a similar catastrophe.

Incident Command System

Not every event of disastrous proportions will involve only your police agency. As a matter of fact, *most events will require the close cooperation of many agencies and other organizations.* As a field officer, you may not be involved in planning at this level, but administrators and managers of a great many organizations must set into place a command system with a predetermined chief and chain of command, and a semipermanent place to establish a command center and to see that it is appropriately equipped and maintained, ready for operation on a continuous basis. The command center may be a section of a public building, such as the basement of City Hall, or it could be a converted motor home with elaborate communications equipment and self-contained to house all the leaders of the various agencies involved. The command network will include police; fire; National Guard; mayors and county supervisors; the governor's office; state police and highway patrol; utilities and transportation; military services; Alcohol, Tobacco, and Firearms; the Federal Bureau of Investigation; other federal agencies; the county sheriff; and the U.S. marshal. The leadership and participation will be very broad-based and include many nongovernmental companies and organizations as well.

Whenever a disaster occurs, the leadership will determine which agencies should be involved, and then they will be called into duty and report to the command center to assume coordination of their particular responsibilities. A predetermined leader will have already been selected, which should reduce the problem of uncertainty and lack of direction by a group of people thrown together who cannot seem to find their way. Periodic mock trials and rehearsals will also tend to keep the command center concept functional and, hopefully, successful.

Logistics and Mobilization

As an emergency public safety agency, the police department should be equipped to meet the usual and unusual demands of various occurrences. The limitations on what a police department could keep on hand are defined only by the limitations of financial resources and the imagination of the officers who prepare the plans. Every contingency should be anticipated, although requests for supplies and equipment must remain realistic.

Local, state, and federal civil defense agencies and their personnel are similarly engaged in preparing for the many disasters that inevitably do occur. Any police department planning or training should definitely be in cooperation with those other agencies involved in civil defense or disaster planning.

Once a disastrous event takes place, there is little opportunity for advance planning. Most procedures should be fairly routine, at least during rehearsals, so that when an actual problem arises, mobilization for disaster control occurs almost automatically. Mutual aid plans and coordination with the various other agencies should be implemented immediately.

The first step to mobilization is to discontinue all nonessential police tasks, such as the routine patrolling and response to miscellaneous calls for service. Adequate personnel will have to be assigned to two locations at the beginning: the site of the event and the site of the complaint board. There will be a considerable increase in telephone and radio communications, and many of the nonessential calls will have to be postponed or "counseled out" by diplomatic desk officers. These officers must make it possible for all available field officers to respond only to emergencies in addition to the disturbance scene. On-duty personnel will probably also be extended an additional four hours, making it possible to assign the entire department to two 12-hour platoons that will alternate on duty as long as the need exists.

Off-duty officers and reserve forces should then be called to duty. To effect this process with the minimal interference with headquarters telephone operations, there should be some form of emergency call system with a pyramid-type procedure. Office personnel should be assigned to call up a few off-duty officers. The call system should then continue from strategic phone locations outside. This system will free both the department's lines and the people who would otherwise have to be making the calls. When mobilizing off-duty officers, it may be wise to have the officers report in uniform to a staging area some distance away from the police headquarters building, possibly nearer to the location where the event is taking place and in a location where the officers' private vehicles will be safe. Using this staging area will keep the movement of the force of officers confidential, and it may add to the element of surprise when the officers arrive on the scene, especially a riot scene. If there were any organization to the agitation at the crowd scene, it would be possible for someone with a small two-way radio or telephone to watch police headquarters for personnel movement. In the absence of such organization, this remote staging process at least reduces confusion at the headquarters building.

Mutual Aid Agreement

In the years since World War II, many contiguous jurisdictions have had rather elaborate machinery for immediate coordination of combined forces under mutual aid compacts and agreements. In California, for example, the entire state is divided into mutual aid zones, and most of the cities in each county have mutual aid pacts. Whenever there is an alert of "limited peril," and the local police forces cannot adequately handle the problem, the alert is broadcast, and officers from the contiguous jurisdictions respond to assist. The jurisdiction having the problem maintains the authority for coordination and supervision. When the situation involves a larger area, such as two or more cities, coordination is assumed by a predesignated administrator, such as the county sheriff. If the problem calls for more assistance than the county's police forces can provide, the authority and responsibility for coordination then goes to a zone commander, who is probably one of the sheriffs of the several counties in the zone. The chain of reinforcement continues to expand until the situation obviously calls for statewide coordination. At that point, the governor declares martial rule.

Martial Rule

Martial rule is a military state, and during its existence all constitutional provisions are suspended. There is no local control, and the objective of putting down the riot becomes a military objective for the National Guard, or state militia, under the control of the commander in chief, who is the governor, and his adjutant general. Because the condition of military rule is alien to a free society, the decision to impose martial rule is an extremely grave one, and the governor must use this power only when the local forces cannot handle the situation. Requests for the imposition of martial rule must come from the chief executive officer of the local government or from some other official source, such as the magistrate or the sheriff. The governor may also make the decision independently. The mechanics for the request and imposition of martial rule depend on the various state laws.

Once the local government officials see the need for additional assistance beyond the forces that they may utilize within their own jurisdiction, it is advisable to alert the governor's office and the National Guard so that they may plan for the contingency of martial rule. In the meantime, it is wise to activate the mutual aid plan and to proceed according to the needs dictated by the situation. When the governor authorizes the use of the National Guard, the first step in the military assistance is to place this force under the supervision of the local police administrator in an assisting capacity.

The governor imposes martial rule only when there is no alternative. During that time when martial rule is in existence, the military commander is in complete charge of the situation. The objective is to restore sufficient order to enable the local police to reassume control of the situation. The minute that objective is achieved, the governor orders the martial rule at an end. The National Guard then reverts to its "support" role until the governor and the local officials determine that it is no longer needed.

Federal Troops

If the situation gets out of hand and reaches such proportions that the local police must relinquish control of the state National Guard, state martial rule is not sufficient. The governor must then request assistance from the president of the United States. The president then goes through a process similar to that of the governor, and he may impose federal martial rule. The state National Guard becomes federalized, and additional federal military troops are sent into the jurisdiction. Once the president determines the need for federal martial rule, he makes the determination and proclaims it to be in effect. In the absence of presidential order, the military troops may be placed at the disposal of local law enforcement administrators when there is a grave need for such assistance. Actually, this determination of grave need may be made by local military commanders and the assistance rendered, but it must then be followed by satisfactory justification to the president through the appropriate levels of command.

The entire system of mutual aid and martial law is designed to provide for local control until all possibilities of quelling the disturbance have been attempted and have failed. Only then may the governor step in and impose martial rule, and he may keep it in effect only as long as the immediate need exists. The same procedure applies to the president of the United States. Local law enforcement has long been recognized as the primary law enforcement body in the country, and the laws have been passed with that concept in mind.

Assignment of Responsibility

If there is any advance warning about an impending disaster or civil disturbance of major proportions, and if planning may be accomplished in advance, such planning should include some serious consideration of which officers will be given the initial assignment to attempt to control the crowds and prevent riots and looting. The following factors should influence the administrators in selecting the officers for this duty. The officers should be in perfect physical condition and should maintain an immaculate appearance in uniform. In addition to being physically capable of doing an excellent job, the officers selected for a special problems detail should also "look the part." They should be cool and reflective, mature, and emotionally stable under stress conditions. They must have a certain degree of social sensitivity and be optimistic about their goal of restoring order through persuasion if possible, force only if and when absolutely necessary.

Intelligence Assignments. A staff officer should be assigned independently to define and measure the field problem in a detached manner, free of the emotional strain of making immediate decisions. This officer should report to the police chief and other command officers so that their decisions may be based upon the evaluation and the reports from the field commander. To assist in this information gathering operation, the intelligence officer may use a team of "scouts" and informants, who enter the field to observe and report on everything that comes to their attention from their points of vantage. When making intelligence assessments, the assigned officer will consult with various specialists to aid the staff in making judgment decisions about situations such as natural disasters, floods, earthquakes, hurricanes, or forest fires, which may accompany the civil disturbance. Utilize the valuable resources among the ranks of your community.

Logistics. An officer should be assigned to plan in advance for the accumulation and proper dispensation of supplies and equipment and to handle distribution details during times of actual need. If a sudden need should arise to feed and provide rest areas for 2000 officers, for example, this officer should be ready to act at once to meet the emergency. A logistics officer must be ready for any contingency.

Public Information. An officer with sufficient rank to make judgments concerning information releases under various circumstances should be assigned to a post somewhere removed from the immediate scene of the event and also far enough away from the center of communications and headquarters operations to avoid interfering with those operations. The information officer should be the only one authorized to release information concerning the event. All units should be required to keep the information officer posted on changing events. The information officer will actually be the best informed of the noncritical operating personnel and can keep the news media informed on events as they happen. If such an officer is assigned, and the policy for "no news except through the information officer" is enforced, the press and other people who have a need to know about the situation will go the information center to satisfy their needs and remain outside the critical operating areas.

Staging Area

The staging area may be at the headquarters building or, to reduce confusion and add to the elements of secrecy and surprise, at some high school or shopping center or any large industrial complex in the general vicinity of the event. Consider restroom facilities, which may not be adequate at a grammar school. Also, a large kitchen might come in handy in the event that the problem continues for an extended period of time. Secure parking facilities are also necessary.

Identification of Disaster Victims

The coroner or medical examiner is in charge of the deceased and their personal effects, but your responsibility will include assisting those individuals and their deputies in locating and identifying the victims. You will have the additional assistance of military personnel if military vehicles or aircraft are involved. Because of their expertise in such matters, as well as their scientific resources, agents of state and federal departments will be involved. If the vehicle is engaged in interstate transportation, or you are working with an airplane crash, federal agencies are required to investigate. These are a few basic procedures in identification of the victims:

All bodies should be fingerprinted (in some cases, as with infants, they will also be footprinted) regardless of any other means of identification.

The locations from which bodies were removed should be staked or located with another identifying device such as a traffic cone, and each location given a number. The body or body part will be given a corresponding number. These will be located on a master sketch and on finders' individual field sketches.

Prepare a field sketch, indicating all items found during the search. These should later be incorporated into a master sketch, and eventually a prepared chart, to aid investigators in reconstructing the disaster. (Parts of the vehicle or aircraft are handled similarly.)

Items of personal property should be placed with the body if they are still affixed to the body, such as in a pocket. Otherwise, found items will be itemized and filed separately, with their locations identified as are the bodies and body parts.

Photos taken by friends and relatives, including those taken at the time of departure, will help identify bodies by personal appearance as well as articles of clothing.

Pathologists will identify the bodies by the following: dental charts, body build and measurements, hair, and physical abnormalities. Scars, marks, and tattoos as well as surgical scars and body repair items, such as plates and screws in repaired body parts, will aid in the identification. The sex of the victim; physical condition, such as pregnancy; repaired fractures and missing body parts, such as a kidney or appendix; and vasectomies and hysterectomies will further aid in the identification process. Clothing and accessories will also help, including religious medals, jewelry, contact lenses, eyeglasses, cosmetics, and other grooming devices. No matter what the item may be, it should be collected and itemized, and its location of discovery charted so that the experts will eventually be able to complete as much as possible of this identifying task.

UNLAWFUL ASSEMBLY AND RIOT CONTROL

Operations

Once the mobilization of officers and the enactment of the plan for special action occurs, the senior patrol officer on duty must serve the dual purpose of attacking the problem and assuaging the people in the rest of the city by restoring some semblance of police patrol in those other areas as quickly as possible. In some departments, the patrol commander will turn authority and responsibility over to an operations officer, who will then coordinate the police control of the special problem. The patrol commander can then adjust to the situation and provide continuity in patrol coverage throughout the rest of the city as best as can be done with the resources remaining. The operations officer should be completely familiar with the overall planning and training for the problem and assign personnel in the strongest possible positions to implement the emergency operations. That officer must also have sufficient rank to command the immediate cooperation and compliance of all other involved personnel.

Civil unrest seems to be indigenous to civilization, although there are times when it is apparent only in isolated situations or among small numbers of people. Since the end of World War II, civil unrest in the United States has become increasingly widespread. Laborers, students, and minority groups have been most prominent and dramatic in their efforts to effect immediate changes in social practices and standards. They conduct demonstrations, sit-ins, teachings, and nonviolent civil disobedience, which usually begin as noncombative and nondestructive incidents but sometimes end in violence and bitter combat. Some movements include mass criminal conspiracies for the purpose of interfering with lawful processes. Others produce spontaneous riotous outbursts arising out of ostensibly peaceful assemblies.

The continually recurring conditions of civil unrest and lawlessness throughout the country make it apparent that it is possible for a major disturbance to occur any place and time there are enough people for a "quorum." Given the right combination of factors, any situation involving large numbers of people may evolve or explode into an unlawful assembly. Without immediate, decisive police action, the situation could quickly evolve into a full-scale riot.

Although reliable intelligence sources for your particular department may report to your command personnel that there is no impending large-scale unlawful assembly or similar confrontation with your forces, the same intelligence sources will report that the potential is almost always there. There are certain individuals and organizations that watch for potential situations with some "promise" for their own selfish motivation to gain sudden power and wealth under the guise of some seemingly selfless purpose. If the situation appears as though it will be newsworthy and the participants will gain sufficient publicity to serve their needs, there is little doubt that they will appear on the scene and make whatever capital they can out of an unfortunate situation.

Most unlawful assembly situations involve local problems. With quick action, they can be quelled and order can be restored with a minimum of property damage and injuries.

Warning Signals

Sometimes it is possible to determine in advance the potentiality of a civil disturbance of major proportions. Although it may not be possible to predict exactly where or when such a situation may occur, some of the following warning signals should cause you to be more attentive to any event at which large groups of people gather for any purpose. The most volatile are those that are attended by groups of people with a common purpose in mind, such as a rally or an advertised demonstration for some single cause.

1. An increase in the recurrence of the same rumor, or the sensationalism of rumors of similar design, such as alleged police abuse of people in certain neighborhoods, or of students, or other alleged defenseless persons.

2. An increase in threatening or insulting signs or pamphlets in commercial or other public places. There may be an attempt to make it socially acceptable to ridicule or display openly contempt for the field patrol officers, thereby reducing the general effectiveness.

3. An increase in the number of incidents of violence or threats of violence. In one incident, a self-appointed champion of a cause made frequent public statements that "if any policeman gets in my way, he should expect to suffer the consequences." One night, during a routine field interview situation, a lone police officer was killed by a single bullet. The next day the newspapers carried a story indicating that a suspect had been taken into custody for the fatal shooting. It was the same individual who had made the threats.

4. Disturbances at various locations that appear to be of a similar nature as if designed to test the capabilities of the police department, or the decisiveness in the official in charge of an institution, such as a school, as a prelude to more serious action later. This "testing" process may go on for weeks or months, sometimes for the purpose of stimulating interest and support. Minor confrontations planned for the purpose of causing an officer to become angry and take some injudicious action may be the object of such confrontations. The unjustified use of the police baton, or excessive force in an aggravated arrest situation, or use of a particular restraining technique, such as the carotid hold or neck arm bar, can be cited by any individual or organization that chooses to point to that incident as a visual aid to prove their claim that *the police* are brutal or abusive. Sometimes it is possible to gain the support of a great many well-meaning dupes in such a movement.

5. More than the usual number of disturbances at places of entertainment or sporting events. Again, the disturbances may be a form of "testing" and "baiting" to keep a cause growing. A "movement" must continually have something to stimulate its participants, or it dies of lack of interest.

6. Factional gang fighting or warfare or a series of raids on parties and places of peaceful congregation. These incidents create a dissipation of the police department's effective strength at a single location.

7. Threats and attacks on private property. Such attacks may be engineered to appear as a popular cause, and they may be used to draw the police into private affairs that are noncriminal in nature, placing the officers in an unpopular position. Sometimes the incidents are designed to appear politically oriented so that the police are condemned for acting as "political oppressors."

8. An increasing need for the use of force in effecting arrests, as though there were a planned effort to "bait" the police.

9. An accompanying increase in the number of complaints about abusive practices of the police, and continuing claims that such complaints are receiving no satisfactory action.

10. Public name-calling and a general attitude of contempt and disrespect for police officers.

11. Significant increase in the amount of graffiti observed throughout the jurisdiction, indicating an increase in intergang conflict.

12. Court cases involving police use of force, such as the police beating of Mr. Rodney King by the officers of the Los Angeles Police Department, and the subsequent state and federal trials that angered large segments of the population throughout the United States.

Police Purpose and Objectives

At the scene of a disturbance—major or minor—the police purpose is constant: to protect human lives and personal property and to restore order and peace in the community. The police officer is a *peace officer,* and it is your responsibility to maintain peace where it exists and to restore peace when there has been a breach. Restoration of the peace is accomplished by persuasion when possible and by force if necessary, but by that degree of force that is necessary, no more.

The objectives of the police department at the scene of an unlawful assembly are prevention, containment, dispersal, prevention of reentry, arrest of violators, and operation according to some system of priorities.

1. *Prevention.* If at all possible, you want to prevent the situation from getting to the point where it becomes necessary to continue steps 2 through 6. Your department may anticipate escalation of criminal behavior on such occasions as holidays, high school or college victory celebrations. Instead of turning a blind eye toward minor infractions and "kissing them off" as if there were a moral holiday, this may be the time to apply your "zero tolerance" enforcement. When you might otherwise send home a bunch of rowdy revelers who have been drinking (and may have a beverage or two in their hands), in this situation you will make immediate arrests and continue to do so until you reduce the numbers of revelers who will get drunker and rowdier as the day or night goes on. Minor infractions are handled while they are small. Several beach cities in California, particularly Huntington Beach, have been having extremely large summertime crowds, and Huntington Beach also hosts a very large parade on the Fourth of July, attracting hundreds of thousands of spectators who drink heavily and get into a festive mood early in the day. For several years, the city has had to cope with some pretty nasty riots with many injuries to police and guests alike. In the summer of 1996, Chief Ron Lowenberg and his staff decided to aggressively enforce the law as each violation occurred and not to wait for the inevitable escalation to take place. Their efforts worked like a charm, and praise for their actions drowned out the complaints, which principally came from the people who were breaking the law—or about to do so—and who were either arrested or told to go to their homes.

2. *Containment.* Unlawful assembly and riot situations are as contagious as the bubonic plague unless they are quarantined from the unaffected areas of the community. Once the specific area is identified, it should be closed off and contained until the problem has passed.

3. *Dispersal.* Any large crowd that has formed that acquires the characteristics of an unlawful assembly must be dispersed. Although the original purpose of the gathering may have been lawful, the current nature of the assembly at the time of the officer's arrival may clearly distinguish it as being unlawful. Once that is determined, it is your sworn responsibility to command the people to disperse. Once you have given the order, allow them a realistic amount of time to leave and provide avenues by which they may leave.

4. *Prevention of reentry.* Once the people have been moved out of an area and dissipated into smaller groups, protect the area against their return.

5. *Arrest of violators.* Whenever practicable, one of the first acts of the first officers to arrive on the scene of a disturbance is to locate and isolate the individuals who are inciting the crowd to more positive action and those who are flagrantly violating the law. Once these individuals are removed, the problem is often solved. If you do arrest such violators, immediately remove them.

6. *Establishment of priorities.* Whenever you arrive on the scene of any sizable crowd disturbance, you will be outnumbered considerably. It is always necessary to establish a system of priorities depending upon the circumstances at the moment of the action, then to proceed according to those priorities.

Although you have given the order to disperse and must give the people time to leave the area, it may still be necessary to rescue people in the crowd who are under attack or have some other urgent need to be rescued. In that case, you may have to resort to a "flying wedge" formation on foot or by cars and/or motorcycles, backed up by horse patrol units to get into the crowd and back out as quickly and safely as possible with the person to be rescued. The use of officers on horseback works very well for crowd control. Avoid the use of police dogs in these situations, as they could become confused and not be able to distinguish the "good guys" from the "bad guys" with the large crowds of noisy and unruly people.

Psychological Influences

The agitator, or leader, who attempts to incite a riot, or who assumes control of a riot already in progress and directs it to serve his purposes, has several factors working for him in such a situation. He may use rumors and propaganda techniques that will give the lagging riot impetus by passing the word that someone has been killed by a police officer or that some reprehensible act has been committed by the opposing faction. In the mass confusion that is taking place, the "inciter" may actually create his own incidents; for example, he might bait an officer to use force upon him and then use his injuries as "visual proof" of police brutality. Gaudy bandages or self-imposed head wounds, which are often superficial but bleed profusely, are not unusual in some riotous situations.

The novelty of the situation works for the inciter, as the new and strange circumstances become a "fun thing" or a "happening" for the thrill seeker. The anonymity works equally well for the agitator, or inciter, who remains in the background and directs others to carry out his orders in the "everyone is doing it" atmosphere. Under the guise of group behavior, the riot allows the individual to release inhibitions that he would contain under normal conditions. Consider the testimony of suspects in cases where brutal gang killings have occurred in mob actions. The suspects interviewed say such things as: "I hit him on the head too. . . . Everyone else was doing it. . . . Besides, he was probably dead already. . . . If I didn't hit him, somebody would'a hit me."

There is always the feeling in a crowd disturbance situation that there is strength in numbers, and even the timid individual sometimes assumes the posture of the ferocious beast when backed up by several protectors. Suggestibility works to the advantage of the inciter in a crowd; the crowd is more likely to accept his ideas as their own and act on them than when its members are alone. Consider the situation in which a child molester is arrested after a chase and a tense neighborhood scene is created. The victimized child is screaming, the enraged parents are demanding action, the officer is attempting to talk to the suspect rationally and the suspect's obscene epithets are reaching the ears of the people in the crowd; suddenly, someone shouts, "Get that b————d!" This situation could quite easily evolve into a riot.

Stages in the Formation of a Mob. Many experts on mob psychology say that there are certain perceptible stages that manifest themselves during the formation of a riot. As a field police officer, I have felt or sensed these stages. They are more subtle than they appear on paper, but they can be recognized. To deal effectively with a crowd, it is imperative that you make an effort to ascertain what point of development the crowd has reached and determine whether it has yet reached mob proportions. A mob will have to be handled differently from a crowd, since there is little value in attempting to reason or debate with a mob. Only some sort of dramatic action will jolt the mob members back to the reality that they are individuals and that dramatic action should not assume the characteristic of an "overreaction" by the police officers.

Mob psychology experts have used various titles to identify the progressive stages in the development of a mob. For the purpose of this discussion, these stages are referred to as stage 1, stage 2, and stage 3.

Stage 1. At this stage, the crowd is still functioning as a conglomeration of individuals. There is some milling about, but any fighting or pushing taking place occurs in independent and unrelated events. The atmosphere is charged with some common feeling of impending activity that seems to act as a form of gravity that pulls the people together, but at this stage it is difficult to define the source of the feeling. It may be some widely spread rumor that a specific event, such as a gang fight, is about to take place.

At stage 1 it is possible to move spectators and disinterested bystanders away from the scene and to begin counteracting the problem by arresting individual law violators, removing them from the scene, and generally taking effective and decisive enforcement action. If you locate any anticipated agitators, divert them from the scene.

Stage 2. In the second stage, the crowd members lose their individuality and begin to function as a single unit. The agitators have assumed their positions and are beginning to see the results of their suggestions. Opportunists or confederates of the leaders may be circulating in the crowd, getting it moving and thinking as a single unit.

Stage 3.   By now, the mob is functioning as a single unit and its leaders are in control. Any event is likely to precipitate violent action. Some officers have appropriately referred to stage 3 as the "riot just waiting to happen."

At this stage, the most effective action is decisive police movement in a show of force to move the people out of the area and to cause them to break down into small groups. Little reasoning, if any, is likely to be effective at stage 3. All three stages could probably be classified as unlawful assembly. Fortunately, it is possible to deal effectively with the majority of crowd control situations and thus prevent devastating riots.

Procedure for Handling an Unlawful Assembly

1. *Assess the situation.* Before you take any immediate action, except for a lifesaving rescue, see what you have. Determine how much assistance you are going to need, and where. If the crowd is large and getting larger, at least some of the officers should be assigned around the perimeter to "peel off" the crowd by diverting them away, and by closing the area and keeping additional vehicle and pedestrian traffic from coming in.

2. *Communicate.* As in the case of other types of major police problems, getting the information to your home base and other officers you are going to need to assist—opening up communications—is more important than attempting to tackle the problem yourself when it is obvious that additional help is needed. Keep this line of communication going, even if it means that you do nothing until help arrives. If you must leave to rescue someone from a brutal assault or to attempt an immediate arrest that cannot wait, make use of noninvolved bystanders to handle the radio while you are away from it. It is better than having no communication at all.

3. *Establish a command center and wait for help to arrive.* Try to position yourself and your unit close enough to the crowd so that you can see the activity and they can see and hear you when you give them the command to disperse.

4. *Take immediate rescue and rescue action once your help arrives.* Lives and property are always predominantly important. As for the persons you will arrest first, you should concentrate on the people who are causing the disturbance, if possible.

5. *Give the dispersal order and help the people leave the scene.* At this point your primary concern is to reduce the size of the crowd, hopefully to break it up completely, but at least reduce it to a core group of uncooperative participants whom you are going to arrest for failing to comply. The procedure should be similar to the following:

    a. Assign witnesses at strategic locations who can testify that they saw and heard you issue the command to disperse. Use reliable witnesses for this purpose, including news reporters, judges, and public officials. Television crews and news photographers are ideal for witnessing the event, and their assistance should be solicited.

b. Order the crowd to disperse. Use amplification equipment, if available. The order should be in accordance with the laws of your state and should include a statement of your identity and the authority for the order. It is an order, not a threat. Give the crowd a realistic time limit within which to disperse.

c. Order all assigned officers to stand ready, guarding the perimeter, but making it possible for the people to leave as directed. Officers who are carrying batons should hold them with both hands at port arms position, never in a menacing manner, such as in a waving position.

d. Expedite the departure of the people who are commanded to disperse.

e. Repeat the order at least three times so that as many people as possible can hear you. Be sure that all the people understand you. Use interpreters, if necessary.

f. Wait until the expiration of the time limit. Do not use a "countdown," or "baiting," technique with the people. Merely wait the stated time.

g. At the end of the time limit, arrest the offenders. If the crowd is complying but for some reason there is a slowdown in traffic, it may be necessary to use a "long count" for the time limit, but do not make a game of it.

Crowd Control Formations

Three crowd control formations are shown in Figure 10–1.

To Assemble the Squad.   The command is: SQUAD, FALL IN. At the command "FALL IN," the members of the squad form a line according to height. The tallest officer, referred to as the "Point," stands at the right end of the formation. As each officer falls in to the left in descending order of height, each officer except the one at the left and extends the left arm laterally at shoulder height, palm down, fingers extended and together, touching the shoulder of the officer to the left.

The point officer looks forward, while all others in the line turn their heads and eyes to their right and adjust position as necessary to make sure the right shoulder is touching the extended fingers of the officer to the right. As soon as the line is correct, all officers promptly drop their arms to the side and face forward.

To Align the Squad.   The command is: DRESS RIGHT, DRESS. At the command, each officer except the one on the left repeats the procedure followed when the members fell in. The squad leader steps to the end of the line and faces down the line to see that it is aligned. If necessary, the squad leader directs any officer to move who is not aligned. When the alignment is correct, the command is "FRONT." and all squad members drop the arms to the side and turn their heads to the front.

To Count Off.   The command is: SQUAD, COUNT OFF. At the command "COUNT OFF," the squad leader, who is standing and moving to be in the best position outside the line, will call out, "ONE." On command of "COUNT OFF," all officers except the point on the right will turn their heads to the right. Starting with the

Figure 10–1 (a) Wedge, (b) diagonal, and (c) line formations.

point officer, who calls out "TWO," each officer in line will call the next number in sequence and turn the head forward as the number is called. This counting-off procedure is necessary when the squad leader is going to designate different officers by number to different assignments.

The Squad. A police squad is approximately 12 officers, including the leader, but it is not mandatory. In a 12-officer squad, the leader is number 1 and the assistant is number 12 (see Figure 10–2). If special weapons or tear gas is used, the next-to-last, or number 11, officer carries the weapon. More than one officer may carry special weapons, which is optional with the squad leader.

Squad, Single File (Column or Line). The verbal command is: SQUAD, FALL IN, SINGLE FILE. The hand signal is: hand above the head with index finger extended vertically.

2 3 4 5 6 7 8 9 10 11 12

1

Line of movement

Squad, Column of Twos. The verbal command is: FALL IN, COLUMN OF TWOS. The hand signal is: two fingers extended vertically from the fist held above the head. (As a general rule, a single column is used to move the squad through a nar-

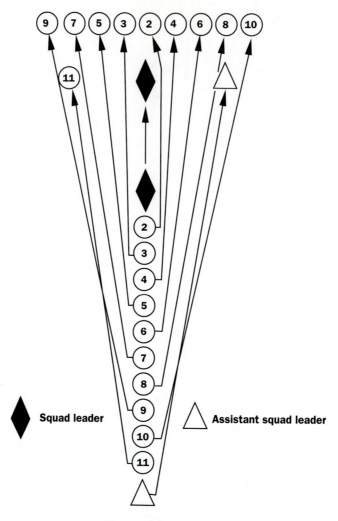

Figure 10–2 Squad line.

row passage, and the column of twos is the formation from which crowd formations evolve.)

2 4 6 8 10 12
3 5 7 9 11 odd numbers on left
1
Line of movement

Squad Column Change: Single File to Column of Twos. Marching in a squad column, the squad leader now wants a column of twos in preparation to form other formations. The command is: COLUMN OF TWOS, MARCH (two fingers). At the command, the even-numbered officers will "mark time," or march in place. The odd-numbered officers will take one step to the left and one step forward, then "mark time" while aligning themselves. All officers will continue marking time until the squad leader commands them to "HALT" or move into another formation.

Squad Column Change: Column of Twos to Single File. The command is: SQUAD COLUMN, MARCH (one finger). At the command, the squad will continue to move at the normal pace unless ordered to "DOUBLE TIME." The odd-numbered officers will find their respective places and move back into the single line and check to be sure they are in a straight line and continue to move until they receive another command.

Squad Diagonal. The verbal command is: SQUAD DIAGONAL, MARCH. The hand signal is: hand circled above head as one would use the "assemble" signal, then pointed in the direction the diagonal is to go. The number 2 officer moves to the location designated by the squad leader, and the other officers follow in the same direction, assuming a position one-half step to the rear and left (or right) of the officer immediately in front (see Figure 10–3).

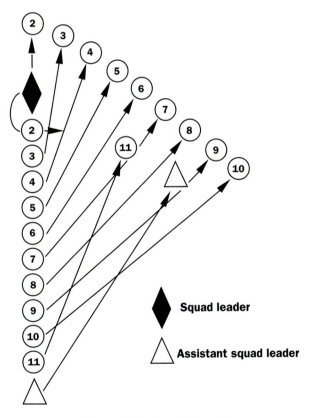

Figure 10–3 Squad diagonal.

Squad Wedge. The verbal command is: SQUAD WEDGE, MOVE. The hand signal is: hands above head with fingers meeting in an inverted V. The number 2 officer moves to the spot designated by the squad leader, with the even-numbered officers on the right and the odd-numbered officers to the left diagonally off the number 2 officer (see Figure 10–4).

Drawing Batons. Batons should be drawn prior to moving the squad into a crowd formation. The most effective position for batons in most crowd situations is the PORT position. The command is: PORT ARMS. The squad leader signals by drawing the baton and placing it in the port position, making sure that the thong is

◆ **Squad leader**   △ **Assistant squad leader**

Figure 10–4 Squad wedge.

securely in place. The thongs are positioned on the command "PORT" and drawn on the command "ARMS."

Strike Duty

The key to effective police action at the scene of a labor–management conflict is to be completely fair and objective. It is not your role to assume that either side is right or wrong. The police responsibility is to establish contact with both the company being struck and the leader of the strikers and to point out the police role to enforce the law and to protect life and property. Ask for the cooperation of all parties on both sides of the dispute. The police concern is compliance with the laws and protection of the people from personal injury or property damage.

When working at the scene of a strike, provide for the free flow of pedestrian and vehicle traffic on the streets, the driveways, and the sidewalks. Whatever you do, handle the matter in such a way that it does not indicate any alliance or sympathy with either side of the dispute. In one strike situation, officers erred by using the company parking lot for their personal vehicles. In another, some of the officers used the company cafeteria to eat their lunch, and in still another, one or two of the assigned officers took advantage of discount prices to buy hams. None of these actions can be condoned any more than can an officer be allowed to carry one of the picket signs for an elderly worker who may have stopped to rest his or her feet.

Injunctions are often obtained to keep the pickets to a minimum number. Enforcement of injunctions is handled by bailiffs of the court, such as the sheriff, marshal, or constable. The municipal police officer cannot generally enforce injunctions. Arrests should be made for flagrant violations, but any situations that have personal animosity involved as well should be referred to an office conference on the following day. Take all the necessary information and prepare a complete report. After a night of calm deliberation when the parties can discuss the matter away from the picket line, a more appropriate course of action can be worked out. Of course, this is limited to nonaggravated situations and should not include cases in which it is clearly obvious that an arrest is necessary.

Demonstrations and Protests

Although peaceful assembly is guaranteed by the First Amendment to the Constitution, many protesters and demonstrators seem to have a different "spin" on how they intend to go about their "peaceful" demonstration. Many conspire to break the law, actually going to the places to demonstrate while armed with sticks and stones, and deliberately violate trespass and forcible entry laws, oftentimes getting into violent confrontations with other people at the same scenes with opposing points of view. As you know, freedoms collide, and compromise is made to assure that all people present are afforded the opportunity to be heard, even the speaker that they try to drown out with their loud protests.

Your primary responsibility is to protect all of the people against attack and to assure that their freedom to express themselves does not violate another person's freedom of expression. Separate the opposing factions to prevent physical contact, such as pushing and shoving that will escalate into punching and attacking. Move the loud protestors just far enough away from a scheduled speaker so that he or she may also exercise the right to free speech. Pointed questioning and heckling are natural at an event like this, but do what you can to assure that no one gets hurt, and arrest those who break the law.

AIRCRAFT CRASHES

An aircraft crash involves police response similar to that response that would follow any disaster of the same proportions.

Injuries and damage are usually of great magnitude because of the large number of passengers involved and the size of the airplane falling from great heights. Aviation is increasing in importance as a mode of commercial and personal travel as well as an integral part of our military defenses. Aircraft crashes—as with railroad and motor vehicle crashes—are going to happen. Certain procedures should be followed when they do occur.

Military aircraft accidents are the primary concern of the military service concerned. Aircraft accidents are the concern of the Federal Aviation Authority and the National Transportation Safety Board and are covered by the Federal Aviation Regulations for pilots. Methods for responding to an accident involving either type of aircraft—military or civilian—are the same as for medical aid and rescue operations, but there are other important differences. Once the immediate emergency needs are met, yet while they are still underway, certain critical factors must be borne in mind. Victims and debris may be dispersed over a wide area surrounding the accident scene, and the danger of fire may be great. Approach the scene with extreme caution. As quickly as you can, take immediate steps to close the area to everyone except those whose presence is absolutely essential.

When approaching military aircraft, stay clear of the front and rear of any tanks or pods that are carried externally on the wings or fuselage. They may contain missiles or rockets. Establish a *no smoking* rule to help reduce the possibility of fire. The following information has been taken from a Department of Defense booklet *What to Do and How to Report Military Aircraft Accidents.*[1]

How to Use Access Hatches, Rescue Point, and Exits

Locations of escape hatches, doors, and exits from all military aircraft are indicated by orange-yellow markings on the outside of the aircraft. On jet aircraft a red rescue arrow will indicate the rescue points. Instructions are stenciled at this arrow for the jettisoning of canopies or hatches. Use care in jettisoning these cartridge-actuated devices as they are displaced violently. When operating jettisoning controls always position yourself well to the side.

(The booklet depicts an inverted triangle inscribed warning, which gives instructions for jet aircraft equipped with ejection seats. The marking is placed on the side of the aircraft.)

1. *Push button to open door.*
2. *Pull "T" handle out (distance will be specified for various aircraft) to jettison canopy.*

Do not raise, move, or tamper with arm rests or crewmembers' seats, or any controls painted yellow and black as these activate the ejection seats and are extremely dangerous. Never move any handle, lever, or device inside the cockpit if you are not thoroughly familiar with the canopy jettison and seat ejection mechanism for that particular aircraft.

Before removing survivors, always unfasten the seat belt, shoulder and/or parachute harness, and oxygen mask as well as radio cords and oxygen lead.

Checklist: How to Report

Tell the operator (or radio dispatcher) that you wish to report a military aircraft crash, collect, to the nearest military installation.

When the call is answered, state that you are reporting an aircraft crash, and include at least the following basic information in your conversation:

1. *Give your name and location where calling from.*
2. *Report that a military aircraft crashed at (time) and that there (is) (is not) a fire.*
3. *Give accurate geographical location, road net, distances and/or compass directions on how to reach the crash site. (Prominent ground and air landmarks can be useful to both military ground vehicles and rescue and fire fighting helicopters.)*
4. *Crew parachuted (or landed with airplane).*
5. *Medical help needed.*
6. *Crew believed to be dead (give number).*
7. *Report damage to private property or civilian injuries.*
8. *Report any of the following:*
   a. *Number on tail of aircraft*
   b. *Type or model of aircraft*
   c. *Where someone will meet the rescue team*
   d. *Nearest suitable helicopter landing area (flat open field, free of poles and wires)*
9. *Make sure the report is understood.*
10. *Any other information of possible immediate value.*
11. *Please wait for any questions before hanging up.*
12. *Leave number for possible callback, if possible.*

The press may be represented and such personnel may be collecting data for their media. The military team that will be dispatched to the scene will have a press relations officer who will handle all information releases. Except for injured persons, leave everything as you find it and wait for the military to assume control of the site. If there is some distance to the nearest military installation, certain rescue operations may continue, including the extinguishing of a fire or prevention of further damage, but nothing else should be disturbed for any reason.

In the event of a civilian aircraft crash, perform whatever rescue operations are necessary and evacuate the immediate vicinity as a precautionary measure. Notify the nearest office of the National Transportation Safety Board: Anchorage, Alaska; Chicago, Illinois; Denver, Colorado; Fort Worth, Texas; Kansas City, Missouri; Los Angeles, California; Miami, Florida; New York, New York; Oakland, California; Seattle, Washington; and Washington, D.C. If the field office is some distance away, notify the nearest airport that has a control tower and request that the crash be reported to the Federal Aviation Administration. The actual reporting of any aircraft accident is the responsibility of the pilot of the involved aircraft, but notification should be prompt. If the pilot had filed a flight plan while flying under visual flight rules or was flying under instrument flight rules, his failure to report in within a prescribed period of time will cause a search for his whereabouts to be instituted by the agencies concerned.

When reporting a civilian aircraft accident, be sure to provide the airplane identification number and its exact location. As with the military aircraft, close the area to spectators and allow only authorized personnel. The National Transportation Safety Board or Federal Aviation Administration investigators will assume responsibility for any of the wreckage, cargo, records, or any other items they deem necessary for their investigation. They are the only persons who may release any of those items. According to Section 430.10(b) of the National Transportation Safety Board regulations, wreckage, mail, or cargo may be moved prior to the time the board or an authorized representative takes custody of such articles only to

1. Remove persons injured or trapped.
2. Protect the wreckage from further damage.
3. Protect the public from injury.

Whenever it is necessary to move any items, if possible arrange to have photographs taken of the scene, prepare a sketch, and make sufficient notes so that you may be able to reconstruct as accurately as possible the scene as you found it.

BOMBS AND BOMB THREATS

Anarchists have been known to use bombs quite effectively to destroy lives and property and to cause a demoralizing effect on people. Sometimes as devastating as the actual detonation of a bomb is a telephoned threat that there will be a bombing. Although you may be reasonably sure that a bomb will not go off as announced, you are probably in no position to decide to "call the bluff" by telling the caller to go ahead and blow up the building named in the threat. The call must be handled as though you expect to find a bomb, and your search must be so exhaustive that you are reasonably sure you have not overlooked a single possibility (see Figure 10–5).

There are two reasons why it is of tremendous importance to identify the party who telephones someone to notify them that a bomb has been planted in a particular location. One is that the threatening call itself is a crime whether an actual bomb was planted or not. The second is that in the event that a bomb has been planted, the caller is a key person to locate and question. He may be the individual who planted it, or he may have participated in the crime, or he may have information concerning the crime and want to do what he can to preserve lives without having to identify himself. If possible, determine what type of bomb was planted. Sometimes the caller will tell what it is and where it is.

In the event that the telephone operator who receives the bomb threat call has a tape recorder attachment, now is the time to activate the recorder. It may be possible to match voices later when a suspect is located. This is an excellent reason why all police lines should have recording capabilities to tape incoming messages.

Figure 10–5 Handling and disposing of bombs is a task for specialists. [(a) and (b) Courtesy New York City Police Department; (c) and (d) courtesy Chicago Police Department.]

Upon arriving on the scene where the bomb is purported to be, contact the calling party—if he or she is at the scene—and locate the device reported to be a bomb, if its location is known. Immediately report to the dispatcher that you have arrived, and report also the progress of your investigation to date. If one is available, consider the use of a telephone for the call because you might have a radio-activated device in the vicinity. Keep in continuous communication with the dispatcher if possible so that any progress reports may be made as the need arises. If the bomb has not been located, take immediate steps to begin a search and protect the people who may be injured from any blast.

Establish a perimeter within which you believe the bomb may be found. Request additional assistance to help keep the area closed, if any need exists. Decide whether to evacuate the premises or to conduct your search without the knowledge of the people who occupy the premises. If the bomb threat involves a school or some other building where infrequent and unannounced fire drills are held, consider having a fire drill to evacuate the building without fanfare. If you must evacuate, do so quickly but in an orderly manner. Evacuation should be to a distance of at least 300 feet (or half a city block).

Your own calm manner under situations such as this may be the deciding factor in whether or not other people at the scene will panic. Keep cool at all costs.

Search the premises for the device, with one officer in charge of the search. Be sure to search every available part of the premises, including those where you believe no bomb would be planted. When searching for a bomb or anything that is foreign to the place being searched, take along someone who is familiar with the place to be searched. If any item is unfamiliar to that person, then it should be considered suspect.

A bomb may be *any* size or shape, and it may be placed inside *any* kind of container. When you find any object that looks as though it may be what you are looking for, evacuate that portion of the building and isolate the device. Allow no one to enter the area or to handle the object. At this point you should have someone contact the nearest military installation or one of the larger neighboring police departments— unless your department is that one—and request the services of an explosive ordinance disposal team. If such a team is at your service, protect the area and wait for its arrival; then continue according to its instructions.

If no bomb disposal team is available and the task of removing the suspected bomb from the premises falls to you, proceed carefully with the operation yourself. Have gas and electric utilities shut off, if possible. Set up a *no smoking* policy immediately. Remove any flammable or explosive substances from the vicinity of the suspected object to avoid a more serious problem than would occur if only a suspected bomb would go off. Do not attempt to open any container or twist any mechanism. If you must remove the device from the premises, do so with extreme caution. Some explosives may detonate quite readily, while others require another explosive to cause a chain series that results in the final explosion of the more powerful material. Move the device to an open area and place it under guard; then contact bomb experts by radio or telephone and follow their instructions.

SUMMARY

It seems as though major disasters come all at once when they do occur. No place is safe from some sort of disaster at any time, such as a major airplane crash caused by pilot error or equipment malfunction or an act of terrorism. In the United States we believed that we were more secure from acts of terrorism than our unfortunate friends and neighbors in other countries. The bombing of the Federal Building in Oklahoma

City, the World Trade Center bombing in New York City, and the murderous acts of the Unabomber are just a few of the incidents that have awakened us from our complacency. *It can happen here* or there or anywhere.

Natural disasters, such as fires, floods, hurricanes, earthquakes, and drought, also occur almost anywhere and are not restricted to those places where they are more commonplace than others. You and your department must have a plan for dealing with all of these types of situations, whether or not anyone wants to believe that they can happen. In this chapter we have covered some of those types of situations that your department's community policing and problem-solving efforts should be devoted to so that you will be ready to deal with the emergency, whatever it is, and not be caught completely off guard as some of us have been in the past.

Although civil disturbances and mass demonstrations may not be as common as in the 1960s, they do still occur now and then. For that reason, we have covered some of the basic concepts of crowd and riot control.

EXERCISES AND STUDY QUESTIONS

1. Describe the equipment that your department has at its disposal for disaster response.
2. What special types of training would you recommend for your department, keeping in mind the geography, topography, and other unique characteristics of the area?
3. What type of unexpected disaster could occur in the jurisdiction where you live?
4. List the locations and types of disasters that could occur in the jurisdiction where you live that might be anticipated as a once-in-a-century event or that might occur any year.
5. Describe in sequence how you would respond to the scene of an aircraft crash.
6. What is the purpose for using the term "Mayday" in a radio transmission?
7. If you are the first officer at the scene of a disaster, what is the advantage of your staying with your unit and radio rather than running in and immediately attempting to begin rescuing the survivors?
8. What other agencies or companies might you call upon for additional transportation and communications needs to aid in disaster response?
9. What personnel assignments would you make with the officers already on duty so that you might adequately cope with an unexpected disaster, such as a broken dam or a volcanic eruption?
10. What can the field officer do to address the problem of unfounded (you believe) rumors being circulated about police abuse?
11. List and discuss the five police objectives at the scene of an unlawful assembly.
12. Define "mob psychology."
13. What kind of a gathering of people would lend itself to the possible formation of a mob?
14. What is the difference between a crowd and a mob?

15. Describe how a crowd may turn into a mob.
16. Describe the three stages in the development of a mob.
17. List and explain the several steps in handling an unlawful assembly.
18. Devise a disaster-riot mobilization plan for your department, and submit it to your field unit commanding officer.
19. What is the advantage of having a staging area away from police headquarters?
20. Describe martial rule and how it is put into effect in your state.
21. At what point do federal troops get involved in local martial rule?
22. Check with your local military air base and compare its recommended procedures regarding a military aircraft accident with the information outlined in this chapter.
23. Describe the procedure for responding to a bomb threat phone call when one of the building's occupants has found what appears to be a bomb.
24. If the police officers who respond to a "keep the peace" call at the scene of a labor–management dispute happen to be members of a union related to that of the strikers, what must the officers do to assure fairness in their enforcement of the law?
25. Describe the incident command system in place in the jurisdiction where you live or work.
26. Is a mutual aid agreement in place in the county where you live? Do the businesspeople and other residents know of its existence?
27. How would you use informants during and prior to a riot?
28. What is *zero tolerance* and how does it work?

REFERENCES

Federal Aviation Regulations, 1988 (annual).

INTERNATIONAL CITY MANAGERS' ASSOCIATION. *Training and Equipping Police Crowd and Riot Control Officers and Units.* Chicago: International City Managers' Association, 1966.

LOS ANGELES COUNTY SHERIFF'S DEPARTMENT. *Crowd and Riot Control Instructional Guide.* Los Angeles: Sheriff's Department, 1963.

_____. *Supervisor's Role in Emergency Operations.* Los Angeles: Sheriff's Department, 1967.

LOS ANGELES DISTRICT ATTORNEY. *Civil Disturbance Manual for Law Enforcement.* Los Angeles: D. A. Evelle J. Younger's Office, 1967.

U.S. DEPARTMENT OF DEFENSE. *What to Do and How to Report Military Aircraft Accidents,* Joint Service Booklet 1. Washington, D.C.: U.S. Department of the Navy, 1968.

FOOTNOTES

1. U.S. Department of Defense, *What to Do and How to Report Military Aircraft Accidents,* Joint Service Booklet 1 (Washington, D.C.: U.S. Department of the Navy, 1968). Available from U.S. Naval Aviation Center, Naval Air Station, Norfolk, Va.

CHAPTER 11

TRAFFIC DIRECTION AND ENFORCEMENT

*I*NTRODUCTION

Depending on which department you work for, your traffic responsibilities will vary. Traditionally, the police and sheriff's departments were already in place enforcing the laws and investigating crimes and other incidents, so they were charged with the task since the automobile first appeared on the scene in large numbers in the early twentieth century. As highways started to connect the urban areas and began to crisscross the states and the entire country in the late 1920s and 1930s, state highway patrol divisions were created.

In order to ensure enforcement uniformity, the state forces were either assigned or asked to assume primary responsibility for all traffic matters on the freeways and expressways throughout the states even when they entered city limits. For some cities, giving up their traffic responsibilities was a reduction in the workload of their officers, but it also meant giving up to the states a lucrative source of revenue from traffic citations. Actually, one of the cities in California that held out the longest before relinquishing its freeway enforcement duties to the California Highway Patrol was Los Angeles, which finally asked the CHP to take over the freeways for enforcement and investigation about 30 years after the CHP was formed in 1937.

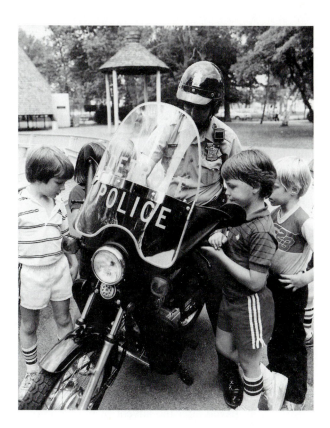

Figure 11-1 (Courtesy Detroit Police Department.)

In the rural areas outside the incorporated cities, where sheriff's departments have the policing responsibilities, traffic enforcement was added to their already heavy burden along with their responsibilities as keepers of the county jail and providing bailiff services in the superior courts. Since a great many of the county roadways crisscrossing the states were also designated state highways, it was only logical that some of the states took over the sheriff's traffic function and added it to the state highway patrols in place by that time. This assures greater consistency in enforcement philosophy throughout the states.

In cities where the sheriff contracts to serve as the police department in lieu of their creating their own police departments, the deputies sheriff function as city police officers and, for all practical purposes *are* city police officers in spite of the color of their uniforms and the title "deputy" on their badges.

This chapter is devoted to the duties and responsibilities of these urban policing agencies. Pursuit driving, car stops, and the DUI will also be covered, as they are traffic related even when the pursued turn out to be wanted felons. In most departments of any size at all, there is a separate individual or division of officers specifically assigned to specialize in traffic. But whether or not there is a separate unit, the field patrol officers will still be charged with total policing in their assigned beats, and this includes traffic enforcement and investigation. You may be "preserving the scene" of a collision, as you would a crime in the larger departments, but even that will change from time to time and you will have to handle the entire situation. In the smaller department, you as a "generalist" will be required to handle traffic matters as you do all others.

THE POLICE TRAFFIC FUNCTION

There are five principal facets of the police traffic function: movement, investigation, enforcement, education, and design. We will cover the first three in this chapter. The fourth and fifth, education and design, will be covered in other texts in greater detail. (See Figure 11–2)

Movement

The police responsibility for assuring the safe and efficient flow of pedestrian and vehicular traffic is probably your most important task. More people are killed each year in traffic accidents than almost any other cause of death. The statisticians have said that more Americans have been killed in automobile collisions in the past one hundred years than have been killed in all of the wars in which the United States has been involved for the past two hundred years.

Traffic Flow.   The streets in many cities were designed for considerably less vehicular traffic than they are now having to accommodate. Many of those streets were paved after the advent of the automobile but have not been widened since the days of the horse carriage. In some places roads are the same as they were in the days of the ox cart and the chariot. It is no wonder that we have horrendous congestion problems.

It is essential that you keep the traffic lanes open and the vehicles and pedestrians moving with maximum efficiency under the conditions that vary with the time of day, the day of week, and the seasons. In order to assure the maximum flow, be on the alert for stoppages caused by left turners in the middle of the block and people who double-park where they hold up traffic unnecessarily. They are probably not breaking the law, but most of these people just simply do not think about the world around them and are oblivious to the backups they are causing. You must direct them to move on to break up the bottlenecks.

You may be able to solve a transient congestion problem by simply getting out of your vehicle, stepping out into the street, and directing traffic for a while until the steady flow resumes. If the problem is more than temporary or regularly occurs at the same time, as if on schedule, then notify your supervisor so that more permanent assignments may be made. You may have an engineering design problem that should be addressed by the traffic engineer.

Whenever you assume a traffic control assignment, consider the entire picture of traffic flow in all directions around you. Bear in mind that overriding a traffic signal may solve the problem at your intersection but may cause bigger problems

Figure 11-2 Traffic control includes inspection of commercial vehicles for safety and load limits. (Courtesy Pennsylvania State Police.)

down the street, where the signals can't cope with the extra load you are putting on them. On one occasion when I was in a strange city, there was a traffic collision ahead. The patrol officer correctly got out of his car and started diverting traffic away from the scene. He directed all cars going west on the boulevard in the direction of the accident to turn right at the intersection where he set up shop. He really had a problem when all of those cars went to the end of the cul-de-sac and had to return to his intersection again because they had nowhere else to go. Had he backed up a block or two, then diverted traffic north onto a through street, he would have certainly made his own job easier and the tempers of those he diverted a few degrees cooler.

If traffic control in the street is a regular or occasional part of your patrol assignment, equip yourself with high-visibility protective gear. I have a fused spine because I was inappropriately attired when many years ago—as a sergeant—I stepped out into the street to direct traffic and was struck down by an intoxicated driver just a few days before Christmas.

Channel the streets to meet the changing needs of the traffic, such as using cones and changing a four-lane, two-way street into three lanes one way during the morning rush and three lanes in the opposite direction during the evening rush. For rush hour, make the parking lanes into no parking towaway lanes, and be sure that those lanes are clear during the scheduled hours. Check on your traffic control signals frequently and immediately notify the appropriate department when you have non-normal-functioning equipment so that your job will be easier.

In some parts of the world, traffic on those ancient streets is so heavy that private vehicles are allowed on the streets only on alternate days of the month, depending on the odd or even last number on their license plates. This may even include commercial vehicles, which are restricted to specific hours to avoid the rush hours of the private vehicle drivers. Carpooling is strongly encouraged, and some companies are heavily fined when they do not provide for carpooling or staggering their employees' work hours.

Traffic Control Hand Signals

When you step out into the street to direct traffic, it is imperative that both you and the drivers know from your signals exactly what it is that you want them to do with each movement. There is no room for vague and uncertain movements that will confuse the drivers and cause collisions. Voice control is out of the question, although I have known some officers who tried it, and hands swinging like a windmill also does not work, as I have seen as a field supervisor. The whistle gets attention, but it says nothing about what you want the motorists, pedestrians, and other vehicle operators to do. Use broad and distinctive hand signals that express your directions to those people. Try these signals if you have not been instructed otherwise in your academy training.

Stand in the intersection where the greatest number of people can see you. Wear a reflector vest or other high-visibility clothing with white gloves. At nighttime use white gloves and signal cones, cyalume rods, or specially designed flashlights, preferably one for each hand.

1. *Ready position* (Figure 11–3 (a) and (b). You are in charge and your presence should be that of the orchestra leader with the baton. It is a serious function and you are *directing* traffic, not just standing there as a spectator. The people must feel through your signals that you are in charge. This is an example of "command presence."

2. *To stop traffic* (Figure 11–3 (c)–(f)). With your arms outstretched, point your finger and look directly at the driver of the vehicle you intend to stop. Continue pointing until you are sure the driver sees you; then raise up the palm of the hand as if you were placing it flat up against the front of the car. Once that vehicle and the others behind it are stopped, turn your head toward the vehicles coming in the opposite direction and repeat the process with your other hand. Once vehicles coming from both directions are stopped, the opposing traffic may proceed. If necessary to get the attention of the driver you wish to stop, blow one short blast with your whistle.

3. *To start traffic* (Figure 11–3 (g)–(h)). Turn so that you are facing the stopped traffic, and your right and left sides are addressing the traffic you are going to signal to go. With your outstretched hand and arm, point directly at the driver of the vehicle you are directing to go. When the driver sees you, swing your hand up and over your chin, bending the arm only at the elbow. To get that driver's attention, blow short blasts with your whistle. Once that vehicle has started, repeat the same procedure with your other hand to start the traffic going the opposite direction on the same street. Repeat the movements for slow or timid drivers and to indicate to all moving vehicle drivers that they still have the right of way. Do not swing your arms in a full arc like a windmill. It is both tiring and confusing. The arms bend only at the elbow. Use the whistle only for attracting the attention of drivers and not to scold them. Avoid shouting directions.

4. *Right turn* (Figs. 11–3 (i)–(k). Signals for the right turner are not usually necessary, unless the driver needs reassurance that it is okay to turn. There is no opposing traffic. With your arm closest to the driver, swing your arm to point in the direction he or she intends to turn. This reassures the driver that the turn meets with your approval.

5. *Left turn* (Figure 11–3 (l)–(n)). In order to allow a left turn, it is necessary to first stop the traffic coming in the opposite direction. For that purpose, use the stop signal described in step 1. Once you have waited for a gap to appear and have stopped that traffic, you then move the left turner. While you are waiting for the gap in the oncoming traffic that you are going to stop, bring the left turner toward you to get into position in the intersection, allowing the vehicles behind to pass around the turner's right side without having to stop. Motion as in Figures 7 and 8 to get the driver in the left-turning position, then give the stop signal (Figure 11–3 (o). When you have stopped the opposing traffic and are ready for the turn, make your signal to authorize the turn. The reason why we say "authorize" here is that you are in charge, and drivers should follow your directions implicitly. If left turners would slow down traffic too much for the heavy volume you have at a particular time, you may not allow left turners at all. Those drivers will just have to find a way to get to their destinations by going around the block and crossing the intersection by going straight on the street onto which they would have turned left.

RIGHT   WRONG

Ready for business   Just waiting   Point
(a)   (b)   (c)

Stop   Point   Stop
(d)   (e)   (f)

Pointing   Starting   Point at the driver
(g)   (h)   (i)

Figure 11-3

Arm swing

(j)

Point where driver is to go

(k)

Halt opposing traffic
with right hand

(l)

Hold opposing traffic
and point to turning driver

(m)

Give turn signal
with left hand

(n)

Direct driver
into intersection

(o)

Figure 11-3 *(Continued)*

TRAFFIC COLLISION INVESTIGATION

Purposes for Investigating Collisions. Collision investigation is definitely not the same as taking a report when someone comes into the office and fills in the blanks. That is nothing more than a traffic report, which is sufficient in many cases when the insurance companies need evidence of the event. When you investigate a collision (see Figure 11–4), the purpose is to go beyond simply filling in the blanks. Your intent is to inquire into the cause of the collision, which may be mechanical, human error, engineering, or an act of some supreme being. Most collisions are not accidents; they are caused events.

Figure 11-4 Courtesy California Highway Patrol.

If there has been a mechanical fault of one or more of the vehicles, then you may have developed data that should be reported to the manufacturer so that its engineers can recall the vehicles or make improvements for future models. If the problem is one of street design or faulty placement of signs or road markings, then your information should go to those engineering specialists so that corrections can be made where appropriate. If the collision involved driver error, then you have an education problem that must be addressed, or it may also require that the cause of the collision was a traffic law violation. The violator learns in two ways not to repeat the violation that led to the citation: the cost of the fine and/or jail time and the increased cost of one's insurance policy at the next renewal. In order to protect the driving record, many violators are allowed to attend a traffic school in lieu of paying a fine and having the violation stand on their driving record.

Types of Accidents. There are three basic types of traffic accidents, which are classified according to what action took place while the vehicle was on the roadway. The first type is "running off the roadway." It is classified as such even though it may strike another vehicle or object after leaving the roadway. A second type of accident is "noncollision on road," which includes an overturning vehicle or noncollision event, such as a person getting injured when brakes are applied suddenly. The third type, the most common of the three, is the "collision with. . . ." This type includes collisions with pedestrians, other vehicles, a train, a bicycle, an animal, or some other object.

Parts of a Collision. The first part of the collision is the "point of surprise," when the driver suddenly realizes that something is going to happen. At about the same time, sometimes concurrent with the surprise, is the "point of no escape," when the collision is inevitable. Once in motion at that point, the only hope is that the result will not be too catastrophic. The "key event" is usually the most noticeable part of the collision, such as the automobile without a driver behind the wheel racing down a hill, or a vehicle entering the wrong way onto a freeway loaded with vehicles going in the opposite direction. The fourth part of the collision is the "maximum engagement," which occurs when the careening vehicle strikes another vehicle or a solitary object, such as a traffic signal pole. The "final position" is where the vehicle(s) comes to a complete stop. You usually arrive at this part of the collision and must investigate and identify the other parts.

The Investigation Procedure. Varying circumstances will dictate occasions when you must deviate from established procedure, but you should develop a sequential guideline to follow as closely as possible to assure that you perform a complete investigation. Make your own checklist and check it carefully before you complete your investigation to ensure that you have done everything you set out to do.

1. Go to the scene as quickly and safely as possible. Depending on your department's policy, your response should hinge on the seriousness of the damage, the injuries, and the hazard to other traffic. The communications operator who receives the initial call from the scene usually has the best information. Code three is used for injury accidents and continuing life-threatening situations. You will usually be assigned the code of your response. If you are not, follow the established policy. Sometimes turning on the red lights and siren only to expedite your movement through an intersection causes more problems than it solves because the traffic may suddenly freeze in place and block your way.

2. Carefully observe and make mental notes about descriptions of vehicles and people who appear to be hastily leaving the scene as you approach. Upon arrival, you may discover that you have a hit-and-run situation. Notify other follow-up units of your observations about possible suspects leaving the scene.

3. While responding to the scene, call for assisting units to post themselves at intersections approaching the actual scene so as to divert traffic onto alternate routes and to keep the way clear for other emergency vehicles if they are necessary. You may be well advised to stop and lay flare or reflector patterns to alert other vehicle operators of the hazard ahead so that they may realize there is a problem to avoid. Flares are widely used, but longer-lasting devices are available and might prove more practical if your department has stocked them.

4. Park your vehicle correctly and safely to avoid further collisions. If vehicles, victims, and/or debris are on the roadway and in the way of traffic, position your vehicle with emergency lights flashing to attract the attention of other motorists and to divert them away from the hazards. Once the roadway is cleared, park your own vehicle off the road and turn off the lights. Have you ever noticed that flashing red and other lights on an emergency vehicle actually draw motorists toward them like a moth is attracted to flames? This seems particularly true when a driver has consumed alcohol or is in a state of fatigue.

5. Immediately locate all drivers, passengers, and any other people who might have been involved in the collision and ascertain what medical attention, if any, they need. Administer what first aid that you can and utilize volunteer services

if they are offered. There are times when doctors or nurses pitch right in and help but they will not identify themselves as medical professionals for fear of malpractice suits later. Don't push for their identity if they are willing to assist.

6. Notify communications of your needs for medical emergency personnel, fire and rescue services, ambulances, tow trucks, and additional police personnel. They should all be on the way as you continue with your investigation.

7. Locate and separate the drivers. Identify them immediately by asking for their driver's licenses, and hold on to the licenses until you have finished questioning them. Give each of them something to write on, such as a notepad on a clipboard, and have them fill in the information that they should exchange to provide to their insurance companies. While you are talking with one driver, it should be out of the hearing range of the other driver. You want their unrehearsed statements before either of them is able to fabricate a story. When you have finished with one driver, question the other one. Have them describe as much as they can about their involvement in the event.

8. Locate and question witnesses separately. To keep them separate, you may hand them some paper and a pen and have them write their names and addresses and a brief account of what they witnessed while they await their turn to be questioned. When you talk with them, avoid the use of the word "witness." You are more apt to get a better response by asking what each of them saw, heard, and otherwise perceived. You should avoid asking "What happened?" because they could tell you their opinion without actually having seen anything. If you ask if they witnessed anything, the word "witness" reminds them that they will probably have to lose time from work or other enterprises to go to court. After you have completed your investigation, take the time (if you have it) to go back to the location from which each witness is said to have perceived the event and determine for yourself whether such perception was actually possible.

9. Note and record all damage to the vehicles involved in the collision, and all other property that might have also been involved in the event. Take photos if you have a camera, which should be standard equipment.

10. Note and record all physical conditions at the scene: locations of vehicles, evidence, weather conditions, and anything else that might have a relationship to the collision. Pay particular attention to short-lived, or transient, evidence. Measure and record skid marks, water, grease, blood spots. Look for vision obstructions, such as vegetation, buildings, walls, or other vehicles that might have interfered with one of the drivers' capacity to operate his or her vehicle safely.

11. Test the vehicles' brakes, steering, broken windshield or windows, when a malfunction or faulty equipment might possibly have been a cause of or contributory factor in the collision.

12. Using chalk or other marking material, mark the location and position of each victim, every item of evidence, the point of impact, and the final resting place of the vehicle(s). Take measurements and make your rough field sketch. You can later prepare a more detailed diagram if all of your measurements and field sketch are accurate.

13. Arrest or cite the law violators, if you have sufficient cause at the time. You will check for whether one or more of the drivers are under the influence of alcohol or drugs. If misdemeanor violations might have caused the collision, such as failing to stop at a red light, the follow-up investigator will handle the charges by filing a complaint and securing a warrant for later arrest.

14. Search the immediate area for any discarded items, such as containers of alcohol or drugs, or weapons, or contraband of some sort that may have caused one of the drivers to be driving erratically.

15. Arrange for disabled vehicles to be removed and have the streets cleaned up. Usually, this is the responsibility of the tow truck driver, but it may require street sweepers and a wash down by the fire department in the case of larger spills.

16. Pay a visit to the hospital if there were injuries that required victims to be taken to the hospital, and take additional statements to complete your investigation, if necessary.

17. Notify relatives and survivors, when necessary.

18. Complete your report.

PURSUIT AND EMERGENCY DRIVING

Pursuit and emergency driving involve the same driving skills that the field officer should master for normal driving, with an extra emphasis on defensive driving techniques. For this type of driving, you must be at your peak efficiency and extremely alert, a condition that is actually enhanced by the increased activity of the nervous system and other body functions that are stimulated by the excitement of the situation. However, most police vehicle accidents occur during "normal" patrol driving, and it is imperative that you be equally alert at all times to avoid serious injury and property damage.

A prime consideration when making the decision to begin a high-speed "code three" run is the nature of the situation. The decision may be made by the dispatcher in accordance with established policies when it is in response to a call for service or help, such as a "no detail" accident (injuries, if any, are unknown) or an armed robbery in progress. The situation in the field that arises in your presence requires your individual decision as to whether or not to pursue. You must immediately evaluate the situation and decide whether it is imperative that an apprehension be effected.

Relative locations of the police unit and the vehicle to be pursued play a significant role in the evaluative process. Can you get into position for the chase without causing an accident or jeopardizing the life of pedestrians? Think ahead. Where is the pursuit going to take you? Is there a school or playground down the street? a dead end? a cross street? What is the estimated speed of the violator, and how fast will the police car be required to go to overtake him or her? Is another police unit in a better position to apprehend the violator if it is notified by radio of the wanted vehicle approaching its location? These questions must be repeated throughout the pursuit in a continuing process of reevaluation. Also, what condition is your police unit in?

If it appears that the pursuit is not possible, it is better to use your time and efforts to alert another unit to the description, the direction of travel, and any other pertinent information that will enable the other unit to locate and apprehend the violators. By means of radio, it is possible to pursue actively the individual in coordination with other police units.

Once you make the decision to pursue, get into position as quickly and efficiently as possible. Notify the dispatcher of your pursuit, the nature of the situation, the direction of travel, your location, and a description of the pursued vehicle. The information that is most critical at the beginning of the pursuit is the direction of travel. Other units in the area may be in a position to assist in the pursuit, or they may clear traffic on side streets to reduce the possibility of traffic collisions involving the police car or the pursued vehicle. During the chase, make frequent broadcasts to keep headquarters and other police units advised of your changing location and any additional need for assistance. Some departments tape all pursuits, and the dispatcher will periodically broadcast the time for later reference, if necessary.

If you use the red light and siren as warning devices, *use* them. Using a siren and turning on the lights only at intersections is unwise and generally illegal (there are exceptions, of course). An emergency vehicle is authorized to violate the rules of the road only when functioning in a code three situation, which requires red light and siren. Never assume that anyone will see the lights or hear the siren, particularly when you are approaching intersections, but use them nevertheless. When you turn on the siren, look for nearby motorists who will be startled by the sudden noise and who may do strange things, such as stop suddenly or swerve into your vehicle. At extremely high speeds and on roads where there are no side streets, such as a freeway or expressway, the siren may serve no useful purpose once the driver of the pursued vehicle clearly understands it is he that you are chasing and it is apparent that he has no intention of stopping.

Depending on the type of siren equipment you have, be sure to utilize it to the maximum, also using the horn, and use the headlights, blinking the high and low beam alternately. Use your seat belts, safety helmets, shoulder harnesses, and any other safety devices provided by the automobile manufacturer and your department (see Figure 11–5).

Shooting any type of weapon at a fleeting vehicle is not advisable and should be limited to extreme cases when there is absolutely no other way to save a human life. In both of these situations, however, it is more logical to assume that the pursued vehicle will be caused to go out of control and someone may die or be seriously injured as a result. Drivers of other vehicles, pedestrians, or occupants of buildings in the area may become the innocent victims of an officer's poor judgment. Pursuing another vehicle is almost the same as if you were pushing it, even though you may be hundreds of feet behind the other vehicle.

Consider this liability problem. A police officer and his department were being sued for several million dollars and an "expert" was consulted by the attorneys for the defense. What do you believe to have been the result of this case?

It was late in the evening. The weather was cool and the sky was moonless. The officer had pulled into the parking lot of a business-industrial area and was slowly checking out the doors and windows for signs of burglaries. His headlights were off and he used the hand brake so that the flash of a brake light would not alert anyone

Figure 11-5 The standard police pursuit vehicle is usually the basic patrol unit, such as this one. (Courtesy North Carolina State Highway Patrol.)

to his presence. While he was cruising the lot, he heard the squeal of tires and looked around as a sedan took off from the intersection at a high rate of speed.

The officer decided to follow the car to see if the tire squealing was accidental or deliberate. As he pulled out into the street and proceeded in the same direction as the car in question, his headlights were still turned off. He followed the car, which kept speeding up. He began the pursuit, turned on his headlights, and by the time he turned on his red lights and siren the suspect vehicle was traveling at least 85 miles per hour on this residential street, which had a 35 mph speed limit. The suspect car continued at about the same speed for about two miles with the officer in hot pursuit, but as the suspect vehicle sped through two intersections that fortunately were not busy at the time, going against the red light in both instances, the officer had to slow down so that he could safely get through the intersection. He was about a half-mile behind the suspect vehicle when the car went through the second intersection. As the officer sped to catch up, the suspect suddenly turned north. The officer continued in the same direction through the intersection. He turned off his red lights and siren, turned around, then turned north to follow the suspect.

The officer was accelerating on this street, which had no traffic, and had not yet turned his lights and siren back on. By that time, the suspect vehicle approached a fairly busy intersection and did not slow down. He went against the red light and ran broadside into a small car containing two elderly women. The impact was so great that the violator totaled the car he struck plus his own. He was slightly injured, but both women were killed instantly.

The prosecution in this civil lawsuit contended that since this uninsured offender was being pursued by the police, he was actually being "pushed" into the accident, causing the fatal injuries. He stated that the officers should have abandoned the chase, and that if they had, the young man being pursued would have slowed down and the accident would not have happened. Do you believe that the officer was liable under the circumstances presented here?

The "expert" reviewed the reports, visited the scene of the chase and the accident, and mentally re-created the event. His opinion, presented in a deposition, was that the officer was not responsible, that he had actually discontinued the chase when he overshot the street where the suspect vehicle had turned, and that the officer had actually turned off the red light and siren. The expert added that even had the officer not overshot the street and had had the emergency equipment turned on, the officer would not have been at fault in this case. The police department did not lose the case. (The expert was a former police lieutenant who writes textbooks and teaches criminal justice classes.)

While driving under pursuit or emergency conditions, approach each intersection with extreme caution, slowing down to avoid an accident with someone who may not hear or heed the warning siren of the approaching police car. Never pass a vehicle on the right with your red light and siren on. You may encounter another individual who is completely oblivious to your proximity until you start passing, when the other driver suddenly sees or hears you and does what is required by law: to immediately drive to the right side of the road and stop to allow the emergency vehicle to pass.

Caravans of several pursuing vehicles should be avoided (see Figure 11–6). There is no need for more than two or three cars to be directly involved in the chase of even the most dangerous criminal. Consider the driver who pulls over to the side of the street to allow the police unit to pass, then immediately returns to the traffic lane and follows the police car to see where it is going. Such a driver normally returns to the traffic lane at about the same time that the second police car reaches the same spot. The second police car is probably not operating with red light and siren,

Figure 11-6 The helicopter is an excellent backup unit to assist in pursuits. (Courtesy North Carolina State Highway Patrol.)

thereby placing the officer in a civilly liable position, not to mention the hazards involved at the time.

Roadblocks may be utilized, but they should seldom, if ever, involve the placement of police vehicles directly in the traffic lane to present a physical, impassable barrier. Barricades, flares, and other objects may serve the purpose without assuming the risks of causing loss of life or destruction of property. Portable spike bars, similar to those used at the exits of parking lots and apartment complexes where you are warned of severe tire damage if you back up, are effective as roadblocks when they cause tires to deflate.

Other devices are being developed, such as electronic sensors in a pad that looks like a large electric blanket that the officer would place on the roadway in the path of the approaching suspect vehicle. As the vehicle passes over the sensors, they send a signal to the motor of the suspect car that shuts it down and the vehicle slows down to a complete stop. Sound farfetched? So did other devices, such as the LoJack, which is activated at the police station when the vehicle is reported stolen. It then sends out a radio signal that is picked up by field units, and it is tracked as it moves and the officers can locate the vehicle pretty much the same way a pilot on a plane or a boat can tell where it is by a navigation process known as triangulation.

Always consider the possibility that the pursued vehicle will stop suddenly and without warning. The driver may not actually be aware of the chase or may be under the influence of alcohol or drugs. The subject may suddenly realize the futility of attempting to lose the police vehicle. Another possibility is that the driver of the pursued vehicle may make a sudden stop to gain strategic advantage by stopping earlier than the police vehicle, placing the officer in front. The subject could then either attack the officer from this position of advantage, or escape by making a quick U-turn or, by alighting from the vehicle, get away on foot. Keep some distance between your vehicle and that of the subject you are pursuing to avoid the possibility of collision when the subject stops suddenly and to avoid placing yourself at a position of disadvantage in front of him.

When you are pursuing another vehicle, you will probably find that you will have a tendency to stay too close. Back off enough to leave a "cushion of space" between the vehicles in case the other driver crashes or stops suddenly or does something that jeopardizes your safety. Consider also the possibility of a blowout, a crash from the front or rear, a fire, or being forced off the road. In case of a blowout, take your foot off the accelerator and slowly without braking, steer firmly and in a straight line until you are almost stopped; then pull off to the side of the road. In the case of an imminent crash from the rear, take your foot off the brake and lie across the seat to avoid whiplash; then apply the brakes immediately following impact. A head-on collision is likely to be fatal, so try to run off the road or strike another vehicle going the same way. In case of a fire, pull over and stop as quickly as possible, use sand or dirt if you have no extinguisher, and get away from the vehicle if the fire is out of control.

Whenever pursuing another vehicle, there may be a time when it is strategically sound judgment to abandon the pursuit. During a high-speed chase when it appears futile to assume that the pursued vehicle will stop for any of a number of reasons, there is always the danger that the chase will become a matter of personal pride to the officer driving the pursuing vehicle. It may be a matter of competition in driving skill, and the officer may become so intent on winning that the objective of the chase is no longer clear. Under conditions that develop during such a contest, any subsequent actions during the chase and eventual capture of the suspect may be quite injudicious. Intelligent and professional police officers cannot lose control of their faculties to the extent that they lose their objectivity.

Protection of life and property, which applies to the high-speed chase, includes the lives and property of the individual being pursued, the officer, and any innocent people who might become involved in a traffic collision as a direct result of the chase. At some time during the chase, it may be necessary to abandon the chase to uphold this police responsibility. The decision to abandon the chase involves factors such as the seriousness of the situation precipitating the chase in the first place, the possibility of identifying the driver and the vehicle for a later arrest with a warrant, and the road conditions at the time of the chase. What is the weather condition? Are there other vehicles, pedestrians, or children nearby that might be injured if the chase continues? Consider also the likelihood that the driver of the pursued vehicle will slow down to a normal speed once he makes good his escape. Or will he continue jeopardizing the lives and property of everyone who gets in his way until he collides with something, runs out of gas, or is apprehended? There are many times when circumstances may dictate the abandonment of the chase.

Ramming Vehicles

Ramming is done only in extreme cases and only when the calculated risk indicates that lives of innocent persons would be saved by such action and that danger to the officer driving the ramming vehicle is not imminent. Running into another vehicle from behind or from the side, or in any other way attempting to push the vehicle off the road, is extremely dangerous with unpredictable results, sometimes even suicidal. There are very few times when such action is worth the risk of your life or that of another person, particularly innocent third parties who have the misfortune to be nearby at the time.

A very skillful driver may succeed in pulling alongside another vehicle, locking the two together, then edging the other vehicle to the side of the road. Or the skillful driver may actually brake both vehicles to a stop, taking advantage of the other driver's hesitancy to accelerate and his willingness to allow himself to be stopped in this manner. Ramming has about the same value as shooting at a car in the hope of puncturing a tire or rupturing the gas tank. The chance of ricochet is greater than either of these two hoped-for effects.

With special training on the track, it is possible to develop skill in ramming a pursued vehicle by striking the rear bumper to one side of the middle when the pursued vehicle is turning. If it is turning right, the ramming is done on the left rear so that the ramming motion causes the struck vehicle to spin in the direction of the turn. This must be done very carefully, however, and not at extremely high speeds or where other vehicles may become involved in a collision as a result of the rammed vehicle spinning out of control. We have probably all seen an effective ramming operation at the conclusion of one of the many high-speed chases caught on television by a news helicopter flying overhead. When the result is successful, it is pretty hard to argue against all ramming under all circumstances.

Code Three

In an urban community of any size, there may often be more than one emergency vehicle traveling along the streets in response to different and unrelated emergencies. The possibility of their colliding always exists, particularly when the emergency vehicles belong to different agencies that have no idea of what the other is doing. At best, the situation is complicated and hazardous, but the danger can be compounded if more than one vehicle is responding to a single emergency. In this case, the vehicles' convergence is imminent. Several agencies may be involved in a single incident, or only one. For example, a routine injury accident involving gas spillage will require code three response by a police unit, at least one fire unit, and an ambulance. Each is a separate and distinct agency and may be on a different radio frequency.

Considering the hazards involved in code three, the following guidelines should be established and followed:

1. Only one police unit will use the red light and siren on any one emergency call.
2. The unit responding to the assignment, or initiating a pursuit, will identify the unit and broadcast by radio the location at which you begin the pursuit.
3. The dispatcher should repeat the acknowledgment and broadcast to other units the location and direction of travel, if known.
4. The assigned unit will broadcast an "arrived on scene" (10-97) transmission to indicate the conclusion of the trip.

Escorts

In traffic of any type at any time of the day or night, driving a police vehicle with red light and siren is extremely hazardous. To drive a police vehicle with red light and siren for the purpose of clearing the way for a following vehicle is generally unwise and places too many lives in jeopardy. The officer driving the police vehicle is actually driving both of them, and you are assuming responsibility for the skill and judgment of the other driver as well. You will be specifically liable if there is a collision.

The driver of the escorted vehicle may be emotionally upset or physically incapable of performing under these conditions. It may be that the driver should not be driving even under normal conditions. He or she may not be skilled enough to maintain a safe distance behind the police vehicle and may either get lost or follow too closely. Since the escorted vehicle would not be equipped as an emergency vehicle, it would appear to others as just any other car that might be following a police car on an emergency call.

Consider the possibility of the police vehicle clearing the way for itself and the car following. The drivers of other vehicles must yield to the emergency vehicle, pull over to the side of the road, and wait until the police car passes. They then immediately pull back into the street and resume driving with the normal stream of traffic. The escorted vehicle speeding along behind the police vehicle may be forced to stop because of congestion that is caused by the resumption of the traffic flow or because of a traffic control sign or signal.

What of the legal consideration? Under no circumstances does the escorted vehicle become an emergency vehicle. The driver does not become exempt from the traffic laws, and he cannot be exempted from any civil liability in an accident that may occur during the escort operation. In most jurisdictions, state law prohibits any type of escort with the use of red light and siren. Any justification for a breach of the law allowed by a police officer would have to concern an extremely grave situation. The exception would have to be justifiable not only in your own eyes at that moment but also in the eyes of your superiors, the courts, and the other private persons who enjoy no such immunity and who would expect the escorted vehicle's driver to be held to answer for breaking the law in the same way as they would be held to answer.

In view of these considerations, it would seem that the best method of operation is to decline the request to serve as an escort and to either call an ambulance or transport an injured person in the police vehicle, which is an emergency vehicle when operating with red light and siren. Another option, of course, is for one officer to drive the victim in his or her own car with the other officer following behind—or in front—as an escort. What you have here is actually an Oliver North situation: If everything turns out okay, you will be a hero, but if something goes wrong and you get into an accident, you are in deep trouble.

Transporting Injured Persons in Police Cars

A police vehicle is *not* an ambulance. There are times, however, when there is no other feasible means of transportation available under certain emergency conditions. In such cases, use of the police vehicle for this purpose is not improper. Consider these hypothetical situations, and you be the judge as to what course of action you as the officer should follow.

- While parked near an intersection, you see a two-door late-model sedan speed through an intersection while the traffic signal for his direction of travel is red. The car narrowly misses another car, which had just started with the green light. You pursue the violator and chase him for about two blocks before you get him to stop. As you alight from the patrol car, citation book in hand, you meet an extremely agitated middle-aged man. The man literally shouts at you that he must get to a hospital because he has been stung by a bee, and he will suffer serious consequences because he is allergic to bee stings. He hopes to reach the hospital before he loses consciousness, and he asks you to please get out of his way so that he can resume his fateful journey. What would you do?
- A young man and woman drive up to you where you are parked alongside the street, bringing your activity log up to date. The man says: "My wife is having a baby. Will you escort us to the hospital?" Will you perform the requested service?
- In response to a call for service in an "unknown trouble, see the woman," call, you meet a woman with a small child in her arms. The child is unconscious and seems to be losing its normal color. The woman hysterically screams that the child had lost consciousness while eating a piece of beef, and she cannot revive him. You begin cardiopulmonary resuscitation and determine that there is a possibility that life still exists in the child but that he will probably die without immediate medical attention. No ambulance is available because of a major traffic accident on the highway in which several people were killed and others injured. The child is dying and needs attention. What is your decision?

If your department has not already done so, you should formulate a set of standards so that you make value judgments. Ask yourself the following questions before making your decision: Would transporting the individual increase the severity of the injury? Is the service in direct competition with another agency's service that is available and actually better prepared to handle the matter? Is the need really an emergency? Is it wise to allow a person to drive a vehicle when it is possible that the person may lose consciousness at any moment? Is another emergency service available? Is the individual under arrest? What are the alternatives? The decision you make each time a situation arises is actually based upon consideration of the alternatives, and selection of the right one.

Legal Aspects of Emergency Driving

Basic laws in virtually every jurisdiction provide for the emergency operation of appropriately equipped and authorized vehicles, including police vehicles. For your consideration, five examples of such laws follow:

1. Whenever an emergency vehicle approaches while displaying legally authorized red lights and sounding a siren, the drivers of other vehicles shall yield the right-of-way and wait for the passage of that vehicle. Although most laws are quite specific about *both* red light *and* siren operating, some case law has been generated because of the impracticability of operating a siren on a freeway at extremely high speeds, and under certain conditions it may be permissible to use red light only. These are exceptional cases, however, and the need rarely manifests itself.

2. Emergency vehicles are exempt from most regulations, such as speeding, right-of-way, stop signs and signals, and other rules of the road when responding to an emergency, engaged in rescue operations, in actual pursuit of a violator, or when responding to a fire *if* the driver is sounding the siren and displaying the red light.

3. Emergency vehicles are generally exempt from civil liability when operating in accordance with the emergency provisions and when properly using the legally required red light and siren clearly indicating "emergency vehicle" character.

4. The driver of an emergency vehicle under any conditions, including emergency conditions, is not relieved from the duty to drive with due regard for the safety of all persons using the streets and highways. Moreover, the law does not protect the driver-officer from the consequences of an arbitrary and unnecessary exercise of the privileges granted in the exempting sections. The officer is thus limited to real emergency needs and is prohibited from using the red light and siren to avoid a traffic signal because of impatience rather than actual necessity.

5. Emergency vehicles are forbidden to use the siren or to drive at an illegal speed when serving as an escort *except* for the preservation of life or when escorting supplies and personnel for the armed forces during a national emergency.

CAR STOPS

The Approach by Automobile

Prior to making the stop, communicate by radio your location, the place where the stop will occur, the license number of the vehicle, and any other pertinent information that you have time for. Other information should include the number of occupants, clothing descriptions of occupants if you believe a pursuit is about to take place when the occupants alight, and a statement to the effect that you have reason to believe they are armed. Also, if you anticipate the need for follow-up units, request them. A follow-up should be automatically assigned, but the dispatcher may be compelled by a personnel shortage to assign units on a priority basis. Yours would be at the top of the list.

When approaching the suspect car, be on the alert for any sudden movements by the people in the car. There may be a sudden panic stop by a timid individual who suddenly realizes that it is he whom you wish to stop. The subject may attempt to ram the police car, or try some evasive action to avoid the contact. If the subject appears to be armed and it looks as though he may shoot at you, back off and follow at a safer distance until follow-up units arrive and you can make the stop with the aid of several additional units. At this time, also watch for any objects that the vehicle's occupants may throw out the window. Narcotics, dangerous weapons, and other contraband are often disposed of in this manner.

Making the Auto Stop

Pick your location where there is adequate lighting and where you will not be at too great a disadvantage should the subject or any of his passengers choose to attack you. You should try to see the people at all times. Signal the driver to pull over to the side of the street, and point to the location where you wish him to go. Use the red light and horn—or siren—to attract the driver's attention and to signal other vehicles to make room for you and the vehicle you are stopping. The object of the maneuver is to stop the other car as quickly as possible, then issue the citation or conduct the field interview while attracting the last amount of attention from other people.

Once you have the vehicle stopped and the cars are not parked in a hazardous location, turn off the overhead red lights to avoid setting up a distraction for passersby. If necessary to divert traffic away from your vehicle and the one that you have stopped, or to alert other police units to your exact whereabouts, do not hesitate to use the lights. Sometimes the blinking lights cause the curious to slow down and drive without paying attention to anything but the blinking lights and collision scene, which creates an additional hazard.

In some cases when you have information or reason to believe that the subjects in the vehicle you are attempting to stop may have committed a felony, you may choose to draw your revolver, pull alongside the other vehicle, and order the driver to stop while pointing your revolver at them. This is extremely dangerous. Many officers have been killed or seriously wounded attempting to hasten a stop in this manner.

If time and circumstances permit, it is wise to refrain from attempting to make contact until a follow-up unit arrives on the scene to cover you while making the stop.

When stopping felony criminals, consider the following points. Some felons actually believe they are being stopped for a minor traffic violation, and they will "play it cool" to receive their citation and avoid the arrest for the felony they had committed, hoping to avoid the detection of the officer. Other felons may consider the gun a challenge that must be met with violence, and they may begin firing at you. Let the circumstances indicate your course of action, but first try the red light and siren or the horn and hand signal. If the suspect shoots at you, attempt to back off and avoid a gun battle while you are operating your vehicle. Shooting firearms at a moving vehicle while operating a vehicle yourself is highly inadvisable and not likely to yield very accurate results. The hazards would probably be greater than any advantages.

The final stopped position for maximum safety to both occupants of the suspect vehicle as well as yourself is with the suspect vehicle pulled to the curb as far as possible and your vehicle directly behind and/or slightly to the right. Of course, if the suspect vehicle is against the curb, you have no choice but to park likewise, unless you can drive safely up on the curb or on the shoulder to the right. When there is little or no traffic, and when the stop is in the daytime and/or it is clear to you that the hazard does not seem to be present, you may offset your vehicle to the left and provide for yourself a safety lane along the left side of the vehicle you are stopping if you choose to address the driver from that side of his or her vehicle (see Figure 11–7). When there is heavy traffic, or you think that the driver may present a problem, approach the vehicle from the right, or passenger side. This is better strategy, as a suspect is more likely to expect an officer's approach from the left. With the police unit offset to the left, there is the problem not only of possible collision by partially blocking off one lane of traffic but also of the vehicles suddenly changing lanes to the

Figure 11-7 The police car should be parked about 3 feet farther from the curb to provide a "walking line" for the officer. This is for the solo officer routine vehicle stop. (Courtesy Ohio State Highway Patrol.)

left, which may cause a collision while all the motorists are straining to see what the police are up to this time.

Leave about 15 feet to a full car length between the vehicles, and set your emergency brakes to avoid an out-of-control vehicle. You will not be able to slide across the seat of your vehicle because of computers and consoles and other paraphernalia, so you will have to alight from the driver's side. When you get out, stand there with your door as a shield until a follow-up unit arrives or, if you are going to handle the matter alone, make your move cautiously to the suspect vehicle. If you are dealing with a dangerous fugitive and you are not yet aware of it, you must take care lest the suspect attempts to avoid the police contact and assault.

The space between vehicles is out of bounds for standing. There is a danger of another motorist slamming into your vehicle. Therefore, if you must cross that spot, cross it quickly. At nighttime, leave your headlights on unless you are going to cross in front of them, making yourself a silhouette target. Aim your spotlight into the rear window and point at the rear view mirror inside the car so that the light reflects from the mirror and illuminates the interior.

The Approach

Two Officers. This procedure may be used for a two-officer unit or the lone officer working one unit with a solo follow-up (see Figure 11–8). Hopefully you will have a two-officer team to handle all but the most routine car stops. While the driver officer of the first unit remains standing at the unit just outside using the door as a shield, the second officer approaches the suspect vehicle from the right. The reason for staying with the unit if you are that first officer is to remain close to your car so

Figure 11-8 A solo officer may choose the approach from the driver's side in a routine stop for a traffic citation, or as the second officer in a two-officer stop. Note the space provided for the officer's protection against passing cars by parking the unit outside to the left. (Courtesy Ohio State Highway Patrol.)

that you may get back in and take off in immediate pursuit should the suspect suddenly decide to flee. If you are the officer approaching from the right, take a position at the right rear of the suspect vehicle and look inside to ascertain if there is any hazard. Tap a part of the vehicle (be careful not to damage a thousand-dollar paint job), or make some sort of a noise to let the occupants of the vehicle know of your presence. Once the officer on the right sees that there appears to be no immediate danger, the first officer may approach the vehicle and issue the citation or handle the field interview.

One Officer. Alight from your vehicle and pause to determine that the driver has completely stopped and has turned off the engine. Approach the car from the right side, and at the same time direct the driver to lean across and open the window on the right side. This will keep the driver off guard and permit you to observe any movements inside the vehicle. You will also be able to see more of the interior of the car, including the glove box if it is opened. If the driver attempts to get out of the car while you are issuing a citation, instruct the driver and other occupants, to stay inside the vehicle, thereby avoiding getting struck by passing vehicles (see Figure 11–9).

Whatever method you use for the routine vehicle stop for a citation or warning for some type of violation, or for a field interview, keep your suspects in plain view at all times and watch them continuously. Most of the hundreds or thousands of people you encounter in this manner will be cooperative and absolutely no danger to you, but you will never know until it actually happens if, and when, one of them proves to be a danger.

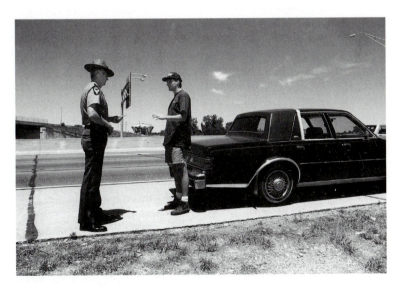

Figure 11-9 Position for interrogation. (Courtesy Ohio State Highway Patrol.)

Approach, Suspects in Vehicle

Assuming that all persons in the vehicle could well be felons, use extreme caution when approaching such persons in any situation in which you anticipate making arrests. Whenever possible, whether you are solo or with a partner, call for a backup unit and wait for its arrival before taking any action beyond the car stop. If you are working alone this is particularly critical. Solo patrol was never intended to be carried into the potential arrest situation.

The driver officer alights from the left side of the unit and stands there, instructing the driver to stop the engine. Stay there until you are sure the other vehicle is not going to suddenly take off. The passenger officer—or follow-up officer, if the first unit on the scene is a solo unit—stands behind the passenger door of the same police unit. If follow-up units are on the way, take as much time as possible to give the other units time to arrive. Sometimes this is not possible because the occupants of the car don't have a copy of the script and will not know what you intend for them to do without your telling them.

If you have a public address system in the unit, use the outside speaker and communicate with the occupants of the suspect vehicle so that they may hear you more clearly. If you have no PA, speak very loudly and clearly so that there will be a greater chance that everyone will hear what you have to say. Only one officer gives the commands. Usually, this will be the driver officer of the first unit on the scene. Although the script may vary, you must immediately notify the occupants of the suspect vehicle that you are in charge and that they are to do exactly what you tell them to do. Your command may be as follows:

> Police officers. All of you, remain in the car. Driver, turn off the ignition. Move very slowly and you will not get hurt. All occupants, let me see all of your hands. Driver, take the ignition key and drop it outside the window so that I can see it. You, in the front seat, put both of your hands up against the windshield with your palms up against the glass. You, in the back seat, move very slowly and put your hands on the back of the seat in front of you with your palms up. Remain in that position until I tell you to move.

Your objective is to keep all occupants of the vehicle under control. You want the vehicle stopped and the keys outside so that someone cannot suddenly drive it away, and you want to see the hands of all the occupants of the vehicle. You don't want them to be fumbling around under the seats or elsewhere in the vehicle and coming up with weapons they might have concealed. If these particular subjects have been through the routine before, they might be totally cooperative, or they might also have weapons conveniently stashed for defense in just this type of an event. Be careful! With occupants under your control in this type of situation, you should have your handguns and/or shotguns in your hands pointed at the suspects, but not in a cocked position.

At this point, wait for your follow-up unit(s) if they have not already arrived. Once you are sufficiently covered, you will want to get the suspects out of the vehicle and immobilized so that you may search them and their vehicle with the least amount of danger to yourself, the other officers, and the suspects. Your next objective is to take them out of the car one at a time, and according to your instructions.

Removing the Occupants from the Vehicle

Both officers in the leading unit should maintain their position of advantage behind the door for maximum safety. While one officer is giving the commands to the vehicle's occupants, the other officer is covering the suspects with the shotgun or handgun in a two-handed position.

Since most modern vehicles have consoles and gear shift controls and possibly bucket seats, instead of the older bench seats that one could slide across from one side to the other with little or no difficulty, you will have to instruct the driver of the vehicle to get out from the driver's side. You will usually get the driver out first so that the vehicle will remain motionless. Once out of the vehicle on the traffic side of the vehicle, you will then instruct the driver to come around the car to the curb side where you will eventually have all of your suspects in a row.

The object is to get the occupants out of the vehicle, all except the driver, from the right-hand side away from traffic. Tell each one—passenger on the right front, driver, passenger on the right rear, and others—to get out of the vehicle one at a time, and continue until they are all out. Direct each one to step outside the vehicle, then lock their hands above and behind the head, kick the door closed, and then to walk backward to a position where the passenger officer will instruct each suspect to stop, kneel in a cross-legged position, or lie prone. The passenger officer will handcuff each suspect and search him or her. This routine is continued until all occupants are out of the vehicle.

Now that all suspects are still handcuffed on their knees or are lying prone on the ground, the passenger officer should use one of the handcuffed suspects as a shield and advance to the vehicle to see that all occupants have left the vehicle. As a precaution to avoid having to resort to deadly force, shout to the vehicle and any possible occupant that you are coming up to the car and that you have one of their compatriots that they will be shooting if they are foolish enough to try. Using that person as a shield, check the trunk; then advance to look inside the vehicle. You should be satisfied that no one remains in the vehicle and that you have all the suspects in custody. As you bring them back from their vehicle, bring them all the way behind the first police unit, using the assistance of your backup officers (if any). At this location, you will then be able to complete the activity most appropriately for the circumstances.

Car Stops—Legal Considerations

A temporary detention or vehicle stop is an act of authority by a police officer that is something less than an arrest but more substantial than a simple contact or consensual encounter. The detention occurs the moment you turn on your red light or otherwise stop a vehicle to investigate a possible crime or to issue a traffic citation. Once you start writing the citation, it is an arrest until the subject signs the promise to appear and is on his or her way. As you know, if the subject refuses to sign the promise to appear, the officer is empowered to book the person for the traffic violation. Signing the citation is a form of posting bail (own recognizance) with a promise to appear in court at a later date to answer the charges.

To make your car stop, you must have a reasonable suspicion that (1) something relating to crime has just happened, is happening, or is about to happen; and (2) the vehicle or person in the vehicle you are about to detain is connected with that activity.

When deciding whether to order the detainee to get out of the vehicle, consider the circumstances. If it is strictly for a traffic citation, there is no need to. Otherwise, if you are going to investigate a possible DUI or other crime, you will get the person(s) out of the vehicle.

A thorough search is not warranted for the person or the vehicle. You can enter the vehicle to search for registration or to retrieve a driver's license. It is also reasonable to conduct a frisk, or patdown, of a person for a weapon, or the car for a crime-related situation, as described in Chapter 10.

Federal rules allow a full body search, including any container, incident to any kind of custodial arrest, from murder to outstanding traffic warrants (*Rn,* 1973, 414 U.S. 218). Your jurisdiction may be more stringent. A car passenger compartment may be searched incident to an arrest, but not the trunk. However, you may have sufficient reasonable cause to search the entire car for specific evidence if you can show that you believe what you are looking for is inside those portions of the car to be searched.

A motor home is a vehicle when it is being operated on the highways or is capable of such use and is found stationary in a place that is not regularly used for residential purposes. If the motor home is hooked up in a campground or other residential park, particularly if the plumbing is connected, the vehicle is treated as a private home and a warrant is needed.

Stopping and Citing the Violator

Whenever you observe a traffic violation, as with any other violation of the laws you are sworn to enforce, you must make contact with the violator if your assignment and the circumstances permit it. For example, if you have been assigned an urgent call to respond to a robbery in progress, you will not stop and cite a person who is speeding five miles over the speed limit. Another example would be that you witness a violation, but traffic is so heavy that you will not be able to negotiate your way through the traffic to safely get to the violator; you would let that one go or radio ahead to another officer to look out for that vehicle to see if there are additional violations. As a rookie patrol officer, I would point out traffic violations to my senior officer, and his reply was: "Let the motor officers get them, that's not our job to enforce traffic laws." How wrong he was. A few years later I had the pleasure of being that man's sergeant, and he was charged with the new task of enforcing traffic laws (in addition to visiting the canning companies every night and mooching for free vegetables so that he would not have to buy them at the produce market). Traffic enforcement is a part of the patrol function of the police department; don't be mistaken about that. It may not be your primary responsibility, but many traffic laws are criminal violations and must be enforced the same as thefts, burglaries, and robberies. When you let a violator go without stopping him or her, you are sending a message to the violator as well as all others who see your inaction that it is okay to disregard traffic laws.

Stop the violator as soon as possible, but choose the right spot for making the stop to avoid causing accidents or unnecessary congestion. There are several considerations in the decision when and where to stop. In heavy traffic, such as during a rush hour, extra lanes are opened up to expedite movement. If you decide to stop a violator in one of those lanes, all traffic behind you must stop and wait until you are finished writing your citation, or they can find a break in the next lane and go around you. Don't you get angry when a bus stops to take on or drop off passengers and brings your lane to a standstill?

If you direct the violator to turn onto a side street to stop and receive a citation, you are helping the other drivers, but doing no favor to the violator, who will then have to figure out a way to make a U-turn (which is another violation) and get back to a homeward-bound route. Follow the violator too far and you will be criticized for following such a distance to have him or her "rack up" more violations for you to cite; stop too soon and you may cause panic stops. Choose your place and make your stop, and try your best to get the best stop, which should not be at a blind curve, hills, or where large groups of people are likely to congregate.

When making your stop, signal the cars behind you of your intentions to stop, and motion for them to slow down and/or go around. Check with the traffic to assure yourself that those cars are following your lead. Use your rear warning lights and forward red lights (unless your department prefers blue), and usually it will take only a tap or two on the horn to get the attention of the violator, who you can then motion with your hand to pull over and stop. The siren may startle not only the violator but also many other motorists, but by all means use the siren if you must clear the way during your chase and stop. Position your vehicle so that the violator can see that it is a police car, and not a possible mugger or drive-by shooter. If you are using an unmarked vehicle in heavy traffic, you may be better advised not to attempt a stop. Convincing everyone that you are operating a police vehicle may cause more trouble than it will solve. When you are stopping a violator, you are actually operating both vehicles throughout the stop. Plan ahead for a place for both vehicles to have room to stop, and when you do stop, try to get both vehicles out of the traffic lanes. Once you are stopped and out of the traffic lanes, turn off your emergency lights, resorting instead to your blinking hazard lights to alert other motorists of your vehicle which may be out farther from the curb than normal, but does not draw their attention to a police car stop which leads to the spectator sport of watching someone get a traffic ticket.

Before contacting the violator, when you have no idea of the sex, race, or age of the violator inside that steel shell, make your initial decision whether to cite or not. This will reduce the claims that you issued citations because you are a sexist, a racist, or hate kids. Exceptions to this standard are obviously when you encounter a person under the influence of drugs or alcohol who you thought was only sleepy and your stop was to suggest that the driver pull over to the side and sleep for a while. A speeder may turn out to be a husband taking a wife giving birth to a hospital, or a doctor rushing to perform emergency surgery. The point here is that the decision whether to cite or not should be based on the violation, not the attitude of the violator when stopped. How many times have you heard officers joke about citing a person because of failure to pass the "attitude test"?

Your attitude on the approach to the violator should be businesslike, courteous, and decisive. Maintain self-control over any personal feelings or animosities that you might have, such as "road rage," also known as "high speed pursuit syndrome," which sometimes "kicks in" when the adrenaline rush accompanies your "must win at all costs" competitive mode.

Before you approach the violator, stop and regain control of your emotions and "regroup" emotionally. Take your time. If you continue to function in this intense emotional condition, a little thing someone says or does may provoke you to react violently and you are certain to regret it the rest of your life.

Once you approach the violator's vehicle, consider the possibility that as long as the driver is behind the wheel with the engine running there is a possibility of flight to avoid being cited or questioned. It is possible that the speeding and/or erratic driving behavior may be because the driver is fleeing the scene of a crime, such as a robbery or hit and run, or may be wanted in another state for some offense. Approach with extreme caution.

As you walk up to the violator's vehicle, continue to keep your emotions under control and then go about the business of issuing the warning, citation, or some instruction about hazards in the roadway ahead. Never turn your back on the violator or any passengers in the vehicle at any time during your encounter for obvious safety reasons.

Prior to issuing the citation, be sure that you have an ample supply of citation forms or that your citation computer is functional. (The officer fills in blanks and makes check marks in the appropriate places on this hand-held computer, which automatically prints out the citation, storing the information so it can be downloaded into a master computer at the end of your shift. The citation computer is appearing slowly because of its expense, but it will be a welcome replacement for the old citation books, with or without carbon.) Have your vehicle code violation list and the book handy.

When you ask for the driver's license, do not accept anything except the license itself. (See Figure 11–10.) If the violator attempts to hand you a wallet or container

Figure 11-10   Ask for the license only, not the wallet containing the license. (Courtesy Ohio State Highway Patrol.)

including the license, do not extend your hand to accept it, but instruct the driver to take out the license and hand only that one item to you. Some violators have a tendency to offer money along with the license to help convince you that the citation is not necessary. If a bribe is offered, you may then arrest for that law violation, but it must be a clean charge, one that does not appear that you trapped the violator into offering.

Special Vehicle Violations

Police, fire, ambulance, and certain other emergency vehicles are exempt from the rules of the road, such as speeding and violations of signs and signals while they are operating their emergency lights and sirens, and actually performing an emergency function as long as their drivers use "due caution for the safety of others" while operating those vehicles. There are other vehicles that do not have the emergency equipment nor the waiver from the rules while operating on the road, such as tow trucks, buses, U.S. mail vehicles, and armored cars. However, when you observe the operators of one of those vehicles violate a traffic law and your first inclination is to stop and cite, consider this: It is against the law for you to interfere with the U.S. mails, and the only way you can cite the driver of such a vehicle is to make a note of date, time, location, violation, vehicle identification number, and description of the driver and go to the post office and get the name of the driver. Then you must file a complaint with the prosecutor and get a warrant for the arrest of the violator when he or she is not operating a U.S. mail vehicle.

The tow truck driver may be rushing to an accident scene to clear vehicles off a roadway so that traffic can be moving again. Speeding there, although against the law, might mean that more accidents may be prevented by having the roadway cleared. The tow truck driver often makes unusual turns and drives on the wrong side of the roadway to get into position. Consider giving this driver slack when you do not have a deliberate and flagrant violation. The bus driver has a schedule, and many passengers depend on that schedule to make transfers to other buses and to get to appointments on time. The armored car driver is usually carrying large amounts of money or other valuables and will not stop for any other vehicle under any conditions, except to obey the rules of the road. When pursued, the vehicle may violate traffic signals and signs to avoid being robbed. It has happened that robbers disguise themselves as police officers and use vehicles that resemble police cars. Don't expect an armored car to stop for you. With these three violators, when you have a bona fide violation that you wish to prosecute, get the vehicle identification and license number, description of the driver, and all other relevant information concerning the violation, and go by way of the complaint and warrant route for best results. This is not to suggest that these drivers should be given free reign to violate traffic laws; my suggestion is that you just use more discretion and restraint when dealing with these violators.

DRIVING UNDER THE INFLUENCE, THE DUI

For many years, the statisticians have said that approximately one half of all fatal traffic collisions involve alcohol and/or drugs, and more than half of the drivers killed have a blood alcohol level of 0.08 or higher, which is considered presumptive evidence in most states that a person is under the influence of alcohol to the extent that they cannot safely operate a motor vehicle. Although the individual may not be in a state of what one might consider intoxication, that percentage is sufficient to sustain a conviction for DUI.

Although the percentage point of 0.08 blood alcohol is a presumptive indication of guilt of DUI, other evidence is also helpful in sustaining a conviction. Testimony about the manner in which the person was maneuvering the vehicle in traffic helps the court and the jury understand what it is that called the officer's attention to the violation in the first place. Your testimony that the vehicle was drifting over the center line on the street, that the stops and starts at signal lights indicated lack of adequate responses to those stimuli, and recounting any traffic violations that occurred during your observations before you stopped the violator help nail the conviction in place. There are some people whose driving is seriously impaired with much less than 0.08% blood alcohol content.

Detection of the DUI may occur in several different ways. They include (1) direct observation by the officer of the person while operating a motor vehicle; (2) a call from a concerned witness such as another driver or a bartender who advised a person not to drive, even a friend or family member; (3) observation of a driver at the scene of a collision; or (4) while stopping or after stopping a driver for some other type of violation. However the driver comes to your attention, be sure to include all observations and information on your report because you will be asked to justify your cause for the arrest. (See Figure 11–11.)

While observing drivers in your district, keep these indicators in mind. They might alert you to the DUI:

Figure 11-11 Many agencies set up roadblocks to look for the dangerous DUI. (Courtesy Ohio State Highway Patrol)

1. Slow reactions to traffic signals when stopping or starting, sometimes suddenly "waking up" and making a quick move to compensate, such as slamming on the brakes at the last minute
2. Overcompensating or exaggerating a turn or lane change
3. Inability to maintain a consistent, or appropriate, speed
4. Apparent confusion in coping with traffic, the lights of oncoming cars, or passing cars
5. Indications of faulty judgment, or dumb moves in traffic
6. Weaving, drifting, or changing lanes without apparent reason
7. A fixed stare straight ahead with apparent disregard for peripheral sighting, or turning to look before turning or changing lanes
8. Jerking driving movements from side to side or slowing and speeding up
9. Cutting in or giving too much clearance after passing another vehicle
10. Overshooting or disregarding traffic signs or signals
11. Driving at night without lights, or delay in turning them on after starting from a parked position
12. Failure to dim lights or to turn them on after opposing drivers have signaled the problem
13. Unnecessary use of turn indicators
14. Straddling lane-divider lines or hugging the curb
15. Windshield wipers working when they are not needed
16. Driving with head sticking out the window
17. Unusual situation, such as open windows when it is cold or raining outside.
18. Subtle movements after you stop the suspect violator, such as falling down when getting out of the car, or fumbling while looking for the driver's license in the wallet, or losing balance while turning around

Once you identify the problem, you should not allow the person to move the vehicle, not even to park it. If such suspects cause physical injury or property damage because they are following your directions, you may be found liable.

Where to Locate the Drinking Driver

"Almost everywhere" may sound like an incorrect answer, but is it? A U.S. Bureau of Justice Statistics publication[1] reported that overall consumption of 95 percent of alcoholic beverages in the United States is by approximately one third of the population (5 percent of those consume about half of all the alcoholic beverages consumed). That publication estimated that the average person over 21 drinks about 34 gallons of beer each year, 3 gallons of wine, 2 gallons of hard liquor, 27 gallons of coffee, 26 gallons of milk, and 42 gallons of soft drinks.

The most likely place you will find the drinking driver will be at the scene of a collision. Study your traffic division's maps and records pinpointing the locations of the accidents and their causes, and those are the places where you should look first. Your department may set up roadblocks, which the courts have ruled legal, near the bars and nightclubs at "happy hour" and bar closing times, and during holiday seasons on the streets where people might be going home from company parties. Resorts and recreational areas are usually full of partygoers who have consumed too much alcohol.

Stopping the Suspected DUI

Use the car stop techniques covered earlier in this chapter, but with more caution because you are dealing with a person whose behavior may be unusually bizarre and totally without apparent reason, such as suddenly stopping in the middle of the street or running into your car when you pull alongside. Watch for the behavior of the suspected driver and the passengers during the stop, including some of the following behaviors:

1. Sudden stopping or slow response to your signals to stop, indicating slow reaction time
2. Attempt to evade by turning suddenly or by speeding up
3. Unusual behaviors that were described in the preceding list
4. Driver switching places with passenger, or some other movement within the vehicle as though to hide alcohol or drugs
5. Driving at excess speed without realizing that the vehicle was moving so fast when asked
6. Inconsistent speeds, such as slowing and speeding up with no other traffic to cause such behavior
7. Lingering at signs or signals after stopping, and the driver may simply stare at the changing lights
8. Taking too long to go back into original lane after passing another vehicle
9. Swerving as if the driver noticed an obstacle at the last moment
10. Exaggerating a turn or other driving movement
11. Drifting over the center line or straddling lanes
12. Unusual swerving and driving on the wrong side of street
13. Appears to be "aiming" the vehicle rather than steering it, grasping steering wheel with eyes fixed in a stare
14. Driving unusually slow for the flow of traffic
15. Driving without lights or high beams when approaching other vehicles
16. Very slow reaction when responding to your signal to pull over and stop

Once you stop the suspected DUI, you are going to use all your senses to see if you can detect the reasons for the suspected driver's behavior. Ask questions to determine if there is an injury or illness involved, or some problem other than alcohol or drugs. You will be able to smell what might be alcohol, and you will see the person's bloodshot eyes and hear the slurred speech. By this time you have probably made a determination that the motor vehicle operation has been impaired by something the subject has ingested. Later you are going to give the subject the choice of a blood-alcohol test via blood, breath, or urine, but now you will perform the field sobriety test. (See Figure 11–12.) It is useful as a guide to keep in mind information regarding the ascending effect of alcohol while performing the test and determining level of alcoholic influence.

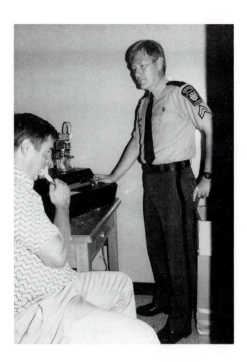

Figure 11-12 The suspected DUI driver most often chooses the breath test. (Courtesy Pennsylvania State Police.)

The following information provides guidelines only; precise, scientifically accurate information is readily available elsewhere. Here, one beer is one 12-ounce bottle of 3½ percent alcohol content beer, a glass of wine is one 3-ounce glass (most bars will serve a 10- to 12-ounce glass which equals four), and one cocktail is 1 ounce of 0.86-proof "hard liquor" (many bars pour "heavy"—about 1½ to 2 ounces of alcohol per mixed drink and sometimes as much as 4 ounces at "happy hour"). The list applies to a person who weighs about 150 pounds, and the amount of alcohol is that remaining in the body. This is dependent upon physical condition, how much and when the person last had something to eat, and how often he or she is taking each of these drinks, plus other variables.

- *One drink: 0.02 BA.* Loss of restraint and awareness, overconfident, careless, underestimates road hazards.
- *Two drinks: 0.04 BA.* Loss of concentration, has tendency to drift into daydreams, inattentive to traffic around him, unpredictable and impulsive.
- *Three drinks: 0.06 BA.* Loss of judgment, unreasonable, argumentative, indecisive, may begin slurring speech. The person is beginning to get sensitive to light and sound. May complain that your flashlight in the face causes pain.
- *Four drinks: 0.08 BA.* Reduction of depth perception and peripheral vision, loss of some muscle coordination.
- *Five drinks: 0.10 BA.* Presumptively under the influence, but the law might be different in your state. Operation of a commercial ship or airplane calls for a much lower level of BA for a violation. By this point the person's driving is impaired to the extent that it is probably obvious to the observer, but may not be.

- *Six to ten drinks.* Driver gets progressively worse with obviously impaired driving and extreme hazard to others.
- *Fifteen drinks: 0.30 BA.* Stupor. If you do not have the subject off the street at this point, and there is a collision, the person is a time bomb.
- *Twenty drinks: 0.40 BA.* Coma.
- *Twenty-five drinks: 0.50 BA.* Death.

Field Sobriety Tests

You will need a level surface for these tests. Be sure that the subject understands you (of course, if she or he is too intoxicated, you may have a problem here), and demonstrate all the physical tests. In your report you will describe how the subject performs each test. (See Figure 11–12.)

1. *Finger to nose.* The subject stands erect with the feet together, eyes closed, and arms outstretched. Alternating right hand, then left hand, and by direction of the officer, the subject swings his arm, bending at the elbow and touching his nose with the tip of the index finger. The purpose of this test is to determine ability to coordinate movements, follow directions, and retain balance.

2. *Modified position of attention.* The subject is instructed to stand at "attention" position, arms at side, heels and toes together, eyes closed, head tilted back slightly. The purpose of this test is to determine ability to retain balance.

3. *Heel-to-toe walking on straight line.* Direct the subject to walk in a straight line, placing one foot before the other in succession (see Figure 11–13). Then turn

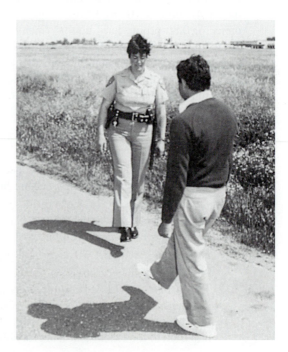

Figure 11-13 Heel-to-toe test. (Courtesy of the California Highway Patrol.)

around and walk back to the starting point. The purpose of this test is for balance, ability to walk a straight line, and ability to retain balance while turning.

4. *Pronunciation.* Have the subject repeat the alphabet. Be sure that the subject has mental capacity and/or language skills, plus the absence of a serious speech impediment. The purpose of the test is to show that a normal, sober person should be able to recite the alphabet.

5. *Dexterity.* Have the subject count on his or her fingers, counting them one at a time, then reversing the order. Test is to determine if the subject can coordinate finger movements with thought process.

6. *Lateral gaze nystagmus test.* For this test an officer completes a short course on DART (Drug, Alcohol Recognition Training). The officer has the subject stand facing him or her (see Figure 11–14). The officer holds up a finger directly in front of and a few inches away from the subject's nose. Directing the subject to follow the officer's finger with his or her eyes without turning the head, the officer moves the finger to the right, then to the left. An officer with the training and expertise can determine that at about 40 degrees the eyeball begins to flutter, which means that about the time the finger has moved to a point even with the subject's ear, the fluttering moves. This indicates that the subject is either under the influence of alcohol or has some serious medical problem with the eyes. Experienced officers claim to be able to determine approximately what the BA is by this test, although the courts will accept it only as indicative of alcoholic influence.

7. *Other tests will be used by various departments, which you will encounter while in the academy.*

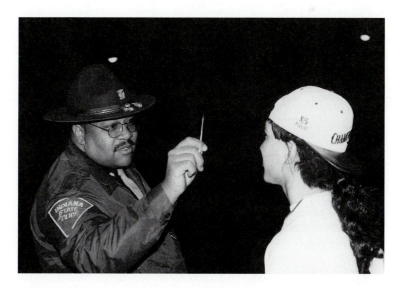

Figure 11-14   Lateral gaze nystagmus test. (Courtesy Indiana State Police.)

☐ **Original Report**

☐ **Supplement to Collision Report**   **DRIVING UNDER INFLUENCE**

1. Incident — Traffic Driving Under The Influence	☐ Day ☐ Night	2. Section	3. DR No.		Dist.	DP

4. Location of Occurrence		5. R.D.	6. Time Occurred	7. Mo/Day/Year	8. Day of Week	TTY	Card

9. Suspect's Name — Last, First, Middle	10. DOB	11. Age	12. Race	13. Sex	14. Hair	15. Eyes	16. HT	17. WT

18. Residence Address	19. Phone	20. Business Address	21. Phone

22. S.D.L.	23. Social Security No.	24. Vehicle	25. Year	26. License	27. State	28. Color	29. Model

30. Location of Vehicle or Impound: ☐ At Request of Driver   No. of Passengers
    ☐ Vehicle Secured at Scene   M ___ F ___

31. WITNESSES Name	Address – City – State – Zip Code	Age	Sex	Phone

32. AREA FIRST OBSERVED   ☐ Traffic Collision

Street _____ Direction _____ Lane _____

Posted Speed Limit _____ ☐ Traffic Condition ☐ None ☐ Light ☐ Medium ☐ Heavy

WHAT ATTRACTED YOUR ATTENTION TO SUSPECT:

☐ Speed _____ ☐ Weaving ☐ Lane Straddling ☐ Following Too Close ☐ Other _____

HOW WAS DRIVER IDENTIFIED?   ☐ CDL   ☐ CA I.D.   ☐ Other

33. TRAFFIC VIOLATION OBSERVED: ☐ None

_____ CVC _____ Location _____

_____ CVC _____ Location _____

DISTANCE TRAVELED FROM POINT FIRST OBSERVED _____

LOCATION SUSPECT STOPPED _____

SUSPECT'S DRIVING ACTIONS DURING STOP:

☐ Sudden Stop   ☐ Parked Illegally   ☐ Attempted to Evade   ☐ Struck Curb   ☐ Other _____

34. SUSPECT'S PHYSICAL ACTIONS EXITING VEHICLE:

☐ Slow   ☐ Staggering   ☐ Unable to Stop   ☐ Fell   ☐ Other _____

35. SUSPECT'S VISUAL APPEARANCE (Please Check Off Boxes)

Breath	Eyes	Speech	Coordination	Appearance	Behavior	Clothing	Following Instructions
☐ Alcohol	☐ Bloodshot	☐ Slurred	☐ Unsteady Gait	☐ Unkempt	☐ Anger	☐ Disheveled	☐ Good Retention
☐ Marijuana	☐ Red	☐ Loud	☐ Staggered	☐ Vomitus	☐ Crying	☐ Stained/Dirty	☐ Fair Retention & Response
☐ Ether/PCP	☐ Watery	☐ Soft/Quiet	☐ Used Support	☐ Hair Mussed	☐ Laughing	☐ Wet	☐ Poor Retention & Response
☐ Strong	☐ Droopy	☐ Mumbled	☐ Fell	☐ Dry Mouth	☐ Belligerent	☐ Neat	
☐ Moderate	☐ Pupils Dilated	☐ Spitting	☐ Fumbled ID	☐ Normal	☐ Aggressive	☐ Urinated	☐ Nuisance
☐ Weak	☐ Pupils Const.	☐ Rapid	☐ Lax Face/Jaw	☐ Other ___	☐ Arrogant	☐ Type of Shoes	☐ Interrupting
☐ None	☐ Clear	☐ Sure	☐ Other ___		☐ Remorseful		☐ Evasive/Question
☐ Other ___	☐ Nystagmus Present?	☐ Correct			☐ Indifferent		☐ Attempt Tests Before/During Instructions
	Present?	☐ Talkative			☐ Fluctuating	☐ Other ___	
	☐ Other ___	☐ Other ___			☐ Cooperative		
					☐ Other ___		

36. SUBJECT'S SPONTANEOUS STATEMENTS and RESPONSES TO INITIAL INVESTIGATIVE QUESTIONS:

_____

_____

_____

_____

PCR #	Helicopter Used ☐ Yes ☐ No	37. Connecting DR Nos.	38. Det Evid Tech ☐ Patrol CSI ☐	39. Detective Utilitized

40. Approved By	41. Date and Time	42. Reporting Officer's Signature	43. Further Action: ☐ Yes ☐ No Copy To:

44. Continuation Report Attached ☐

APD-444 Rev. 10/95

Figure 11-15   DUI report (Courtesy Anaheim Police Department.)

---

45. INTERVIEW (MIRANDA WARNING NOT REQUIRED IF NON-CUSTODIAL AND PRIOR TO ARREST)

1. What is your name? _____

2. Are you sick: (If yes, what is your illness?) _____
   ☐ Diabetic   ☐ Epileptic

3. Are you taking any pills, medication, or drugs?_____

   (If yes, what type and for what reason?) _____

4. Do you have any injuries? (If yes, what is the nature of the injury?)

   _____

5. Do you have any physical disabilities?_____

   (If yes, what are they?) _____

6. What year, make and model vehicle are you driving?

   _____

7. What have you been drinking? _____

8. Where have you been drinking? (What city?) _____

9. What time did you start drinking? _____

10. What time did you stop drinking? _____

11. How much did you drink during that time? _____

12. How much did you drink within
    the hour before you were stopped?_____

13. What time is it now? (Actual time_____) _____

14. Where are you now? (Actual location_____)_____

    _____

15. Have you ever been issued a California Driver's License? _____

16. Is your privilege to drive a motor vehicle suspended or revoked? _____

17. If yes, why was your driving privilege suspended or revoked? _____

18. Do you feel any effects from the alcohol/drugs? _____

    _____

19. Anything mechanically wrong with your vehicle?   ☐ Yes   ☐ No

    Describe _____

20. How long were you driving the vehicle before being stopped?_____

    _____

21. Where did you start driving from?_____

22. Time started driving? _____

---

46. COORDINATION TEST:
#1 Feet together, arms out-stretched, palms up, eyes closed tight, head tilted back:
☐ satisfactory   ☐ unsatisfactory   ☐ unable to perform   ☐ refused   ☐ too drunk to perform
RESULTS: ☐ weaved   ☐ fell   ☐ lost balance   ☐ wouldn't keep eyes closed   ☐ Other _____

_____

---

47. #2 Standing on either foot (right, then left), 6"-12" above ground and out in front, arms at side:
☐ satisfactory   ☐ unsatisfactory   ☐ unable to perform   ☐ refused   ☐ too drunk to perform
RESULTS: Right/leg, number of times foot down _____   ☐ fell   ☐ lost balance   ☐ put arms out to balance
        ☐ Other _____
        Left/leg, number of times foot down_____   ☐ fell   ☐ lost balance   ☐ put arms out to balance
        ☐ Other_____

---

48. Walking straight line, heel to toe: ☐ satisfactory   ☐ unsatisfactory   ☐ unable to perform   ☐ refused   ☐ too drunk to perform
RESULTS: ☐ couldn't stay on line   ☐ feet not heel to toe   ☐ used arms to balance   ☐ fell   ☐ lost balance   ☐ left
☐ Other _____   ☐ right
☐ Alphabet Test   ☐ Digital Count Test   ☐ Finger to Nose Test   ☐ Other _____

---

49. TRANSPORTED TO: ☐ Anaheim City Jail   ☐ O.C. Jail   ☐ Hospital_____   ☐ Other _____
Transported By _____   Badge No._____

---

50. ADVISEMENT OF CVC 13353   ☐ Yes   ☐ No   By Officer _____   Badge No._____
Chemical Test: ☐ Blood   ☐ Breath   ☐ Urine   ☐ Refused   Filed on for CVC 13353   ☐ Yes   ☐ No
Chemical Test Conducted By _____   Date _____   Time _____
Chemical Test Witnessed By _____   Vial # _____   Vial # _____

---

51. PRIOR CONVICTIONS: _____
_____
_____
_____

---

52. NARRATIVE: (Use a Page 3 Continuation Report for Narrative)

Now that you have performed your field tests and have decided that you have a bona fide DUI, the next step is to take the subject into the station for a BA test, using the subject's choice of blood, breath, or urine. The blood specimen is taken by a licensed physician or technician and analyzed by a laboratory; the urine is taken in the presence of the arresting officer and is sent to the lab; and the breath test is made at headquarters or in the jail and is operated by a trained operator, usually a fellow officer. The results of the breath test are available immediately. These tests are covered in greater detail in a traffic text and course.

The DUI Report

Your department will have standardized forms to use for this arrest (see Figure 11–15), and at points of the interview with the subject, you will be required to admonish him or her about the implied consent to take blood-alcohol tests under these conditions as a condition of retaining an operator's license. You may repeat the field sobriety test to be sure that your test is fair and on level ground with professional witnesses, and your report should recount every observation that you make from the time of your first contact up to—and including—the booking. The thoroughness of your report may lead the subject later to plead guilty, particularly if the blood-alcohol report comes back showing 0.08 or more, which is accepted as proof of "influence." Although it may be more difficult to get a conviction with a BA of less than 0.08, the driving and the field sobriety tests might have been so poorly done that you will still get a conviction.

SUMMARY

In this chapter we have covered those facets of policing that directly involve you as a field officer. One of your primary responsibilities with regard to traffic is to facilitate the safe and efficient movement of traffic in, and through, your district with a maximum amount of safety and a minimum loss of lives and property.

The purpose of traffic investigation is to determine the causes for collisions so that enforcement action can be taken against the violator, and educational programs may be devised by the department's traffic specialists to reduce the number and severity of such collisions and to identify problems in traffic engineering and design for the responsible agencies to correct the problems you have identified.

Enforcement should be selective and your efforts should be devoted to warning and citing those violators who are causing the accidents. Times, locations, and accident-causing violations are prioritized so that your enforcement efforts yield positive results.

EXERCISES AND STUDY QUESTIONS

1. Explain the types of situations when a police vehicle may violate the rules of the road as an emergency vehicle.
2. Write a general order for your department to use regarding escorting vehicles with nonpolice personnel driving.

3. Give one good reason for abandoning a police pursuit.

4. Is it acceptable police practice to abandon a pursuit?

5. For what reason might you decide *not* to pursue a traffic law violator?

6. How could an officer be held liable for pursuing a violator?

7. How many vehicles should use red light and siren when following a violator?

8. What does the author say about ramming a pursued vehicle?

9. Under what circumstances would you transport an injured person in your police vehicle?

10. When you stop a car for a citation, why would you park your vehicle behind and about three feet farther out into the street than the suspect vehicle?

11. Why would you park your vehicle parallel with, or to the right of, the suspect vehicle?

12. Describe what instructions you would use to get four suspects you believe to have been involved in an armed robbery out of their car.

13. When you stop a person for a routine traffic citation, are you justified to search him and his vehicle?

14. What is the BA level at which a person is presumed to be "under the influence"?

15. List and discuss five types of behavior that might alert you to the presence of a DUI.

16. Describe the field sobriety tests that are used in your jurisdiction.

17. Approximately how much alcohol must a person have in his or her system to have a BA of 0.10 according to the list in this chapter?

18. Which of the several field sobriety tests described is conclusive proof that the driver is "under the influence"?

19. Take the field sobriety test yourself and describe how well you did with absolutely no alcohol in your system.

20. In the unincorporated areas of the county where you live, does the local sheriff or a state highway patrol force have primary jurisdiction for traffic enforcement and investigation?

21. If you wish to stop a violator on a busy thoroughfare during rush hour, how would you go about making the stop?

22. Picture yourself in the middle of the intersection directing traffic. The north-south traffic has been moving for a while and you see a break. How do you stop that traffic so that you can let the opposing traffic have its turn? Now, the north-south traffic is completely stopped. You then want to direct an eastbound driver to turn south and the next vehicle to turn north. Next, start all east-west traffic going both directions.

23. How do you describe the *point of no escape*?

24. What is a *maximum engagement*?

25. Describe how you would approach a witness to a traffic collision and what you would ask about his or her involvement in the event.

26. Describe at what point you decide whether to cite or warn a violator.

27. What should you do when the violator hands you the entire wallet when you have asked for only the driver's license?
28. Is a roadblock legal? constitutional?
29. List three places where you would most likely find a DUI.
30. List five behaviors that signal a possible DUI.
31. How would you cite the driver of a U.S. mail truck? an armored car driver?

REFERENCES

California Vehicle Code (annual).

FALES, E. D., JR. "New Facts about Skidding: They May Save Your Life." *Law Enforcement Bulletin,* May 1965, pp. 13–16.

Various training bulletins from Los Angeles Police Department, Santa Ana Police Department, California Highway Patrol, Golden West College, Orange County Sheriff's Department, academy training outlines, and various other sources were used for the compilation of this chapter.

FOOTNOTES

1. *Drunk Driving* U.S. Government Printing Office, (Washington, D.C.: 1992).

C H A P T E R 1 2

ARREST, SEARCH, AND CUSTODY

*I*NTRODUCTION

Among the many critical discretionary decisions you make every day of your career as a police officer, the decision to arrest is one of the most significant for you as well as for the person you arrest. Although laws may read as though they are cut and dried and that you have little choice in deciding whether or not to arrest, you are the only person who can—and should—actually make that ultimate decision. At the moment you announce to the person that you are making the arrest, you are in great peril. At that point, you may meet violent resistance or an attempt to escape.

The decision to take a person into custody for arrest or for questioning involves the deprivation of that person's freedom of movement and affects that person's life from many aspects. You may be in great peril, but you will probably not know it until the arrestee's actions alert you to the danger you are in.

In this chapter we cover some general laws of arrest, some of which perhaps vary from those of the jurisdiction in which you work; then we cover some procedures and guidelines in arrest, searching, transportation, and custody.

LAWS OF ARREST

The laws providing for arrest by peace officers may vary from one state to another, but for the purpose of discussion, we shall use California laws. Where there is a variance with the laws of your state, make the appropriate adjustments. Generally, a peace officer may arrest on authority of a warrant for either a felony or a misdemeanor with the only restrictions on the arrest conditions differing on time of day when the arrest may be made.

For example, all felony warrants provide for the arrest at any time of the day or night. Misdemeanor warrants are for a wide range of lesser offenses, from minor parking and license infractions to more serious assaults and drug offenses. For that reason, many warrants restrict the hours of arrest to daytime only (sunrise to sunset), or between the hours of 6 A.M. and 10 P.M. Historically, a warrant was a warrant and before changes were made in time of day restrictions, it was not unusual for many misdemeanor warrant arrests to be made at 3:00 or 4:00 A.M. Many old-timers will tell you that they would check out a parking warrant on someone they suspected of dealing in drugs or stolen property, and would carry the warrant in their pocket (hence the nickname "hip pocket warrants") until they could spot their suspect at home. With no strong evidence to sustain a search warrant for contraband, the officers would make their arrest for the minor misdemeanor and then make their search of the individual and his or her premises for the stolen or forbidden goods. Once in a while they would come up with the evidence they were looking for, and this practice was continued for many years until the courts began restricting the hours for these arrests and the scope of searches coincidental with arrests.

The amount of force that may be used depends on the amount of resistance that is offered by the person being arrested or other persons who might be attempting to help him or her evade arrest. When in immediate pursuit of the subject to be arrested, the officer is empowered to continue the pursuit until the subject is in custody, and this involves entering private property and breaking into—and back out of—places where the subject has fled and into other geographical jurisdictions. These laws are covered in more detail in the police academy and are directly related to state law and department policies.

Section 836 of the California Penal Code provides for three conditions when a peace officer may arrest without a warrant. They are

1. Whenever he or she has reasonable cause to believe that the person to be arrested has committed a public offense in the officer's presence
2. When a person arrested has committed a felony, although not in the officer's presence
3. Whenever the officer has reasonable cause to believe that the person to be arrested has committed a felony, whether or not a felony has in fact been committed

In the matter of misdemeanor arrests, the first factor in the "reasonable cause" consideration is that you should be reasonably familiar with the laws in the various codes that you enforce. Assuming that you have a better than adequate base of knowledge in that area, the next step is to determine whether or not you can deduce from your observations that an act—or a failure to act—on the part of the person to be arrested is a violation of the law. Is the individual crossing that white line after the signal light has clearly turned to red? Is the man striking the woman with his fist? Is the woman being touched on a very personal part of her body actually offended by that touching, or are they involved in "lovers tag"? Are those very loud and boisterous noises that you hear coming from that wedding party actually disturbing someone who is willing to sign a complaint for disturbing the peace, or are all the neighbors also at the party with no complainants available? In short, are you actually perceiving the act? What is your "presence," as far as the law is concerned? Let's look at some court decisions.

A federal court in 1924 noted that "presence" continues to be a requirement for a police officer to make a warrantless arrest "only if he had reasonable cause to believe it had been committed in his presence."[1] "In presence" means that which is directly perceived by any of the senses.[2] Of the senses by which law violations are perceived, eyesight is most common and the use of binoculars or a telescope is permitted.[3] Eyesight aided by a flashlight is acceptable.[4] Hearing without artificial aids was ruled as being in the officer's presence in *People* v. *Goldberg*.[5] Smell was similarly ruled in a 1922 case.[6]

The sense of touch is considered in shakedown or patdown searches when the officer detects an object through the clothing that feels like an automatic pistol, or a knife. Taste usually accompanies sight and smell, such as the person who might have the expertise to taste a suspected powder to determine if it is cocaine or heroin (although I do not recommend this taste test procedure because it could contain poison), or for the alcoholic nature of a beverage, such as beer or wine. Perception may also be accomplished through a team effort to qualify for the "presence" requirement, such as the 1968 case when one officer observed a burglary and described the fleeing suspects in a radio broadcast. Another officer heard the broadcast and stopped the suspects on the basis of the description.[7]

The second subsection of the arrest laws, which states "when a person arrested has committed a felony, although not in his presence," also presupposes that you are familiar with the felonies in your state and the elements of the corpus delicti necessary to prove for a conviction. This, too, would depend upon your perceptual abilities; your presence would not have been required, but you would be required to explain to the court how you knew the person had committed a felony. Perhaps you were informed by the detectives working burglary or by radio broadcast or by reading a bulletin listing wanted felons.

The third subsection is more complex and is principally what distinguishes a private person arrest from an arrest made by a peace officer. By the very nature of your work, you are trained and are required to be more suspicious of questionable activities. You are charged with protection of life and property in your assigned district. You must be diligent and must constantly exercise an inquiring mind. Based on your observations, your interpretations of those observations, your reasonable cause to believe certain things that you presume to be true as related to other facts, and the requirement that you act as a police officer, whenever the situation calls for it, you may arrest on the basis of this portion of the law. Later, it is affirmed or disaffirmed that the person arrested did in fact (or did not) commit a felony as you suspected. Let's consider two examples.

- While cruising in your district, you are passing a restaurant when you observe a crowd gathering inside. Several of the people appear to be watching some sort of struggle inside a circle of onlookers. As you break through the crowd, you ask several people what is happening and receive no answer. They just point to a man lying on the floor and another man kneeling over him with a butcher knife in his hand. The person with the knife is cutting the other man's throat. Acting on the belief that what you are observing appears to be an attempted murder, you immediately disarm the man with the knife and place him under arrest. You are then informed by several people in the crowd and the man with the knife that what you actually observed was a choking victim with a piece of meat lodged in his throat and a doctor who is performing a tracheotomy on the victim to save his life. After you release the doctor and allow him to continue the emergency surgery, you ask yourself "was I legally correct in what I did, based on the information I had to operate under?" The answer is "yes."

- Under circumstances that lead you to believe that a group of people in a car is cruising an area where there have been numerous burglaries at that particular time of night, you stop the car and conduct a field interview. The occupants of the car choose not to answer any of your questions designed to explain their presence in the area or any of their activities, and you observe several household items in the car, such as stereo speakers and components, a portable television set, and three small radios. You ask the occupants about the items, and their response is that it is none of your business. You check records on the occupants and discover that three of the four have extensive records for burglary. You sincerely believe that you have probable cause for an arrest. You arrest all four of the subjects for suspicion of being in possession of stolen property. You impound their car, book the suspects, put the property you believed to have been stolen in the evidence locker, and prepare your reports. The next day, detectives working burglary check out the property and the suspects and find out that none of the property was stolen and that their only crime was failing to cooperate with you. The detectives release the suspects and return their property to them. Did you commit a false arrest? No.

WHAT CONSTITUTES AN ARREST?

Actually, there are many different types of situations when an officer makes contact with a person which may appear to be an arrest but is not. According to the courts in various situations, the contact may be a "contact," a "consensual encounter," a "detention," or an "arrest."

In the "contact" situation, the person contacted remains totally free to leave or not to cooperate with you. In the encounter, you may not restrain the person or exert any authority over him or her (*Roger,* 1983, 460 U.S. 491). You may continue to ask for the subject's cooperation, but do not demand it. If necessary, tell the person you are not detaining him and that he is free to leave, but you would like to ask a few questions. Once you start giving orders, the contact becomes a "detention."

A detention is something less than an arrest, but it is more than a "consensual encounter." In this situation a reasonable person would believe that he or she is not free to leave, and it is under conditions when an officer believes that the person is in some way involved in a criminal activity (*Terry* v. *Ohio,* 1968, 392 U.S. 1). You should have sufficient facts, coupled with your unique training and experience as a police officer, to be able to articulate to the court a reasonable suspicion that something related to crime has happened, is happening, or is about to happen and you believe the person to be connected with that activity.

Police actions in a detention situation would include:

1. You may question the person about his or her identity, conduct, and reason for being at this particular location at this time. You may ask for some type of documentary proof of identification, such as a driver's license. If he or she states that he or she has ID but is not going to produce it, you may conduct a limited search for it.

2. You may detain the subject while you contact other persons to confirm the information given by the subject, to verify the identification, or to determine if further investigation or an arrest is warranted.

3. You may detain the subject while checking premises at or near the place of contact, or contact residents or businesses nearby to determine if a crime has been committed, or to check out suspicious items that might be stolen merchandise.

4. You may detain a subject for the purpose of bringing a victim or witness to that location for a field "showup."

Avoid using any type of physical restraints such as handcuffs when detaining a person, because it then takes on the characteristics of an arrest. Survival is essential, however, and you may take whatever precautions are necessary to avoid injury to yourself or the subject. Move the subject under detention only when absolutely necessary, such as from a hostile crowd.

ARREST PROCEDURES

Use of Force

"Only that force which is necessary" or "no more than is reasonable" are two phrases describing how much force you may use in effecting an arrest. You may ask: "How much is necessary?" or "What is reasonable force?" Those questions are easier to ask than to answer. Since most of the decisions that you make about use of force in any police situation are dependent upon a unique situation that is unlike any other, and your action is a reaction to whatever the person to be arrested takes, it is impossible to develop a simple formula. Consider the Los Angeles officers charged with using too much force on parolee Mr. Rodney King, a young African-American on whom the officers testified they had to use so much force because they "feared for their lives" and that they believed that he was continuing to attack even though he was down on the ground and appeared to be going nowhere on the videotape that was televised around the world.

Although the criminal codes of your state cover the laws of arrest and define how much force you may use, do not take those words at face value. For example, consider the California Penal Code sections that cover the use of deadly force:

Sec. 834a. Resistance to arrest.   If a person has knowledge, or by the exercise of reasonable care, should have knowledge, that he is being arrested by a peace officer, it is the duty of such person to refrain from using force or any weapon to resist such arrest.

A problem with this section is that the person who resists arrest may plead that he had no idea that the badge the officer was wearing was real, or that he believed he was being pounced upon by a gang of cab drivers, or that he was so full of drugs or narcotics that he was out of his mind and did not know what he was doing.

Sec. 835. Method of making arrest; amount of restraint.   An arrest is made by an actual restraint of the person, or by submission to the custody of an officer. The person arrested may be subjected to such restraint as is reasonable for his arrest and detention.

What about the level of training and experience of the officer; the relative sizes of the officer and the suspect; the appearance of the person to be arrested (threatening, massive, extremely agitated, may be in possession of a weapon), and the individual officer's perception of danger from the subject? What is "reasonable"?

Sec. 835a. Use of force to effect arrest, prevent escape, or overcome resistance.   A peace officer who makes an arrest need not retreat or desist from his efforts by reason of the resistance or threatened resistance of the person being arrested; nor shall such officer be deemed an aggressor or lose his right to self-defense by the use of reasonable force to effect the arrest or to prevent escape or to overcome resistance.

Here we see the word "reasonable" again. What is reasonable depends on the independent judgment of the officer at the moment of decision. A lot depends on the skill of the officer and his or her own confidence in the use of that skill in a given situation. Unless the officer has been in contests with the arrestee before, the officer has no idea of the skill and experience, or intent of the arrestee.

Sec. 196. Justifiable homicide; public officers.   Homicide is justifiable when committed by public officers and those acting by their command in their aid and assistance, either:

1. In obedience to any judgment of a competent Court; or
2. When necessarily committed in overcoming actual resistance to the execution of some legal process.
3. When necessarily committed in retaking felons who have been rescued or have escaped, or when necessarily committed in arresting persons charged with felony, and who are fleeing from justice or resisting such arrest.

The first part applies to carrying out a legal execution, but the next two parts ask the officer to decide what is "necessary."

None of these sections are self-defense situations. That problem is addressed by the justifiable homicide sections that cover all persons, including peace officers, and are based upon life-threatening situations—the person's fears of imminent death or grievous bodily harm to himself or another person. These justifiable homicide situations also depend on whether such action was reasonable under the circumstances.

"Reasonable" is determined by the officer who responds to the call, or by the supervisor in case the defender is a peace officer, by a prosecuting attorney or a grand jury, and eventually by a judge or a jury.

Consider the *Garner* case[8] when the police officer, responding to a prowler call, observed the suspect leave the house which he had broken into earlier. The officer described him as 17 or 18 and 5'5" to 5'7" tall, but he was actually 5'4" and 15 years old. The boy ran across the back yard and, when he did not stop when commanded by the officer's "Police. Halt!" the officer believed that he would escape if he were to get over the fence. In order to stop the boy before he got over the fence, the officer shot him in the back of the head, killing him. In that case, the Supreme Court said that use of deadly force to prevent the escape of all felony suspects, whatever the circumstances, is constitutionally unreasonable. In this case, the suspect posed no real threat to the officer, and by shooting and killing him, the officer violated the civil rights of the suspect. Had the suspect threatened the officer with a gun or in some other way been an imminent threat to the officer's personal life, the law would have been applied correctly. This renders invalid the old common law rule that allowed the use of deadly force in many felony situations without requiring that the officer be in jeopardy of great physical harm or death to himself/herself. According to Tennessee law, the officer was justified in killing the suspect after he ordered the suspect to halt and did not get the appropriate response.

In your own mind, and within the policies of your department, there must be some guidelines for you to follow when it comes to the use of force. As a general guideline, it seems to me that taking a person into custody is absolutely essential for the ends of justice to be met. That said, now let's look at reality. We are dealing with human beings, who are entitled to be treated as humans. Depending on the actions of the person to be arrested, your actions are reactions. When you tell a person that he or she is under arrest, and the person willingly complies with your directions and submits to custody, handcuffing and transporting would normally be no problem. But we know that nothing is normal in police work. If the subject gives token resistance or verbal indications that there is going to be some resistance, then some degree of force is necessary to control the arrestee. If there is forceful resistance or you have the sense that the forcible resistance is imminent, you must use whatever force you believe at that moment to be adequate to continue to maintain control over the arrestee. As the forceful resistance escalates, so will be your degree of force, with the arrestee actually calling the shots. If you anticipate deadly resistance, your use of deadly force is justified.

As you can see, there are no "exacts" in the use of force, because it is difficult—if not impossible—to predict precisely what the arrestee is about to do. When it comes to making an arrest of someone who is not an imminent threat to your life or that of another person, deadly force is never justified. It is better to let the fleeing felon get away than to take that person's life. If the felon is pulling a bloody knife out of the chest of his victim or is stepping away from a dead or dying victim that he or she just shot with the smoking gun in hand, and you believe that his or her escape is going to lead to the death of another person the moment the suspect rounds the corner or gets over the fence and makes an escape, your use of deadly force may be reasonable and necessary. If there is no sense of imminent deadly consequence of the suspect getting away from your custody, better to let the person go and get him or her at a later time. This should be the same as your decision when to abandon any pursuit. It is not a contest, and you will not be judged no longer champion if you let one get away.

Breaking into a Building to Arrest

You may break into a door or window to gain entry into any place where you know or believe that a person you have legal cause to arrest is sheltered. In most situations, you must first identify yourself as a police officer to establish your authority to enter and then demand admittance and state your reason for the demand. In general, you will need an arrest and a search warrant when you are entering a person's private residence. If there is no response, or the people inside refuse to admit you, you may then make the entry. An exception to this rule would be if such announcement and delay in gaining entry would further endanger someone's life, if critical evidence would probably be destroyed during the delay, or if it would otherwise frustrate the arrest. Once inside, and if, for some reason, you are trapped inside, you have the same authority to break out to free yourself.

Resistance to Arrest a Crime

When you are making an arrest, be sure to identify yourself so that there can be no question as to your authority; then make it clear to the person you intend to arrest what you are going to do and for what charge. If he knows that he is being arrested, according to law he must submit to the arrest without offering resistance. If he claims innocence of the crime, or positively knows that he had nothing to do with a criminal matter that would lead to his arrest, he should present his case at a more appropriate time. It is your responsibility to act on valid information and good faith, assuring yourself that the arrests you make are valid.

Warrant Arrests

A warrant is usually directed to any peace officer with jurisdiction in the state. One of the most important aspects of a warrant arrest is to make sure that the warrant is valid. There have been occasions when the arrest had already been made in the warrant, but for some reason, it was not removed from the files. If you are in doubt as to the validity of the warrant, it is usually wiser not to make the arrest.

The warrant must state the specific charge for which the person is to be arrested, such as "Criminal Code Section 123, Loitering." There must be a description of the person to be arrested. Generally, a person's name is considered his identification, but there is room for error when arresting by name only. You must be sure that you are arresting the individual for whom the warrant is intended. There are several principal "identifiers" useful for a warrant, including name, address, driver's license number, date of birth, place of birth, sex, color of hair and eyes, height and weight, race, nationality descent, and visible scars and marks.

The warrant must also bear the signature of the issuing judge or magistrate. If the warrant is for a felony, the arrest may be made at any time. In the case of misdemeanors, however, the warrant must specifically state that it is for nighttime service or that it can be used as a basis for arrest only during daytime.

The warrant requires that the person named be taken to the judge who issued the warrant or to the court of issue. In your own jurisdiction, it may be a standard procedure to take the arrestee directly to jail to go through the "booking" process. He then posts bail and receives a specific time to report to the court. In these cases, the arrestees are not generally taken directly to the judge unless they demand it. Once the subject named on the warrant has been arrested and processed according to its instructions, the officer signs that portion of the document known as the "notification (or certification) of service," and the document is returned to the court.

Arrests without a Warrant

Except when it is obvious that you are arresting the subject for a crime that he is committing at the time of arrest, or are arresting him immediately following a pursuit, it is mandatory that you identify yourself, that you announce your intention to arrest him, and that you state the crime for which you are arresting him. Review the facts that you have and make sure that your justification for the arrest is valid.

Prepare for the arrest by arranging for adequate support if time permits. Use common sense and distinguish between bravery and foolhardiness. A single-handed arrest accomplished by a brave officer looks good in the personnel jacket, but do not risk it at the expense of possibly losing the suspect or causing yourself to sustain an injury or death because of your failure to call for assistance. Charisma, or command presence, is essential. Make it clear to the suspect that you are arresting him or her by your actions, your appearance, and your command voice. Give clear and concise orders. Use only that force that is necessary. Maintain constant visual and physical control of the arrestee. If the situation is serious enough to call for an arrest, it should be standard procedure to consider the possibility that the suspect may try to attack you or attempt to escape. Never turn your back on the suspect; always "keep on your guard."

DIPLOMATIC IMMUNITY

The FBI *Law Enforcement Bulletin* of August 1973[9] presented an updated set of guidelines entitled "Procedures and Policies Relating to Diplomatic and Consular Officials." The guidelines that follow reflect the amended rules enacted at the Vienna Convention on Diplomatic Relations of December 13, 1972. The guidelines were explained by the Office of the Chief of Protocol, U.S. Department of State.

The Chief of Protocol defines "diplomatic immunity" as

the freedom from local jurisdiction accorded to duly accredited diplomatic officers, their families, and servants. Diplomatic officers should not be arrested or detained for any offense, and foreign career consular officers should not be arrested or detained except for the commission of a grave crime. Family members of diplomatic officers, their servants, and employees of a diplomatic mission are entitled to the same immunities under current U.S. law (22 U.S.C. 252), if they are not nationals of or permanently resident in the receiving state.

Associated with this personal diplomatic immunity is the inviolability enjoyed by the premises of the mission of the sending state and the private residence of a diplomatic agent, his property papers, and correspondence.

What this means, essentially, is that diplomatic officers and their families, official staff, and servants who are not citizens of, or permanent residents of, the United States, are totally immune from arrest, detention, or prosecution for any civil or criminal offense. They are identified by credentials issued by the State Department, and although their offices are located in Washington, D.C., or New York City, they may be encountered almost anywhere.

Consular officials are accorded some limited immunities, but their families and other members of their household or other entourage are not covered by the immunity. As with all individuals you encounter in any given situation, they should be treated fairly and courteously. Credentials for consular officials are also issued by the State Department.

A foreign career officer may not be arrested or held pending trial for any criminal charge except a grave crime, defined by the State Department as a felony offense that would endanger the public safety and "pursuant to a decision by the competent judicial authority."[10] The guidelines further point out that this immunity to criminal prosecution involves only "acts performed in the exercise of consular functions and is subject to court determination."[11] From that statement, it would appear that consular officials other than those protected by diplomatic immunity would be subject to the same law enforcement as any other persons in your jurisdiction, although there might be some delicate international issue in balance. If in doubt, contact your local prosecutor or judge for guidance.

A consular office or building and official papers and documents of such a consulate post and in possession of consular officials are protected by diplomatic immunity. Entry of such official premises that are used exclusively for work may be done only with permission of the head of that post or the head of that diplomatic mission or without permission if there is an urgent need to put out a fire or provide some other protective service.[12]

ENTRAPMENT

Sooner or later, the entrapment issue will be raised when you make an arrest, particularly when the arrest involves some sort of undercover or decoy operation. Because you were not standing directly in front of the violator at the time in full uniform, you may be accused of entrapment. The issue was addressed in the *Sorrells* case in 1932, when the Supreme Court stated: "Society is at war with the criminal classes and courts have uniformly held that in waging this warfare, the forces of prevention and detection may use traps, decoys, and deception to obtain evidence of the commission of crime."[13] Although there has been some erosion by rules involving interrogation and lineups, that statement still carries considerable weight. Undercover activities may include placing an informer among criminal ranks to build a case and collect evidence, having officers pose as "hit men" to gather evidence against people who are looking for someone to kill a friend or relative for insurance purposes, having an officer pose as a prostitute or a "john" on the streets to arrest solicitors, or having a team of officers go out on the streets posing as derelicts and drunks so that they may draw the muggers to them as potential victims.

Undercover operations, plants, informants, and decoys are all used at one time or another in this "war with the criminal classes." And it's legal. The test as to whether entrapment occurred is "with whom did the idea to commit crime originate?" The narcotics dealer, or the mugger, or the prostitute are all plying their trades on the streets, and the officers working such clandestine assignments are not putting the ideas to commit crime in the offenders' minds. They are merely increasing the odds for protecting other people and in catching the offenders at their occupations. Whenever you work such an assignment, the key to prosecution free of entrapment is to make yourself available for the criminal to operate in your presence and not to induce him or her in any way that could be interpreted to mean that the idea to commit crime was yours and not the offender's.

In a 1979 California case, the California Supreme Court in *Barraza* gave its definition of entrapment:[14]

> Entrapment—which is a defense, not a crime—means inducing a person to commit a crime which was not contemplated by him, for the purpose of prosecuting him.

> The current judicial test for entrapment is whether your conduct was likely to induce a mythical, innocent, normally law-abiding person to commit the offense. If it was, then you have gone too far, and the defense is available.

> On the other hand, if you just provided the opportunity for the crime to be committed by someone who was already of a mind to commit it on his own, then there has been no entrapment.

INVESTIGATIVE DETENTION

There are many occasions when you will temporarily detain a person in the field or possibly transport the person to the station for a short period of time to investigate the individual and circumstances that seem to warrant further inquiry. The field interview situation or the field identification of all people who happen to be in the vicinity of a crime are just two examples of such temporary detention. In *United States* v. *West*[15] and *United States* v. *Allen*,[16] the courts stated, "The local policeman . . . is also in a very real sense a guardian of the public peace, and he has a duty in the course of his work to be alert for suspicious circumstances and, provided that he acts within constitutional limits, to investigate whenever such circumstances indicate to him that he should do so."

In 1968 the U.S. Supreme Court ruled that

> where a police officer observes unusual conduct which leads him reasonably to conclude in light of his experiences that criminal activity may be afoot and that the persons with whom he is dealing may be armed and presently dangerous, where in the course of investigating this behavior he identifies himself as a policeman and makes reasonable inquiries, and where nothing in the initial stages of the encounter serves to dispel his reasonable fear for his own or others' safety, he is entitled for the protection of himself and others in the area to conduct a carefully limited search of the outer clothing of such persons in an attempt to discover weapons which might be used to assault him. (*Terry* v. *Ohio,* 392 U.S.1)

A temporary detention for additional investigation beyond the frisk may be necessary, according to the courts. The Fourth Amendment is not so restrictive that a police officer should allow a crime to occur or a criminal to escape apprehension just because the officer lacks the precise amount of information necessary to show probable cause for an arrest. For example, an officer may have probable cause to search a person but at that moment not have enough cause for an arrest. Then, during the search, the officer finds a weapon or contraband and now has the probable cause for an arrest. With the continued validity of court decisions reinforcing age-old police procedures of stopping persons for investigation and searching for weapons and the constitutionality of temporary detention upon reasonable cause, officers may perform their jobs when they can show probable cause for their actions at each step along the way.

SEARCHING TECHNIQUES

Officers who sustain injuries while searching persons are apt to be those with several years of experience. They have probably made hundreds, or thousands, of arrests without incident and have grown confident that they are doing everything right. Actually there is a possibility that those officers are developing bad habits without realizing it. One way to counteract this development of bad habits is to approach each arrest and each search as an entirely new experience, and strictly according to an established procedure.

There are two essential aspects to search and seizure: law and procedure. The following section covers the procedure. It is extremely important that an armed and potentially dangerous suspect be disarmed as quickly and efficiently as possible.

Types and Methods of Search

The patrol officer conducts three basic types of searches: the frisk, the field search, and the strip search. Each has its own distinct procedure.

Frisk, or "Patdown."   The frisk is the cursory search. It generally accompanies a field interview and is not considered an exploratory search. The only objects for which you can search during the frisk are weapons. However, if the frisk reveals other contraband and it can be truly shown that the discovery was incidental to the frisk, rather than the frisk being used as an excuse to look for some objects, the discovery of the contraband is sufficient cause to conduct the more thorough search. Start at the head and work the hands along the outside of the clothing wherever weapons may be found. Do not place your hands inside the clothing unless the outside patting process reveals something that feels like a weapon, in which case you may search inside to verify your suspicions. Then have the subject face you while you examine the mouth, nose and ears, and the female's bra area.

Field Search.   This search may be conducted on reasonable cause to search without an arrest or prior to an arrest, and it should be routine whenever you perform an arrest. If you are alone and you have more than one suspect, the wiser course of action would be to have them all lie prone side by side and apart from each other with their hands stretched out above the head with the palms flat on the surface until backup officers arrive. Then conduct your search.

1. Keep the person off balance. This can be accomplished by three basic methods: the standing search position, kneeling search position, and prone search position.

For the standing position, have the subject stand with fingers locked together. Have the subject lean back while you maintain complete control. (See Figure 12–1.)

For the kneeling search position, have the subject kneel on both knees, and cross his legs behind him. As you search him from behind, it is possible to exert a slight pressure on the top of the crossed legs to maintain control. Have the subject hold his hands above his head and lock his fingers behind his head.

For the prone search position, have the subject lie face down on the ground or floor surface with arms and legs outstretched. This position of disadvantage makes it very difficult for the subject to assume a combative position.

2. Handcuff each subject prior to conducting the search when possible.

3. Maintain your own balance on your toes, and always keep your eyes on the subject. While your backup officer assumes a cover position, the best place for the searching officer's weapon is securely fastened in a holster. It is not unusual for a suspect to attempt to attack an officer during the initial phases of an arrest and search.

4. Search with one hand. Use the other hand for defense and to place on the small of the suspect's back during the search. You can hold him off-balance with this hand.

5. Start at the head, running your hands through the hair, and watching for straight-edged razor blades that might have been planted for the purpose of injuring the searching officer. (Other places for planted razor blades are inside small trousers pockets and along the inside of the waistband.) While standing to the right rear of the subject, run your hands around the collar of his jacket or shirt, down the front of the shirt, and starting at the shoulders, down the inside of the sleeve up to the armpits. The armpit area of a bulky jacket or coat is a favorite hiding place for pistols or

Figure 12-1 The objective while searching a person is to keep him or her off balance to maintain your advantage. (Courtesy Ohio State Highway Patrol.)

revolvers. Run your hand down the outside of the arm, feeling the sleeve, then around the waistband. At the waistband, feel for any string that may be hanging from the belt and be holding a gun or knife at the other end for easy access. Loosen the belt or remove it entirely, if necessary.

Search the legs, starting at the crotch area and working down from the outside and the inside. One popular hiding place for weapons is inside the shorts in the area of the genitals, because of the knowledge that there will be a natural reluctance to touch the private parts. If you want to live long enough to retire, you had better get over that squeamish attitude. Another popular place is on the inside of the calf of the leg, where a garter or elastic part of a sock may be used to hold a weapon. Feel inside the subject's shoes or boots. After completing one side, go to the other side and repeat the operation. Remove boots or shoes and socks and search thoroughly.

6. Make all your commands and instructions clear and brief.

7. When other officers are assisting you in the search, have them stand off to one side opposite the side you are working on. If there is more than one subject, search each one in turn, starting with the one on the left while your "cover officer" is standing at the opposite side of the line. Search the first subject from the left; then move him and yourself to the right end of the line and search him from the right. Repeat this procedure with each subject. By using this method, it is possible to search as many people as there are in the line without ever placing yourself between two of the subjects you are searching. By having the "cover" officer move to the opposite side of the line whenever you move, you are assuring maximum coverage of the subjects during the entire searching process. If you have enough officers, each suspect may be searched by a different officer at the same time.

8. Never turn your back on a subject.

9. Do not be timid when searching an individual, but do not use abusive methods or abusive language.

10. Do not get too close to any subject before you have him at a position of disadvantage.

11. Your search is for weapons, tools or implements used to commit crime, evidence relevant to a crime, or the fruits of a crime.

Strip Search. This search is conducted in the privacy of headquarters and eventually in jail during the booking process. The most efficient means of searching an individual's person and clothing is to have the person remove all clothes and then perform a systematic and thorough search of the body and of each item of clothing. Carefully examine the individual's body from head to toe, looking for any item that may be attached to the body by means of tape, a bandage, chains, straps, or various types of jewelry. Favorite hiding places are the hair, bottom of the feet, in the mouth, near the genitalia, and in the body crevices. If necessary to search the interior of the body cavities, call upon the services of a physician or nurse to conduct the examination under clinical conditions. Be sure of your legal limitations in this type of search.

Search of Women.   There is no legal distinction between searching a man and searching a woman, and searches may be conducted by police personnel of either sex. However, propriety should prevail unless the life of a person is endangered. When a search is essential for the protection of life, it must be conducted, but it must be justifiable in the eyes of many other persons at a later time. The most acceptable arrangement for a search of a woman is to have a woman conduct it. In the absence of a woman who may conduct the search, handcuff the female suspect with her hands behind her back, and place her pocketbook or purse where she cannot get her hands inside. You may roll the police baton across any suspected bulges, particularly in the breast, pelvic, and buttock areas.

To ascertain if bulges are caused by some hard object such as a weapon, a cursory search may be made by any woman in the immediate area if she is willing, but a thorough search must be made by a female employee of a law enforcement agency who has been adequately trained in the art of self-defense and in searching techniques.

As with the male suspect, search of body cavities should always be made by a medical doctor or other qualified person under dignified and sanitary clinical conditions.

Searches of Persons at Airports.   Skyjacking is not new. Actually, the first commercial aircraft to hold the distinction of being taken over forcefully was a Peruvian airplane in 1930.[17] Since then, there have been several hundred similar crimes. As the crime became more frequent, the Federal Aviation Act of 1958 was amended to include a possible death penalty for the crime. In the years that followed, security at airports became more and more critical. Until February 6, 1972, airport security was voluntary. On that date, the Federal Aviation Administration made it mandatory that all airline passengers be screened by one or more screening devices, such as the electronics weapons detector, interview by airline personnel, interview by law enforcement personnel, or a patdown or frisk for weapons. Now it is a routine preboarding experience for all passengers to pass through a metal-detecting unit or to be searched with the aid of a portable metal-detecting unit and to have carry-on luggage and other items searched and/or x-rayed.

In addition to the routine gate procedures, airport personnel are trained to look for individuals who appear to match a "profile" of potential skyjackers and drug dealers. The exact nature of the profile is kept secret. Whenever suspicions are aroused by a person matching the profile, or by some other behavior, the search and personal attention is considerably more intense. Luggage that is being sent through may be searched as well as the carry-on luggage. Such a search is usually conducted by airline personnel and is then continued by law enforcement personnel if the initial search reveals material of significance.

Since January 5, 1973, every air carrier is required to inspect all carry-on baggage and to screen all passengers through a metal detector or, if no such detection device is available, to require a consent to search prior to boarding. According to those regulations, issued under Federal Regulations 25934-35 of December 6, 1972, the airline personnel actually do the screening, but law enforcement personnel will be present to assist when necessary. From that point on, probable, or reasonable, cause justification dictates how you may proceed with further searches.

During the years since the 1970s, the airlines and airport security personnel have been continuously updating and improving their procedures in screening passengers, luggage, and employees. Sophisticated x-ray equipment and metal detectors, as well as specially trained dogs to sniff out explosives and other contraband (including the Agriculture Department's dogs who sniff out fruits and vegetables unlawfully brought into our ports of entry), are constantly upgraded. Spot checks and searches are made of individuals who match "profiles" (who fits those profiles are closely guarded secrets).

Luggage, especially carry-ons, must be under constant control of their owners; any items that are standing alone in the terminal or on an airplane that do not have an owner are immediately taken to an isolated location and disposed of, sometimes by the bomb squad. Many security measures are secret and cannot be published in a book such as this for obvious reasons.

The courts generally give wide latitude to officers and airport personnel who conduct searches at transportation terminals because of the urgent need for safety of large numbers of people at these locations.

Vehicle Searches. Not all occasions on which a police officer looks through a vehicle are necessarily considered searches. For example, when you must have someone's automobile stored because it was parked in a hazardous location, or was recovered stolen, or was being held for some other legitimate reason, it should be routine for someone to *inventory* the automobile. Because you will be held responsible for the vehicle and its contents, you should conduct a careful inventory of the condition of the vehicle and itemize all contents while taking steps to provide for the safekeeping of those contents. It is also possible that you might be looking through an abandoned vehicle and find something that will later prove to be of evidentiary value. Another occasion might be when you approach a vehicle and look inside to determine that there is no one hiding in the back seat who might be a threat to your safety. What is in plain sight, even when illuminated by flashlight, is not being searched.

The issue of whether you may search a vehicle has been addressed in many court decisions, and the usual guideline is that, whenever an officer has reasonable cause to conduct a search and whenever it appears that such a search is consistent with good police work, you may search a vehicle without a warrant, whether under suspicious circumstances or whether incidental to an arrest. Automobiles and other vehicles that are highly mobile could be moved so easily and quickly that evidence could be destroyed or taken completely away from its original location before you could get a warrant. As with any other searching procedure, these are merely guidelines and are subject to change by rapidly changing court decisions.

Whenever possible, you might consider trying for a consent search. By merely asking a question such as "You don't mind if I search your car, do you?" or "I would like to look in your trunk. You have the right to refuse. May I look?" you may receive blanket approval. Situations that may negate any consent include the use of restraint, a display of force or weapons while you are asking, the number of officers present, the issuance of threats or promises, or the use of trickery or deceit in gaining the consent. To show consent, you must prove the following:

1. The person was informed of or indicated a knowledge of the right to refuse admittance to the search.
2. The person consenting understood his or her rights and knowingly consented to the search.
3. The waiver was given in a clear and positive manner.
4. The waiving party was in a legal position to give consent.
5. The consent was free of duress or coercion.

Whenever you search a vehicle incidental to an arrest, conduct the search when it is contemporaneous with the arrest and when the subject is present. While searching, you may show the subject certain items and ask for a statement of ownership or other knowledge about their presence in the vehicle. Also, the subject will be witnessing the search and discoveries you make and will be less likely to claim that you planted evidence in the vehicle.

You may move the vehicle prior to searching under certain conditions; for example, poor lighting conditions at the scene, gathering hostile crowds, severely inclement weather, traffic congestion or road hazards, or lack of special searching equipment—vacuum, ultraviolet light—at the place you are conducting the search.

The method for searching vehicles should be as thorough and as imaginative as possible. The most effective means is to begin at the front and work systematically to the back on one side and then work back to the front of the vehicle on the opposite side. If two officers are working together, they should conduct the search independently of each other, with each officer conducting a complete search in succession. In this manner you are getting a "second opinion," so to speak.

This procedure is far more efficient than having each officer search a portion of the vehicle. There are so many hiding places that it is easy to overlook one, and two complete searches are better than one partial search.

Where to Search

This is a real challenge to the inquiring officer. Evidence and contraband have been found in virtually every place where anything may be concealed. Consider the places where objects have been found by other officers. Where would *you* hide something?

In the bumper and grill areas, certain items may be concealed by the use of masking tape or wire. Look for boxes, which may be welded in, that serve no functional purpose for the operation of the vehicle. The area under the hood provides many excellent hiding places; for example, inside the air cleaner, the vents, or the air conditioner. Certain accessories may be inoperable and the housing parts may be used to store items such as smuggled marijuana or other narcotics.

Under the dashboard, there are several places that may hold evidence; for example, the area above the glove compartment, the fuse box, or the underside of the dash. Use a flashlight and a mirror to search this area. Under the floorboard may be a good place for a built-in carrying case. In one smuggling case, an officer lifted the floor mat and found a trap door. Opening it, he found a large storage box welded to the underside of the car. The box was full of narcotics.

Look for torn places in the upholstery, in the headliner, and in the side panels; these may signal the presence of a hidden pocket for carrying a concealed weapon. The area inside the dome lights and similar empty places are accessible for hiding, and they should also be searched.

Move everything that is movable and look inside, behind, and under it. Ask yourself where you would hide a weapon, narcotics, or stolen merchandise, or whether you would hide it at all. One burglar carried his stolen merchandise right out on the seat of the car and was stopped for routine questioning on several occasions. When asked about the merchandise, he stated that it was his. When asked about his success, he explained that his secret was to remain calm and cool when questioned, because his natural manner did not arouse any of the officers' suspicions. He added that some officers erroneously believe that a thief or burglar will become very nervous in the presence of an officer, obviously for fear of being found out.

Generally, when searching an automobile for evidence, it is good practice to be familiar with the particular body designs and to look for modifications or deviations from those designs. Conduct a thorough search and use your imagination. Pickups with campers may have false walls, with the outside and inside appearing to correspond, while there may actually be a foot or two of space between the inside and outside walls. Vans and trucks may be similarly designed.

Search of the Premises

Except under conditions when you pursue someone into a house or apartment or other private place, or when contraband or other evidence is in plain sight while you are lawfully inside the place, or when you can show that you did not have time to get a warrant prior to the search because the delay would result in destruction of the evidence, your best option is to seek permission for the search from a person who has a legal right to give consent to search the place or person you wish to search.

Whenever there is time, particularly if you know when and where you are going to make the arrest, what evidence you intend to look for, and that you will probably find it, secure a warrant for the search before you go to the place you wish to search. Your search may then be much more methodical and complete.

According to the *Chimel* decision,[18] a search that is coincidental to an arrest requires that the arrest must have been based upon a warrant and upon reasonable cause (or probable cause, whichever term you prefer), and the search must be contemporaneous with the arrest. You may search only that portion of the premises where the subject is located at the time of the arrest (his sphere of influence or control) where the subject may have deposited or disposed of what you are searching for. Your search will be limited to only those areas that were within the sphere or the area where the subject may have placed or deposited evidence or other contraband along his route of travel or where he is located at the time. You may search only for weapons that were used in the crime in question or with which the subject might attack you, tools or instruments with which the subject might have used to commit the crime, fruits of the crime or evidence taken from the crime scene, or contraband that is unlawful to possess such as drugs or counterfeit money.

Notebook Entries Regarding Searches

Whenever you discover items of evidence during a search, record in your field notebook an accurate description of the item, and describe exactly where and under what conditions you found it. If the owner or driver of the vehicle is present, ask for a state of ownership for each item you find, and record his response. Handle the items as you would handle any other evidence.

Review of Legal Considerations

The rules of search and seizure are principally court-made rules developed over the past 200 years, with the major thrust having begun in the 1960s. The courts review cases brought before them on a case-by-case basis and determine which evidence should have been suppressed, or "excluded"—hence the "exclusionary rule." Reasonableness or unreasonableness of the search made by the police or their agents is determined in light of the provisions of the Constitution and the Bill of Rights, which restrict their activity.

A person's place of residence, personal property, and personal places within a person's place of business present an expectation of privacy. For example, a paying guest in a hotel room has a greater expectation of privacy than does one of his casual visitors to whom the room has not been rented, and the driver of a vehicle has a greater expectation of privacy than does his passenger, unless, of course, the passenger is the owner of the car. The private office of the manager of the insurance company has a greater expectation of privacy than do persons in the adjoining general office area. The general rule is that before an officer may search any place or person, a search warrant must be issued by a judge who has reviewed an affidavit signed by a witness alleging facts supporting the need for a search of a certain place or person, describing what the search is expected to turn up, and what it is expected to prove.

Searches conducted without warrants are based on "good faith" exceptions to the rule. According to the Court in a 1979 case (*Sanders,* 442 U.S. 753): Warrantless searches are presumed to be illegal and will be upheld only if the prosecution can prove that the police conduct came within one of the few "carefully circumscribed and jealously guarded" exceptions to the warrant requirements. Examples of such exceptions include (1) consent searches, (2) emergency searches permitted because of exigent circumstances, and (3) searches conducted incident to arrest. Loosely defined, an exigency is an emergency.

According to the ruling made in the *Chimel* case (1969, 395 U.S. 752), after a lawful arrest you may search the arrestee and the immediate area around him or her incidental to the arrest. A full search of the person is admissible, plus the immediate area, that within arm's reach and the space from which the suspect could reach for a weapon or to destroy or conceal evidence. The search may be for (1) instrumentalities used to commit the crime, the fruits of that crime, and other evidence thereof which will aid in the apprehension and conviction of the criminal; (2) articles whose possession is itself unlawful, such as contraband or goods known to be stolen; and (3) weapons that can be used to assault the arresting officer or to effect an escape.

It is unreasonable for a police officer to enter physically into an area where a person has a "reasonable expectation of privacy" in order to conduct a search or for the purpose of seizing something unless (a) you have a warrant, or (b) emergency circumstances exist, or (c) you have obtained a valid consent.

If you are already inside legally, there is no rule which says that you have to shut your eyes. If you are outside a house and see something inside, secure a warrant unless the criterion (b) or (c) is present. A driveway has no privacy, and a back yard deserves more privacy than does a front yard. It is permissible to look through an open window, but it will be ruled unreasonable if you peer through a hole in a blind or a drape.

Walls or fences pose different problems. If you can see across a fence without climbing on something to see, such as if you are in a next-door neighbor's second-floor room and you can plainly see into the yard, there is no intrusion. You may use binoculars or zoom lens on a camera to enhance your observation, as such an observation is in plain sight.

When flying overhead in a fixed-wing airplane or in a helicopter, what you observe below is generally admissible, unless your flight is for the purpose of looking into a specific enclosed residential yard which is not otherwise open to ground level view for suspected evidence of a crime within that yard. In the latter case, the observation may be inadmissible in your state. Because of the drug epidemic in the country, many of the courts are relaxing rules in this respect, and the rules change from day to day.

Who has authority to consent to a search varies from state to state, but these are general rules: Joint occupants may consent to search of that area which is jointly occupied. Husband–wife consents are generally admissible, except if the one spouse has a private space or room that is not available to the other spouse, such as a workshop or office in the house, or a private storage area. Children have limited authority to consent to a search, while parents have considerably more authority to consent to searching a child's room or space, unless the child pays rent and the parent does not regularly go into the room and clean. Also, the parent cannot consent to searching the personal effects of the child, such as a suitcase.

Searches with Search Warrants

Unless justified by an exception, such as consent, incident to an arrest, emergency and there is no time to get a warrant, vehicle search, and other exceptional cases, a search of private property may lawfully be conducted *only* if authorized by a search warrant. The rule also applies to commercial property, except where open to the public.

Searches made with a warrant are presumed to be lawful, principally because they have been subjected in some degree to judicial scrutiny. You have developed sufficient information and have either filled out an affidavit yourself based on your personal observations, or the affidavit is sworn to by a person with personal knowledge about what the warrant seeks to find as a result of the search. This puts you well ahead of the game in getting the fruits of the search introduced into evidence.

Even with a warrant, it is always a recommended practice to ask for consent before presenting a warrant. Then, if consent is given, you may then show the warrant and proceed with the search.

In the *Leon* case[19] it was ruled that under a "good faith" exception to the exclusionary rule, evidence obtained with an arrest or search warrant will be admitted even if the warrant is later found to be defective.

Prisoner Control And Transportation

Specific techniques will be covered in your academy, but these are some of the general procedures for handcuffing and control of the prisoner and transportation of both male and female subjects.

Once you have the suspect in the hands-over-head position, this is the most logical time to handcuff the suspect, and it should be prior to the search. Place one cuff on the wrist of the subject, make it sufficiently tight so as to maintain control. Instruct the subject to keep the other hand in place until you tell him to move. With the cuffed hand under control, bring it down in an arc to a position behind his back with the palm out. Then, while holding onto the one hand tightly, instruct the subject to slowly move the other hand down to a similar position with the palm out. Attach the other cuff. If you have a control problem, quickly tighten the one cuff that you have already attached. You will usually discover that this is sufficient to regain control. A tight handcuff can be painful. Once you have both hands cuffed, you might want to adjust the pressure slightly if you had to tighten one or both of the cuffs while getting them on. Do not release; merely turn the key while quickly loosening the cuff one notch at a time and quickly turning the key back to the locked position. Use the double lock so as to prevent the subject from tightening the cuffs later, cutting off the circulation, and working on your sympathy to get you to loosen the cuffs, giving him an opportunity to get away.

Whether to handcuff or not, and under what conditions, depends on your own department's policy. Whatever the policy, there are good reasons for using the handcuffs. Don't hesitate to use them in arrest situations, keeping in mind that they are for the safety of the suspects as well as yourself.

Once you have the subject cuffed, make your search. As presented earlier, do not hesitate to make a thorough search. Each time a different officer assumes custody of a subject from another officer, it should be standard operating procedure to search the subject again. Never take another person's word that there is no need to search again.

Whenever you receive custody of a prisoner from another officer, conduct a thorough search for your own satisfaction. This should be a department requirement. It is not a surprise to hear that the second officer who searches a suspect comes up with some weapon that had been somehow overlooked on the previous searches. In one case a subject had been arrested for driving while under the influence of alcohol. He was a jovial fellow, but he was going to jail because he had violated the law. He did not resist, and he had all the appearances of a harmless drunk. He was first taken to a local police station to be held for transfer to the county jail. He was searched in the field by the arresting officer, searched by the booking officer at the jail, and searched again when another officer took him out of the cell and placed him inside a transportation unit to take him to the county jail.

While they were en route down the highway, the suspect pulled a small-caliber automatic pistol out of his undershorts and fatally shot the officer. When the officer died, he lost control of the vehicle and the car crashed into a retaining fence. The killer was still in the back seat after the accident, but his gun had been thrown from his hand and had slid under the front seat where he could not reach it. There was a steel mesh case between the front and rear seat. A passerby discovered the accident. The suspect pleaded to be let out, but the man observed the officer with the bullet wound and the gun on the front floorboard and presumed that the suspect had committed the murder. He used the police car's radio and called for assistance. Thanks to his presence of mind, the suspect did not get away and was held to answer for his crime. Three complete searches and the gun was not discovered! A terrible price to pay for a slipshod series of searches.

Maintain visual supervision of every subject in your custody until he has been thoroughly searched and securely held in jail or a holding room. Whenever you place a prisoner in a cell containing other prisoners, first instruct the others to step back away from the door. This will prevent any rushing movement by the prisoners inside when you place the new prisoner in the cell.

Female Prisoners

Female prisoners pose special problems. They may attempt to use their charm and femininity on the gullible male officer. They may use tears and attempt to elicit sympathy for their plight or speak of their importance in the social, political, or economic structure of the community. A woman may also become sullen and uncooperative. Some females may charge that a male officer has taken improper advantage of them and attempt to bargain to drop their charges of rape in exchange for the officers' dropping criminal charges against them.

Use courtesy and diplomacy with all prisoners. When making an arrest, it should be perfectly clear that any placing of the hands on the person is to accomplish the arrest. If you adopt a policy of handcuffing all arrestees, the female should be handcuffed. In addition to adding to the safety of the situation, the handcuffs will also serve to show other people that the woman is in custody of police officers and that her charges of "rape" are probably false, even though the officers are not in uniform.

Self-defense by the officer against a woman who violently resists arrest or who attacks the officer should consist of the same basic techniques that are used against attacks by male protagonists. "Necessary and reasonable force" is justifiable against an attack by either sex. Be extra cautious that nothing you do while defending yourself and maintaining control of the prisoner can be misinterpreted as an undue amount of liberty taken under the guise of self-defense. Avoid making any injudicious remarks that may later be taken out of context and quoted, or misquoted. Use no statements that have double meanings. A double entendre may sound quite funny at a party or in a barroom under social conditions, but in an arrest situation, it can sound insidious and evil.

Transportation of Prisoners

At the beginning of the tour of duty, when you assume control of your vehicle, you should search the entire vehicle, particularly that portion that is used for transporting prisoners. When making an arrest, each subject should be thoroughly searched prior to being placed in the vehicle. Additionally, it should become routine to search the vehicle again after each time a prisoner is transported, to be certain that the subject did not hide something in the unit. Items such as revolvers and knives are occasionally found, but other items of value to an investigation may likewise be disposed of, such as narcotics, pawn slips, slips of paper containing names and addresses of accomplices, or stolen documents used for false identification.

If the transportation unit is equipped with a screen or shield separating the driving compartment from the rear of the vehicle, the prisoner should ride in that compartment alone or with other prisoners, with the officers in front. If the unit does not have this equipment, place the prisoner in the right portion of the rear seat and the second officer immediately behind the driver. If there is any indication that the prisoner will attempt to kick out the windows or kick at the transporting officers, remove his shoes. For additional safety to the prisoner during this trip, fasten his seat belt. With his hands cuffed behind his back and the seat belt fastened and looped around at least one arm, the prisoner's likelihood of escape is lessened (Figure 12–2). If the prisoner has any apparent injury, or makes any complaint of pain, be sure to see that he gets appropriate medical attention prior to booking at the jail.

If the situation occurs when there is one officer and one prisoner, and the police unit is not equipped with a screen between the front and rear compartments, consider placing the arrestee in the front seat with the seat belt securely fastened and his hands cuffed behind his back. Watch his feet; but if he is securely fastened, he will not be able to reach your feet or the car's foot pedals. If necessary, use restraining devices on the feet as well. A triangular bandage placed on a mouth might serve as adequate protection against those subjects who try to spit on you.

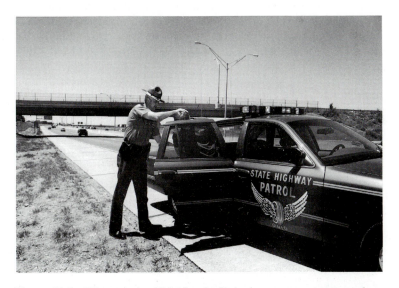

Figure 12-2 Prisoners should be handcuffed whenever you transport them. (Courtesy Ohio State Highway Patrol.)

Transporting Female Prisoners. Two officers, one preferably a female, should be used to transport a female prisoner. If a female officer is not available, consider the use of a woman volunteer from the scene of the arrest, who will accompany the officer and the prisoner to jail or headquarters and then be returned to her home. Seating while transporting a female prisoner is the same as that when transporting a male prisoner.

At the beginning and completion of each trip involving custodial transportation, indicate in your field notebook the exact time, the mileage to the tenth of a mile, and the location. Radio in this information to the dispatcher at the same time. The dispatcher should use a time-stamp machine or some other means to indicate the time the trip begins and ends, and record the locations and the mileage readings that you call in. A convenient aid for this process would be a printed form that the dispatcher would fill out correctly, time stamp, and then forward to you at the time you file your report concerning the arrest. The "trip" card could be attached to the original of the report and become a permanent record. If your department continuously records all radio traffic, you will have this additional support, with the dispatcher periodically stating the time of day throughout the recording.

SUMMARY

Arrest, search, and custody are three very important topics in your training as a police officer. Personal safety for yourself, your fellow officers, and the subjects you are dealing with is paramount. It cannot be emphasized too strongly that there is no simple arrest situation. You are dealing with the personal lives of the individuals you are arresting, and how they may react at any moment is totally unpredictable. Be constantly aware that you must act judiciously, diplomatically, and with extreme caution.

Not only must you be aware of the proper mechanical procedures for arrest, search, and custody, but it is your responsibility to keep abreast of the changing laws and court decisions that affect those areas of your job. Never underestimate the suspect.

EXERCISES AND STUDY QUESTIONS

1. In your state, what is the basic difference between an arrest by a peace officer and an arrest by a private person?
2. Is there any difference in procedure for making an arrest for a felony in your department than there is for making a misdemeanor arrest? If so, what is the difference?
3. Give at least one example of how a witness might be considered in the presence of an event when using each of the following senses: (a) sight, (b) hearing, (c) smell, (d) touch, (e) taste.
4. Describe a situation in which an officer may have cause to arrest for what appears to be a crime in progress, yet it is actually not a crime at all.

5. Give an example of a situation when an officer may have cause to arrest a person for a felony, although the crime was not committed in the officer's presence.

6. How much force may an officer use to make an arrest and/or to provide self-defense?

7. Give an example of a situation in which a peace officer may use deadly force.

8. In your jurisdiction, may a person forcibly resist arrest legally if that person knows that there is no probable cause for the arrest?

9. What difference, if any, is there between making an arrest with a warrant and without a warrant?

10. Describe the correct procedure for stopping a traffic violator on a busy street and how you would approach the vehicle to make your initial contact with the driver.

11. May an ambassador's spouse be protected under the diplomatic immunity laws?

12. Give an example of police entrapment. Give an example of a situation that a person with less knowledge of police procedures than you might misinterpret as entrapment.

13. What did the officer do wrong in the *Garner* case?

14. List at least 20 places in a passenger car where you might expect to find hidden contraband.

15. Describe a searching technique that is used in your area but is not described in this text.

16. Draw a chart showing the escalation of use of force based on the actions and reactions of a person being arrested.

17. What is *reasonable use of force?*

18. What are the laws in your state that correspond with those in California, and how do they compare?

REFERENCES

California Penal Code (Annual).

FRICKE, CHARLES W., and ARTHUR L. ALARCON. *California Criminal Law,* 11th ed. Los Angeles: Legal Book Corp., 1977.

JONES, DAVID A. *The Law of Criminal Procedure: An Analysis and Critique.* Boston: Little, Brown, 1981.

KLEIN, IRVING J. *Constitutional Law for Criminal Justice Professionals.* North Scituate, Mass.: Duxbury, 1980.

LENN, PETER D., THOMAS F. MASER, and R. BRYCE YOUNG. *Arrest, Search, and Seizure.* San Francisco: American Analysis Corp., 1973.

RUTTER, WILLIAM A. *Criminal Procedure.* Gardena, Calif.: Gilbert Law Summaries, 1981.

WADDINGTON, LAWRENCE C. *Arrest, Search, and Seizure.* Beverly Hills, Calif.: Glencoe, 1974.

WELLS, KENNETH M., and PAUL B. WESTON. *Criminal Procedure and Trial Practice.* Englewood Cliffs, N.J.: Prentice Hall, 1977.

WESTON, PAUL B., and KENNETH M. WELLS. *Criminal Evidence for Police,* 2nd ed. Englewood Cliffs, N.J.: Prentice Hall, 1976.

See also the numerous cases referred to in the footnotes.

FOOTNOTES

1. *Garske* v. *United States,* 1 F.2d 620, 86th Cir. (1924).
2. *Beck* v. *Ohio,* 379 U.S. 89 (1964).
3. *People* v. *Steinberg,* 148 Cal. App. 2d 855, 307 P.2d 634 (1957).
4. *Dorsey* v. *United States,* 372 F.2d 928, C.A.D.C. (1967).
5. *People* v. *Goldberg,* 280 N.Y.S.2d 646, 19 N.Y.2d 460, 277 N.E.2d 575 (1967).
6. *McBride* v. *United States,* 284 F.416, 5th Cir. (1922).
7. *Robinson* v. *State,* 4 Md. App. 515, 243 A.2d 879 (1968).
8. *Tennessee* v. *Garner,* 471 U.S. 1, 9, 10 (1985).
9. Federal Bureau of Investigation, *Law Enforcement Bulletin,* August 1973.
10. Ibid., p. 14.
11. Ibid.
12. Ibid.
13. *Sorrells* v. *United States,* 287 U.S. 435 (1932).
14. 23 Cal. 3d 675 (1979).
15. 460 F.2d 374, 5th Cir. (1972).
16. 472 F.2d 145, 5th Cir. (1973).
17. David G. Hubbard, *The Skyjacker and His Flights of Fantasy* (New York: Macmillan, 1971), p. 258.
18. *Chimel* v. *Calif.,* 395 U.S. 752 S. Ct. 2034 (1969).
19. 468 U.S. 897 (1984).

STRESS SURVIVAL AND THE USE OF FORCE

*I*NTRODUCTION

In this chapter we consider the general area of survival under normal and abnormal police field work. Because there is so much variance in departmental policies, as there is in various methods of using the revolver, in weaponless defense, in the baton of traditional style and the sidearm, and in the various martial arts, what we shall attempt here are some basic guidelines that will follow something of a "middle-of-the-road" posture. Depending on the agency that employs you, there will be considerable variations in rules and techniques of self-defense. Public and political pressures, as well as the attitudes and philosophies of your own administrators and supervisors, will dictate policy in those areas. As a writer of textbooks, a college professor, and a former police administrator, it seems to me that I would be somewhat presumptuous if I were to try to tell those professional colleagues of mine what their policies should be. It is they, and not I, who will be on the mat when the referee makes the count.

This chapter is divided into five parts: (1) stress, (2) officer survival, (3) rules of self-defense, (4) choice of weapons, and (5) use of firearms. In the section on stress we address the common everyday stresses as well as the unusual events, and give a few suggestions on how you might address the stress problem that plagues all police officers. In the survival section we present a few guidelines on alertness and state of mind while you perform your field duties that might help you stay alive and healthy. The third section, rules of self-defense, deals with your rights and liabilities as a police officer and as a reasonable person in preserving your own life and that of others. Next, we discuss some of the more traditional weapons and give a few suggestions as to when to use them (*how* to use such weapons should be the academy's responsibility, and the subject is covered extensively in texts exclusively devoted to the subject). The fifth and final section of the chapter is devoted to firearms, some pointers about their use, and a suggested policy statement on the use of deadly force.

STRESS

As a police officer, you do not have a monopoly on stress. Many of your fellow officers, instructors, supervisors, and people outside police service will emphasize the amount of stress that a police officer must sustain. While this is so, it is important that we keep the subject of stress in its proper perspective and deal with it as we would any other job-related problem.

Some of the situations that cause your stress, however, are unique. You are exposed to death and violence in real life, which is a world of difference from the violent scenes you encounter in the movies and television. Those are real people losing real blood and body parts, and they do not collect their residuals and get up to appear in the next feature. You are required by the job to be dispassionate and to hide your own emotional reactions to these situations because you cannot do your job while crying or getting hysterical. You will be called "cold" and "heartless" for shielding your personal emotions from the people you deal with, and that takes its toll as time goes on.

Some of the major causes of stress are that you are not suited for the position in which you find yourself, that you are not comfortable in the position, that you find the position frustrating, that you lack adequate training, and that the position is emotionally disturbing. Selection of police officers must include a complete psychological workup, including testing as well as a thorough background investigation. Some individuals cannot handle stress well, no matter what they do for a living. Although a person may display traits that appear desirable for a police candidate to have, such as aggressiveness, such an outward display of what appears to be good may actually simply be bravado that compensates for an inferiority complex that will fall to pieces when that person's true strength is called upon to manifest itself. The result is a police officer who is totally unqualified to perform with self-assurance and considerable restraint. The person who should not be on the job in the first place will continue to perform behind this facade, hoping that no one will find him or her out. The bravado continues, but so do the insecurities. The result may be hypertension or alcoholism, overreactions to stressful confrontations, or all three. The result is a sick officer who is prematurely retired from service because of stress.

The police officer is not the only person whose personal and professional life is stressful. Although it is true that not many other professions call upon a person to face a crazed gunman or a burglar inside a building, or an unknown situation when you don't know what or who is inside a darkened building with a broken window, those situations do not make up the police officer's total career. Police work has been described as "hours of sheer boredom interspersed with moments of stark terror." There are some risk takers, including police officers, who consider it a necessary part of their lives to jump out of airplanes, to race cars or boats, to climb mountain peaks, or to perform other death-defying feats. There are also some psychologists who will say that such peaks of emotion are essential to the healthy psyche.

For comparable stressful situations, consider the entertainer who waits in the wings to go on stage in front of an audience of 3000; the student who just completed three years of law school who is taking the bar exam that only 40 percent will pass; the airline pilot whose plane has just lost part of its skin and nine of its passengers were sucked out, who now must safely land with the remaining 237 passengers aboard; the computer programmer with an insoluble problem that must be solved within minutes or the space shuttle crew will be lost in space forever. Perhaps you remember how much stress you felt before your first date, or the day of your marriage and the wedding night, or that important baseball game when your base hit would win the game. Those are all stressful situations that will have the same effect on your system as a "man with gun" call.

If you are well matched to your work, and if you like your work so much that you look forward to going to work every day, no matter what it is, chances are that the accompanying stresses will not seem half as bad nor will they have the same debilitating effects.

The stress confronting you as a field officer includes supervision, conflict, too much work, not enough work, inactivity, responsibility for others, crisis situations, real danger, imagined danger, frustrated anger, a feeling of helplessness, tragedy, inadequate equipment, lack of recognition by superiors, inadequate pay, disrespect from citizens, negative attitudes of fellow officers, unusual and long hours, having to testify in court, having to speak in public, and self-consciousness. Other types of stress that compound on-the-job stress include marital difficulties, family problems, family tragedy, negative image of police by friends and/or relatives, financial problems, alcoholism, pregnancy, sex problems, acquiring a new home, and outside employment.

In this text, we shall address just a few of the stresses of the job and suggest a few activities that might help you deal with stress.

Stress Causes

Trauma. Responding to an accident or a crime scene and finding dead, beaten, and dismembered bodies of what once were walking and talking people in perfectly good health is not a normal part of our growing up and going to school and college before becoming police officers. There are no courses to prepare you for that, except on-the-job exposure and perhaps a trip or two to the morgue to witness autopsies while in the academy. It becomes more personal, though, when you are actually on the scene trying to administer aid and comfort to those victims. In your training you will have been schooled in what signs of life and death to look for and efficiently and dispassionately going through the routines. Once you are in the field and experiencing these events up close and firsthand, the emotions sometimes go haywire inside while you must show no outward signs of it bothering you. These pent-up emotions need to be released. Department and volunteer psychologists and psychiatrists are—or should be—provided for you and your colleagues during break and debriefing sessions. When many of your senior colleagues went through these events in the past, they were expected to "take it like a man." I was present during and immediately following a tragic shooting event between officers and suspects, when one of the officers who fired a fatal shot broke down and cried. A very high-ranking superior officer taunted him and told him that "grown police officers do not cry like babies." (I have and I'm not ashamed of having cried.)

Officers involved in two shootings, whom I counseled following the episode, never did recover. One turned devoutly religious and seemed to be coping until he committed suicide 10 years later. The other officer, who was only in his mid-twenties at the time of the shooting, drastically increased his intake of alcohol and within a few short months had to be fired because his alcoholism rendered him useless as a police officer. Today, those people might still be viable police officers if they had had appropriate attention and follow-up treatment given many officers following such traumatic events as a firefight or other tragedies. Look at the psychological counseling given the rescue workers and investigators following the bombing of the World Trade Center in New York and the Federal Building in Oklahoma City.

Crisis Situations.   Many of the crises you encounter do not involve you personally, and you are not expected to inject yourself into the situation. You should have empathy, or the ability to understand why a person cries, but you are not required to cry too. Professional detachment is essential. When you go to the accident scene and find three children with arms and legs severed and crushed, your effectiveness in getting those children the best care will be seriously decreased if you find yourself grief-stricken and unable to think and act clearly. Set those feelings aside and remember that you do not have the "luxury" of getting emotionally involved. This professional aloofness is not "callousness." Resiliency in being able to "bounce back" and put those unfortunate experiences into the past and keep them there is essential to your role.

Real and Imagined Danger.   At the time you are approaching a house and you have been told of a sniper inside who threatened to kill the first police officer he sees, the danger is real. It only becomes imagined after you have secured the scene and have found that the person was inside sleeping off a drunken interlude and there was no gun after all. This is a hazard that goes with the job. You must understand the dangers when you are first hired and should not forget them throughout your career. Every officer copes differently. Whenever you sense that any of these situations is having a negative effect on you, arrange to see your department's psychological counselor, or one who is privately contracted, who has experience in dealing with police emotional crises.

Frustrated Anger.   This will occur more frequently if you take it personally whenever someone calls you names or questions your legal status at birth. Two ways to cope with this problem are to counsel yourself and learn to ignore the name-calling and to get involved in some type of physically exerting activity. Racket ball or tennis may help you overcome the urge to strike out at someone. Other sports, such as running or swimming, may help you work out some of the built-up anxiety.

Feeling of Helplessness.   This occurs when you watch someone whom you are attempting to rescue die or when you do not succeed in saving the life of a drowning victim. There are also feelings of helplessness when you arrest someone and later see that individual go free. The best way to cope with that stressful situation is to remember that you are not superhuman and that you have no control over the results of most of the things you do. This also applies to those tragedies you witness and later feel that there is something more that you should have done. You cannot "Should Have."

Road Rage, or Pursuit Syndrome.   Either we are having more frequent occurrences, or perhaps more are getting caught on tape, but road rage experienced by operators of motor vehicles and officers losing their head at the end of high-speed chases is an extremely volatile and serious situation. Many people who get into their automobiles seem to go through metamorphosis, and take on the aggressive attitude of the powerful engines under the hoods of their cars. Shielded in anonymity inside all that fiberglass, steel, and tinted glass, there seems to be no reason to behave like courteous human beings while operating those vehicles. Those individuals vent their frustrations and feelings of helplessness while stuck in traffic by making wild and angry gestures at other drivers, and often when there is even a minor collision, the built-up pressures explode into violent confrontations. Police officers who carry over these attitudes into their police vehicles are doubly cursed. They are also frustrated and feel helpless when people they are chasing with red lights and siren on full blast, who should pull over to the side of the street and stop, just keep on driving.

The officer's rage keeps building up to the point of exploding by the time he or she is finally able to get the driver of the pursued vehicle to stop and follow orders. By assuming the mantle of authority and making the chase a personal matter, the officer's objectivity is gone. This is no longer an objective officer merely carrying out his or her duties. This is an outrageous insult in the mind of the officer, whose "supreme authority" as *the man* or *the law* has been held in contempt. Sometimes the violator adds insult to injury by smirking or giving the officer a disrespectful glare, sometimes making an obscene gesture or turning a back on the officer and being slow or noncooperative when ordered to get out of the car or move from one place to the other. This all continues to build the officer's rage, which must be held in check by the officer taking time out to come back down and under control. If not able to bring the rage down, we have seen the result on videotape. The officer cannot get personal and take the action of the violator as anything but perhaps a contempt or disrespect for the law and not the officer as an individual. It is the badge, not the wearer, that is being held in contempt. The police officer is neither an executioner nor the individual assigned the task of punishing miscreants.

Supervision.   Keep in mind that supervisors and administrators may have greater pressures on them for your performance than you have. A technique used by some supervisors is fear, which is quite effective when used on a subordinate whose tenure depends on that supervisor. They might threaten and impose sanctions for virtually anything but perfect performance. The supervisors may fear for their own tenure or believe that they must outperform their competing supervisors to gain promotions. You can survive in this environment only by doing the best that you can. If the situation becomes unbearable, document the incidents of abuse by recording times, dates, people present, and the exact nature of the situation. It may be possible to go to the next higher supervisor, if there is an open-door policy in your department.

Conflict.   Some people try to avoid conflict. You may be a person who finds any kind of conflict depressing. Look at yourself. Are you able to put these conflicts in their proper perspective as being the natural part of your job, or do you internalize them and take them as personal affronts? If there are conflicting personalities on the job, only a transfer or a resignation will likely resolve the problem. If you find that arguments and physical confrontations between yourself and other people cause you to have headaches and suffer from fits of depression, you are probably in the wrong profession.

Too Much Work.   When the demands are for more than you can handle, and when such demands exceed what is customary for the position you fill, ask for an audience with your supervisor and discuss the problem. Do the best that you can and make it apparent to your supervisors. If it becomes clear that you simply cannot keep up because of your own inadequacy, change assignments or professions.

Not Enough Work.   Sometimes assignments do not demand enough of your time. In that case, discuss the situation with your supervisor and point out that you would like to have additional work. You may be assigned to conduct special surveys or compile statistics or maintain pin maps. Bring along with you to work study materials that are related to your assignment. Try to devise some way to make your job more of a game. For example, how many buildings have telephone poles next to walls that provide access to roof burglars? How many buildings have skylights? Which buildings and apartment houses in your district have names inscribed on their fronts? What are the names? Compile a directory of various types of information that will make your work easier and more interesting.

Inactivity.   The best way to cope with this stressful situation is to make activity, but not meaningless "make-work" activities.

Responsibility for Others.   This may take some attitude adjustment. It is true that you are responsible to do the best that you can to protect people and their property. You cannot prevent violent crimes that are committed by friends or members of the victim's family in the privacy of their homes, and you cannot stop a burglar from breaking into a house unless you are standing alongside him, and even then you might not be able to stop him. People are responsible for their own lives and must make their own decisions. Your way to cope with your feeling of responsibility is to devote your full attention to what you are doing while on duty and to make the best possible effort to make the right decisions and to be in the most appropriate places; then you must let happen whatever happens. The doctor in surgery does not save every life, but he or she does the best possible. If the patient dies, it is no fault of the doctor, who will perform many more surgeries when patients will not die. You will probably never live to see a crime-free society no matter how hard you try. Although many do not make it, the salmon still swim upstream every year. The big league baseball batter has more strikeouts than he has home runs, but he still plays the game and sets new records for the team.

Inadequate Equipment and Insufficient Pay. These are matters for personnel negotiations. You should be fully aware of these conditions when you apply for the job. Although it is a real problem, the situation reminds me of the famous television personality who decided he could not afford to run for Congress because he could not afford the cut in pay. He is still in the entertainment business—never did run for office.

Lack of Recognition by Supervisors. This is a two-way situation. Perhaps a little work on complimenting your superiors and recognizing them for their good work will result in their reciprocating. Try it. The same suggestion applies to the complaint about lack of respect by the public. By showing respect, you might receive some in return. At least, you know that you are okay and that you are doing a good job. Don't expect to be complimented for doing a good job, as many people believe doing a good job is what you are getting paid for.

Speaking in Public. Having to speak in public or testify in court are fears known to everyone. Be prepared, gain competency and self-confidence in what you are doing, and you will find that these stressful problems will lessen with time. Some professional entertainers never overcome stage fright, and those individuals are among the first who will tell you that the anxiety makes them better performers.

Dealing with Stress

Involvement in outside interests, such as family matters, boys' and girls' organizations, church or community activities, sports, hobbies, or other avocations may be so distracting that they have the effect of putting the pressures of the job into a different perspective. For example, the anxiety of facing a flight test for a pilot's license during your day off next week, or the opening night of a play in which you have the leading role, or a showing of your paintings at a gallery in a major city will give your life more breadth, so that the "chewing out" you received last night for writing a "substandard" report does not seem so humiliating. Moreover, you will know that your next report will be up to par and that the world will not have stopped turning because you "screwed up."

Some of the activities suggested by psychologists and other stress specialists as diversions from pressures of the job include biofeedback, meditation, yoga, good nutrition, running, bicycling, contact and other competitive sports, exercise, music, acting, art, water sports, camping and other outdoor activities, high-intensity sports such as sky diving, hang gliding, mountain climbing, or automobile racing. Although there may be disagreement among specialists, some "workaholics" do not do better or more work than do some of those individuals who spend half the time in the same occupations. Worrying more about the job does not necessarily produce better results. For many of the individuals I have encountered, I have had to advise them to wait to see what happens, that their worrying about an outcome will have absolutely no effect on the success or failure of the project or the event. I have even offered my services to worry for them (for an hourly fee, of course).

Critical Incident Debriefing

Emergency service agencies have to recognize that police officers, paramedics, fire-fighters, emergency medical technicians, and other emergency and rescue workers suffer emotional pain when working disasters and tragedies involving broken and dead bodies and body parts of fellow humans. No matter how emotionally strong a person is, there is only so much baggage one can carry before there is a partial or complete breakdown. Many departments are recognizing the need for emotional debriefing of these workers at regular intervals during the rescue operation as well as after it is all over, and this parallels the informational debriefing necessary for investigative purposes to determine the causes of these situations and what training and preparation can be done to make similar operations in the future easier to handle. Psychologists, psychiatrists, and counselors help all of the workers as they accumulate the emotional baggage, and they are often able to help the officers and others unload some of it before it becomes such a problem that it negatively affects their work. Then they do follow-up counseling after the event for as long as they deem necessary.

As a participant in any type of police or rescue activity that causes you to suffer emotional trauma, it is wise to seek counseling as soon as possible after the event and not to consider it some kind of a sign of weakness to seek such help. Covering up your emotions is like covering up any other kind of injury without applying the appropriate medication or therapy. If your department does not provide such services, your health insurance most probably will. If you are worried about your "secret" getting out, that somehow you feel that others will consider you weak and not fit for the job, remember that it is unethical for any of those counselors to discuss your personal situation with anyone but you. It is a privileged communication, the same as if you had a personal conversation with a spiritual advisor. Even if you do choose to seek help from your priest, rabbi, minister, or other religious mentor, consider the fact that many of them do not have the experience or adequate training to perform psychological counseling or handle severe emotional problems.

OFFICER SURVIVAL

Throughout your tour of duty, you should always be alert for any activity that seems out of the ordinary and that arouses your suspicions. The most important life that you are charged to protect is your own, because without you and your fellow officers, there is no one to do the protecting. Paranoia will not help, but you should be wary of any situation that might lead to an open or ambush attack. Even normal-looking people might take advantage of the opportunity to assault a police officer. Common sites for attacks on police officers are lunch and refreshment stops, places where officers park their cars, places where officers gather at the scenes of disturbances or other calls where there are several officers, where an officer is called to an isolated area for a nonexistent problem, and places of officer recreation. Usually, the attackers' success depends on the element of surprise. Your awareness of what is going on around you might be the factor that will save your life and cause the would-be assailant to choose another time, another place, and possibly another victim.

The routine traffic violator, hitchhiker, transient, lovers in a lovers' lane location are all potential hazards. You are also, no doubt, highly aware of the hazards involved in responding to family and neighborhood disputes, when tempers are always unpredictable. The arrest situation is also dangerous, no matter how docile the arrestee appears to be. Be wary of the individual who immediately alights from his vehicle and approaches you when you make a stop or when several people appear to be converging upon you from two or more directions at once.

Many individuals are at the brink of desperation when they happen to be interrupted by a police officer who stops them while they are walking or driving, or just standing around, and they may react violently for no apparent reason as the officer can see at the moment. An individual may be a wanted felon and one more arrest may mean life imprisonment or the death penalty if caught and prosecuted for the crime(s) he or she committed. As far as you are concerned, the only reason you are approaching the individual is to conduct a routine field interview or to cite for a minor traffic violation. Although you may have no idea whatsoever of the individual's other transgressions, he or she does not know what information you have, and may act on the belief that you have finally caught your suspect for that murder and robbery spree in six eastern states.

If a police officer can experience the "high-speed pursuit rage," so can the person being pursued. If the emotions are working in overdrive at the time you stop a traffic violator after a long and dangerous chase, the person stopped may become enraged over having been stopped and may strike out at you whether you are wearing a uniform or not. At the moment you are an adversary that must be beaten down or killed. Usually the most that will happen will be that traffic violators will scream and swear at you, calling you "gestapo," demanding that you should be chasing "real criminals," demanding that you provide your name and badge number so that they can have your jobs (although they probably could not do it if they had it), even then risking the ire of the officer and having the "book thrown at them" for "contempt of cop." Some gang leaders may have to kill a police officer to show their "homies" that they are not going to be dominated by the police.

Terrorists and other people who have to "get even" with the police for whatever their reasons use sniper or ambush tactics. Both types of assault require planning, tactical advantage, and surprise. If you were to commit one of those types of assault, where and how would you do it? Sniping requires a clear line of vision to the victim from some place of concealment: consider the phony call for help to get the officer to the scene, an attack from a place of concealment may be the approach, and then a hasty and safe escape.

Situations you might watch for and suggested countermeasures include the following:

1. You are approaching a location to which you have been summoned by a call for service, such as a neighborhood disturbance, but it appears that the call was false, and people appear to be leaving rapidly, as though some invisible person had told them all to leave. This may be a setup. Call for assistance and proceed only when the assistance has arrived.

2. You are pursuing someone who jumps out of a vehicle and runs into a building. It appears as though he is making it too easy for you to catch him, but you have to go into the building to apprehend him. Wait for a follow-up and cover possible avenues of escape; then invite the person to come out as you would with a crime-in-progress situation.

   The individual you chase may actually be running away to draw you away from the vehicle, which may contain contraband or a fugitive, such as a jail escapee. When you chase the fleeing person—which seems to be a natural animal instinct—the vehicle or the people whom you should really be checking out are getting away free. It may be the wiser course of action to stay with the vehicle and the other occupants and have a follow-up unit cautiously search for the individual who fled. It may be the registered owner of the vehicle and registration papers may lead you to his or her place of residence where you can make an arrest later, after you check out the vehicle and remaining occupants.

3. You are inside your car and someone throws a firebomb at your car. The device breaks and ignites on the top of your car. Immediately roll up all the windows, close the door, and leave the scene. If the fire is entirely outside the car, you will find that the temperature inside will not change appreciably and you will leave most of the fire behind you.

4. If the same situation in case 3 results in the fire bomb igniting inside, you will have about 1 second to get out of the car before it turns into a funeral pyre.

5. If objects are thrown at you, or if you are fired upon, immediately drive out of the street, such as up a driveway, toward the source of attack. As soon as you can, get out of the car and away from it. In a police car in the middle of the street, you are a target. If you have time, radio for help.

6. If under attack while not in a vehicle, start yelling and making as much noise as you can. Consider running toward the source of the attack because you have a better chance of seeing and counterattacking your assailant than if you are predictably running away and making an excellent target with your back and unable to return fire. Use ammunition wisely and fire only at a target.

7. If you are being held at gunpoint, you can guess that the person holding the gun had some reason for not having already shot at you. If you are immediately facing the suspect and are within reach of the weapon, consider grabbing the cylinder of a revolver, which cannot fire a second time if already cocked and cannot fire at all if not cocked yet. Some automatic pistols cannot be fired if the barrel is jammed back. These measures are extreme and should be tried only as a last resort or when there is no other alternative.

8. If a suspect demands that you give him your gun, there is no assurance that you will not be killed with that gun. You may have a better chance for survival if you decide to counterattack.

9. If fired upon, jump to your left. Most people are right-handed, and when a right-handed person fires a gun, there is usually a sharp pull to his or her left. If you see the gun in the person's left hand, jump to your right.

10. Any kind of a loud noise and sudden defensive movement may be all you need to gain an advantage because of the suspect's slow reaction to the surprise. Strike the subject with something if you can grab a handful of dirt or sand, a handful of coins, your baton, spray of aerosol tear gas (CN or CS) or pepper spray.

11. Try the old trick of shouting to the imaginary officers behind the suspect, an old trick that might buy you a second or two.

12. Immediately drop to the ground and roll toward the suspect; then attack him however possible. You have only one chance and you are probably fighting for your life.

13. If there is a chance while you are being led from one place to another, such as to a place around the corner where you know the suspect is going to kill you, run. He might miss, or the gun might misfire. Your only alternative is to be killed.

14. Maintain a positive attitude and a strong will to live.

15. If you are so inclined, prayer might help, but do it quickly.

RULES OF SELF-DEFENSE

When you add any weapon to your personal arsenal, you have the very serious and very real responsibility to know how and under what conditions you may use the weapon. You must develop considerable skill in its use as well and be ready and willing to use the weapon without hesitation when the times comes for you to use it. Above all, you are required to assume responsibility for the ultimate consequences that use of such a weapon may cause. I know of no officer who has a *desire* to kill, but you have no business carrying any type of firearm if you do not carry it with a *will* to kill. The baton, when applied to a suspect's head, may cause brain damage or death, and you have no business striking anyone on the head unless you are willing to accept responsibility for the consequences. Most of the weapons and techniques of restraint and self-defense that are provided you as a police officer can result in someone's death. That is a serious responsibility.

In this section of the chapter, we shall cover the basic rules of self-defense—that is, defense of yourself and others you have sworn to protect. Whenever you are using any amount of force to take a person into custody or to recapture someone who attempts to avoid arrest, or when you are restraining that person while holding or transporting him (or her), the force that you use should only be "that which is necessary," according to the rule and law books. If the individual resists or counterattacks, you are then in the position of defending yourself, and possibly others. It is not you who is the aggressor, but the suspect who chooses to force you to react. Therefore, the following rules generally apply when you use any degree of force, including deadly force.

1. The amount of force that you use may be in direct proportion to that force or degree of injury you believe is about to be used on you. As a police officer, you will be considered a *reasonable* person unless proven otherwise in court. As a reasonable person, it is also understood that you are charged with the responsibility of preserving lives and arresting people and that the choice is not yours as to whether you should act as a police officer or run away to avoid a bad situation. There is no legal reason why you must retreat or first notify the attacker that you are going to defend yourself. It is at that moment when you—in your own mind and using your own logical thought process—*believe* that you are going to suffer attack unless you immediately defend yourself. This also applies to defense of another person. This belief that you have of impending attack may be used on actual fact, or it may be based on your assumption of what you believe to be fact. For example, a suspect alights from a car you have stopped for a routine traffic violation. As the suspect approaches you, he states in a very threatening manner, "————ing cop. I am going to kill you," while he reaches in the direction of his right waistband. He pulls something out of that location and you see the reflection of metal. At that instant you see a gun. You shoot the suspect to stop his attack. He falls to the ground and dies. As you approach the suspect you see that he actually has in his hands a handful of keys. You saw a gun, you acted on the belief that he was going to kill you because he said that he intended to, and you had no reason to believe that he was not telling the truth.

You have no legal or moral obligation to wait to see if the suspect has a gun, or if he really intends to use it, or if his aim is any good before you defend yourself. Self-defense has never been intended to be a contest, and you are supposed to survive. If you believe that the suspect is going to strike you with a fist or a stick and you have no reason to believe that the blow will be fatal, you will have no justification to kill the suspect. In that case, your defense will have to be another of your alternative choices. If there is mere pushing or shoving, you may use only enough force to stop the pushing or shoving. However, you are not expected to enter a pushing and shoving match; therefore, your defense may be one well-placed kick or blow to some part of the anatomy that will cause so much pain that the fight is ended.

In this type of situation, you are not fearing a mortal assault, but it is quite likely to inflict pain and injury should your assailant succeed. Use of force may be met with force in anticipation and/or return. At this point, restraining holds may work, but in order to control the subject so that you can place that hold upon the person, use of your fists may be replaced or accompanied by a spray of aerosol tear gas (some call it mace) of the CS or CN variety, or pepper spray. Another option would be the electric weapons, the taser or the stun gun. If you have some other nonlethal weapon at your disposal, you may use that as well, but not one intended to produce lethal results.

2. Fear is a personal matter. To defend yourself, you have to be operating under the belief, or *fear,* that you are about to be attacked. This fear element does not mean that your heart rate or blood pressure has to change or that you have to be shaking or in a state of panic. Exactly what and when and how to *fear* is hardly something that one can learn. It is something that someone experiences. Fear may be influenced by previous similar experiences, such as an earlier attack with a gun that had a certain result, or simulated training experiences in the academy may stimulate certain responses. Your state of awareness of the event, or the amount of importance you place upon it, influences your actions. An event immediately preceding this one may magnify or dwarf the fears because you are comparing situations.

Because of the individuality in perception and interpretation, you as an individual must make a personal assessment of the situation and then act in whatever manner you believe appropriate at the moment. Later, your peers, your supervisors, and others who will be judging your actions must put themselves in your shoes and try to evaluate the uniqueness of the specific situation that caused you to interpret the event and to act as you did.

3. The danger must be imminent. There must be a clear and present danger of an immediate attack that calls for a decisive act of self-defense. If an attack has ended, there is no justification for a counterattack, because you would no longer be defending yourself. You would be "getting even." However, if the attack has paused momentarily and it is obvious that the assault on you or someone else is going to continue unless you do something to stop it, you are still acting in self-defense.

4. Your next step is to make the arrest. Now you must use all force that is necessary to make the arrest, but no more. Exactly how much force is enough or too much to accomplish the arrest with no further injuries is largely dependent upon how much resistance the arrestee puts out. If the resistance is verbal, then your force may have to be nothing more than strong verbalization on your part. If the resistance amounts to pushing and pulling, then you are going to have to resort to take-down and come-along holds. If the arrestee attempts to become violent and cause you grievous bodily harm, then your weapons such as your baton, tear gas or pepper spray, striking weapon, or your own physical use of hands and feet comes into play. If the resistance escalates to deadly force, then your use of deadly force will be necessary for you to survive.

5. You must pass the "reasonable person" test. Not only must your actions be justifiable in your own mind, but there may be witnesses whose assessment may differ from yours. Your supervisors, your peers in shooting boards and internal affairs investigations, coroners, prosecuting attorneys, and the administrators of your department must all agree that what you did was "reasonable." If, for any reason a decision is made that what you did was a prosecutable offense and not—in their opinion—self-defense, you may be subjected to criminal prosecution or disciplinary action. In that case, the judge or a jury will decide whether your actions were those of a "reasonable person" and whether you exercised good judgment in accordance with the professional "standard of care" required of you in your position as a police officer.

Consider the following scenarios and decide whether the officers passed the "reasonable person" test.

Scenario 1.   It was a balmy afternoon on the bluffs overlooking the American River. There were several homes under various stages of construction, with some of the homes already occupied. Most of the occupants were away at work during the day, but there were workers from the various utilities and construction companies performing their respective jobs. While connecting the telephone at a neighboring house, the worker observed two young males crawl into a side window of one of the homes. It appeared as though the window had been left open, so it could have been an occupant who had lost his key crawling in so that he could open the front door from the inside, or it could have been two burglars. The witness called the sheriff's department and reported what he saw.

The deputy assigned to the area responded to the call. When he arrived he called in that he was on the scene, then approached the front door. Two young males burst out the front door, almost knocking the deputy down. The deputy called to the two young men, who appeared to be in their middle or late teens. The deputy saw something in their hands, but could not describe whatever it was that they were carrying. The boys did not stop. The deputy chased them across several lawns, through backyards, and over a couple of six-foot backyard fences. He lost them. He returned to the house and verified that the place had, in fact, been broken into. The boys who ran were apparently running to avoid apprehension. The deputy called for backup, then resumed his search for the suspects.

As the deputy was continuing his search, the original witness described what he saw, and added that when he saw the boys run away from the site, one of them was carrying what looked like a "gun with a long barrel." The deputy inquired of several other witnesses along the route of his search, which led him to the edge of the granite cliffs, which rose about 100 feet above the American River. Two other witnesses, each questioned separately and out of earshot of each other, pointed out the direction of travel and said that one of the boys was carrying a weapon; one described a rifle and the other thought it was a shotgun.

The officer was met at the top of the cliff by fellow deputies. They saw the boys climb down the cliff, which had paths, considerable scrubs and weeds, and some shallow caves where someone could hide. At the top, the officer had a fellow deputy drive to the edge, where they tied a rope to the bumper. The deputy used the rope to rappel down the side of the cliff along the treacherous paths. He was down about halfway, or 50 feet from the water below, when he saw one of the boys. The other boy was out of sight. The boy he did see had something in his hand, and the officer believed that it was a rifle or shotgun, and it was pointed at him. Keep in mind the statements by three independent witnesses that one of the suspects was carrying a gun.

When the deputy saw the boy with the gun, he shouted at least three times. He shouted loud enough that some witnesses across the river heard him. He shouted that the boy should drop the gun or that he (the deputy) would shoot. Receiving no response but the boy continuing to point the gun at him, the deputy believed that the boy was going to shoot him. The deputy fired several shots, apparently striking the suspect. The boy and his companion, who must have been right there with him, both fell to the river below. At the same time the deputy lost his footing and he, too, fell into the river. He holstered his weapon and swam to the two boys. The boys were unable to swim, but the deputy was able to rescue both of them and hold them up against the cliff while still in the water. He held onto the boys until rescuers arrived with a boat and pulled the three of them into the boat. At that time they discovered that the one boy had been shot in the shoulder, with the bullet going down (into the heart, it was determined during the autopsy). By the time the ambulance arrived, the boy had died.

Question: Based on the preceding information, is it your opinion that the officer met the "reasonable person" requirement for self-defense, or was he wrong? (See the last page of this chapter for the answer determined by a federal court jury.)

Scenario 2.   This is a city in northern California. The time was November in the early evening hours, and the weather was cold, dark, and drizzling. It was a miserable night for both human and beast. During the previous several weeks, a gang of young black youths was terrorizing the neighborhood beer bars where factory workers and day laborers cashed their checks on Friday night and spent half of their pay buying beer and wine before going home. These places were excellent targets because of the extra cash they carried to cash the paychecks. These youths had already robbed six or seven of the establishments and it appeared that they were going to hit every one at least twice. During each robbery, which were committed with the use of shotguns, shots were fired and several victims had been shot. The more serious ones included a bartender who moved too slowly and lost the use of his hand because of a shotgun wound; another victim was a pregnant woman in the ninth month who was sitting at the bar when one of the robbers made some vicious remark, then shot her, causing her to lose half of her right thigh. (Fortunately, the unborn baby did not get hurt.)

All the bar owners in the neighborhood were in a state of near hysteria, to say the least. They had set up a system whereby if anyone were to see what appeared to be the suspects at or near their establishment, they would immediately telephone a predesignated neighbor, say: "This is 23. They're here!" then hang up. The neighbor would then call the police and give the location of the suspects. The MO of this particular band of robbers was that they would usually shoot anyone who was on the telephone. On this particular evening, two sergeants of the city police department just happened to be within blocks of the location when the dispatcher stated: "Possible armed robbery suspects observed at. . . ." What had actually happened, but was not known to witnesses or the police, was that two youths who had heard of the robberies and the hysteria that they had created decided that they would have some fun with those frightened people. They cut down a couple of broomstick handles to resemble shotgun barrels, then painted them black. These boys then went to one of the bars in the neighborhood where the robberies had occurred, stood outside the front window, and stood there displaying their weapons (actually not weapons at all) until they saw the woman inside look in their direction, then dash to the telephone. The boys ran to the alley, apparently feeling satisfied that they had done what they set out to do: scare someone. They meant no harm, one of them said later. They were just having some fun.

The two sergeants converged at the scene, each one at opposite ends of the alleyway they thought the boys had probably entered. Both officers were armed with shotguns. They had been advised that their suspects were similarly armed. The two suspects ran directly toward one of the officers with what looked like shotguns. The sergeant shouted to them to drop their guns or that he would kill them. They did not, but kept coming toward him. As he shot one of the suspects, the other one ran the opposite direction into the arms of the other waiting officer. When the sergeant approached the suspect that he had shot, he turned the boy over on his back, and it was then that he discovered two things: The boy was quite young (although about 5'11", 150 pounds) and the weapon was nothing more than a stick painted black.

The second sergeant was able to disarm his suspect and bring him to where the other suspect was shot. By the time the paramedics had arrived, the one suspect had died.

Question: Did the officer who shot and killed the suspect in this case meet the "reasonable person" criteria? (See the last page of this chapter for the answer determined by a superior court judge.)

CHOICE OF WEAPONS

As a recently appointed "rookie," or as a future officer, whatever your current status, you will have little or nothing to say about what weapons your agency authorizes you to carry. You will have certain weapons specifically prescribed for you to carry, and there may be some "optional weapons."

For the sake of uniformity, interchangeability, and many other reasons, the department will either provide your weapon for you or will require you to purchase and carry specific weapons while on duty. The weapons may be optional as far as whether you carry a pistol or a revolver, but the caliber and size and manufacturer are decided by the chief executive and his or her staff. When you work plainclothes, you may have an additional optional weapon, such as a smaller and lighter gun to make it easier to conceal. For your off-duty weapon, the department may leave that up to you, but each time you make a selection, it must be approved by your superiors, and you will be required to shoot it frequently at the range and to qualify with it periodically the same as you do with your duty weapons. Whatever weapons you use on a regular basis or only once in a while, you must be trained well and practice frequently. Without the correct training, your weapon of any choice will be virtually useless.

Special weapons and assault or hostage teams are carefully selected, usually by invitation from the team leader on recommendation of superior officers who have observed their candidates under various types of field situations. Once you are assigned to one of those units, your range of weapons will probably be different than you would use otherwise. In this chapter, we intend to cover the weapons and their use, and leave specific choices or assignments to the specialists.

Automatic and Semiautomatic Rifles. Special weapons teams are armed with rifles because of the unusual nature of their assignments, such as dealing with barricaded felons with hostages. These types of weapons are not a part of your regular equipment. Many of your suspects may be thusly armed, however.

Shotguns. For short-range person-to-person assault, the 12-gauge shotgun with 00 buckshot is extremely effective and standard equipment in many departments. Not only does the weapon have a dramatic effect on a suspect, but it is extremely effective when used by an officer with no great marksmanship skills. There is also less danger to surrounding neighborhoods because of its limited range. It is to be used only for felony situations or when there is reasonable cause to believe that a suspect may attempt a fatal assault. For greater range and accuracy, the shotgun may be loaded with rifled slugs.

Handguns. Whether to carry a revolver or semi-automatic pistol is usually a matter of policy in your department. Each has its merits, and proponents for each will extol those virtues. These are the traditional and most common of all police weapons and will be covered in more detail in the next section of this chapter.

Tasers. This weapon consists of a barrel through which two small barbed darts are shot and penetrate the suspect's skin. Wires leading from the darts go back to the handle of the dart gun. When both darts are attached to the suspect, the officer pushes a button, which activates an electrical charge that arcs and gives the suspect an electrical jolt that temporarily immobilizes the suspect. The circuit has to be complete and both darts attached for the taser to work. The effect is similar to the cattle prod or the electrically charged baton that shocks the suspect to immobilize him or her. Two or more officers should be present to allow the officer using the weapon to get an accurate shot or to fire again until both darts penetrate the suspect's body.

Stun Guns. A stun gun looks like a flat flashlight and has a nine-volt battery and two prongs extending from one end. By touching an assailant with the two probes and pushing a button on the side of the weapon, the operator is able to send a high voltage charge of electricity (but very low amperage) giving the recipient a terrific shock that causes muscle spasms and disorientation. The feeling is about the same as if you were to stick your finger in a light socket.

Another weapon sometimes called a stun gun uses the shotgun with a powder charge that projects a wad that opens up and strikes the target like a beanbag with a great amount of force. This beanbag stun gun is used in jails and prisons as a type of nonlethal weapon to restore order in a jail riot or an unruly crowd that is throwing stones and small objects, which amounts to less than a felony and would rule out your use of lethal weapons.

The Hand-Sap and Sap Gloves. Although not authorized by most departments, these weapons are still sold by uniform and police equipment stores. They are very ineffective weapons, in my opinion, and more of a hindrance than a help. The hand-sap is much more effective. It is made of two strips of leather which resemble an elongated eight with a strip of spring steel that runs its length. At the striking end of the sap are weights or beads of lead placed between the steel and the leather, which adds weight and more body to the weapon. The sap is used to strike the wrist bone, shin bone, or clavicle and will cause some pain when used correctly. The sap gloves consist of leather gloves with the knuckles and fingers reinforced with lead buckshot to give them extra weight and body when the officer strikes someone while wearing the gloves. It is an effect similar to carrying a roll of dimes in your fist when punching someone. They are uncomfortable when trying to operate a motor vehicle.

The Baton.   This weapon comes in two forms: the traditional straight stick and the baton with a side arm, usually referred to as a PR 24. (See Figure 13–1.) The baton not only is effective in striking an attacker in either a defensive or offensive mode but also serves as a pry tool and come-along device. It can be used to keep an animal or another person at a distance, or to move things without touching them with your hands, such as contaminated materials. In the United States, the baton is about one meter long, but some of our fellow officers in other countries use a shorter version called a truncheon, and they become very efficient in their use.

Tear Gas and Pepper Spray.   CN tear gas (chloroacetophenone) was invented in the 1890s and CS (orthochlorobenzalmalononitrile) was developed in the late 1920s. Both were used extensively by the police and military services, principally in grenades which burst and expelled tear gas fumes along with smoke. In 1966 two aerosol forms of tear gas appeared on the scene with the trade names of Chemical Mace and Federal Streamer. These two CN gases were supplemented by aerosol

Figure 13-1   Non-Lethal weapons training includes the police baton. (Courtesy North Carolina State Highway Patrol.)

CS gas produced by many manufacturers in the late 1970s. Pepper spray, or oleoresin capsicum (OC), has been produced for use by park rangers, postal carriers, and bicyclists as a defense against belligerent dogs and other animals, such as bears. By the early 1990s the pepper spray manufacturers began repackaging and marketing their material as effective against humans as well as animals. Which material is more effective than the other is subject to debate, largely stimulated by competing product manufacturers and distributors, but my recommendation is to try them all without relying on marketing claims, then have your department adopt the spray formula and device that best suits your needs. They all work essentially the same. You spray your attacker (it is not to be used to enforce behavior or to punish) directly in the face and eyes, then take the person into custody while he or she is incapacitated by the tearing eyes and intense burning. The only treatment for any of these chemicals is copious flushing with water and exposure to fresh air.

USE OF FIREARMS

Carrying and using the firearm should never be taken lightly. A firearm is an instrument of death, and when you carry it as part of your uniform, you are doing so with the awesome realization that whenever you fire the gun, someone may die. For that reason, never fire the gun unless you sincerely believe that you have legal and moral justification to do so and you are willing to accept responsibility for someone's death. Contrary to the fictional image of the police officer using the firearm on a daily basis, you will actually have rare cause to use it, considering the many thousands of potentially dangerous situations you will be facing throughout your career.

The police mission is to preserve life, including that of the people you are required to arrest. Although your primary purpose is to preserve life, the time may come when it will be necessary for you to take the life of another in order to protect yourself or another victim of criminal assault. You must decide when you accept the position as a police officer and the gun that goes with it that you can and will kill, if necessary, for the purpose of preserving life (see Figure 13–2). That "will to kill" in *no way* should ever be interpreted as anything but acceptance of the responsibility that goes along with carrying the firearm. In most situations you will have to make a split-second decision to shoot in self-defense; that will not be the time to search your conscience to determine whether or not you are willing to take a human life.

"Why not shoot to disarm, or shoot the person in the leg?" Since criminal offenders have easy access to firearms and may have had extensive training in their use in or out of the military service, you may have only one chance to shoot to save your life or that of someone else. In the highly emotional situation, you will be lucky if you hit any part of your target. Therefore, you have to aim for the biggest part of the target, or where the target is going to be when the bullet reaches it. No one is such a good shot that he or she can shoot a gun out of a hand under a sudden attack situation. Even when you strike the center of the target, bullets in the heart sometimes do not even stop an approaching attacker. A bullet in an arm or leg is certainly not going to stop that person. Your goal is to shoot to stop and expect that the attacker may die.

Figure 13-2 Mastery of skill in using a weapon develops the officer's confidence that he or she will be prepared to use it when necessary. (Courtesy New York Police Department.)

Here are a few basic rules to follow when handling firearms:

1. Never take another person's words that a gun is not loaded. Handle the gun as though it were loaded, and examine it yourself.
2. While examining a firearm, or cleaning or handling it for any purpose, keep the action or cylinder open, the muzzle pointed in a safe direction, and your finger off the trigger.
3. When carrying the gun in your hand outside of a holster, have the action or cylinder open and hands off the trigger.
4. Be careful where you store a firearm. If you have it stored for self-protection, it must be in an accessible place, but weight the hazards of children and the curious getting hold of the gun against the benefits of the gun as protection.
5. Whenever you fire a gun, know your target, consider ricochets, and be aware of the route the bullet will probably travel.
6. If you "dry fire" your gun for practice, be sure that the gun is not loaded and point it only in a safe direction even though it is empty.
7. Keep the gun in a perfect state of repair and be sure the trigger pull is not so light that it could be considered "hair trigger."
8. *Think safety.*

When to Shoot

State laws and your own department's policies will dictate when you may use deadly force. Consider also the following as your personal policies.

As a police officer, you will never be exempt from the legal and moral responsibilities of using good judgment when resorting to the use of a firearm. Its use is usually irreversible. Never remove the weapon from its holster unless you believe that you have cause to use it. Never point it at anyone unless you believe that you will be legally and morally justified to use it if you have to, and never shoot anyone unless you are willing to accept responsibility for that person's death (see Figure 13–3).

If you intend to make loud noises, find some means other than shooting a firearm. Warning shots are a waste of ammunition. You should never point a gun at someone for the purpose of frightening the person. Your pointing should be so that you will be ready to fire if you have to.

Use of deadly force may be justified only when defending yourself or someone else from what you believe to be an attempt at deadly force. Although the law may provide for deadly force in taking a felon, or retaking a felon who has escaped, or someone who has committed a serious felony, your consideration will be whether it is morally justifiable. There are other means for arresting the felon or someone who has escaped. The firearm is the last resort, not the first. Your role is that of protector, not executioner. The general rule should be "self-defense" as discussed earlier in this chapter.

As a police officer you may use reasonable force to make an arrest. What is reasonable depends on the specific set of circumstances that present themselves to you, and you must consider the overall picture when making your decision as to how much force to use. A misdemeanor certainly does not justify deadly force. If you are making a felony arrest, no matter what the crime, and if you are meeting no resistance, then any force at all beyond merely restraining the subject is too much force. "As much force as necessary" depends on what the suspect does. Whether a felon or misdemeanor, if the suspect pulls a gun out of his or her pocket and starts shooting at you, you are now in a self-defense situation.

After any police shooting, immediately isolate the officer who did the shooting. The last words an officer wants to hear at that moment is any kind of praise, such as "that was great, you sure blew that guy away." Provide a time for the

Figure 13–3 All officers must become proficient in the use of many weapons. (Courtesy Indiana State Police.)

officer to be alone. If a department chaplain or psychological counselor is available, and the officer wants to talk to someone, let it be one of those individuals. Human life is so delicate and so precious, and probably no one appreciates that more than a police officer.

Additional Guidelines for Officers' Use of Firearms

Policies and procedures for officers' use of firearms, or any other statement of policy for that matter, are guidelines on standards of practice. They do not relieve the individual officer from making the ultimate decision and taking appropriate action that will be judged retroactively by others. It is the officer's discretionary prerogative to assess the situation personally and to act decisively.

The value of human life is paramount in any life-threatening situation, including the life of the suspect, no matter how heinous his or her crime. The officer's life—yours—should be right at the top of the list when it comes to the preservation of life. There is nothing in the regulations or code of ethics that requires an officer to have suicidal desires.

The threat of life that leads to the officer's defensive action must be evaluated carefully, taking into account the total picture, such as the danger of wild shots striking innocent bystanders, the age of the offender, and whether moving vehicles are involved. Statistically, the younger person with a gun is more likely to shoot than an older person who has lived long enough to respect life more. Shooting at or from a moving vehicle is extremely hazardous, actually foolhardy except under extraordinary circumstances.

Shots to destroy animals should be only (1) for self-defense, (2) to prevent substantial harm to the officer or another, or (3) when an animal is injured so badly that humanity required its relief from suffering. The first consideration should be whether animal control personnel are available to handle the situation. If so, the decision is theirs. In any event, disposal of any animal should be made out of the presence of children when possible.

Warning shots are not justifiable except in a correctional situation when a violent assault takes place when the officer is too far from the assailant and the victim to intercede. The first shot may be into the ground, with the next shot in rapid succession into the body of the assailant in case the first shot did not stop the assault.

Secondary weapons carried on the officer's person, whether in uniform or plainclothes, makes sense to me, but depends on the policy of your department. If a secondary weapon is authorized, it must be of the caliber and type that is approved by the chief executive officer, and the officer must qualify with the weapon at the range.

Off-duty weapons may be optional, particularly for such activities as beach parties, out-of-town trips, participative sports events, but officers should be encouraged to carry firearms whenever there is a possibility that they may be called upon to use them.

Duty weapons should be standardized and officers required to qualify at least once a quarter. If ballistic samples of bullets fired by the weapon are kept on file by the department, new samples should be collected occasionally to update their validity. The barrel interior changes drastically when a large number of bullets have been fired through it.

Personnel Services Following an Officer-Involved Shooting

Immediately following a shooting, the officer should be required to be separated from all other department personnel until he or she has had an opportunity to go through a counseling session with a psychologist and/or spiritual counselor and consultation with an attorney of the officer's choosing. The attorney should be present when the officer is questioned by department and other agency personnel to assure protection of the officer's rights. An officer placed on administrative leave immediately following a shooting should not be considered prejudicial.

SUMMARY

Stress is a very real and serious problem for police officers and you must develop a program to cope with your own personal problems with stress, whether it be competitive sports or other physical activities, performing in community theatre or playing an instrument in a local orchestra.

In this chapter we have discussed some of the causes for your stress, and offered a few suggestions on how to cope with them. In this chapter we have also discussed your choices of weapons and some basic rules of self-defense and your use of the weapons you are authorized to carry. The guiding principle in your use of force should always be REASONABLE FORCE AS NECESSARY.

EXERCISES AND STUDY QUESTIONS

1. Describe the various types of stressful experiences encountered by such nonpolice practitioners as the following: (a) musicians, (b) students, (c) teachers, (d) attorneys, (e) operating room nurses, (f) ambulance drivers, (g) bartenders, (h) used car salespeople, (i) escrow officers, and (j) auto mechanics.

2. Expanding on the list of stressful situations confronting a peace officer, add at least 10 types of stress that are jointly experienced by *both* peace officers and the people in those other walks of life.

3. List and discuss at least five different activities that you believe would help you with your personal stress problems, if you have any.

4. Look over each of the sources or causes of stress listed in the text, and list which ones directly involve you. Write a paragraph on what you intend to do to relieve the stresses of each one.

5. What has your department planned to handle terrorist activities, should terrorists strike with little or no advance warning?

6. List as many types of unexpected occurrences you can think of that are not given in the section on officer survival. Next, describe what you should do to lessen the danger to yourself and other officers.

7. List and explain the five basic rules of self-defense. Give an example of how each would be applied to real-life situations.

8. What is the greatest advantage of the shotgun as a police weapon?

9. What new weapons have been recently developed for the police arsenal? Describe how they work.

10. Write a policy statement on police use of firearms.

11. What is road rage?

12. Is road rage different from *high-speed pursuit syndrome?* How?

ANSWERS TO SCENARIOS

1. The jury found the officer not civilly liable for the shooting. It did not have a happy ending, however. The officer went to trial six years after the shooting, and the shooting must have weighed heavily on him for that time. Two weeks before the trial began, the officer was confronting an armed suspect and did not shoot when the situation called for it. The officer was shot and killed by the assailant.

2. The judge directed a verdict of *not guilty* but did state in open court that whereas the officer was justified in taking what action he did, he was *not* justified in using the racist language that he used while firing his weapon. Since then, all personnel in that department receive very intensive instruction on the appropriate use of language in all racially sensitive situations.

C H A P T E R   1 4

COMMUNITY POLICING AND PROBLEM SOLVING

*I*NTRODUCTION

The police and sheriff's departments—the local police—cannot separate themselves from the communities they serve (Figure 14–1). They are inseparable. Policing problems are community problems as well. All problem-solving efforts must be made as a cooperative effort including the various segments of the communities. We say "communities" because there are actually many within one city or county. We have the minority community, the business community, the academic community, the neighborhood communities, and so forth. The professional model of policing held the police aloof from the public to create a certain element of mystery to the police operations. One very high-ranking administrator told me that he did not think it wise for the people to know our "police secrets," as much of our success depends on not letting the people know how much we know about police work. I hasten to add, "How much we do not know as well."

There should be no secrets about how you do your job. You will certainly keep secret certain bits of information concerning an ongoing investigation to protect the privacy rights of the people involved, including the suspects. However, you need to and should solicit help from everyone in your community that you can if you hope to solve the "gang problem" or the "graffiti problem," which may involve the same gangs or two separate types of gangs or both.

Figure 14-1 Community policing must involve the community. (Courtesy Chicago Police Department.)

To get at the root of the problem, your contacts will be with present and past gang members and taggers.

You were selected from the community you serve, or from a neighboring community, and you are an integral part of the community. As you participate in church and athletic and youth organizations, so should your fellow members of those groups participate in your police activities. That's the heart of community policing. You reflect the habits, cultures, social pressures, economic conditions, and prejudices and so do your neighbors. In short, police and community problems are interchangeable.

When you are on the job, you play the role of police officer, which is just one of your many roles. You do not lose your identity as a police officer while you are playing all those other roles, and the way in which you play those other roles as well as that of police officer influences the attitudes of the people you encounter.

The police department is not generally looked upon as a single unit. It is many individuals who are viewed by other individuals in a variety of ways. To the mayor or the city manager, the *police department* is the chief, possibly also the captains or deputy chiefs. To the service club member, the *"police"* is the officer who also belongs to the same club. To the lodge fellows, the officer is just another one of their brothers or sisters. Each individual in the community perceives the police department through a different set of eyes, and the police department is no stronger or greater than the officer who is its weakest link. The *"police"* may be viewed as the married man with two teenage children, who sits in the backroom of the neighborhood tavern after closing hours and drinks beer while on duty, and makes passes at the divorcée who works in the doctor's office down the street. To the average person, the police department is the patrol officers who patrol the streets and perform the many hundreds of police services in their own quiet, efficient manner. The police department is what the people see it as being, and what the police officers are, not what the city charter says they are. The police department must be above reproach, which means that every one of its members should likewise be above reproach.

You must have impeccable manners, you must be unquestionably honest, your moral standards must be almost cherubic, your bravery must be undaunting, and you must have all those qualities that are described in your Code of Ethics and in the laws that relate to your job. More important than *having* all those attributes, you must have them *in the eyes of others*. In short, you are on display no matter what you are doing or where you are.

We shall approach police–community interaction from the viewpoint that you as a field officer are involved in this relationship constantly. In this chapter we shall also take a look at the various responsibilities and activities of the police department in its role as the most highly visible branch of the criminal justice system.

The second half of this final chapter is devoted to community-oriented policing in its many forms as practiced by many police and sheriff's agencies throughout the country. Although not a new concept, it is getting renewed attention by departments that have decided the best way to address growing community problems is to do so by getting everyone involved.

THE FIELD OFFICER AND THE COMMUNITY

Your real authority is actually little more than that of the average citizen, but your responsibilities are far greater. You are compelled by law, by court decisions, and by the department's policies to take decisive action whenever a criminal law violation comes to your attention. You are limited in that you may arrest for misdemeanors only when they are committed in your presence, and you may make suspicion arrests for felonies based upon reasonable cause, which is narrowly interpreted by the courts to assure the accused of their constitutional guarantees of the "due process" clauses. Every arrest or law enforcement action that you make must be justified in the eyes of your superiors, the prosecuting attorney, the courts, and eventually the U.S. Supreme Court.

You must develop considerable skill in using the correct choice of words at all times, according to the situation. Sometimes poorly—or accidentally—chosen words may cause unexpected conflict. Words are spoken by attitude and innuendo as well as by actual utterance. Choose them wisely. Any antagonism that arises during a citizen–officer contact should not be a reflection of your poor attitude. Virtually every ethnic and religious minority has at least one nickname that is considered insulting when it is directed by some nonmember toward a member of that minority in a disdainful manner. These words are sometimes referred to as "trigger words." It is the responsibility of every police officer to learn what those words are, and then to make it a point not to use them even during friendly locker room kidding. Take them out of your vocabulary.

Overfamiliarity with the people in your district may result in difficulties caused by a lessening of their respect for you. You should be friendly in your field contacts with the people in your district, but not to the point where you lose your police "image" or objectivity. Consider the "good Joe" officer who was such a nice guy and wanted everyone to like him. He would drive through a certain neighborhood and smile and wave at the kids, and sometimes even stop awhile and "chew the fat" with them before going on about his patrolling. The young children loved him. So did the young delinquents and some of the young adults, who were in the habit of playing poker for money on the street corner, and who committed various types of minor crimes without having to worry about "good old Joe." When asked about how they were able to get away with such obvious law violations, several of the people questioned replied: "Oh, good old Joe? He wouldn't arrest us. We weren't hurting anyone, and Joe didn't mind as long as we were minding our business and not hurting anyone."

Avoiding overfamiliarity does not mean that you should keep aloof and isolated from the people in your district. It just means that you must play your role as law enforcer as well as Good Samaritan. The shopkeeper does not give away any of his or her merchandise to friends but asks the same price. The doctor and dentist provide the same medical services to friend and stranger alike and charge their fees. Giving away their goods and services makes no sense for those professionals. Your services take on a different form, but the rule still stands: You are not doing your job by giving away something, such as an arrest that should have been made. You are not doing anything good for the crime victim when you let criminals get away. Enforce the law and let the courts handle the punishment, or lack of it, as they see fit.

In community policing, involve the people in your district in addressing these problems. If it is vandalism, the vandals must be the children of people who live in the neighborhood, and their victims are the merchants who cater to those children and their parents. All three segments of that community problem should be drawn into your problem-solving discussions and actions to solve the problem. The merchants should report infractions and clean up the damage as soon as possible; the parents should keep their children under control and help stop the vandalism. The vandals should pay for their crimes by repairing and cleaning up the damage and be put to work to pay for the money their parents and the merchants lost in the situation. Religious and educational leaders should direct some of their efforts toward trying to instill a sense of responsibility in those vandals.

You should never limit your organization membership exclusively to police-oriented clubs. You are a part of the larger community and should not isolate yourself from that community. When someone finds out that you are a police officer, they may want help in "fixing" a ticket, or they may just want to "gripe" about the "bum tickets" they received the last four times they were stopped. Doctors are plagued with requests for free diagnoses or a tip; electricians are expected to provide free installation services. Unfortunately, the nature of the work and the strange hours that usually accompany employment as a police officer preclude an active participation in community organizations. But social interactions as an individual and as a family member are important.

Youth groups, parent organizations, religious clubs, lodges, and service organizations all have memberships from all segments of the population. Participation in these groups yields results, not only for the individual but also for the community. They allow you and the people you contact while on duty to interact as social equals and to gain an insight into each other that could not be gotten otherwise.

As a part of the community, your own family unit is just as important as all the others. Don't sacrifice your own family life for that of the department and the other communities you serve. The job is a compelling force which constantly tugs at you for your time and attention like a hungry puppy, but remember that your family needs care and nourishment too.

Your personal appearance and grooming must be acceptable to the majority of the population. Adopting current fads in facial and head hair, makeup, and jewelry is not advised; the people who live in your community want their police officers to represent "middle America." Your uniform must be immaculate and have a semimilitary appearance. Personal cleanliness must also be above average. You must be free of offensive body odors, which may include too much cologne or perfume. You cannot have foul breath or dirty fingernails, and you should use a handkerchief when you sneeze.

Your contact with the traffic violator should be pleasant and friendly, yet not overly familiar. Sometime following the experience of receiving the citation, the individual will see for himself the violation that he committed and will agree that he should have received the ticket, providing his contact with you was pleasant (see Figure 14–2). If there was an unpleasant scene, the same individual will relive the experience and build his own case for his innocence. In addition, he will find good cause for growing angry over your unprofessional attitude and conduct.

You may be a member of an ethnic minority, but once you become a police officer, you lose that individuality. You become a faceless badge and uniform. You must guard against developing strong prejudices and not allow any of your intense feelings *for* or *against* any individual or group of people to influence your decisions to act as an ethical police officer.

Figure 14-2 Every contact with the police need not be a bad experience. (Courtesy Missouri Highway Patrol.)

When dealing with your people in any type of police action, you should always avoid attempts at intimidation through your language or your attitude. The juvenile should be dealt with positively and with respect if you are to expect any respect in return. Kindness and understanding are sometimes received by some youngsters with contempt and you may find it extremely difficult to hold your temper. In such cases, a positive and firm approach in the manner of a benevolent but strict parent may be the better approach. Never resort to losing your temper or name-calling, thereby denigrating the objective status of the law enforcement officer.

You are judged by many people on the type and quality of service you perform. You can perform a tremendously important crime prevention service for the merchants and business owners in your district by making an occasional inspection visit. You should drop in and ask the owner or manager if there is any objection to your making a few observations about his building security. You will probably find the front doors in good shape. However, the back doors, through which burglars would rather enter, are more likely to need improvement. You may suggest that the merchant put the safe in a location where the patrolling officer can see it from outside or that a silent burglar alarm system is installed. Dead bolt locks are excellent devices for slowing down burglars, providing that the doors and frames are well constructed.

While on patrol, you are in an excellent position to develop informants. Contrary to popular belief, your most frequent source of information is not the underworld "rat" or "snitch." Most of the people who give you information are those in whom you have developed a feeling of pride and respect by keeping their neighborhood crime-free. You will have also given them a feeling of confidence that any information they give you about known or suspected crime violations will not immediately get back to them as a source of the information. By your own courteous service, you create in the people you contact a feeling of obligation to help you continue

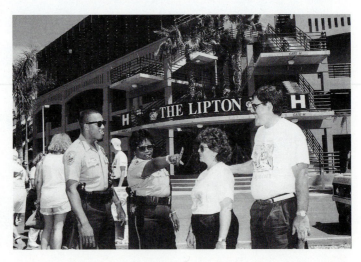

Figure 14-3 Officers direct citizens at the Lipton Tennis Open. (Photo by Brian Clay; courtesy Metro Dade Police Department.)

to perform an exemplary job. While on patrol, never accept, or expect, any free or cut-rate refreshments, gasoline, or services.

One of the community interaction programs that many police departments have established on a more formal basis during recent years has been the "lunch bag," or "adopt-a-cop," or "officer-on-campus" program.

This is an assigned function, established in cooperation with various schools, colleges, or organizations, at which one or two officers meet with several people in an informal setting while having lunch or refreshments together. The meeting is generally an unstructured affair, with the officers attempting to "break the ice" with some of the people they may meet on the street under different conditions (see Figure 14–3). Many of the group's questions are answered in such a way that the rapport extends far beyond their informal meetings. It is not uncommon for officers to find that a great many of the questions asked of them are based on misinformation or complete lack of information about the police role in the community.

POLICE DEPARTMENT COMMUNITY RELATIONS ACTIVITIES

Every police department in the country is involved in community relations or police–community interaction. The police department is a service organization, and its service involves a direct interaction with the community it serves. During recent years, the trend has been to formalize many of the functions that had previously been conducted on an informal basis (see Figures 14–4 and 14–5). Some departments have created special bureaus or divisions with staff responsibility and full-time, assigned personnel to coordinate the community relations activities of the department. Others have added this function to the list of responsibilities of one or more of the staff officers, to be

Figure 14-4 The police officer's community relations activities involve more than formal prepared speeches to large audiences, and often the audiences are small. (Courtesy Chicago Police Department.)

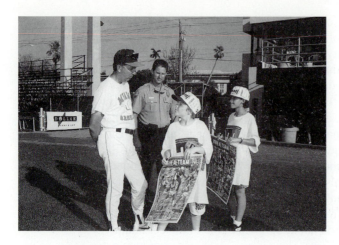

Figure 14-5 "Join a team, not a gang program." (Courtesy Metro Dade Police Department.)

handled along with a number of other assignments. Often the various programs of interaction with the public that are not directly related to law enforcement or crime repression activities are cataloged, and an effort is made to measure their effectiveness in terms of public acceptance and changes in crime and accident trends. The following deals with some of the police department's community interaction programs and activities.

Community Relations Unit

Someone within the organization should be charged with the responsibility for the department's community relations activities. That person should possess commensurate authority to implement techniques and programs, both formal and informal, that will create and maintain a better community understanding of the police role and a better police understanding of the various peoples and their cultural backgrounds and respective roles in the community (see Figure 14–6). The program must have the complete endorsement and participation of the police chief, because some of the activities break with years of tradition, and they may be rejected at the level of execution without such backing. This community relations unit may function as a rumor control center in times of turmoil. At all times it should operate as a communications vehicle between the people and their police department whenever and wherever there is a need for the communicating process.

Community Relations Policies

The police department must have a set of workable, and working, community relations policies. If your department does not have a human relations statement of philosophy, consider this one:

> The mutual advantages of a friendly relationship between the people of a community and their police force should be widely understood and more fully appreciated. The success of a police department in the performance of its duties is largely measured by the degree of support and cooperation it receives from the people it serves. It is of paramount importance, therefore, to secure for this department the confidence, respect, and approbation of the public. The cultivation of such desirable attitudes on the part of the public is dependent upon reciprocal attitudes on the part of this department. These poli-

Figure 14-6 Police officers make the community relations unit work by going into the community instead of waiting for it to come to them. (Courtesy Metro Dade Police Department.)

cies are designed to enhance good public relations and [we] anticipate active participation therein by every member of the department.

This statement is based on three major premises.

1. The attitude of the people in the community is affected by the degree of efficiency demonstrated by their police officers in the performance of their duties.
2. There must be a mutual understanding between the people of all backgrounds and ethnic origins and the officers who comprise their police department.
3. There must be a continuous, free flow of information about the activities of the police department to the public through the news media. The information must be honest and frank.

COMMUNITY-POLICE PARTNERSHIP

One excellent method for developing a closer working relationship with the community is to assign officers on a permanent or semipermanent basis to designated districts. By breaking down the department into smaller units, sometimes in such a way that most police activities, including juvenile, detective, traffic, and patrol, are all handled by this "neighborhood police force," the people in each district have the feeling that they have their own police department (see Figure 14–7). This concept is usually well received by the people, and their cooperative efforts with the police usually improve. The people are constantly reminded by their regular police officers that crime prevention and the apprehension of criminal offenders depends on citizen and police cooperation. Taking the concept a little farther, some departments organize neighborhood "watch" groups, sometimes naming the project "community-oriented policing."

Figure 14-7 Community Watch Meeting. (Courtesy Hawaii Police Department, Hilo.)

Community–police partnership (CPP) depends on mutual trust and respect between the community and the police. Continual dialogue is essential, and we must be honest and candid with each other during that dialogue. Neighborhood meetings are held to identify local problems, committees are formed, and each committee elects its own leader, or "block captain." The neighbors get to know one another and develop methods for watching the neighborhood for unusual events and for immediately notifying the police department. They know and feel that the partnership will enhance the police department's effectiveness and that they are participants.

Fair and Equal Treatment for All Persons

Selection of the men and women who comprise the ranks of the organization is significant in setting the tone for a department that operates free of bias or prejudices. Everyone has the constitutional right to be prejudiced, but police officers relinquish the right to let any prejudices be reflected in their official actions. If they are so colored by prejudice that they lose their objectivity in their personal contacts with people, they will not be effective as police officers. Police action should be dictated by the circumstances, and the officers' discretion in taking police action must be without regard to the individual's ethnic, religious, or moral characteristics.

Understanding the People in the Community

Seminars and conferences may be specifically programmed to bring together in educational debates police officers and people from various minority groups or philosophical organizations, political or religious. The aim of such debates is to promote a free exchange of views on various community concerns. They allow the police officer to explain the purpose and intent of the laws and the philosophy of his particular department, thereby reducing the amount and degree of misunderstanding of the police role.

Community Leadership Participation

It has been said that a camel is a horse put together by a committee. I agree, particularly if the committee is formed to accomplish a specific job. However, committees do serve a purpose if their goal is to develop a broader base of understanding among the people in the community of the many problems confronting their police department. A committee could be established, for example, for the purpose of disseminating information about the juvenile laws of the state and the community, and the police department's enforcement attitude toward those laws. The committee could present their opinions and representative views as citizens of the community at a meeting with the police chief and juvenile officers, and the police department would establish its own policies using the committee's suggestions as guidelines rather than mandates. The police department would then disseminate to the general public, through the committee and the press, the department's policies and enforcement program. This procedure could be effective in dealing with various major problems confronting law enforcement and the community. Some jurisdictions use a more formal approach by creating citizens crime commissions, which have more authority in developing police policies.

Police Reserve Corps

There are many outstanding ladies and gentlemen who might have been excellent police officers or other police department employees, but who decided to enter other lifetime pursuits. By establishing a reserve program, it is possible to create in a segment of the population a greater sense of involvement in their police department's activities through actual participation. Under normal conditions, the reserves train and serve alongside the regular officers once or twice weekly. Then, in case of a sudden emergency calling for personnel far in excess of that which the department could provide, the full complement of the reserves could be called into action to handle the immediate problem. Men and women could be used for a variety of functions, including actual field duties, such as operating a patrol unit, protecting a crime scene, directing traffic at the scene of an accident, or handling an unruly crowd. There are many other functions that need equal attention during times of emergency, such as preparing meals for officers who cannot leave their posts, staffing telephones and radio equipment, maintaining radio and automotive equipment, and sketching robbery suspects. These and myriad other functions could be performed by people from a variety of occupations and professions.

Auxiliary and Volunteers. There are many men and women in the community of all ages who would willingly give their time and talents to the police or sheriff's department but could not or would not devote the time and physical exertion required to go through a reserve academy to wear the uniform and other accouterments of the job and to function as enforcement officers. They would willingly give of their time and talents to work in the office performing public relations, training, docent, technical, and clerical functions. This is another facet of the community policing concept. Former welfare recipients and other people in need of an income could be paid salaries greatly inferior to that of sworn police officers and at the same time free the officers for field duties instead of getting stuck in the office performing what they consider nonpolice tasks, and probably at a subpar level because they feel overqualified for the job.

Public Information

There should be some means for keeping the public informed about new laws and procedures, enforcement policies, and crime statistics. It is no secret that the police department cannot survive as an effective instrument of the government without the cooperation and support of the people, as we have already stated, but the public's support should be based on knowledge gained from accurate information. The department should neither ask for, nor expect, blind faith. Through the medium of personal appearances before every organization that will listen, the police chief and his direct representatives must appear and discuss frankly the actions and intentions of the police department. It is essential that we overcome some of the apathy which is expressed by lack of intercourse with the people. The people and their police department should be discussing the important problems of today and the ways in which these problems can be solved through mutual cooperation.

Press Relations

Whenever anything in the field occurs that appears to be newsworthy, such as an accident or a human interest story, it should be standard operating procedure to call it to the attention of the press. The "exclusive" should be avoided by adopting a standard department procedure for news releases and sticking to the procedure. An information officer may be assigned on a permanent, full-time basis, or one should be assigned each time a newsworthy situation occurs. If the department utilizes this practice, it should then be a department policy for all members of the department to adhere to it by referring any inquiring reporters or press people to the single individual who is responsible for releasing the information. Such a procedure reduces the disparity between stories emanating from several officers about the same case, and avoids what might be a legitimate complaint of "reliability gap."

The department philosophy should be one of complete cooperation with the press. All information that will not directly hinder the ongoing progress of a case currently under investigation should be released. Withholding information concerning some cases is essential, but in most cases it is not. As a matter of fact, it may be wise to discuss even the confidential information with the press representatives, explaining to them why the release of such information is harmful to the case. They then will act as responsible people should and refrain from releasing the information. This candid approach may be wiser than withholding certain facts and running the risk of their discovering the information through other means and inadvertently releasing their "inside" or "exclusive" that may ruin the case. If the news reporters are truly serving the public as they claim, they will respect the request and withhold printing of certain details until given clearance from the department. As a result, both the police and the press will improve their efficiency.

COMMUNITY-ORIENTED POLICING

In a concerted effort to get the people of the community more directly involved in police problems and challenges, many police agencies have gone back to the drawing board and have come up with a myriad of ideas to get all the communities involved. They have developed police–community partnerships with the beat officers working in their neighborhoods with greater autonomy and incentives to work with people rather than taking the somewhat aloof approach some of us were using during the "professionalism" era of the 1950s and 1960s. Working apart from the community created chasms that led to problems and suspicion, sort of an "us versus them" philosophy, with the result that considerable alienation developed.

Lieutenant Christopher M. Robertson of the Cincinnati (Ohio) Police Department wrote in an unpublished paper in the spring of 1992:

> Community-Oriented Policing (C.O.P.) is a nontraditional, proactive approach to crime control, order maintenance, crime prevention and basic service delivery. C.O.P. utilizes modern problem-solving techniques to identify and correct conditions which contribute to an atmosphere conducive to criminality, thereby expanding the traditionally narrow definition of police responsibility.

> Fundamental to the concept of C.O.P. is the formation of a cohesive, working partnership between the police and the community to address both crime problems and quality of life issues which may impact, indirectly, on the crime situation. C.O.P. aggressively solicits input from the citizenry regarding their perceptions of neighborhood problems, both individually, through one-on-one street contacts, and collectively through regular community council meetings, church groups, schools, recreation centers, etc. This connection is crucial, as the police tend to overlook the more subtle aspects of neighborhood life which may be of major significance to the community.

Chief of Police Phil Green of the twin cities of Corte Madera and Larkspur, California, in a personal letter dated March 23, 1992, wrote: "Community policing means different things to different people. Also, some people have put the name of Community Policing for what many of us have been doing for years."

Williams and Wagoner made this assessment: "Community policing requires a substantial change in both structure and form, including attitudinal, organizational, and subcultural change. It represents a 'new' philosophy of policing whereby police officers and the community work together to solve community problems of crime and related social ills. This means giving citizens . . . a direct say in the solutions and activities that regulate crime."[1]

In the Fall/Winter 1988 publication *Footprints,* Robert C. Trojanowicz wrote:

> Community relations and team policing are only two of the most obvious recent examples [of well-intentioned modern policing reforms that have faltered and died]. . . . Community policing means freeing the officer from the isolation of the patrol car and putting the same officer into direct, face-to-face contact with the same community residents every day. It means allowing that officer the freedom to explore new ways the police and community residents can work together to solve the problems of crime, fear of crime, and physical and social disorder.[2]

Actually, in my search for a definition of community policing and descriptions of some of the activities that comprise community policing, I received approximately 60 different answers from 80 different police and sheriff's departments. I am of the opinion that there is no definitive answer and that each community and its police or sheriff's department will continue to find its own way of meeting its unique needs. Some of my colleagues in criminal justice education would prefer to have a single definition like the answer to "What is organized crime?" but at this time I am not prepared to cast the definition in bronze while the metal is still in a molten state. In January 1993, the Honorable Edwin Meese, former U.S. attorney general and distinguished fellow of the Heritage Foundation in Washington, D.C., wrote: "As the emphasis and methods of policing change, the position of the police officer in the organization changes also. Instead of reacting to specified situations, limited by rigid guidelines and regulations, the officer becomes a thinking professional, utilizing imagination and creativity to identify and solve problems. Instead of being locked in an organizational straightjacket, the police officer is encouraged to develop cooperative relationships in the community, guided by values and purposes, rather than constrained by rules and excessive supervision."[3]

Now that we have seen what the experts say about community policing, let's take a look at what the many police and sheriff agencies are doing about implementing some of their programs that fall into the category of community policing. They are not listed in any order of importance of priority, and what may be attributed to any one department does not in any way mean that their program is theirs exclusively or originally.

Neighborhood Watch (Santa Fe, New Mexico, Police Department). This is a program of neighbors watching each other's property while they are absent, such as during working hours, while on vacation, or other absence. The neighbor who sees someone or some event that does not seem appropriate at the neighbor's residence, such as strange vehicles or people who have never been seen before around the residence, calls the police to check it out.

Target Area Program (Jackson, Michigan, Police Department). An officer is permanently assigned to a specific area to work exclusively on foot or on a bicycle. The officer is equipped with a beeper and is available to the people as their personal police officer. The officer maintains a close working relationship with the residents (see Figure 14–8) as well as other city departments such as Community Development, Building Inspection Division, Fire Department, Parks and Recreation, and the Department of Public Works. The officer serves as a link between the public and whichever of their needs can be addressed by the police or other agencies.

Citizen Volunteer Program (Merced County, California, Sheriff's Department). Citizens are recruited to work for no compensation to aid sheriff's deputies and other employees in their many nonconfrontational duties, such as warrants, records, greeting and directing people at the information desk, assisting officers in patrol, detective, identification divisions, dispatch, and patrolling in sheriff's cars, serving as extra sets of eyes and ears in a nonpolice capacity.

Figure 14-8 Officer A. Hart and the Airlie Neighborhood Watch group following a street parade. (Courtesy of the Police Department, Charlotte, North Carolina.)

SAFE (SAFety for Everyone) Program (Minneapolis, Minnesota, Police Department). Citizen volunteers assist the police department in identifying and attempting to solve such problems as property crimes, undesirable housing conditions, garbage and litter, noisy neighbors, drug houses, landlord–tenant issues, and animal control problems.

NEON (Neighborhood Enhancement Operation Network) (Miami, Florida, Police Department). A roving force of 100 officers are used to "saturate" a quadrant of the city to fight severe crime problems for 30 days, then move to another location for saturation patrol.

In a letter from Assistant Chief Arnold Gibbs dated April 21, 1992, the program works like this:

> Beginning August 23, 1991 a roving force of 100. . . . Its primary objective is to educate and empower residents and allow them fuller participation in making their neighborhoods safer. The operation also involves the Department of Sanitation, Code Enforcement, the Fire Department, Nuisance Abatement, the Parks Department, Public Works, and the State Attorney's Office. On its first night of operation, 61 arrests were made, 220 citations were written, 24 cars were confiscated or towed, and 1 crack house was demolished.

Combat Auto Theft (CAT) Program (Widespread Use, Many Cities). People who do not usually operate their personal vehicles between 1 A.M. and 5 A.M. volunteer to have a decal put on their vehicle and sign a waiver that gives an officer probable cause to stop such a vehicle because anyone driving it will most likely be a car thief.

Business Crime Watch (Metro-Dade Police Department, Miami, Florida). This program is similar to the neighborhood watch in residential areas, but the participants are neighboring business establishments. The idea is the same, looking out for the neighbor's property at all times, especially when the tenant is away from the place.

Drug Abuse Resistance Education (DARE) and ADAPT (Alcohol and Drug Abuse Prevention Training) (Many Agencies). Officers are placed in the schools and present intensive educational programs on alcohol and drug resistance in grades 5 and 6, in some cases in the lower grades, and then carried on through the junior and senior high school years.

Community Police Officer Program (San Francisco, California, Police Department). This is principally a goal-directed foot beat program designed to bring officers and public closer together so that they may discuss and attempt to work out mutual problems.

"Dear John" Letters (Des Moines, Iowa, Police Department). Residents in neighborhoods where there is considerable unwanted prostitution activity, with the prostitutes standing around waiting on the street to be picked up by their "Johns," take down license numbers of vehicles cruising the area and/or picking up male and female prostitutes. They secure names and addresses of car owners from the Department of Transportation and send "Dear John" letters to those owners.

> Mr. and/or Mrs. _____ Your *(Vehicle Description)* was seen picking up a prostitute in the vicinity of *(Area)* in Des Moines on *(Date)* at approximately *(Time)*. We hope you realize that by participating in such behavior you risk criminal prosecution, as well as exposing yourself—and possibly your family—to public humiliation and a host of diseases, including the deadly AIDS virus. Prostitution is unacceptable and it will not be tolerated any more in our neighborhood. A detailed description of your vehicle, complete with the license number, has been circulated to area residents.

It is signed by "area residents," and copies are sent to the vice squad of the police department and the prosecuting attorney.

The Des Moines police also have a unit called S.C.A.T. (Strategic Complement Against Thugs) consisting of nine officers who work from 8 P.M. to 4 A.M. and mainly work foot patrol in specific target areas where gangs are known to congregate. They keep themselves familiar with gang members and drug dealers with their "GOOD BOOK," a file of mug shots and bios on all known gang members, which they share with officers on the beat throughout the city.

Operation C.A.R.E. (Combined Accident Reduction Effort) (Kentucky State Police in Cooperation with Local Police). Accompanied by a media "blitz," a D-Day is designated when all agencies set up roadblocks and sobriety checkpoints with a combined effort to remove alcohol- and drug-impaired drivers from the roads.

AT&T Language Line (Carmel, California, Police Department). In diverse communities of many languages, it is often difficult to find someone who can interpret when it is critical. In this community the agency has arranged for instant access via telephone to an interpreter in any language. Another resource not to be overlooked is the language department at your local college or university. Many language instructors are fluent in several languages other than the ones they teach, and many other faculty members travel widely and study languages.

Graffiti Busters (Costa Mesa, California, Police Department). Business owners volunteer to sign agreements that they will have graffiti removed within specified periods of time after discovery and to report all graffiti problems. The city has purchased graffiti removal equipment, consisting of sand-blasters, chemical paint removers, and paint-over paints. Using volunteers and Explorer Scouts, the mobile graffiti blaster goes out into the community and removes the unwanted symbols and messages. Many cities provide graffiti removal services and attempt to remove the graffiti on the day it is reported.

Building Security Standards (Orange, California, Police Department). Written into their building codes are minimum requirements for locks, gates, doors, and security devices that must be installed for code compliance. Citations are issued for violators.

Cellular Phone and Citizen Band Watch (Many Agencies). People who have their vehicles equipped with these convenient devices are encouraged to call in anything they observe that calls for the attention of the police or any other agency in the city, including crimes, graffiti, accidents, lots overgrown with weeds, abandoned buildings, and other problem items.

"I've Had Enough" Coupons (Manteca, California, Police Department). Coupons are printed in the local newspapers and are to be clipped out and mailed to the police department with reports and complaints about drug and other activities in the neighborhood that the complainant is tired of putting up with. This is similar to the WE TIP telephone call-in programs, where a person may report activities and suspicious people anonymously to the police.

Project Cuddle (Many Agencies, Including Highway Patrols). Children who are victims of traffic accidents, child abuse, and other emotionally traumatic situations are taken aside for personal attention and given teddy bears or Raggedy Ann dolls of their own to help ease the pain.

Crime Prevention Column in Newspaper (Many Agencies). Local newspapers are recruiting police and highway patrol officers to write columns addressing the problems of crime and accident prevention and to answer questions asked by the reading public. This is an excellent forum for the agency to use to get messages to the public about items of mutual interest.

Operation Identification (Many Agencies). This project provides the residents of the community with decals to attach to windows notifying would-be burglars that all valuable items inside are marked for quick identification, and assisting people in affixing those marks of ownership with labels and engraving equipment.

Operation Cul-de-Sac (Many Agencies). Streets that have heavy traffic through the neighborhood by people dealing in drug trafficking have been closed to through traffic by barricades or curbs to eliminate some of that traffic.

Coordinated Neighborhood Policing (Dallas, Texas, Police Department).
Utilizing neighborhood police officers working with the community as discussed in other places throughout this chapter, Dallas describes their program thus: "The problem-solving approach represents a significant evolutionary step in helping law enforcement work smarter, not harder. Rather than approaching calls for service as separate unrelated incidents, problem-oriented policing emphasizes analyzing groups of incidents and deriving solutions that draw upon a wide variety of public and private resources. Law enforcement has evolved from a reactive process to a proactive process, and now to a coactive process."

Coordinated Neighborhood Policing (Dallas, Texas).   A neighborhood liaison officer meets regularly with various community groups in his or her district and determines with the help of those groups where patrol units are needed and the emphasis of patrol (juvenile curfew, loitering groups, gang activity, frequent crimes). As a storefront operation, it is a place for residents to come in and discuss problems and concerns and to make reports of minor crimes and nonemergency situations.

Department Ranger Corps (Huntsville, Alabama).   Youths 16 to 20, similar to Explorer posts of Boy Scouts, are recruited and trained in traffic control and assisting at large gatherings, and various other nonhazardous assignments to supplement patrol force. Rangers also work in the office and go on ride-alongs for orientation and training. Huntsville also has a Community Officers Resource Team (C.O.R.T.) in some neighborhoods where foot beat officers work with the community in solving local problems, including better lighting, trash problems, and juvenile delinquency prevention.

Target Area Program (Jackson, Michigan).   With the cooperation of the Fire, Inspection, Community Development, Public Works, and other departments, the purpose of this program is to improve the quality of life in the target area by addressing drug activity, housing code violations, deterioration of public facilities, health and safety code violations, and other problems not necessarily involving criminal activities. Officers patrol on foot and bicycle and encourage citizen involvement in addressing the problems in the community that affect their quality of life.

Problem-Oriented Policing.   Spelman and Eck[4] wrote that problem-oriented policing is the culmination of 20 years of research into police operations that came upon three main themes: *increased effectiveness* by attacking underlying problems that affect patrol and investigative time, *reliance upon the expertise and creativity of line officers* to study the problems and come up with solutions to these problems, and *close involvement with the public in dealing with them.* The strategy consists of four parts: (1) scanning, (2) analysis, (3) response, and (4) assessment. The scanning process involves looking closely at the problem as more than just a robbery problem, but robberies committed by prostitutes upon their "johns," whom they met in certain bars. Then the officers work on the bars, the prostitutes, and the robberies, prevailing upon the businesspeople to cooperate by keeping the prostitutes out of their bars, the public by making them aware of the problems with those prostitutes, and by aggressively arresting the prostitutes, reducing the number of robberies. The assessment portion involves follow-up to see if the officers' efforts actually had an effect on the problem.

Cable Access Television.   Taking advantage of free time available on cable television, many police and sheriff's departments are putting on programs similar to *Unsolved Mysteries* and *America's Most Wanted,* both excellent programs that have been instrumental in solving many crimes and locating many fugitives. Television viewers swell the ranks of police volunteers manyfold. These programs are used for crime prevention as well as to seek those who have already committed the crimes.

World Wide Web Sites.   Criminal justice agencies at all levels of government are going—or have gone—on their own web sites to disseminate information and seek cooperation of the public.

C.A.P. (Community Activist Policing) (Monrovia, California, Police Department).   The C.A.P. task force officer serves as an ombudsman who cuts through red tape and coordinates police activity with all other city departments, such as Code Enforcement, Fire, Building Inspection, Health Services, and others. Some dimensions of this multifaceted program are: (1) organizing neighborhood groups of citizens to work toward deterrence of crime; (2) working with code enforcement people to identify roach- and rodent-infested and run-down properties that are unfit for habitation and are centers for criminal activity; (3) videotaping of unfit homes, with the tapes used to inform property owners of their condition and to encourage them to improve the properties; (4) encouraging owners to rehabilitate their properties and, with their cooperation (or not) locating and eliminating gang activities and narcotic rock houses, and (5) enforcing all applicable laws.

"Are You OK?" Program for Seniors and the Infirm (Pleasanton, California).   This is an automated system for making daily contacts with people in their homes to confirm their well-being. At a predetermined time each day, the computer automatically places a call to each subscriber's home. If answered to confirm that the person is fine, there is no further contact. If there is no answer and the person has not called ahead of time to announce that he or she would not be home, an alert is sent to a dispatcher, who directly calls the person by phone. If still no answer, a police officer is dispatched to the residence for a personal "welfare check."

SUMMARY

As you can see, policing in the United States is moving toward development of a partnership with the communities that we serve. As the cities grew and departments got larger, the trend was to draw away from the community in a stand-off position, a process of "us serving them," and never the twain shall meet. As time passed and budgets became skimpier, the police community began to realize that the better approach to the problems of increased criminal activity and decay of the moral fiber of our citizens was to get the community involved in a partnership. Hundreds of police and sheriff's departments have developed community policing models, each with a different twist, but the common thread in the fabric has been this partnership that is so essential to our success. This is the wave of the future, and we shall see more of it as time goes on. Within a few short years, the old-timers will no longer recognize their police departments. You as a young "beginner" in the profession are in for the ride of your life as the whirlwind takes you into the twenty-first century.

EXERCISES AND STUDY QUESTIONS

1. Outline a five-point plan for your department's community relations program as you think it should be.
2. What is a trigger word, and what should be the police attitude toward usage of such words?
3. Why must a peace officer take an active part in nonpolice-related activities, according to the author?
4. What should your own personal policy be concerning acceptance of free refreshments and other handouts while on duty?
5. What is the difference between being friendly and *overfamiliarity* with the people whom a police officer serves in the community?
6. To what extent is your local police department involved in *community policing*? your sheriff's department?
7. Prepare a police–press policy that you think would be most appropriate for your department.
8. Define "community-oriented policing."
9. Name and describe at least five separate community policing models listed in his chapter.
10. What departments other than the police are involved in community policing programs?

REFERENCES

ADAMS, THOMAS F. *Introduction to the Administration of Criminal Justice,* 2nd ed. Englewood Cliffs, N.J.: Prentice Hall, 1980.

BENT, ALLAN E., and RALPH A. ROSSUM. *Police, Criminal Justice, and the Community.* New York: Harper & Row, 1976.

BRANDSTATTER, A. F., and LOUIS RADELET. *Police and Community Relations: A Sourcebook.* Beverly Hills, Calif.: Glencoe, 1968.

CROMWELL, PAUL F., JR., and GEORGE KEEFER. *Police–Community Relations.* St. Paul, Minn.: West, 1973.

HOLLINGSWORTH, DAN. *Rocks in the Roadway.* Chicago: Stromberg-Allen, 1954.

INTERNATIONAL ASSOCIATION OF CHIEFS OF POLICE AND ANTI-DEFAMATION LEAGUE OF B'NAI B'RITH. *The Police and the Civil Rights Act.* New York: International Association of Chiefs of Police and Anti-Defamation League, 1959.

KRETCH, DAVID, RICHARD S. CRUTCHFIELD, and EGERTON L. BALLACHEY. *Individual in Society.* New York: McGraw-Hill, 1962.

RADELET, LOUIS A. *The Police and the Community.* Encino, Calif.: Glencoe, 1980.

TROJANOWICZ, ROBERT C., and SAMUEL DIXON. *Criminal Justice and the Community.* Englewood Cliffs, N.J.: Prentice Hall, 1974.

FOOTNOTES

1. Frank P. Williams III and Carl P. Wagoner. *"Making the Police Proactive: An Impossible Task for Improbable Reasons," Police Forum,* A.C.J.S. Police Section, Vol. 2, No. 2, June 1992.
2. Robert C. Trojanowicz, *"Serious Threats to the Future of Policing" Footprints,* Community Policing Newsletter published by the National Neighborhood Foot Patrol Center, Michigan State University, Vol. 1, No. 3, and Vol. 2, No. 1, pp. 1–3.
3. Community Policing and the Police Officer, *Perspectives on Policing* U.S. Department of Justice, Washington, D.C.: (January 1993), pp. 1, 2.
4. William Spelman and John E. Eck, *Problem Oriented Policing* Department of Justice, N.I.J. Washington, D.C.: Research in Brief publication, January 1987.

INDEX

snapshots of, as set-up protection,
252–53
waiting outside, 250, 251
closer-unit reassignment to, 133
computer records of, 125
entry for, discovering, 250–51
gang activity, responding to, 257–59
investigations of, preliminary, 19–21
against persons, responding to,
247–49
prevention follow-up for, 66, 78
in progress,
coordination of, 259
dispatching units to, 244–45
field-unit response to, 245–47
follow-up units at, 247
informants of, instructing, 244
information on, obtaining, 244
against persons, 247–49
plainclothes assistance in, 261–62
against property, 249–57
response plans for, 242–43
searches during, 259–61
by prowlers, responding to, 254–47
reference on, 263
reported, back-up for, 133
reports on,
of law violated, 166–67
of time, 167
of victim, 167–68
repression of, 7
responding to, 249–57
reviewing, 49–50
scenes of,
copying, 292
protecting, 292
sketching, 285
"trademarks" in, 170
Criminals:
computer records of, 125
incomes of, 7
See also Interviews: in the field.
Crises: police responsibility in, 10–11
Crowd control:
during disasters, planning for, 309
references on, listed, 331
zero tolerance in, 314
See also Demonstrations. Riots.
Strikes. Unlawful assembly.
Custody:
See Arrests. Detention.

D

Daily logs:
notes for, 53–54
purpose of, 150
scope of, 150–51

Danger: See Stress: from danger.
Survival.
Death: determining, 290–91
Debriefings:
from counselors, for stress relief,
406
from fellow officers, 51–52
notes for, personal, 145
Demonstrations: response to, 323
Detentions:
defined, 376–77
investigative, 383–84
Diplomatic immunity: discussed,
381–82
Disasters:
access to,
assuring, 305
limiting, 306
aircraft crashes, 324–26
area of, containing, 305
command posts for, setting up, 304,
306–7
communications during,
interagency, 305–6
to public, 305, 310
responsibility for, 304
intelligence assignments during, 310
logistics of, 310
martial rule during, 308–9
federal, 390
mobilization in, 307–8
mutual-aid agreements for, 308
planning for, 301–2, 307, 309
recording, 306
references on, listed, 331
response to, 302–11
evaluating, 306
stage area for, 310
victims of,
evacuating, 305
identifying, 310
Discretion:
guidelines for, 34, 35–36
prerogatives in, 32–33
See also Bill of rights: for police.
District:
learning, 50–51, 242–43, 245
orientation inspection of, 53–54
responsibility to, 61–62
See also Community.
Dogs:
in riots, disadvised, 315
for searches, at airports, 388
uses of,
for building searches, 252
in lost-child cases, 212
Domestic arguments: police
responsibility in, 14

Domestic disputes: See Civil disputes:
domestic.
Drug abuse:
community informant program for,
439
laboratories for, investigation of,
293–94
police education, groups against,
437
roadblocks against, 438, 439
Drunks: See Alcohol: abuse of.
Due process: variability of, 9
Dune buggies: computer records of,
125

E

Elderly: neighborhood watch over, 441
Entrapment: discussed, 382–83
Evidence:
ballistic, value of, 275
biological-fluid, 277
chain of custody of, 154, 280–81
collection of, 21, 39, 270–71
DNA, accuracy of, 274–75
fabric, 278
fingerprint,
identification systems for, 272–73
most valued, 271–72
taking, kit for, 274
types of, 271
footprint, value of, 272
of gambling, gathering, 295
latent, collecting, 272, 273
marking, 280
miscellaneous, 279–80
paint, 279
perishable, handling of, 281
photographs as, 281–83
preservation of, 21, 39, 270–71
priority of, 266–67
safe-insulation, 278
searches for, 292
shoeprint,
taking, 275
value of, 275
short-lived, preserving, 267
sketches as, 283–86
soil samples as, 275
tireprint,
taking, 275
value of, 275
tool-mark,
taking, 275
value of, 275
toothmark, 277
transfer theory of, 270
videographs as, 283